AN INTRODUCTION TO LAND LAW

The rules of land law are numerous, complex, and in some cases baffling to students. The study of land law is also often portrayed as dull. Too frequently those who find success in working out how the law operates in other areas find themselves defeated by land law. Even the great jurist Blackstone, while maintaining that 'there is nothing which so generally strikes the imagination, and engages the affections of mankind, as the right of property', also concluded that the study of land law 'afforded the student less amusement and pleasure in the pursuit' than the study of crime and tort.

This book tries to help with that problem. It aims to tell the rules' story: to talk about them in terms of the work they do, in a way that will allow readers to understand and engage with them. And through the example it offers, it aims also to give students the confidence, spur and tools to go on to develop such perspectives for themselves.

The book covers the main points of land law found in the syllabuses of law schools in England and Wales. While it is not intended as a comprehensive textbook on the topic, it offers sufficient detail for anyone reading it to gain an overview of the subject, and for those seeking more the footnotes offer plenty of pointers. As well as bringing the coverage up to date, this new edition adds chapters about two especially challenging aspects of the subject: the human rights dimension, and the nature of 'ownership'.

As one reader of the first edition commented, 'it shone light where none had shone before, and lit a clear path to understanding'.

D0294368

An Introduction to Land Law

Third edition

Simon Gardner

with

Emily MacKenzie

·HART·
PUBLISHING

OXFORD AND PORTLAND, OREGON
2012

Published in the United Kingdom by Hart Publishing Ltd
16C Worcester Place, Oxford, OX1 2JW
Telephone: +44 (0)1865 517530
Fax: +44 (0)1865 510710
E-mail: mail@hartpub.co.uk
Website: http://www.hartpub.co.uk

Published in North America (US and Canada) by
Hart Publishing
c/o International Specialized Book Services
920 NE 58th Avenue, Suite 300
Portland, OR 97213-3786
USA
Tel: +1 503 287 3093 or toll-free: (1) 800 944 6190
Fax: +1 503 280 8832
E-mail: orders@isbs.com
Website: http://www.isbs.com

© Simon Gardner and Emily MacKenzie 2012

British Library Cataloguing in Publication Data
Data Available

ISBN: 978-1-84946-236-5

Typeset by Hope Services, Abingdon
Printed and bound in Great Britain by
TJ International Ltd, Padstow, Cornwall

Preface

Like previous editions of this book, this one aims not just to state the law, but to paint its portrait, or write its biography, or something of that kind; an enterprise whose success demands a careful, thoughtful, honest and critical (but not unsympathetic) inspection of it, from a number of directions.

This portrait or biography is offered both for such interest as it may possess in itself, and also – indeed, more especially – as an example of the sort of thing that readers may like to undertake for themselves.

The principal substantive changes from the previous edition consist in coverage of an important new Supreme Court decision on family property (*Jones v Kernott* [2011] 3 WLR 1121), and the addition of two chapters, one on human rights in land law, the other on 'ownership' (this title being, however, only the tip of a very important, and intriguing, iceberg). These chapters are principally the work of Emily, though Simon contributed to some of the initial blocking-out and revision of the drafts, and the ownership chapter does incorporate a certain amount of text from the previous edition. Partly as a result of introducing these new chapters, we also decided to change the arrangement of some of the book's remaining other content.

We are more than happy to acknowledge the generosity shown to us in many quarters in producing this edition. Specific mention must be made of the assistance given with its content by Susan Bright, Elizabeth Cooke, Eoin Daly, Katharine Davidson, Liz Fisher, Joshua Getzler, Gerwyn Griffiths, Noam Gur, Mike Macnair, Kai Möller, Roger Smith, and especially Amy Goymour, who helped unstintingly with the human rights dimension; but no less appreciated has been the more general support and encouragement that we have had from these same colleagues and also from our families and friends. We must of course express our thanks also to the publishers, with a special mention for the cover designer; and to the Oxford University Law Faculty and the Michael Zilkha Trust at Lincoln College, whose financial assistance made possible Emily's involvement.

Simon Gardner
Emily MacKenzie
Dydd Santes Dwynwen 2012

Contents

Table of Cases

Australia

European Court of Human Rights

United States of America

Table of Legislation and International Conventions

United Kingdom

Statutory Instruments etc

Canada

European Union

United States of America

International

Part 1

The Basic Ideas

This book aims to give an account of that part of English[1] law known as 'land law'.

This label is, however, misleading. It suggests that the topic is the whole set of English law's rules relevant to land. This in turn could mean various things. At its widest, it could mean the set of all the rules applicable to someone using land. Since legal rules are propositions about human behaviour, and nearly all human behaviour takes place on land, 'land law' in this sense would comprise almost the entire law, excluding only the special rules applicable to activities on water or in the air. Less widely, it could mean, within that set, the subset of all the rules making some particular reference to the land dimension. So while the first meaning would take in the rules about pollution generally, the second meaning would include only those rules focusing specifically (though perhaps inter alia) on pollution of the soil. And while the first meaning would include the whole law of contract, the second would take in only those contract rules aimed specifically at arrangements involving land, such as room rental agreements.

One certainly could address such subjects, though the enterprise would be a huge one, because land is in these senses an aspect of so many rules. Even the less wide of the two meanings would, for example, take in areas as distant from one another as agricultural law, planning law, domestic violence, and the crime of burglary.

In practice, the label 'land law' is more often used much more narrowly: as referring, out of all the rules involving land, only – or at any rate principally – to the rules that establish rights in land, of two kinds: 'rights in rem' as recognised by English law (indeed, traditionally, 'land law' consisted only of these), and (a more recent accretion) those rights in land that arise under the

---

[1] Traditionally, 'English and Welsh', in that the two countries formed a single jurisdiction with a single set of rules; but devolution has created the possibility of divergence. To date, however, the rules in the area of 'land law' remain very largely common – indeed probably entirely so, at the level covered in this book. References to 'English' law should therefore be read as very probably extending to Welsh law too.

European Convention on Human Rights. Attention to these two kinds of rights will be the focus of this book.[2]

The book is divided into three parts. The first, comprising Chapters 1 to 4, concentrates on the basic ideas: the two kinds of rights in land, and how they behave. Parts 2 and 3 contain more detail regarding specifically rights in rem. Part 2, comprising Chapters 5 to 9, looks at the ways in which rights in rem can be acquired. Part 3, comprising Chapters 10 to 17, reviews a number of different sorts of rights in rem. There currently seems less to be said about these matters in regard to rights in land arising under the European Convention on Human Rights . . . though this statement may turn out to require adjustment in future editions.

---

[2] This is not to say that other foci are unworthy of attention. For a reminder of how important the *lack* of rights to land may be, see D Cowan and J Fionda, 'Homelessness' in S Bright and J Dewar (eds), *Land Law – Themes and Perspectives* (Oxford, 1998) ch 10.

Rights in Rem

As already stated, this book focuses on two kinds of rights in land: 'rights in rem' as recognised by traditional English ('domestic') law, and those additional rights that are declared in the European Convention on Human Rights. This chapter introduces the former, Chapter 2 the latter.

1.1 The Idea of a Right in Rem

1.1.1 'Rights in Personam' and 'Rights in Rem'

Say I own a house, but then something occurs which, according to the rules of English domestic law, means that you now have a right to live in it. The 'something' might be that I make a contract with you to this effect; or that I give you a share in the ownership; or that I marry you; or various other significant happenings. Say then that I sell the house to John. In terms once again of English domestic law, there are two possibilities.

One is that your right cannot affect John. That is, it is effective only against me, and if you want to enforce it you will have to look to me, not to John. It follows, now I have passed the house to John, that you will not be able to insist on living there: as it is said, to maintain your right '*in specie*'. Only a right effective against John could allow that. Because your remedy can only be against me, it will have to take the form of a money payment, from me, compensating you for *not* now being able to live in the house. Rights which behave in this way are called 'rights in personam'. Prominent among the rules dealing in rights of this kind are those comprising the ordinary law of contract. Contract has a feature called 'privity', whereby a contract between *A* and *B* cannot bind *C*.[3] That is another way of describing the fact that rights arising under the law of contract alone are in personam.

The other possibility is that your right can affect – bind – John. If your right is of this kind, and the conditions for John being affected are indeed satisfied, your remedy is no longer against me alone: you can enforce the right against John. Just because your right is effective against John does not necessarily mean that you will be able to maintain it *in specie*, ie insist on living in the house: your remedy might still take the form of money compensation for not being able to live in it, though this time against John rather than me. However, effectiveness against John is certainly a precondition for your being able to claim *in specie* protection, and commonly this will indeed be forthcoming. If the law treats your right as having the potential to affect John in this way, your right is called a 'right in rem'.[4]

Your right to live in the house might be of either kind. To know which, we need further information. For example, if you simply rent the house from me, your right will be a 'lease', and in rem; but if your right is to live in it with me, as my lodger, it will be a 'licence', and in personam. There are various other possibilities, some of each type. We shall review many, though not all, of them in the course of this book.

1.1.2 'The Potential to Affect John'

The previous section spoke of a right in rem as one 'having the potential to affect John', and noted that John will in fact be affected by it only if certain conditions are satisfied.

In principle, the law could say that rights in rem *will* affect John, full stop. In practice, contemporary English land law takes a more complex position, whereby John will commonly be affected only if certain circumstances are present. The rules on this point have varied over the years, but currently are for the most part stated in the Land Registration Act 2002. We shall look at these in detail in Chapter 3, but, for example, the position may be that John will be affected by your right in rem only if, before he bought my land, your right had been registered at the Government's Land Registry. (A right in personam cannot be registered at the Registry, and even if somehow it were, it

---

[3] Distinguish this meaning of privity from another, whereby a contract between *A* and *B* cannot *confer a right* on *C*. This too was a feature of the law of contract, but the relevant rules have been substantially amended by the Contracts (Rights of Third Parties) Act 1999. On privity generally, see eg M Chen-Wishart, *Contract Law* (4th edn, Oxford, 2012) ch 4.

[4] An argument has been made that, of the rights which this book treats as in rem, some lack certain of the features of a true right in rem, and so should be segregated out and considered instead as 'persistent' rights. This argument is explored in § 1.3.2. Even if there are two categories of non-in personam rights in this way, however, they certainly share the characteristic of 'having the potential to affect John', so can be bracketed together so far as this matter – our present focus – is concerned.

would still not bind John. Registration, and certain equivalent phenomena,[5] constitute the circumstances under which rights capable of binding John will actually do so. So they apply only to rights in rem. A right in personam is by definition not capable of binding John, so will not do so, no matter what.)

The idea of a right in rem is sometimes conveyed in the Latin expression *nemo dat quod non habet*, ie no one can give what he[6] does not have. Say I purport to sell John a house, but in fact it belongs not to me but to you. John does not become owner of the house, because I did not own it previously, so did not have it to give. Equally if I do own the house but have leased it to you for five years, thereby giving you a right in rem over it for that period. If I purport to sell the house to John, what I have to give is the ownership minus your leased interest, so the picture is painted of him acquiring the ownership minus your interest. Which, in both cases, explains why John must respect your interest: he never acquired (because I never gave him, because I never had) the ability to do otherwise.[7] Whereas if your right is only in personam – as where you are my lodger – your claim is against me personally, so all the rights in the house remain mine to give, and I can successfully transfer them to John. If John chooses to evict you, all you can do is sue me for breaking my contract with you.

But this picture does not fit with the fact that English land law's rights in rem affect someone like John *only if certain conditions, such as registration, are met*. I may own a house subject to a lease in your favour, but if that lease is not registered, John may not be affected by it: I will thus have given him the house unencumbered, despite not owning such an unencumbered house myself. So the actual law regarding the behaviour of rights in rem is not in fact fully described by the *nemo dat* image. How should we think about this discrepancy?

A quick answer might be that *nemo dat* is only a metaphor, and its imprecision therefore unimportant. That is not good enough, however. The idea underlying *nemo dat* is that when something 'belongs' to a person, as the house in the above examples belongs wholly or in part (to the extent of the lease) to you, that person's entitlement to it is absolute, impregnable. This idea has a powerful appeal.[8] The fact that the actual law departs from it, in the manner under discussion, therefore requires explanation and justification.

---

[5] That is, the cases in which the law regards a right in rem as an 'overriding interest': § 3.1.1.

[6] Here, and (unless the context indicates otherwise) throughout this book, masculine pronouns are used to refer to both sexes.

[7] Likewise if, rather than selling the house to John, I go bankrupt and the house is to be taken and sold to help pay my creditors. If the house is not mine but yours, this cannot happen. If it is mine but you have a lease over it, it can and will happen, but when the house is offered for sale, the offer must be subject to your lease.

[8] It is an aspect of the paradigm conception of property, or ownership. For further discussion of the latter (the reasons why it has a powerful appeal, and the reasons why we may nonetheless not espouse it), see Ch 10.

The key is that, for all its appeal seen from your perspective, the pure *nemo dat* idea creates dangers for others such as John. Dealing with me, he may believe that I have the house to sell, and that there are no derogations from this, for example a lease in your favour; and he may proceed on the basis of this belief, most especially by paying me for the house's whole value. If this belief turns out to be ill founded, John will suffer. He may well have a claim against me for his money, or the relevant fraction of it, but this is distinctly second best to not encountering the problem at all.

Of course, John's mistake may be entirely his own fault, with the result that we may have little sympathy for him. But equally, he may have taken all the care in the world, so that there is a sense in which the emergence of your right against him genuinely upsets the understanding he could reasonably have of his position. To put it more pointedly, the pure *nemo dat* idea, allowing you to insist on your (in this situation) undiscoverable right against John, permits you in that way to exert 'arbitrary domination' over him. And the precepts of republicanism – a very important political tradition treating liberty as the absence of such domination, or of any scope for it – invite us to organise the law so as not to permit such a thing.[9] That is, they invite us to stop the law short of the pure *nemo dat* idea.

And consider finally the possibility that John took, not all the care in the world in failing to discover your rights, but all the care that we should wish him to. For the market in an asset to operate most effectively, so that the asset can move to the person able to extract the greatest profit from it, we need to minimise the 'transaction costs', ie the costs involved in procuring this move-ment. The more care we expect of John, or that is in effect demanded by our rules about when a right in rem will bind him, the higher will be his transac-tion costs, frustrating these boons.

From these points of view, then, it makes sense for the law to make John bound by a right in rem only when it ought to be easily discoverable. Hence the rule whereby John will in many cases be bound by your right only if the latter has been registered: registration makes for easy discoverability.[10] The literal idea of *nemo dat quod non habet* is sacrificed to the extent required by such countervailing considerations. But that idea's essential appeal remains, so the rules embodying the departures from it require the most careful design. Those currently in force will be examined and evaluated in Chapter 3.

---

[9] For republicanism, see F Lovett, 'Republicanism' (2010) in *Stanford Encyclopedia of Philosophy* (http://plato.stanford.edu/entries/republicanism/), and further references there.

[10] An older rule provided that certain rights bound John only if he was not a 'bona fide pur-chaser for value without notice' of them. The key element in this, the idea of 'notice', in theory referred to the possibility of discovery by a 'reasonable purchaser'. As such, it was apparently sympathetic to the value under discussion. But the concept of a 'reasonable purchaser' was itself interpreted in various ways, including some quite demanding on John: leaving the concept not so sympathetic after all.

1.1.3 Two Difficulties with the Terminology

Two difficulties with the terminology, 'in rem' and 'in personam', need exploration.

First, one often encounters other terminology, dividing the universe of rights into 'real', or 'proprietary', or 'property' rights on the one hand and 'personal' rights on the other. Unless it seems that the writer intends otherwise, it should be assumed that 'personal' is a synonym for 'in personam', and that 'real', 'proprietary' and 'property' are synonyms for 'in rem' . . . as are 'a right in (or relating to, or affecting) the land', 'an interest in (or relating to, or affecting) the land', or even 'an interest' without more.

These other labels may be preferred because 'in rem' and 'in personam' were originally used in the law of ancient Rome, whose rules gave them specific meanings; and the writer wishes to make clear that the meanings of the corresponding concepts in modern English law are not necessarily quite the same. Those who, like the present writers, use the Roman terms are, however, usually clear that they do so simply for convenience, with no intention to treat the terms as having the Roman or any other particular meaning. The Roman terms are generally used in this book precisely because, unlike their synonyms, they are not ordinary English words. Their very strangeness, by arresting the mind, helps to flag up the fact that the concepts in question are crucial, and involve technical rules.

Second, a writer will sometimes draw the line between rights in rem and in personam in a different place from that sketched in § 1.1.2, insisting that a right counts as 'in rem' only if it affects John without further ado, unconditionally, without need of registration or whatever; and that all other rights are thus in personam, *including* those that have the potential to affect John, but will do so only if certain conditions are met.

This issue arises because there are in fact three classes of right – (i) those that will affect John without further ado; (ii) those that will affect John, but only if certain conditions are met; and (iii) those that cannot affect John – but only two labels (whether Roman or English). A solution would be to adopt a third label, and some take this path, though the third label often chosen – and used for category (ii) rights – is '*sui generis*', meaning 'in a class of their own', which is hardly illuminating. But say we restrict ourselves to only two labels, as is more usual, and treat rights in category (i) as certainly in rem, and those in category (iii) as certainly in personam. We need to group those in category (ii) with one of the other categories. Which? Either answer could be defended, but in practice it is more useful to group category (ii) with (i) than with (iii). The rules creating the boundary between categories (ii) and (iii), ie determining whether a right is capable of binding John at all, are rather firm and long lived;[11] whereas the rules

---

[11] These rules comprise the '*numerus clausus*' effect, and there are reasons for it, discussed in § 1.2.2.

creating the boundary between (i) and (ii) – ie the precise details about when a given right, capable of binding John, will actually do so – are relatively superficial and ephemeral. Hence the decision in this book (and in most lawyers' parlance) to treat rights in category (ii) alongside those in category (i) as rights in rem, regarding those in category (iii) alone as in personam.

In short, this book uses the term 'right in rem' to mean a right that is capable of affecting John, and will do so under the conditions prescribed by the law's prevailing rules on the matter, whether these make it affect him without further ado or (as in the current state of English registered land law) only under certain conditions.

1.1.4 Rights in Rem as Effective against 'Disponees'

So far we have seen that a right in rem over my land is one that can affect John, to whom I sell that land. We need to be a little more precise about the kind of person that can be affected.

To put it abstractly, a right in rem over a piece of land is a right (to use the land in some way, and) effective not merely vis-à-vis the person against whom the right arose in the first place, but also, potentially, vis-à-vis people subsequently acquiring rights in the land in question.

There is no definitive term for people of this latter kind, but in this book they are referred to as 'disponees'. Disponees thus include someone who becomes owner of the land in my place, such as John: as owner hitherto, I give John all my rights. They also include those to whom I give only some of my rights, while remaining owner myself. So if I give you a right in rem to live in my house, and then merely rent my house out to Kate, Kate too is a disponee. If the conditions for your right affecting Kate are met, therefore, she will be affected by your right.

In this example, your right's 'effect' on Kate is likely to be immediate and obvious. She will probably want to occupy the house herself, or to allow someone else to do so, and your right to do so will frustrate this desire.

Sometimes, however, the effect will be less immediate or obvious, but nonetheless there. Say I give you a right – in rem – to get from your land to a certain road by crossing my land that lies between the two: a 'right of way'. Then I mortgage my land to a bank, to secure my overdraft. As a disponee of the land, the bank will (assuming the relevant conditions for this are met) be affected by your right. But at any rate to begin with, there will be no practical impact on the bank: your crossing my land is quite compatible with the bank's having its security right. The picture changes, however, if I default on my repayments and the bank repossesses my land so as to sell it and recoup the outstanding debt. Being bound by your right to cross the land, the bank will be able to offer the land for sale only subject to your right, and that will mean fetching a lower price than would otherwise be attainable (since a buyer will be to that extent deprived of the land's use: he will not, for example, be able to build across your route).

Equally, if I mortgage the land to the bank first, then later give you your right of way. A mortgage is a right in rem, so assuming the necessary conditions are fulfilled, you – as a disponee – will be affected by it. But at any rate at first, there will be no practical impact on you. The impact will appear if the bank repossesses and sells. Being 'affected' by the mortgage means that you cannot insist on your right of way so as to cut down the bank's rights. So the bank can offer the land for sale free from your right to cross it, and thus attract a higher price.

Sometimes again, the nature of the two rights will be such that even a delayed impact of this kind cannot occur. Say I give you the right to cross my land following route X, then give Liam the right to cross it following route Y, and that the two routes do not cross one another. Assuming the necessary conditions are met, Liam, as a disponee, will be affected by your right, but given the topography it is hard to see how this could ever matter. So when we say that a right in rem is one that is potentially 'effective' against a later disponee of the land in question, we mean that it takes priority – precedence – over the later disponee's interest; but whether this makes a concrete difference will depend on the two rights' specifications, and the ways in which they are in practice used.

As already stated, this book refers to a person who acquires a right in land – such as Kate, the bank, Liam, and indeed you in these examples – as a 'disponee'. The word 'disponee' has only recently come to be generally used to describe a person of this kind. Until 2002,[12] the usual term was 'purchaser'. But that term was misleading in suggesting (at any rate to lay ears) someone who *bought* the *ownership* of the land. Neither of these limitations reflected the actual rule, which has always been as described in this section. The word 'disponee' avoids giving such an impression, correctly capturing someone to whom I give any kind of right in my land (like Kate, the bank, Liam and you), and whether for payment or gratuitously.[13] This book will use the word 'disponee', but given the relative recentness of the change, the word 'purchaser' will still be found in many sources.

---

[12] The change occurred in the language used by the Land Registration Act 2002.

[13] There are, however, variations between different classes of disponee in respect of the precise circumstances in which pre-existing rights in rem, capable of affecting them, will actually do so. See § 3.1.1.

1.2 The Kinds of Rights in Rem

So far we have talked about rights in rem in the abstract, though some concrete examples of them – ownership, leases, rights of way, mortgages – have cropped up. Now we shall develop a firmer understanding of the kinds of rights in rem that the law recognises.

1.2.1 The *Numerus Clausus*

Notice the key assumption in this: that the law recognises only rights of certain kinds – ie with certain contents – as able to exist in rem. This contrasts with the position regarding the in personam rights[14] that can be generated by making a contract, which can be given almost[15] any content. So I can effectively contract with you (in personam) for you to occupy my house on a temporary basis in more or less any manner we choose. But if you are to have the relevant right in rem, a lease, we must conform our arrangement to the law's template for the latter. As we shall see in § 11.2.1, this requires the arrangement to give you the right to 'exclusive possession' of the land (so, not sharing with me); for a defined period (so, not simply for as long as you like); and, supposedly but perhaps not correctly, in return for some sort of payment.

There are only a certain number of such templates, and they are not exhaustive of all possible rights. So it is not a matter simply of finding the correct label for the right we wish to create. Many rights will not fit any of the templates, and so cannot exist in rem at all. Say we try to create a right allowing you non-exclusive possession of my land, in return for rent, for a defined period, and having the potential to bind a disponee of my land. We shall fail, for there is no such right in rem. We shall succeed only in creating a right in personam (a licence), which cannot bind a disponee.

So a right can be in rem only if it positively matches the demands of one of the limited number of defined templates, and otherwise can be in personam only. To put it another way, rights in rem, as defined by their respective tem-

---

[14] But also, it has been argued, with the position regarding 'persistent rights', which (according to the argument) are not in personam but which, like in personam rights, are exempt from the *numerus clausus*. This argument is considered in § 1.3.2, but rejected. It seems quite clear that all non-in personam rights have to conform to the *numerus clausus* principle, so that for at least these purposes, there is no reason to differentiate 'persistent rights' from (other) rights in rem.

[15] The sole exceptions are where the right would give a claim to something that is against the law (eg the supply of illegal drugs), or otherwise contrary to public policy (eg an unacceptable restriction on trade).

plates, form a finite subset of all possible rights, the remainder being capable of existing in personam only. The idea that rights in rem are limited to this finite subset is known as the '*numerus clausus*' (closed number) principle.

The *numerus clausus* principle operates at two levels. Hitherto, this section has focused on only one: that concerning individuals who might wish to create rights in rem of their own devising, but who (the principle dictates) cannot.[16] The other concerns the design of the law. When we say that, to be in rem, a right must conform to one of the recognised templates, we do not necessarily say that the law should be shy of enlarging the class of templates. But in fact, the *numerus clausus* principle seems to operate at this level too. The class of rights in rem is small. There are problems about how to count them, but one could certainly defend an assertion that the number of rights in rem recognised by English land law barely reaches double figures; over the last couple of centuries, arguably four new rights in rem have been recognised,[17] but certain others have been lost.[18] And the principle may even have received statutory statement, instructing the courts not to develop new rights in rem on their own.[19]

1.2.2 Why the *Numerus Clausus*?

Why does the law operate this *numerus clausus* principle? Essentially, to ensure that rights can operate in rem where, but only where, this does more good than harm.

It seems fair to say that rights in rem always do at least some harm. Say I own some land over which you have a right of way, which is one kind of right in rem. If I transfer the land to John, given your right's in rem status, he will probably be bound by it. This will ordinarily reduce the land's usefulness and attractiveness to him. This in turn should of course be offset by a reduction in the price he will pay me for it, but that may not be a complete answer: your right of way may altogether prevent him from using the land in the particular way he hopes to, and the same may well go for many other potential

[16] The principle is stated in this form in certain decisions, most famously *Keppell v Bailey* (1834) 2 My & K 517, 535–6 (Ch).

[17] The restrictive covenant (Ch 14); the right of pre-emption and the 'mere equity' (Land Registration Act 2002 ss 115, 116(b)); and the 'home right' dealt with in the Family Law Act 1996 s 30 (though the conditions under which the latter will bind a disponee – s 31(10) – are unique to it, and somewhat restrictive).

[18] Until 1925, it was possible to divide up the ownership of land, using a variety of more limited estates which were themselves rights in rem: eg a life estate and an entail. By the Law of Property Act 1925 s 1(1), such interests can no longer exist in their own right (§ 10.1.3). They can, however, still take effect as beneficial interests under trusts. The latter are traditionally conceived as rights in rem, but § 16.8.2 concludes that the combined effect of a number of contemporary rules is substantially to deprive them too of their effect in rem.

[19] Law of Property Act 1925 s 4(1). 'May', because although this appears to be the provision's literal meaning, many refuse to accept it, finding it a little too strong a reading of the principle. See further § 17.3.3.

transferees. Moreover, John will naturally wish to know about your right – or any right you or anyone else may possibly have, even if actually there is none – before agreeing a price and taking the transfer: and meeting this wish will obviously involve the harm of a cost (known as a 'transaction cost'), whether this be large or small, and whether borne by John himself, or me, or indeed the public at large, if the method of discovery is via a state register that is financed from taxation. It may further be possible to say that the idea of inflicting your right on John at all, when he was not party to its creation, is an injury to him.

Given the ill-effects that they thus engender, one might think it right to prohibit all rights in rem other than unrestricted ownership (ie to have a *numerus clausus* consisting only of that one type of right).[20] Then John could acquire the land with the freedom to enjoy it as he might wish, and could do so without needing even to worry about the matter, or without costs arising in allaying that worry. But this would be to overlook the counter-arguments, in favour of allowing rights to operate in rem. Rights in rem have positive value in at least two ways. If I, the owner of the land, wish to give you such a right, allowing me to do so vindicates my wish, so enhancing my liberty. (And so also allowing the generation of wealth: the possibility of giving you such a right in return for payment offers me another way of extracting value from my land.) And the fact that your right is in rem gives you the opportunity to enforce it against John (not merely against me, as where it is in personam) . . . and so, in turn, the possibility of maintaining it *in specie* after the transfer to him, rather than seeing it lost *in specie* and become merely a claim to compensation from me. It is thus the means of preserving your right as such, safe from the vicissitudes that other dealings with the land in question (such as my transfer of it to John) would otherwise introduce. Say the right is, or connects with, your entitlement to your home, such as a right of way without which you cannot even reach your door: the possibility of maintaining it *in specie* – and so, its operation in rem – will be of enormous importance to you.

The *numerus clausus* principle represents the law's effort, or one of the law's efforts, to reach a settlement between such opposing considerations – essentially, by allowing rights to operate in rem where the arguments for their doing so outweigh those against, but forbidding them otherwise. But how is the necessary calculation actually performed?

Given how basic the *numerus clausus* is, one would expect the answer to be clear. In fact, it is speculative and contentious.[21] A number of commentators have sought it in economic terms, hypothesising that rights are admitted to

---

[20] Another way of seeing this scenario would be as one in which ownership cannot be fragmented (as by the generation of other rights in rem from within it), but could exist only in the unitary form known as *dominium*. This idea is explored further in § 10.1.

[21] For a reflection of this, see B Rudden, 'Economic Theory v Property Law: The *Numerus Clausus* Problem' in J Eekelaar and J Bell (eds), *Oxford Essays in Jurisprudence, Third Series* (Oxford, 1987) ch 11.

the *numerus clausus* – permitted to operate in rem – where the (financially expressible) costs of their doing so are less than the costs of their not doing so, and excluded from the *numerus clausus* where the reverse is the case.[22] The efforts in this vein, however, differ strikingly over the kinds of costs involved, and their relative magnitude, and thus, ultimately, over the correctness or otherwise of the hypothesis. It seems fair to regard them as having conspicuously failed to wrap the matter up.

It is more promising to view the calculation as one which should and does take into account all the considerations that might, for any good reason, bear upon the matter.[23] The precise mix of these considerations might very well differ from one right's case to another; that is to say, there is probably more than one set of units in which to perform the calculation, ie reasons for deciding whether a right merits admission to the *numerus clausus*. So these reasons might include relevant economic effects, if any could be satisfactorily identified, but they would certainly not be confined to the latter. They would appropriately include considerations valued rather for their political sake, such as the liberty of an owner such as me to do as he likes with his property, and, conversely, the liberty of a disponee such as John to do as he in turn likes with it.

A particularly important and rewarding prism through which to think about such liberties may be, certainly ought to be, the republican one. As explained in § 1.1.2, republicanism asks us to design our institutions – such as 'property', ie the class of rights in rem – so as best to guard against the possibility of some people exercising arbitrary domination over others. If your right of way were in rem, enabling you to insist on it against John, you would have the means to exercise arbitrary domination over him, for your right would permit you to act in your own interests to the suppression of his.[24] To protect John and other disponees from the possibility of arbitrary domination of this kind, we might therefore incline to deny in rem status to rights such as yours. But of course this solution would come at the price of allowing

---

[22] See especially R Epstein, 'Notice and Freedom of Contract in the Law of Servitudes' (1981–2) 55 *S Cal LR* 1353; T Merrill and H Smith, 'Optimal Standardization in the Law of Property: The *Numerus Clausus* Principle' (2000) 110 *Yale LJ* 1; H Hansmann and R Kraakman, 'Property, Contract and Verification: The *Numerus Clausus* Problem and the Divisibility of Rights' (2002) 31 *JLS* S373.

[23] This is the vision proposed by, especially, J Harris, 'Reason or Mumbo Jumbo: The Common Law's Approach to Property' (Maccabaean Lecture in Jurisprudence) (2002) 117 *Proceedings of the British Academy* 445, 470–4; B Edgeworth, 'The *Numerus Clausus* Principle in Contemporary Australian Property Law' (2006) 32 *Monash U LR* 387; N Davidson, 'Standardization and Pluralism in Property Law' (2008) 61 *Vanderbilt LR* 1597; J Singer, 'Democratic Estates: Property Law in a Free and Democratic Society' (2009) 94 *Cornell L Rev* 1009; A Dorfman, 'Property and Collective Undertaking: the Principle of *Numerus Clausus*' (2011) 61 *U Toronto LJ* 467.

[24] We do not trouble so much over the fact that, before the transfer to John, you could exercise such domination over me. That is because I, in granting you the right in the first place, consent to the relationship between us that it creates. Though *cf* H Dagan, 'The Craft of Property' (2003) 91 *Cal LR* 1517, 1565–71.

John to wield arbitrary domination over *you*, and to prevent that, we find ourselves inclining to accept your right as in rem after all. To address this conundrum, it seems we need to decide whether it is more important to protect John's interest or yours. We might readily prefer John's ownership where your right is to, for example, turn cartwheels over his land (appealing though the contrary thought may be); but we might very well lean the other way in at least some cases where what is at stake is your home. The task of prioritising competing interests in this way is one of land law's more important and challenging preoccupations, and receives further attention in Chapter 10. The point for the moment is that the *numerus clausus* principle, policing the ability of rights to bind disponees or otherwise, is one of the tools (though not the only one) by which it is performed.

In each chapter dealing with a particular right in rem later in the book, we shall have to think in this sort of way about the case for accepting it as such.

1.2.3 The Rights

The chapters in Part 3 of this book consider a number of the rights in rem that can exist over land in English law, ie are members of the *numerus clausus*, namely:[25]

—— Ownership (Chapter 10): the grandest of all rights. Everyone has a ready intuitive sense of its import, but there is much to be said about its exact significance and place in English land law, and also by way of challenge to that intuitive sense.

—— Leases (Chapter 11): rights allowing one person (or a group) to have exclusive possession of land belonging to another, for a defined period. If say you rent a house, or shop or field from me for 10 years, you will probably do so by way of a lease.

—— Mortgages (Chapter 12): rights securing obligations, principally debts. If I owe you money, and grant you a mortgage over my land, you thereby acquire the right to recoup the outstanding debt by seizing my land and selling it.

—— Easements (Chapter 13): rights that one piece of land be used in a certain way, for the benefit of another piece of land. An example is a right

---

[25] Others are profits (rights allowing one person to enter and take certain things – eg coal, timber, game – from land owned by another); rentcharges (rights allowing someone to own land in return for periodical payments to someone else, but since the Rentcharges Act 1977 usable only in rather exiguous circumstances); rights of entry (rights connected with leases and rentcharges, allowing the land to be taken from its tenant or owner respectively if the required rent is not paid); estate contracts (rights arising where the parties intend to create, or purport to have created, some other right, but have not yet done so: see § 6.2); options and rights of pre-emption (rights to demand a right under certain circumstances); 'mere equities' (rights to rescind a transaction, if it is vitiated by eg misrepresentation); and 'home rights' (occupation rights arising by virtue of a family relationship).

of way, ie a right allowing the owner of one piece of land to access it by crossing another that adjoins it.

—— Restrictive covenants (Chapter 14): a further class of rights that one piece of land be used in a certain way, for the benefit of another piece of land: for instance, a right that you have, as owner of your house, requiring me not to build on my garden, lest this interrupt your view. Restrictive covenants and easements evidently have similarities; their relationship is considered in § 14.6.

—— Rights under trusts (Chapters 15 and 16): rights entitling their owners ('beneficiaries') to the benefit of land nominally held by others ('trustees'), who themselves are not allowed to derive benefit from it. This distinguishes trust rights from the other rights in rem short of ownership itself, for in the case of these other rights the owner of the land clearly retains, for his own benefit, all remaining rights in it. The point underlying this is in fact that the beneficiaries can be said to collectively enjoy the very ownership of the land. So trusts can be used to divide the ownership between two or more people. This is perhaps their principal importance.

—— Licences coupled with an interest (§ 17.4): rights allowing someone to enter the land of another so as to gain access to some asset that he owns and that is located there. But § 17.4.3 queries whether this class of right exists as a distinct species, or whether it is better understood as a type of easement.

Additionally, Chapter 17 deals with licences in general, which are the rights in personam that may exist in respect of land thanks to its owner's consent. (Others again may exist without the owner's consent, but this book does not extend so far.) Given what was said about the *numerus clausus* principle in § 1.2.1, it will be appreciated that such rights – unlike the specific rights in rem – can have any content their parties wish. It is, however, always possible that licences with a particular type of content will, on account of evolving social perceptions of that content, come to be seen as sufficiently valuable to merit recognition as in rem (ie be added to the *numerus clausus*), notwithstanding the harm that this would entail. In § 17.3.3, we shall see how the courts have experimented with giving in rem status to a certain class of licence in this way, though without producing an enduring change in the law to that effect.

1.3 'Persistent Rights'

An argument has been made that, properly speaking, the rights which this book treats as rights in rem fall into two separate categories: rights in rem proper, and a less powerful and less tightly controlled kind labelled 'persistent rights'. We shall need to examine the features which are claimed to distinguish two categories one from another. This examination will follow in § 1.3.2.

There is a preliminary issue, however. The argument claims that the distinction between rights in rem proper and persistent rights tracks another distinction, that between 'common law' and 'equitable' rights; maintaining that whilst common law rights can be in rem, equitable rights can only be persistent. So we must begin by understanding this latter distinction.

1.3.1 Common Law and Equity

English law, together with other legal systems derived from it, has a peculiarity: it comes in two varieties, 'common law' – alternatively called simply 'law' – and 'equity'.[26]

Common law is the set of rules developed by the courts of King's (or Queen's) Bench, Exchequer and Common Pleas, and equity is the different set of rules developed by the court of Chancery, during the period when these all existed as separate courts: the late middle ages to the end of the 19th century.[27] The different courts were merged by the Judicature Acts 1873–5, but the rules for which they were historically responsible continue to be identifiable by their distinct origins.

Equity operates as a supplement to the common law. That is, it takes the common law's answer to a given situation, and adjusts that answer if it seems inappropriate. So say the common law courts had a rule saying 'In situation *ABC* you must do *X*'. If the Chancery agreed, it added nothing, and the rule operated without complication. But if the Chancery disagreed, it ruled 'In situ-

---

[26] There are two possible sources of confusion here. First, the word 'law' is also used – as in the phrase 'English law' at the start of the sentence in the text – to refer to the set of rules comprising *both* common law *and* equity: ie the entirety of English jurisprudence. Indeed, it is probably used more often in this sense than in contrast to equity. Second, 'common law' is also contrasted with 'statutory' law. In this sense, 'common law' means the law made by the judges in their decisions, while 'statutory' law is that enacted by Parliament. This latter meaning of 'common law' includes both common law, in the sense used in the text, and equity. (Conversely, both law and equity, as explored in the text, contain both judge-made and statutory rules.) Despite the manifest scope for confusion, it is usually clear from the context which meaning a writer intends.

[27] For the history, see eg A Simpson, *A History of the Land Law* (2nd edn, Oxford, 1986) ch 8.

ation *ABC*, you must *not* do *X*: instead you must do *Y*'. The Chancery did not pretend that the common law required anything but *X*, but it imposed its own requirement of *Y*. In concrete terms, if your adversary sought to enlist the help of the common law courts to make you do *X* – as was his right, in their eyes – you could respond by having the Chancery order him not to, and to accept *Y* instead. The conflict between the two rules would have been intolerable unless one took priority over the other. In fact, it was the Chancery's rules that had priority:[28] so the law's overall bottom line was that you had indeed to do *Y*. And when the courts themselves were merged, that remained the case.

Sometimes, equity's answer will flatly contradict the common law's, with the result that the latter will drop out of the picture altogether, and be forgotten about. For example, say you and I make what looks like a contract, but you mislead me about some relevant issue, though you do so innocently. The common law regards the contract as nonetheless valid, but equity regards it as invalid. Because the two answers straightforwardly contradict one another, there is no reason to recall the common law's: for the bottom line, we can – and do – generally refer simply to equity's. In the land law context, this is the case with the type of right known as a restrictive covenant, explained in Chapter 14. A restrictive covenant arises in circumstances which the common law regards as requiring no response, but equity treats as meriting the imposition of an obligation. Here, then, equity is generally seen as overriding the common law's position, the latter being thenceforth forgotten or ignored.

But sometimes the relationship between the legal and equitable answers is less straightforward, and then it will be right to continue to be aware of and to speak of both. So if, again, you and I have a contract, and you break it, I can certainly sue you for damages. That is the common law's rule. There is a different equitable rule. It does not however say that I cannot have damages. Instead, it allows me, in certain cases, to claim an injunction or an order for specific performance against you as an alternative: something that the common law does not.

The classic instance of this latter kind is the trust. We shall explore the idea of a trust in greater depth in Chapters 15 and 16. For present purposes, the point is that if we say 'I hold this property on trust for you', we are saying that the common law regards me as owning the property, while equity obliges me to use it not for my benefit but for yours.[29] At first sight, the fact that I cannot use the property for my own benefit seems to leave me very far from owning it. Nonetheless, we do not simply omit all reference to the common law position, and say that you own the property, full stop. There are certain

---

[28] This rule is sometimes ascribed to the Judicature Acts 1873–5, but it is much earlier. King James I's ruling in favour of equity in connection with *The Earl of Oxford's Case* (1615) 1 Ch Rep 1 (Ch) reflects it, but again did not create it. In truth, though its universal acceptance took some time, it is a function of the essential relationship between common law and equity: equity cannot operate as a supplement to the common law without it.

[29] For further discussion of the significance of trusts being equitable concepts, see S Gardner, *An Introduction to the Law of Trusts* (3rd edn, Oxford, 2011) 18–25.

respects in which (equity agrees) the property does and should continue to rest in my hands. For example, I have to keep the property so as to look after and manage it; and if the property is to be sold to someone else, only I – not you – can make a valid transfer of it. Essentially, it is not that the ownership rights are simply taken away from me; rather, I continue to have them, *but must use them only for your benefit.*

In cases of this latter kind, then, it can be useful and indeed important to speak of the respective common law and equitable positions, though only to the extent needed to explain matters properly. As well as to capture the idea of a trust, for example, such talk is needed to explain the rules regarding the conferral of rights. As the law stands, if I am to confer a right – say, an easement – on you so that both equity and the common law will recognise it, I must usually use a deed; while equity alone will recognise me as having done so also if I use only writing. (These rules are discussed in detail in Chapters 5 and 6.) So if I use a deed, you acquire a 'legal easement'; but if I use only writing, you acquire an 'equitable easement'. Given equity's claim to the last word, we might think of saying simply that you acquire an easement in both cases . . . except that traditionally, the two kinds of easement have behaved somewhat differently as regards their effect on a subsequent disponee of the land to which they relate,[30] and although the differences have now been reduced by the registration rules, some still remain, at any rate for the time being.[31] To this extent, then, it remains useful to make explicit reference to 'common law' and 'equity'.[32]

1.3.2 Equitable Rights as 'Persistent'

As noted above, it has been argued[33] that there is a further reason for attending to the provenance of a right in the common law or in equity: that whilst

[30] For example: historically, a legal right (eg a legal easement) normally bound a disponee without further ado, but an equitable right (eg an equitable easement) bound a disponee unless he was a *bona fide* purchaser of the land without notice of the right.

[31] Nowadays, as detailed in Ch 3, both legal and equitable rights in rem can normally be registered so as to bind a disponee, and under certain circumstances (when they qualify as 'overriding interests') will bind a disponee despite not being registered . . . but those circumstances can vary between legal and equitable rights. For example, while a legal easement can sometimes operate as an overriding interest in its own right, an equitable easement can do so only in the (rather unlikely) event that its holder occupies the land over which it obtains: § 13.3.

[32] The matters discussed in the text are details in a much larger picture, the question at stake being whether (or to what extent) the law's various 'common law' and 'equity' rules have been, or should be, 'fused'. The literature is voluminous. See perhaps especially A Burrows, 'We Do This at Common Law but That in Equity' (2002) 22 *OJLS* 1; S Degeling and J Edelman (eds), *Equity in Commercial Law* (Pyrmont NSW, 2005).

[33] See principally B McFarlane, *The Structure of Property Law* (Oxford, 2008) 21–39; B McFarlane and R Stevens, 'The Nature of Equitable Property' (2010) 4 *Journal of Equity* 1; B McFarlane, 'The *Numerus Clausus* Principle and Covenants Relating to Land' in S Bright (ed), *Modern Studies in Property Law, Volume 6* (Oxford, 2011) ch 15. For further discussion, see S Gardner, ' "Persistent Rights" Appraised' (forthcoming).

common law rights can be rights in rem proper, equitable rights can only be 'persistent', or, as it is alternatively put, 'rights against rights'.[34]

According to the argument, persistent rights are capable, like rights in rem proper, of binding disponees of the property in question (and do so, likewise, under whatever circumstances the law stipulates, as explained in § 1.1.2). Hence the label 'persistent'. But rights in rem proper have a further character-istic: they are capable of binding not merely disponees, but all other outsid-ers, third parties, too. 'Persistent' rights differ in *not* being capable of binding non-disponee third parties in this way.

To illustrate: say I give you a *lease* over my house. A lease will usually be a common law right. You can enforce it, not only against me, but against two other kinds of people. If I transfer the house to John – a disponee – you may be able to enforce your right against him. If, rather, some arsonists – not dis-ponees – burn the house down, you will be able to enforce your right against them, suing them for their wrong. Your ability to enforce your right against third parties in both these ways, against both disponees and non-disponees, earns it the title of a right in rem.

In contrast, however, say now that I hold land *on trust* for you, meaning that you have an equitable right. If I transfer the land to John,[35] once again your right may bind John. But if some arsonists burn the house down, you cannot enforce against them. Only I can do that, though if I do so it will be on your behalf (so the damages I recover will go to you), and indeed you can require me to do so. Because your right is enforceable only against a disponee (such as John), and not this time against a third party of any other descrip-tion (such as the arsonists), the argument denies it the title of a right in rem. More positively, because you can enforce your right only against a disponee – that is, only against someone who acquires a right in the land by way of derivation from my right (for example, who succeeds me as owner) – it is a 'right against a right'. The kinds of third parties against whom you cannot enforce your right, such as the arsonists, do not themselves acquire a right deriving from mine (indeed, a right of any kind), so your 'right *against a right*' cannot affect them.

As well as asserting this distinction between the two kinds of rights in terms of their range of enforceability, the argument attaches a particular cor-ollary to it. It maintains that, whilst rights in rem can exist only in so far as they are recognised within the *numerus clausus*, this is not the case for persis-tent rights. That is to say, persistent rights, like rights in personam, are exempt

---

[34] Authoritative statements can be found to the effect that (at any rate) trust rights are in rem, or proprietary (see eg *Tinsley v Milligan* [1994] 1 AC 340, 371 (HL); *Westdeutsche Landesbank Girozentrale v Islington London Borough Council* [1996] AC 669, 705 (HL); *Foskett v McKeown* [2001] 1 AC 102, 108, 127 (HL)). These might be thought immediately conclusive against the argument, but that would be too hasty a conclusion, for they show no sign of having considered the alternative that the argument proposes.

[35] More precisely, if I do so in circumstances such that your right does not detach from it, as is sometimes the case with trust rights: see §§ 16.4–16.8.

from the *numerus clausus*, and so can be given any content (short of illegality) that their creators choose.

In short, the argument thus makes two assertions about equitable rights that require to be tested. One is that these rights cannot be enforced against non-disponee third parties in the way that common law rights can. The other is that these rights are exempt from the *numerus clausus*.

The first assertion is certainly not without foundation, but nor is it completely solid. In support of it is a set of old rules whereby holders of equitable rights could not access the kinds of remedies (mainly, common law damages) that would have allowed them to enforce these rights against non-disponee third parties such as arsonists.[36] More positively, but perhaps ultimately for the same reason, there is authority to the effect that, as noted above, your trust right does not entitle you to sue non-disponee third parties such as arsonists: that only I, the trustee, can do that.[37] On the other hand, this is not the whole story. The old rules have been challenged and to a considerable extent abandoned, giving holders of equitable rights access to the relevant remedies after all.[38] Where enforcing an equitable right against a non-disponee third party does not require access to such remedies anyway, it is certainly possible.[39] And if I, your trustee, do sue the arsonists, the damages I recover will reflect your, not merely my, losses.[40] So, for example, if you in fact used the house for your business, and its destruction meant not merely the loss of the building itself but also a loss of profits, I will recover the latter as well as the former, despite the impossibility of saying that I suffered it myself. It is hard to see why that should be so, unless the law does, after all, regard the arsonists as owing duties to you; or, to put it the other way round, unless it regards your right as in essence (in some core sense) enforceable against persons such as the arsonists.

The second assertion, that equitable rights are exempt from the *numerus clausus*, is contrary to authority.[41] It is also implausible as a matter of princi-

---

[36] See S Gardner, 'Equity, Estate Contracts and the Judicature Acts: *Walsh v Lonsdale* Revisited' (1987) 7 *OJLS* 60, 81–7. And see further § 6.2.3.

[37] For rulings to this effect in analogous cases see *MCC Proceeds Inc v Lehman Bros International (Europe)* [1998] 4 All ER 675 (CA); *Leigh and Sillavan Ltd v Aliakmon Shipping Co Ltd, The Aliakmon* [1986] AC 785, 812 (HL).

[38] See Gardner (n 36) 87–91. And see further § 6.2.3. Notice too the recent abandonment of some old rules about the availability of certain remedies, limiting them to holders of common law interests: see eg *Manchester Airport plc v Dutton* [2000] QB 133 (CA); *Mayor of London v Hall* [2011] 1 WLR 504 (CA) (though cf *Hunter v Canary Wharf Ltd* [1997] AC 655 (HL)).

[39] *Re Nisbet and Potts' Contract* [1905] 1 Ch 391 (Ch D), affirmed [1906] 1 Ch 386 (CA). This held that an equitable right known as a 'restrictive covenant' (see Ch 14) was enforceable against a squatter on the relevant land, despite his being a non-disponee. On the facts, this outcome required no access to common law remedies.

[40] *Pan Atlantic Insurance Co Ltd v Pine Top Insurance Co Ltd* [1988] 2 Lloyd's Rep 505 (QBD), affirmed [1989] 1 Lloyd's Rep 568 (CA); *Chappell v Somers & Blake* [2004] Ch 19 (Ch D); *Shell UK Ltd v Total UK Ltd* [2011] QB 86 (CA).

[41] See *Keppell v Bailey* (1834) 2 My & K 517 (Ch) and *Haywood v Brunswick Permanent Benefit Building Society* (1881) 8 QBD 403 (CA), in both of which judges declared themselves unable, or at any rate unwilling, to allow the parties to create new types of equitable right. In other words,

ple. As § 1.2.2 shows, the *numerus clausus* principle is treated by all who have written about it as aimed – for whatever reason, whether for better or for worse, and whether or not inter alia – at controlling the impact of rights on disponees. Since everyone agrees that equitable rights, whether we think of them as in rem or 'persistent', can certainly be enforced against disponees, this vision of the *numerus clausus* principle clearly requires their subjection to it. (It is, however, fair to make one counter-point. There may be a difficulty in seeing that, specifically, trust rights do in fact conform to the *numerus clausus* principle; and if they do not, this provides evidence that at least they, and perhaps other equitable rights too, are exempt from it. This problem has however received attention, and seems to have been dispelled, along the lines that the supposed difficulty is no more than an illusion, closer examination revealing that trust rights do conform to the principle after all.[42])

In short, the suggestion that equitable rights cannot be enforced against non-disponee third parties, such as the arsonists in our example, has some basis, though not a wholly secure one; while the suggestion that such rights are (therefore) exempt from the *numerus clausus* seems incorrect. So for the purposes of this book – which attends to the in rem status of different rights more or less entirely in terms of their effectiveness against disponees, and so their place within the *numerus clausus* – there is no very good reason to split equitable rights off into such a separate category as 'persistent rights'. They will therefore be generally treated, along with common law rights, as rights in rem.

1.4 Why Focus on Rights in Rem in Land?

Why should we concern ourselves, as this book invites us to, with those rights that exist in respect of land, and are recognised as in rem (or as persistent) by English law?

if equitable rights are persistent as opposed to in rem, they are nevertheless subject to some form of *numerus clausus*, rather than for the parties to generate as they please.

[42] See R Nolan, 'Equitable Property' (2006) 122 *LQR* 232; Gardner, *An Introduction to the Law of Trusts* (n 29) 214–15. The apparent difficulty arises from the fact that trust rights may vary widely in their content (see further § 16.1) . . . which rights in rem cannot, since their very acceptance into the *numerus clausus* depends on a judgement that, *with their particular content*, they do more good than harm (§ 1.2.2). The apparent difficulty is dispelled by the reflection that trust rights' impact on a disponee is very limited. The disponee must recognise that the property in question is trust property and probably at some fairly low level look after it, but nothing more. Only this much of the trust right is therefore in rem. Such further obligations as the trust may demand (and it usually does; this is where trusts' variety becomes visible) do not bind the disponee; he must simply transfer the land to a proper trustee (whether the original trustee or one newly appointed for this purpose), who will then perform them. These further obligations are thus only in personam.

To begin with the focus on *land*. From as long ago as we can see, English law's rules regarding land have been different from its rules regarding other entities. (A similar observation can probably be made about the rules of other legal systems.) Land is not unique in this: there are myriad differentiations between the rules relating to other classes of entity too. Such differentiations occur wherever the class of entity in question has some particular quality requiring regulation of human behaviour regarding it. Thus, for example, there are special rules detailing how we can or must behave towards animals, reflecting inter alia the fact that, as animate creatures, we should be concerned with their welfare, in a way that we are not in the case of inanimates; and, for another example, there are special rules concerning firearms, reflecting their unusual potential for harmful use. So when we observe that land has in fact been made the subject of distinctive rules, we should be able to ascribe their distinctiveness to particular distinctive qualities that land possesses. What are these qualities?

Most basically, land is uniquely vital to sustaining animal, including human, life. Such life is ultimately powered by the consumption of plants, and most plant life is in turn supported by nutrients extracted from the soil, ie land. Given the make-up of the planet, things could hardly have evolved otherwise. Also vital to plants and animals is a supply of suitable water, and by far the most accessible sources of water as principally needed (both directly and indirectly) by humans are those to be found on or in the ground, ie land.[43] So a legal system centred (as legal systems always are) on human fulfilment can hardly not seek to ensure that the land within its jurisdiction delivers these goods, and to address the conflicts to which securing them may well give rise. At not much less basic a level, and thus also attracting dedicated rules, land is the unique resource from which we extract most of our raw materials (timber, stone, clay, metals, oil), and upon which, given gravity, we must live our lives: make our homes, do our jobs, run, dance, play, and so on. Much else follows: land is thus indirectly essential to economic activity and 'standard of living' (and via these, to the maximisation of human happiness), and also to power. Land is also special in perhaps less obvious ways. In particular, it is more or less indestructible, making it a basis for long-term or indefinite arrangements; and it remains for practical purposes in one place, which can be helpfully reassuring (rights connected with a piece of land are much less prone to frustration by its disappearance than those connected with other assets: a point vital to the supply of finance via mortgage arrangements). The latter feature in turn also means that any given plot of land has a fixed spatial relationship with any other plot, creating both opportunities (for joint exploitation) and problems (of nuisance) to which the law does well to react.

---

[43] On the rules developed around this, see J Getzler, *A History of Water Rights at Common Law* (Oxford, 2004).

Now the interest in *rights in rem*. A right relating to land is essentially a mechanism for allowing humans to exploit that land in some way (such as to source food, water or other raw materials, or to provide a place to live, work, run, dance, play, etc). And a right in rem relating to land is such a mechanism, with the distinctive quality of remaining in force while other rights relating to the same land are reconfigured (ie of 'affecting disponees' of the land). Given the essential nature of many of the uses to which land can be put, it is unsurprising that rights with this quality should be wanted, and should be thought valuable enough to merit acceptance despite the damage it means they entail – this, as explained in § 1.2.2, being the condition for a right's ability to operate in rem. Rights in rem in land thus represent some of our most valued ways of facilitating the exploitation of our most valued resource. It is thus understandable that they should attract substantial attention. (§ 2.6 explains that relevant human rights have similar importance, and so deserve our attention too.)

Human Rights

2.1 Human Rights in Land

2.1.1 The Focus

We come now to review the human rights relevant to land law. We could draw on various enunciations of such rights.[1] However, this chapter will focus on the rights that arise under the European Convention on Human Rights (ECHR). For British citizens and British courts, these are the most directly accessible human rights. The rights conferred in the ECHR were brought into this country's law by the Human Rights Act 1998. This means that there are now two mechanisms for invoking them here. In the first instance, they can be relied upon directly in the national courts via various provisions of the 1998 Act. Beyond this, they can be relied upon in front of the European Court of Human Rights in Strasbourg.[2]

The following section considers the place of human rights in land law. Section 2.2 reviews the mechanics of relying on them. Sections 2.3 and 2.4 examine the two rights that will most often be invoked in this context: Article 1 of the First Protocol to the ECHR (the right to peaceful enjoyment of one's possessions, or property), and ECHR Article 8 (the right to respect for private and family life, home and correspondence).

---

[1] For example the Universal Declaration of Human Rights Arts 10 and 17, and the International Covenant on Civil and Political Rights Art 17.

[2] The interaction between Strasbourg case-law and domestic case-law is a highly complex area, which is not the subject of this book. In this section we will look only briefly at the different ways in which the Human Rights Act 1998 allows human rights questions to arise in land law cases. For a more comprehensive discussion it would be wise to consult specialist works on the matter.

2.1.2 A 'Reservoir of Entitlement'

Say that you and I are involved in a dispute because you are my tenant and I wish to evict you. In practical terms, we will each care about human rights to the extent that they help us to forward our respective positions. They can do so in the sense that they form a 'reservoir of entitlement',[3] a further set of claims to which you can have recourse beyond the protection given by domestic law.[4] So if you can invoke your human rights in order to defeat my attempt to evict you, even though you would have no defence in domestic law, you are drawing on this 'reservoir of entitlement'. Similarly if I am able to evict you on the basis of my human rights, when I would not be able so to do relying purely on my domestic entitlements.

The 'reservoir of entitlement' idea thus means that human rights can be relied upon to disallow claims that would succeed under domestic law, or to allow claims that under domestic law would fail. There are in fact two elements to the idea. It supposes, of course, that human rights go beyond domestic law in terms of the entitlements they provide. But it also (pre-)supposes that such rights are 'justiciable', ie capable of being invoked, in a court, at all. Section 2.2 will look at the latter element, while §§ 2.3 and 2.4 will deal with the former.

2.2 Justiciability

In addressing the question whether human rights can be invoked in a court, we must distinguish between two different courts: the European Court of Human Rights, in Strasbourg, and the domestic courts of England and Wales. This is because the rules governing their invocation differ between the two. We shall begin with the Strasbourg court.

---

[3] This term was first coined by Wilson LJ in *Pirabakaran v Patel* [2006] 1 WLR 3112, [41] (CA). He described this as a reservoir 'upon which the occupier of a home can draw in order to resist an order for possession when domestic law leaves him defenceless'. The idea is taken up by A Goymour, 'Proprietary Claims and Human Rights – A "Reservoir of Entitlement"?' [2006] *CLJ* 696.

[4] 'Domestic law' is used here to describe the law apart from human rights, although the term is technically inaccurate as the Human Rights Act 1998 makes ECHR rights part of domestic law.

2.2.1 In the European Court of Human Rights

The Strasbourg jurisprudence[5] regarding the invocation of ECHR rights distinguishes between 'vertical' and 'horizontal' disputes. A 'vertical' dispute is one where you seek to invoke your ECHR rights against the acts or omissions of the state (which includes public authorities); while a 'horizontal' dispute is one where you seek to invoke them against the acts or omissions of another private party (generally an ordinary person, or a private company). The Strasbourg court regards itself as able to implement the ECHR only vertically, ie against the state.[6]

This apparently simple account would be misleading, however. It is in fact possible for a dispute to be both horizontal and vertical at the same time. The question then is, which characterisation will the court adopt? The answer is, unfortunately, murky.

To understand the issue, consider a case where you are my tenant and I am trying to evict you – in your contention, in violation of your ECHR rights. Given the account so far, one might suppose that if I am, say, a local authority, and so count as part of the state of the UK,[7] our case will be a 'vertical' dispute, which the Strasbourg court will thus entertain. But that if I am a private party, it is a 'horizontal' dispute, which the court will not entertain.

There is certainly no doubt that our dispute is vertical in the situation where I count as part of the state. We shall refer to this kind of scenario as the 'straightforward' vertical case. Your claim in respect of my treatment of you is plainly against the UK.

Take now the situation where I am your private-sector landlord. You are seeking to invoke your human right against the acts or omissions of a private party, so your case is a horizontal one. *But it may simultaneously be vertical*, ie against the state, too: on the ground that you are also complaining against the acts or omissions of the state, in maintaining a state of domestic law in which I can behave as I (domestically legally) have towards you, thereby violating your human rights. Certainly, our original, domestic, battle – in which I, a

---

[5] See A Goymour 'Property and Housing' in D Hoffman (ed), *The Impact of the Human Rights Act on Private Law* (Cambridge, 2011) ch 12, 253–8.

[6] *Marckx v Belgium* (1979) 2 EHRR 330, [20] (ECtHR); *Niemietz v Germany* (1993) 16 EHRR 97, [31] (ECtHR). This is because the ECHR is an international treaty, and the Strasbourg court is an organ established under it, with the role of adjudicating compliance or otherwise with it by the states which are party to it.

[7] Note the crucial step, embedded here, of regarding public agencies beyond central government, such as local authorities, as 'part of the state', so that the latter (eg the UK) is responsible for their activities. This is not self-evidently right; certainly, it involves 'piercing' certain domestic 'veils', which may domestically be rather important. For example, a state may – generally will – *distinguish between* its central government and other (more or less) 'public' entities such as the country's courts, local authorities and utility corporations, and indeed do so very sharply, often as required by a constitutional imperative such as the separation of powers, or federalism/localism/subsidiarity. The idea that all such entities 'count as' the state for present purposes should certainly be recognised as a tendentious one.

private landlord, evict you – was a horizontal one. In raising a human rights challenge against my ability to evict you, however, you can be seen as *vertically* complaining of the UK's laws that produce that ability.

In other words, 'vertical' and 'horizontal' are not mutually exclusive categories. A case that is horizontal in the sense that it is a domestic law dispute between private parties is *also* vertical in the sense that it involves a complaint under the ECHR against the law of the state concerned. To put it another way, to say that a case is horizontal does not mean that it is not vertical; on the contrary, it is, in the sense just explained; it means rather that it is horizontal *as well*, in the sense of originating in a domestic law dispute between two private parties.

Given this, we could decide no longer to make reference to the horizontal aspect at all. We could say that, since Strasbourg is concerned only with verticality, but verticality is always present, whatever the domestic origins of the dispute, there is no more to be said. This would be a justifiable stance, but it is a less than completely helpful one. It is useful to be able to distinguish cases with a horizontal dimension from those without, ie from those where your complaint is straightforwardly against a public body. This is so for two reasons.

One is this. Say your human rights complaint in the non-straightforward type of case is upheld – ie it is held that the UK domestic law allowing me to evict you violates your ECHR rights. The implication of this is that the ECHR does in practice impinge on the domestic rules governing a basically private, inter-personal issue, ie 'operate horizontally'. This will be an important thing to know, certainly for our purpose of discovering the part ECHR rights play in English land law ... whether they provide the kind of 'reservoir of entitlement' sketched in § 2.1.2. For this reason, this book does distinguish this type of case, and uses the label 'horizontal' in reference to it.[8]

The other reason for distinguishing this type of case from a 'straightforward' vertical dispute is that, despite its unmistakable vertical dimension, the Strasbourg court itself approaches it differently. Certainly, the court will often recognise a case of this type as one against a state, in the way described above, and address it accordingly.[9] *But not always.* The court perceives some cases of this kind as 'purely private', and on that basis refuses to get involved in them.[10] The key tool it seems to have used for doing so has been the idea of

---

[8] As does Goymour (n 5) 252 and generally.

[9] eg *James v United Kingdom* (1986) 8 EHRR 123 (ECtHR); *Pye v United Kingdom* (2008) 46 EHRR 45 (ECtHR).

[10] See eg *H v United Kingdom* (1983) 33 DR (ECtHR); *Bramelid and Malmström v Sweden* (1985) 5 EHRR 249 (ECommHR); *A v United Kingdom* (1986) 10 EHRR CD149 (ECommHR). Goymour (n 5) 256 implies that a state will always be responsible for the condition of its statute law, only common law issues being treated as (sometimes) purely private; but the *H* and *Bramelid* decisions treated statutory issues this way too, and the *A* decision involved a mix of common law and statute, though it is fair to say that the reasoning appears to focus principally on the former.

'positive obligation': the state is responsible for the results thrown up by its domestic rules only if it has a 'positive obligation' to ensure different (more ECHR-compliant) results.[11] At any rate in our area,[12] however, it has declined to intimate when (let alone why) we should, and should not, detect such a 'positive obligation'.[13] This is of course a disappointing thing to have to report of a body charged with implementing an instrument, one of whose core values purports to be the Rule of Law. Putting the matter more positively, however, it thus appears that the court will sometimes, invoking the 'positive obligation' idea, require compliance with the ECHR in respect of otherwise purely private cases. In other words – and this is what matters for our present purpose – ECHR rights have some, albeit unpredictable, horizontal effect at the Strasbourg level.

2.2.2 In the Courts of England and Wales

Now let us consider the position regarding the invocation of ECHR rights in the English and Welsh domestic courts.[14] It is rather different. It is controlled by the Human Rights Act 1998. Essentially, the Act requires the courts to apply the ECHR ... but allows them to do so only in the particular ways that it identifies in section 3 (interpreting legislation in such a way as to leave it compliant with the ECHR); section 4 (declaring legislation that cannot be so interpreted incompatible with the ECHR); and section 6 (insisting on ECHR-compliant behaviour from public authorities, including courts).

The position is simple where our dispute is a vertical one in the straightforward sense. So where, for example, I am your public-sector landlord and I am seeking (in conformity with the domestic rules) to evict you, this set of rules certainly allows you to invoke your ECHR rights against me.[15] I am a public

---

[11] See eg *A v United Kingdom* (1988) 10 EHRR CD149 (ECommHR).

[12] See more generally A Mowbray, *The Development of Positive Obligations under the ECHR by the European Court of Human Rights* (Oxford, 2004).

[13] In *A v United Kingdom* (1986) 10 EHRR CD149, 155 (ECommHR), for example, one finds: 'It is not necessary for the purposes of the present decision to attempt an exhaustive description of the circumstances in which such an obligation may arise.' In this case, moreover, the sorts of points that might enter into a 'positive obligation' reckoning seem – interestingly – to have been handled not as affecting justiciability at all, but as the basis of a conclusion that the claimant's rights were not violated as a matter of substance. (The rights in question were those protected under ECHR First Protocol Art 1, and under Art 8. As to the former, there was said to be no interference; as to the latter, a proportionate interference.)

[14] See Goymour (n 5) 258–73; A Young, 'Mapping Horizontal Effect' in *ibid* ch 2.

[15] This is now clear from *Pinnock v Manchester City Council* [2011] 2 AC 104 (SC) and *Hounslow London Borough Council v Powell* [2011] 2 AC 186 (SC), but the previous law made it doubtful. See *Harrow London Borough Council v Qazi* [2004] 1 AC 983 (HL); *Kay v Lambeth London Borough Council; Leeds City Council v Price* [2006] 2 AC 465 (HL); *Doherty v Birmingham CC* [2009] 1 AC 367 (HL). These older cases diverged from the position in the text via a complex set of propositions, some addressed to the issue under discussion (ie the invocability of the ECHR in domestic proceedings), others to the substantive significance of the ECHR itself (especially Art 8, the right to one's home). They were at odds with the Strasbourg decisions *Connors v*

authority, and the court is required by section 6 to insist that I, likewise on account of section 6, respect your ECHR rights; if any statutory rule appears positively to prevent me from doing so (which will probably be quite rare: usually I will have had a choice whether to evict you or not), the court must either re-interpret it so that it does not, under section 3, or else declare it incompatible with the ECHR, under section 4.

The question is more complicated in the horizontal case, ie where I am a private party. We do not in this context need to concern ourselves with Strasbourg's question of 'positive obligation'. Instead, however, we have to discover the import of the Human Rights Act 1998 – whose treatment of the issue is however also, in its different way, not altogether easy to discern.

Matters are reasonably straightforward if I am asking the court to exercise a discretion in my favour. Section 6 of the 1998 Act requires the court, as itself a public authority, to exercise its discretion in a way that respects your ECHR rights. This will be the case, for example, where you and I are co-owners of our house, and we disagree whether it should be sold, and approach the court to decide, in its discretion.[16]

Likewise if, on the other hand, I am asking the court to assist me by apply-ing a mandatory[17] statutory rule, and that rule or its application to my case appears not to respect my ECHR rights. The court must either re-interpret the rule in such a way that my rights are respected after all (section 3), or, fail-ing that, declare it incompatible with the ECHR (section 4).

But say I instead invoke a mandatory common law rule – which is quite likely in the land law context. Although it is not easy to see why, as a matter of substance, the answer here should be any different from that prevailing in the statutory context, Goymour tells us that the extent to which the Convention might in fact be invoked against such a rule is 'far from certain'.[18] Some land law cases have indicated that it can be,[19] but others have refused to take a position on the issue.[20] To this extent, we are still waiting to learn the horizontal reach of the ECHR into the domestic understanding of land law.[21] (It is once again disappointing that one should be reduced to awaiting a

United Kingdom (2005) 40 EHRR 9 (ECtHR); *McCann v United Kingdom* (2008) 47 EHRR 40 (ECtHR), with which the present law is more aligned. See generally Goymour (n 5).

[16] Under the Trusts of Land and Appointment of Trustees Act 1996 s 14. See §§ 16.2.2–16.2.6.

[17] Note the very naive dichotomy between discretions and mandatory rules that this conven-tional account of the structure of the Act requires.

[18] Goymour (n 5) 272. Goymour suggests that the rule might be attacked via s 6, requiring the court, as a public authority, to act in compliance with the ECHR. Since common law rules are of judicial creation and sustaining, the courts thus have a duty to 'manipulate [the rules] to give effect to Convention rights'.

[19] eg *Aston Cantlow Parochial Church Council v Wallbank* [2004] 1 AC 546 (HL).

[20] See especially *Manchester City Council v Pinnock* [2011] 2 AC 104, [50] (SC).

[21] For treatments of the domestic horizontal effect issue more generally, see eg *X v Y* [2004] ICR 1634 (CA); *Douglas v Hello! Ltd (No 3)* [2008] 1 AC 1 (HL); *Campbell v Mirror Group Newspapers* [2004] 2 AC 457 (HL); J Howell, 'The Human Rights Act 1998: Land, Private Citizens, and the Common Law' (2007) 123 *LQR* 618.

judicial announcement as to the state of the law in this way, rather than having a reasonable opportunity to deduce it, and so converse with the judges about it, oneself.)

2.3 Article 1 of the First Protocol

We saw in § 2.2 how human rights arguments can be raised in land law cases. Sections 2.3 and 2.4 look at the substantive content of these arguments: adding content to the idea of a 'reservoir of entitlement' by seeing to what extent human rights guarantees go beyond the guarantees afforded by domestic law.

We shall look specifically at the two rights that are most commonly invoked in land disputes. This section will consider Article 1 of the First Protocol to the ECHR, which protects 'possessions', or property;[22] § 2.4 will look at ECHR Article 8, which guarantees respect for one's home.[23]

2.3.1 The Article

Article 1 of the First Protocol to the ECHR states:

> Every natural or legal person is entitled to the peaceful enjoyment of his possessions. No one shall be deprived of his possessions except in the public interest and subject to the conditions provided for by law and by the general principles of international law.
>
> The preceding provisions shall not, however, in any way impair the right of a State to enforce such laws as it deems necessary to control the use of property in accordance with the general interest or to secure the payment of taxes or other contributions or penalties.

Establishing a violation of this Article involves two stages. First, the right must be engaged ... which in turn raises the questions whether 'possessions'

---

[22] It is in fact contentious whether the right to one's possessions or property should be seen as a *human right* at all. While it is thus protected under the ECHR, and also the Universal Declaration of Human Rights (Art 17), and the United States Constitution (Fifth Amendment), it is omitted from the Canadian Charter of Rights and Freedoms. The literature is considerable. See eg J Waldron, *The Right to Private Property* (Oxford, 1988); J Harris, *Property and Justice* (Oxford, 1996) (especially Pt II), and 'Is Property a Human Right?' in J McLean (ed), *Property and the Constitution* (Oxford, 1999). But see also eg C Gosden, *Prehistory – A Very Short Introduction* (Oxford, 2003) ch 3, for the sort of highly illuminating empirical – here, palaeoanthropological – observation on the subject that is generally absent from, or at any rate muffed in, the legal and philosophical discourse.

[23] A number of other Convention rights can also be relevant, including the rights to a fair hearing (Art 6), to free expression (Art 10), to free association (Art 11), and to be free from discrimination (Art 14) (eg *Ghaidan v Godin-Mendoza* [2004] 2 AC 557 (HL)).

have been affected (§ 2.3.2) and whether what happened to them constitutes an 'interference' (§§ 2.3.3–2.3.4). Second, the interference must be unjustified. This will be dealt with in § 2.3.5.

2.3.2 Possessions

In order for the right to be in play, you have to show that your 'possessions' have been affected.[24] As with many terms used by the ECHR, this has an autonomous meaning, such that we cannot rely on our understanding of the term in domestic law.[25] It is uncontroversial that existing domestic interests in land, ie rights in rem, count as possessions. The category may, however, extend wider, so as also to embrace contractual rights over land, including licences, which to domestic law are in personam.[26] The main limitation is that your right must already exist: an expectation of getting a right over property in the future, for example by gift or inheritance, does not count.[27] However, if you are presently entitled to have a right in the future,[28] this entitlement should count as a possession too, though as yet no case has clearly confirmed this.[29]

2.3.3 Interference

Once you have shown that it is your 'possession' that is at stake, you next have to show that what has happened to it constitutes an 'interference'.

For this purpose, an 'interference' is a wide idea, meaning something that entails a restriction upon the normal exercise of your rights associated with

---

[24] One of the first confusions that arises regarding this Article is the inconsistency of its wording here. Note that the first paragraph uses the term 'possessions', whereas the second uses the term 'property'. In practice this has not given rise to interpretive difficulties. The two are treated as having the same meaning and are given a broad interpretation. See T Allen, *Property and the Human Rights Act 1998* (Oxford, 2005) 29.

[25] *Gasus Dosier und Fordertechnik GmbH v Netherlands* (1995) 20 EHRR 403, [53] (ECtHR).

[26] §§ 17.2.3, 17.3.3. The position regarding licences and other contractual rights is however unsettled. *Wilson v First County Trust Ltd (No 2)* [2004] 1 AC 816 (HL) indicates that a contractual right (there, a credit agreement) certainly can count as a possession; but *JLS v Spain* (1999) App No 41917/98 (ECtHR) holds that a contractual licence over land does not. See Allen (n 24) 75.

[27] See *Marckx v Belgium* (1979–80) 2 EHRR 330, [50] (ECtHR), asserting that First Protocol Art 1 'applies only to a person's existing possessions and . . . does not guarantee the right to acquire possessions whether on intestacy or through voluntary dispositions'.

[28] As eg where you sign up to a lease taking effect not immediately but at some future date; or you are a 'remainderman' under a trust (§ 15.2.1); or I promise to leave you my house in my will, and you act in reliance on this promise in such a way as to become entitled to the house via proprietary estoppel (Ch 8).

[29] Pointing in this direction is, however, *Stretch v United Kingdom* (2004) 38 EHRR 12 (ECtHR), holding that a legitimate expectation which has been relied upon constitutes a 'possession'.

the 'possession' in question.[30] Say the government decide to build a new high-speed train line through the countryside. The normal exercise of the right to property will be affected by this in many different ways: people may lose their property entirely, if it is expropriated; they may in practical terms be unable to sell it or develop it; they may lose substantial enjoyment of it because of the noise and vibrations.

Something that one might otherwise view as an interference does not, however, count as such if it merely picks up on an 'inherent limitation' in the relevant possession in the first place. The 'inherent limitation' idea is, however, a difficult one.[31]

The most obvious understanding of it runs as follows. An event picks up on an inherent limitation where the affected possession (right) is qualified in the relevant way at the time when you acquire it; as opposed to where the possession is not so initially qualified, meaning that the event supervenes upon it.[32] So the key is to find out whether the alleged interference has a basis that already existed when you acquired the right. If you buy some land over which I already have a right of way, for example, my using this right of way by walking over your land – to your annoyance – would not count as an interference with your possession in the land for the purposes of First Protocol Article 1, because your possession was always the ownership of the land *minus* the right of way. Whereas if I behave in the same way on the strength of the law's giving me a right to do so *after* you have acquired the land in question, that would (other things being equal) be an interference.

One can describe two key decisions in these terms. In *Aston Cantlow Parochial Church Council v Wallbank*,[33] it was held that when someone acquires land to which is already attached the responsibility to repair the chancel of a nearby church, the responsibility is an inherent limitation on his right, so that its invocation by the church does not count as an interference with his possession. Whereas *Pye v United Kingdom*[34] took it that when a squatter destroys the previous owner's title to the relevant land by adverse possession, the destruction does not pick up on an inherent limitation in the previous owner's rights, but is an interference with his possession.

This understanding of the distinction can, however, be easily subverted. It seems perfectly sensible to regard the destruction of the owner's title in *Pye v*

---

[30] *Sporrong and Lönnroth v Sweden* (1983) 5 EHRR 35, [58]–[60] (ECtHR). The import of this will vary with the nature of the 'possession' in question. The illustrations given in the text make unproblematic sense where the possession in question is people's ownership of the affected land. Where it is say a short lease of the land, they may not (there may have been no real chance of sale or development in the first place, for example); but the question will be whether there is nonetheless a restriction upon what can be expected from such a right.

[31] For an excellent account, see Goymour (n 5) 276 ff.

[32] *Pye v United Kingdom* (2006) 43 EHRR 3, [51] (ECtHR Lower Chamber).

[33] [2004] 1 AC 546 (HL).

[34] (2006) 43 EHRR 3, [53] (ECtHR Lower Chamber); (2008) 46 EHRR 45, [63] (ECtHR Grand Chamber).

United Kingdom[35] as, on the contrary, picking up on an inherent limitation: on the basis that when he acquired the land in the first place, the pre-existing law of adverse possession already made this out-turn a possibility. This latter approach would leave the 'inherent limitation' exception very wide. Everyone's ownership of their land is always subject to the operation of, for example, pre-existing planning, environmental and compulsory purchase laws, and understanding the 'inherent limitation' idea in this way would mean that their operation would never constitute an interference. The approach's width is not, however, really an objection to it. We cannot rule out the possibility that, whether by its drafting or by its application, Article 1 of the First Protocol really does have a scope as narrow as this approach would leave it.[36]

Rather than striving (vainly) to prove that one or other of the above approaches is 'correct', the message we should take away from this discussion is that the 'inherent limitation' idea is inherently unstable. Rather than tracking a real-world difference between an event amounting to an 'interference' and one picking up on an 'inherent limitation', the distinction actually reflects an ambiguity regarding what a property right is in the first place.

This is a question to which we will return in more detail in Chapter 10. For now, suffice it to say that we routinely see the Article's 'possessions' – property rights like 'ownership' – in two ways. We quite sensibly see them as absolute entitlements (*'dominium'*), from which bits may end up being taken away in the cause of competing projects (this taking away amounting to an 'interference'). But we also, and equally sensibly, see them as never constituting more than the sum total of whatever is left once, as time goes along, the needs of such other projects have been subtracted (and so as 'inherently limited', the subtractions merely picking up on this). The business of seeing an event as one that interferes with possessions, or instead as one that picks up on an inherent limitation in them, can thus be reduced to nothing more than the making of a choice as between these two visions of property. Progress might nonetheless be possible if such a choice had to be made, but in fact there is truth in both visions, such that choosing between them would be an act of destruction. The 'inherent limitation' idea thus quite naturally and inevitably defies all attempts at a principled construction.[37] The concepts of

---

[35] (2006) 43 EHRR 3 (ECtHR Lower Chamber); (2008) 46 EHRR 45 (ECtHR Grand Chamber).

[36] Goymour (n 5) 277 comments that if 'inherent limitation' is viewed in this way, First Protocol Art 1 loses 'any sensible meaning'. This assumes that an 'inherent limitation' is to be found not only in rules pre-dating the owner's acquisition, but also in the possibility of such rules being introduced after his acquisition, and indeed the possibility of his rights being invaded without any legal basis at all. Such a reading of 'inherent limitation' is not inconceivable, but neither is it inevitable; there is clearly at least one step-change involved; a less extreme reading would leave the Article with *some* 'sensible meaning' after all.

[37] Goymour suggests that Art 1 only bites if there has been a 'shift in the beneficial incidents of proprietary entitlement': *ibid* 278. So in *Aston Cantlow Parochial Church Council v Wallbank* [2004] 1 AC 546 (HL), the 'shift' occurred when the repair responsibility was originally created – carved out from the title to the relevant land – which was before the present owners acquired

'interference' and 'inherent limitation' do not describe two different kinds of event, as the courts pretend, but are simply different ways of describing exactly the same real-world phenomena.

2.3.4 The Three Types of Interference

To the extent that an event does constitute (or is viewed as) an 'interference', we need to take one further step. The case-law has settled that there are three types of interference, and so three different 'rules' within Article 1 of the First Protocol. In the early cases[38] the Strasbourg court treated this as an aspect of justification because, as explained in § 2.3.5, it is there that the classification matters. Logically, however, it makes more sense to deal with the issue at the stage of determining whether the Article is engaged at all, and in later cases[39] the court has come to address it in this way.

If we consider the Convention text, the first rule[40] appears to be that, prima facie, any interference with peaceful enjoyment of property breaches the Article. The second and third rules then read as statements that, in the particular kinds of situation that they respectively cover – though not otherwise – it is possible to depart from this prima facie position after all. So by the second rule,[41] a person can be 'deprived' of their property, if this is in accordance with the public interest. And by the third rule, a person's 'use' of their property can be 'controlled', if this is in accordance with the general interest.[42]

This is not, however, the Strasbourg court's understanding of the three rules.[43] The latter understanding shows two differences from the picture given in the previous paragraph. First, it treats the three rules as mutually exclusive; the first rule deals only with interferences *other than* those covered by the second and third rules.[44] Second, interferences falling not just under the second and third rules, but under the first rule too, can be justified, where they are in the general interests of the community.[45]

---

that land. By contrast, in *Pye v United Kingdom* (2006) 43 EHRR 3 (ECtHR Lower Chamber); (2008) 46 EHRR 45 (ECtHR Grand Chamber), the 'shift' was the squatter's adverse possession depriving the owner of his title to the land, which obviously occurred after he acquired it. Goymour herself remarks, however, that this rule is 'easier to state than to apply'; she goes on to survey a number of types of case where she regards it as difficult to say whether there has been a shift in entitlement or not.

[38]   eg *Sporrong and Lönnroth v Sweden* (1983) 5 EHRR 35 (ECtHR).
[39]   eg *James v United Kingdom* (1986) 8 EHRR 123 (ECtHR).
[40]   See the first sentence of the first paragraph of First Protocol Art 1.
[41]   See the second sentence of the first paragraph of First Protocol Art 1.
[42]   See the second paragraph of First Protocol Art 1.
[43]   The court's understanding was first and most fully articulated in *Sporrong and Lönnroth v Sweden* (1983) 5 EHRR 35 (ECtHR).
[44]   *Sporrong and Lönnroth v Sweden* (1983) 5 EHRR 35, [61] (ECtHR).
[45]   *ibid*, [69].

Let us illustrate this account. Since, under the court's treatment, the first rule is residual, we need first to see what fits into the second and third rules. A paradigm example of a 'deprivation' (second rule) is an expropriation. So when the government requisitions your property in order to make space for a new school, you can challenge the expropriation (only) under the second rule. A paradigm example of a 'control of use' (third rule) would be a planning law. Such a law does not deprive you of your property, but may prevent you, say, from adding an extension, or from converting it for use as a hotel. Then, any other kind of event amounting to an interference should fall into the first rule. An example might be your affliction by noise pollution to the extent that you cannot sleep in your property, there being insufficient domestic regulation to prevent this.

The account does, however, present difficulties.

It is clear that the borderline between the second and third rules is problematic. Consider *Pye v United Kingdom*,[46] where squatters gained rights over a property by adverse possession, destroying the previous owner's title. The Strasbourg court ultimately classified what had happened to the owner as a control of use (ie as attracting the third rule), rather than a deprivation (attracting the second rule). It did so on the basis that the adverse possession doctrine was 'not intended to deprive paper owners of their ownership, but rather to regulate questions of title'.[47] This analysis serves very well to highlight the problem in question. The fact is that the two descriptions ('intended to deprive paper owners of their ownership', 'rather to regulate questions of title') are not antithetical, as the court pretends; some interferences – such as the impact of adverse possession – clearly 'deprive paper owners of their ownership', within the second rule, at the same time as they can *also* be perfectly accurately said to 'regulate questions of title', for the third. Furthermore, the Lower Chamber of the court had earlier fallen into exactly the same conceptual error – on its way, moreover, to reaching the opposite conclusion. In its view, the rules of the adverse possession doctrine

> *do not involve the control of the use to which land is put* and are in this respect different in aim and effect from the provisions of, for instance, planning legislation. They are *instead* concerned with the entitlement to land where there has been a period of adverse possession and their cumulative effect, where the statutory requirements are met, is to transfer beneficial ownership of the land from one individual to another. (emphasis added)[48]

One might, however, respond that while the decision's judgments certainly expressed themselves poorly, matters can easily be patched up, by saying that any regulation of title going so far as to *deprive* an owner of his possession

---

[46] (2006) 43 EHRR 3 (ECtHR Lower Chamber); (2008) 46 EHRR 45 (ECtHR Grand Chamber).

[47] *Pye v United Kingdom* (2008) 46 EHRR 45, [66] (ECtHR Grand Chamber).

[48] *Pye v United Kingdom* (2006) 43 EHRR 3, [60] (ECtHR Lower Chamber).

attracts the second rule, while any of a less invasive nature attracts the third.[49]

This vision of the rules' relationship is in fact to be found in *Sporrong and Lönnroth v Sweden.*[50] One alleged interference in that case was the government's grant of expropriation permits over the property in question (ie its designation of the property as liable to expropriation at some future point). Addressing itself to the second rule, the court first found that there had been no *formal* deprivation, because the permits still left the applicants with the right 'to use, sell, devise, donate or mortgage their properties'.[51] Going on to inquire whether there had nonetheless been a de facto deprivation, it found that there had not, because the applicants remained able to 'utilise', ie use, the property.[52] So the test for 'deprivation', of both kinds, focuses on the question whether the applicant can still use the property; a 'deprivation' is simply a particularly serious form of a 'control of [ie reduction of the freedom of] use'.

On this account, then, the difference between a 'deprivation' (for the second rule), and a (mere) 'control of use' (for the third), emerges as a question of degree. This sounds entirely plausible ... but as such, it leaves it difficult or impossible satisfactorily to present the two 'categories' as distinct 'types' of interference, attracting two distinct 'rules', as the ECHR and the court insist. At the very least, a lucid indication needs to be given of the line separating the two; and if this ever could be forthcoming, it has not been.[53]

Matters become worse still, of course, when we remember that there is also the first rule to be factored in. This requires us to be able to say, with fair assurance, that a particular event *is* (for example) a (mere) 'control of use', and *is not* a 'deprivation' *or indeed* 'some other kind of interference'. Sometimes perhaps we shall be able to; but often enough we shall not.

Remember the example where the government intends to build a new high-speed railway. Imagine the tracks will run right past (though not encroach upon) the grounds of a fine manor house that you own. It may fairly be assumed that the construction and operation of the new railway will have a major negative impact on you, and that this will amount to an 'interference' with your possessions. In which category – under which rule – does this inter-

---

[49] By this reckoning, however, the correct classification of the event here in question was obviously that reached by the Lower rather than the Grand Chamber, ie a deprivation; perhaps the Grand Chamber resorted to the analysis disparaged in the text precisely so as to obscure this. For a possible explanation of the Grand Chamber's conclusion, see n 72.

[50] (1983) 5 EHRR 35 (ECtHR).

[51] *ibid*, [62].

[52] *ibid*, [63].

[53] In the United States, it is understood that a control of use amounts to a 'taking', so as to attract the protection of the US Constitution's Fifth Amendment, if it deprives the owner of all economically beneficial use of his property: *Lucas v South Carolina Coastal Council* 505 US 1003 (1992) 798 (US Supreme Court). (However, there is only reckoned to be such a deprivation/taking at all if the 'use' in question counted as part of the owner's 'property' in the first place, raising raises issues akin to 'inherent limitation'. For discussion, see L Underkuffler, *The Idea of Property: Its Meaning and Power* (Oxford, 2003), especially 46–51, and further references there.)

ference belong? If we focus on the use of your property that lies in its monetary value, the project may well de facto rob you of this use altogether, or certainly a very large proportion of it indeed, seemingly leaving the interference a 'deprivation'. Looked at from another perspective, the interference 'controls' the way you can use the land; again de facto, it amounts to a prohibition on your turning the manor into something like a country house hotel, or even perhaps comfortably using it as a domestic home. It can also be argued that neither of these perspectives fully captures the full nature of the interference, and that really we are looking (instead or as well) at something less specific, a 'general disruption of peaceful enjoyment', which would have to attract the first rule. The point is that lawyers could argue for each interpretation ad nauseam. But their doing so would not lead us to learn anything about the interference that we did not know already. No one, certainly not the Strasbourg court, has ever successfully explained *why* the three-rule categorisation is either theoretically meaningful or practically helpful. It would be better to recognise that interferences come not in discrete categories, but in all sorts of forms and degrees of intrusiveness; quite simply, that interferences come in all shapes and sizes, but nonetheless ultimately remain . . . interferences.

2.3.5 Justification

To establish a violation of your First Protocol Article 1 right, once you have shown an interference with your possessions, you must show that the interference was not justified.[54]

There are three stages to determining whether an interference is justified.

—— First, the interference must be lawful. This requires both that there is a law in place under which the action was taken,[55] and that that law passes the 'quality of law' test.[56]
—— Second, the interference must be in the public interest. From the text of the First Protocol Article 1, it would appear as if there was intended to be a variation between its component rules on this score, as the second rule (deprivation) refers to the *public* interest while the third (control of use) refers to the *general* interest;[57] while, as we saw in § 2.3.4, the first

---

[54] For a helpful exposition of this see Goymour (n 5) 284–9; and Allen (n 24) chs 3, 5, 6.

[55] Allen gives *Akdivar v Turkey* (1997) 23 EHRR 143 (ECtHR) as an example of a case where the interference was not in accordance with national law, because Turkish security forces illegally destroyed property. He asserts that where the national court rules that the state has complied, Strasbourg will normally accept this. Allen, *ibid*, 94–5.

[56] This involves reference to classic Rule of Law considerations, such as that the law in question must be prospective, accessible and clear.

[57] Allen points out that the expressions used in the French version of the text – 'pour cause d'utilité publique' and 'conformément à l'intérêt général' respectively – certainly have precise and different meanings. See Allen (n 24) 29.

contains no such reference at all. Ignoring the text, Strasbourg has held that all three rules share the same requirement.[58]

—— Third, it must be asked whether the interference struck a 'fair balance' between the demands of the general (or public) interest and the protection of individual human rights.[59] This has subsequently been described as the search for a 'reasonable relationship of proportionality'.[60]

It is the third of these elements that causes the most difficulty. When we try to see how the 'fair balance' question is to be answered, we find ourselves unable to do much more than to recognise the factors that the court takes into account. There is little or nothing to see regarding how these factors are to be handled; the Strasbourg decisions jump from broad statements of principle directly to specific conclusions, with no account of the reasoning in between. We quickly descend from an attempt to offer a principled account[61] to providing a mere catalogue of facts and results.

Three observations about the reasoning can be made, however.

First, the approach to the proportionality question under this Article is less structured than in cases under the other 'qualified rights' (ie Articles 8–11, which explicitly allow the right in question to be outweighed by other sufficient considerations). As used in the latter, the classic proportionality formula under the ECHR asks four questions. Was the interference done in pursuit of a legitimate aim? (This question corresponds to the first two of the First Protocol Article 1 questions identified above.) Then, was it capable of achieving that aim? Was it necessary to achieve the aim? And finally, did it impose burdens disproportionate to the benefits attained? Although traces of these latter questions arise in First Protocol Article 1 judgments, there is no four-fold analysis as such. Indeed, the third of the classic questions – whether the measure taken was necessary to achieve the aim – has been said by the Strasbourg court not to apply as such in cases under this Article.[62] Rather, the availability of alternative solutions (which would render the measure not necessary) is one factor to be taken into account in the overall assessment of fair balance. In terms of the

---

[58] *James v United Kingdom* (1986) 8 EHRR 123, [43] (ECtHR).

[59] *Sporrong and Lönnroth v Sweden* (1983) 5 EHRR 35, [69] (ECtHR), addressing itself to the first rule; *James v United Kingdom* (1986) 8 EHRR 123, [50] (ECtHR) extended the test to all three rules. Allen has argued that it is not at all clear that any such test was supposed to be used in First Protocol Art 1, because the formulation 'necessary in a democratic society', which is used in some form in ECHR Arts 8 to 11, is conspicuously absent. Instead, it appears from the text that First Protocol Art 1 claims to have worked out the correct balance in advance; ie that (at any rate in the case of the second and third rules) where the first two elements are present, the interference is ipso facto justified (Allen (n 24) 123).

[60] *James v United Kingdom* (1986) 8 EHRR 123, [50] (ECtHR).

[61] Goymour (n 5) 284–6 offers three 'rules of thumb': that consensual interferences will not violate First Protocol Art 1; that where there is a strong public interest, the deprivation is readily justified; and that a deprivation will normally be justified only on payment of compensation. But even if we accept these, they clearly do not come close to comprising a set of principles guiding us through any and every case that might arise.

[62] *James v United Kingdom* (1986) 8 EHRR 123, [51] (ECtHR).

classic questions then, the fourth, which is a balancing test and so analogous to the 'fair balance' idea, assumes unusual prominence.

But this prominence is deceptive; it is rather analytical than real. For the second observation to be made about the approach to 'fair balance' is that the doctrine of the 'margin of appreciation' is deployed particularly heavily in the context of this Article.[63] This means that when the court is answering the question whether a given interference with property strikes a fair balance, it will pay considerable deference to the views of national legislative and executive bodies (as encapsulated, for example, in the decision to enact the law generating the interference in the first place). The margin of appreciation is particularly wide in the context of this Article because interference with property is a classic example of an area of regulation that is both nation-specific and political; think for example of tax laws, town planning laws, and laws (re-)configuring social security rights. Certainly, the Strasbourg court, as both a judicial and a supranational body, is ill equipped to determine the way to handle such issues.[64] A domestic court does not suffer from the same problem of supranationality, but there is still the fact that, as the judicial limb of the state, it may well not be the best forum for the resolution of policy questions.[65]

Combining this second observation with the first, then, we find that although in this context the proportionality analysis is unusually heavy on 'balance', the wide margin of appreciation means that the balance is, in effect, presumptively tilted from the outset in favour of finding the interference to be proportionate and so justified. In other words, the court is looking only for positive *dis*proportionality. The resultant question has also been described as not whether the national solution struck the *best* balance, but whether it represented an *acceptable* balance;[66] and as whether the rights-holder has been subjected to a 'disproportionate and excessive burden'.[67] In short, in this context the proportionality hurdle is not a difficult one to overcome.

The third observation is that where an interference counts as a 'deprivation' (ie attracts the Article's second rule: § 2.3.4), it will not normally be justified as proportionate unless those affected are paid compensation reasonably related to the market value of the property in question.[68] Less than full compensation has been found to satisfy the proportionality test where it is associated with fundamental constitutional changes taking place in a country,[69] or

---

[63] See eg *Sporrong and Lönnroth v Sweden* (1983) 5 EHRR 35, [69] (ECtHR).

[64] See *Blecic v Croatia* (2004) 41 EHRR 185, [65] (ECtHR).

[65] As recognised in eg *R (Prolife Alliance) v British Broadcasting Corporation* [2004] 1 AC 185, [76] (HL).

[66] *James v United Kingdom* (1986) 8 EHRR 123, [51] (ECtHR).

[67] *Scordino v Italy* (2009) 48 EHRR 9, [99] (ECtHR).

[68] *James v United Kingdom* (1986) 8 EHRR 123, [54] (ECtHR).

[69] *Former King of Greece v Greece* (2001) 33 EHRR 21 (ECtHR). In *Jahn v Germany* (2006) 42 EHRR 49 (ECtHR), deprivation involving no compensation at all was allowed, in the context of German reunification.

where there is some other particularly compelling public interest argument.[70] But such cases are regarded as exceptional.[71] This position regarding deprivations contrasts with that regarding the other two categories of interferences: 'controls of use' (attracting the third rule), and more general 'interferences with peaceful enjoyment' (attracting the first rule). In these cases, there is no presumption that compensation must be paid. Rather, the provision or otherwise of compensation is merely one factor to be entered into the balance when conducting the proportionality review.

At first sight, we might feel that this discrepancy in the treatment of compensation is appropriate: being *deprived* of your property is so objectionable a form of interference as, surely, normally to demand proper compensation, while a less absolute position is probably warranted as regards less objectionable forms. And this reflection might lead us after all – against the position to which we were attracted in § 2.3.4 – to accept the law's maintaining of its second rule, relating to deprivations, as distinct from its first and third rules, relating to other kinds of interference. (Though there is no reason from the present point of view, and appears to be none from any other point of view either, for distinguishing the first and third rules from one another.) On further examination, however, this line of thought breaks down, leading us after all to revert to what was said in § 2.3.4, that it would be preferable to see interferences as a genus, reacting to their evident individual differences ad hoc.

This is so partly because of the truth we discovered there: that it can be very hard, and sometimes even nonsensical, to have to say that something is (or is not) a 'deprivation' *as opposed to* some other form of interference.[72] It is so

---

[70] See eg *Lithgow v* United *Kingdom* (1986) 8 EHRR 329 (ECtHR), where less than full compensation was found justified when aircraft and shipbuilding, industries of strategic national importance, were nationalised, bringing organisational and economic improvements and a greater degree of public control and accountability. See too *R (SRM Global Master Fund LP) v HM Treasury Commissioners* [2010] BCC 558 (CA), where Northern Rock, a failed bank, was taken into public ownership, its shareholders being paid (at any rate in their view) less than full compensation. This was held justified by the public interest in quickly stemming any more general loss of confidence in banks.

[71] *Scordino v Italy* (2009) 48 EHRR 9 (ECtHR); see particularly [102].

[72] One could say that an interference counts as a 'deprivation' where, and only where, it appears prima facie to demand compensation. But to define the kinds of interference in this way, while admittedly not distracting from the real issue and so doctrinally harmful, is circular and thus redundant. It can of course also do violence to the word 'deprivation'. It may however essentially explain the decision of the Strasbourg Grand Chamber in *Pye v United Kingdom* (2008) 46 EHRR 45 that the adverse possession doctrine, which clearly deprived the previous owner of his title to the relevant land, nonetheless involved *not* a 'deprivation', but a control of use. The doctrine's rules did not provide for the payment of any compensation. If their effect were regarded as a 'deprivation', therefore – as indeed was held by the Lower Chamber, (2006) 43 EHRR 3 – it would virtually certainly have been found unjustified; treating it instead as a 'control of use' enabled the Grand Chamber to avoid this outcome. While semantically dubious, in realpolitik terms the adjustment was an unsurprising move. Many ECHR member countries had similar laws on adverse possession and, had the Lower Chamber's ruling stood, it would therefore have set the Strasbourg court at odds with all their governments simultaneously, doubtless a discomfiting prospect: see Goymour (n 5) 286. For all that, however, why should compensation *not* have been appropriate? This question is considered a little in § 7.2.4.

also because when a court is considering whether an interference of any kind is justified, it will inevitably ask whether the sum of compensation offered – or the absence of such an offer – comes across as adequate. And its metric for this is, indeed more or less has to be, the impact of the interference in question in monetary terms.[73] Take again our example where a high-speed rail line is to be built just beyond your grounds. However we view it, the interference here has reduced the value of your land. And a reduction is a reduction. There seems no reason why the law should address the case via different analyses – as the singling out of the second rule entails – depending on whether the reduction is a *partial* one (reflecting the unpleasantness caused by the adjacent line) or a *total* one, ie a reduction to zero (as would occur if the line were simply driven straight through your property, completely absorbing it). So we return after all to the view that it would be better to group all interferences together, taking the question of compensation into account in the overall proportionality assessment, but doing so ad hoc, rather than constraining matters by an artificial pre-categorisation. It would remain quite clear that something that can naturally enough be called a 'deprivation' will usually need proper compensation if it is to be justified; but there would be nothing in this platitudinous remark to cause linguistic or conceptual headaches.

Finally, although it seems impossible to say how, in general terms, the balancing exercise is conducted by the courts, one might seek some understanding of the reason(s) for that, and consider whether it ought to be possible to do better. Section 2.5.2 assesses the current position, and begins to consider these questions.

2.3.6 Impact

So – subject always to issues of justiciability, § 2.2 – does Article 1 of the First Protocol provide any protected interests over and above the entitlements to which one can already lay claim in English domestic land law, and so contribute anything of substance to the 'reservoir of entitlement'? At the time of writing, it appears that an affirmative answer cannot confidently be given; there is reputed to be no area of English property law that has yet been unequivocally found to violate the Article.[74] But not every stone has yet been properly turned. Where a possible concern has been identified,[75] it may yet

---

[73] This seems implicit in *James v United Kingdom* (1986) 8 EHRR 123, [54] (ECtHR).

[74] Goymour (n 5) 286.

[75] Goymour, *ibid*, 287–8 sees three 'potential violators' of the Article in the rules on the sale of mortgaged land, on the overreaching of trust rights, and on the implied grant of easements. These and some possible others are considered in the relevant places in subsequent chapters of this book.

turn out to be well founded; and new areas of difficulty may come to light, or indeed be introduced into the law.[76]

2.4 Article 8

2.4.1 The Article

The commonest human right invoked in land law cases is the right to respect for a person's home. This right is protected under Article 8 of the ECHR, which states:

> (1) Everyone has the right to respect for his private and family life, his home and his correspondence.
>
> (2) There shall be no interference by a public authority with the exercise of this right except such as is in accordance with the law and is necessary in a democratic society in the interests of national security, public safety or the economic well-being of the country, for the prevention of disorder or crime, for the protection of health or morals, or for the protection of the rights and freedoms of others.

The task of determining whether someone has the benefit of this protection has structural similarities with its counterpart in relation to the protection of the right to possessions under Article 1 of the First Protocol, which we have just explored. First we must determine whether the right to home is engaged, which involves asking whether the entity in question is a 'home' (§ 2.4.2) and then whether it has been interfered with (§ 2.4.3). If the right is engaged, we must secondly ask whether the interference with the home was nevertheless justified (§ 2.4.4).

2.4.2 Respect for One's Home

Article 8 affirms a right to respect for a person's home.

It does not, therefore, give you a right *to* a home; it is of no help to you if you are simply homeless. But if you already have a home (or had one, until the alleged interference deprived you of it), the Article demands that it be respected.[77] The first thing to know, therefore, is what counts as your 'home'.

---

[76] As could occur if 'electronic conveyancing' were introduced insensitively: see §§ 3.2.4–3.2.5.

[77] *Selçuk and Asker v Turkey* (1998) 26 EHRR 477 (ECtHR).

This is once again a term with an autonomous meaning under the ECHR.[78] Importantly, something can be your home even if you do not have a domestic legal right to call it so.[79] What matters is whether you have 'sufficient and continuous links' to the place in question.[80] The kinds of factors that will be relevant include the length of time in which you have had ties with the land,[81] and whether you have established a home elsewhere.[82] At the same time, the idea of a 'home' has been interpreted broadly: it can even include business premises.[83] Given this, the Article 8 right to respect[84] for home will be very often engaged by the operation of domestic land law rules, as most of these have the potential to interfere with someone's home in some way. Most of the interesting discussion therefore takes place instead under the rubric of justification (§ 2.4.4).

2.4.3 Interference

The matter of interference is normally straightforward and thus has generated little discussion. It may of course consist in eviction itself,[85] but also in erosion of one's ability to access and occupy the place in question.[86] There can additionally be an interference when your peaceful enjoyment of your

---

[78] *Buckley v United Kingdom* (1996) 23 EHRR 101, [63] (ECtHR).

[79] *ibid.*

[80] *Gillow v United Kingdom* (1986) 11 EHRR 335 (ECtHR); *Hounslow London Borough Council v Powell* [2011] 2 AC 186, [33] (SC). This rule is striking. It means that Art 8 protects those who have roots, while neglecting those who do not: the 'haves', rather than the 'have-nots'. We want to be clear, therefore, about the rule's function. It might be seen as a pre-weighting in the balancing exercise (§ 2.4.4), the idea being that someone's interest in a transient short-term home is never going to be of sufficient significance to outweigh the considerations that are served by the interference. It might be otherwise, however, if the loss of a temporary home – or indeed, looking at the matter in this way, even the lack of a home in the first place – is sufficient to amount to inhuman and degrading treatment under ECHR Art 3 (see *R (Limbuela) v Secretary of State for the Home Department* [2006] 1 AC 396 (HL)). Combining these two perspectives, the idea seems to be that there must be a minimum severity of harm, either because what is lost is a home which is settled and established (this seen as being worse than the loss of a short-term home), or because personal circumstances render the loss of even a temporary home detrimental to an individual's humanity.

[81] See *Leeds City Council v Price* [2006] 2 AC 465 (HL), in which insufficient ties were found to exist when gypsies were evicted only two days after commencing occupation of the site in question.

[82] *Gillow v United Kingdom* (1986) 11 EHRR 335, [46] (ECtHR).

[83] *Niemietz v Germany* (1993) 16 EHRR 97 (ECtHR). One reason for the broad interpretation is that the French text uses the word 'domicile', which has a wider meaning than does 'home' in English.

[84] Note that there is no right 'to' one's home, merely a right to 'respect for' one's home. This is taken to both enhance and reduce the rights under Art 8. On the one hand it has been used as a foundation for establishing positive obligations on the part of the state to protect the home. On the other hand, however, it is also used to justify widening the margin of appreciation that the state enjoys in determining what interferences with homes are justified. See *Abdulaziz v United Kingdom* (1985) 7 EHRR 471 (ECtHR), which demonstrates both phenomena.

[85] *Cyprus v Turkey* (1976) 4 EHRR 482 (ECommHR).

[86] *Wiggins v United Kingdom* (1978) 13 DR 40 (ECommHR).

residence is interrupted either physically, by someone else's entry, or non-physically, for example by pollution or noise.[87]

2.4.4 Justification

Like Article 1 of the First Protocol, Article 8 gives a qualified right. There is a requirement that any interference be 'in accordance with the law', which once again requires that the interference be provided for by a law that meets the 'quality of law' test. The rest of Article 8(2) follows the standard pattern of qualified rights under the ECHR. The four proportionality questions outlined in § 2.3.5 must be answered. For the purpose of the first of those four questions, the ECHR text itself provides a list of the aims that the interference may legitimately pursue, but this is not very restrictive, as the listed aims are broad in nature; in particular the 'economic well-being of the country'. When it comes to the fourth of the questions – whether the interference imposes burdens disproportionate to the benefits attained – we see similar features to the First Protocol Article 1 'fair balance' cases. The margin of appreciation is again in play, and indeed has been said to be as wide as under the latter Article. Once more, then, we are looking for *dis*proportionality, rather than the optimum balance in the eyes of the court.[88]

As regards the assessment of (dis)proportionality, *Manchester City Council v Pinnock*[89] is the most important recent case. Although instrumental in securing the current in-principle availability of Article 8 against public authorities in domestic courts (§ 2.2.2), its position on proportionality[90] nonetheless continues in the previous domestic tradition of limiting the real impact that the Article can have. So the court states that 'in virtually every case' where a local authority is domestically entitled to possession against its tenant, there will be a 'very strong case for saying that making an order for possession would be proportionate'.[91]

The first reason given for this statement is that 'unencumbered property rights . . . are of real weight when it comes to proportionality'.[92] That is to say, where the Article 8 right is inconsistent with, and so has to be weighed against, the domestic property interest of the owner of the property in question, very considerable importance will be accorded to the latter . . . perhaps

---

[87] *Hatton v United Kingdom* (2002) 34 EHRR 1 (ECtHR).

[88] *Blecic v Croatia* (2004) 41 EHRR 185, [65] (ECtHR); *Manchester City Council v Pinnock* [2011] 2 AC 104, [34] (SC).

[89] [2011] 2 AC 104 (SC).

[90] Amongst other things. In particular, Art 8 will be considered only when specifically raised by the occupier and should initially be considered summarily, on the ground that a more proactive approach would demand uncomfortably much of the courts dealing with what are otherwise rather routine and straightforward cases: [2011] 2 AC 104, [61]; also *Hounslow London Borough Council v Powell* [2011] 2 AC 186, [35] (SC).

[91] [2011] 2 AC 104, [54].

[92] *ibid.*

even to the extent of creating a presumption, ie pre-weighting the proportionality exercise, in favour of the property right. It would then be an uphill struggle to show that in the particular case, the considerations supporting the Article 8 right were sufficiently weighty to rebut this presumption. Importantly, too, this position affects the potency of the Article 8 right not only against a public authority, such as the local authority landlord involved in this particular decision, but also against a private owner (eg landlord) of the property in question.[93] Accordingly Goymour[94] praises the decision for its recognition of the importance of the right to property, as allaying (understandable) fears that Article 8 could destabilise property rights.

The second basis given in *Manchester City Council v Pinnock*[95] for the ease with which the proportionality test can be satisfied, when a local authority landlord legitimately seeks to evict its tenant, is the authority's public law duties; in particular its duty to decide who should occupy its property.[96] (On top of this, the authority 'should, in the absence of cogent evidence to the contrary, be assumed to be acting in accordance with its duties', so that, unless proved otherwise, the appropriateness of its aims will be taken as read.[97])

Obviously, this latter consideration arises only where the Article 8 right is invoked against a public authority, rather than a private owner. According to Goymour, the implication is that the proportionality scales are weighted even more heavily in the public authority's favour than they are in the private owner's; the latter can point only to the court's first ground for presuming proportionality, whereas the former can point to both grounds.[98] This is probably incorrect, however. The reasons why we value ownership are less strongly present where the owner is a public body. We will discuss these reasons in

---

[93] In a case involving a public authority landlord, it would be inappropriate to refer to the latter's ownership interest as being protected by Article 1 of the First Protocol, because public authorities cannot lay claim to human rights. But in the case of a private landlord, such reference would be entirely appropriate . . . leading us to think of the dispute as involving a conflict between the tenant's right under Article 8, and the landlord's under Article 1 of the First Protocol. The position taken by the court implies that in this event, there is a rebuttable presumption that the latter takes priority over the former.

[94] Goymour (n 5), 294.

[95] [2011] 2 AC 104, [52], [54], [128] (SC).

[96] Notably ([2011] 2 AC 104, [52]) 'its duties in relation to the distribution and management of its housing stock, including, for example, the fair allocation of its housing, the redevelopment of the site, the refurbishing of sub-standard accommodation, the need to move people who are in accommodation that now exceeds their needs, and the need to move vulnerable people into sheltered or warden-assisted housing', as well as 'the need to remove a source of nuisance to neighbours'.

[97] [2011] 2 AC 104, [53] (SC); also *Hounslow London Borough Council v Powell* [2011] 2 AC 186, [37] (SC). If the authority's act occurs, as it commonly will, in the context of a statutory scheme shaped around the national legislature's perception of 'general social and economic policy considerations', this may add further to the act's immunity from close scrutiny, since such considerations tend to generate a margin of appreciation: *Connors v United Kingdom* (2005) 40 EHRR 9, [82] (ECtHR).

[98] Goymour (n 5) 295.

detail in § 10.2.2, but for now it is sufficient to know that to a substantial extent they are based upon the benefit that 'ownership' represents for the owner. As public bodies do not own things for their own benefit, but rather on a 'fiduciary' basis[99] for their stakeholders the public,[100] the reasons why we value property rights cannot apply to them in the same way; so the court's first ground, the importance of ownership *per se*, is much muted here.[101, 102]

As well as these two explicit reasons for loading the proportionality question in favour of the owner/public authority, a third source of such loading emerges from the court's detailed treatment of the question. The key individual factor referred to as supporting the proportionality of the local authority's actions was the extraordinary history of 'crime, nuisance and harassment' on the part of the tenant's family, sustained even despite the warning shot of a 'demotion order' in respect of his tenancy; 'in the light of the history, the demotion order, the interests of their neighbours, and the council's rights and duty to manage and allocate its housing stock, the decision [to evict the tenant] cannot be characterised as unreasonable or disproportionate'.[103] This is of course a very intelligible evocation of material that was clearly germane to the court's proclaimed vision of the proportionality question, especially its second axis. But notice the absence from the reasoning of any reference to the fact that the property in question was, after all, the tenant's (and his family's) *home*. It was as if, having (because a threat to a home engages Article 8) formally launched the proportionality question in the first place, this factor then drops out of sight, playing no part in the process of answering that question.

This cannot be right. The proportionality exercise must involve a weighing of the considerations supporting interference with someone's home *against the reasons for protecting that home*. And the latter must comprise *both* any reasons specific to the individual case, *and* reasons for protecting homes generically. Speaking hypothetically, the court in fact clearly accepts the rele-

---

[99] That is, as if on trust; the point being that a trustee can have no personal interest. For public bodies operating as 'trustees' for their stakeholders in this way, see S Gardner, *An Introduction to the Law of Trusts* (Oxford, 2011) 6–7.

[100] *Bromley London Borough Council v Greater London Council* [1983] 1 AC 768, 815, 818 (HL).

[101] This appears to be recognised by the court, in its remark that 'unencumbered property rights, *even* where they are enjoyed by a public body such as a local authority, are of real weight when it comes to proportionality' ([2011] AC 104, [54]; emphasis added). The implied residual significance of such rights in this context (hence 'much muted', and 'less strongly present', in the text, rather than simply 'irrelevant') is their instrumental economic importance; they entail that the property in question is freely commerciable, which is as valuable when it is owned publicly as privately.

[102] It may, however, be the case that the second basis is more powerful than the first per se; ie that a public authority, relying (principally) on the second basis, will as a generality find it easier to outweigh a given set of countervailing factors than would a private owner, relying on the first basis. Assessing this suggestion would require a clear fix on the rationalia and power of the two bases: not an easy ask.

[103] [2011] 2 AC 104, [112], [118]–[123], [126] (SC).

vance of specific factors where they are to be found, which they were apparently not in this particular case.[104] What is lacking is any recognition of the relevance of generic factors, which were of course as present in this case as in every other. Perhaps we should not take this particular decision as positively affirming their irrelevance, however.[105] On its individual facts – the considerations supporting eviction being especially strong – maybe the proportionality exercise could not, even if more satisfactorily framed, have gone in the tenant's favour, and the account of the exercise was rather short-changed merely for that reason.

Even after eradicating such infelicities, however, it seems once again – as with our consideration of the same issue regarding Article 1 of the First Protocol – impossible to say in general terms just *how* the (dis)proportionality assessment is made. Section 2.5 takes a more general perspective on this.

2.4.5 Impact

So, subject of course to issues of justiciability (§ 2.2), does Article 8 provide any protected interests over and above the entitlements to which one can already lay claim in English domestic land law, and so contribute to the 'reservoir of entitlement'? The cases regarding the eviction of tenants from local authority housing, culminating in *Manchester City Council v Pinnock*[106] *and Hounslow London Borough Council v Powell*,[107] show that the answer in that context is certainly 'yes'. Beyond this, there could be further instances. Certainly, the question has been meaningfully raised in judicial and academic treatments of a number of areas of the law. It will be addressed in the relevant places in subsequent chapters.

---

[104] 'The court will . . . be concerned with the occupiers' personal circumstances', [2011] 2 AC 104, [53]; '*in some cases* there may be factors which would tell [against allowing the eviction]', *ibid* [54], emphasis added; see also *ibid* [64], accepting that an occupier's special vulnerability could and should potentially make a difference (as in *Connors v United Kingdom* (2005) 40 EHRR 9 (ECtHR)).

[105] As does Goymour, describing the court as ruling that Art 8 'only prevents the vindication of existing rights where to do so would result in *significant personal hardship*': Goymour (n 5) 294, emphasis added.

[106] [2011] 2 AC 104 (SC).

[107] [2011] 2 AC 186 (SC).

2.5 An Overview

2.5.1 The Law's Practical Operation

What we have seen in §§ 2.3 and 2.4 is that it is not at all clear, in the context both of Article 1 of the First Protocol and of Article 8, just what the ECHR protections actually mean in practice. Above all (though it is not the only source of difficulty), the proportionality test is extremely opaque. It is all very well to take decided cases and explain their results, but it can be very difficult to describe – and above all, satisfactorily justify – the way in which the assessment should be conducted, and concluded, on a new set of facts.

To illustrate this, and more especially explore it, let us go back to the example of the construction of a new high-speed railway line, already introduced. The line is aimed at allowing journeys between major cities to be made in the shortest possible time. This requires that, as far as possible, it must follow a geographical straight line between the cities. In order to build it, the government will have to acquire and demolish many properties that lie along the route, including historic houses and people's homes. Many other properties will be badly affected by noise and obstruction of views. In addition, the line will pass through rural areas previously renowned for their tranquillity and natural beauty. It will also affect sites known to be environmentally important, say as habitats for some endangered kinds of bats.

The project will obviously engage both Article 1 of the First Protocol and Article 8 in respect of its impacts on the property rights and homes of the people affected by it. The latter have then to be justified by reference to the project's (legitimately aimed) benefits, which might include the direct boon of improved rail travel, together with the indirect ones of the stimulation of the national economy, the generation of employment, the development of new technology, and perhaps the prestige of having high-speed rail travel in Britain. The weight of this set of justificatory benefits may, however, have to be adjusted – potentially even reduced to zero – by taking account of associated disbenefits (that is, disbenefits other than the damage to the ECHR rights themselves), such as the harm to the bats.

To move from this rather vague account of the general mix to an actual answer, however, one would need to grapple with questions such as the following. What level of gain in terms of rail travel improvement do we need to see to justify the cost to those whose rights will be interfered with? (If we shave half an hour off a journey that currently takes two hours, is that enough? What if it is only 15 minutes?) Does it matter that those who are asked to suffer the project's impact, by in some sense losing their properties and homes, reap none of the direct benefits, because the train will not stop in between the cities? How much weight should we place on the fact that while the project may improve the national economy, no one is sure of this? How significant is it that alternatives could be pursued, which would result in a very similar reduction in journey times whilst disrupting far fewer houses, and not requiring new technology? Do we count the negative impact on the environment at all, and if so do we assess it purely in terms of its significance to humans, or do we try to respect it – say, value the bats – per se?[108]

The answers to such questions are plainly not self-evident, but depend strongly on one's notions of what is important. For example, one person might say that it will never be justifiable to knock down a building of high historical and cultural importance in order to build a railway. Another might say that environmental factors are the most important. Yet another might weight the economic factors most heavily. And, of course, another again might go – as, prima facie, the ECHR itself invites us to – with the interests of those whose properties and homes are detrimentally affected.

So far as the case's handling in the courts goes, we can say with reasonable assurance that the judges – whether domestic or in Strasbourg – will not go into any of this. They will simply see themselves as in no position to deal with the enormous and complex balancing exercise that should thus in principle be involved. In practice, the outcome will almost certainly be that, since Parliament and the government want the project, they will basically – give or take some incidental skirmishing (usually over 'how' rather than 'what' or 'whether') – get it. The sibling ideas of the 'margin of appreciation' and of 'judicial deference' will be deployed heavily so as to account for this result.

2.5.2 An Appraisal

This may come as a shock. The human rights project is commonly depicted as transporting us to a paradise where it is possible to judge whether actions or initiatives of the kind under discussion are positively justified, ie *right*. The 'proportionality' concept is presented as the key vehicle for arriving at such judgements. In reality, however, they are either ducked, as we have just seen; or, to the extent that they are made at all, the difficulties involved in making them (such as, how do we tell whether your home matters more than my ownership, or vice versa?) are brushed under the carpet.

On this account, then, all that human rights jurisprudence really provides in practice is a rather clunky means of identifying fairly gross *dis*proportionality; a blunt tool for screening out events that more or less everyone would readily intuit as infringing a minimum level of guarantee.

---

[108] Do not underestimate the difficulty of assessing the impact on the bats itself (*cf R (Morge) v Hampshire County Council* [2011] 1 WLR 268 (SC)), even before netting it off against other considerations.

Indeed, having moved past any initial disappointment, one could find something positive in this. We may not be talking about paradise, but there is still value – quite a lot of value – in being able to invoke the law against the kind of excesses just referred to.

Moreover, while this rather basic jurisdiction may be the extant reality, it may not represent the best that can ever be achieved. By thinking carefully about the ideas involved, we may – though let us be clear, we may not – succeed in sharpening the tool it gives us. If so, it would allow the judges defensibly to make (appropriate) deeper incursions into what currently stands as the political space, and so provide a more ample level of guarantee.

Insufficient work has yet been done on this.[109] We are fortunate, however, in the context presently under discussion. The material we are concerned with involves a balancing with *property*. (In the case of the First Protocol Article 1, property lies on the threatened side of the balance; in the case of Article 8, it lies on the threatening side.) And a good deal of reflection has already taken place about how to approach such balancing, so as to understand the accommodation there must always be between the claims of owners and opposing considerations, on a wide variety of fronts. This experience is chronicled in Chapter 10, especially § 10.2. It can very helpfully be fed back into our reflection about the particular business of human rights balancing, with which we are presently concerned.

2.6 Why Focus on Human Rights in Land?

This section twins § 1.4, which examines why rights in rem in land form an important subject for study. Why is the same true of human rights relating to land?

The answer is essentially simple. In § 1.4 we saw that rights in rem matter because, by definition, they represent a set of legal mechanisms, of especial social worth, for facilitating human exploitation of (the rather important resource of) land in some way. The same can be said of the human rights discussed in the present chapter.

The ways that both types of right facilitate the human exploitation of land are plain. In various respects, they put flesh on the key ideas of allowing people to have their own particular means of exploiting land, and protecting these means from interference by others.

---

[109] For a potentially important contribution, see K Möller, *The Global Model of Constitutional Rights* (Oxford, forthcoming).

It is in respect of their being of especial social worth that they differ. We see them thus for divergent reasons.

To be sure, the difference is not absolute. There is an overlap between the justifications for rights in rem, explored in § 1.2.2, and those for human rights. Both kinds of rights can stand upon considerations of individual liberty . . . most notably the republican ideal of safeguarding some against arbitrary domination by others. But rights in rem can also be justified by reference to their economic value and contribution to the socially optimal use of land. For example, we shall see in § 13.1.6 how easements – rights of way and the like – take the form they do on account of such considerations. By contrast, human rights are generally understood to arise solely in recognition of their owner's claim to be treated with dignity and respect, simply by virtue of his existence as a human being.

Moreover, the analysis that goes into justifying some right's recognition as in rem is more relative than that which announces human rights. As we saw in § 1.2.2, a right cannot qualify as a right in rem within the *numerus clausus* unless its social worth outweighs the harm that its in rem status will certainly also entail, for example others' ability to use the land, and to the market. Human rights can also entail harm. Say you are prevented from selling your property because you have a tenant who can claim that to evict him would be a disproportionate interference with his right to home. His ability to assert this right harms both your property right and the public interest in its ready marketability. But unlike rights in rem, human rights have been described as 'trumps' over public interests and collective goals,[110] as belonging to individuals 'simply by virtue of their humanity, independently of any utilitarian calculation'.[111] So, unlike rights in rem, they are recognised as such *regardless of* their downside.

Of course, in the case of most human rights – certainly including those under discussion here – this account omits the rather important information that interferences with them can in appropriate cases be allowed, as justified; and that the justification exercise can undoubtedly make reference to others' interests and the public good. As a result, real-time human rights, and certainly the shapes they take on the ground in individual cases, have to be understood less idealistically, and in fact as not ultimately dissimilar to rights in rem. In their different ways – rights in rem as a matter of initial design, human rights as a matter of the bottom line – both will be permitted to exist, in the sense of 'to concretely affect what happens in the world outside legal thought', only in the same circumstance: where their downside does indeed not outweigh their upside. Moreover, we saw in § 2.5.1 that it will in practice be assumed, indeed almost necessarily assumed, in human rights cases that this is so. And thus, that the putative right does not 'exist', in this sense, after all.

---

[110] R Dworkin, *Taking Rights Seriously* (Cambridge MA, 1977).
[111] *R (Alconbury) v Secretary of State for the Environment* [2003] 2 AC 295, [70] (HL).

But a distinction remains. It is reflected in the different ways, just referred to, in which the two kinds of rights are given permission to 'exist' in the sense used there. Put more positively, it is that the idealistic, non-qualified, conceptions of human rights do count for something. In the business of deciding whether they should concretely affect what happens in the real world, their origin (in their owner's claim to be treated with dignity and respect, simply by virtue of his existence as a human being) does, or should,[112] matter, *in opposition to* all contrary considerations.

---

[112] In § 2.4.4, we saw that this appears to have been overlooked in *Manchester City Council v Pinnock* [2011] 2 AC 104 (SC), in the context of the justification exercise under Art 8.

3

When are Disponees Bound?

We now revert to rights in rem, to go into more detail about their behaviour as such.

In § 1.1.2 we saw that rights in rem are rights which are in principle capable of binding disponees ... but that they will actually bind a particular disponee only if certain conditions are present. This chapter looks at the rules telling us what those conditions are, when the rights are ones that concern land.

There are two sets of such rules: one for 'registered land' (or 'land of registered title') and one for 'unregistered land'. The question whether a disponee of a piece of registered land is affected by a right in rem relating to it is decided solely by the rules contained in the Land Registration Act 2002. No other rules are relevant.[1] In the case of unregistered land the same question is decided partly by rules in the Land Charges Act 1972, and partly by some non-statutory rules. Much the greater part of the land in England and Wales is now registered land.[2] This book will therefore go on to look in detail only at the provisions of the Land Registration Act 2002, relating to registered land.

---

[1] Sometimes a disponee will incur an obligation by reason of a rule not supplied by the Act, but this is an essentially different matter from becoming the subject of a pre-existing right in rem, which is our present focus. A rule of the former kind is that generating a 'constructive trust' against a disponee who, as part of the disposition transaction, promises to do something he would not otherwise have to: see § 9.2.

[2] When the registration regime was originally introduced, in 1925, it was made applicable only to certain areas. The number of areas was increased over time, until eventually the whole of the two countries was covered. Even when a piece of land is located in an area to which registration applies, however, the registration regime becomes applicable to it only when its title has been entered on the register: and that need occur only when it is involved in a prescribed kind of transaction (though it can also occur without such a transaction, being registered voluntarily). The list of prescribed transactions has lengthened over time, bringing increasing areas of land within the scope of the regime. For the current law relating to initial registration, see the Land Registration Act 2002 Pt 2 and Sch 1.

3.1 The Registered Land Regime

3.1.1 The Principles

The key principle of the Land Registration Act 2002 is that a right in rem will affect a disponee of the land in question in two, and only two, sets of circumstances:[3] if it appears on the register, and if it operates as an 'overriding interest'.[4]

The Act makes detailed provision for the recording of rights in rem on the register.[5] Nearly all types of right in rem either must or can be registered;[6] only a few are not registrable.[7] The most important of the non-registrable types is an ordinary lease for three years or less (including therefore a weekly, monthly or yearly tenancy[8]), which can therefore affect a disponee only via the alternative route, as an overriding interest.[9]

---

[3] Land Registration Act 2002 ss 29–30. As these sections indicate, however, this key principle does not apply if the disponee (i) does not give valuable consideration for the disposition, as where he receives it as a gift; or (ii) takes an interest in the land other than (approximately speaking) ownership, a lease, an easement or a mortgage, ie (again approximately speaking) those interests which must be conferred by a 'registrable disposition' (see § 5.4.1). Where the key principle does not apply, the rule is instead that the disponee is affected by any extant right in rem pre-dating his own, whether or not it is registered or overriding: s 28. So if I own land, and for example I sell you an option to buy it (this being a right in rem), but then I transfer it as a gift to John, John will be affected by your option over it *even if your option is not registered, nor counts as overriding*. Even though thus exceptional (albeit bizarrely described by s 28 itself as the 'basic rule'), this rule appears rather a sell-out of the logic of registration. Its ambit will further diminish if, with the possible eventual advent of electronic conveyancing (§ 5.4.5), registration comes to be required in respect of more interests than at present, such as, let us imagine, your option in the example. But it is questionable whether registration would ever be required of all interests, in which case the rule will continue to have at least some application.

[4] The expression 'overriding interest' was used in the Land Registration Act 1925; the 2002 Act avoids it, coming closest with the phrase 'unregistered interests which override', but the shorter form remains in common usage and will be adopted here.

[5] Land Registration Act 2002 Pt 4.

[6] ss 27, 32, 40 (s 32 being the catch-all provision, its word 'interest' – meaning right in rem – referring to all such rights except those which are specifically excluded). Technically, only those rights whose conferral is a 'registrable disposition' – ie which have to be recorded on the register in order to exist at all (see § 5.4.1) – are said to be 'registered' when so recorded. The remainder are said to be 'protected by', or 'the subject of', 'entry on the register', or similar. But this linguistic differentiation is commonly ignored, the word 'registered' being used in all cases.

[7] s 33.

[8] See § 11.4.2.

[9] The rules about registering rights under trusts (ss 33(a), 40) are also special, reflecting a preference that such rights, though in some sense rights in rem and so capable of binding a disponee, should not actually do so, but should instead be 'overreached': ie detached from the land at the moment of the disposition, and thenceforth attached instead to the purchase money. This phenomenon is explored more fully in §§ 16.5–16.6.

A right in rem that has not been registered (despite the fact that, usually, it could have been) will nonetheless bind a disponee if it operates as an overriding interest. And it will do so if it fits the description in Schedule 3 to the Act.[10] This lists 14 kinds of circumstances in which a right can be overriding.[11] In 13 of them, the right qualifies as overriding simply by being a particular kind of right, as named in the Schedule. The most generally important of such rights are ordinary leases of up to seven years' duration,[12] and some kinds of easement (an easement is a right such as a right of way).[13] The 14th, enormously important, case is that described in Schedule 3 paragraph 2. By this, almost[14] *any* right in rem concerning a piece of land operates as an overriding interest if the person to whom it belongs is in actual and apparent[15] occupation of that land at the time of the disposition (though not if the disponee asks that person about the right, and he does not reveal it[16]). The idea of 'actual occupation' is explored in more detail in § 3.1.2.

So in theory, almost all rights in rem can be registered, which is one route by which they can bind a disponee; but, if not registered, they can almost all (so long as they are either one of the 13 named rights in Schedule 3, or accompanied by actual and apparent occupation) bind a disponee nonetheless, as overriding interests.[17] In practice, however, the range of overriding interests is not quite so wide. Some kinds of rights in rem do not themselves entitle their owner to occupy the land to which they relate, and will thus rarely, and coincidentally, satisfy paragraph 2. So unless they are among the 13, they will not normally qualify as overriding interests.[18] But many important rights can still

[10] Sch 3 explains when rights will count as overriding against a disposition of land, title to which is already registered. When the disposition is one as a result of which the land's title will become registered for the first time, rights against it will count as overriding under the slightly wider, but essentially similar, rules in Sch 1.

[11] A 15th is added by s 90, giving overriding interest status to PPP leases over the London Underground: a very specialised category.

[12] Sch 3 para 1: see § 11.7.1. So leases that cannot be registered, as being for three years or less, are thus covered, together with some that can be registered. Registration of the latter can thus be regarded as optional.

[13] Sch 3 para 3: see § 13.3.

[14] Two kinds of right are excluded (Sch 3 para 2(a) and (d)), namely beneficial rights under the Settled Land Act 1925 and leases with a start date three months or more after their grant, where the start date has not yet arrived; but the former type is not truly a right in rem anyway, and a tenant under the latter type would be unlikely to be in occupation.

[15] The word 'apparent' is used here and throughout this book as shorthand for the statutory words 'obvious on a reasonably careful inspection of the land at the time of the disposition'.

[16] If 'inquiry was made [of him] before the disposition and [he] failed to disclose the right when he could reasonably have been expected to do so', unless the disponee actually knew about it anyway.

[17] At one time, some people seem to have thought that, under the Land Registration regime, any given type of right in rem could be capable *either* of registration, *or* of operation as an overriding interest, but not both. But there was never a basis for this view in the relevant statutory wording, and it was authoritatively denied in *Williams & Glyn's Bank Ltd v Boland* [1981] AC 487 (HL).

[18] For example, a restrictive covenant: a right that you may have, as my neighbour, forbidding me from, say, erecting additional buildings on my land (see Ch 14). When I sell my land to John, and the question arises whether he is bound by your right, it is unlikely that you will be able to

be seen as realistically able to bind disponees *either* via registration, *or* by being overriding.

There is, however, no third alternative. This rule represents a choice: before 2002, there was a third alternative, but the 2002 Act has eradicated it. It can be seen in the pre-2002 case of *Peffer v Rigg*,[19] holding that a right which was neither registered nor overriding nevertheless bound a disponee who actually knew of it. This conclusion was reached on the basis of the wording of the then prevailing Land Registration Act 1925,[20] which certainly could be read to this effect.[21] But it arguably also embodied a view that such a disponee ought to be bound, as a matter of general principle. That view was considered by the Law Commission during the design phase of the 2002 Act, and rejected,[22] principally on grounds of its incompatibility with the idea that a right in rem will not bind a disponee unless it is registered. The provisions for overriding interests are thus the only route by which rights in rem can bind despite not being registered. As part of our appraisal of those provisions in § 3.2.3, however, we shall consider whether the law is right to draw the line there, or whether another such route – the alternative here under discussion – ought to be added.

3.1.2 'Actual Occupation'

As we have seen, Schedule 3 paragraph 2 gives overriding status to almost any right in rem whose owner is, at the time of the disposition of the land to which it relates, in actual and apparent occupation of that land. Say you have a right in rem over a house which I own, and that I transfer the house to John.

---

rely on its operating against him as an overriding interest, because a restrictive covenant is not among the 13 named rights, and by the nature of it you are unlikely to have been in occupation of my land at the time, so as to bring it under Sch 3 para 2.

[19] [1977] 1 WLR 285, 293–4 (Ch D).

[20] ss 20(1) and 59(6). The two sections described the circumstances in which a disponee was bound and not bound in differing terms. The judge's ruling was one of a number of possible readings of their combined effect. Under s 59(6), read with s 3(xxi), a disponee took free of unregistered and non-overriding rights only if he was in good faith. The judge held that a disponee was not in good faith if he knew of the right but went on to buy the land ostensibly free from it.

[21] This was the decision's second ratio decidendi. It had two others. The first pointed out that the rules (ss 20(1) and 59(6)) required the right to be registered or overriding only if the disposition was for valuable consideration, and held that, on the facts, the disposition in the particular case was not for valuable consideration. This is a narrow issue, on which the result would be the same under the Land Registration Act 2002: ss 29(1), 132. The third ratio was that the disponee was bound (not by the right itself, operating in rem, but) by a 'constructive trust' generated by the circumstances of the transaction. This involves an idea of considerable general importance, discussed in § 9.2.4.

[22] Law Commission, *Land Registration for the Twenty-First Century – A Consultative Document* (Law Com No 254, London, 1998) paras 3.44–3.46, and *Land Registration for the Twenty-First Century – A Conveyancing Revolution* (Law Com No 271, London, 2001) para 5.16; Land Registration Act 2002 ss 28, 29.

If you are, and are discoverable as being, in actual occupation of the house at the time of that transfer, you can claim that your right binds John as an overriding interest in this way. This section looks at the idea of 'actual occupation'.

In many cases, applying the concept of 'actual occupation' poses no problem. (As a consequence, authority regarding these cases is sparse, but there appears no reason to doubt one's commonsense instincts.) If you live in a house, you will normally be in actual occupation of it. This remains so notwithstanding that you may be physically absent from it at the precise moment of the disposition. You may be out for a few hours (at work, on a walk, shopping, etc), or away for a longer spell (on business, on holiday, in hospital,[23] etc). It probably need not be your main home (so you could be in actual occupation of your weekend cottage as well as your flat in town), or even your 'real' home at all (as where you are living with me for the time being, but have no expectation that this will be a permanent arrangement). On the other hand, 'mere fleeting presence' is not enough; 'some degree of permanence and continuity' is required:[24] so the fact that you happen to pay me a quick visit at the moment of the disposition will not avail you. There are, however, bound to be marginal situations, in which it will be impossible to give a confident answer either way. As, perhaps, where you have a number of homes, and move between them . . . at the time of the disposition of one of them, you happen to be there . . . this is your first visit to it for six months, and you plan to stay for a fortnight.[25]

Some of the pre-2002 interpretations of 'actual occupation' slanted it to cover only situations in which the disponee could readily discover the putative occupant, or perhaps the occupant's right.[26] This tendency has now been institutionalised in the requirement of Schedule 3 paragraph 2 that the occupation be not only actual, but also apparent: 'obvious on a reasonably careful inspection of the land at the time of the disposition'. Under this formulation, it is not necessary (or sufficient) for the right itself to be obvious, or discoverable from the occupation alone. Rather, insisting that the occupation – and so the occupant – be discoverable, the formulation ensures that the disponee is in a position to make enquiries of the occupant, which in turn should lead to discovery of the right. Paragraph 2 rules that if the disponee makes such

---

[23] As in *Chhokar v Chhokar* [1984] FLR 313 (CA). In *Link Lending Ltd v Bustard* [2010] EWCA Civ 424 (CA), a person was found to be in actual occupation of her house despite having been detained in a psychiatric care institution for over a year, returning to the house only once a week for a brief visit under supervision – on the basis that she still regarded it as her home, and hoped to live there once more some day.

[24] *Abbey National Building Society v Cann* [1991] 1 AC 56, 93 (HL).

[25] In *Stockholm Finance Ltd v Garden Holdings Inc* [1995] NPC 162 (Ch D) the visit to the residence in question was the first for over a year, and was held *not* to represent actual occupation.

[26] *Epps v Esso Petroleum Co Ltd* [1973] 1 WLR 1071, 1080G–H (Ch D); *Kling v Keston Properties Ltd* (1984) 49 P & CR 212, 221 (Ch D); *Lloyds Bank plc v Rosset* [1989] 1 Ch 350, 379, 394, 405 (CA); *Abbey National Building Society v Cann* [1991] 1 AC 56, 88 (HL). See further P Sparkes, 'The Discoverability of Occupiers of Registered Land' [1989] *Conv* 342.

enquiries (they have to be addressed to the owner of the right, not merely say to the disponor), and the right is not disclosed when disclosure could reasonably be expected, the disponee is not bound by the right, unless he knows about it anyway.

Some decisions treat you as in actual occupation of a house on the strength of facts other than your own personal presence there. So you might qualify as in actual occupation, despite not being there yourself, on the basis that John is there ... and John is your employee, there to do his job for you,[27] or perhaps if he is your spouse[28] ... but apparently not if he is your tenant,[29] or your guest.[30] You might also qualify as in actual occupation on the basis that your belongings are there[31] ... but apparently not if they have been there for only a short time when the disposition occurs.[32] It is hard to understand why you should thus count as in actual occupation in circumstances where, in ordinary terms, you are not. Perhaps the thinking is that in these circumstances the disponee should be able to discover your right. This is problematic (as we saw in the previous paragraph, the legislation focuses not on discoverability of the right itself, but on the occupation of the right-owner, from whom information about the right may then be elicited), but even if it is correct, it does not fully account for the various distinctions. These seem not consistently to reflect the discoverability of the right, or even of the 'occupation'. The contrasting treatments of belongings may perhaps be understood in that way, but not those regarding the presence of other people.

Sometimes you do *not* count as in actual occupation of a house even if, without complication, you *are* present there at the relevant time, living in it as your home. In some old decisions, where a husband owned a house, and lived in it with his wife, she was nonetheless regarded as not in actual occupation of it.[33] In *Williams & Glyn's Bank Ltd v Boland*[34] this approach was abandoned, in favour of one whereby 'actual occupation' means what (or at any rate not less than) it appears to. But the earlier view has been revived, in a ruling that children under 18 living in their parents' house do not count as in actual occupation of it.[35] Perhaps this ruling too was intended to ensure discoverability (one certainly hopes that it rests on more than a mere sense that

---

[27] *Lloyds Bank plc v Rosset* [1989] Ch 350 (CA): occupation via builders.

[28] *Strand Securities Ltd v Caswell* [1965] Ch 958, 984–5 (CA). Would any other relationship suffice? Perhaps the presence of a child would amount to actual occupation by a parent ... but in that decision, the presence of a step-daughter was not regarded as actual occupation by her step-father.

[29] The Land Registration Act 1925 did treat a landlord as in actual occupation via his tenant (s 70(1)(g)), but this has not been carried forward into the Land Registration Act 2002 Sch 3 para 2.

[30] *Strand Securities Ltd v Caswell* [1965] Ch 958, 984–5 (CA).

[31] *Chhokar v Chhokar* [1984] FLR 313 (CA).

[32] *Abbey National Building Society v Cann* [1991] 1 AC 56 (HL), where the time between the arrival of the belongings and the disposition was 35 minutes.

[33] See especially *Bird v Syme-Thomson* [1979] 1 WLR 440 (Ch D).

[34] [1981] AC 487 (HL).

[35] *Hypo-Mortgage Services Ltd v Robinson* [1997] 2 FLR 71 (CA).

children do not count). If so, it ought not to prevail in the law as configured by Schedule 3 paragraph 2. As we have seen, the latter demands only discoverable occupation. A child's occupation is probably no less discoverable than an adult's, and certainly cannot be said to be always undiscoverable. After that, it is for the disponee to make appropriate enquiries. In the case of a young child, the disponee may not be protected by the rule whereby a right that is *not* disclosed on enquiry to its owner does not bind, because the rule demands that it be reasonable to expect such disclosure, and in the case of a young child it would often not be reasonable. But the disponee will normally be able to ensure that the right *is* disclosed, by enquiring of the child's parents.

The foregoing paragraphs focus on actual occupation of a house. Land put to other uses can of course be the subject of occupation too. What counts as 'occupation' will vary with the use. For example, to show that you are in actual occupation of my warehouse, you would point out that you keep your goods there: no one would expect you to live there. Actual occupation of a garage will usually consist in keeping a car in it,[36] and actual occupation of a farm will presumably consist normally in farming it.

3.2 The Appropriateness of the Registered Land Regime

3.2.1 An Argument for Registration

The provision for rights in rem to bind when they are registered is generally welcome. Say I own some land, and you have a right affecting it (say, a right of way), then I transfer it to John. From your point of view, the advantage of being able to bind John by registering your right is that if you proceed in this way, you cannot lose your right.[37] And from John's point of view, the advantage is that he can discover the rights by which he will or may be bound (yours and others) relatively easily, by consulting the register. The difficulty and cost of the transaction should therefore be diminished, and the market in land therefore lubricated; and the threat of people being bound by rights of which

---

[36] As in *Kling v Keston Properties Ltd* (1983) 49 P & CR 212 (Ch D). Apparently inconsistently, *Epps v Esso Petroleum Co Ltd* [1973] 1 WLR 1071 (Ch D) held that parking a car on an open but nonetheless defined piece of land did not amount to actual occupation of it. For a broadly similar case, see further *Chaudhary v Yavuz* [2011] EWCA Civ 1314, [28]–[32] (CA).

[37] As you might under some other approaches, such as the old non-statutory rule whereby John was sometimes bound unless he was a bona fide purchaser without notice. This meant that John was not bound by your right if he was justifiably ignorant of it, and in that case you lost it.

they do not even know ahead of time, and so of having their liberty damaged, largely eradicated.

But it is more controversial whether the law is right to allow rights in rem to affect disponees alternatively as overriding interests. Indeed, this alternative provision has been widely criticised. The central criticism is that it runs counter to the key aim of a registration regime. This, it is asserted, is accurately to reflect all aspects of the title to a given piece of land. 'All aspects of the title' means all the legal rights by which a person acquiring an interest in the land could be affected: in short, all the rights in rem germane to the land. The idea that the register should display all these rights is generally referred to as the 'mirror principle'.[38] Evidence for its authoritative influence on thought in this field can be found in the words of judges,[39] in publications by those connected with the Land Registry,[40] and in Law Commission reports.[41] These texts (of course) acknowledge the provision for overriding interests, but not as something to be applauded. For it is clearly inconsistent with the mirror principle that rights in rem should – as they do with overriding interests – subsist, and be capable of binding purchasers, despite not being registered. From this perspective, overriding interests have been described as a 'cavernous crack' in the mirror.[42]

Historically speaking, this assertion about the key aim of a registration regime is mistaken. Before the land registration regime was introduced, some rights affecting land were generated in transactions on paper, the collection of such pieces of paper being known as the 'deeds' to the land. But other rights arose in other ways, as where a right of way arose by prescription, ie on the basis of 20 years' usage.[43] When registration was first introduced, it was clearly understood that the register was to reflect only rights in the former of the two classes. That is, it was to be a 'mirror' of the paper title, but only the paper title.[44] Rights not shown on the paper deeds were to continue operating on a non-formalised basis: that is, as overriding interests.

---

[38] Reference is also made to the 'curtain principle'. In its original guise, this seems to have consisted in the idea that putative disponees should not have to concern themselves with beneficial interests under a trust on which the land might be held (that such interests existed 'behind the curtain'), because in the event of a disposition these interests would be overreached and so would not affect the disponee (see § 16.5). More recently, however, the 'curtain principle' seems to have become the counterpart of the 'mirror principle' in a composite thesis to the effect that a disponee is bound by all interests shown on the (mirror of the) register, but only by those interests (any others being curtained).

[39] eg *Abbey National Building Society v Cann* [1991] 1 AC 56, 78 (HL).

[40] eg J Stewart-Wallace, *Introduction to the Principles of Land Registration* (London, 1937) 32; T Ruoff, *An Englishman Looks at the Torrens System* (Sydney, 1957) ch 2.

[41] eg Law Commission No 271 (n 22) paras 1.5, 8.1, 8.6. This report was the basis of the Land Registration Act 2002 itself. The latter may therefore be perceived as having moved the law towards the mirror, at the expense of overriding interests. But the appearance to that effect may be superficial: see M Dixon, 'Protecting Third-Party Interests Under the Land Registration Act 2002: To Worry or Not to Worry, That is the Question' in M Dixon and G Griffiths (eds), *Contemporary Perspectives on Property, Equity and Trusts Law* (Oxford, 2007) ch 2.

[42] D Hayton, *Registered Land* (3rd edn, London, 1981) 76.

[43] See § 7.3.

[44] Commission on Registration of Title, *Report* (1857) HCP xxi 245 (London, 1857) para 63.

This is not a full answer to the criticism, however. It remains arguable that in principle the aim should be for the register to reflect ('mirror') *all* rights in rem germane to the land. That is, that the old fact of life – that not all rights were shown on the papers – was a defect which registration should be calculated to cure: that a mature registration regime should be expected to deliver this aim. On this view, we return to the argument that providing for overriding interests is a bad thing, because it prevents the achievement of this aim.[45]

A full mirror can hardly be an end in itself, however. It must be desired as a means to some more fundamental end(s).[46] Thus: a full mirror is needed so as to promote the market in land, by reducing the difficulty and cost of transactions involving it. As already noted, the fact that a right concerning a piece of land is recorded on the register has this effect. But the argument's logic requires *all* the relevant rights to be registered. If any can bind a disponee without being registered, as overriding interests do, costs will be reintroduced as the disponee seeks to discover whether this will occur in his case. And the costs involved in searching for even one such right are likely to be no less than those generated by having to search for many. So from the viewpoint of promoting the market, nothing would have been gained.[47]

This argument for a full mirror, and so against overriding interests, must clearly be taken seriously. It would be wrong, however, instantly to conclude that the law must not provide for overriding interests. It is possible to point to a rival argument, in favour of providing for overriding interests.

3.2.2 An Argument for Overriding Interests

The argument is that the overriding interest provisions cater to those rights in rem that arise in disorganised ways, as a result of which it would be unrealistic to require their registration.

---

[45] See C Harpum, 'Property in an Electronic Age' in E Cooke (ed), *Modern Studies in Property Law, Volume 1* (Oxford, 2001) ch 1.

[46] Another possible end is transparency, ie a concern that as much information as possible should be in the public domain: Law Commission No 271 (n 22) para 2.9. This is a reasonable goal for a democratic society, as empowering individuals. But in broad terms, potentially countervailing concerns, also ascribable to the empowerment of individuals, are also worthy of attention: in particular privacy, and the freedom not to have to bother. The accommodation between the two sets of concerns has to be worked out sensitively to the nature of the information in question. It has certainly never been demonstrated that the proper accommodation in this context demands a full mirror.

[47] A further important argument for registration in general is the republican one of seeking to ensure that a disponee is not exposed to arbitrary domination – as he would be if he could be bound by a right without knowledge of it and so the opportunity to avoid it. But this argument does not demand a full mirror. It is satisfied if the disponee can (must, before he is bound) reasonably acquire knowledge of the right in any way; it supports registration merely as a particularly good way of delivering such knowledge. The ensuing discussion is therefore framed around the market argument, which by contrast does demand a full mirror, for the reason explained in the text.

The rights in rem over land recognised by English law arise in two ways. The distinction between the two ways is not officially made, so there is no established pair of terms for referring to them. We shall call them 'organised' and 'disorganised'.

A right arises in an *organised* way when it is acquired as a result of someone intending, indeed planning, to confer it: as where I transfer my house to you in fulfilment of our contract for you to buy it, or grant you a mortgage (Chapter 12), or make a restrictive covenant in your favour (Chapter 14). When someone is involved in a transaction of this kind, he will know that he is dealing in rights in land. And, land being the valuable and notoriously sophisticated commodity that it is, he will if he has any sense use lawyers to ensure that everything is done properly. The lawyers will know what right is in play, will know the law's rules about how to create or transfer it, and will follow these rules. So if the law requires these rights to be registered, in the nature of things they normally will be registered. Indeed, they normally will be even if the law does not require them to be, ie even if the law does also allow for overriding interests. Except for a saving of the small registration fee, there is certainly no advantage in not registering them. And there is likely advantage in registering them, as cutting out all scope for argument over such matters as whether their owner was in actual and apparent occupation at the relevant time.

In contrast, however, English law also allows rights in rem concerning land sometimes to arise in *disorganised* ways. That is, they are acquired in circumstances where the parties do not realise, or have only a vague idea, that they are dealing in legal rights at all; or, if they do realise any of this, assume that the law itself will 'see them right'. As a consequence, they do not normally enlist the services of a lawyer. Rights of this kind include those arising by the doctrine of proprietary estoppel (Chapter 8), or under a constructive trust (Chapter 9). Take a characteristic example. I own some land adjoining yours. You believe that it too belongs to you, and cultivate it. I know all this, but do not bother to correct you. The law will probably award you some sort of right in rem over the land in question, under the doctrine of proprietary estoppel. But you will likely not realise this, or not with any clarity. Moreover, it is of the very nature of a situation like this that we are not using lawyers: otherwise, we would not have got into such a muddle. And without lawyers, there is nobody to know about, and comply with, any technical rules that the law may impose.[48] So even if the law were to require rights acquired in such a way to be registered, in the nature of things the requirement would not normally be complied with.

---

[48] It is sometimes suggested that campaigns should be undertaken to educate the lay public about land registration. The suggestion seems unpromising in itself, but moreover, education about registration would be useless without education also about the circumstances in which rights can arise requiring registration – which seems even less feasible.

The law does not have to recognise both modes of generating rights. In a strongly individualistic political context, we should expect rights to arise only where people are organised enough to arrange them, with no support for people who do not look after themselves. On the other hand, in certain other kinds of political context, such as an extremely communitarian one, the law would impose its own solutions, to the extent of taking no account of any efforts that people did make to settle their own rights. Unsurprisingly, English law in reality supposes it appropriate to allow those who can to settle their own rights, and to support those who fail to do so but deserve them nonetheless. So it recognises both modes. In consequence, it produces the situation in which lawyers, who alone know about registration, will only sometimes be involved: and so, the situation in which only some of its rights in rem will in practice normally be registered. We shall look at the organised creation of rights (in effectuation of their creator's wish) in Chapters 5 and 6, and a variety of ways in which rights are recognised as arising in a disorganised fashion (for important reasons of justice or utility) in Chapters 7 to 9.

So whilst rights arising in organised ways typically will be registered, those arising in disorganised ways typically will not. If the latter are to survive, then there must be provision for them to affect disponees without registration: that is, as overriding interests. This way of accounting for overriding interests underlies the Law Commission's apologia for them: that, owing to the nature of rights of this kind, it is 'neither reasonable to expect nor sensible to require any entry on the register'.[49] It also connects with the historical fact, noted above, that the register was originally intended only to reflect those rights which appeared in the paper title to the land in question. These would have been the rights created in an organised way. Those not shown in the paper title would have arisen in disorganised ways: so the decision not to require their registration was based on just the argument presently under discussion.

To understand the full strength of this argument for overriding interests, remember the fundamental point of this chapter: to look at the rules (including the provision for overriding interests, if one is to exist) establishing exactly when a right in rem, ie a right capable of binding a disponee, will actually do so. Given that they have this role, these rules are connected not merely adjectivally, but intrinsically, with the rights in rem themselves. The rules' design therefore must be sympathetic to the qualities of the rights in rem that the law maintains. (They are, if you like, the fuel on which the in rem engine runs . . . it being obvious that the fuel and engine must work together.) As we have seen, the law in fact provides for rights in rem to arise in disorganised ways. It cannot properly then design the rules for the operation of rights in rem along such lines that rights arising in disorganised ways cannot fulfil their mission of binding a disponee. Rules sympathetic to these rights' qualities are

---

[49] Law Commission No 271 (n 22) para 8.53.

required. That is, rules allowing them to bind despite not being registered; in other words, rules providing for them to operate as overriding interests.

3.2.3 A Compromise between the Two Arguments

This argument in favour of providing for overriding interests is a powerful one. But we have not finished yet. In § 3.2.1 we noted the argument for promoting marketability, and so making no provision for overriding interests; and it too was impressive. What position should the law in fact take?

There is no difficulty about rights arising in organised ways. The market argument in favour of a full mirror obviously operates here, but there is no opposition to it. As explained in § 3.2.2, those involved in the conferral of such a right – who will almost necessarily include lawyers – will know of the possibility of registering it, and will naturally do so, because of the advantages of improved security that this will bring. The question is what to do about rights arising in disorganised ways, where the market argument in favour of registration remains the same, but now runs up against the counter-argument we have identified.

One might contend for the complete victory of either argument over the other, so that such rights either always bound despite not being registered, or never did so. Such an outcome would be unsatisfactory, however, as failing to reflect the truth behind one argument or the other.[50] The best outcome has to involve some kind of compromise between them. The Land Registration Act 2002 has in fact adopted such a compromise. Its shape is to be found in the terms of the rules about overriding interests, in Schedule 3.

To be sure, Schedule 3 is not explicitly confined to disorganised rights (on the face of it, it allows almost any right in rem to become overriding, regardless of how the right arose[51]). But this is its scope in reality, for, as already noted, those involved in a right's organised conferral will in practice register it. However, the Schedule does not give overriding status to all disorganised rights under all circumstances. To qualify for overriding status, the right must meet the Schedule's stipulations. That is, it must fall within one of the 13 listed categories, or be accompanied by actual and apparent occupation.

This is the key point, the nub of the compromise: these stipulations are calculated to ensure that even disorganised rights achieve overriding status only if they are readily discoverable by a disponee. So, for example, certain leases and

---

[50] Indeed, a regime which made no provision for disorganised rights to operate in rem without registration might well infringe the European Convention on Human Rights, First Protocol, Art 1: it would deprive the rights' owners of their 'possessions', admittedly in a legitimate cause (protecting the market in land), but surely – given the argument in the text – in a disproportionately vigorous manner.

[51] Exceptionally, the combination of the Land Registration Act 2002 s 27(2)(d) and Sch 3 para 3 has the effect of preventing expressly granted – ie organised – easements from operating as overriding interests.

easements are allowed to be overriding, but certain others are not:[52] both sorts can be equally disorganised, but the former are at least represented as being more easily discoverable than the latter.[53] So too, perhaps above all, with the rule that almost any kind of right will be overriding if its owner is in actual and apparent occupation of the land to which it relates. The idea is that the right should be discoverable ... not simply in the abstract, for that could mean by way of tortuous and expensive inquiries in all manner of directions, but via the specific, pregnant, and by definition unmissable fact of its owner's actual and apparent occupation. The right is thus *readily* – easily, cheaply – discoverable.

This restriction of overriding status to those rights that are not only disorganised but also readily discoverable makes the compromise a soundly principled one. (In contrast, say, to a rule giving disorganised rights overriding status, but only on Mondays, Wednesdays and Fridays.) The concern of the argument against overriding interests – in favour of demanding registration without exception – is, as we have seen, a worry about increasing disponees' costs and so damaging the market in land. By accepting the case for having overriding interests at all, the law has brought this problem to life. But by ruling that a disponee need trouble only about those unregistered rights that are readily discoverable, it has ensured that he incurs only a quite limited amount of extra cost, and so has contained the extent of the problem.

It would be wrong, however, to think that this ruling firmly positions the law at some notional point mid-way between those advocated as ideals by the competing arguments. The concepts used in the ruling – ie in Schedule 3 – are often malleable. (In § 3.1.2, for example, we discovered considerable instability in the idea of 'actual occupation'; and schedule 3 paragraphs 2 and 3 both use the expression 'obvious on a reasonably careful inspection of the land', which is obviously highly indeterminate.) A court especially impressed by the argument for or against overriding interests will thus find it easy to bend the compromise towards its preferred position.[54] The pre-2002 case-law certainly shows this effect.[55] There is no reason to think that it will no longer occur.

---

[52] Sch 3 paras 1 and 3. Briefly, the rights excluded under these provisions are a lease taking effect more than three months after its creation; a disorganised easement not 'obvious on a reasonably careful inspection of the land', unless actually known to the disponee, or used within the last year; and an equitable easement. See §§ 11.7.1 and 13.3.

[53] See Law Commission No 271 (n 22) paras 8.10 and 8.65. But withholding overriding status from equitable easements cannot be justified in this way, and appears ill-judged and in violation of ECHR First Protocol Art 1: § 13.3.

[54] See N Jackson, 'Title by Registration and Concealed Overriding Interests: The Cause and Effect of Antipathy to Documentary Proof' (2003) 119 *LQR* 660.

[55] Pro-market decisions, constructing their concepts on lines unsympathetic to the protection of disorganised rights, include *Abbey National Building Society v Cann* [1991] 1 AC 56 (HL). Decisions constructing their concepts more sympathetically to the protection of disorganised rights include *Williams & Glyn's Bank Ltd v Boland* [1981] AC 487 (HL). (Discussions of these and related decisions sometimes, however, overstate their room for conceptual manoeuvre and therefore their impact on the shape of the law. See M Conaglen, 'Mortgagee Powers Rhetoric' (2006) 69 *MLR* 583.)

One final point. Since the compromise aims to allow a disorganised right to bind a disponee, despite non-registration, when the disponee could easily – cheaply – discover it, one would expect it to contain a rule whereby a disponee who *actually knows* of such a right is bound by it, without more. Indeed, such a rule should be a stronger candidate for acceptance than the overriding interest rules themselves. As we have seen, the latter create an incentive for the disponee to incur costs in finding out about the right, though they are designed so as to limit the extent of these costs. But a rule reacting only to a disponee's actual knowledge creates no such incentive: if anything, the reverse. As we saw in § 3.1.1, a rule on these lines existed in the pre-2002 law,[56] but does not feature in the Land Registration Act 2002.[57] The reason is a concern that if disponees could be bound by actual knowledge, the law might drift into their being bound by less than actual knowledge, so reintroducing incentives to investigate.[58] This seems a weak argument: the concepts used for expressing such a rule would be no more malleable than those apparently found acceptable for stating the overriding interest rules.

3.2.4 The Future of Overriding Interests

There exist plans to reduce the profile of overriding interests, via two principal strategies.[59]

First, the Land Registration Act 2002 provides that, of the 14 kinds of right on the current list of overriding interests, the five most esoteric shall remain on the list only for 10 years, after which they will bind disponees only if registered.[60] The case for this change is that, however unreasonable and unrealistic it may be to expect and require these rights to be registered, they are relatively difficult for a disponee to discover. So in terms of the accommodation we have identified between the arguments for a full mirror and those for overriding interests, their claim to overriding status is

---

[56] *Peffer v Rigg* [1977] 1 WLR 285 (Ch D).

[57] ss 28–29. (The sections do not explicitly deny the rule, but are phrased in such a way as not to admit it.) For discussion, see E Cooke and P O'Connor, 'Purchaser Liability to Third Parties in the English Land Registration System: A Comparative Perspective' (2004) 120 *LQR* 640. Contradictorily of the general position, however, an easement will operate as an overriding interest if the disponee of the relevant land actually knows about it: Land Registration Act 2002 Schedule 3 para 3(1)(a).

[58] See Law Commission No 271 (n 22) para 5.16; Law Commission No 254 (n 22) paras 3.44–3.46.

[59] A third consists in provisions requiring the Land Registry to register most hitherto overriding interests which do come to its attention (Land Registration Act 2002 s 37), and allowing it to require people applying for registration to disclose, for registration, overriding interests of which they are aware (s 71). These provisions are uncontroversial, but of limited impact.

[60] s 117. The rights in question are those in Sch 3 paras 10–14, namely: 'A franchise. A manorial right. A right to rent which was reserved to the Crown on the granting of any freehold estate (whether or not the right is still vested in the Crown). A non-statutory right in respect of an embankment or sea or river wall. A right to payment in lieu of tithe.'

relatively weak. They were included in the Act's list merely so as to give their owners the benefit of a notice period before their (essentially merited) discontinuance.[61]

Second, it was planned that, at a point in the future, at least some rights that the current regime leaves as overriding would require registration for their very creation.[62] Thus registered in order to exist at all, there would be no question of their being able to bind disponees without registration.[63] So, at present a lease for more than seven years can be made only by a registered transaction,[64] but an ordinary lease for seven years or less can be overriding.[65] If the seven-year threshold for compulsory registration were lowered, say to three years, leases only for less than that would be capable of being over-riding.[66] Unless registered, a lease for more than three years would not exist, and so necessarily would not be able to form the basis of an overriding interest.

The Land Registration Act 2002[67] provides for statutory instruments to be made adding rights to the list of those required to be registered, and so una-ble to operate as overriding interests, in this way. It was envisaged that such instruments would be made in the context of the introduction of 'electronic conveyancing'. Whereas under present arrangements, parties' lawyers send physical paperwork concerning their transactions to the Registry for the Registry to make the appropriate entries on the register, under electronic con-veyancing – explained in detail in § 5.4.5 – the lawyers would themselves make the entries online.[68]

In terms of the principles involved in the present compromise, why should this make a difference? One can undoubtedly argue that it should *not* make a difference. The feasibility of registering organised transactions online would not in the least make it more reasonable to expect rights arising in disorgan-ised ways to be registered too, whether online or otherwise. The disorganised nature of the ways in which they arise itself rules this out. Equally, the possi-bility of searching the register for organised (registered) rights online would not make it less easy to make the quite different inquiries that the design of Schedule 3 makes relevant to disorganised (unregistered) rights. So long as the law continues to have disorganised rights in land at all, the advent of

---

[61] See Law Commission No 271 (n 22) paras 8.35–8.46 and 8.81–8.89. The Commission believes that immediate termination of their overriding status would have violated the European Convention on Human Rights (*cf* n 50 above), but that the notice period will prevent this result.

[62] On registration for a right's creation, see further §§ 5.4.4–5.4.5.

[63] Law Commission No 271 (n 22) paras 8.2, 8.74.

[64] Land Registration Act 2002 ss 4, 6 and 7.

[65] Sch 3 para 1.

[66] The significance of three years is that, below this duration, a lease can – under the present law – validly be made without any formality at all: Law of Property Act 1925 s 54(2) (§ 5.5).

[67] s 93.

[68] As noted in § 5.4.5, the project to introduce electronic registration has recently been discon-tinued indefinitely, though not necessarily permanently.

electronic conveyancing should make no difference to the correctness of allowing them to operate as overriding interests.[69]

One might, however, challenge this view, by pointing to a trend to align our way of living with the possibilities offered by information technology. The latter, of course, are continually evolving, and recent developments have made the idea of such an alignment more plausible than it was even recently. Our smartphones can, by scanning our discourse, know our tastes, interests, friends[70] and so on, and by drawing on this knowledge, and combining it with the knowledge they can also have of our position, suggest courses of action, without our even needing to ask: perhaps presenting us with a personalised offer from a nearby shop or restaurant, or the idea of a rendezvous with an acquaintance who happens also to be in the vicinity. And (this being the alignment) we, presumably, sometimes take up these suggestions, content to do so in substitution for taking a path of our own devising. It is imaginable, therefore, that our communications devices will come to be able to perceive the aspects of our dealings entitling us to a disorganised right ... or, more likely, *some of* those aspects, whereupon, as part of the alignment, we shall be content to revise our ideas about disorganised rights so as to recognise these aspects alone as mattering[71] ... and then (this part would be easy) to register the right in question on our behalf.[72] At which point, comprehensive electronic conveyancing would have come about, and overriding interests would deservedly exist no longer.

---

[69] At one time the Law Commission appeared to accept this, remarking 'rights that could arise without express grant or reservation or by operation of law, interests under trusts and short leases which were overriding interests would not be subject to the "creation by registration" requirement': Law Commission No 254 (n 22) para 2.47. But the Commission's more recent discussion of electronic conveyancing in Law Commission No 271 (n 22) Pt XIII contains no such statement.

[70] Concepts – especially that of 'friends' – that have themselves altered in meaning as part of this trend.

[71] Take for example the acquisition of a constructive trust right in a family home: see § 9.3. As explained there, any number of factors may currently bear upon the question whether you acquire such a right in a house registered in my name, and if so of the right's size. Of these factors, some will be more easily perceived by our communications devices than others. Broadly speaking, quantitative factors (such as your contributions to the mortgage repayments) will be more easily captured than qualitative ones (such as the essential nature of our relationship), though the latter might be approachable via quantitative proxies (such as the fact that only one of us has an income, suggesting that our relationship is 'materially communal', indicating that you should have a half share in the house). To the extent that some factors are nonetheless uncapturable, the argument of the text is that, as part of our alignment of real life with the possibilities offered by our IT, we should, or at least will, come to see these as unimportant.

[72] There is a possible difficulty, however. At least some disorganised rights, perhaps all of them, arise only if, or to the extent that, a judicial discretion is exercised in the claimant's favour. On the face of it, this discretion could not be supplanted by an IT program: meaning that the registration would be only of a claim to a right. But the alignment under discussion might mean the excision of such discretion, or the acceptance of an algorithmic replacement for it.

3.2.5 Human Rights

The question arises (subject to issues of horizontal effect: § 2.2): is the picture described in this group of sections compliant with the ECHR?[73]

At first sight, one might say that, if your rights in rem have to be registered before they can operate as such, we are looking at an interference with your 'possessions', engaging ECHR First Protocol Article 1. And on appropriate facts, an interference also with your home, engaging ECHR Article 8.

On closer inspection, it is not so clear that there is always such an interference with your possessions (though there seems no equivalent reason to doubt that there is an interference with your home). As noted in § 3.1.1, while some rights in rem have to be registered before they will bind a disponee, others have to be registered in order to exist as such at all.[74] And while the registration requirement in the former case may indeed 'interfere' with your right, in the latter it may not, for the reason that it contributes to the right's very constitution: the right simply does not come into being, to be interfered with or not, unless and until the requirement has been complied with. Whether this analysis is correct, or whether we are looking at an interference in this case too, is a difficult issue, on which the courts have not yet taken anything like a definitive position.[75]

To the extent that there is an interference, whether with your possessions or with your home, it may, however, be justified if it displays 'proportionality', ie represents a well-calculated means to deliver a proper end. And this seems generally likely. The arguments for registration which we considered in § 3.2.1 represent perfectly (if not of course unchallengeably) proper ends, and the specific registration rules seem broadly apt to deliver them.[76]

We should immediately note, however, that the latter statement can be regarded as true only to the extent that there exists provision for overriding interests alongside the registration rules themselves. Taken alone, the registration rules would be disproportionate, as failing to do justice to the countervailing considerations discussed in § 3.2.2. It is the overall mix between registration and overriding interests, structured in some such way (not necessarily exactly) as described in § 3.2.3, that strikes one as apt, proportionate, give or take the odd infelicity.[77] In particular, in according overriding interest

---

[73] For a fuller and more general treatment of the ECHR's impact on land law, see Ch 2.

[74] The creation of a right of the latter type is known as a 'registrable disposition'. Registrable dispositions are discussed further in § 5.4.1.

[75] See *Wilson v First County Trust Ltd (No 2)* [2004] 1 AC 816 (HL). This decision addressed an issue analogous to that discussed in the text, but in a different context. Of the five judges involved, two considered that there was an interference; one that there was not; one that there might have been; while the fifth avoided the point altogether.

[76] Any interference arising from the registration rules will presumably be of the 'control of use' variety, which can be justified even without compensation: § 2.3.5.

[77] Such as the withholding of overriding interest status from equitable easements: n 53.

status to registrable[78] but unregistered rights accompanied by actual and apparent occupation, the current law does much to abort any interference with homes, which, given the deep importance of the latter, would be especially difficult to regard as justified. Such ideas regarding the role of overriding interests in securing the alignment of the registration regime with the ECHR will need, of course, to be borne in mind as the future of such interests is considered, as discussed in § 3.2.4; though of course the social realignments noted in that section could put a different complexion on the prevailing matrix, as explained there.

3.3 Registration More Generally

3.3.1 The Act's Wider Impact and Essential Thrust

This chapter has been about the circumstances under which a right in rem, ie a right capable of affecting a disponee, will actually do so. Addressing only registered land, it has explained that those circumstances are defined by the rules in the Land Registration Act 2002 (and are that the right must either be registered, or qualify as an overriding interest under Schedule 3).

For clarity's sake, it is worth noting that this is not the only task at which the Act is aimed. In particular, it also makes provision regarding the circumstances in which rights can arise in the first place. It does so in two principal ways.

First, it contributes rules – and paves the way for the possible introduction of more in the future, via the electronic conveyancing project discussed in § 3.2.4 – about the formalities that must be used in order for certain kinds of rights to come into being (not simply for them to affect a subsequent disponee, though of course that follows). These rules are considered in Chapters 5 and 6, which deal with that topic. And secondly, it makes large changes in one doctrine allowing rights to arise in a disorganised way, namely 'adverse possession', whereby (to put it broadly) a landowner can find himself supplanted by a squatter after 12 years' occupation by the latter. This topic is covered in more detail in § 7.2, but for the present, the important point is that, as a result of the changes made by the Act, rights can arise by adverse possession much less readily than they used to (and still do, in the case of unregistered land); this enhancement of the landowner's protection being founded on the very fact that his title is registered, meaning that the squatter – like everyone else – should know about it and respect it.[79]

---

[78] But not of course those rights which have to be registered in order to exist at all.
[79] Law Commission No 254 (n 22) para 10.11; Law Commission No 271 (n 22) para 14.3.

These two further sets of rules have a common theme. This theme is to the effect that the registration project per se (obviously, overriding interests continue to reflect variant considerations) is best envisaged in terms of the state of the title regarding a given piece of land being *that which the register asserts*. In other words, the idea is that the register should no longer passively track a reality obtaining in the outside world; instead, it should actively constitute that reality. So the 2002 Act is said[80] to provide not for 'registration of title' but for 'title by registration'.[81]

3.3.2 Amendment of the Register

At the same time, however, the Land Registration Act 2002 provides also for amendment of the register.[82]

Of course it is unthinkable that the register should impede ongoing human life. So amendment must be possible so as to allow for new conferrals of rights: as where I, owning the land, rent it to John, or give a right of way over it to Kate, or sell it to Liam, or die leaving it to Meg; or where a lease or a mortgage over it comes to an end. It is therefore quite unsurprising that the Act's rules[83] allow for amendment of this kind.

The Act goes further, however, and allows also for abandonment of the information shown on the register where that information contains a 'mistake'.[84] The case for such a provision is easy to see: one would not wish people's substantive rights to be determined by clerical errors or indeed frauds. But allowing for the correction of 'mistakes' is troublesome, for two reasons. First, because the meaning of 'mistake' is not made clear. Apparently the intention was for it to refer to a situation where the register asserts something which, if the full true facts had been known to the Registry, the Registry would not have allowed it to assert.[85] *Quaere*, however, how far this clarification in

---

[80] Law Commission No 254, *ibid* para 10.43. See also Law Commission No 271, *ibid* para 1.10.

[81] Indeed, the Land Registration Act 2002 s 58(1) declares: 'If, on the entry of a person in the register as the proprietor of a legal estate, the legal estate would not otherwise be vested in him, it shall be deemed to be vested in him as a result of the registration.'

[82] Land Registration Act 2002 Sch 4. See further D Fox, 'Forgery and Alteration of the Register under the Land Registration Act 2002' and P O'Connor, 'Registration of Invalid Dispositions' in E Cooke (ed), *Modern Studies in Property Law, Volume 3* (Oxford, 2005) chs 2, 3.

[83] Land Registration Act 2002 Sch 4 paras 2(1)(b), 5(b) and (d).

[84] Sch 4 para 5(a).

[85] C Harpum, 'Rectification' (unpublished paper to Chancery Bar Association seminar on Land Registration, 9 May 2011). *Cf Baxter v Mannion* [2011] 2 All ER 574 (CA). Mr Baxter applied to the Land Registry to be registered as owner of some land on the basis of having adversely possessed it for 10 years. (For adverse possession, see § 7.2.) The Registry notified Mr Mannion, in whose name the land in question had until then been registered, giving him the chance to block the application. Mr Mannion failed to respond within the allowed time, so registration was made in Mr Baxter's name. All this was procedurally correct, but Mr Mannion then pointed out – accurately – that Mr Baxter had never adversely possessed the land in the first place. The court accepted that, given this, the registration in Mr Baxter's name involved a

fact takes us. The reference point of the Registry's hypothetical reaction to the full true facts is hardly transparent, and neither is it normatively respectable: the law should be shaping the Registry's behaviour, rather than vice versa. And second, because the whole idea of correcting 'mistakes' seems to run counter to the idea that the facts relating to the land should be those shown by the register. For if title is whatever the register states it to be, how – by definition – *can* the register contain a 'mistake'?[86]

Where correcting the mistake will not injure the registered owner, the rules provide for it to be done almost automatically.[87] But where correction will injure the registered owner, it is called 'rectification',[88] and then, if the registered owner is *not* in possession of the land, the correction must likewise be made almost automatically;[89] but if the registered owner *is* in possession of the land,[90] it must not be made unless the mistake was the registered owner's own fault,[91] or it would be unjust not to correct it.[92] So, if I am registered as owner but you ought to have been, correcting the mistake will plainly injure me: I will lose the land. If I am in possession of the land, I shall probably be safe, whereas otherwise I shall very probably suffer. However, where rectification occurs and I do suffer (or indeed where it is refused and so you suffer), compensation – 'indemnity' – will normally be payable out of state funds.[93]

This complex of arrangements appears generally compatible with the ECHR. First consider matters from the point of view of the registered owner, benefited by the mistaken registration. The rectification rules ensure that there will be no correction injurious to his home (for Article 8) unless there is a very good – and so proportionate – reason why there should be. The rules

---

'mistake'. This decision thus fits with the understanding of 'mistake' described in the text: the Registry would not have registered the land to Mr Baxter if it had known that he had never adversely possessed it. The court's own focus, however, was on the question (at [1]) 'Does the machinery of the Land Registration Act 2002 allow a party to take some else's land by operation of a bureaucratic machinery which trumps reality?' *Quaere* whether the reference to 'a bureaucratic machinery [trumping] reality' represents merely a robust way of expressing the same idea, or something narrower.

[86] For thoughtful consideration of this question, see A Nair, 'The Normative Limits of the "Principles of Land Registration"' in S Bright (ed), *Modern Studies in Property Law, Volume 6* (Oxford, 2011) ch 13.

[87] Except in 'exceptional circumstances': Land Registration Rules 2003 (SI 2003/1417) r 126. The statement in the text, however, relates only to alteration ordered by a court. The position regarding alteration at the Registry's own initiative appears not to have been so firmly settled.

[88] Land Registration Act 2002 Sch 4 para 1.

[89] '. . . unless there are exceptional circumstances which justify . . . not doing so . . .': *ibid* paras 3(3), 6(3).

[90] This has an extended meaning, additionally covering various situations where one is not personally in possession but permits another to be: *ibid* s 131.

[91] '. . . unless . . . he has by fraud or lack of proper care caused or substantially contributed to the mistake . . .'.

[92] Land Registration Act 2002 Sch 4 paras 3(2), 6(2).

[93] The provision for this is contained in the Land Registration Act 2002 Sch 8: see especially para 1(1)(a) and (b). Exceptionally, if I suffer rectification because, despite being in possession, the mistake was wholly or partly my own fault, I lose my indemnity to the extent of that fault: Sch 8 para 5.

also ensure that where (usually where his home is not at stake) a correction does occur, whilst this will certainly be injurious to his 'possessions' (for the First Protocol Article 1), he will normally receive compensation, once again securing proportionality. Take now the point of view of the 'true' owner, disserved by the mistaken registration. A refusal of correction – which in any case will usually occur only where the registered owner is in possession of the relevant land – will doubtless (contrary to the rhetoric of 'title by registration') interfere with his 'possessions', though presumably not his home. But the normal availability of compensation should mean that this interference is justifiable as proportionate.

Consenting Out of a Right

4.1 The Rule in *Bristol and West Building Society v Henning*

4.1.1 The Rule

Say you have a right over land which will in principle bind a disponee of that land, in one of the ways explored in Chapter 3: it is a right in rem, and either it is registered or it qualifies as an overriding interest. If, however, you consent to the disponee not being bound by the right after all, he will not be bound by it. This was established in *Bristol and West Building Society v Henning*,[1] a decision in the context of unregistered land which was soon applied to registered land in *Paddington Building Society v Mendelsohn*.[2]

Imagine, for example, that you and I live together in a house which I own, but in which, we have agreed, you should have an interest too. The law accords you that interest; it is a beneficial interest under a constructive trust,[3] and so a right in rem. You may have registered it, but if not (which is more probable), it will be an overriding interest on the basis of your actual and apparent occupation. Now I sell the house to John. If you were unaware of the sale, your interest will bind John.[4] But that is an unlikely scenario. More likely is that I sell the house because we have decided to move home, and you go along with the steps I take to that end. When the sale goes through, you cannot change your mind and claim to keep your right in the house after all. You consented to John not being bound by it, and must abide by that. Your interest is 'postponed' to his, meaning that you still have it, but instead of ranking ahead of

[1] [1985] 1 WLR 778 (CA).
[2] (1985) 50 P & CR 244 (CA).
[3] See § 9.3.
[4] For the (complicated) law on the effectiveness of trust interests against buyers, see §§ 16.4–16.8.

his right, it ranks after his right. In a straightforward case, this means simply that, now that the house belongs to John, you no longer have rights in the house.

The same principle applies if the transaction is not to sell the house, but to mortgage it. Say again that you and I live in a house that I own but in which you have an interest. Then, instead of selling the house, I 'release the equity' in it: ie borrow money against its value, by giving the lending bank a mortgage over it. As your interest is in rem, and you are (let us suppose) in actual and apparent occupation at the time of the mortgage, your interest will in principle affect the bank as an overriding interest. Then, although I have purported to grant the bank a mortgage over the entire value of the house, your interest – binding the bank – has to be subtracted from what the bank actually gets. That is to say, the mortgage will be effective only to the extent of my interest in the house. This may well be discomforting for the bank.[5] But loans raised in this way are often used for purposes in which we are both involved, such as home improvements. In such a case you will normally know what is going on and consent to the mortgage, so postponing your right and allowing the mortgage to apply to the house's full value after all. On the other hand, such loans are also sometimes used for purposes in which you are not necessarily involved, such as to put extra money into my business. Then, it is not unknown for me to act without you realising it and thus without your consent,[6] meaning that your right will operate as an overriding interest and bind the bank after all.

4.1.2 The Underlying Analysis

In *Bristol and West Building Society v Henning*,[7] the court explained this rule in a particular way. This explanation was not satisfactory, however.[8] Although there has been no explicit discussion of the change in the cases, the more recent ones have replaced the original explanation with a new one. It is said

---

[5] Say I have a 67% share in the house, and you have the other 33% share. The fact that the mortgage is effective only to the extent of my interest means that, if I default on the loan and the bank repossesses the house to recoup itself, the bank can take only 67% of the house's value, and must give the other 33% up to you. So if my loan was for more than 67% of the house's value, the bank will lose. For a more detailed account of the relevant law, see Ch 16, especially § 16.8.1.

[6] As apparently in eg *Williams & Glyn's Bank Ltd v Boland* [1981] AC 487 (HL).

[7] [1985] 1 WLR 778 (CA).

[8] It involved – in terms of the example given in § 4.1.1 – recalling that you acquired your right in the house via an agreement with me, and continuing to assert that built into this agreement was an understanding that your right would be postponed as described in the text. This account had two deficiencies. First, the alleged understanding about postponement would be quite fictitious, aimed at fulfilling some other agenda, which had better be identified more transparently. Second, the consent principle should apply not only to rights arising from an agreement between us, but also to rights arising in other ways, which would be impossible under the explanation given.

now that, if you go along with my steps to sell or mortgage our house, you will be prevented from setting up against the disponee any interest that would otherwise bind him, on the basis that you are estopped from doing so.[9] By going along with my steps, you have impliedly represented to the disponee that you will not set up your right against him; and the disponee has relied on this representation to his detriment, by undertaking his part in the disposition; so you may not go back on your representation.

4.2 What Counts as the Necessary Representation?

To be estopped from setting up against a disponee a right of yours which would otherwise bind him, you must represent that you will not enforce it, and he must act in reliance on that representation in such a way that it would be inequitable for you to enforce it after all.

4.2.1 Finding the Necessary Representation

When will you be regarded as representing that you will not set your interest up against the disponee? The case-law contains very little discussion of this question, but we can suggest some answers on the basis of general principles.

Fundamentally, whatever language or behaviour you use, whether it counts as the required representation depends on its objective appearance: ie whether it would be interpreted as such by a reasonable bystander.

An appropriate explicit statement will suffice, of course.[10] But so should an implication, such as going along with the steps I take to sell or mortgage the house, so giving the impression that you are not going to put obstacles in the way. Most of the cases involve a mere omission to object to the disposition, and treat it as enough. In principle, however, such an omission to object should suffice only if you could have been expected to object. Contrast two illustrative scenarios.

The first, which is the one addressed by the cases, is that where I sell to John – or mortgage to a bank – the house, which I hold on trust for myself and you and which is our home. In this scenario, it normally would be rea-

---

[9] *Skipton Building Society v Clayton* (1993) 66 P & CR 223 (CA); *Woolwich Building Society v Dickman* [1996] 3 All ER 204 (CA).

[10] According to *Woolwich Building Society v Dickman, ibid*, the disponee can rely on your consent only if (presumably, your consent has been given explicitly, and) *it has been noted on the register*. There is no warrant for this view, however, and it has attracted no attention in other decisions.

sonable for John or the bank to reckon that you know what I am doing, and to interpret silence on your part as a promise to postpone your right. So your omission to object does qualify as the required representation. In the second scenario, however, I sell to John a piece of land over which you, living next door, have a right of way. Even if John has reason to think that you know of the sale, he has no reason to expect you to take an interest in it. So here your failure to object to the sale, or to assert your right, ought not to be seen as a representation that you will postpone your right.

The contrast between the two scenarios arises from the difference in the relationship between you and me. Crucial to the first scenario is the fact that the house is our shared home. This suggests that I am acting on behalf of both of us. It makes it reasonable to suppose that you share my aim of making the disposition on the basis that the disponee will be unconcerned with your right. In the second scenario, however, your position is quite independent of mine, so it is not reasonable to see you as aligning your position with mine: even though, evidently, I plan to make way for the disponee, there is no reason to suppose that you do too.

4.2.2 Vitiation

Even if your words or behaviour are read as the required representation in that way, this representation should as a matter of principle not bind you if, when you made it, you were under pressure, or did not know or understand what you were doing.

But the precise ground regarded as covered by these phenomena varies between different areas of law, to reflect variations in the policy considerations prevailing in them. The circumstances in which saying 'yes' to sexual intercourse fails to represent consent for the offence of rape,[11] for example, are clearly different from those in which someone's apparent agreement will be regarded as invalid for civil law purposes. The latter must normally qualify as 'duress', 'undue influence', 'misrepresentation' or 'mistake'. And there are differences within the civil law itself. A mistake will vitiate a *gift* whenever it causes the giver to make the gift,[12] but a *contract* only when it is shared by both parties, and is 'fundamental'.[13] The less sensitive contract rule tracks the concern that the more invalidity one finds among apparently valid agreements, the greater the damage to commercial certainty, and so to trade. The more sensitive gifts rule reflects the fact that commerce is less affected by the

---

[11] See the Sexual Offences Act 2003 ss 74–76.

[12] *Barclays Bank Ltd v WJ Simms Son & Cooke (Southern) Ltd* [1980] QB 677 (QBD).

[13] *Bell v Lever Bros Ltd* [1932] AC 161 (HL); *Great Peace Shipping Ltd v Tsavliris Salvage (International) Ltd, The Great Peace* [2003] QB 679 (CA). A mistake is 'fundamental' if it makes the thing, service, etc contracted for 'essentially different from the thing [etc] as it was believed to be': [2003] QB 679, [154].

treatment of gifts in this respect, so the law can afford to be readier to see the giver's consent as vitiated by the mistake.

To turn to our context, exactly when will your consent to a disposition, so as to postpone your right, be regarded as vitiated? Probably, when you gave it in circumstances of duress, undue influence, misrepresentation or mistake; but what meanings do these concepts have here? The cases offer scant discussion of the matter, but a view can be deduced from their facts and outcomes. In the leading cases,[14] the person held to have given agreement seems to have been far from fully informed about what was at stake, and probably also had little real choice whether to go along with the disposition, if their family was not to disintegrate. But the courts treated the agreement as self-evidently valid, not even considering the contrary possibility. That is, they tacitly constructed the idea of valid agreement, for the purposes of the present context, on relatively insensitive lines. The likeliest reading of them is that your agreement to a disposition will be treated as vitiated only in the circumstances in which a contractual undertaking would have been.

At first sight, this is odd, because the contractual understandings of the phenomena apply – obviously – when the parties between whom they arise are the parties to a (putative) contract: which you and I are normally not. In the scenario we have been considering, you and I live together in a house that I own but which you have helped pay for. Our relationship is probably therefore a family one. If the question of my consent's vitiation arose purely between ourselves, then a contractual construction of the relevant rules would be inappropriate. The key, however, is that this question does not arise purely between us. By definition, it is aimed at determining whether my right is to bind a third party, John: who very probably does come into the picture via a contract (the disposition from me). It is presumably to safeguard that contract that this rather insensitive reading of the vitiation concepts has been adopted.

Even if your consent does count as vitiated, however, John is not automatically affected by this, so as to be unable to rely on the apparent postponement. Some additional rules govern the question whether or not he is so affected.

4.2.3 Do Flaws in your Consent Affect the Disponee?

So imagine that your apparent consent to postpone your right to John's is vitiated – probably, as just noted, on the basis of mistake, misrepresentation, duress or undue influence, as these ideas are read in the law of contract. When exactly will this affect John?

---

[14] *Bristol and West Building Society v Henning* [1985] 1 WLR 778 (CA); *Paddington Building Society v Mendelsohn* (1985) 50 P & CR 244 (CA).

If your consent to postpone is vitiated by a *mistake*, John will not be able to rely on it. The source of the mistake does not matter, but (assuming the contract approach) it must be shared between you and either me or John. Either way, it will prevent John from relying on your agreement, as the effect of a mistake is to make an agreement void, ie of no legal effect at all.[15]

It is different, however, if your consent is affected by misrepresentation, duress, or undue influence. These render an agreement voidable rather than void: that is, of legal effect until set aside ('rescinded'). It can normally[16] be set aside against the author of the misrepresentation, duress or undue influence. In our context, this will usually be me, the disponor: it is I, rather than John, who am likely to have lied to you or put pressure on you to get you to agree to the disposition. But there is little or no gain for you in being able to set aside your consent as against me alone, certainly once the disposition has gone through and the question has therefore arisen whether or not your right binds John. Your concern will be rather that you can set your agreement aside as against John too, so that your apparent postponement of your right is reversed, and the right will bind him after all. The law is that if your consent to a disposition is vitiated by duress, undue influence or misrepresentation on my part, you will be able to set it aside also as against the disponee only if, when acquiring his interest in the land, he *had notice of* the duress, undue influence or misrepresentation.[17]

4.2.4 'Notice'

To say that someone has 'notice' of some fact means that a reasonable person would have known or discovered that fact. A 'reasonable person' is one who acts with the care and perspicacity required by the law in the context in question. In different contexts, and at different times, the law has, as a matter of policy, raised and lowered its required standard of care and perspicacity.

For the purposes of the rule under discussion, the authorities suggest that notice means actual knowledge: ie that John can rely on your apparent consent to the disposition, notwithstanding that I have obtained that consent by (say) misrepresentation, unless he actually knows that fact.[18] These decisions are antique, and may not be reliable. But since their effect is largely to protect

---

[15] *Great Peace Shipping Ltd v Tsavliris Salvage (International) Ltd, The Great Peace* [2003] QB 679 (CA).

[16] Unless a 'bar to rescission' is present: eg laches, impossibility of *restitutio in integrum*. For details, see M Chen-Wishart, *Contract Law* (4th edn, Oxford, 2012) 231–7.

[17] *Bridgman v Green* (1757) Wilm 58 (Lords Commissioners); *Turnbull v Duval* [1902] AC 429 (PC).

[18] *Cobbett v Brock* (1855) 20 Beav 524, 528 (Rolls); *Kempson v Ashbee* (1874) LR 10 Ch App 15, 21 (CA in Ch); *Bainbrigge v Brown* (1881) 18 Ch D 188, 197 (Ch D); but *cf Bank of Credit and Commerce International SA v Aboody* [1990] 1 QB 923 (CA), which seems to contemplate notice in its more usual sense of 'the ability to discover'.

the disponee, it would be unsurprising if they were indeed adhered to, making this the general vision of notice for present purposes.

There is, however, a very important exception to that general vision. It consists in the special rule about notice that was developed in *Barclays Bank plc v O'Brien*[19] and *Royal Bank of Scotland plc v Etridge (No 2)*.[20]

This rule applies only where two conditions are met. First, the relationship between you and me must be a non-commercial one: we must be, for example, a married or unmarried couple, or parent and child. And second, the transaction – the disposition by me to which you have given (vitiated) consent – must be[21] 'not to your advantage'. A case clearly satisfying this condition would be that where I release the equity in our house to finance my gambling habit. On the face of it, releasing the equity so as to expand my business is to your advantage in that it may well produce a better standard of living for both of us, meaning that the condition is not met; but the courts disregard this indirect advantage, regarding such a transaction as to your advantage only if you play an active part in the business itself. It is, however, assumed that my simply selling our house to John, so that we can move for any of the usual reasons (say, for the sake of my new job: but why is this not equivalent to a mortgage for the sake of my business?), is a transaction to your advantage and so does not attract the rule. It can be seen that these conditions effectively limit the scope of the rule to (certain) dispositions in favour of banks and the like.[22]

Where your consent to postpone your right is flawed because I have obtained it by misrepresentation, duress or undue influence, and these two conditions are met, a disponee bank will *automatically* have notice of the flaw in your consent ... unless it arranges for you to receive independent, one-to-one legal advice before you commit yourself. The automatic nature of notice here is justified because the presence of the two conditions (the combined facts that you and I have a non-commercial relationship, and that the transaction in question is not to your advantage) should itself alert the bank to the possibility that my behaviour in obtaining your consent has been such as to render it flawed. But if the bank arranges for you to receive advice, it can assume that your consent is satisfactory after all, for the advice session should ensure that you know your legal position and have more space to reach your decision (though total freedom from pressure cannot be achieved).

---

[19] [1994] 1 AC 180 (HL).

[20] [2002] 2 AC 773 (HL). See further Chen-Wishart (n 16) 345–51.

[21] So far as appears to the disponee: *UCB Group Ltd v Hedworth* [2003] EWCA Civ 1717, [121] (CA).

[22] The rule was originally applied only to a guarantee given by you to my creditor, underwriting my debt (*Turnbull v Duval* [1902] AC 429 (PC)). It was extended to the case where you and I jointly own our house, and you join with me in mortgaging it so as to secure my debt (*Barclays Bank plc v O'Brien* [1994] 1 AC 180 (HL); *Royal Bank of Scotland plc v Etridge (No 2)* [2002] 2 AC 773 (HL)); or where you alone own the house, and mortgage it to secure my debt (*Castle Phillips Finance v Piddington* [1995] 1 FLR 783 (CA)). It was then applied also to the context with which we are concerned, where I own the house but you have an interest in it, and you agree to postpone your right so as to allow me to mortgage it (*Scottish Equitable Life plc v Virdee* [1999] 1 FLR 863 (CA)).

4.3 Consent to a Replacement Mortgage

Say that I own a house in which you have an interest. With your valid consent, I mortgage it to secure a loan from bank *A*. But then I replace this mortgage with a new one from bank *B*. If you know about and consent to this replacement mortgage, you will of course be held to have postponed your interest to it in the usual way.

But say now that I have taken out the bank *B* mortgage behind your back, so that on the face of things you do not consent to it. So long as the bank *B* mortgage is on terms no more onerous than the bank *A* one, your consent to the latter is carried forward, and your interest is postponed to the bank *B* mortgage after all.[23]

This result was originally explained in the same unsatisfactory way as the basic rule,[24] but is now regarded as occurring on the basis of subrogation. By this, when *X* (me) owes money under a mortgage to *Y* (bank *A*), and *Z* (bank *B*) pays *Y* the sum in question, *Z* steps into *Y*'s shoes, ie becomes *X*'s creditor for the same amount and enjoys the same mortgage over *X*'s property – all regardless of *X*'s knowledge or consent.[25] The idea of stepping into the previous creditor's shoes is taken to mean that, when I replace the bank *A* mortgage with the bank *B* one, bank *B* can take advantage of your consent to the bank *A* one. Conversely, if your consent to the bank *A* mortgage was flawed, and the flaw affected bank *A* in the way explained in §§ 4.2.3–4.2.4, bank *B* is affected by it too.[26]

Now say instead that, in transacting the replacement mortgage with bank *B*, I not only acted without your knowledge, but also arranged more onerous terms. Most obviously, perhaps, the sum I borrow from bank *B* is larger than that which I owed to bank *A*: for example, I owed bank *A* £200,000, but my new loan from bank *B* is of £250,000. Your consent to the bank *A* mortgage once again avails bank *B*, but only to the extent of the sum owed to bank *A*, ie £200,000.[27] Subrogation allows bank *B* to take advantage of your earlier consent because bank *B* is stepping into bank *A*'s shoes, but it is doing so only to the extent of the loan that it is taking over.[28]

---

[23] *Equity and Law Home Loans v Prestidge* [1992] 1 WLR 137 (CA).
[24] See n 8.
[25] *Butler v Rice* [1910] 2 Ch 277 (CA).
[26] *Yorkshire Bank plc v Tinsley* [2004] 1 WLR 2380 (CA).
[27] *Equity and Law Home Loans v Prestidge* [1992] 1 WLR 137 (CA).
[28] Analogously, in *Castle Phillips Finance v Piddington* [1995] 1 FLR 783 (CA), the wife mortgaged a house that she owned to secure her husband's debt, and although subsequent lenders increased the amount of the debt, their rights by subrogation against the wife were limited to the outstanding balance on the original mortgage.

Part 2

Acquisition of Rights in Rem

In Part 1, we looked at the nature of rights in rem, and also human rights, in relation to land. Noting that there is a lot of detailed law regarding the former, we went on to look in more detail at the rules governing their behaviour as such.

It may be helpful to recap the key points. We have seen that:

—— a right in rem is one that is *capable of* binding a disponee of the land to which it relates; but

—— for a right in rem *actually* to bind a particular disponee (in the context of registered land), the rules in the Land Registration Act 2002 must be complied with, ie the right must either have been registered or qualify as overriding; but

—— the disponee will nevertheless *not* be bound by the right if the right's owner validly consents to the transaction by which the disponee acquires his interest in the land.

Now, in Part 2, comprising Chapters 5 to 9, we go on to look at the rules controlling how such rights can be acquired.

Part 2

Acquisition of Rights in Rem

5

Conferment

5.1 Acquisition by 'Conferment'

5.1.1 Conferment as a Vindication of Choice

As the law stands, there are two broad ways in which you can acquire a right in rem in my land. One is on the basis that I, the owner of the land[1] hitherto, intend you to acquire the right, and set out to confer it on you. The present chapter and Chapter 6 are concerned with acquisitions of this kind. Chapters 7, 8 and 9 focus on the other way: acquisition on grounds other than the owner's intention. These grounds will be detailed in due course, but they include ideas such as 'squatters' rights', and the phenomenon where I lead you to believe that you have, or will get, a right in my land, and you rely on that belief to your detriment, giving rise to rights under the doctrine of proprietary estoppel.

These two ways of acquiring rights are respectively the 'organised' and 'disorganised' ways referred to in § 3.2.2. As was explained there, the law does not have to recognise both approaches. It does so because of a perception that there are important values behind each. The values behind the rules covered in Chapters 7, 8 and 9 will be explored there. Behind the subject matter of this and the next chapter – acquisition on the basis of the hitherto owner's intention – is the idea that respecting my hitherto ownership of the land means, among other important things, respecting and so effectuating my choice to confer some or all of my rights on you. That I am able to make such a choice, and have it thus respected and effectuated by the law, is part of what it means to say that I am an 'owner' at all, and protecting this ability is

---

[1] Or of some interest in it from which yours could be derived. For example, if I am the tenant of some land (the owner – my landlord – being John), I might intend to give you a sub-tenancy, or a right of way over it lasting only as long as my tenancy.

therefore something that modern English law has signed up to in maintaining the idea of ownership (over land) at all.

5.1.2 Choice and the ECHR

There is, however, a surprising relationship between the idea of conferment as a vindication of choice and the ECHR.

Approaching matters from the perspective adopted in § 5.1.1, we have no difficulty in understanding and accepting the key points. First, if I – hitherto owner of the land – 'confer' a right in the land on you, then unless something goes quite sharply wrong,[2] you will assuredly get that right. Second, you will do so precisely because that is what I have chosen should happen. And third, this in turn is so precisely because it is a facet of the very fact that I am hitherto owner, that I can make such a choice and thereby make the chosen result happen.

Of course, there is room for thought about the next – fourth – step, namely the reason(s) *why* the law should and does take my choice so seriously, and so, as regards my relationship with 'things', maintain the idea of ownership. There are in fact probably multiple such reasons (as explored in § 10.2.2). Some have an intrinsic flavour, such as the idea that the ability effectively to make choices about one's affairs is an aspect of human dignity, and to be valued as such. Others are more instrumental, such as the idea that being serious about choice and the assumptions behind it is a precondition for a 'market', which in its turn is a central mechanism for developing human happiness. But such further thought is rarely found substantially to disturb our acceptance of the three key points identified in the previous paragraph.

If we now think about the conferment of rights from the point of view of the ECHR, however, we struggle to recognise the perspective just described. Take the very simplest case where I have hitherto owned a house, and now transfer it to you – which thousands of people do every day, as they buy and sell properties, and move in and out of them, all without anyone imagining for a moment that there is, or even could be, anything intellectually problematic about it. In the language of the ECHR,[3] however, we find ourselves immediately entertaining the thought that the transfer from me to you interferes with my enjoyment of my possessions, so engaging the First Protocol Article 1, and (where the house has been my residence, or indeed place of work) with my home, so engaging Article 8. If these Articles are engaged, the

---

[2] Notably in the nature of there being something illegal about my choice. But in fact, it is striking that even in this event, the law as often as not vindicates my choice to confer the right, while reacting to the illegality in other ways. See eg *Bowmakers Ltd v Barnet Instruments Ltd* [1945] KB 65 (CA); *Singh v Ali* [1960] AC 167 (PC).

[3] Subject to questions of the ECHR's horizontal effect: § 2.2.

transfer will be permitted efficacy if, but only if, such efficacy is proportionate, ie represents a well-calculated means of securing a proper end.[4]

Doubtless this will commonly be the case. The 'proper end' will be 'taking ownership seriously', with all that this assumes and entails; and treating the transfer as efficacious will absolutely be a well-calculated means of securing this end. But sometimes it may be suggested, and perhaps even concluded, that the latter proposition is untrue. Say I transfer my home to you, but before actually vacating it I find myself with nowhere else to move to, or so gravely ill that a move would be significantly injurious to me; while you would suffer no great hardship if the move were not to occur. In these circumstances, the interferences with my possessions and home represented by upholding the transfer as valid, and so evicting me, might be judged disproportionate – all things considered, over-enthusiastic – means of taking my ownership seriously. (Though one cannot say for sure, or anything like it: for as explained in § 2.5, 'proportionality' is a very opaque notion.)

The quarrel being raised with this analysis is not so much a substantive one: that, contrary to the sketched position, my transfer to you must necessarily be effectuated, come what may. It is rather an epistemological one: that, in introducing the value of 'ownership' into the equation only at the proportionality stage – ie very downstream – the analysis is very substantially at variance with the manner in which we actually do, and quite properly may or should, make reference to 'ownership', which is much more upstream. That is to say: we do not in reality think of ownership, and more especially its set of underpinnings, as a condiment, applied so as to confirm or challenge the conclusions we might otherwise have prima facie reached by reference to other values such as the right not to suffer interference with one's possessions and home. We think of it and its underpinnings as at least as important, fundamental and worthy of respect as such other values.[5]

Searching therefore for a more upstream locale for ownership, we might reconsider whether, in our example, ECHR First Protocol Article 1, and Article 8, are indeed truly engaged, given that I have chosen to deprive myself of my possession and home. There are grounds for saying not. One might regard the rule effectuating my choice to transfer my house not as an 'interference' with my possession in respect of it at all, but as picking up on an 'inherent limitation' in my possession (§ 2.3.3). That is, view my 'possession' as, by its very definition, profiled by reference to my ability to choose what to

---

[4] This analysis is adopted by A Goymour, 'Property and Housing' in D Hoffman (ed), *The Impact of the Human Rights Act on Private Law* (Cambridge, 2011) ch 12, 285.

[5] Interestingly, where ownership, and especially its aspect of choice, is attacked by domestic law – as opposed to neglected by the ECHR itself – the ECHR (First Protocol Art 1) is routinely invoked in its support. See eg *Marckx v Belgium* (1979–80) 2 EHRR 330, [63] (ECtHR); *Sporrong and Lönnroth v Sweden* (1983) 5 EHRR 35, [60] (ECtHR); *Chassagnou v France* (2000) 29 EHRR 615, [74] (ECtHR).

do with it.[6] This is the way in which, for example, it has been held that the sale of a mortgaged house by the lender does not represent an interference with the borrower's possession: the borrower chose to subject his house to the mortgage, and so, in the circumstances which eventuated, to lose it in this way.[7] As things stand, however, it is doubtful whether the 'inherent limitation' idea is at all applicable to interferences with homes, under ECHR Article 8[8] – even though in the context under discussion, the two Articles are both engaged (or not) for apparently identical reasons.

It would in any event be more transparent, and intellectually satisfactory, to place choice more upstream still: to deal with it as a value demanding to be taken seriously in its own name and right, rather than buried in 'inherent limitation' and similar ideas, even where the latter can be invoked. After all, it can without the least difficulty be regarded as a (very important indeed) facet of human dignity, which is said to be the ECHR's focal concept.

But the ECHR is firmly understood as not going this far. To be sure, the Strasbourg court said in *Pretty v United Kingdom*[9] that 'the notion of personal autonomy is an important principle underlying the interpretation of [Article 8's] guarantees' – Article 8 being the Article that protects the right to a 'private life'. But so far as concerned a domestic rule effectively denying Mrs Pretty the choice whether to end her own life, the court's explication of these remarks was merely that it was 'not prepared to exclude that [the rule] constitutes an interference with her right to respect for private life as guaranteed under Article 8(1) of the Convention'.[10] The restricted scope of this

---

[6] Not, however, by reference to the contours of my ownership *as in all respects constituted by domestic law*. Under domestic law, for example, my ownership of my house terminates if the house is compulsorily acquired by the state. Although one could thus intelligibly see the liability of citizens' property to compulsory acquisition in this way as an aspect of the very terms on which the domestic law recognises me as the house's owner in the first place, it is clear that for ECHR purposes, such acquisition counts not as picking up on an 'inherent limitation' in my possession but as an interference with it, engaging First Protocol Art 1. For present purposes, it appears to be crucial that the transfer is rooted in the aspect of my ownership that is my *choice* to retain or dispose of the house as I will.

[7] *Horsham Properties Group Ltd v Clark* [2009] 1 WLR 1255, [34]–[40] (Ch D); see § 12.4.1. Likewise the termination of a lease by notice given in accordance with its terms: *Sheffield City Council v Smart* [2002] EWCA Civ 4, [46] (CA); see too *A v United Kingdom* (1988) EHRR CD149, 155 (ECommHR).

[8] In the context of mortgage sales, a positive answer was given, simply tracking the position adopted as regards First Protocol Art 1, in *Horsham Properties Group Ltd v Clark* [2009] 1 WLR 1255, [13] (Ch D); but in the context of mortgage repossessions (which ought to be treated no differently), a negative answer was implied in *Wood v United Kingdom* (1997) 24 EHRR CD69 (ECommHR) and *Barclays Bank plc v Alcorn* [2002] EWHC 498 (Ch D) (the former dealing not only with Art 8, but indeed with First Protocol Art 1 as well) (see § 12.5.1). In the context of the termination of leases, the assumption seems to be that there is no 'inherent limitation' boundary to the Art 8 right: *McCann v United Kingdom* (2008) 47 EHRR 40 (ECtHR); *Kay v United Kingdom* [2011] HLR 2 (ECtHR); *Manchester City Council v Pinnock* [2011] 2 AC 104 (SC); *Hounslow London Borough Council v Powell* [2011] 2 AC 186 (SC); see § 11.5.2. In *A v UK* (1988) EHRR CD149, 155–6 (ECommHR), however, facts of the kind under discussion were said to make a termination proportionate.

[9] (2002) 35 EHRR 1, [61] (ECtHR).

[10] *ibid*, [67].

treatment was not lost on the House of Lords in *R (Countryside Alliance) v A-G*,[11] reading it as showing that Article 8 protects choice only in respect of 'very personal and private concerns', 'the choices that a person makes about his or her body or physical identity', matters 'integral to [a person's] identity'.[12] Even where attraction was expressed to a wider understanding, moreover, the proposed understanding was not the respecting of choice per se, but the protection of the freedom to undertake particular 'activities' or 'pursuits', 'central to [their adherents'] well-being' or 'all-important' to them.[13] The idea of respecting choice as such was mentioned, but as a matter of background interest, rather than as something that the ECHR itself set out to deliver.[14]

So when the Strasbourg court, in *Pretty v United Kingdom*,[15] avers that 'the very essence of the Convention is respect for human dignity and human freedom', it uses these concepts, along with 'personal autonomy',[16] in a distinctly republican sense, ie as protecting people against (the possibility of) arbitrary domination,[17] rather than a libertarian, ie choice-oriented, one. (More positive confirmation of the same impression is given by a survey of the particular rights and freedoms that *are* identified for protection by the ECHR.) Given the roots of the ECHR in a reaction against the atrocities of Nazism – the principal complaint against which was clearly their quality of arbitrary domination rather than their neglect of choice – this emphasis, focus, is obviously explicable. But it leaves us with an instrument falling considerably short of what, in less appalling times, we might hope and indeed expect from it. The republican vision of liberty merits protection, certainly, but surely the libertarian vision does too.

5.2 Expression and Formalities

To recall § 5.1.1, then, my conferment[18] of the right on you is based in my choice – wish – that you should have the right. But the law does not treat my

---

[11] [2008] 1 AC 719 (HL).

[12] *ibid*, [15], [54], [101] (HL). See too *R (Razgar) v Secretary of State for the Home Department* [2004] 2 AC 368, [9] (HL).

[13] [2008] 1 AC 719, [139], [140] (HL).

[14] *ibid*, [112]; compare [115], [116].

[15] (2002) 35 EHRR 1, [65] (ECtHR).

[16] *ibid*, [61].

[17] For republicanism, see F Lovett, 'Republicanism' (2010) in *Stanford Encyclopedia of Philosophy* (http://plato.stanford.edu/entries/republicanism/), and further references there.

[18] This chapter uses the word 'conferment' or 'conferral' to denote a transaction by which I voluntarily cause you to have a right over land which has (at least hitherto) been mine. These words are not technical legal terms, and are chosen for that reason. The relevant technical terms, which include 'conveyance', 'grant', 'transfer' and 'disposition', all have particular connotations not relevant to the present discussion.

wish alone as sufficient. My wish certainly needs to be *evinced*: the law has no means of reading my mind, and even if it had, it ought not to attach consequences to what remains merely an internal thought – people need the space to think what they will, and if they like to un-think it again, without it having legal significance.

Moreover, in order for my wish to be effectuated, the law requires that in most cases, I must have evinced that wish *in a particular way*: using certain formalities. The required formalities vary from one context to another, and the detailed rules will be explained in a moment, but the main kinds of formality that the law uses in this area are:

—— *writing*, signed by the conferor (or on his behalf, by an agent), with or without a requirement of witnesses;

—— a *deed*, which nowadays[19] means a piece of writing that declares itself to be a deed, and that is signed by the conferor (or, with certain caveats, by an agent), witnessed, and 'delivered' (essentially, accompanied by some overt acknowledgement of binding effect, either immediate or conditional);

—— *registration* at the Land Registry.

Like most legal formalities, those required for the conferment of rights in land serve a number of purposes.

One is the promotion of *certainty*. One aspect of this is certainty that the transaction has occurred at all. This is provided by its being recorded in permanent form. Another aspect is clarity as to what the transaction comprises. This is provided by its details too being recorded in permanent form, but also by the fact that having to make such a record will make those involved focus more sharply on just what these details should be, and so avoid contradictions, crucial omissions and so on.

A second purpose is to improve *the quality of the intention* on which the transaction is based. The need to use formality will encourage those involved to give serious thought to what they are about to do, and perhaps also – as where the supplying of the formality is a semi-public event, eg when witnesses must be present – make it less likely that they are under objectionable pressure.

A third purpose is to make the transaction more *visible* to persons or bodies not involved in its making, but having an interest in knowing about it or its effects. These persons or bodies might include the tax authorities, as where the transaction or the interest conferred is dutiable, or the environmental authorities, who might need to discover the owner of a piece of land that is the source of pollution. They might include those considering subsequent dealings with the property or parties involved: where I am hoping to buy a piece of land from you, for example, I will want to be sure that you are indeed its current owner, and that there are no problems for me in the make-up of

---

[19] Law of Property (Miscellaneous Provisions) Act 1989 s 1.

your rights. Perhaps they also include the general public: there may be a public interest in being able to discover the owner of every inch of the country, on the ground that the country's citizens all have a stake in its physical form ... and perhaps also in being able to discover the various rights less than ownership there might be over it, though this is less plausible.

The three kinds of formality used for conferring rights in land all deliver the first two of these purposes, though they do it to varying extents. Writing and deeds do not themselves provide visibility, however, though one who is on the brink of taking a right from someone claiming to have the means to confer it would naturally be normally able to demand to see the documents supporting that claim. Visibility has been much better promoted by registration, since the register became a public resource.[20]

Underneath these purposes are deeper-lying considerations explaining why they count as valuable. The first and second of them principally reflect a liberal concern to maximise autonomy: the concern that people should be neither prevented from achieving what they want to, nor made to be involved in transactions which they do not genuinely want. The considerations underlying the third purpose, promoting visibility, are more various, ranging from the desirability of an efficient market (where it is a question of visibility to those considering subsequent dealings with the property concerned), to the aims of whatever tax is at issue (where it is a question of visibility to the tax authorities), to the communitarian notions yielding the idea that a country's citizens all have a stake in its land.

At the same time, formality requirements can be injurious to these or other values. An interest in privacy is evidently sacrificed in achieving full visibility. And most especially, if a person wishes to achieve a certain end, but is prevented from doing so by his non-compliance with a formality requirement, the frustration of his wish will offend the liberal desideratum that he should be able to do as he likes. Here, then, we find a paradox: formality requirements can cut both ways in liberal terms. As we saw a moment ago, they can help someone achieve an end; but as we see now, they can equally frustrate him.

Whether it is overall a good or a bad idea to require formality[21] therefore depends significantly on the likelihood of people complying with that requirement. It is fair to say that people will generally comply with formality requirements applying to transactions involving rights over land. There is a general understanding that land is 'special', such that a person, realising that he is conferring a right in his land, will actually expect to do so formally: and not

---

[20] Under the Land Registration Act 1988 s 1. Access was previously confined to registered proprietors and others authorised by them, which in practice obviously included those to whom they hoped to sell rights. In the case of conferrals on death, visibility is achieved by placing all wills on public display.

[21] See further P Critchley, 'Taking Formalities Seriously' in S Bright and J Dewar (eds), *Land Law – Themes and Perspectives* (Oxford, 1998) ch 20.

merely in some formal way of his own devising, but as indicated by the law. He is unlikely to know the content of the relevant law, but his general understanding will lead him to consult a lawyer, who will supply what is needed. The same is true whether the conferral is to take effect during his lifetime (*inter vivos*) or on his death, ie under his will. (Indeed, the same general understanding probably applies to all dispositions on death, even those not involving land.)

Certainly from this key point of view, then, the balance of advantage lies in favour of requiring conferrals of rights in land to be made using formality.[22] As we are about to see, the law reflects this, and in doing so it is therefore broadly compliant with the ECHR. That is to say, to the extent that formality requirements interfere with the possessions (and potentially also the homes) of those affected by them,[23] so engaging ECHR First Protocol Art 1 (and Art 8), they will generally be justified as proportionate in doing so, as being apt means of achieving proper ends.[24] The relevant rules do, however, have some surprising features, which may create exceptions to this statement. Where these features are not only surprising but actually dysfunctional, they may leave the rules not proportionate after all, as being no longer aimed at proper ends, and/or not apt means of achieving such ends.

The rules differ according to whether I am seeking to confer the right on my death, or *inter vivos*.

5.3 Conferment on Death

If I try to give you a right in my land in a way that takes effect on my death, I must do so using a will. And in order for my will to be valid, it must normally be in writing, signed by myself, and by two witnesses.[25]

---

[22] It is of course quite different where the acquisition of rights in a disorganised way is concerned. By definition, in this case, those involved do not understand the legal significance of what they are doing. They would therefore not comply with a formality requirement, and the law, in providing for the right, would be self-defeating if it required them to do so. Unsurprisingly, then, it does not. But this chapter is concerned only with organised conferrals.

[23] It is not completely clear that formality requirements always do so interfere with possessions; sometimes they may instead be considered constitutive of the possessions in the first place. This is a difficult topic, not yet firmly addressed by the courts: see *Wilson v First County Trust Ltd (No 2)* [2004] 1 AC 816 (HL).

[24] Interference arising from the formality rules will be of the 'control of use' variety, which can be justified even without compensation: § 2.3.5.

[25] Wills Act 1837 s 9, amended by the Administration of Justice Act 1982 s 17. (Further rules exist about the details of these requirements.) There is a well-known method of leaving property on death without using a will, and so without having to comply with these formalities: the 'secret trust'. Properly understood, however, secret trusts are in principle (though not necessarily in

These rules, which have prevailed for a long time, seem apt. They are well calculated to promote thoughtfulness on the testator's part about what he is doing, clarity in his description of it, and also freedom from immediate (though one cannot say more than that) pressure. A further element of the law of wills, 'probate', involves opening a deceased's will to public inspection, so additionally giving visibility to what he has done.

5.4 Conferment *Inter Vivos*

5.4.1 The Rules

If I am trying to give you the right *inter vivos*, the requirements vary according to the type of right in question.

—— To give you a *legal* right in my land (ie one recognised by the common law),[26] I must usually[27] use a deed,[28] and (in the case of registered land) in most[29] such cases the conferral must also be registered with the Land Registry.[30]

—— To give you an *equitable* right (ie one recognised only by equity), I must do so in writing,[31] with no further requirement of registration.

So, say I wish to give you an easement or a mortgage over my land, or indeed to transfer the freehold ownership to you.[32] These are all legal rights, and their conferral requires a deed and registration. Whereas say I wish to give you a restrictive covenant or a beneficial interest under a trust I shall create in your favour.[33] These are equitable rights, and their conferral requires only writing.

practice: there is a problem) a vehicle for the acquisition of rights on a basis other than intentional conferment. As such, they do not belong in this chapter.

[26] For the distinction between legal and equitable rights, see § 1.3.1.

[27] The main exception is a lease for up to three years, which does not normally require a deed, and can indeed be made orally: Law of Property Act 1925 s 54(2).

[28] *ibid* s 52(1). This refers to 'legal estates'. The Act had already defined that term to include rights properly speaking less than estates, such as mortgages and easements: s 1(4).

[29] The main exception is a lease for up to seven years. If for more than three years (and sometimes if for less), the lease must be made by deed, but it need not additionally be registered. The special rules about leases are explained in § 5.5.

[30] Land Registration Act 2002 s 27.

[31] Law of Property Act s 53(1).

[32] For easements (eg rights of way), see Ch 13. For mortgages, see Ch 12.

[33] For restrictive covenants (essentially, a restrictive covenant is a right enjoyed by you as my neighbour, preventing me from doing something – eg erecting further buildings – on my land), see Ch 14. For trusts, see Chs 15–16.

Where a right's conferral requires not only a deed but also registration, its conferral is known as a 'registrable disposition'.[34] In the case of a registrable disposition, the conferral of the right must be registered *in order to take effect at all*.[35] All other kinds of rights in rem in land – rights which are not the subject of registrable dispositions – can be registered too, and ideally should be, so as to ensure that they bind a disponee of the land, as explained in § 3.2.1. But unlike the rights which are the subject of registrable dispositions, a failure to register them does not leave them simply ineffective. Even if, remaining unregistered, they fail to bind a disponee of the land (and that will depend on whether they can operate instead as an overriding interest), they will normally still be valid against the person who conferred them.

Take a restrictive covenant. As noted above, the conferral of a restrictive covenant is not a registrable disposition. Say I make a restrictive covenant in your favour over my land (using writing, as required), but you do not register it against my land; and then I transfer my land to John. Your failure to register the right means that you cannot use this route to enforce it against John. But you still have it, and can enforce it against me ... and against John too, if you can show that it operates as an overriding interest.[36] Contrast this with an easement, the conferral of which is a registrable disposition.[37] Say I purport to confer an easement on you (using a deed, as required), but we omit to register it; and then I transfer the land in question to John. This time, you cannot enforce the easement against John, even as an overriding interest: for, lacking registration, the law simply does not recognise the easement as existing at all. Nor can you enforce it even against me: again, lacking registration, the law simply does not recognise it as existing at all.[38] Registration is as much a precondition for its valid existence as the deed which is also required to confer it.

5.4.2 The Distinction between the Legal and Equitable Rules

So the rules draw a marked distinction between legal and equitable rights, normally requiring a deed and registration for the former but only writing for the latter. Is this distinction supportable?

[34]   Land Registration Act 2002 s 27.

[35]   That is to say, in order for the conferral to take effect at all as the conferral of the *legal* right in question. If the conferral is not registered as required, it will usually operate instead to create the *equitable* version of the right, in the manner described in § 6.2.4 – but criticised in § 6.2.5.

[36]   In the case of a restrictive covenant, this would have to be on the basis that you are in actual and apparent occupation of my land at the time of the transfer to John: which is in practice rather unlikely. See § 16.4.

[37]   Land Registration Act 2002 s 27(2)(d); § 13.2.8.

[38]   These statements relate only, however, to the *legal* easement that we purported to create. As explained in n 35, although no legal easement has arisen, an *equitable* easement may well have done so. An equitable easement does not require registration in order to exist, so you will be able to enforce it against me; and also against John if you later register it, or as an overriding interest, in the again unlikely event that you are in actual and apparent occupation of my land at the time of my transfer to him: § 13.3.

At one time, there were significant differences in the behaviour of legal and equitable rights. In particular, a legal right would bind any disponee of the land in question, without further ado, while an equitable right would bind a disponee only so long as he was not a 'bona fide purchaser for value without notice' of the land in question.

It is doubtful whether these differences ever justified the disparity in the formality rules for the two kinds of rights. This disparity arose historically, from other differences between the approaches of the common law and of equity.[39] The common law has always (that is, since mid-medieval times) demanded a deed. Indeed, to say 'demanded' may give a misleading impression of the original idea: early on, acts done in a certain stylised way, ie by deed, were seen as possessing an intrinsic dispositive significance, capable of production in no other way. As equity developed, however, it required no formality at all. (An oral expression, or even apparently a gesture, sufficed.) It took this position as a corrective to what it now constructed as the obtuseness of the common law in demanding a deed, appealing instead to conscience, ie how a person stood vis-à-vis divine justice: God, it was reckoned, neither needed nor was interested in formal proofs. The divergence was captured by the saying 'equity looks to the substance, not the form'. Eventually, however, it came to be thought that equity's preference for informality was doing more harm than good: transactions were apparently being falsely alleged on a substantial scale. So the Statute of Frauds 1677 required the conferment of equitable rights in land to be proved in writing. Hence the modern rule (though the additional requirement for legal rights, alone, to be registered was introduced much more recently). Coming at the matter today, however, whatever we may think of the relative merits of the common law and equitable approaches to proof (formality), there is nothing in the difference between legal and equitable *rights* to imply that they should attract different kinds of formality.

Indeed, the substantive differences between legal and equitable rights have largely disappeared. In particular, in place of the old division over the need for 'notice', nowadays both legal and equitable rights in registered land will bind a disponee only if they have been registered, or qualify as an overriding interest. The rules about the possibility of registering a right and of its qualifying as an overriding interest preserve a few distinctions between legal and equitable rights,[40] but these are relatively few, largely unjustifiable, and surely destined for eventual extermination.[41] At that point, the distinction between

---

[39] For their relationship, see § 1.3.1.

[40] For example, only legal leases (for not more than seven years) can be overriding interests under the Land Registration Act 2002 Sch 3 para 1 . . . though an equitable lease accompanied by actual and apparent occupation will qualify as overriding under Sch 3 para 2. There is also a difference as regards easements: § 13.3.

[41] It is still just possible to assert that different remedies are available for the breach of a legal and an equitable right. Sometimes this difference may be warranted by the substantive nature of the specific kind of right, but often it springs solely from a historical disparity between the

legal and equitable rights will have disappeared, and the idea that they should have different formality requirements will become wholly unsustainable.

Having concluded that the formality rules for the conferral of a right in land should certainly not differ according to whether the right in question is legal or equitable, we need to consider what shape they should actually take. As explained in § 5.2, it seems right to require that the conferral of a right in land be attended with some kind of formality. It would be possible to devise completely new kinds, but we shall confine ourselves to those currently in play, appraising the choice between a deed and writing, and the demand for completion by registration.

5.4.3 Deed or Writing?

Consider first the choice between a deed and signed writing.

A deed used to be a piece of writing 'signed, sealed and delivered' by the conferor. But since 1989,[42] the requirement of a seal has been dropped – instead, the writing must merely assert itself to be a deed – and although the requirement of 'delivery' remains, it adds little. A deed does have to be witnessed,[43] however, and this is therefore the principal contemporary difference between it and the kind of writing demanded by the law's current rule for equitable interests, which must be signed but need not be witnessed.

The involvement of witnesses does add a degree of assurance that the transaction supposedly underlying the formal documents actually took place, and perhaps that its maker was acting voluntarily. But the contrary possibilities seem not to be a significant problem in practice, and in any case, whenever the necessary writing is arranged by a solicitor, the solicitor will normally make sure it is indeed witnessed, precisely so as to provide this kind of assurance.

Today, then, the distinction between a deed and writing is very small indeed, and could very easily be collapsed into a single, uniform requirement. This uniform requirement might be of signed writing, which need not be witnessed but in practice very often would be.

5.4.4 Completion by Registration?

As noted in § 5.4.1, the current rule is that where the conferral of a right requires a deed (but not otherwise), it is usually also a registrable disposition, ie requires registration in order for the right to exist at all.

---

remedial equipment of the common law and equity courts (*cf* § 1.3.2). In the latter case, it too has become unsupportable and destined for extermination. (See further A Burrows, 'We Do This at Common Law but That in Equity' (2002) 22 *OJLS* 1.) In any event, it once again does not warrant a difference in the formality requirements for the two kinds of right.

[42] Law of Property (Miscellaneous Provisions) Act 1989 s 1.

[43] *ibid* s 1(3)(a).

Is the law right to demand completion by registration in this way? Yes. In essence, the rule ensures greater visibility for the right: obviously, greater than if it were not registered at all, but also greater than if the right could come into existence without registration, and needed to be registered only before the moment of a subsequent disposition, so as to bind the disponee. If John is interested in buying my land, he will find it helpful to know the rights against it (including the fact that I am indeed its owner) not merely at the moment before it becomes his, but at a much earlier stage. In order to calculate the price he is willing to pay for the land, and more generally to decide whether it is suited to his needs at all, he needs to know about complications such as problematic rights from the moment he begins to contemplate his purchase. If he can only find out about them later, his time, and quite possibly his effort and money, could be wasted. It follows that a right should, as the registrable disposition regime has it, be made visible as part and parcel of its entry into existence.

But although it is thus essentially commendable, there are three weaknesses to this regime.

First, it applies only to conferrals of a limited set of rights, rather than to *every* conferral to which formality requirements are appropriate at all. Remember that it applies only to legal rights, such as easements, and not to equitable rights, such as restrictive covenants and trust rights. But visibility to potential disponees is just as important, and just as achievable, in respect of the latter as of the former. The regime ought to be applied to both.

Second, the registration of the conferred right is the responsibility of the conferee. So while it yields the desideratum of visibility, it does not provide the boons that § 5.2 tells us to expect internally to the conferral process, such as clarity, and a good quality of intention on the part of the conferor. To address this deficiency, the law – rightly – requires that the conferral of the right not only be registered, but *also* done by deed (though, as we argued in § 5.4.3, writing should really be enough).

Third, the right's registration is something that happens in and through the actions of the Land Registry, some time after the transaction between the parties themselves: so even if there are no complications, a time lag (known as the 'registration gap') occurs as the transaction queues in the Registry's in tray.[44] During this time, the benefits that registration in principle delivers are

---

[44] A solution might be to rule that the conferral has no effect until registered, but that cannot be countenanced: it would smack of the bureaucratic tail wagging the substantive dog. The Land Registration Act 2002 s 27(1) nonetheless toys with the idea, making the right take effect *at law* only when the conferral is completed by registration: impliedly meaning, however, that in the meantime – from the moment it is given by deed – the right will take effect, but *in equity*, on the basis (as an 'estate contract') explained in § 6.2.4. This interim adjustment to the right's quality does not affect the right's operation as between conferor and conferee: for them, it has full immediate effect. It impacts only, and to a limited extent, on the circumstances in which the right will bind a subsequent disponee. Not being registered, it can bind only if it qualifies as an overriding interest: and some rights (leases and easements) qualify as overriding interests without more only if they are legal . . . though their equitable forms will qualify if accompanied by actual and apparent occupation.

not forthcoming. The continuing requirement of a deed removes part of the problem, giving the conferor and conferee themselves an immediate marker to the transaction. But the deed is far from guaranteed to make the right visible to third parties. So, to take an extreme case, having sold my land to you, I have during this period the opportunity to 'sell' it over again to John. Your right should nonetheless prevail against John;[45] certainly both you and John will have claims against me for any loss suffered; and I shall very likely have committed a crime. But at best I – aided and abetted by the registration gap – will have caused a great deal of trouble.

These three weaknesses of the current registrable disposition regime would, however, fall away if an electronic conveyancing regime were introduced.

5.4.5 Electronic Conveyancing

'Electronic conveyancing' means a system under which the parties – or rather their lawyers, on their behalf – effect the conferral of the right by registering it online, directly accessing the Land Registry computer files.[46] The Land Registration Act 2002 contains provisions enabling the system's introduction.[47] Practical progress has been slow, however. The steps taken to date have been aimed at only restricted parts of the conveyancing spectrum, notably mortgages, and received without widespread enthusiasm by the lawyers involved; and the Land Registry has now decided to delay the system's wider introduction, in particular its application to the core matter of transfers of ownership between private individuals. But it appears to remain the long-term goal.[48]

Under the electronic conveyancing system, the right's registration would be immediate, so removing the registration gap and the problems it gives rise to. The registration would also be under the conferor's control as much as the conferee's, meaning that the system would deliver the especial benefit of a formality rule to the former, namely to safeguard the quality of his intention. Both the reasons for demanding a deed as well as registration would therefore

---

[45] Though the Land Registration Act 2002 itself does not make this clear.

[46] For a full account of the ideas involved, see Law Commission, *Land Registration for the Twenty-First Century – A Conveyancing Revolution* (Law Com No 271, London, 2001) paras 2.41–2.68 and Pt XIII. For concerns, see R Smith, 'The Role of Registration in Modern Land Law' in L Tee (ed), *Land Law: Issues, Debates, Policy* (Cullompton, 2002) ch 2, 34–42. In particular, there might be qualms about the robustness of the system's IT arrangements, which need to be accessible enough to guarantee operability by conveyancing lawyers up and down the country, but also secure against abuse. My illicitly transferring your house – or, say, the Olympic Stadium – into my name is only the most obvious of the manifold ways in which an insecure system could imaginably be misused. The issue has begun to attract the attention of the press, and it is acknowledged by the Land Registry: see www1.landregistry.gov.uk/propertyfraud/.

[47] ss 91–95 and Sch 5.

[48] See Land Registry, *Report on Responses to E-Conveyancing Secondary Legislation Part 3* (London, 2011; www1.landregistry.gov.uk/upload/documents/econveyancing_cons.pdf) para 5.2.

vanish, and the demand is accordingly dropped for conferrals effected via this system.[49]

The 2002 Act does not itself state which rights would need to be conferred by electronic registration: they are left to be identified by future subordinate legislation ('rules').[50] But it may be confidently anticipated that all the rights whose conferral is currently a registrable disposition would be subjected to this regime. The system can also be applied to equitable rights,[51] in which case the registration could count as any signed writing that would otherwise be required.[52] We noted in the previous section the inappropriateness of the existing registrable disposition regime's confinement to legal rights. Applying the electronic registration system to both legal and equitable rights would bring about the assimilation between the two for which we argued in § 5.4.2. The most contentious issue would be whether, or to what extent, the system should be applied to the rights which presently count as overriding, meaning that they can currently bind transferees – and so, obviously, arise in the first place – without being registered. As we saw in § 3.2.2, the existence of overriding interests can be justified on the basis that the rights in question are disorganised. That is to say, the rights are acquired in circumstances where the parties do not realise, or have only a vague idea, that they are dealing in legal rights at all; or, if they do realise any of this, they assume that the law itself will 'see them right'; and, as a consequence, do not normally enlist the services of a lawyer. At first sight, to rule that such rights could in future be acquired only by electronic registration would simply be to abolish them, for with these characteristics they never would be registered, electronically any more than manually. But the matter may be less straightforward than that, as §§ 3.2.4–3.2.5 explain.

5.5 The Special Case of Leases

We shall deal with leases in Chapter 11. The rules regarding their conferral have certain unique features, and so require a short account of their own.

---

[49] Land Registration Act 2002 s 91(5), stating that the right's electronic registration shall itself count as the deed which would otherwise be required: a roundabout way of saying that a deed is no longer required.

[50] s 93(1).

[51] s 93(1) provides for the regime to be applied to 'a disposition of . . . a registered estate'. At first sight, these words may seem to restrict it to the conferral of a legal right in rem (Law of Property Act 1925 s 1(4)). But the Land Registration Act 2002 uses the word 'disposition' to cover the conferral of any right in rem (this emerges from the phrasing and content of s 27(1) and (2)), so 'a disposition *of* . . . a registered estate' comprehends the conferral of any right in rem, legal or equitable, *over* a registered estate.

[52] s 91(4).

5.5.1 The Formality Rules

Leases are legal (ie common law) rights. In accordance with the general rule stated in § 5.4.1 for legal rights, therefore, they must be conferred by deed and registration[53] ... save that:

—— with certain exceptions, leases for up to three years do not require a deed, or even writing, but can be made orally;[54] and
—— with certain different exceptions,[55] leases for up to seven years are not required to be registered.[56]

Note the way 'periodic tenancies' connect with these rules. Periodic tenancies are leases which nominally last only for say a week, or a month, or a year, but which are automatically renewed each week, month, year unless steps are taken to prevent this (§ 11.4.2). They thus have the potential to run on indefinitely. But for these purposes they count as lasting only for a week, month, year ... so, for less than three years (let alone seven) ... and can validly be made orally.

5.5.2 An Appraisal

The general idea behind these rules is that short leases are commonly made in a somewhat disorganised way, and so cannot appropriately be made the subject of formality requirements.

The stereotype is of a person renting residential accommodation from a private landlord, probably on a monthly or yearly basis. To be sure, the transaction will not be so markedly disorganised as some. English law recognises some rights as arising over land when the people involved might well not realise that anything of the kind is happening: rights arising under the doctrine of proprietary estoppel are of this type. Short leases are not like that: the parties to them undoubtedly realise that they are entering into a legal relationship, and can probably say a certain amount about its implications. But those making these leases commonly act without legal advice, and without a sense of this being a stupid thing to do, probably assuming that the law will sort out any problems in a fair way. It is these leases' dissociation from legal

---

[53] Law of Property Act 1925 s 52(1); Land Registration Act 2002 s 27.

[54] *ibid* s 54(2). The exceptions are that a lease of less than three years requires a deed if it has a delayed start (is not 'taking effect in possession'), or if it is paid for by lump sum in advance or by a nominal rent (is not 'at the best rent which can be reasonably obtained without taking a fine').

[55] A delay of up to three months is allowed, but no longer; there is no stipulation as to rent; but there is an exception if the lease is 'discontinuous', ie giving the tenant a right to possess the land not every day, but only for certain days (as with a timeshare). There are further exceptions of more specialised significance.

[56] Land Registration Act 2002 s 27(2)(b).

advice that is the reason why they cannot aptly be subjected to a formality requirement. Without lawyers to relay it, the need for registration or a deed, perhaps even writing, would not very reliably occur to the parties.

That is the background idea, but where should the line be drawn between the leases that are to be regarded in this way, and so exempted from the formality requirements, and their more organised siblings, for which formality is rightly demanded?

A reasonable case could be made for restricting the exempt category to the very type of case just sketched, namely a periodic (up to yearly) tenancy of residential accommodation between two private individuals. Give one or both of the parties, or the nature of the premises, a business character, and it becomes more reasonable to expect that legal advice will be taken. Likewise, probably, if the tenancy is non-periodic, even if it does not exceed three years.

So even the current exemption from the deed requirement for most leases of up to three years is arguably over generous, though perhaps that is the right side on which to err. The seven-year exemption from the registration requirement, however, is hard to defend even in that way. It is best regarded as an interim arrangement. Before the Land Registration Act 2002, registration was required only of leases of 21 years and more. The 2002 Act substituted seven years. It was explained that the previous rule exempted even most business tenancies, which are commonly of up to 21 years,[57] but no positive justification for the choice of a seven-year limit seems to have been offered. There is provision for reducing the limit further, however,[58] and the Law Commission has suggested that under the proposed electronic conveyancing regime (under which registration takes the place of a deed[59]), the line would be drawn for registration where it currently is for a deed, ie at three years.[60] That would make the law internally consistent, and, as explained above, more or less defensible.

5.5.3 Implied Periodic Tenancies

Say I purport to give you a 10-year lease of my land, but we fail to use a deed (as required for a lease above three years) or to register (as required above seven years). The upshot is that you do not acquire the lease I purported to give you. Say, however, that you go into possession of the land nonetheless, and begin to pay me rent. The law will often take you to be my tenant after all, with a periodic tenancy reflecting the basis on which you are paying rent.[61]

---

[57] Law Commission (n 46) para 3.16.
[58] Land Registration Act 2002 s 118(1)(d).
[59] *ibid* s 91(5): see § 5.4.5.
[60] Law Commission (n 46) para 3.17.
[61] If, for example, you pay on a monthly basis, you will be taken to have a monthly tenancy. But the presumption is that periodic payments are made on an annual basis, yielding a yearly tenancy, even if money actually changes hands at more frequent intervals.

As explained in § 5.5.1, this periodic tenancy, counting as one for less than three years, will be valid despite its lack of any formality.

But a periodic tenancy will be found in this way only if the parties believe themselves to be landlord and tenant. So if you and I know that our purported lease is ineffective (as may be shown, for example, by our continuing to negotiate over it), we will regard ourselves as *not* (yet) landlord and tenant. It will therefore be inappropriate to find a periodic tenancy instead, and one will not be found.[62] One should be found, however, where we are unaware of the invalidity of our original purported lease.

But although a periodic tenancy is thus implied only where not incompatible with the parties' own perception of their position, it is nonetheless a right imposed on a disorganised basis by the law, rather than transacted by the parties themselves. This is emphasised by the fact that the periodic tenancy implied will not have the same content as the lease which I unsuccessfully purported to give you: obviously, it may be terminated earlier, and it will contain only such terms of that lease as make sense in the periodic context.[63] It serves to correct the unsatisfactory discrepancy that would otherwise exist between the parties' legal position and the way in which, in bona fide reliance on their assumed legal position, they conduct themselves in practice. In particular, if we both think our purported lease is valid, and you set yourself up in the premises on that basis, and I lend myself to this (especially by accepting your rent), it would be unfair to allow me, discovering the invalidity, to say you have no right at all to stay. The periodic tenancy that the law imposes is the minimum needed to prevent this unfairness.[64]

So although the requirements of a deed and of registration for our purported 10-year lease are in a sense undercut by the finding of a valid periodic tenancy in its place, the undercutting is the result of the appropriate operation of a disorganised acquisition rule, and so is defensible.

---

[62] *Javad v Aqil* [1991] 1 WLR 1007 (CA).

[63] Covenants requiring the tenant to redecorate at intervals longer than a year would be dropped on this basis, for example.

[64] But see J Morgan, 'The Rise and Fall of the Implied Periodic Tenancy' in S Bright (ed), *Modern Studies in Property Law, Volume 6* (Oxford, 2011) ch 6 for discussion of whether the disorganised right thus required should be a periodic tenancy, or could be some other kind of right.

Contracts to Confer

Chapter 5 described the ways in which I may confer on you a right in rem in my land, and the formality requirements relevant to those ways. But it is very common for the conferral to be something I am obliged to do under a contract I have with you. There are formality rules concerning such contracts too. This chapter looks at these rules. It looks also at an additional matter: a rule whereby a valid contract to confer a right can operate as a quasi-conferral of that right.

The observations made at the end of § 5.2 about the relationship between the law's formality rules and the ECHR are broadly, *mutatis mutandis*, applicable to the contents of this chapter too.

6.1 Pre-conferment Contracts

When you set out to buy a house, and have decided that you would like to buy mine, the ordinary sequence of events is this.

First, you and I agree on the sale orally, whether through an estate agent or in person. So far as the general law of contract goes, nothing more is needed to make a binding contract. But where the contract's subject matter is land,[1] an oral contract will not be valid: the contract must be in writing, and signed by both of us (or by agents acting on our behalf).[2] At the oral agreement

---

[1] That is, it is 'a contract for the sale or other disposition of an interest in land': Law of Property (Miscellaneous Provisions) Act 1989 s 2(1).

[2] *ibid* s 2.

stage, then, you and I may regard ourselves as morally committed,[3] but no legal obligation will have arisen. The 'For Sale' board outside my house will be changed to read 'Sold', but there will be the additional words 'Subject to Contract', meaning that we still await the making of a legally binding, ie written, agreement.

You and I now instruct our solicitors to prepare the necessary written contract. Our solicitors will commonly correspond with each other, but in order that these letters do not become the written contract before everyone and everything is ready, they too will contain the words 'subject to contract', which are recognised as preventing the letters from having contractual effect.[4] Eventually, everything will be settled, and the solicitors will have you and me sign the actual contract documents.

At this point, we are legally committed to the agreed sale; the 'Subject to Contract' rider should come off the board, though estate agents often do not get round to this. All that now remains is the stage known as 'completion', which means the actual transfer of the house from me to you (this is when you get the keys), and your payment of the price to me.[5] Completion is the fulfilment – performance – by each of us of the obligations which we undertook in the contract. It includes my conferring the ownership of the house on you, which is a transaction of the sort dealt with in the previous chapter. As explained there, to make it effective, I have to use a deed, and you have to register yourself as the new owner.[6]

---

[3] Or we may not. This is the point at which, in a rising market, 'gazumping' may occur: ie the seller, having accepted an offer from one buyer, now accepts a better offer from a second buyer – leaving the first buyer disappointed, or obliged to enter into a bidding war. Unless there is something unusual in the circumstances, there is nothing illegal about this practice.

[4] *Tiverton Estates Ltd v Wearwell Ltd* [1975] Ch 146 (CA). This decision disapproved another (*Law v Jones* [1974] Ch 112 (CA)) which had held that written memoranda 'subject to contract' could be turned into a binding contact by an oral agreement to that effect. The current, more recent, version of the formality requirement would itself make that reasoning impossible, as it requires the contract to be '*made* in writing': Law of Property (Miscellaneous Provisions) Act 1989 s 2(1). The oral agreement, if acted upon, might however be the basis of a claim in proprietary estoppel (as in *Waltons Stores (Interstate) Ltd v Maher* (1988) 164 CLR 387 (High Court of Australia)); but it is controversial whether that doctrine can be used to circumvent the formality requirements for contracts in this way: see § 8.4.3.

[5] Often you will have raised part of the price by way of mortgage. Mortgages are explained in Ch 12. Briefly, what technically happens is that you are loaned the money in question by bank A; you use this money to pay me; and you simultaneously give bank A a right over your new house, entitling it to repossess the house from you if you fail to keep up your repayments of the loan. But although in theory the loan is to you and the payment to me, in practice bank A will forward the money to your solicitor, who will pay it to my solicitor, who will use it to pay off the remainder of the mortgage I currently have on the house in question with bank B. Simultaneously, my solicitor will receive the new loan I have arranged with bank C, enabling me to pay for the new house I have contracted to buy from John: and so on.

[6] The process can evidently take some time. It can also be precarious, with the parties breaking away for all sorts of reasons. It is sometimes said that the former spawns the latter, and various reforms aimed at speeding matters up have been made or advocated. It seems likely, however, that the problem (if it is a problem) is deeper rooted.

That is the sequence of events leading up to the sale of a freehold, but essentially the same process generally occurs whenever someone buys any kind of right in another's land. If you want a right of way across my yard, for example, you will normally first agree on it with me orally; then have solicitors create an appropriate written contract; then proceed, with me, to the performance of this contract, by paying me the agreed price while I grant you the right of way, using a deed, and you register yourself as now having it.

The rule, then, is that a contract for the conferral of a right in land must usually[7] be made in writing, and signed by each of its parties, or agents on their behalf.[8] This formality requirement seems justified, as ensuring that the parties are helped – they are unlikely to want it otherwise – to take care over what is likely to be a very major (valuable, complicated, implication-laden) transaction for them, and that the transaction is given clarity for the benefit of others who may have to engage with its impact (other members of the 'chain', for example). Of itself, however, a requirement merely of signed writing does not give the transaction any external visibility, so outsiders who might be affected by it are not alerted. Under the current law, it is possible to register the effect of the contract with the Land Registry,[9] but this is not normally done, it presumably being felt that the effort is not worthwhile, given that the completion of the transaction, which must be registered (§ 5.4.1), should follow soon after. But there is a proposal to include the contract stage in any electronic conveyancing regime that may be introduced (§ 5.4.5).[10] Then, the contract would have to be made (no longer by signed writing but) in the form of an electronic document, with electronic signatures, via the Land Registry website. Like the application of the regime to the completion stage, this would not only preserve the benefits of the current formality rule, but – assuming it worked well – also give the contract the visibility that the current rule cannot deliver.

---

[7] One exception is a contract for a lease of up to three years: Law of Property (Miscellaneous Provisions) Act 1989 s 2(5)(a). This is justified on the same basis that formality is not required for the *conferral* of such a lease: § 5.5. Another exception is a contract made at a public auction: s 2(5)(b). It is in the very nature of an auction that the contract is made orally, and the stylised and public nature of the event is a kind of formality in itself, obviating the mischiefs that may otherwise beset oral contracts: participants should be fully focused on the implications of what they are doing, and there should be plenty of witnesses to what is agreed.

[8] Law of Property (Miscellaneous Provisions) Act 1989 s 2.

[9] As explained in § 6.2, the contract normally generates a right known as an 'estate contract', which is essentially an equitable anticipation of the right contracted to be conferred, and thus itself a right in rem, and capable of registration as such.

[10] Law Commission, *Land Registration for the Twenty-First Century – A Conveyancing Revolution* (Law Com No 271, London, 2001) para 2.54. Moreover, para 2.52 depicts the Registry as facilitating the transaction more generally – eg by keeping the various members of a chain informed of each other's progress towards completion.

6.2 Estate Contracts

6.2.1 The Doctrine of Conversion

Say I validly (so, in writing) contract with you to confer on you a right in rem over land that I own. As explained in § 6.1, we are then supposed to perform ('complete') this contract by my actually conferring the right on you, using whatever formality (deed, registration) is required for this step.

In the meantime, our positions might be expected to be governed simply by the law of contract. So if, for example, I refuse to perform after all, you could claim an order for specific performance obliging me to do so, but you would still not actually acquire the promised right until I comply with this order and confer it on you. But this is not the case. Instead, the law applies a notion called the 'equitable doctrine of conversion', whereby 'equity looks upon as done that which ought to be done'. That is to say, we each *automatically* move into more or less the position we would occupy if we had already completed the contract: so you are regarded as acquiring the right as soon as the contract is made, and without me having actually to confer it at all. Actual conferral remains a good idea and normally occurs, however, because (as we shall see in §§ 6.2.2–6.2.3) the right yielded by this automatic effect is only *more or less* the same as that which we contracted for: conferral is needed to put the finishing touches.

So say you and I have a contract obliging me to confer on you, and you to accept from me, a 10-year lease. Given this contract, actually conferring the lease (by deed and registration) is something that 'ought to be done'. Because of conversion, equity will look upon it as already done. That is, in the eyes of equity, I have already made myself your landlord, and you my tenant, under a 10-year lease.

The set of rights you acquire under this doctrine is known as an 'estate contract'. The term sounds most appropriate in the case of the conferral of a freehold or lease, but extends also to conferrals of other rights, such as easements and mortgages. In the case of a lease, there is an alternative term, having the same meaning: an 'agreement for a lease'.

In the abstract, the doctrine of conversion is rather baffling: *why* should equity look upon as done that which ought to be done?[11] But for all that estate

---

[11] There is in fact an answer, but it is obsolete. The effect that we call conversion was the reasoning by which, in the 15th century, the law began to think that a putative buyer of land could sue a seller for non-performance of the agreement: on the footing that the agreement made the land in some sense immediately the buyer's. (See S Gardner, 'Equity, Estate Contracts and the Judicature Acts: *Walsh v Lonsdale* Revisited' (1987) 7 *OJLS* 60, 74–7.) Nowadays, of course, we allow the buyer to sue (for breach of contract) simply on the basis of the agreement itself.

contracts arise in this mysterious way, they may be functionally valuable. They order our rights in the potentially problematic transition period (especially in the freehold case) between contract and completion, establishing what may be appropriate default rules on such matters as which of us must insure the property and which of us shall receive any profits it generates.[12]

6.2.2 The Nature of Estate Contracts

As we saw in § 1.3.1, where the common law and equity give conflicting readings of a situation, the equitable reading takes precedence. So when the common law says that you do not have a 10-year lease, but equity says you do, the bottom line is that you do. But your having an estate contract does not mean that you *actually have* the 10-year lease (or whatever) that we contracted for: that was a 10-year lease *recognised by the common law*. What you have is the position of *being treated by equity as* having that lease. This is usually translated into 'What you have is a 10-year *equitable* lease';[13] but this somewhat overstates the nature of your rights.

It is an overstatement partly because some statutory rules do in fact treat the two kinds of right – equitable and common law – differently, whether or not they have any good reason to do so.[14]

But it may be an overstatement also because of two further, more fundamental, factors. First, equity itself may not treat you as having the relevant right – eg the 10-year lease – in absolutely every case where we have a valid contract for its conferral: it may regard you as having the 10-year lease only if the contract is not only valid, *but also capable of specific performance*.[15] And

---

[12] For details, see A Oakley, *Constructive Trusts* (3rd edn, London, 1997) ch 6; for analysis, see P Turner, 'Understanding the Constructive Trust between Vendor and Purchaser' (2012) 128 *LQR* (forthcoming).

[13] Or, as the case may be, 'equitable easement', 'equitable mortgage', etc. And where freehold ownership is involved, therefore, 'equitable ownership'. (If I am the legal owner of land but you are its equitable owner, I necessarily hold it on trust for you. So in this case, the freehold estate contract can also be described as a trust: *Shaw v Foster* (1872) LR 5 HL 321, 338 (HL); *Lysaght v Edwards* (1876) 2 Ch D 499, 506 (Ch D). But to say merely that it is a trust is to omit reference to some important aspects of it. See Oakley, *ibid*.)

[14] In particular, the rules whereby common law rights must commonly be registered (see especially the Land Registration Act 2002 s 27(2)), while their equitable counterparts generally can be (s 34) but need not. There are also some differences in the treatment of common law rights and their equitable counterparts in terms of their ability to operate as overriding interests (Sch 3 paras 1 – *cf City Permanent Building Society v Miller* [1952] Ch 840 (CA) – and 3). But compare the Landlord and Tenant (Covenants) Act 1995 s 28(1), governing some central aspects of the law of leases, which expressly defines 'tenancy' as including 'an agreement for a tenancy', ie an equitable lease.

[15] If the contract is not capable of specific performance, so that you do not have the equitable right, all may not be lost. If the contract was for a lease, you may be able to fall back on a (common law) periodic tenancy, as explained in § 5.5.3. But if the purported grant was of some other type of right, eg a freehold or mortgage or easement, you may be left only with an action for breach of contract. Depending on the surrounding facts, however, a disorganised acquisition doctrine such as proprietary estoppel (Ch 8) may be relevant.

second, even in 'treating you as having' the lease (or other right), equity may not accord you exactly the same protection as you would enjoy under a genuine – ie common law – lease of the same kind. Purists therefore assert that your right does not amount to an 'equitable *lease*' at all.[16] That expression would suggest a straightforward anticipation of the legal lease which was due to be conferred on you, whereas these two factors, if we take them seriously, mean that your right falls somewhat short of that. But should we take them seriously?

6.2.3 The Two Factors

The first factor was the demand that, for conversion to occur, the contract must be one of which a court would grant specific performance, as between the parties to the dispute that has arisen, and in the current circumstances.

It must immediately be said that, even if it does represent the law, this demand will usually be met, so equity will usually regard you as having the right. In particular, specific performance is the ordinary remedy associated with contracts to grant a right in land. It will be available in such a case unless there is some reason why not. Such a reason might be, however,[17] that you have breached one of the terms of the purported lease: this would disable you from claiming specific performance against me ('he who comes to equity must come with clean hands', and yours would not be), and so from relying on conversion against me.[18]

But does the requirement for specific enforceability really represent the law? Or will equity treat you as having the lease or other relevant right, full stop, as soon as a valid contract for its grant exists between us? There are certainly some well-known judicial statements saying that the specific enforceability requirement is part of the law,[19] and few explicitly asserting that it is not.[20] But the alleged requirement is often tacitly ignored, in that the law takes positions irreconcilable with it. These positions include the fact that equitable leases, and other types of estate contract, are in rem at all. Take the

---

[16] *Swain v Ayres* (1888) 21 QBD 289, 295 (CA).

[17] See *Coatsworth v Johnson* (1886) 54 LT 520 (CA). It might be asked whether your inability to claim specific performance, and so rely on an equitable lease, makes any difference to the bottom line: even if you had been able to rely on the equitable lease, would not your breach have meant you lost ('forfeited') it? Not necessarily: the rules about forfeiture are complex (see § 11.5.2), but they do give tenants quite a lot of leeway before the whole lease is lost in the way that it is if your breach simply prevents you claiming specific performance.

[18] Though not vice versa: if *I* wanted to rely on an equitable lease against *you*, I should be able to do so, for your breach should not prevent me from claiming specific performance against you.

[19] See eg *Coatsworth v Johnson* (1886) 54 LT 520 (CA); *Swain v Ayres* (1888) 21 QBD 289, 295 (CA); *Manchester Brewery Co v Coombs* [1901] 2 Ch 608, 617 (Ch D).

[20] Perhaps the only explicit statement unequivocally to this effect (as opposed to loose talk where greater precision was unnecessary) is by Denning LJ in *Boyer v Warbey* [1953] 1 QB 234, 245 (CA).

scenario where I contract to grant you a 10-year lease. If I then transfer my freehold to John, can John be bound by your right? Not if you have to be able to claim specific performance of our contract against him, for he is not a party to it.[21] But it is quite clear that the law is to the contrary: your right is in rem, ie can bind John (and will do so if you have registered it or are in actual and apparent occupation of the land). This is explicable only on the basis that the right arises as an equitable lease *at the outset*: its nature as a lease makes it in rem (for leases are in rem), and thus capable of binding John when the land in question is later transferred to him.[22]

Now the second factor,[23] that equity may not accord you exactly the same rights and remedies as you would enjoy if you genuinely had a common law right of the same kind. Specifically, equity may not allow you to protect yourself in any way that would have involved your suing in a common law court.[24] Say I contract to grant you a lease. You can certainly prevent me from evicting you as having no right to be on the land at all: the remedy that that requires is an injunction, which equity itself can grant. But if this factor represents the law, it means that you cannot sue me for damages if I breach my obligation, as landlord, to repair the premises: for this form of relief is available only from a common law court, and thus available only if you have a true common law lease, so as to merit protection by such a court. Nor, likewise, can you claim damages from someone who trespasses against you on the land.[25]

For a long time, there was no reason to doubt that this was the position. It was the upshot of some central, if not nowadays widely appreciated, learning about the practical manner in which equity handled its relationship with the common law, via a device known as a 'common injunction'. Briefly, equity

---

[21] This was recognised in *Purchase v Lichfield Brewery Co* [1915] 1 KB 184 (KBD), holding that the obligations in an equitable lease cannot therefore be enforced against an assignee from one of its original parties.

[22] See further Gardner (n 11) 60; R Chambers, 'The Importance of Specific Performance' in S Degeling and J Edelman (eds), *Equity in Commercial Law* (Pyrmont NSW, 2005) ch 17.

[23] On this, see further Gardner, *ibid* 81–91. The claim is made there (at 86–7) that the first factor is in fact rooted in the second: so if the argument against the second factor succeeds, the first inevitably falls too.

[24] The discussion in the text is put in terms of the remedies you might obtain in the different (common law and equity) courts. It is true that, since the Judicature Acts 1873–5, there are no such separate courts: all remedies can be had in the same court. The traditional view, however, is that this streamlining of court business had no impact on the question what remedies are available in vindication of what rights: in particular, equitable rights (such as estate contracts, and also trusts) continue to attract only equitable remedies. This traditional view is, however, subject to arguments about 'fusion', whereby all remedies are in principle available in support of all rights. If this is correct, the factor under discussion in the text would certainly not represent the law. See further § 1.3.1.

[25] Your inability to claim damages against a trespasser might be viewed as the result of your having, in your *equitable* lease, only a 'persistent' right, not a true right in rem; the point being that, unlike true rights in rem, persistent rights are enforceable only against disponees, not against non-disponee third parties such as trespassers too. The concept of a persistent right is considered in see § 1.3.2. It is suggested there that, to the extent that it is valid at all, it may be not an independent insight, but an upshot of the issues discussed in the text below.

would grant a common injunction to prevent someone – such as me, in our example – *enforcing* common law rights against a person whom it, equity, saw as having a contrary right – such as you, with your estate contract right. But equity would *not* grant a common injunction to prevent me *defending* a common law action that you brought against me on the footing of your equitable right. If you could have had a common injunction in the latter case, you would in effect have been able to access common law relief on the basis of only an equitable right. But the enduring view was that you could not do so. Hence the rule presented here as the second fundamental factor in the way of treating estate contract rights as practically identical to the fully granted rights that they anticipate.

This appreciation of the operation of common injunctions was not inevitable, however. There was no technical reason why equity could not issue them in the way just described, and so make its rights emulate their common law counterparts – so that, for example, your rights under our agreement for a lease would have amounted to an 'equitable lease' after all. The reason it chose not do so is not well understood. And in fact, there are clear indications that it ultimately started to review that choice, and take the opposite path, producing rights such as 'equitable leases' after all.

The headline insistence, nevertheless, on the traditional view of common injunctions – and also on the traditional view regarding our first factor, the demand for specific enforceability, in the teeth of the reasons for rejecting it too – seems to have been the result of nothing more elevated than a demarcation dispute amongst elements of the Bar at the end of the 19th century. That aside, there seems no good reason not to reject these two impediments to seeing estate contracts as truly generating equitable copies of the fully granted rights they anticipate. With the caveat that this position is unorthodox, and the reminder (see § 6.2.2) that some statutory rules, sensibly or not, treat the two kinds of rights differently, we should therefore conclude that estate contract rights are in fact true copies of their common law counterparts.

6.2.4 'Discovered' Contracts

So far, we have supposed the contract from which the estate contract arises to be a real one: the contract to confer a right that normally precedes the actual conferral. But there is another possibility.

As explained in § 6.1, the conferral of the right commonly represents the completion of a preceding contract. If the conferral is made using the required formalities, it will take effect; otherwise, the conversion of the preceding contract will normally give you an estate contract, in the way described in § 6.2.1. But sometimes the conferral will not be preceded by any contract: the conferral itself will represent the totality of the transaction between us. That is often the case with leases, in particular: we may omit the contract stage (at any rate, the written contract stage) and instead declare ourselves there and then to be giving and taking the lease itself. Again, if the conferral is made using the required formalities, it will take effect; but if not, on the face of it there in this case appears to be no contract to be converted so as to produce an estate contract.

The law, however, supposes otherwise. In such a case it will after all 'discover' (the discovery is by definition fictitious), in the failed conferral, a contract to make the conferral.[26] Of course, to be of further help, this contract must itself be valid. So it – that is, the purported conferral in which it is 'discovered' – must have the formality necessary to contracts for the conferment of rights in land, ie (as explained in § 6.1) be in writing, signed by each of us.[27] But given such validity, the contract can be sued upon for damages, or for specific performance, ordering the conferral actually to be made, properly. And it will also be the subject of conversion, so as immediately to create an estate contract over the land, corresponding to the right with whose actual conferral, failing for want of formality, we began.

So, for example, if I purport to confer on you a legal lease for 10 years, but we do not use a deed or register the lease, the purported conferral will fail as such but will be treated as a contract to confer. And, so long as the purported conferral is in writing, this contract will be converted so as to give you an 'equitable lease' on the same terms. This combination of conversion with the 'discovery' of the required contract in a failed conferral is known as 'the doctrine in *Walsh v Lonsdale*'.[28]

6.2.5 Estate Contracts as Undercutting Legal Formality Requirements

To sum up what we have learned about estate contracts. The relevant situation is one in which a legal conferral has not taken place, for want of a deed or (where relevant) registration. This may be the case either where the transaction has not yet reached the stage requiring a deed or registration at all; or where it has reached that stage, but the required deed has not been used, or the required registration has not occurred. So long as there is an underlying contract (genuine or 'discovered') in writing, an equitable right – an estate

---

[26] *Parker v Taswell* (1858) 2 De G & J 559 (Ch).

[27] Law of Property (Miscellaneous Provisions) Act 1989 s 2. Previously, the contract could under certain circumstances have been valid even if only oral, and some of the older cases thus involved only oral transactions. Nowadays, if the transaction is merely oral, while not generating the effect discussed in the text, it may nonetheless ground the finding of a periodic tenancy, as explained in § 5.5.3.

[28] (1882) 21 Ch D 9 (CA). This decision involved a lease. Other decisions, on the same lines, apply to further kinds of right whose conferral requires a deed, and nowadays also registration: eg *Shaw v Foster* (1872) LR 5 HL 321 (HL) (freehold); *McManus v Cooke* (1887) 35 Ch D 681 (Ch D) (easement); *Mason v Clarke* [1955] AC 778 (HL) (profit à prendre); *Ex parte Wright* (1812) 19 Ves 255 (Ch) (mortgage).

contract – will arise; and although its effect will not be quite the same as that of the intended legal right, it will be similar.

As we saw in § 6.2.1, estate contracts may be functionally sensible devices, for the structure they give to the parties' rights in the transition period between contract and completion. But this role is more or less confined to the case where the contract in question is a genuine one, and the parties are proceeding to a proper completion. If the parties do not proceed to a proper completion, which will almost certainly be the case where the required contract is 'discovered' in the manner explained in § 6.2.4, estate contracts instead operate (to the large extent that the equitable right does replicate the intended legal right) in lieu of the right purportedly conferred. They thus undercut the formality requirements that the conferral does not meet, making it the law's bottom line that the right's conferral requires only writing, not a deed and (where relevant) registration, after all.

Is this undercutting effect acceptable? It might be, if the generation of estate contracts were a disorganised mode of creating rights, for then it would rightly proceed without reference to the formality rules that would otherwise apply. It is fair to regard the generation of an estate contract as disorganised in the sense that the parties do not always intend specifically this right, as opposed to the legal right whose conferral has not (yet) occurred. But estate contracts arise only within the context of an organised transaction for the conferral of a legal right, and they operate substantially to effectuate that conferral. The effect must therefore count as an essentially organised one. In principle, therefore, the law ought to demand formality in respect of it. Indeed, it does so, by requiring the contract from which they arise to be in writing. It ought also, however, to make that formality no less than it properly demands for the conferral of the legal right itself, as discussed in Chapter 5.

'Properly' is important, however. Consider first the contrast between the requirement of writing for the estate contract, and that of a deed for the conferral. Although the undercutting is unacceptable, it is the demand for a deed that is misplaced. As was argued in § 5.4.3, there is insufficient justification for the respects in which a deed requires more than writing. Writing ought therefore to be enough for both the estate contract and the grant.

Consider then the contrast between the requirement of writing for the estate contract, and that of registration (under the registrable disposition regime) for the conferral. Again, the undercutting is unjustified in principle. But this time, it is the estate contract's lack of a registration requirement that is unsatisfactory. As was argued in § 5.4.4, a requirement of registration is justified because it makes the right visible to prospective disponees of the land to which it relates, enabling them not to waste time and resources exploring transactions in which, discovering the full picture, they lose interest. From this point of view, writing alone – which does not deliver such visibility – is not enough. Registration should in principle be required for estate contracts just as much as for conferrals.

There are practical reasons why such a rule could not be expected under the land registration arrangements that have existed hitherto. Registration is too sluggish a process to be sensibly required in respect of transitory rights, which estate contracts arising from genuine contracts (though not 'discovered' ones) are: they exist only until the performance of the contract by the conferral proper. But this problem would fall away if electronic conveyancing were brought into operation, with its feature that registration takes place simultaneously with – indeed, as a very component of – the transaction itself.

As noted in § 6.1, the enabling legislation for electronic conveyancing[29] clearly envisages that contracts for the conferral of rights in land would need to be made via the register, just like the conferral itself. Estate contracts would continue to arise from the contract, and this might be all to the good, for the sake of the transitional effects that we have noted. But because the formality requirements for estate contracts would be aligned with those for conferral, the latter would no longer be undercut by the arising of estate contracts. Many centuries of dysfunction would have come to an end.

---

[29] Land Registration Act 2002 s 93(2). As noted in § 5.4.5, there is no current plan to progress with its introduction.

Adverse Possession and Prescription

7.1 Disorganised Acquisition

In Chapters 5 and 6, we focused on the possibility of your acquiring a right in my land for the reason that I intend you to, and set out to confer it on you. We are calling acquisition in this way 'organised'. But at the outset (§ 5.1), we noted that this is not the only way in which you may acquire a right in my land. Factors of other kinds may equally mean that you ought to have such a right. In fact the law has a number of rules giving you a right in this alternative – what we are calling 'disorganised' – way. This chapter looks at some of these rules; Chapters 8 and 9 look at some others.

7.1.1 'Factors of Other Kinds'

When it is said, above, that 'factors of other kinds' may mean that you ought to have a right in my land, what might these factors be?

There is certainly no pre-ordained template for them. But, on the plane of principle, nor is there simply a blank page on which any idea may be written as validly as any other. To merit acceptance, and implementation by the law, a possible factor needs a satisfactory moral or political justification. Recognising this does not, of course, constrain the answer very tightly, for there is room for debate over what moral and political arguments are satisfactory. This book will not attempt significantly to engage with that issue. It will confine itself to identifying some of the main plausible arguments reflected in English law, and explaining the rules in which they are reflected.

Some useful basic mapping can be done. First, there is a distinction between arguments about justice and those about other forms of good, often utility.

Many rules exist, or have existed, based on considerations of the latter kind. The law on compulsory purchase is a major example. This permits land to be acquired by bodies of various kinds, to allow them to pursue purposes regarded by Parliament (which creates the facility) as of value to the nation. Thus, land can be compulsorily purchased to create new roads: this being thought valuable for such ends as giving citizens more freedom to get about, and lubricating trade.

Rules aimed at doing justice work to correct unfairness between individuals (or groups). The unfairness may be an embedded one: that is, one which was not, or not at all directly, the result of events for which an identifiable person is responsible. In this case, the unfairness will lie simply in the fact that two people ought (there is a lot of baggage beneath this 'ought', of course) to enjoy equivalent or in some other way comparable advantages, but do not. A rule may then be made aimed at delivering such equivalence or comparability. A project of this kind is said to promote 'distributive justice'. English law's taxation rules are partly of this kind: although the reason for raising the money at all is generally a utilitarian one (to finance the NHS, etc), the incidence of the liability to pay varies to some extent with wealth, identifying and seeking to redress an unfairness in the way this is distributed.

But such a broad mission cannot be pursued between two parties at a time, as in the sort of litigation we are accustomed to. If distributive justice is to be done in such litigation, it must be on the basis that the parties' relationship requires equality (or some other goal) specifically between the two of them. So, when a couple are divorced, and the judge is called upon to make a 'fair'[1] redistribution of their property between them,[2] the approach is to minimise the material impact of the divorce on any children, to secure the parties' 'reasonable requirements' and to divide any remaining assets equally between them.[3] The theory underlying these operations seems to be that the parties owe each other and their children the level of wealth in question, by virtue of their marriage and their status as parents. I might be ordered to transfer my house, or a share in it, to you on this basis.

Or the unfairness may have come about as a result of events for which an identifiable person (or group) is responsible. Then, achieving justice – redressing the unfairness – will consist in transferring goods[4] from the person (or

---

[1] *White v White* [2001] AC 596, 599 (HL).

[2] Matrimonial Causes Act 1973 ss 24, 25. These provisions require the judge 'to have regard to all the circumstances', and list some which are not to be overlooked. The majority of these consist in the problems that the divorce may cause for the parties' future standard of living. So although it expresses no particular goal, the statute does seem to hint that the parties' assets should be reallocated so as to secure their future material well-being in some way.

[3] *White v White* [2001] AC 596 (HL); *Miller v Miller, McFarlane v McFarlane* [2006] 2 AC 618 (HL).

[4] Generally property (especially money, but also for example rights in land), but sometimes alternatively liberty (as with imprisonment) or bodily well-being (as where, if I am responsible for injuring you, you are permitted to injure me in return). At first sight, a regime of this alternative kind seems not to *transfer* anything, but that may be an insensitive appreciation. Where you

group) responsible to the person (or group) whose position has suffered through those events. Adjustments of this kind pursue 'corrective justice'.[5] An example of corrective justice is the relief given for torts or breaches of contract. Rights in land are conferred on this type of basis under the doctrine of proprietary estoppel. Say you believe that you have, or are going to have, a right in my land, and I am in some way responsible for that belief, most notably because I told you so. Then you act (perhaps you spend some money) in reasonable reliance on your belief, and suffer a detriment as a result. Because I am responsible for your belief, I am also responsible for this detriment you have suffered. There is thus an unfairness between us. The law may correct this unfairness by conferring on you a right in my land.[6]

So these three – utility, distributive justice and corrective justice – are the main bases on which the law may confer on you a right in my land for reasons other than the fact that I intended you to have such a right. In this and the following two chapters, we shall look at a collection of doctrines which, between them, exhibit all three of these bases. These doctrines are adverse possession; prescription; proprietary estoppel; and two doctrines said to give rise to constructive trusts. They are selected for coverage here simply because they commonly feature in the syllabus of the subject called land law, at which this book is directed. There is no essential difference between them and the areas of compulsory purchase and allocation of assets upon divorce, referred to above as instances of the general phenomenon at which this chapter is aimed. These latter areas of law are not discussed further here simply because they are not normally included in the land law syllabus.

7.1.2 Disorganised Acquisition and Formality

In Chapters 5 and 6, we saw how, if a right in rem over land is to be acquired in an organised way, its conferral, and any preceding contract, must normally be effected using some degree of formality (writing, deed, registration). What happens in this respect if such a right is to be acquired in a disorganised way?

As we saw in § 5.2, the goals of a formality requirement include improving the quality of the intention behind its conferral. This is irrelevant to the disor-

---

and I exist in close proximity, or where I have harmed the overall well-being of society (a group), levelling my position down may be a way of restoring fairness between us.

[5] The division of justice-based claims between 'distributive' and 'corrective' in this way was first suggested by Aristotle. A considerable literature has grown up discussing what exactly Aristotle meant by 'corrective'; in particular, whether he wished to say that non-distributive claims are justifiable only in certain circumstances, narrower than we might otherwise think. In this book, the word 'corrective' is used simply to refer to all non-distributive claims, the question of their justifiability to be addressed independently of Aristotle's views.

[6] For proprietary estoppel, see Ch 8. As we shall see there (§ 8.4), however, this doctrine is a protean one, arguably representing more than one corrective project, and indeed a distributive one.

ganised generation of a right, as this does not rest on intention. But the other goals we discussed were promoting certainty that the right has been acquired at all, clarity as to its details, and its visibility to the outside world. These goals are in principle no less important if the right arises in a disorganised than in an organised way. In particular, being in rem, the right is no less capable of binding disponees, so those contemplating a deal involving the land will certainly be helped if they can easily find out where they stand regarding it.

So there is a case for saying that rights arising in disorganised ways should be given some kind of formal mark. But in general, the law does not take this position. It allows them to arise quite informally, and this is indeed the more appropriate answer. If a formality requirement were imposed in the disorganised sector, it would hardly ever be complied with. Since, by definition, a disorganised right arises against the (hitherto) owner of the land for reasons other than his wanting it to, one certainly could not rely on him to meet the requirement. Nor, however, could one rely on the person acquiring the right, for in the nature of disorganised acquisition, he might well not even realise that he is acquiring it; and even if he does, he will not have the help of a lawyer, and so access to information about the formality rule. (If it were otherwise, the story would not have been a disorganised one in the first place.) So if formality were required, the law's very object in generating the right would normally be immediately frustrated by the invalidity attendant upon the predictable failure to comply with that requirement.

Visibility remains an issue, of course. Although a right in rem arising in a disorganised way can be registered (not as a pre-condition to its existence but) in order actually to bind a disponee, it commonly will not be, for the reason just discussed: the person holding it will often neither personally know that the right exists or can be registered, nor have reason to discover this via a lawyer. As explained in § 3.2.2, therefore, its route to binding a disponee will rightly be normally as an overriding interest. But as we found in § 3.2.3, the law generally permits it to operate as an overriding interest only where, in its own nature, it is reasonably visible.

One could get past the difficulty preoccupying us, and require formality for disorganised rights after all, by arranging for them to arise only when declared to do so by an official organ, such as a court. (The court would obviously know to comply with a formality rule, such as a demand to register the right.) Something of this kind is in fact now the case where a right in registered land arises by adverse possession (§ 7.2): in this case, the right is only clinched through an alteration of the register, by the Land Registry.[7] It is also the case where the property of former spouses or civil partners is reallocated under the Matrimonial Causes Act 1973. It may or may not be the case, but should be, where a right arises under the doctrine of proprietary estoppel.[8]

---

[7] Land Registration Act 2002 Sch 6 paras 1–9.
[8] *ibid* s 116(a); § 8.5.1.

The argument for preferring the rival approach – that is, for allowing the right to arise from the key facts themselves, rather than requiring an official order – is that this would give the people concerned more autonomy (treating their rights and obligations as in essence theirs, to be recognised rather than conferred by the court). But taking such a rival approach can be counter-indicated if the rule under which the right arises needs to take account of a complex set of factors, such that its result in a given case can only be satisfac-torily elicited by the exercise of a discretion by a judge ... or, even without this complication, if the desirability of formality is thought too important to allow the right to arise without an official order.

7.2 Adverse Possession

You can acquire the freehold ownership of my land[9] via the doctrine of 'adverse possession'.[10] This doctrine has two elements. The first is that you must take adverse possession of the land. This is considered in § 7.2.1. Before 2002 (and still today, in the case of unregistered land), the second was that you had to remain in adverse possession for 12 years. Since the Land Registration Act 2002, however, the second has become (so far as registered land is concerned) – roughly speaking – that your adverse possession must have lasted for 10 years, and must either be followed by certain proofs of my having abandoned the land, or have occurred on land adjoining our common boundary, with you reasonably believing it to be yours throughout. We shall explore this second element in § 7.2.2.

7.2.1 The First Element: 'Taking Adverse Possession'

To acquire an interest by adverse possession, then, the first thing you have to show is that you have taken adverse possession of the land in question. What counts as 'taking adverse possession'?

'Possession' is essentially the set of things that an owner has the right to do with the land.[11] These can be instanced, but cannot be exhaustively enumer-

---

[9] Or a lease over it, if that is the interest I myself have. However, certain complications arise in this case, which are not detailed in this book.

[10] See further A Clarke, 'Use, Time, and Entitlement' (2004) 57 *CLP* 238.

[11] The Latin root of 'possession' means something like 'having power over', and one judicial rendition speaks (losing something of the true amplitude?) of the exercise of 'custody and con-trol': *JA Pye (Oxford) Ltd v Graham* [2003] 1 AC 347, [40] (HL). The most illuminating para-phrase is perhaps 'dealing with the land in question as an occupying owner might have been

ated, for the set is open-ended: it comprises everything that is physically possible, minus those things that are prohibited.

The idea of 'taking' possession means *behaving as though* you have this set of rights.[12] This has two aspects.

The first is that you must have the mindset known as '*animus possidendi*', ie intention to possess. That is, you must envisage yourself doing not necessarily all the things an owner might do (obviously), but as many of them as you may fancy, rather than a limited class of them.[13]

So in principle, you should need to envisage excluding anyone unwelcome, including me, and living on the land gratis; these being two of the things an owner can do. But it has also been ruled that you can have *animus possidendi* even though you realise and concede my ownership, and, therefore, even though you concede the possibility of not excluding me, or of needing to pay me rent in order to stay.[14] It is hard to see how this ruling can co-exist with the fundamental idea of *animus possidendi*. The courts have fudged the difficulty. They have decided that you have *animus possidendi* so long as you reckon to exclude me 'so far as is reasonably practicable and so far as the processes of the law will allow',[15] ie so far as you can get away with it. Likewise as regards rent: you have *animus possidendi*, despite a mere mental preparedness to pay, so long as you do not actually offer to do so.[16] The distinctions being made here are clearly unstable, so will be difficult to apply in practice, making the law unpredictable in its effect.

Then, as the second aspect of taking possession, you must put your *animus possidendi* into effect. Since (as explained above) the set of an owner's rights is open-ended, you necessarily can be found to have done so even though

---

expected to deal with it': *Powell v McFarlane* (1977) 38 P & CR 452, 471 (Ch D), approved in *JA Pye (Oxford) Ltd v Graham* at [41].

[12] 'Using the land in the way one would expect [you] to use it if [you] were the true owner': *JA Pye (Oxford) Ltd v Graham, ibid* [71].

[13] That is, you must have 'an intention to occupy and use the land as [your] own': *JA Pye (Oxford) Ltd v Graham, ibid*. A claim to adverse possession failed on this ground in *Powell v McFarlane* (1977) 38 P & CR 452 (Ch D), where the claimant, aged 14 at the relevant time, used the land to graze his cow: especially given his age, he probably did not aspire to a broader range of use.

[14] *JA Pye (Oxford) Ltd v Graham, ibid* [42]–[43]. Regarding an argument for the contrary view (ie a demand that you should actually believe yourself owner of the land), see L Tee, 'Adverse Possession and the Intention to Possess' [2000] *Conv* 113; O Radley-Gardner and C Harpum, 'Adverse Possession and the Intention to Possess – A Reply' [2001] *Conv* 155; and L Tee, 'Adverse Possession and the Intention to Possess – A Rejoinder' [2002] *Conv* 50. This argument would narrow the scope of adverse possession substantially. As we shall see in § 7.2.2, it is now reflected in the only case where, in registered land since 2002, you can rely on your adverse possession alone, rather than your adverse possession together with my failure to object.

[15] *Powell v McFarlane* (1977) 38 P & CR 452, 472 (Ch D), approved in *JA Pye (Oxford) Ltd v Graham* [2003] 1 AC 347, [43] (HL).

[16] *JA Pye (Oxford) Ltd v Graham, ibid* [46]; *cf Pavledes v Ryesbridge Properties Ltd* (1989) 58 P & CR 459 (Ch D). For unregistered land, there was a statutory sibling for this rule in the Limitation Act 1980 ss 29–30, whereby there is no *animus possidendi* if you 'acknowledge' my ownership, but only where you put your 'acknowledgement' in writing.

your actual deeds fall short of the entire set. Something fairly substantial is nonetheless demanded, presumably in that it would be unsafe to extrapolate too narrow a base of behaviour to the required conclusion that you rule out nothing. So the question is whether you are 'dealing with the land in question as an occupying owner might have been expected to deal with it',[17] ie whether you are making reasonably full use of the particular piece of land concerned. You can take possession of a house by living in it; of a garden by tending it; of an arable field by ploughing it; and so on.[18] But your use of the land need not match the use to which I previously put it, or to which someone else might put it.[19] Judgments on this issue are often impressionistic. This, combining with the difficulties over *animus possidendi*, leaves the law in this area highly discretionary... and more especially with no clear guiding principle(s).

Finally, you must take – and retain – possession in an 'adverse' manner. There are two aspects to this too.[20] First, you must be a trespasser: your possession cannot be adverse if I consent to it, permit it.[21] (So there is no question of adverse possession if you possess my land by virtue of a lease I have given you.) Second, before your possession without my consent can tell against me, I must have had the opportunity to give concrete effect to my lack of consent, by suing to evict you... and have failed to do so.[22] So if your possession is undetectable,[23] or I have only a future interest in the land,[24] or I am

---

[17]   *Powell v McFarlane* (1977) 38 P & CR 452, 471 (Ch D), approved in *JA Pye (Oxford) Ltd v Graham, ibid* [41].

[18]   *Powell v McFarlane, ibid.* Fencing the land in, or locking its gates, is sometimes treated as conclusive (see eg *Seddon v Smith* (1877) 36 LT 168, 169 (CA)), but this seems implausible, if you do nothing further.

[19]   So in *Buckinghamshire County Council v Moran* [1990] Ch 623 (CA), where the council left the land alone, intending to use it for road improvements, the defendant took possession by using it as a garden. But in *Boosey v Davis* (1988) 55 P & CR 83 (CA), where the land in question had development potential, the grazing of goats on it was held to be too limited to amount to taking possession of it.

[20]   There is no further requirement that you forcibly evict me – *JA Pye (Oxford) Ltd v Graham* [2003] 1 AC 347, [35]–[38] (HL) – though I must be excluded or at any rate absent from the land, otherwise it will remain in my possession, rather than come into yours. Nor need your user actually incommode me: *ibid* [44]–[45].

[21]   *JA Pye (Oxford) Ltd v Graham, ibid* [35]–[38]. So, in *BP Properties Ltd v Buckler* (1987) 55 P & CR 337 (CA) the owner stopped the possession from being adverse by writing a letter to say that it was permitted. The permission may of course be implied as well as express. But it cannot be inferred from the mere fact that, despite being aware of your presence on my land, I fail to evict you: Limitation Act 1980 Sch 1 para 8(4), reversing a contrary position taken in *Wallis's Cayton Bay Holiday Camp Ltd v Shell-Mex & BP Ltd* [1975] QB 94 (CA). It is difficult to fault the logic of the latter decision (a licence would readily be found under such circumstances if adverse possession were not at stake), and its statutory reversal seems a (possibly ill-advised) policy initiative aimed at restoring the potency that would otherwise have drained from the doctrine of adverse possession.

[22]   To prevent you relying on adverse possession, before the end of the qualifying period I must either (obviously) actually evict you, or have a court judgment not more than two years old entitling me to do so, or be suing you to this end: Land Registration Act 2002 Sch 6 para 1(3). It is not however enough if within the last six months I evict you otherwise than through court proceedings: Sch 6 para 1(2).

[23]   *Rains v Buxton* (1880) 14 Ch D 537 (Ch D).

[24]   Land Registration Act 2002 Sch 6 para 12.

disabled from attacking your possession for a number of other reasons,[25] I lack the necessary opportunity, and you should fail. But if I am merely absent, or take no interest in the land, the law regards me as still having the necessary opportunity, and your possession as therefore adverse.

7.2.2 The Second Element

Before the Land Registration Act 2002, you acquired my land if, having taken adverse possession of my land, you remained in possession of it for 12 years.[26] Under that Act, however, the 12-year rule no longer applies.[27] Instead, you acquire my land only if, in addition to taking adverse possession of it:

—— after remaining in adverse possession for at least 10 years,[28] you apply to be registered as owner;[29] then, when the Registry notify me of your application:

—— *either* I fail to object;[30] *or* I do object, but two further years pass without my proceeding to evict you;[31] *or* (whether I object or not) we own neighbouring pieces of land, and the area in question, while hitherto part of my land, adjoins our boundary, and you reasonably thought it yours.[32]

Put shortly, these additional requirements mean that, having adversely possessed my land for 10 years, you now become owner of it in only two scenarios. One is where I have in effect abandoned the land – as shown by my failure to object, or to press my objection. The other is where the land lies on our boundary, and you reasonably believed it yours.[33] (The latter scenario's restriction to boundary land and its demand that you reasonably believe yourself owner are in fact connected. In general, the register shows me as owner, so a contrary belief cannot be reasonable. But the register does not indicate exactly where a property's boundaries lie, so in this respect a reasonable error can occur.)

Where one of these two scenarios is made out, you are entitled to be registered as owner of the land in place of me.

[25] *ibid* para 8.
[26] Limitation Act 1980 s 15, following the Real Property Limitation Act 1874, before which the law used longer periods.
[27] Land Registration Act 2002 s 96.
[28] The change from 12 to 10 years reflects a general proposal to reduce limitation periods: see Law Commission, *Limitation of Actions* (Law Com No 270, London, 2001).
[29] Sch 6 para 1.
[30] Sch 6 para 4.
[31] Sch 6 para 6.
[32] Sch 6 para 5(4). Para 5(2) and (3) purport to add two further cases: where you deserve the land in question under the doctrine of proprietary estoppel, and where you are entitled to it for some other reason. These, however, are free-standing reasons why you can claim the land, nothing of substance being added by your having also adversely possessed it.
[33] In order to apply to be registered as owner, you must of course have discovered your error. The demand is thus that you must have been in adverse possession for 10 years before doing so.

7.2.3 The Pre-2002 Doctrine's Basis and Acceptability

We now turn to consider why the law should make you owner of the land in these circumstances, if indeed it should at all.

Before the changes in 2002, the doctrine achieved its effect in the following way. The first element, the demand for adverse possession, represented English law's ancient position that taking possession of land itself gave you an entitlement to it.[34] You became owner of the land except to the extent that someone else could show a better entitlement. This would be someone who, or whose title derived from someone else who, had possession before you. As it was normally impossible to know the first person ever to possess a piece of land, this relative kind of entitlement was as good as you or anyone else could hope to have: unqualified ownership did not exist. But if in reality, for one reason or another, you were reasonably safe from such eviction, for practical purposes your relative entitlement was not too different from the non-existent unqualified ownership. Picking up on this last reflection, the law added the doctrine's second element: the rule whereby, if you stayed in possession for 12 years, all who might otherwise have evicted you lost the ability to do so,[35] and indeed lost their own rights in the land.[36] The invulnerability this gave you to earlier claims meant that you acquired something even more like unqualified ownership of the land (though of course you in turn could lose the land to someone who later adversely possessed against you).

At any rate from the 19th century on, the basis for the doctrine seems to have been a desire to facilitate the marketability of land, to utilitarian ends.[37] If in due course you found yourself trying to sell the land to John, John would want to feel reasonably sure that he was not wasting his money, as he would have been if someone with a better right to the land than you could show up and eject him. And if John could not feel reasonably sure of this, he would be less eager to engage in land transactions at all . . . to the detriment of the nation's economy, for then land would not find its way to the person valuing it highest, and the projects for which they so valued it would never be put into operation, and so on. From this point of view, the idea behind the first element, that entitlement rests upon possession, posed a problem as much as it offered a solution. The solution lay in the second element. This operated to reassure John and so correct all this. So long as you had been in possession

---

[34] Hence the demand that you 'take possession', ie behave like an owner: if you presented yourself as anything less than an owner, the law would have no reason to treat you as one. (Though initially, the key idea was not possession, but the similar, though not identical, concept of seisin.) For an account, see eg A Simpson, *A History of the Land Law* (2nd edn, Oxford, 1986) ch 2 (especially 37–40), and also 150–55. For the assumptions embedded in the construction of 'possession', see further K Green, 'Citizens and Squatters: Under the Surfaces of Land Law' in S Bright and J Dewar (eds), *Land Law – Themes and Perspectives* (Oxford, 1998) ch 9.

[35] Limitation Act 1980 s 15.

[36] *ibid* s 17.

[37] See M Dockray, 'Why Do we Need Adverse Possession?' [1985] *Conv* 272.

for the relatively short period of 12 years, or you derived your title from one who had, John had no need to concern himself with what might have gone before.

This utilitarian project may have provided a sufficient justification for the original form of the second element, given the problem created by the first. But any such justification disappeared when the law simultaneously[38] set about stabilising land titles in a different way. This involved eradicating the first element – the idea that possession in itself gives someone a title to the land – and replacing it with registration: the idea that title belongs to the person registered as having it (§ 3.3.1).[39] Given the latter, a rule transferring title to someone who adversely possessed the land for 12 years was no longer needed to provide stability, and indeed in general (we shall note an exception in a moment) had the opposite effect. John, wanting to buy land registered in your name, would actually be injured by the possibility that some other person had acquired title to it by having adversely possessed it. Certainly in its then form, therefore, the doctrine of adverse possession was no longer needed for the utilitarian task which had previously justified it, and indeed from the point of view of that basis had in general become positively malign.

For a time, it was thought that, in thus giving in effect uncompensated transfers without sufficient justification, the doctrine violated the ECHR First Protocol Article 1, whereby 'No one shall be deprived of his possessions except in the public interest . . .', and in a manner proportionate to the particular interest in question.[40] That position was later reversed, it being held that the doctrine's infelicities did not exceed what was allowable under the margin of appreciation.[41] The doctrine was nonetheless unsatisfactory, and was given the overhaul it needed in the Land Registration Act 2002.

7.2.4 The Post-2002 Doctrine's Basis and Acceptability

The doctrine was not, however, simply abolished by the 2002 Act. Instead, as we have seen, it was retained, but narrowed by adjustments to its second

---

[38] But not coincidentally: the 19th and 20th centuries saw many new rules aimed at the same end. Most were complementary, however, rather than mutually antagonistic, in the manner of those explained here.

[39] Though of course the initial registration would naturally be made on the basis of the traditional possession theory.

[40] *JA Pye (Oxford) Ltd v United Kingdom* (2006) 43 EHRR 3 (ECtHR Lower Chamber). *Beaulane Properties Ltd v Palmer* [2006] Ch 79 (Ch D) temporarily rescued the old rules by reinterpreting them (under the Human Rights Act 1998 s 3(1)) so as in effect to demand the original owner's consent to the transfer, thereby giving a transfer under them the additional, legitimising, support of that consideration.

[41] *JA Pye (Oxford) Ltd v United Kingdom* (2007) 46 EHRR 1083 (ECtHR Grand Chamber). The reversal was eased by a recharacterisation of the nature of the 'interference' (see § 2.3.4) from 'deprivation' (Lower Chamber) to 'control of use' (Grand Chamber), so avoiding the rule (§ 2.3.5) that a 'deprivation' can be proportionate only if compensated ((2006) 43 EHRR 3, [73]–[74]), which loss by adverse possession is not.

element. In its new form, it comprises two distinct rules, each having its own basis.

The first of these rules is that whereby you can acquire boundary land by adversely possessing it for 10 years, even if I object. The basis for this continues to be the stabilisation of titles. Remember how, above, it was said that adverse possession is *in general* inimical to this goal. There is an exception. The register is not designed to give an accurate statement of properties' boundaries. When you offer land for sale, then, there is still a need to ensure that the exact area you are offering is indeed yours to sell, to the market's benefit. Hence the rule. The rule's demand that you should have reasonably believed the land to be your own is a new one, however: as we saw in § 7.2.1, the traditional view of adverse possession involves no such demand.[42] But the demand is appropriate – an improvement on the old approach – as ensuring (very properly, for a utilitarian project) that the good done by stabilising title is not outweighed by a countervailing harm. There would be such a countervailing harm if you could acquire boundary land despite knowing or suspecting it to be mine, for then there would be an incentive to the theft of such land.[43]

The other of the new law's rules is that whereby you acquire my land if you adversely possess it for 10 years and I then abandon it. The consideration behind this version of the rule seems to be a different utilitarian goal: promoting the active use of land. This is seen as desirable because, certainly in England, land has become a rather scarce resource, relative to the size of the human population and to that population's aspirations, so that the common good requires its reasonably intensive exploitation.[44] The rule's first element – adverse possession itself – tracks this goal in only the crudest way. In two fairly recent decisions, the original owner, while not using the land at the time, intended it for road improvements[45] or house-building,[46] while the squatter used it for a garden or for grazing respectively. Transferring the land on this basis alone (as the pre-2002 rule did, after 12 years) does not intensify the land's use, except in the short term. Crucially, however, the rule now demands that I must also have abandoned the land, as shown by my failure to oppose its transfer to you, or to evict you. This element makes it highly likely that transferring the land to you will intensify its use. Under the new arrangements, the original owners in the two decisions just mentioned, for example,

---

[42] *JA Pye (Oxford) Ltd v Graham* [2003] 1 AC 347, [42]–[43] (HL).

[43] For other ways of dealing with mistakes about boundaries, see P O'Connor, 'An Adjudication Rule for Encroachment Disputes: Adverse Possession or a Building Encroachment Statute?' in E Cooke (ed), *Modern Studies in Property Law, Volume 4* (Oxford, 2007) ch 9.

[44] This is not beyond challenge, of course. One might argue that a fuller understanding of the common good (or some higher value, capturing more than the human common good alone) demands that land be exploited less intensively. If adverse possession has the opposite effect, this argument might require its abolition.

[45] *Buckinghamshire County Council v Moran* [1990] Ch 623 (CA).

[46] *JA Pye (Oxford) Ltd v Graham* [2003] 1 AC 347 (HL).

would surely oppose the transfer and evict the squatter. The same element also ensures that the good done by promoting more intensive use is not outweighed by the harm involved in creating an incentive to land theft: even if you take adverse possession of my land deliberately so as to acquire it, you will rarely succeed, for I will normally oppose the transfer.

The post-2002 rules thus rest upon arguments from utility that are respectable, and indeed, given the rules' design, significantly stronger than before. Given that even the old rules were eventually held proportionate for the purposes of the ECHR, as we saw in the previous section, the new rules' compliance may be assumed too. A worry of principle remains, however. The rules continue to take my land away from me without compensation. Although the argument from utility alone may justify this in the case of boundary land, it is probably insufficient where the whole area is at stake: if the public interest demands taking the land from me so as to put it to better use, I should at least be compensated. The argument's deficiency may be corrected, however, by the element of consent that must also be present under the new rules concerning this case. The requirement that I be given the opportunity to oppose the transfer to you, and fail to take it, tends to show not only that I have abandoned the land in question, so as to confirm the advantage in transferring it to you, but also that I accede to the transfer. The degree of consent thus displayed is insufficient to justify an uncompensated transfer on its own (it shows that I do not object to the transfer, rather than that I positively will it), but it and the argument from utility together may claim to do so.

One final point. Strictly, there is no reason why the post-2002 rules should continue to use the concept of 'adverse possession' at all. In unregistered land, the concept was key because, as explained in § 7.2.3, it encapsulated English law's traditional basis for the ownership of land. Given your adverse possession, you had a claim to the land only one degree less strong than mine: so extinguishing mine, as policy was thought to require, necessarily left yours in its place. In registered land, however, this is not the case. Title to land is more a function of the state of the register. If policy requires provision for sometimes adjusting title for utilitarian reasons (as we have seen it may), the adjustments can be shaped in whatever way the same policy indicates. They do not have to proceed from adverse possession. At the same time, however, the concept of adverse possession formed the traditional basis of title not accidentally, but because the happenings covered by it – 'behaving like an owner' – generated reasons for the effects the law ascribed to it. It is reasonable for today's rules to find what is significant for them in broadly the same sorts of happenings: that is, for the projects of stabilising boundary titles, and of promoting the intensive use of land, likewise to focus on someone's behaving like the owner of the land in question.

7.3 Prescription

Prescription[47] is a means of acquiring easements.[48] Easements are dealt with fully in Chapter 13, but to explain prescription let us take one instance of an easement, namely a right of way: a right entitling you to cross my land on your way to and from yours. You can acquire an easement by my conferring it on you;[49] or by prescription, on the basis, roughly speaking, that you have behaved as though you had it – ie you have crossed my land – over a period of 20 years.

Prescription can occur under three different rules, or families of rules. They are 'prescription at common law', 'lost modern grant', and prescription under the Prescription Act 1832. Each rule was developed not so as to reform its predecessors, but to allow prescription in meritorious cases which it was thought fell outside the earlier rule(s). The result, however, is at best unnecessary complexity.

The rules ask us to suppose that your behaviour occurs under an easement that was conferred at some time in the past (hence the very label, 'lost modern grant'). But the supposition of a genuine historic conferral is largely a fiction. We are to overlook the absence of evidence actually showing any conferral, and indeed the presence of evidence negating it[50] ... though there can be no easement if the supposed conferral would have been positively impossible, as where the supposed conferor lacked the capacity or power to make it.[51] This limitation apart, the rules generate rights on the basis of your behaviour, and my reaction to it.

---

[47] See further J Getzler, 'Roman and English Prescription for Incorporeal Property' in J Getzler (ed), *Rationalizing Property, Equity and Trusts – Essays in Honour of Edward Burn* (London, 2003) ch 11.

[48] With some differences, it is also a means of acquiring two other kinds of rights – profits and commons – but we shall focus only on easements. Several of the leading cases, however, come from those other contexts. They will be referred to here as relevant. (The Law Commission has recommended that profits should no longer be capable of acquisition by prescription: *Making Land Work: Easements, Covenants and Profits à Prendre* (Law Com No 327, London, 2011) paras 3.3–3.9.)

[49] In the context of easements, the law on conferral has some special features (some striking rules regarding especially *implied* conferral), which require extended treatment: see § 13.2.

[50] *Dalton v Angus & Co* (1881) 6 App Cas 740 (HL); *Tehidy Minerals Ltd v Norman* [1971] 2 QB 528, 552 (CA).

[51] *Rochdale Canal Co v Radcliffe* (1852) 18 QB 287 (QB); *Proprietors of the Staffordshire and Worcestershire Canal Navigation v Birmingham Canal Navigations* [1866] LR 1 HL 254 (HL); *Dalton v Angus & Co* (1881) 6 App Cas 740 (HL); *Neaverson v Peterborough RDC* [1902] 1 Ch 557 (CA); *Tehidy Minerals Ltd v Norman* [1971] 2 QB 528 (CA); *Oakley v Boston* [1976] QB 270 (CA); *Housden v Conservators of Wimbledon and Putney Commons* [2008] 1 WLR 172 (CA). Exceptionally, under the Prescription Act 1832 s 3, an easement of light can arise despite impossibility of conferral. And see N Piška, 'Granting Capacity to the Fiction of Presumed Grant' [2009] *Conv* 349 regarding the impossibility rule (or at least the capacity version of it) generally.

Your behaviour – your crossing my land, say – must be 'as of right', meaning that, to external appearances, you seem to be acting lawfully[52] (though
neither of us need believe that you actually are[53]). It must be '*nec vi, nec clam,
nec precario*': that is, peaceable, rather than involving force against me; open,
rather than of a kind which I could not detect; and on your own account,
rather than with my permission.[54] It is sometimes said (indeed, it appears to
be the current ostensible law[55]) that the two requirements, 'as of right' and
'*nec vi, nec clam, nec precario*', are the one and the same: that the former is
proved exclusively via the latter. In principle, however, this seems unlikely, at
any rate unless '*nec vi, nec clam, nec precario*' is given some strained connotations. If you cross my land peaceably, openly, and without my permission, but
positively proclaiming yourself to be a trespasser, you surely do not do so 'as
of right'. Likewise, one would think, if in any other way your behaviour
shows an acceptance that you have no right.[56] In particular, this might be the
case if you 'defer' to me while on my land. On the other hand, one should
take care not to find such 'deference', and so conclude that you do not act 'as
of right', in every situation where you do not in practice trouble me. Our
respective usages of the land may simply be such that, even if you do act 'as
of right', we can co-exist without friction anyway, as for example where you
cross my golf course without coming into conflict with the golfers, there
being plenty of room for everyone.[57] The demand is essentially that you
appear, to external appearances, to be acting on the footing of a right to
behave as you do.[58]

In appraising the prescription rules, the starting point is the fact of your
having acted historically in accordance with the alleged easement. This is
taken to create a reason why you should in future have the right to do so. That
reason seems to be a utilitarian one: a desire, as in one version of adverse
possession,[59] to promote the more intensive use of land. As explained in
§ 13.1.6, easements allow for the cross-exploitation of land, precisely so that
it can be used more intensively than would otherwise be possible. Your having
used my land in the manner in question for an extended period suggests that
this particular instance of cross-exploitation may in fact be valuable.

---

[52] So your behaviour cannot be prescriptive if you commit an offence while you are about it:
Cargill v Gotts [1981] 1 WLR 441, 446 (CA); presumably because *ex turpi causa non oritur actio*.

[53] *R v Oxfordshire County Council, ex p Sunningwell Parish Council* [2000] 1 AC 335 (HL).

[54] The case-law goes into considerable detail about the exact meaning of these demands, in
particular dealing with the hazy borderlines that each possesses.

[55] *R (Lewis) v Redcar and Cleveland Borough Council* [2010] 2 AC 70, [63]–[70], [87], [107]
(SC).

[56] *ibid*, [112] (SC).

[57] *R (Lewis) v Redcar and Cleveland Borough Council* [2010] 2 AC 70 (SC). The various statements identified in n 55 above, to the effect that '*nec vi, nec clam, nec precario*' is the only test of
'as of right', are in fact embedded in a full consideration of this issue.

[58] *ibid*, [36].

[59] That which applies where you adversely possess my land for 10 years, apply to have it transferred to you, and I do not effectively oppose this: § 7.2.4.

But an easement might be equally valuable even without such prior user, yet not arise, except under some statutory provision having its own more specific utilitarian basis. This suggests that the argument from utility is insufficient on its own to warrant your acquiring an easement against me. That is plausible. The cross-exploitation in question may be valuable, but it is unlikely to be vital, as would be needed to justify such a confiscation of my property without compensation (which a statutory provision would normally provide). Hence the doctrine's remaining requirements, which allow us to find an element of consent[60] (in this area normally referred to as 'acquiescence') on my part to your acquiring the easement,[61] which – as in adverse possession – combines with the argument from utility, and may justify the prescription.

This element of consent is relatively weak, compared with the case where I willingly confer the easement on you; so (as in the corresponding aspect of adverse possession) it is not enough to warrant your acquiring the easement on its own. But it is discernible. One of its ingredients is the demand that your behaviour must be open, and apparently based on a right. This means I can know both that you are doing what you are, and that it is adverse to my own interests, so as to have a fair opportunity to stop you before you acquire an easement.[62] Another ingredient is the demand that you must not have used force: any such force may not quite deprive me of a fair opportunity to stop you, but it colours my failure to do so, making it less consent than submission. Another ingredient again is the requirement that your behaviour must not be permitted by me. Though at first sight puzzling (surely I consent the more if I do permit your behaviour?),[63] this helps on the basis that, if I consent to your *behaviour from time to time*, I do not consent to your acquisition of *an easement whereby, in future, you will need no such consent*. If I fail to

---

[60] See eg *Dalton v Angus & Co* (1881) 6 App Cas 740, 744 (HL); *Oakley v Boston* [1976] QB 270, 284–5 (CA); *R v Oxfordshire County Council, ex p Sunningwell Parish Council* [2000] 1 AC 335, 351, 353 (HL).

[61] See *R v Oxfordshire County Council, ex p Sunningwell Parish Council* [2000] *ibid*; *R (Lewis) v Redcar and Cleveland Borough Council* [2010] 2 AC 70, [36], [94], [116] (SC).

[62] There is a difficulty, however. It is wrong to assume that the openness of your behaviour necessarily gives me a fair opportunity to stop you. The assumption works if your behaviour involves a tort against me – a trespass or nuisance – such as where you go to and from your land across mine. Then I can stop you by legal action against you, or perhaps self-help. But some easements ('negative easements') involve only your passive and entirely legal reliance on a state of affairs prevailing on my land: such as where your building's foundations, while contained within your own land, would collapse if I excavated my neighbouring land. The only way for me to stop such 'behaviour' is actually to negative the state of affairs on which you rely, eg to excavate my land. My failure to do so can hardly be regarded as acquiescence in your reliance. Responding to this, where your reliance is on the light reaching your window across my land, the law has created a special way for me to stop it, by notice under the Rights of Light Act 1959 (see further M Barnes and J Bignell, 'The Rights of Light Act 1959 and a Fiction too Far?' [2009] *Conv* 474); and the courts have strictly limited the kinds of negative easements that can exist (*Phipps v Pears* [1965] 1 QB 76 (CA); *Hunter v Canary Wharf Ltd* [1997] AC 655 (HL): see § 13.1.4). But otherwise the problem remains.

[63] Compare the discussion in *R (Beresford) v Sunderland City Council* [2004] 1 AC 889, [76]–[81] (HL).

oppose your behaviour when I do not consent to it in its own right, that suggests I do consent to your acquiring such an easement.

However, is the combination of this degree of consent and the argument from utility sufficient to warrant your acquiring the easement? Quite possibly not. The problem lies in the relative weakness of the argument from utility. As we have seen, it takes your protracted use of my land in the manner in question as evidence that such a use is a valuable instance of cross-exploitation. But unlike the rule about adverse possession in the context of abandonment, which we saw in § 7.2.4 also to operate on the combined basis of utility and consent, prescription is not actually confined to the case where giving you the right will fairly clearly mean a more advantageous use of the land. Some other rules[64] generating easements on the same combined basis are so confined, demanding that the new easement be needed or at least useful. Without such a restriction, even with a modicum of consent, the prescription rules seem to provide insufficient reason to impose the easement on me. If prescription is not to be abolished outright,[65] therefore, it should be restricted to cases where some degree of need for the easement can be shown.[66]

Subject to any issue as to horizontal effect (§ 2.2), analysis via the ECHR First Protocol Article 1, prohibiting interference with my 'possessions' except where the interference is a proportionate means of promoting a proper interest, points the same way. Even given a modicum of consent, achieving the low level of utility that is required for prescription may well not amount to such a proper interest as will justify the inroad into my ownership.[67]

---

[64] See §§ 13.2.2, 13.2.4. But one such rule, that in the Law of Property Act 1925 s 62, suffers from the same weakness as prescription, and is similarly criticised: § 13.2.5.

[65] As proposed by the Law Reform Committee, *Acquisition of Easements and Profits by Prescription* (14th Report, 1966); but not, more recently, by the Law Commission, *Making Land Work: Easements, Covenants and Profits à Prendre* (n 48) paras 3.71–3.187, recommending the retention of essentially the present law, with some rationalisation of its details. (The Commission's account of the argument for retention – paras 3.74–3.81 – is superficial, however.) See further S Bridge, 'Prescriptive Acquisition of Easements: Abolition or Reform?' in E Cooke (ed), *Modern Studies in Property Law, Volume 3* (Oxford, 2005) ch 1; F Burns, 'Prescriptive Easements in England and Legal "Climate Change" ' [2007] *Conv* 133.

[66] For alternative visions of the ideas underlying prescription, see C Sara, 'Prescription – What Is It For?' [2004] *Conv* 13; Clarke (n 10). Additionally, for a critical overview of the law's whole gamut of rules whereby rights can be acquired through long usage – including both adverse possession and prescription, but others too, such as that whereby private land can become a village green – see A Goymour, 'The Acquisition of Rights in Property by the Effluxion of Time' in Cooke (ed) (n 43) ch 8.

[67] Indeed, if the interference is a 'deprivation', one would expect justification to be impossible in the absence of compensation (*JA Pye (Oxford) Ltd v United Kingdom* (2006) 43 EHRR 3, [73]–[74] (ECtHR Lower Chamber)), but in the parallel context of adverse possession the interference was characterised as a 'control of use', so avoiding this rule. See n 41 above.

Proprietary Estoppel

8.1 An Outline

This chapter looks at your acquiring a right in my land via the doctrine of proprietary estoppel.

There is no definition of proprietary estoppel that is both comprehensive and uncontroversial (and many attempts at one have been neither), but the following outline of the doctrine is offered. As will emerge over the course of the chapter, however, there is uncertainty, in some sense and/or at some level, about virtually all of its aspects.

If I encourage you to believe – or if I acquiesce in a belief you already hold – that you have a right over my land, or else that I will confer such a right on you; and you then, in reliance on that belief, act to your detriment; you will be entitled to relief. This entitlement is itself a right in rem, capable of binding any subsequent disponee of the land in question.

An illustration will help. Say you and I are neighbouring landowners. Included in my land is a strip in which I take no interest (perhaps it is cut off from the remainder by a hedge). You, however, see value in it. In a conversation with you one day, I tell you that you can have the strip, or even that I believe it to be yours already. You, taking me at my word, begin to cultivate it. Under the doctrine of proprietary estoppel, you thereupon become entitled to a remedy against me. And if, before you in fact claim the strip, I transfer it to John, then so long as your entitlement is registered or counts as an overriding interest, you will be able to claim your remedy from him instead.

8.2 The Requirements for an Estoppel

8.2.1 The Requirements

The headline requirements for claiming an estoppel are thus:

—— You must firmly believe either that you already have a right over my land, or that I will confer such a right on you.
—— You must act to your detriment.
—— You must suffer your detriment in reasonable reliance on your belief, which in turn must be the reasonable product of an assurance (whether by way of encouragement or acquiescence) on my part.

We must now examine these requirements in more detail.

8.2.2 Your Belief

According to the statement above, you must firmly believe that you either already have, or are going to acquire, a right over my land or other property.[1]

So you must believe that you *definitely* have the right, or that I shall *definitely* confer it on you.[2] This requirement is easily explicable. If you act upon what you realise is only a possibility, I am not responsible for your doing so: it is for you to clarify matters first, or to decide to take the risk anyway. A claim can readily fail on this basis, especially where your belief is as to the future. You will have no claim if I promise to give you the right but you think 'I'll believe it when I see it'. For example, if I say I shall leave you the right in my will, that might well be what you think (or at any rate what the court will be persuaded you think). You surely know that, even if I make a will to this effect, I can always revoke it.

A contrary tendency is visible in some cases about wills, however. A leading decision is *Gillett v Holt*.[3] The court there concluded that the claimant's belief was sufficiently definite. In favour of this answer was the fact that the

---

[1] In most cases the right has been over land, but there is authority that it can be over any form of property: *Re Basham* [1986] 1 WLR 1498 (Ch D); *Jennings v Rice* [2002] EWCA Civ 159 (CA); *Cobbe v Yeoman's Row Management Ltd* [2008] 1 WLR 1752, [14] (HL); *Thorner v Major* [2009] 1 WLR 776 (HL).

[2] *Ramsden v Dyson* (1866) LR 1 HL 129 (HL); *A-G for Hong Kong v Humphreys Estate (Queen's Gardens) Ltd* [1987] AC 114 (PC); *Cobbe v Yeoman's Row Management Ltd* [2008] 1 WLR 1752 (HL).

[3] [2001] Ch 210 (CA). *Re Basham* [1986] 1 WLR 1498 (Ch D), *Jennings v Rice* [2002] EWCA Civ 159 (CA) and *Thorner v Major* [2009] 1 WLR 776 (HL) are similar.

defendant not only promised the claimant that he would leave certain property to him by will: he also announced this promise to his family on important family occasions, which was especially significant as they would have expected to inherit the property otherwise. Yet this did not quite prove that the claimant believed his inheritance to be in the bag: 'I'll believe it when I see it' would still have been a natural reaction. The court tried to bolster its reading with more general reasoning. It asserted that the law itself, in the shape of the estoppel doctrine, would make the promise irrevocable and so definite. But this argument is circular: it tries to use the estoppel doctrine to make the promise be definite, when correctly, the doctrine does not bite in the first place unless the claimant's understanding is definite in itself. The decision's conclusion, that the claimant's belief was sufficiently definite, therefore seems questionable. The case really stands for an attenuation of the very requirement that you have a definite belief.

According to *Cobbe v Yeoman's Row Management Ltd*,[4] your belief must be in a 'certain interest'[5] which is also a 'proprietary right'.[6] But this does not accurately state the law.

A 'certain interest' seems to mean a defined right over defined property. The suggestion therefore seems to be that if, in the illustration in § 8.1, I had said merely 'we'll sort something out for you', an estoppel would not have arisen in your favour: I should have needed to say something more focused, such as 'you can have the strip', or 'you can use the strip'. This requirement is overstated, however. You must certainly believe in a right *over my property*, but greater specificity than that seems not to be required:[7] even 'we'll sort something out for you' should be enough, if it implies that you should have a right over my land.[8] Nor need the right in question be identified with any precision;[9] and it commonly will not be, for by definition, estoppel cases will not normally involve formal documentation, so the particular words used are likely not to have been carefully chosen, and also to be difficult of proof.

---

[4] [2008] 1 WLR 1752 (HL). (See J Mee, 'Proprietary Estoppel, Promises and Mistaken Belief' in S Bright (ed), *Modern Studies in Property Law, Volume 6* (Oxford, 2011) ch 8.)

[5] *ibid* [18]–[23].

[6] *ibid* [14]. Or 'proprietary claim': [16].

[7] In *Thorner v Major* [2009] 1 WLR 776 (HL), the claimant's belief seems to have been that he would inherit the defendant's 'farm'. There was obviously room for debate as to what, if anything, the 'farm' comprised, beyond the land itself. The judge took it to cover the farm buildings, live and dead stock, other assets of the farming business, and £24,000 in the defendant's business account. The House of Lords had no difficulty with this; see especially at [98].

[8] There is, however, a potential difficulty where I promise to leave you some asset in my will (eg 'my farm') . . . it being understood that, in view of the time-lag before you are due to have it, I may in the meantime lose the asset, or alter its substance (eg I may expand or shrink my farm, or exchange it for a new farm altogether). This difficulty is noticed, and some lines of approach suggested, in *Thorner v Major* [2009] 1 WLR 776, [9], [18], [20], [62], [88], [95] (HL).

[9] *Ramsden v Dyson* (1866) LR 1 HL 129, 171 (HL); *Plimmer v Mayor &c of Wellington* (1884) 9 App Cas 699, 713 (PC); *Thorner v Major* [2009] 1 WLR 776, [64], [97] (HL). Likewise, in *Crabb v Arun District Council* [1976] Ch 179 (CA), the defendant promised the claimant a right of way over its land for a price to be agreed; the court awarded the claimant the right of way, untroubled by the indeterminacy as to its price.

When *Cobbe v Yeoman's Row Management Ltd*[10] demanded that you must believe in a 'certain interest', it did so as a proxy for the requirement that you must (reasonably) believe in a right over my property.[11] That decision involved commercial parties. They did not precisely specify the right in question because they never settled that the claimant should have any right at all; fundamentally, it was for the latter reason that the claimant could not establish an estoppel claim. If you and I are non-commercial parties, however, it is perfectly possible, and reasonable, for you to believe in a right over my property, yet for that right to remain vague.[12]

The further demand that your belief be in a 'proprietary right' is not to be taken very literally. This phrase ordinarily means 'right in rem'. So, apparently, an estoppel can arise if I say you can live in my house on your own, since the right to do this is in rem;[13] but an estoppel cannot arise if I say you can live there with me, since the right to do that is in personam.[14] But a demand for a belief in a right in rem would run counter to established authority.[15] It seems clear that an estoppel can indeed arise if I say that you can live in my house with me, or, to revert to our original illustration, that you can make use of my strip of land alongside me. The requirement thus seems to be that you believe in a right, whether in rem or in personam, over some piece of land (or other property) of mine, as opposed to a right that I will do something for you. A belief in a right to live in my house would therefore be enough; but a belief in a right to be housed by me, in some unspecified location, would not.[16]

8.2.3 Your Detriment

According to the account in § 8.2.1, you must then act to your detriment. Actions of any kind will suffice.

To show 'detriment', it is not enough that you are worse off (unless you win redress from me) than my assurance led you to expect to be. That will

---

[10] [2008] 1 WLR 1752, [18]–[23] (HL).

[11] *Thorner v Major* [2009] 1 WLR 776, [96]–[99] (HL).

[12] Indeed, the author of the 'certain interest' requirement – Lord Scott – subsequently indicated that, while cases failing it may not succeed in proprietary estoppel, they should succeed by way of 'remedial constructive trust': *Thorner v Major* [2009] 1 WLR 776, [20] (HL). For discussion of this proposal, see § 8.5.1.

[13] It is a lease: § 11.2.1.

[14] It is a licence: §§ 11.2.1, 17.1.

[15] *Plimmer v Mayor &c of Wellington* (1884) 9 App Cas 699 (PC); *Inwards v Baker* [1965] 2 QB 29 (CA) – decisions cited, with apparent approval, in *Cobbe v Yeoman's Row Management Ltd* [2008] 1 WLR 1752 (HL). See also eg *Greasley v Cooke* [1980] 1 WLR 1306 (CA).

[16] Likewise, a right to a particular investment, owned by me, would be covered; but a right to be paid some sum of money from my assets at large would not. Thus in *Re Basham* [1986] 1 WLR 1498 (Ch D), the claimant successfully relied on proprietary estoppel in a case where she believed that she would inherit the defendant's entire estate, ie believed in a right over his specific property.

necessarily be the case. The idea is rather that your reliance on your belief has left you worse off (unless you win, perhaps) than you were *before you acted in reliance on my assurance*: as in the illustration in § 8.1, where you believe the strip of land is now yours, and (expend money and labour to) cultivate it.[17]

There are plenty of cases where this requirement has been applied uncontroversially. In *Gillett v Holt*,[18] however, the Court of Appeal indicated[19] that it is to be applied loosely. The court held the claimant to have suffered detriment when, believing he would inherit the defendant's land, he remained in the defendant's employment; continued living, rent-free, in a house owned by the defendant rather than buying or renting a house for himself; and paid for his younger son to attend boarding school, the defendant having paid for the claimant's elder son to do so.[20] It is not impossible that the claimant became worse off as a result, but concluding to this effect involves speculation about how the claimant would have fared if he had not remained in the defendant's employment and housing, and the taking of the surely dubious view that paying for the younger son's schooling was a 'loss' at all.[21] The best way to see the decision is as, having attenuated the requirement of belief, doing the same to the requirement of detriment.

8.2.4 My Responsibility

The remaining requirements are that I must encourage or acquiesce in your belief; that your belief is a reasonable conclusion for you to draw from that encouragement or acquiescence; that you suffer your detriment in reliance on your belief; and that this reliance too was reasonable. This set of requirements operates to make me responsible for what has occurred. That is: if, but only if, all these requirements are present, a thread of responsibility can be followed through from your detriment, via my encouragement or acquiescence, to me.

The two ideas of encouragement and acquiescence cover the spectrum between your developing your belief because of what I say; and your conceiv-

---

[17] The requirement is that you should be left with a *net* detriment. That is, while you may also have gleaned benefits, this does not block your estoppel claim so long as they are outweighed by your losses: *Henry v Henry* [2010] 1 All ER 988, [51]–[53] (PC). *Quaere* how the calculation is to be performed, however.

[18] [2001] Ch 210 (CA).

[19] *ibid* 232 (approved in *Fisher v Brooker* [2009] 1 WLR 1764, [63] (HL); *Henry v Henry* [2010] 1 All ER 988, [55] (PC)): 'The detriment need not consist of the expenditure of money or other quantifiable detriment, so long as it is something substantial. The requirement must be approached as part of a broad inquiry as to whether repudiation of an assurance is or is not unconscionable in the circumstances.' The same approach was taken in *Campbell v Griffin* [2001] EWCA Civ 990, [23]–[24] (CA), though on the facts there the conclusion reached was less controversial.

[20] [2001] Ch 210, 234–5 (CA).

[21] For discussion of the decision's approach to 'detriment', see R Wells, 'The Element of Detriment in Proprietary Estoppel' [2001] *Conv* 13.

ing it for yourself or because of something you pick up elsewhere, and my not correcting it. The former scenario is straightforward, but in the latter, I must be aware that you hold the belief:[22] otherwise, my failure to correct it cannot make me responsible for it. The law's very acceptance of acquiescence is surprising, however. If you and I were negotiating towards a contract, it would not be enough: you normally[23] have no relief for mistakes which you make and which, even knowingly, I fail to correct.[24] Estoppel is more generous to you: it is unclear why it should be.[25]

I can encourage or acquiesce in your belief in any way that produces the necessary result, ie a belief that you already have the right in question, or a belief that I will confer it on you. Remember the illustration in § 7.1, involving the strip of land. I can encourage or acquiesce in your belief that you own the strip by giving you to think either that the strip has been yours all along, or that I am there and then giving you it. I can encourage or acquiesce in your belief that I will give you the strip either by giving you to understand that we have an enforceable contract to that effect, or else by firmly promising you it. The case-law includes decisions and statements showing that proprietary estoppel reacts to assurances of all these kinds,[26] and that is unsurprising, because my assurance could very easily be ambiguous between them: as for example if I simply say, referring to the strip, 'It's yours.'

But my encouragement of or acquiescence in your belief does not make me responsible for the detriment you have suffered unless the two are linked: that

---

[22] And aware also that you do not already have the right in question: *Taylors Fashions Ltd v Liverpool Victoria Trustees Co Ltd* [1982] QB 133n (Ch D). There is no such requirement if I actively encourage your belief (*ibid*), for in doing so I take the risk of any mistakes.

[23] It is otherwise where our relationship is a special ('fiduciary', or '*uberrimae fidei*') kind, such that I have a duty to look after your interests: but relationships in estoppel cases are not normally such, any more than they are in contract cases.

[24] *Smith v Hughes* (1871) LR 6 QB 597, 607 (QB).

[25] The point could be readily explained if, in estoppel, I were always enriched by your loss: the law does treat receipt of an enrichment as creating a duty to correct any mistake under which that enrichment is being given. (Though this differentiation between the rule where I am enriched, and that where you merely lose, requires justification in its turn. The key is probably that stronger reasons are required to say that I must compensate your loss than to say that I must reimburse you for a gain that I have made at your expense.) But that is not the case: your estoppel claim does not depend on my being enriched: sometimes I will be, sometimes not.

[26] For example, representation that the right is already yours: *Taylors Fashions Ltd v Liverpool Victoria Trustees Co Ltd* [1982] QB 133n (Ch D); purported conferral: *Dillwyn v Llewelyn* (1862) De GF & J 517 (Ch); assurance that we have a contract entitling you to the right: *Ramsden v Dyson* (1866) LR 1 HL 129, 170 (HL); promise of the right: *ibid*, *Crabb v Arun District Council* [1976] Ch 179 (CA); *Thorner v Major* [2009] 1 WLR 776 (HL). (A statement in *Cobbe v Yeoman's Row Management Ltd* [2008] 1 WLR 1752, [14] (HL) describes proprietary estoppel as 'a subspecies of "promissory" estoppel'. Promissory estoppel certainly reacts only to promises; so taken literally, this statement suggests that in proprietary estoppel too, the assurance must be a promise. This cannot, however, be reconciled with the decisions just cited, involving other forms of assurance. Indeed, the statement is more fundamentally ill conceived. A promissory estoppel arises where I promise not to treat certain behaviour on your part as the breach of your obligation to me that it would otherwise be: a domain which is quite separate from that of proprietary estoppel, where I say that you have, or can have, a right over my property. See further *Thorner v Major*, *ibid* [67].)

is, unless you suffer the detriment 'in reliance on' your belief,[27] and that reliance is reasonable.[28]

According to the courts' traditional reading of the requirement of reliance,[29] you suffer your detriment 'in reliance' on your belief if your belief is at least a *but for* cause of what you do. Say I promise you that you can be a part-owner of my house, and you act to your detriment by home-making for us. On this reading, you act 'in reliance' on your belief if your mindset is either 'the only reason I'm doing this washing is my share in the house,'[30] or 'I'm doing the washing because the clothes are dirty, but I wouldn't be doing it if I didn't think I had a share in the house'. It would not be enough if you would have done the washing anyway.

Wayling v Jones[31] shows a wider reading, however. According to it, you also act in reliance if you say to yourself 'I'm doing the washing because the clothes are dirty, and having a share in the house is neither here nor there to that. But you *promised* me a share, and that makes a difference: I'm not washing for someone who breaks his promises to me.' This wider reading represents another attenuation of the traditional requirements for an estoppel claim. It allows you to ascribe your detriment not to your belief in *having a right over my property* at all, but instead to your belief in my trustworthiness. So it works equally well if my promise has nothing to do with you having a right over my property: say, if it is to marry you.

In a further attenuation of this requirement, too, the usual onus of proof is reversed in regard to proving reliance. If a detrimental action by you might plausibly have been made in reliance on the belief in question, it is for me to prove that you did not in fact rely on that belief, rather than for you to prove that you did.[32]

If I say something to you and you put a silly interpretation on it (one which a reasonable person would not have put), that is your problem: I am not responsible for a loss you suffer as a consequence. Likewise if, although your belief is sensible, you decide to take some silly actions on the strength of it. So the traditional position is that your belief and your reliance on it must be reasonable products of my encouragement or acquiescence. Once again, how-

---

[27] See further S Nield, 'Estoppel and Reliance' in E Cooke (ed), *Modern Studies in Property Law, Volume 1* (Oxford, 2001) ch 5.

[28] Likewise, the question whether I have 'encouraged or acquiesced in' your belief is itself judged in terms not of whether I intended to do so, or explicitly or unequivocally did so, but of whether it was reasonable for you, in the prevailing context, to understand me as doing so: *Thorner v Major* [2009] 1 WLR 776 (HL).

[29] Found in *Greasley v Cooke* [1980] 1 WLR 1306 (CA), and probably many other cases.

[30] According to *Coombes v Smith* [1986] 1 WLR 808 (Ch D), this alone qualifies as 'in reliance'. But this approach appears excessively narrow (you would rarely do the washing *solely* because of your belief), one of several devices adopted by the judge to defeat the claim in that case. The decision seems an isolated one.

[31] (1993) 69 P & CR 170 (CA), followed in *Campbell v Griffin* [2001] EWCA Civ 990 (CA) and *Ottey v Grundy* [2003] EWCA Civ 1176 (CA).

[32] *Greasley v Cooke* [1980] 1 WLR 1306 (CA); *Wayling v Jones* (1995) 69 P & CR 170 (CA); *Campbell v Griffin* [2001] EWCA Civ 990 (CA).

ever, the courts' decisions show that this rule is not being taken completely seriously.[33] Take *Gillett v Holt*[34] again. If the claimant there really did believe that his bequest from the defendant was in the bag, he very arguably should not have done. Promises of bequests are notoriously unreliable, however loudly, publicly and frequently they are made (indeed, perhaps the more so for being made loudly, publicly and frequently, as showing a manipulative streak in the testator). Yet the court gave the issue no real attention at all.

8.2.5 A Summary

In this group of sections, we have seen that, for an estoppel claim to arise, the official approach requires that you firmly believe you have a right over my land, or that I will confer such a right on you; that you act to your detriment; and that you do these things in reasonable reliance on my encouragement or acquiescence. But we have also seen that each of these requirements has been compromised, so that an estoppel claim can in fact arise in their substantial absence.

This discussion has not used the word 'unconscionability'. It is more common for accounts of proprietary estoppel to use, and indeed emphasise, this word. While acknowledging the elements of belief, encouragement or acquiescence, detriment, reliance, they tend to wrap everything in the question of whether it is 'unconscionable' for me to see you suffer in this way. In *Gillett v Holt*,[35] for example, it is said: 'the fundamental principle that equity is concerned to prevent unconscionable conduct permeates all the elements of the doctrine'. Statements such as this confirm the impression that the courts are ready to allow estoppel claims where the traditional requirements are less than fully met – or, equally, to disallow them even where those requirements are fully met.[36]

---

[33] This is pointedly so where you believe that I have in fact validly conferred the right on you, or that I am enforceably contracting with you to do so. In both cases, the law sometimes imposes formality requirements, but the courts have never said that your belief could therefore not have been reasonable.

[34] [2001] Ch 210 (CA): see at n 3 above.

[35] *ibid* 225; approved in *Fisher v Brooker* [2009] 1 WLR 1764, [63] (HL). See too *Taylors Fashions Ltd v Liverpool Victoria Trustees Co Ltd* [1982] QB 133n, 151–2 (Ch D): the question is 'whether, in particular individual circumstances, it would be unconscionable for a party to deny that which, knowingly or unknowingly, he has allowed or encouraged another to assume to his detriment rather than to inquiring whether the circumstances can be fitted within the confines of some preconceived formula serving as a universal yardstick for every form of unconscionable behaviour'. But compare another depiction of unconscionability, as 'unifying and confirming, as it were, the other elements. If the other elements appear to be present but the result does not shock the conscience of the court, the analysis needs to be looked at again' (*Cobbe v Yeoman's Row Management Ltd* [2008] 1 WLR 1752, [92] (HL)). This seems a little more hesitant, though also less clear.

[36] See perhaps *Sledmore v Dalby* (1996) 72 P & CR 196 (CA), where an estoppel right arose which would ordinarily have entitled Mr Dalby to remain in a house – but the court regarded this entitlement as having already ended, on the ground that Mrs Sledmore, the owner of the house, needed it more than he did. For disapproval of this kind of approach, however, see *Cobbe v Yeoman's Row Management Ltd, ibid* [17], [28]; *Thorner v Major* [2009] 1 WLR 776, [98] (HL).

This raises the question: if the courts are allowing or denying estoppel claims for reasons other than those embedded in the official approach, what are these reasons? We shall come to this question in § 8.4, after taking stock of the courts' approach to relief, which also needs to be factored into our answer.

8.3 Estoppel Relief

8.3.1 Estoppel Relief is Discretionary

If all these requirements are satisfied, so that you have the benefit of the estoppel doctrine against me, what does that entitle you to? That is, what is your relief?

It is firmly established that the outcome of a successful estoppel claim lies in the court's discretion.[37] For a moment, a non-discretionary view – requiring the outcome always to be the vindication of the claimant's belief – seemed recently to be espoused by the House of Lords in *Cobbe v Yeoman's Row Management Ltd*,[38] but the discretionary position was reaffirmed in *Thorner v Major*.[39]

In the exercise of this discretion, the courts have arrived at a variety of outcomes. It is not easy to account for these,[40] not least because the courts themselves have commonly made little effort to explain them. But Robert Walker LJ in *Jennings v Rice*[41] made an important attempt to illuminate the issue.

---

[37] Decisions highlighting such a discretion included *Pascoe v Turner* [1979] 1 WLR 431 (CA); *Sledmore v Dalby* (1996) 72 P & CR 196 (CA); *Jennings v Rice* [2002] EWCA Civ 159 (CA). But it is spoken of and/or visible in very many more.

[38] [2008] 1 WLR 1752, [14] (HL): proprietary estoppel 'bars [me] from asserting some fact or facts, or, sometimes, something that is a mixture of fact and law, that stands in the way of some right claimed by [you]'. This formulation might even have been thought to mean that proprietary estoppel would operate only where the defendant was estopped from denying the existence of a valid contract to the effect for which the claimant contended (as in estoppel *in pais*: *Amalgamated Investment & Property Co Ltd (in liquidation) v Texas Commerce International Bank Ltd* [1982] QB 84, 131–2 (QBD and CA)). That this was not, however, the intended meaning was shown by the simultaneous approval apparently given to earlier proprietary estoppel decisions where claims succeeded not via contract in this way, but directly on the basis of the estoppel: notably *Plimmer v Mayor &c of Wellington* (1884) 9 App Cas 699 (PC); *Inwards v Baker* [1965] 2 QB 29 (CA); *Crabb v Arun District Council* [1976] Ch 179 (CA).

[39] [2009] 1 WLR 776, [66] (HL). The latter seems even to have been substantially accepted by Lord Scott, the author of the *Cobbe* position, though he preferred to badge it 'remedial construct trust' rather than proprietary estoppel (*Thorner v Major, ibid* [20]–[21]). For discussion of this suggestion, see § 8.5.1.

[40] See S Gardner, 'The Remedial Discretion in Proprietary Estoppel' (1999) 115 *LQR* 438.

[41] [2002] EWCA Civ 159 (CA); see S Gardner, 'The Remedial Discretion in Proprietary Estoppel – Again' (2006) 122 *LQR* 492.

8.3.2 *Jennings v Rice*

According to Robert Walker LJ,[42] the court's award has to be 'proportionate' to the value of the detriment suffered by the claimant in reliance on the defendant's assurance, while also taking account of his expectation.[43] In 'bargain' cases, where the parties had agreed upon the claimant's expectation and how he had to earn it, the claimant's detriment is to be regarded as equivalent to his expectation, and the 'proportionate' outcome is thus the award of that expectation. Otherwise, in 'non-bargain' cases, it is at large.

Robert Walker LJ went on to say that, as well as 'proportionality', the outcome has also to reflect – as and when relevant – the parties' conduct (eg reducing your award if you have been gratuitously horrible to me); the need for a clean break between them (deciding against an order that we share my house, because we now hate each other); alterations in the defendant's circumstances (reducing your award because of my impoverishment); the effect of taxation (choosing between two styles of award on the basis that one would be taxed more heavily, and so be worth less to you, than the other); other claims on the defendant or his estate (reducing your award because I have significant responsibilities, legal or perhaps also moral, to other people too); and possibly other considerations too.[44]

Robert Walker LJ's judgment is an important one, but it is also difficult, for two main reasons. First, it is hard to say what the key notion of 'proportionality' means. The idea is apparently to take some account of both the claimant's expectation and his detriment,[45] but (except in 'bargain' cases) not to give either pure and simple.[46] But that rather negative information is all we have. The suspicion is that, so long as they stay somewhere in the region between the value of the claimant's detriment and that of his expectation, judges are left to decide for themselves on the aim to be pursued. But giving judges discretion to decide the law's very aim, and to do so afresh in each case, would be antithetical to the Rule of Law. Unsurprisingly therefore,

---

[42] *ibid* [45]–[56].

[43] See too *Henry v Henry* [2010] 1 All ER 988, [65] (PC): 'Proportionality lies at the heart of the doctrine of proprietary estoppel and permeates its every application.'

[44] On a strict reading of Robert Walker LJ's judgment (*ibid* [52]), these factors are to be taken into account only in 'non-bargain' cases. This was probably a slip, however. Say we bargained for you to live with me in my house, in return for services. If we now hate each other, a clean break will be just as necessary as in a non-bargain case. *Burrows and Burrows v Sharp* (1989) 23 HLR 82 and *Gillett v Holt* [2001] Ch 210 (CA) appeared to be 'bargain' cases in which relief took account of such factors.

[45] And also, apparently, of any relevant advantage enjoyed by the claimant, such as rent-free accommodation in the period before his expectation is disappointed: *Sledmore v Dalby* (1996) 72 P & CR 196, 204, 209 (CA); *Fisher v Brooker* [2009] 1 WLR 1764, [11] (HL).

[46] *cf* A Robertson, 'The Reliance Basis of Proprietary Estoppel Remedies' [2008] *Conv* 295, arguing that relief is indeed focused purely on detriment.

Robert Walker LJ stated that he envisaged no such thing.[47] But we remain unclear what he did envisage.

Second, there is a puzzle over the significance of the other factors – the parties' conduct, the need for a clean break between them, alterations in the defendant's circumstances, the effect of taxation, other claims on the defendant or his estate, and possible further considerations. The problem is that none of these affects the extent to which estoppel's actual requirements are present – the extent to which your reliance on your belief has injured you, and the extent to which I am responsible for that. If they are relevant, it can only be because, despite appearances, estoppel is not (or not only) about those requirements. In § 8.4, we shall consider what (else) it may be about.

8.3.3 More about the Discretion

In practice, in the exercise of the discretion, awards have been made by reference frequently to the claimant's expectation,[48] and occasionally to his detriment.[49] There has also been a hint that, where the claimant's action in reliance has enriched the defendant, the award may involve the return of that enrichment.[50] Of particular interest, however, is a group of cases in which the award seems to reflect more than anything (the court's perception of) the implications, in the circumstances that had come about, of the personal relationship between the parties.[51]

---

[47] [2002] EWCA Civ 159, [43] (CA).

[48] As in *Dillwyn v Llewelyn* (1862) De GF & J 517 (Ch); *Plimmer v Mayor &c of Wellington* (1884) 9 App Cas 699 (PC); *Inwards v Baker* [1965] 2 QB 29 (CA); *Greasley v Cooke* [1980] 1 WLR 1306 (CA); *Re Basham* [1986] 1 WLR 1498 (Ch D); *Thorner v Major* [2009] 1 WLR 776 (HL). Some of these can be regarded as 'bargain' cases within Robert Walker LJ's analysis, but by no means all of them. See further J Mee, 'The Role of Expectation in the Determination of Proprietary Estoppel Remedies' in M Dixon (ed), *Modern Studies in Property Law, Volume 5* (Oxford, 2009) ch 16, arguing that the award should never reflect the claimant's expectation, except by way of a cap on relief quantified on some other (maybe reliance) basis.

[49] As in *Dodsworth v Dodsworth* (1973) 228 EG 1115 (CA) (though this was criticised as insufficiently generous in *Griffiths v Williams* (1978) 248 EG 947, 950 (CA)); *Burrows and Burrows v Sharp* (1989) 23 HLR 82 (CA); *Baker v Baker* [1993] 2 FLR 247 (CA) (though in the latter the claimant's reliance loss exceeded his expectation interest, and his award was capped at the latter). *Crabb v Arun District Council* [1976] Ch 179 (CA) can also be seen this way. The claimant sold off part of his land, leaving the remaining part with no road access. He did this in reliance on the defendant's promise to give him such access through its own adjoining land. He was awarded the promised access. This could be seen as a vindication of his expectation, but alternatively as a correction of his reliance loss, ie his loss of the opportunity to secure such access more effectively before his sale.

[50] This was the nature of the award sought in *Blue Haven Enterprises Ltd v Tully* [2006] UKPC 17 (PC). The claim failed on the facts, but no objection was taken in principle. See further N Hopkins, 'Estoppel and Restitution: Drawing a Divide' in E Cooke (ed), *Modern Studies in Property Law, Volume 2* (Oxford, 2003) ch 8.

[51] The importance of the parties' relationship is also highlighted in *Thorner v Major* [2009] 1 WLR 776, [12] (HL).

In several of these cases, the claimant had provided live-in care for the defendant after being promised the defendant's house in the latter's will. The awards in these cases were of money, rather than a right *in specie*. In their quantum, they did not track the claimant's expectation (the promised house itself), nor his detriment, nor his enrichment of the defendant (these were not normally even quantified); their basis was in fact never specified. But they may have reflected the cost to the claimant of finding substitute accommodation of the standard he had enjoyed in the defendant's house before the latter's death and to which (it assumed) he continued to be entitled as a result of his estoppel. In *Jennings v Rice*,[52] for example, it was the trial judge's view, approved by the Court of Appeal, that to award the claimant the promised house itself, valued at £420,000, would have been excessive, for he was single, and merely the defendant's employee. He needed only £150,000 to buy a suitable house, and £200,000 sufficed to 'see him all right'.[53] Similarly in *Campbell v Griffin*,[54] where the claimant was awarded £35,000, the court explaining: 'It would not be right to confer on [the claimant] (who began as a lodger with one out of four bedrooms) a right in respect of the whole house … [£35,000] will not by itself enable him to buy a freehold house in [the town in question], but it will assist him with rehousing himself.'[55]

The group extends more widely. It includes *Pascoe v Turner*,[56] in which a claimant was awarded the defendant's house not because he had promised her it, but because it was the best way of giving her a secure future following the breakdown of their relationship as lovers; and *Sledmore v Dalby*,[57] in which, while the claimant was granted a right to remain in the house which the defendant (his mother-in-law) had promised he could occupy, this right was truncated in its duration because the defendant, now an impoverished old lady, needed the house more than he did.

---

[52] [2002] EWCA Civ 159 (CA).

[53] *ibid* [15].

[54] [2001] EWCA Civ 990 (CA).

[55] *ibid* [36]. Likewise perhaps *Ottey v Grundy* [2003] EWCA Civ 1176 (CA). The claimant had a role similar to that of a wife to the defendant for many years. They separated shortly before his death, and he left her nothing. Not having been married to the defendant, she was unable to use the provisions of the Inheritance (Provision for Family and Dependants) Act 1975 aimed at securing an appropriate share in a deceased's estate for his spouse. Having been rejected by the defendant at the time of his death, she was also unable to use that Act's provisions aimed at securing the reasonable needs of dependants and intimate cohabitants. She succeeded however in her estoppel claim, the award being £100,000.

[56] [1979] 1 WLR 431 (CA).

[57] (1996) 72 P & CR 196 (CA).

8.4 What is Estoppel About?

This chapter depicts proprietary estoppel as one of the rules by which the law gives one person rights in the land of another. But what is the theoretical basis on which it does so?

8.4.1 The Problem

A doctrine's theoretical basis – the goal that it aims to promote or vindicate – should, obviously, be reflected in the rules controlling what it does: the situations to which it applies, and the outcomes it yields. To see the basis of proprietary estoppel, therefore, we need to reflect on what we have learnt in §§ 8.2 and 8.3.

Take the rules about outcomes. We have seen that some decisions have granted expectation relief (you get the interest in which you believed). These decisions therefore suggest that the doctrine aims to uphold assurances. But we have also noted some other decisions yielding various other outcomes, notably the recoupment of your detriment, and the vindication of our relationship's implications for the circumstances in question. Such decisions must assert that the doctrine's aim is to deliver these goals as well or instead. In short, the cases about outcomes allow for more than one account of proprietary estoppel's theoretical basis.

Commentators have responded to this diversity by arguing that one basis or another is the true one, and that the others are false (from which it would follow that the courts should not order outcomes in their terms).[58] These arguments can always readily point to aspects of the doctrine evincing the view that they support: unsurprisingly, given the range of views that the cases stand for, as we have seen. In presenting the doctrine's basis as one thing rather than another, however, they all ask us to disregard – or regard as mistakes – other things we know about it.

Another approach is possible, however. Each of the arguments accounts for some but not all of the things we know about estoppel. That need be a problem only if we assume, as the arguments do, that the term 'proprietary estoppel' denotes a single legal project. If the term in fact refers to a collection of different projects, the problem disappears. We need only see whether we can articulate, and justify, accounts of what those different projects are.

---

[58] See eg P Birks, 'Equity in the Modern Law: An Exercise in Taxonomy' (1996) 26 *University of Western Australia Law Review* 1, 60; S Bright and B McFarlane, 'Proprietary Estoppel and Property Rights' [2005] *CLJ* 449; A Robertson, 'The Reliance Basis of Proprietary Estoppel Remedies' [2008] *Conv* 295.

8.4.2 The Projects

The projects apparently in play include the following:

—— The effectuation of otherwise ineffective conferrals of interests in land, or contracts or promises to confer such interests, or representations of the existence of such interests.
—— The correction of reliance loss on your part for which I am responsible.
—— Distributive justice, requiring me to put you into a satisfactory material position, in a context where a fair distribution between us is called for.

We shall look at each in turn.

8.4.3 Effectuation of Otherwise Ineffective Conferrals Etc

The first suggestion, then, is that proprietary estoppel has a project to effectuate otherwise ineffective conferrals of interests in land, or contracts or promises to confer such interests, or representations of the existence of such interests.

Remember the illustration given in § 8.1, and suppose that I say 'OK, have the strip', thus purporting to confer the strip on you. Or that I say 'You can have the strip if you'll do such-and-such for me in return', thereby (if you accept) purporting to contract to confer the strip on you. Or that I say 'I'll give you the strip', thus making a non-contractual promise to confer the strip on you. Or that I say 'The strip's already yours', so representing that this is the case. None of these utterances is in itself enough to give you the strip, or an entitlement to it. The conferral and the contract would have been enough if they had been supported by the necessary formalities, but cannot be effectively made by my spoken words.[59] The bare promise and representation could never have been enough: the law does not give dispositive force to such utterances at all. The first suggested project, however, depicts proprietary estoppel as, in all these cases (so long as you reasonably believe me, and rely on your belief to your detriment), operating to give you the strip nonetheless.

This suggestion connects with some of the courts' estoppel decisions. Certainly, utterances of all these kinds, when accompanied by belief, reliance and responsibility, give rise to estoppel claims.[60] (We should expect the belief, reliance and responsibility to be real, if they are to justify your claim. This project therefore strikes no chord with the attenuation of those requirements, which we noticed in § 8.2; but that may turn out to be evidence of another project.) And the relief required by this project is the effectuation of my

---

[59] §§ 5.4.1 and 6.1.
[60] § 8.2.4.

utterance: which, as we have seen, is one of the measures of relief used in proprietary estoppel.

So it is certainly possible to perceive such a project in what we know about proprietary estoppel. But there are two problems of principle.

First, if my assurance takes the form of a conferral or contract, it will, as noted above, normally be ineffective in itself for want of formality. If – as this project proposes – proprietary estoppel can operate to effectuate my assurance after all, the law appears to subvert its own formality rules.[61] It is hard to see that this can be proper.

In *Cobbe v Yeoman's Row Management Ltd*,[62] Lord Scott took a curious position over this issue. He expressed the opinion (without firmly deciding) that proprietary estoppel cannot be used to effectuate a *contract* despite its informality in this way, since to use it thus would indeed contradict the relevant formality requirement.[63] But the remainder of his reasoning assumes that the doctrine can be used to effectuate an informal *conferral*: I am estopped from setting up my own right against your assertion of the right in which I gave you to believe. There seems no reason why the two should be treated differently in this way: if there is a contradiction in the case of contract, then there is too in the case of conferral.[64] More usually, the courts have not differentiated between informal conferrals and contracts in this way, allowing proprietary estoppel to effectuate both.[65] This avoids the inconsistency of Lord Scott's position, but at the expense of an even greater subversion of the formality rules. If proprietary estoppel is to avoid subverting formality rules in this way, it must not seek to effectuate assurances that fall foul of them: that is, it must not carry on the first project.

---

[61] See further M Dixon, 'Proprietary Estoppel and Formalities in Land Law and the Land Registration Act 2002: A Theory of Unconscionability' in Cooke (ed) (n 50) ch 9.

[62] [2008] 1 WLR 1752 (HL).

[63] *ibid* [29].

[64] Although worded slightly differently, the relevant statutory provisions justify no such difference in treatment of the two cases. Regarding contracts, the rule (Law of Property (Miscellaneous Provisions) Act 1989 s 2(1)) reads: 'A contract for the sale or other disposition of an interest in land can only be made in writing . . .' Regarding conferrals, the principal rule (Law of Property Act 1925 s 52(1)) reads: 'All conveyances of land or of any interest therein are void for the purpose of conveying or creating a legal estate unless made by deed.'

[65] As well as *Ramsden v Dyson* (1866) LR 1 HL 129, 170 (HL), see (in the context of the current contractual formality rule, in the Law of Property (Miscellaneous Provisions) Act 1989 s 2(1)) *Yaxley v Gotts* [2000] Ch 162 (CA); *Kinane v Mackie-Conteh* [2005] EWCA Civ 45 (CA); *Oates v Stimson* [2006] EWCA Civ 548 (CA); and – even after *Cobbe v Yeoman's Row Management Ltd* [2008] 1 WLR 1752 (HL) – *Brightlingsea Haven Ltd v Morris* [2008] EWHC 1928 (QBD); *Halifax Plc, Bank of Scotland v Curry Popeck (A Firm), Pulvers (A Firm)* [2008] EWHC 1692, [26] (Ch D). In some of these decisions it is reasoned that the estoppel claim, rather than effectuating the contract directly, gives rise to a 'constructive trust', to which no formality requirement applies (Law of Property (Miscellaneous Provisions) Act 1989 s 2(5)). It is hard to see that the outcomes in question amounted to trusts at all, so this reasoning seems fallacious: surely the estoppel claim is operating in its own right. Either way, however, the de facto outcome remains the effectuation of the informal contract via an estoppel award, as discussed in the text.

The second problem with this project is more fundamental. It is hard to see why estoppel claims should yield expectation relief at all. To be sure, vindicating an *effective* assurance on my part would require such relief, by definition. But the assurances in question here are by definition (estoppel apart) *ineffective*: either (in the case of conferrals or contracts) for want of formality, or (in the case of bare promises or representations) because in themselves they simply lack legal significance. The basis for estoppel intervention, then, lies not in the assurance itself, but in the belief, reliance and responsibility that the doctrine requires. And these afford no reason for the effectuation of your expectations. If I give you to think that you have or shall have my strip of land, and you, believing me, expend money and/or effort in cultivating it, you certainly deserve a claim against me. But if the basis of your claim is your detrimental reliance, rather than my assurance itself, your remedy ought to be compensation for the loss entailed by this detrimental reliance.[66]

In short, while evidence of this project can certainly be found in the way the courts have used proprietary estoppel, it appears unsustainable in principle.

8.4.4 Correction of Reliance Loss

The second project with which proprietary estoppel may be identified is one aimed at correcting your reliance loss: that is, at making me compensate you for the loss you suffer when you rely to your detriment on your belief, for which I am responsible.

The occasional awards of compensation for reliance loss in proprietary estoppel[67] can of course be ascribed to this project. The project also connects well with estoppel's traditional requirements of belief, reliance and responsibility, using these to show that I ought to compensate your reliance loss.[68] By the same token, this project cannot account for decisions yielding other outcomes; nor for many of the attenuations of the traditional rules regarding 'belief', 'detriment' and 'reliance' that we noticed in § 8.2. But on the supposition that 'proprietary estoppel' refers to more than one project, these points need not be evidence against the present suggestion, merely evidence for some other project(s).

---

[66] Compare the old (abolished by the Law of Property (Miscellaneous Provisions) Act 1989 s 2) doctrine of 'part performance'. In the context of a contract that had not, as required, been put in writing, but given facts similar to those generating an estoppel, this doctrine too gave you a claim against me . . . which was always met by enforcement of the contract. There is the same puzzle as to the remedy.

[67] *Dodsworth v Dodsworth* (1973) 228 EG 1115 (CA); *Burrows and Burrows v Sharp* (1989) 23 HLR 82 (CA); *Baker v Baker* [1993] 2 FLR 247 (CA); perhaps *Crabb v Arun District Council* [1976] Ch 179 (CA). See § 8.3.3.

[68] Proprietary estoppel is also passingly depicted in this way in *Cobbe v Yeoman's Row Management Ltd* [2008] 1 WLR 1752, [48] (HL).

This second project is in broad terms intelligible in principle. It is readily understandable that I should have to compensate you for the loss you suffer in reasonable reliance on a belief for which I am responsible – in short, loss for which I am, therefore, responsible. There are two points requiring discussion, but they turn out not to leave this project unsupportable.

First, the loss you suffer in a proprietary estoppel case is always economic, rather than by way of physical injury or damage. If we take the law as a whole, economic loss is recoverable only in rather special circumstances. Among these are the cases where you incur the loss in reasonable reliance on an incorrect statement that I negligently make within an appropriately close relationship,[69] or a contractual promise that I break. It is appropriate to limit recovery in this way to cases where I have undertaken a particular responsibility towards you, on the basis of which you rely on me; if you could recover whenever you are my 'neighbour',[70] without such encouraged reliance, liability for economic loss would proliferate too widely. The project under discussion could well be seen as aligned with these other special cases, by recalling that in it too, you suffer your loss in reasonable reliance on something I tell you, or at least allow you to believe.

Second, the traditional understanding of proprietary estoppel, confirmed in *Cobbe v Yeoman's Row Management Ltd*,[71] limits it to the case where your belief is in (my statement is about) *an interest over my property*. This limitation appears inapt to a project aimed at redressing reliance loss. It could be explained if it helped show that I have allowed you to rely on me, in the way just discussed: but it obviously does not. Remember, however, the attenuation of the 'reliance' requirement in *Wayling v Jones*,[72] allowing your reliance to be not on your belief in a right over my property at all, but instead on your belief in my trustworthiness. This sidelines the requirement of such a belief, leaving it an arbitrary restriction on estoppel's scope. The logical next step would be its abandonment, leaving an unproblematic fit with the current project.

So a project to correct reliance loss can be discerned in the positions that the judges have sometimes (remember, that is all that is needed) taken regarding proprietary estoppel. It can also be supported in principle, as compatible with what we otherwise want to say about the correction of economic loss suffered by a claimant in reliance on the defendant's statements. This project is thus a possible one. Fully accepting it does, however, require some violence

---

[69] *Hedley Byrne & Co Ltd v Heller & Partners Ltd* [1964] AC 465 (HL).

[70] *cf Donoghue v Stevenson* [1932] AC 562, 580 (HL), Lord Atkin: 'The rule that you are to love your neighbour becomes in law, you must not injure your neighbour; and the lawyer's question, Who is my neighbour? receives a restricted reply. You must take reasonable care to avoid acts or omissions which you can reasonably foresee would be likely to injure your neighbour. Who, then, in law is my neighbour? The answer seems to be – persons who are so closely and directly affected by my act that I ought reasonably to have them in contemplation as being so affected when I am directing my mind to the acts or omissions which are called in question.'

[71] [2008] 1 WLR 1752 (HL): see § 8.2.2.

[72] (1995) 69 P & CR 170 (CA): see § 8.2.4.

to the traditional understanding of proprietary estoppel as focused on rights over property: for a project on these lines, such a focus would be out of place.

8.4.5 Distributive Justice

The third of the projects that can be identified with proprietary estoppel is one aimed at doing distributive justice: that is, at requiring me to put you into a certain material position, on the ground that our (previous or continuing) relationship itself requires that outcome.

The idea of distributive justice was explained in § 7.1.1. An example of a distributive jurisdiction is that providing for the reallocation of a couple's property upon their divorce,[73] which focuses on minimising the material impact of the divorce on any children, securing the parties' 'reasonable requirements', and dividing any remaining assets equally between them: all on the basis that the parties owe each other and their children the level of wealth in question, by virtue of their marriage or civil partnership and, where relevant, their status as parents. There is evidence that the courts sometimes do work of this kind via proprietary estoppel. That is, they use estoppel to reallocate property from me to you where, and to the extent that, this is what our relationship itself requires.

So, the third project provides the best explanation for the treatment of quantum in a number of important decisions.[74] As we saw in § 8.3.3, these decisions appeared to reflect the implications of the parties' relationship, in the circumstances that had occurred. For example, where a claimant had been the defendant's resident carer, and had been promised the defendant's house in the latter's will but had in fact been disappointed, he was then awarded not the house itself, nor his reliance loss, but the cost of finding accommodation of a standard similar to that which he had enjoyed when living with the defendant, before the latter's death.

The third project also helps make sense of Robert Walker LJ's judgment in *Jennings v Rice*,[75] considered in § 8.3.2. As we saw there, this judgment was problematic, for the lack of fit between on the one hand the central idea of 'proportionality', and the various additional discretionary considerations (the parties' misconduct, etc), and on the other hand estoppel's ostensible requirements of belief, reliance and responsibility. This lack of fit becomes explicable if Robert Walker LJ was creating space for a project to do something, such as to achieve distributive justice between the parties, that is unconnected with estoppel's ostensible structure.

[73] Matrimonial Causes Act 1973 s 24; *White v White* [2001] AC 596 (HL); *Miller v Miller, McFarlane v McFarlane* [2006] 2 AC 618 (HL).
[74] *Campbell v Griffin* [2001] EWCA Civ 990 (CA); *Jennings v Rice* [2002] EWCA Civ 159 (CA); *Ottey v Grundy* [2003] EWCA Civ 1176 (CA); *Pascoe v Turner* [1979] 1 WLR 431 (CA); *Sledmore v Dalby* (1996) 72 P & CR 196 (CA).
[75] [2002] EWCA Civ 159 (CA).

In the same way, this project can account for the attenuations we have observed in the requirements for an estoppel claim. For a distributive jurisdiction, it simply does not matter whether you act to your detriment in reliance on a belief in a right over my property, for which I am responsible. Attenuating these requirements allows a claim to succeed despite their real absence.

It is especially noteworthy that the main decisions in which the attenuation took place – *Gillett v Holt*[76] and *Wayling v Jones*[77] – were in cases where the parties had been in long-term relationships which could plausibly be regarded as in themselves creating obligations on the defendants in favour of the claimants; and that the courts attached importance to this. So, in *Gillett v Holt*,[78] the court refers to a number of episodes which, since they antedated any relevant belief on the claimant's part, could not have amounted to detrimental reliance, even in that concept's attenuated form. What does emerge, however, is the establishment of a relationship of patronage between defendant and claimant, in the course of which the defendant promised to bequeath his property to the claimant, before eventually fracturing the relationship and letting the claimant down. And in *Wayling v Jones*,[79] where there was a similar relationship and a similar promise, the claimant had difficulty showing that the services he rendered the defendant were 'in reliance' on the promise: for in his relationship with the defendant, he would have done the same anyway, out of love and loyalty. Reading 'in reliance', however, as focused not on the content of the promise but on the promisor's trustworthiness,[80] the court turned it from a requirement likely to be defeated in such a context to one positively likely to be met: it is in a committed relationship that trustworthiness matters most of all.

A project of delivering the distributive implications of personal relationships is evidently supportable in principle. And there thus seems to be evidence that the judges have treated proprietary estoppel as having such a project, in addition to the first two projects. This evidence consists in the approach some decisions have taken to quantum, and their attenuation of proprietary estoppel's official requirements. But attenuation is not really enough. The project cannot operate coherently without the requirements' complete removal from the picture, and replacement by explicit reference to

---

[76] [2001] Ch 210 (CA). As noted in §§ 8.2.2 and 8.2.3, this decision attenuated the requirements of belief and detriment.

[77] (1995) 69 P & CR 170 (CA). As noted in § 8.2.4, this decision attenuated the requirement of reliance. The same comment can also be made of *Greasley v Cooke* [1980] 1 WLR 1306 (CA), holding (§ 8.2.4) that the onus of proof regarding 'in reliance' rests on the defendant rather than the claimant.

[78] [2001] Ch 210, 234–5 (CA).

[79] (1995) 69 P & CR 170 (CA). The pattern is similar in the other two decisions taking the same line on 'in reliance', *Campbell v Griffin* [2001] EWCA Civ 990 (CA) and *Ottey v Grundy* [2003] EWCA Civ 1176 (CA).

[80] § 8.2.4.

the relevant relationship(s).[81] At which point, the jurisdiction will cease to warrant the title 'estoppel' at all.

8.4.6 A Summary

Let us summarise this group of sections. We have found that each of the three suggested projects succeeds in describing some of what we know about proprietary estoppel, but beyond that the picture is not encouraging.

The first project – the effectuation of otherwise ineffective conferrals etc – has the closest fit with the traditional vision of proprietary estoppel. On the other hand, we found it unsupportable in principle. When you rely to your detriment on my assurance, doubtless you deserve relief. But there is no reason why that relief should be the fulfilment of the assurance.

The second and third projects – relieving your reliance loss, and doing distributive justice between us – are more readily supportable in principle. But while they do strike some chords with what the judges have done in the name of proprietary estoppel, they both demand a substantial rewriting of that doctrine. The second project requires the abandonment of the traditional requirement that you believe in a right *over my property* (if the aim is to correct your reliance loss, there is nothing special about beliefs of that kind). The rewriting required for the third project goes even further, amounting to the abandonment of all reference to belief, detriment and responsibility: the proper driver being simply the implications of our relationship in the circumstances in question.

The conclusion is that none of the three suggested projects provides an adequate justification for what the law has been doing under the name of proprietary estoppel. It follows that, unless it is engaged in some further project(s) more convincing than those uncovered here, the doctrine of proprietary estoppel should be abolished. The second and third projects would be better carried on under their own names, while the first should be seen as unsustainable, and aborted.

This is a troubling conclusion in itself, of course, but it is given extra point if we think about it in human rights terms. Subject usually to issues of horizontal effect (§ 2.2), in giving you rights against me via the doctrine of proprietary estoppel, the law interferes with my enjoyment of my possessions, engaging ECHR First Protocol Article 1, and on appropriate facts also my home, engaging Article 8. These interferences can of course be justified if they represent proportionate means of securing proper ends. But given what we have seen about the projects immanent in the estoppel doctrine, they do

---

[81] For recent proposals for a statutory regime in this direction (though taking effect only on the defendant's death – when the estoppel cases themselves tend to arise, however), see Law Commission, *Intestacy and Family Provision Claims on Death* (Law Com No 331, London, 2011) Pt 8.

not. If the first project is simply unsustainable, it cannot be a proper end. And if the second and third projects are sustainable but would be more appropriately pursued in their own guises than via proprietary estoppel, the latter cannot represent a proportionate means of securing them.

8.5 The Estoppel 'Equity'

One last question requires attention. What is the nature of your rights, under the estoppel doctrine, between the time when the doctrine's requirements are met (you act to your detriment in reliance on a belief, encouraged or acquiesced in by me, in a right over my property), and the judgment of the court to which you bring your case?

8.5.1 When do Estoppel Rights Arise?

Section 116(a) of the Land Registration Act 2002, applying to registered land, declares that 'an equity by estoppel . . . has effect from the time the equity arises . . .'.

Although the wording is unfortunately circular, this provision seems to mean that you have an 'equity by estoppel' immediately the facts generating your estoppel claim occurred. We need, however, to decide what the phrase 'equity by estoppel' means – what in fact you are entitled to from that moment.

There seem to be two possibilities.

One, which we shall call the 'strong' possibility, is that your rights are fixed, immutably, from the time of the key facts. The other, which we shall call the 'weak' possibility, is that although you have your 'equity' from the time of the key facts, its content is not fixed immutably from that time, but can vary as time goes on and circumstances change. That is, your 'equity' is the right to whatever relief is warranted at the moment when the question arises.

To understand the difference between the two visions, consider a case where, in a context apt to give you an estoppel claim, you have for some time occupied my land. According to the strong vision, if the court decides that your occupation should now be protected by the award of some occupation right for the future, the implication is that you already had this right from the time of the key facts. (To put it another way: your award of the right to occupy is necessarily backdated to the time of the key facts.) So, albeit only in retrospect from the time of the award, we can say with assurance that in occupying my land between the time of the key facts and the court award, you were not a trespasser. But according to the weak vision, although your estoppel 'equity' certainly (and as section 116(a) insists) gave you some sort of right from the time of the key facts, this right need not have had the same shape as the eventual court award, and indeed may itself have varied from time to time. So, even by retrospection from the eventual award of an occupation right, we cannot necessarily say whether in occupying my land between the time of the key facts and the court award – or at any given moment during that time – you were or were not a trespasser.

It is possible to find signs of both visions in the case-law.[82] In any event, we need to consider the choice between them as a matter of principle. Which offers the preferable understanding of the idea that you have an 'equity' from the time of the key facts?

It may appear that the strong vision is preferable. Remember, it perceives the position between the time of the key facts and the eventual award as being simply an anticipation of the latter, fixed from the time of the former; with none of the weak vision's scope for variation over this period. It therefore appears to promise greater alignment with the Rule of Law, and so with the liberal desideratum of allowing people to organise their lives without going to court. However, this appearance is deceptive. The problem is that, given the condition of the law regarding proprietary estoppel, one or both of the two data which are together crucial to this effect – the time of the key facts, and the content of the eventual award – are in fact commonly unknowable. To see this, we need to remember the three 'projects' for estoppel that were identified in § 8.4.

In all three projects, there is difficulty pinning down the time, and indeed occurrence, of the key facts. Take the first project (to effectuate otherwise

---

[82] Strictly speaking, in the case-law outside the 2002 Act, but there is nothing in the wording of the latter to constrain a different picture. The weak approach is certainly adopted in *Williams v Staite* [1979] Ch 291 (CA), and in *Sledmore v Dalby* (1996) 72 P & CR 196 (CA). It seems implicit too in the judgment of Robert Walker LJ in *Jennings v Rice* [2002] EWCA Civ 159 (CA), proposing (see § 8.3.2), no doubt partly to reflect these decisions, that estoppel relief should take account of a range of factors, many of which will naturally fluctuate, or come and go, between the time of the key facts and the eventual award – and one of which is, explicitly, 'alterations in the [defendant's] assets and circumstances' (see at [52]). The weak approach is also overtly entertained as a possibility in *Henry v Henry* [2010] 1 All ER 988, [46]–[47], [56] (PC). The strong approach is less clearly evidenced. It is probably visible in three decisions where the eventual award was taken to have operated without qualification from the time of the key facts; but one cannot say for sure, as this position could also be reached under the weak approach, if the circumstances contain no reason for any qualification. The decisions are *Crabb v Arun District Council* [1976] Ch 179 (CA), where the claimant's remedy included compensation for the loss he suffered when the defendant denied his claim for the seven years between the requirements being met and the case reaching court; *Voyce v Voyce* (1991) 62 P & CR 290 (CA), where time began to run against the claimant as soon as the requirements were met, for the purposes of prescription; *Birmingham Midshires Mortgage Services Ltd v Sabherwal* (2000) 80 P & CR 256 (CA), where the beneficial interest to which the court eventually declared the claimant entitled was overreached by a disposition occurring between the time the requirements were met and that of the judgment.

ineffective conferrals of interests in land, etc) and the second (to correct reliance losses). For them, the time of the key facts is not the time of the original assurance; the facts remain incomplete until the necessary reliance has occurred. And it may be impossible confidently to say when this is, or even that it has happened at all, short of a judicial determination. The difficulty is more intense still as regards the third project, aimed at effecting distributive justice between the parties, by vindicating the normative implications of their relationship. Here, as we saw in § 8.4.5, the 'key facts', in the sense of proprietary estoppel's official requirements, are simply irrelevant . . . and so are 'found', or not, in non-realistic ways, by the court, retrospectively. And with all three projects, there is a further difficulty in knowing the content of any eventual court award. This is especially true in respect of the third project, with its focus on the implications of the parties' relationship. It is also true of the second project, aiming to rectify the claimant's reliance loss: identifying and quantifying the latter will often be an inexact business. And on top of all this, of course, the very co-existence of the three projects generates yet further unpredictability.

So the strong vision's apparent promise transparently to fix people's rights between the time of the key facts and the eventual award turns out to be undeliverable. One might however think that, although this difficulty removes the strong vision's prima facie superiority over the weak vision, it goes no further than that; that we could still defensibly choose it anyway. But this would be incorrect.

From the point of view of the Rule of Law, it is positively dangerous to mix the uncertainties we have just noticed, with the unqualified backdating that characterises the 'strong' vision. For it means that the legal situation between us, at the moment we inhabit it, is *already* structured along lines *that we cannot discover until later*. We are thus obliged to conduct our affairs in the dark, at risk of later learning that we have transgressed. Say you occupy my land, but I want to evict you. I have to decide whether to go ahead and try to do so, and you have to decide whether to resist if I do. If the strong vision represents the law, the items of information we require in order satisfactorily to make these decisions are the court's eventual response to our situation, and the knowledge whether the key facts count as yet having occurred at all. Since estoppel's uncertainties mean that these items of information are in reality unavailable to us, we cannot satisfactorily make our decisions. Yet this vision's unqualified backdating of the eventual award means the law treating us as if the contrary were true: scrutinising our decisions and giving consequences to them just as if they had been properly informed.

The most radical cures for this worry would involve substantially removing the unpredictability from the estoppel doctrine; or, coming at things from the opposite direction, allowing the unpredictability to remain, but discarding all thought of backdating. Short of these cures, however, the weak vision at least avoids making things worse in the way that we have just recognised the strong one as doing. It sees the court, in fixing your estoppel relief, as also choosing to what extent, and in what way, its effect should be backdated, as a matter of discretion. Your 'equity' 'has effect from' the time of the key facts, as section 116(a) insists, in the sense that whenever you had brought your claim in the meantime, your rights would have received some recognition. But this hypothetical recognition need not take the same form as any retrospective remedy that you are actually awarded when you do eventually come to court. Indeed the latter can – and should – be designed so as to take sensitive account of the interim position's opacity to those inhabiting it. For this reason, the surrounding context makes the weak vision preferable to the strong one.

The weak vision is in fact a manifestation of an idea more usually known as the 'remedial constructive trust'. The term 'remedial constructive trust' has been given a number of different meanings.[83] Under the dominant one, on which we shall focus here, it refers not necessarily to something that can be described as a 'trust' at all, but to an outcome of any sort, awarded and profiled by the court in an ad hoc discretionary determination.[84] The nature and extent of any backdating represent an aspect of this. (Note here, however, an improvement on the weak vision as we have it. Because of section 116(a), the latter must treat you as having some rights from the time of the key facts, even if not necessarily the same rights as those to be found in the eventual court award. Under the pure concept of a remedial constructive trust, there is a discretion whether to backdate your rights at all.)

Remedial constructive trusts are controversial.[85] But the principal argument against them is not so much that they cannot be usefully applied in this way to discretionary jurisdictions, as that (recalling the precepts of the Rule of Law) discretionary jurisdictions should not exist: that there should be firmly predictable rights, and nothing else.[86] So long as the law does in fact have discretionary jurisdictions,[87] remedial constructive trusts – alias, for present purposes, the weak vision of estoppel relief – allow it to make the best of a (in Rule of Law terms) bad job with regard to backdating.[88]

---

[83] See S Gardner, *An Introduction to the Law of Trusts* (3rd edn, Oxford, 2011) 277–81.

[84] For a full account, see D Waters, 'The Nature of the Remedial Constructive Trust' in P Birks (ed), *The Frontiers of Liability, Volume 2* (Oxford, 1994) ch 13; D Wright, *The Remedial Constructive Trust* (Sydney, 1998).

[85] For their acceptance or otherwise in English law, see Gardner (n 83) 282–4.

[86] See eg P Birks, 'Proprietary Rights as Remedies' in Birks (ed) (n 84) ch 16, and 'The End of the Remedial Constructive Trust' (1998) 12 *Trusts Law International* 202.

[87] Their value to the law is explored in K Hawkins (ed), *The Uses of Discretion* (Oxford, 1992).

[88] In *Thorner v Major* [2009] 1 WLR 776, [14], [20]–[21] (HL) Lord Scott suggested, in effect, that the term 'proprietary estoppel' should be applied only to cases where the response is nothing more or less than the effectuation of the claimant's belief; while cases involving more complex responses should instead be seen as involving remedial constructive trusts. This is a different usage of 'remedial constructive trust' to that advanced in the text. It treats a remedial constructive trust not as a fine-tuned award emerging under an established cause of action, such as proprietary estoppel, but as a cause of action in its own right, with its own components and underlying rationale (which, however, Lord Scott makes no attempt to describe). This is the version of the idea against which the argument identified in the text is most appropriately aimed,

8.5.2 Estoppel Equities as Rights in Rem

Section 116(a) also rules that your equity will be a right in rem, capable of binding anyone who takes a disposition of the land from me during the period between the facts occurring and the court's award.[89] Say the facts on which you rely occur in January; in April, I transfer the land in question to John; and in July, you sue. Because your equity binds John (so long as the usual conditions for this are met[90]), you can bring your action against him.

The exact implications of this depend once again on whether we adopt the strong or the weak view of section 116(a)'s ruling on the question of backdating, discussed in the previous section. If we take the strong view, your eventual relief operates in an unqualified way from the time of the key facts. So when John takes the land, he simultaneously incurs the liability to this relief. Your award against him must therefore take the same form as it would have taken against me, from the day of the key facts onwards. Of course, since the award cannot necessarily be predicted, we cannot say what form this will be until the court makes it. But what we can say is that, whatever else goes into the formation of the award, changes in circumstances after the time of the key facts do not – including the change in the identity of the defendant from me to John, a disponee.

Consider now the weak view, whereby although you certainly acquire an 'equity' from the time of the key facts, its content – and so the form of the award the court will eventually make in your favour – varies with the evolving circumstances. On this view, although John will certainly be liable, his liability will be to whatever award the court thinks right at the time it is called upon to make it: with the transfer from me to John, and John's particular circumstances etc, counting among the 'evolving circumstances' that the court will take into account.

---

and which had indeed previously been declared not part of English law: *Re Polly Peck International plc (in administration) (No 2)* [1998] 3 All ER 812 (CA).

[89] 'An equity by estoppel . . . has effect from the time the equity arises *as an interest capable of binding successors in title*' (emphasis added); *Halifax Plc, Bank of Scotland v Curry Popeck (A Firm), Pulvers (A Firm)* [2008] EWHC 1692, [26] (Ch D). This replicates what was probably the rule anyway, it being taken thus in a number of cases, including *Inwards v Baker* [1965] 2 QB 29, 37 (CA); *Lloyds Bank plc v Carrick* [1996] 4 All ER 630, 642 (CA); *Campbell v Griffin* [2001] EWCA Civ 990, [37] (CA); *Lloyd v Dugdale* [2001] EWCA Civ 1754, [39] (CA).

[90] That is, either the right is registered, which is unlikely, as proprietary estoppel is a disorganised way of generating rights; or it operates as an overriding interest. This will often be the case on the basis of your actual and apparent occupation of the land. But if your right is in the nature of an easement, you may well have a problem. As explained in § 13.3, the Land Registration Act 2002 Sch 3 para 3 allows only a *legal* easement to count as an overriding interest, not an *equitable* easement, which an easement generated via proprietary estoppel – an equitable doctrine – would necessarily be; and in the nature of things, you are unlikely to be in occupation of the land in question (*cf Chaudhary v Yavuz* [2011] EWCA Civ 1314, [28]–[35] (CA)).

The case-law has little light to shed: very few decisions are against a disponee, and useful statements or other indications are even rarer.[91]

As a matter of principle, however, the weak view of section 116(a) is once again to be preferred. In the previous section, we saw how it combines less dangerously than the strong view with the unpredictability of estoppel rights. The weak view (alias remedial constructive trust) does, while the strong view does not, allow sensitivity to the evolving circumstances between the time of the key facts and that of the court's eventual award, and to the very opacity of the situation during this time. This advantage becomes all the more valuable if we now build in the complication that the matter is one of your rights (no longer against me but) against John, whose entry into the picture is likely to make a distinctive difference to 'the evolving circumstances'.[92]

[91] The weak view was aired, and not rejected, in *Henry v Henry* [2010] 1 All ER 988, [46]–[47], [56] (PC). It may be significant that this could be seen as a third project case, ie one where the parties' positions are most difficult to state without an actual court award . . . meaning that the weak vision is at its most attractive.

[92] Since (as noted in the previous section) under a pure remedial constructive trust there is an option not to backdate at all, its use here would permit the court to declare John wholly unaffected by your estoppel rights. Section 116(a) prohibits such a possibility; it would represent an improvement.

9

Constructive Trusts

9.1 Two Constructive Trust Doctrines

This chapter looks at two further doctrines whereby you may gain a right in my land, in an essentially disorganised way. These are the doctrines whereby a right arises against me if I acquire the land after giving an undertaking to allow you to benefit from it; or in some circumstances when you and I are family members together.

The right that arises under these doctrines is a constructive trust. Saying that the trust is 'constructive' means that it arises for reasons other than that I intend it to: which is another way of saying that it arises on a disorganised basis. Our task will be to examine the relevant reasons in more detail, and to assess their merit. Before moving to that, however, let us look at the stipulation that these doctrines generate a *trust*, and only a trust.

9.1.1 The Doctrines' Limitation to Trusts

We looked at the idea of a trust briefly in § 1.3.1, and will explore it fully in Chapters 15 and 16. In outline, a trust is 'a situation in which property is vested in someone (a trustee), who is under legally recognised obligations, at least some of which are of a proprietary kind [ie in rem], to handle it in a certain way, and to the exclusion of any personal interest'.[1] Take the case where I own some land but hold it on trust, for you as the beneficiary of that trust. The land will remain vested in me (ie registered in my name), but I will be obliged to let you, as beneficiary, have all the benefit from it, retaining none for myself ('to the exclusion of any personal interest').[2] This distinguishes a trust right from

---

[1] S Gardner, *An Introduction to the Law of Trusts* (3rd edn, Oxford, 2011) 2.
[2] I can of course hold the land on trust for you and John together, meaning that all the benefit goes to the two of you. And indeed, I can hold it on trust for you and me together, in which case

all other rights in rem short of ownership itself. Where you have such another right over my land it does not absorb all the benefit. All the benefit not absorbed by the right remains with me, as owner. For example, if you have a right of way over my land, you can cross it by the route in question, but nothing else. In all respects not inconsistent with this, the land is mine to enjoy.

Contrast the disorganised acquisition doctrine which we looked at in Chapter 8, namely proprietary estoppel. The latter can generate any kind of right in rem over land:[3] a trust (so that you take all the land's benefit) or some other right (so that you take some benefit, but I keep the rest), as the circumstances warrant. It is striking that the doctrines we shall look at in this chapter purport to generate only trust rights. Assuming we find that they should generate you a right at all, we shall want to think why it should have to be a trust right, and cannot be anything else. In fact, we shall find that, despite assertions that it generates only constructive trusts, the first of this chapter's two doctrines can generate any kind of right. The second of the two doctrines, however, is actually defined in such a way that it produces specifically trust rights – though the fundamental ideas involved could perhaps yield other outcomes too.

9.2 Transfer Subject to an Undertaking

The first of our two doctrines is this. Say I acquire some land from John, promising John that I will allow you to use the land in some way (commonly, to continue to use it as you did in John's time, but this is not essential). The law obliges me to keep my promise, saying that I now hold the land on constructive trust for you.[4]

9.2.1 The Principle

This doctrine originated in two groups of decisions.

One[5] deals with the case where my acquisition of the land is *inter vivos*, and I make John an oral promise to hold the land on trust for you (or indeed

I share the benefit with you: that is to say, while I can derive no benefit *in my capacity as trustee*, I can do so as co-object of the trust with you. This matters especially for the second of our two doctrines, which most commonly operates so as to produce such an outcome.

[3] As well as some other outcomes, including a right in personam over land, a right in rem or in personam over other kinds of property, and a money award.

[4] See further B McFarlane, 'Constructive Trusts Arising on a Receipt of Property *Sub Conditione*' (2004) 120 *LQR* 667; S Gardner, 'Reliance-Based Constructive Trusts' in C Mitchell (ed), *Constructive and Resulting Trusts* (Oxford, 2009) ch 2.

[5] *Rochefoucauld v Boustead* [1897] 1 Ch 196 (CA); *Bannister v Bannister* [1948] 2 All ER 133 (CA).

him). The *inter vivos* creation of trusts of land requires writing,[6] so at first sight my oral promise is ineffective. But John relied on my promise in transferring the land to me, or at any rate in doing so without putting the trust in writing. If I were now to go back on my promise, John would have been injured by this reliance. My obligation to keep my promise arises so as to prevent this injury.

The other group[7] deals with the case (involving what is known as a 'secret trust') where John transfers the land to me on his death. John does not stipulate in his will that I should hold the land on trust for you, which is, as § 5.3 explains, what the Wills Act 1837 requires if he is to make an express trust effective upon death. But he takes a promise from me that I will do so. Again, John's reliance on my promise (failing to use the proper form to make his trust for you) means that he will suffer detriment if I go back on my promise, and, to prevent that, the law obliges me to keep my promise.

The effect seen in these cases is sometimes put as 'equity will not permit a statute [the Wills Act or the *inter vivos* formality requirement] to be used as an instrument of fraud'; my failure to keep my promise, so injuring John, being the (actual or potential) fraud. But this view of the matter suggests that the court is able to abort the application of the statutory rule, which is hard to understand. It is more intelligible to see the statutory rule as stopping any express trust from arising, but the need to prevent my fraud as requiring relief against me, on the corrective grounds just described. As it happens, this relief needs to take the same shape as the express trust would have had, ie an obligation requiring me to keep my promise. It would not suffice merely to return the land to John, so as to give him the chance to impose the trust – using the proper form – for himself. That is because returning the land to John in this way, even if John is still alive, would not allow him to establish the trust from the moment he wanted it; nor indeed ensure that the chance now to establish such a trust is all he receives, as returning the land to him would also allow him to do other things with it, such as keep it for himself. The only way to bring about that the promised trust arises, no less and no more, is for the law, straight away, to hold me to the trust. So the best view of the matter is that the law imposes the promised trust on me[8] as a constructive trust.[9]

---

[6] Law of Property Act 1925 s 53(1)(b): see § 15.3.3.

[7] The principal decision of this kind is *Blackwell v Blackwell* [1929] AC 318 (HL), but there is much other authority.

[8] That is, the trust arises not from John's stipulation alone, but from the combination of that stipulation, my agreement, and John's reliance. The trust so generated is therefore appropriately said, in the secret trust context, to arise 'outside the will'. That truth is sometimes, however, misunderstood as connoting that the trust arises from John's stipulation alone, but is exempt from the Wills Act's requirements: an impossible idea. See further Gardner (n 1) 93–101.

[9] *Rochefoucauld v Boustead* [1897] 1 Ch 196, 208 (CA) may (it is not quite clear, however) have treated the trust as express, but if so, it is probably not supportable. Subsequent decisions have certainly regarded the trust as constructive: see especially *Bannister v Bannister* [1948] 2 All ER 133, 136 (CA). See Gardner *ibid* 95–97.

In subjecting me to a constructive trust in this way, the law interferes with my enjoyment of my 'possessions', and on appropriate facts also potentially my home, so engaging ECHR First Protocol Article 1, and Article 8, respectively. But especially given what has just been said about the basis for these constructive trusts, this uncontroversially appears justified as a proportionate means of securing a proper end.

9.2.2 Must the Outcome be a Trust?

In the original decisions, my promise was always to hold the land *on trust*. Following the reasoning above, my obligation is thus also a trust, and correctly labelled as such. Some further decisions, however, hold that a constructive trust arises in this way also if the promise I make to John is not to hold the land on trust for you, but to allow you to enjoy it in some other way. Say John owns a stately home, and you have a contract with him allowing you to sell refreshments to his visitors. John transfers the house to me. Your rights under your contract are not rights in rem, capable of binding me automatically.[10] But if John takes a promise from me that I will continue with the same arrangement, the cases say that I will be obliged to do so, my obligation being a constructive trust in your favour.[11]

It is correct that I should come under the obligation described, for the reason given above: otherwise, John will have suffered the detriment of failing to provide for you in the way he wished. But calling my obligation a 'trust' is incorrect. As we saw in § 9.1.1, saying I hold land on trust for you denotes that, although I am the land's legal owner, I have no rights to enjoy it myself. That is not the case here. In our example, I must allow you to continue with your refreshment business, but I have the right to enjoy the land in all other respects myself. So if I resell the land, I keep the proceeds. I do not give the proceeds to you, as I would have to if I truly held the land on trust for you.[12]

If my obligation really is a trust, as in the original decisions, it will, as such, be a right in rem, so as potentially to bind someone to whom I in turn

---

[10] You have a contractual licence, which operates in personam: see § 17.3.3.

[11] *Binions v Evans* [1972] Ch 359, 368–9 (CA); *Lyus v Prowsa Developments Ltd* [1982] 1 WLR 1044 (Ch D); *Ashburn Anstalt v WJ Arnold & Co* [1989] Ch 1, 22–27 (CA).

[12] Can it be argued that I hold not the land as a whole, but the specific right (your right to sell refreshments) on trust for you? No, because this right has no separate identity in my hands, so as to allow it to be something that I can hold on trust. It exists only as *your* right *against* John or me. Alternatively, can it be said that I hold the land as a whole on trust for you (to the extent of your refreshment right) and myself (as to the remainder) together? This is a more interesting suggestion. But the conventional wisdom is that where two or more people have trust rights entitling them to benefit from the asset simultaneously, the benefit must remain a single package to be enjoyed on a shared basis (ie on the basis of 'unity of possession'). That is to say, the benefit may not be divided, in the manner of the suggestion, so as to give the different people different pieces of it.

transfer the land.[13] If it is not a trust, its character as in rem or in personam should in principle depend on its content. My obligation to allow you to sell refreshments should be in personam, because there is no such recognised right in rem. But say I promised to allow you a lease or a right of way over the land. These are recognised rights in rem, so my obligation, reproducing them, ought to be in rem too.[14]

9.2.3 Proving the Promise

So if, on acquiring the land in question from John, I promise him that I will let you use it in some way, the law protects John's reliance on my promise by imposing on me an obligation to adhere to it.

In principle, the promise I make to John in your favour can be either express or implied. Whether it is sufficiently evidenced will require a judgment on individual facts.[15]

A word is needed, however, about one type of case: that where John transfers the land to me, and I agree to accept it, 'subject to' your right. This phrase could in principle have two different meanings, only one of which involves the promise on my part needed to create the obligation under discussion.[16]

The contract under which John sells me the land will normally oblige John to give me 'vacant possession' of the land. So – continuing with the example above – if you are still running your refreshment business on the land when it becomes mine, the possession I receive will not be vacant, and John will find himself in breach of contract . . . unless he and I have agreed that he may give me possession that is vacant in all respects except your presence. Making the contract 'subject to' your presence will do that.

The words 'subject to' will always operate in this way. In the first of their two possible meanings, however, that is all they do. Then, they do not oblige

---

[13] More strictly, at least some obligations under every trust are in rem (see § 16.4), but this leaves it fair to say for present purposes that 'a trust is a right in rem'.

[14] The cases have not yet addressed this issue properly; the most that can be said is that they contain nothing inconsistent with the proposition suggested in the text. In *Chattey v Farndale Holdings Inc* (1998) 75 P & CR 298 (CA) the undertaking was to honour a lien, which is a right in rem, and the resulting obligation seems to have been treated as in rem (*ibid* 313–17). No decision has yet been required on the position where the undertaking is to honour a right in personam. There is, however, a hint in *DHN Food Distributors Ltd v Tower Hamlets London Borough Council* [1976] 1 WLR 852 (CA) and, following it, *Re Sharpe (a bankrupt)* [1980] 1 WLR 219 (Ch D) that the obligation in that case is, contrary to the argument here, in rem. But the right in personam in question in those decisions was a contractual licence, which some judges wished to reclassify as a right in rem (§ 17.3.3). The decisions may be seen as influenced by that project, and were (therefore) disapproved in *Ashburn Anstalt v WJ Arnold & Co* [1989] Ch 1, 24 (CA).

[15] *Ashburn Anstalt v WJ Arnold & Co, ibid,* asserts that the promise should not be found by 'inferences from slender materials'. In the secret trust context, there is some authority that a higher than usual standard of proof is required – *Re Snowden* [1979] Ch 528 (Ch D) – but the statement is confused.

[16] For a detailed discussion, see *Chaudhary v Yavuz* [2011] EWCA Civ 1314, [37]–[69] (CA).

me to let you remain: I can evict you, but I cannot recoup the losses I suffer in the process by suing John. But in their second meaning, the words additionally denote a promise by me to let you remain. Then, an obligation to that effect will arise against me in the manner currently under discussion.

How do we tell which meaning the words have in a given case? The short answer is that we cannot always know for sure. But, it is sometimes said, if the land is priced below the figure that it could command with vacant possession, that shows I am promising to let you stay. This is insufficiently sophisticated, however. Certainly, if I have to let you stay, the value of the land is less than it would be if it were wholly vacant, and its price will normally reflect that. But even if I can evict you, the fact that I cannot reclaim any associated losses should also impair the value of the deal and show up in a reduced price. The reduction in the latter case should be smaller than in the former, as my right to evict you allows me eventually to eradicate the reason for the diminution in the land's value. But it will sometimes be hard to be confident which of the two levels of impaired value is reflected in an admittedly reduced price. That matter aside, remember also to think about the contractual language itself, in its context. If the relevant term stipulates that I will take the land from John 'subject to your *right*', rather than merely to 'your presence', it may be thought to indicate that I am indeed promising to let you stay.[17]

9.2.4 An Alternative to a Promise?

So far, we have discussed this doctrine in terms of my *promising* John to allow you to use the relevant land in some way. This is certainly the standard account of it.[18]

But some decisions[19] suggest that such an obligation also arises against me if you have a right against John to use the land in the way in question, and I

---

[17] In *Ashburn Anstalt v WJ Arnold & Co* [1989] Ch 1, 26, 25–26 (CA), it is said that John's making the transfer 'subject to' your right could alternatively be a performance by John of the duty, normally found in his contract with me, to disclose to me any 'incumbrances' affecting the land that are known to him. Explained in this way, the words would again not amount to a promise by me to let you stay. The argument is not clean, however. 'Incumbrances' are properly speaking rights in rem already extant against the land, which *will* bind me, even without a promise. *Ex hypothesi*, the kind of right presently under discussion is not an already extant right in rem, so will not bind me on that basis (only if I promise that it should). So it does not require disclosure as an 'incumbrance' anyway.

[18] The statement of the principle in *Ashburn Anstalt v WJ Arnold & Co, ibid* 22–27 does not commit itself univocally to the requirement for a *promise*, instead demanding an inquiry whether, in all the circumstances, it would be 'unconscionable' for me not to owe you the obligation in question. However, *IDC Group Ltd v Clark* [1992] 1 EGLR 186 (Ch D), *Lloyd v Dugdale* [2001] EWCA Civ 1754, [50]–[56] (CA) and *Chaudhary v Yavuz* [2011] EWCA Civ 1314, [37]–[69] (CA) appear to regard this unconscionability as arising from John having transferred the land to me on the basis of my promise, as described in the text.

[19] *De Mattos v Gibson* (1859) 4 De G & J 276, 282 (LJJ); *Catt v Tourle* (1869) 4 Ch App 654 (CA in Ch); *Luker v Dennis* (1877) 7 Ch D 227 (Ch D); *Binions v Evans* [1972] Ch 359, 369 (CA); *Peffer v Rigg* [1977] 1 WLR 285, 294 (Ch D). (The proposition under discussion forms the third

buy the land from John *knowing of* this right. Other decisions reject this extension, however.[20] Which view is correct?

It must of course be assumed that your right will not bind me of its own accord – that is, as a right in rem, effective against me either through having been registered, or as an overriding interest.[21] In traditional unregistered land law, an equitable right in rem would affect me unless I was a bona fide purchaser of the land in question for value and without notice of the right. In that context, then, if your right was in rem, and I knew of it, it would bind me. But that is quite different from the hypothesis under discussion. This concerns the case where a right will *not* bind me of its own accord, either because it is in personam, or because, although in rem, it has not been registered and does not qualify as overriding. The hypothesis is that I will put myself under a new obligation ('constructive trust') to honour the right if I know about it, just as if I promise to honour it, when I buy the land.[22]

As we saw in § 9.2.1, when I acquire land from John promising John to honour your right, I am bound because an obligation arises to correct the detriment (loss of opportunity for John to protect you) for which I would otherwise be responsible. But there seems to be no reason why I should incur an obligation merely because I know about your right. If John suffers detriment in such a case, my awareness of it is insufficient to ascribe it to me: in the absence of a promise from me to honour your right, any expectation on his part that I shall do so is not of my making. The correct decisions are therefore those[23] which hold that knowledge of a non-binding right does *not* oblige me to honour it.

---

ratio of *Peffer v Rigg*. It is quite distinct from the first and second ratios, which address the possibility that the right in question bound the transferee as a right in rem. For discussion of the latter issue, see § 3.1.1.)

[20] *Formby v Barker* [1903] 2 Ch 539 (CA); *London County Council v Allen* [1914] 3 KB 642 (CA); *Ashburn Anstalt v WJ Arnold & Co* [1989] Ch 1, 26 (CA). *Midland Bank Trust Co Ltd v Green* [1981] AC 513 (HL) is sometimes added to these, but incorrectly. The discussion there was solely of the terms of the Land Charges Act 1925 s 13. That section ruled that I was not bound by a right in rem to which the Act applied if you had not registered it. The question was whether the section contained an exception if I nonetheless knew about your right. The answer was no.

[21] So distinguish the present discussion from the argument, in § 3.2.3, that a disponee of land should be bound by a right in rem against it if he knows of the right, as an alternative to it being registered or counting as overriding under the Land Registration Act 2002 Sch 3. The point of that argument is that the right is in rem – ie exists to bind the disponee – and, given his knowledge, there is no reason why it should not do so.

[22] There is thus no analogy with the obligation which arises under the doctrine known as 'knowing receipt of trust property'. If I acquire trust property and, knowing that it is not mine, lose it again, so causing a loss to the trust, this doctrine makes me liable to the trust for the loss. Properly understood, this doctrine depends on my being bound, as I acquire the property, by the rights in rem which make it trust property: so I become its trustee: and when I lose it, I break my duty as trustee to keep it safe, and so am liable in that way. See Gardner (n 1) 268; *cf* M Conaglen and A Goymour, 'Knowing Receipt and Registered Land' in Mitchell (ed) (n 4) ch 5.

[23] n 20.

Sometimes, however, on top of my knowledge of your right, there is a possible further factor. Does this make a difference? Two kinds of further factor may be considered.

First, where not only do I know about your right, but also John charges me a reduced price for the land, because he believes I will honour your right. Unless my acceptance of the price reduction suggests that I am making an implicit promise after all, this should make no difference:[24] I have done nothing to mean that John's erroneous belief should be ascribed to me, and his acceptance of a lower price on the strength of this belief is simply a mistake on his part.

Second, where not only do I know about your right, but also John transfers the land to me deliberately so as to destroy your right (though this will normally give you a right to compensation from John). If I am merely the innocent instrument of John's scheme, I should not be affected by it any more than by my knowledge alone. But if I cooperate with John in his scheme (and going ahead knowing of the scheme seems necessarily to amount to cooperating in it), I become responsible for the detriment you have suffered, because I lend myself to the wrong by which John brings that about.[25] Correcting that detriment by imposing a corresponding obligation on me appears right.[26]

9.3 Family Property

We now turn to the second of our constructive trust doctrines.

9.3.1 An Outline

Say I own a house, and I wish to give you a share in it. I can do so by intentional conferral. As the creation of a beneficial interest in land, this operation will require writing.[27] If I use writing, however, the upshot will be an *express* trust of the house, I being the trustee, for you and myself in the intended proportions.[28]

---

[24] Compare *Tulk v Moxhay* (1848) 2 Ph 774, 778 (Ch), where it is said that such facts do generate an obligation against me. The obligation is better understood as a right in rem, the restrictive covenant, newly created by that case: see Ch 14.

[25] There is perhaps a connection with the wrongs of inducing a breach of contract, and dishonest assistance in a breach of trust.

[26] Whereas (the third ratio in) *Peffer v Rigg* [1977] 1 WLR 285, 294 (Ch D) apparently imposed an obligation on the basis of knowledge alone (see at n 19), the facts of the case suggest that the true explanation may be the analysis here under consideration.

[27] Law of Property Act 1925 s 53(1)(b); § 5.4.1.

[28] For express trusts, see § 15.3.1.

Say, on the other hand, that I own a house; that you and I are members of a family, probably living together in the house; and that you and I have a 'common intention' that you should have a particular share in it (say, half), but I do not put this in writing. No express trust can arise, but the law gives effect to our 'common intention' nonetheless, recognising it as generating a *constructive* trust. Under this constructive trust, I again become trustee of the house for you and myself, in the proportions indicated by our 'common intention'. It is this constructive trust that is the focus of the present discussion.

This sketch has so far focused on the simple case, where I am the sole registered owner of the house (the 'sole name' scenario). The same principles apply also where you and I are registered as joint owners of the house (the 'joint names' scenario). Unless the registration or other paperwork indicates otherwise, the law assumes that we hold the house for our own benefit, in 50:50 shares.[29] If I wish you to have a larger share, I can confer it on you expressly, by the use of writing.[30] But even without such writing, if it is our 'common intention' that you should have a larger share, the law will again rule that we hold the house on constructive trust in the indicated proportions.

In both scenarios, then, our (unwritten) 'common intention' – that the house should belong to us in such-and-such proportions – gives rise to a constructive trust to that effect. But this statement is only an initial outline of this type of constructive trust, providing a point of departure for a fuller treatment. We shall encounter a number of complexities and difficulties.

9.3.2 Two Questions

At the outset, it is necessary to separate two questions with which the doctrine deals. The first question is whether to depart from the prima facie position. In the 'sole name' scenario, the prima facie position is that the house is entirely mine, so this question is in effect whether you should have a share in it at all. In the 'joint names' scenario, the prima facie position is that the house belongs to us in 50:50 shares, and the question is whether you should have a larger fraction. If the answer to this first question is 'yes', we continue to the second question: how large should your share then be?

These two questions could have been condensed into the single question of whether you ought to have such-and-such a share; this being – obviously – a larger share than that, if any, to which you would otherwise be entitled (ie than the prima facie position). But as the cases currently stand, they require separate discussion. We shall take them in turn.

---

[29] *Stack v Dowden* [2007] 2 AC 432, [54]–[58] (HL); *Jones v Kernott* [2011] 3 WLR 1121, [10], [17], [19], [68] (SC). Note A Briggs, 'Co-ownership and an Equitable Non-sequitur (2012) 128 *LQR* 183.

[30] Law of Property Act 1925 s 53(1)(c).

9.3.3 Departure from the Prima Facie Position

First, then, the question whether to depart from the prima facie position, so that in the 'sole name' scenario you can claim a share at all, and in the 'joint names' scenario you can claim more than 50 per cent.

As stated in the outline above, your ability to do so depends on whether you and I have a 'common intention' that you should. Over the years, the law has taken more than one approach to the exact meaning of this statement.[31] Under the current law, however, it means simply what is appears to.[32]

That is, the judge must find that, at any rate by external appearances (there is no inquiry as to what might have been lurking in our hearts), you and I agreed that you should have such an enhanced share.[33] This agreement might be explicit, as where we have actually discussed the question and expressly concurred in a positive answer to it. In seeking such an explicit agreement, the judge must look at all relevant evidence. Or the agreement might be implicit, as where we proceeded on the basis of a tacit, but nonetheless real, consensus that you should have an enhanced share. In seeking such an implicit agreement, the judge must once again attend to all relevant evidence, which in this case means our 'whole course of conduct in relation to [the property]'.[34]

9.3.4 Quantum

If the first question is answered in the affirmative – that is, it is decided that the claimant deserves more than his prima facie share, if any – the second

---

[31] The most important variations from the current law were: (i) a rule that, if our common intention was implicit rather than explicit, it could be proved only by reference to 'direct contributions to the purchase price [of the house in question] by the partner who is not the legal owner, whether initially or by payment of mortgage instalments' (*Lloyds Bank plc v Rosset* [1991] 1 AC 107, 133 (HL)); and (ii) a rule that, as well as showing a common intention, you must also have relied on it to your detriment (*ibid* 132). These rules were more extensively discussed in the previous edition of this book. Although the authority for them has not been explicitly overruled, they are conspicuously absent from the more recent coverage of this area of the law in *Stack v Dowden* [2007] 2 AC 432 (HL) and *Jones v Kernott* [2011] 3 WLR 1121 (SC), and must sensibly be regarded as having been superseded.

[32] There has existed some reason to wonder whether the statement bears the same meaning in both the 'sole name' scenario and the 'joint names' scenario. This reason was one not of principle (for why should the two scenarios be treated differently in this respect?), but of authority. In one of the key decisions, attention is explicitly focused on the latter, leaving the former aside: *Stack v Dowden, ibid* [63]. A similar impression may be given in *Jones v Kernott, ibid* [16]–[17]. But – fortunately – it is immediately dispelled, to the effect that the two scenarios are to be treated in the same way, ie that stated in the text: *ibid* [51]–[52].

[33] *Jones v Kernott, ibid* [51]–[52].

[34] *Stack v Dowden* [2007] 2 AC 432, [60] (HL). A long but non-exhaustive list of the kinds of material that might count towards this is given at [69]–[70]. It extends all the way from the parties' contributions to the acquisition of the property to the nature of their relationship itself, with all the latter's ramifications.

question arises: what should be the quantum, ie how large a share should he in fact have?

Once again, over the years the courts have experimented with a number of different approaches to this question.[35] The current rule requires effect to be given to any genuine common intention the parties may have had as to the matter (whether explicit or implicit, discovered in the same manner as a common intention to depart from their prima facie shares). But, the rule continues:[36] in the absence of such a genuine common intention, the judge must 'impute' such an intention, ie invent one on the parties' behalf, so as to achieve a 'fair' outcome.

9.3.5 'Fairness'

When the courts impute – invent – a common intention (under the current rules, officially only in establishing quantum), they thus do so in order to achieve 'fairness'. But what does this mean?

The guide is said to be[37] the parties' 'whole course of conduct in relation to [the property]',[38] which in turn means many different aspects of their behaviour.[39]

Notice that the parties' 'whole course of conduct in relation to [the property]' is thus used in two ways: here, to shape 'fairness', but also to prove a genuine common intention.[40] The two uses are, however, quite different. In the latter, the course of conduct is simply evidence, helping reveal the intention the parties actually had; while in the present context, it has a normative role, determining the intention the judge wants them to have had. But it is quite unclear – and the courts have not overtly explained – how it does this; that is, what significance should be ascribed to the various possible kinds of behaviour.

Imagine, for example, that you and I were unmarried partners for 10 years, but have now separated. Our former home together is registered in my name alone, but you are now claiming a share in it. Grant that we agreed – or that a court will be prepared to say we agreed – that you should have such a share; but we had no agreement as to its size, so you are now asking the court to impute one by reference to our behaviour. I was always the sole wage-earner, and so all our outgoings, including the mortgage repayments on the house, came from my earnings – though we operated a joint account, as you needed

---

[35] For the most striking earlier efforts, see *Midland Bank plc v Cooke* [1995] 4 All ER 562 (CA) and *Oxley v Hiscock* [2005] Fam 211 (CA).

[36] *Jones v Kernott* [2011] 3 WLR 1121, [47], [51]–[52], [64], [72], [84], [89] (SC).

[37] *ibid* [51].

[38] *Stack v Dowden* [2007] 2 AC 432, [60] (HL).

[39] *ibid* [69]–[70].

[40] n 34.

to draw on my earnings too, for the shopping etc that you did. You kept house for us, and indeed redecorated the house and remodelled the garden.

The 'whole course of conduct' formula means that all these facts can enter into the imputation exercise. But a court might respond to them in a number of ways. Consider two, though it is possible to imagine others. First, it might give you a half share in the house, on the basis that you and I shared our lives: pooled our efforts and resources, making different but equally valuable contributions, in a way that suited our particular relationship best. For this perspective, it is in your favour that you were not a wage-earner, but depended financially on me: this helps confirm that we must have seen ourselves as sharing. Second, the court might give you a share reflecting your contribution to the acquisition of the house. Directly, in the form of actual mortgage repayments, you contributed nothing, so on that reckoning your share would be zero. You could, however, be seen as having contributed indirectly: by undertaking your work in and around our home, you saved me the cost of hiring a housekeeper, cook, personal shopper, decorator, gardener (therapist, escort, . . .), allowing me to put the saved sums towards repaying the mortgage. If all this was taken into account, your share would be the proportionate value of these savings to the total mortgage repayments.

It is easy to find problems with each of these perspectives. But the more fundamental difficulty is that no decision explicitly tells us which of them – or indeed any others that might suggest themselves – is right. That is, there has been no articulation of the rationale behind the imputation of common intention: what goal it is aimed at achieving. This goal may, however, be constructively identified by considering the way in which the courts have drawn particular outcomes from particular fact situations. As yet there is not a great deal to go on. Especially helpful however, at any rate as a starting point, are the decisions of the House of Lords and Privy Council respectively in *Stack v Dowden*[41] and *Abbott v Abbott*.[42]

In *Stack v Dowden*,[43] the claimant was found entitled to (at least) a 65 per cent share, apparently on the basis that this reflected the contribution her earnings had made to the acquisition of the property in question, relative to that made by the defendant.[44] In *Abbott v Abbott*,[45] the claimant emerged with a 50 per cent share. Although she had made a financial contribution, it was much smaller than this. The outcome seems to have reflected the fact that she was married to the defendant, and that they had pooled their financial resources through a joint bank account[46] – in contrast to *Stack v Dowden*,[47]

[41] [2007] 2 AC 432 (HL).
[42] [2008] 1 FLR 1451 (PC).
[43] [2007] 2 AC 432 (HL).
[44] *ibid* [86]–[88].
[45] [2008] 1 FLR 1451 (PC).
[46] *ibid* [9], [18].
[47] [2007] 2 AC 432 (HL).

where the parties were unmarried, and had kept their financial affairs sharply separate.[48]

It is possible to detect a pattern here. The key question appears to be whether the parties have a materially communal relationship: ie one in which, in practical terms, they pool their material resources (including money, other assets, and labour). If they do (as in *Abbott v Abbott*[49]), the claimant's share will be 50 per cent. In a distributive response, the law follows the relationship's own implication that the house, like the parties' other assets, should likewise be pooled. If, however, the parties' relationship is not materially communal (as in *Stack v Dowden*[50]), the relationship itself will have no particular message as regards the allocation of the property. Instead (again, as there), the claimant's share will be that which reflects his contribution, if any, to the acquisition of the house. This corrective outcome rectifies what would otherwise be the claimant's unjust enrichment of the defendant, who would otherwise be left with a share in the property, wholly or partly paid for by the claimant.[51]

In the illustration given earlier, therefore, we should expect the first of the two suggested outcomes: that is, since we had a materially communal relationship, our shares in the house will be equal. The second outcome (shares reflecting our respective contributions to the acquisition of the house) was driven by unjust enrichment, and would have been apt only if our relationship had not been materially communal.

So this is the basic pattern – and, therefore, meaning of 'fairness' – that, it is suggested, may be discerned in the cases. It does of course face an immediate difficulty: if the law is to respond differently as between the two different kinds of relationships, it must be able to identify them. In some instances, that will be possible; but this will not always be the case. Even if the parties themselves are both clear about and happy with the nature of their individual relationship, the set of possible relationships will form at best a spectrum, and drawing the required line between those that are materially communal and the rest will entail treating quite similar relationships strikingly differently, bringing about substantive injustice. And, of course, it is highly optimistic to suppose that people will always be both clear about and happy with the nature of their relationship, leaving this at best an uncomfortable determinant of the law's response.[52] On the other hand, there may in reality be no better approach on offer.

This account of the meaning of 'fairness' must, however, be developed further.

---

[48] *ibid* [90]–[92].
[49] [2008] 1 FLR 1451 (PC).
[50] [2007] 2 AC 432 (HL).
[51] For further discussion, see S Gardner, 'Family Property Today' (2008) 124 *LQR* 422.
[52] See A Bottomley, 'Women and Trust(s): Portraying the Family in the Gallery of Law' in S Bright and J Dewar (eds), *Land Law – Themes and Perspectives* (Oxford, 1998) ch 8.

9.3.6 Materially Communal Relationships

So the suggestion is that in materially communal relationships, 'fairness' means equality. In *Jones v Kernott*,[53] however, the Supreme Court has elaborated the concept of 'equality'. To see this, we once again attend less to what the judges said than to what they did – the outcome they reached, on the particular facts.

The outcome in that case was that the woman emerged with a 90 per cent share in the house, the man 10 per cent. At first sight, this outcome may appear quite unlike the equal shares that, given the discussion so far, one might have expected. But this appearance is deceptive. The parties' 90:10 shares in the house that was the subject of their litigation in fact equated to 50:50 shares in their overall pool of assets. (The rest of the pool consisting of another, slightly less valuable, house, that was and remained entirely the man's.[54]) So the expected equal shares were indeed forthcoming, on this more comprehensive plane. And on reflection, the latter is the more appropriate one. As already explained, the gist of a materially communal relationship is that the parties 'pool their material resources' ... so the pool, that is the *overall* pool, should be the focus of our attention in delivering the 50:50 split that such a relationship requires. (Though of course, especially where the litigation occurs during or immediately at the end of the parties' relationship, the pool may well consist of only one asset to speak of, namely the one shared house, and in this case its equal division could therefore still mean a 50:50 division of that house.[55])

But while intelligible, this account of *Jones v Kernott*[56] is in fact ambiguous. We could stop with what had already been said: simply, that the gist of the parties' materially communal relationship requires equal division between them of their entire asset pool at the time of litigation. Or we could see this, first, idea in turn as only the predicate of a second: a further, deeper, principle, demanding implementation in its own right. This possible further principle is in fact also found in the (modern understanding[57] of the) jurisdiction to award financial relief upon the divorce of a married couple or civil partners,

---

[53] [2011] UKSC 53 (SC).

[54] Notice that, if the *man's* house had been the more valuable of the two, the same essential reasoning would have required the woman to have the *entirety* of the shared house *plus* a fractional share in the man's house – despite perhaps having never set foot in it, for it was acquired after the breakdown of their relationship.

[55] This is not, however, the explanation for the 50:50 split in *Abbott v Abbott* [2008] 1 FLR 1451 (PC). There, too, there were assets beyond the house: most notably, some investments in the husband's name. Yet these were not taken into account in the reckoning; the house was viewed in isolation in arriving at its equal division. This decision should therefore be seen as using a not yet fully worked-through vision of the 'materially communal' idea.

[56] [2011] 3 WLR 1121 (SC).

[57] That is, since *White v White* [2001] AC 596 (HL); *Miller v Miller, McFarlane v McFarlane* [2006] 2 AC 618 (HL).

under section 24 of the Matrimonial Causes Act 1973. It is that the parties' overall asset pool should be divided . . . not simply into 50 per cent shares, but so as to produce equality between them in their new, separated, situation.

Of course, on appropriate facts, these two visions could involve the same outcome, ie a simple 50:50 split. But this is the case only where the parties' new situation does not leave one of them in a needier position than the other. Where there is a discrepancy in the parties' degree of need, the second vision requires some other split, adjusted for this discrepancy and so calculated to produce equality in this deeper or more global sense. The outstanding (though not the only) situation in which to see the difference between the two visions is that in which the parties have dependent children, who now live with one of them rather than the other. The parent with whom the children now live will of course incur higher housing and other costs than the other, and producing equality between the two parents will thus require their shares in the asset pool to reflect this disparity. The parties in *Jones v Kernott*[58] did not have dependent children at the time of their litigation (nor was there any other factor requiring a similar adjustment), so the difference between the two visions did not arise. In principle, however, the second of them is preferable, as most faithfully capturing the idea of equality that is the core implication of material communality.

This account of 'fairness' in materially communal cases needs to be read against some judicial statements[59] to the effect that there should only infrequently be any departure from the prima facie equal shares found in a joint names case. Now if the suggestions in § 9.3.5 are correct, these statements certainly make no sense in regard to non-materially communal relationships. As said, where the latter are involved, the parties' shares will reflect their respective contributions to the acquisition of the house, which will very commonly be unequal (hence the departure from equal shares in *Stack v Dowden*[60] itself); and this has now been recognised, and the statements to this extent retracted.[61] But nor do the statements make sense in regard to a materially communal relationship, if, as suggested here, the idea of producing 'equality' is to be read in any more sophisticated way than as requiring a simple 50:50 split of the house under litigation. Such a more sophisticated reading will mean that here too, departures from the prima facie equal shares should be commonplace. Hence the departure from equal shares which occurred even in a materially communal context, in *Jones v Kernott*;[62] and likewise in the case, just discussed, where dependent children continue to live with one rather than the other of the parties. In fact, there seems to remain no warrant for the statements.

[58] [2011] 3 WLR 1121 (SC).
[59] See especially *Stack v Dowden* [2007] 2 AC 432, [68] (HL); *Jones v Kernott, ibid* [19].
[60] [2007] 2 AC 432 (HL).
[61] *Jones v Kernott* [2011] 3 WLR 1121, [25] (SC).
[62] [2011] 3 WLR 1121 (SC).

Finally, the suggested treatment of materially communal cases is of course politically contentious. This is especially true of the second of the visions under discussion, which, remember, takes the same approach to these cases – commonly involving unmarried couples – as is taken to the award of financial relief upon the dissolution of a marriage or civil partnership. To the extent that the vision represents the law, it becomes true (rather than false, as usually claimed) that the law does have a concept of 'common law marriage'. This will be comforting to many, above all to those who (it is usually claimed erroneously) rely on it being the case. But it will be discomforting to those who see it as 'undermining the institution of marriage'. Or more accurately, given what has just been said, 'undermining the institution of non-common law marriage' – which may put a rather different complexion on things, perhaps suggesting that those who raise this objection are excessively interested in form, to the neglect of substance. (It surely could not be argued that marriage is, in its true essence, a matter of form rather than substance?)[63]

9.3.7 Non-materially Communal Relationships

The suggestion is, remember, that in non-materially communal cases the law seeks to correct the unjust enrichment to one party stemming from the contributions of the other party. We must examine the fit between the fact-patterns of cases of the kind under discussion and the law's approach to redressing unjust enrichment generally.[64] Put shortly, the latter requires that the defendant be enriched (at the claimant's expense), and that this enrichment be unjust.

[63] If the common law does indeed take this form, it pre-empts the calls that are sometimes made for a *statutory* provision applying matrimonial-style relief to (appropriate) unmarried relationships. See eg Wall P, cited in F Gibb, 'Top Judge's Charter for Unmarried Couples' *The Times* 3.2.2011. Wall P linked his call with a request for the implementation of some proposals by the Law Commission: *Cohabitation: the Financial Consequences of Relationship Breakdown* (Law Com No 307, London, 2007). But these proposals were *not* for the application of distributive, matrimonial-style, equality-oriented relief to unmarried relationships: rather, for a corrective scheme aimed at redressing the economic advantages and disadvantages arising from the parties' contributions to the relationship and experienced on its breakdown. Eg where a couple originally had similar incomes, but the woman paused her career to be their children's carer, protecting the man's future earning capacity but sacrificing her own, a financial adjustment would be made to correct their resultant respective gain and loss. As well as involving the confiscation of the rights of those to whom the common law's approach is more generous (so engaging the ECHR First Protocol Art 1), the proposals have further weaknesses, including their confinement to parties living as a couple in a joint household and having either had children or lived together for a defined period (probably of somewhere between 2 and 5 years), so excluding platonic, inter-generational, inter-sibling, etc, relationships; and their need (overlooked by the Commission) for conceptually as well as factually difficult inquires as to the survival of an economic advantage or disadvantage on the relationship's breakdown ('tracing'). It was therefore good news when, on 6 September 2011, the government announced its intention not to seek the proposals' implementation.

[64] See Gardner (n 51) 437–9. There is also a question whether the law can properly redress unjust enrichment by the imposition of a proprietary rather than a personal remedy (a constructive trust being proprietary): *ibid* 439.

It is accepted that someone receiving money is thereby enriched, but someone receiving some other kind of boon, such as a service, may be able to say that they are not benefited by it, as given the choice they would not have taken it, at least for payment.[65] In our context, the boon will as often be of the latter kind (eg work on the house) as of the former (eg help towards mortgage repayments). But it should nonetheless qualify as an enrichment, since it will usually be freely accepted by the defendant, who will therefore not then be able to deny its value to him. Indeed, the fact that the parties are in an emotional relationship – even if not a materially communal one – should perhaps itself block off any contrary argument.

So there may be no reason in principle why a claimant's non-financial contributions should not count, as well as his financial ones.[66] But viewing non-financial contributions in terms of the extent to which they enrich the defendant may not do them appropriate justice. Consider a case where you run our home and care for me and our children, while I go out to work. Assuming we view these activities on your part as enriching me, how do we quantify this enrichment? Most obviously, by seeing them as saving me the money that I would otherwise have to pay towards hiring someone to do them, giving you a claim equivalent to the latter. But work of this kind is generally not well paid, so your entitlement, calculated on this basis, may well be smaller than you could have gained by going out to work and making a financial contribution.[67] And the market price of your efforts is only one aspect of their full significance: done by you, work of this kind will have qualities different from those brought to it by others, which cannot be well expressed in pounds and pence. So although, as we have seen, your contributions can fairly readily be seen as enriching me, the lens through which they have to be seen for this purpose is not a sympathetic one; and moreover, given societal roles, it is one that tends to present more of a problem to women than to men. We may, however, take some comfort from the fact that these concerns, stemming from differences in the nature of the parties' contributions, are likely to arise most pressingly in cases where the parties' relationship is materially communal, and will therefore require treatment on that basis (ie via a matrimonial relief-style approach) anyway.

To establish an unjust enrichment claim, the enrichment – of whatever kind – has then to be 'unjust'.[68] This requirement is classically met by showing that

---

[65] See generally P Birks, *Unjust Enrichment* (2nd edn, Oxford, 2005) ch 3. But *cf* now *Benedetti v Sawiris* [2010] EWCA Civ 1427 (CA).

[66] They were, however, left out of account in the leading non-materially communal case, *Stack v Dowden* [2007] 2 AC 432 (HL) itself; the outcome reflected only the claimant's respective monetary contributions. In view of the point made in the present paragraph, however, it may have been significant that in that case, the greater such contributions, yielding a 65% share, were made by the woman.

[67] You might do better by pointing not to the value of your contribution to me, but to the cost to you of making it – notably, the loss of your career prospects. But an unjust enrichment analysis privileges the former, as capturing the extent to which *I am enriched*.

[68] See generally Birks (n 65) Pt III.

the claimant conferred it on the defendant by mistake, or under duress, or in some other such circumstance, meaning that his will was not fully behind it. This is not especially likely in our type of case. It is much more likely however, given the nature of the situation, that the claimant conferred the benefit with no particular thoughts at all. It is unclear whether, in general, so doing does or should render an enrichment 'unjust'. When the parties are not in an emotional relationship, an enrichment conferred without thought probably ought not to count as 'unjust': people (claimants) should probably be more alert in their own interests than to enrich others without thinking about what they are doing. But in the present context, the contrary seems very arguable. A claimant's emotional bond with a defendant may well mean that we after all sympathise with (indeed, rather approve of) his readiness to enrich the latter without circumspection, and do not penalise him for it by denying him a claim for unjust enrichment if the relationship should turn sour.

9.3.8 Genuine and Invented Common Intentions

To summarise the suggested understanding of the current law: if you are to have a share larger than your prima facie one (zero in a single name case, 50 per cent in a joint names case), the law requires us to have a genuine common intention that you should; but as to its quantum, will implement any genuine common intention we may have, but otherwise will impute, ie invent, a common intention (in such a way as to achieve 'fairness', as explained in §§ 9.3.5–9.3.7), and implement that.

Notice that the rules use a mix of genuine and invented common intentions, while distinguishing between them. But the business of inventing a common intention can be not so very different from that of discovering a tacit genuine one. The latter is necessarily somewhat speculative; the supposed 'discovery' may lie very much in the eye of the beholder. The similarity has even led some judges to equate the two.[69] Ultimately, they are wrong, as there must always be the possibility that the parties really did not address the issue, let alone agree upon it, even tacitly, yet one may be invented on their behalf.[70] But to the extent that they are right, the implication is not only that the quantum question may often be addressed either way and the same answer reached. It is also that, despite the alleged prior rule requiring a genuine common intention to depart from the claimant's prima facie share at all, in practice this intention too may be an invented one after all.[71] Meaning that

[69] See especially *Jones v Kernott* [2011] 3 WLR 1121, [34]–[36], [65]–[66] (SC). See too N Piška, 'Intention, Fairness and the Presumption of Resulting Trust after *Stack v Dowden*' (2008) 71 *MLR* 120, 127–8.

[70] *Jones v Kernott, ibid* [67], [89].

[71] This was probably the case in *Jones v Kernott, ibid* where the trial judge and the Supreme Court claimed to find a tacit but 'genuine' common intention to this effect . . . despite there being, according to the Court of Appeal, no evidential basis on which to do so: [2010] 1 WLR 2401, [81]–[83] (CA).

although a constructive trust of this kind may indeed arise from the parties' genuine common intentions, in reality it may equally, and probably more often, be effectively imposed by the court.[72]

It remains the case, however, that a genuine common intention, if present, will be effectuated. Why should this be? One might assume, for libertarian reasons: the parties' wishes should be respected, though it may be allowable to support these – as the law does – by filling in blanks on matters of detail, as by inventing an intention if necessary in respect of quantum.

While immediately intelligible at one level, however, this basic vision in terms of vindicating the parties' wishes does have a problem: how to explain the *legal effectiveness* of a common intention viewed thus. As we saw in § 9.3.1, if I had intended you to have a particular share in the house, and had put this intention in writing, I would have made an express trust (or expressly transferred the relevant part of my share to you) to the intended effect. According to the rules we have been considering, however, if I share my intention with you, the law gives effect to it in exactly the same way, but via a constructive trust, without need of writing. But is my sharing of my intention with you a sufficient reason to disapply the requirement of writing in this way?

At one time, the law required not only a common intention, but also reliance upon that intention on your part, to your detriment.[73] Certainly, this detrimental reliance provided a reason for the law to intervene, distinct from the – as we now see, problematic – invocation of the parties' will. But it did so only to the extent of rectifying your detriment. Sometimes this might mean giving you your expectation, ie enforcing the common intention as such. This would be the case where your detriment was the otherwise irrevocable loss of an opportunity which you had to secure your expectation in some other way: as where, in relying upon your agreement with me, you forewent a genuine chance to have a stake in a house of the relevant value by, say, becoming involved with a more reliable partner, or by acquiring such a stake on your own.[74] This would by no means always be the case, however. Where your detriment did not take this form, it afforded no reason to enforce your expectation.[75]

There is, however, a possible other non-will-based way in which to explain why our common intention might itself generate, and be effectuated by, a constructive trust. Even if they are not of the 'materially communal' variety, but all the more so if they are, the relationships that are central to this area of the law are trusting and collaborative – in a word, familial. As we are reminded

---

[72] For a tentative judicial suggestion that this be recognised and accepted, see *Jones v Kernott* [2011] 3 WLR 1121, [84] (SC).

[73] *Lloyds Bank plc v Rosset* [1991] 1 AC 107, 132 (HL).

[74] See Gardner (n 4).

[75] Compare the difficulty of explaining why there should be an expectation remedy in proprietary estoppel: § 8.4.3.

by the arguments of communitarians, there is a major interest in fostering such relationships, as more or less indispensable to human society.[76] One way of fostering them is by helping those involved in them to rely on undertakings given within them, without stopping to inquire whether it is safe to do so, or having to amass proofs of having done so. And a way of doing that is by a rule that such undertakings – our 'common intentions' – will be enforced as such, without further requirements by way of detrimental reliance or indeed writing.[77]

The communitarian perspective just introduced may in fact take us still further. It may lead us to the conclusion that, while we (and the law) should respect family understandings precisely because of their quality as such, we (and the law) should *not* respect them – as the current rules require – if, taking the wider picture into account, they harm the institution of the family. This might be the case, in particular, if they take the parties away from the full idea of 'equality' that, as we saw in § 9.3.6, the law would otherwise use in order to fix a materially communal couple's shares: as, for example, where a less-well-off woman gets into a relationship with a wealthy man, but agrees not to claim a full half share in his assets. The same might also be the case on account of republican arguments.[78] These urge us not to respect the parties' understanding if this perpetuates, or indeed worsens, the possibility of arbitrary domination which their different roles in the relationship – eg bread-winner, home-maker – may commonly engender. Adopting either of these perspectives would very often require the law to seek full 'equality' between the parties, and to do so of its own initiative, without waiting for them to agree, and indeed in disregard of any agreement they might have made to the contrary.[79]

---

[76] For communitarianism, see D Bell, 'Communitarianism' (2009), *Stanford Encyclopedia of Philosophy* (http://plato.stanford.edu/entries/communitarianism/), and further references there.

[77] There is a similarity here with the suggestion (L Fuller and W Perdue Jr, 'The Reliance Interest in Contract Damages' (1936–7) 46 *Yale LJ* 52, 61–2) that contractual expectations, not merely reliance losses, are enforced so as to encourage reliance on them in the context of trade. (See too J Finnis, *Natural Law and Natural Rights* (2nd edn, Oxford, 2011) 181–3.) The argument is all the stronger in our context of family relationships.

[78] For republicanism, see F Lovett, 'Republicanism' (2010) in *Stanford Encyclopedia of Philosophy* (http://plato.stanford.edu/entries/republicanism/), and further references there.

[79] Compare the communitarian and republican objections to the law's (will-based) respect for nuptial agreements: *Radmacher v Granatino* [2011] 1 AC 534, [78], [135]–[137], [187]–[193] (SC). Compare too the proposition (*Goodman v Gallant* [1986] Fam 106 (CA)) that, if the parties have shares under an *express* trust (ie the house has expressly been placed on trust for them both, in whatever proportions), these cannot be adjusted by a constructive trust, arising in the manner under discussion, to different effect; that is, the wish(es) of the person(s) establishing the express trust take precedence over all else. This has, however, now been doubted: *Clarke v Meadus* [2010] EWHC 3117, [42] (Ch D). Especially given the argument in the text, the latter seems the better view in principle. There is, moreover, no technical objection to it; there is nothing about an express trust that should make it immutable by subsequent legally significant occurrences, as much by the emergence of a constructive trust (and of the present, as much as of any other, kind) as otherwise (eg by proprietary estoppel: *ibid* [50], [56]).

9.3.9 The Nature of Family Property Rights

If you and I 'have a common intention' that you should have such-and-such a share in the house, you emerge with that share as a (constructive) trust right. That is to say, in a sole name case, I hold the house on (constructive) trust for you and myself, in our respective proportions; in a joint names case, we both hold the house on trust for ourselves, likewise.[80] The outcome has to be a trust right precisely because what you, and for that matter I, emerge with is a share in the ownership of the house.[81]

It is easiest to see this if we imagine that the house is in my sole name, but that you acquire a 100 per cent share in it. Broadly following the outline of a 'trust' given in § 9.1.1, the house is vested in me (the trustee); but because you now have your entitlement, I am under legal obligations, to the exclusion of any personal interest on my own part, to handle the house for your benefit (ie you are the beneficiary). As explained there, it is this last element that especially distinguishes a trust from other situations. Care is needed to see how it is also satisfied where, for example, the house is in my sole name (but essentially, everything is the same if it is in our joint names), but we have 50:50 shares. Then, I certainly have a personal interest *in my capacity as beneficiary*, alongside you; but I continue to have no personal interest *in my capacity as the legal owner, ie trustee*, which is the requirement under discussion.

A right arising in this way takes effect from the time of the facts generating it, ie from the time of the formation of our common intention. This proposition is firmly implicit in many decisions[82] where the issue at stake was whether the right (which, being a trust right, is in rem[83]) binds a subsequent disponee of the land in question. It is however problematic.

---

[80] Where we both have shares, we will usually do so as tenants in common as opposed to joint tenants. (For the two types of co-ownership, see § 15.2.2.) This will certainly be the case if the shares are unequal in size, for here there is no unity of interest; but also if equal, but arising from different sources, as where the house is in my name but a constructive trust arises giving you half of it, for here there is no unity of title (see § 15.2.4 for the need for these unities). (*Hurst v Supperstone* [2005] EWHC 1309, [11] (Ch D), to the contrary, is mistaken.) We will thus have our shares as joint tenants only if the shares are equal and arise from the same source, something which may occur only in the prima facie treatment of the joint names scenario, where our joint title to the house itself predicates a 50:50 beneficial sharing of it (§ 9.3.1). Such a joint tenancy would of course be severed (§ 15.2.6) by any change in the sizes of our respective shares, the constructive trust effecting this change constituting an 'act operating on' each of our shares, disrupting unity of title.

[81] If our relationship has broken down, your trust right, alias share in the ownership of the house, will most conventionally be vindicated by an order for the sale of the house and the payment of the proceeds to us each in our respective proportions (or sometimes, for the transfer of the whole house to you, probably on conditions reflecting my own interest). But, especially if your right is going to be shaped after the fashion of matrimonial relief (see § 9.3.6), there may in at least some cases be a call for periodical payments rather than a one-off transfer like this. A future question will be whether the constructive trust can be adapted to yield such an outcome.

[82] For example, *Williams & Glyn's Bank Ltd v Boland* [1981] AC 487 (HL); *Lloyds Bank plc v Rosset* [1991] 1 AC 107 (HL).

[83] Though while trust rights are in principle in rem (§ 16.4), in practice there are many impediments to their actually binding a disponee, leaving them not far off rights in personam. See § 16.8.2.

In § 8.5, when we discussed the equivalent issue in the context of proprietary estoppel, we saw that a lack of predictability as to relief is not properly
compatible with a rule that the resultant right is straightforwardly backdated
to the time of the underlying facts, especially as a right in rem: the discretion
means that the outcome is not sufficiently predictable to operate satisfactorily
in this way. We encounter the same problem in the present context. Here too
we find a lack of predictability. This is especially so if the courts maintain
the current opacity regarding 'fairness', as discussed in § 9.3.5. But it is also
the case even if we take it, and the courts make clear, that 'fairness' has the
meaning suggested in §§ 9.3.5–9.3.7. For various reasons considered there,
the latter does not deliver sharp results. Moreover, the results (especially as
regards the sizes of the respective shares) will often change over time, tracking movements in the factors controlling 'fairness', such as the parties' respective needs.

In the context of proprietary estoppel, the solution to such concerns was
suggested (in §§ 8.5.1–8.5.2) to be the use of the 'remedial constructive trust'.
This enables the court, in making its award, to decide whether to backdate
the award's effect to the time of the facts or to impose it only prospectively,
from the time of the decision; and also, if backdating it, to fine-tune its
impact, including on disponees. The same solution would be as appropriate
here.[84]

9.3.10 Human Rights

In reducing my prima facie share in our family home so as to give you a correspondingly larger share in the manner described, the law does of course
interfere with my enjoyment of my possessions, so (subject to issues about
horizontal effect: § 2.2) engaging ECHR First Protocol Article 1; and at least
potentially also with my home, engaging Article 8. So long as a satisfactory
explanation for the interference can be given, however, the interference should
without difficulty be seen as justified. The discussion above has suggested
such a satisfactory explanation – or rather, a set of satisfactory explanations,
some cumulative, others alternative. If they are denied, and no others offered
in their place (eg if one insists that 'fairness' means simply whatever the judge
wants it to mean on the day), then of course we have a problem.

---

[84] T Etherton, 'Constructive Trusts: A New Model for Equity and Unjust Enrichment' [2008]
CLJ 265 (and also 'Constructive Trusts and Proprietary Estoppel: The Search for Clarity and
Principle' [2009] *Conv* 104) contends that *Stack v Dowden* [2007] 2 AC 432 (HL) has already
introduced remedial constructive trusts to this area. In so saying, he appears to focus purely on
the discretionary state in which that decision has left the law as between the two principal parties,
as outlined in the text. The argument here, however, is that that is the problem, rather than the
solution. There is nothing in the current law to suggest that its awards can be fine-tuned as to
their impact, especially on disponees, in the way that true remedial constructive trusts can.

We also encounter a human rights dimension if we look at matters from the other direction – from your point of view. Take the sole name scenario. If the law were to deny you a share in our home despite your being in a materially communal relationship with me, or being in a non-materially communal but still emotional relationship with me and contributing to our domestic economy, it might very well engage and indeed violate ECHR Article 14. This requires that Convention rights – here, your right to your home, under Article 8[85] – be secured without discrimination on any illegitimate ground, including sex and property. There is a strong argument to be made that, in adhering to my prima facie sole ownership, the law would be discriminating against you on both these grounds. Property, because in denying you a share in our home the law would be aligning its bestowal or recognition of that boon too automatically with our prima facie property rights. And sex, because in the nature of these cases, you are likely to be a woman; and not merely coincidentally, but because, no doubt substantially as an incident of child-bearing exigencies, there exist discernible characteristically 'male' and 'female' roles in relationships, the former carrying with it the facility to acquire property rights to the exclusion of the latter.

And although perhaps less obvious, essentially the same could sometimes be said as regards the joint names scenario. If in this case you were limited to your prima facie 50 per cent share despite all the factors that the law does in fact take into account in giving you more, its neglect of those factors might once again involve discrimination against you on illegitimate grounds. Property, since here too the law would be connecting our home shares too rigidly to our prima facie property rights. And sex, because the law would once more be tending to neglect the characteristically 'female' role, which might for example entail dependent children commonly remaining with their mother after a parental separation, raising her need to something more than a half share.

For such reasons, then, the law not only violates no human rights of mine in maintaining rules such as those discussed in this group of sections; looking at the matter from your end, it really has no option but to maintain them.

---

[85] Perhaps also your right to peaceful enjoyment of your possessions, under First Protocol Art 1, *sed quaere*. In one sense, you have no possessions to enjoy: your whole complaint is that the law accords you no share. One might attempt to move past this objection by observing that the autonomous meaning of 'possessions' is wider than the domestic legal incidence of a 'right', but one would still need some basis on which to say that you do in these circumstances have a 'possession', and this does not appear straightforward. However, one might plausibly regard the family home as necessarily the (shared) 'possession' of both parties, regardless of their domestically recognised rights, or lack of rights, in it.

Part 3

The Individual Rights in Rem

In Part 1, noting that this book sets out to focus principally on the rights in rem and human rights that can exist in respect of land, we considered the nature of such rights, and went into some detail about how rights in rem behave as such. In Part 2 we went on to look at the ways in which rights in rem can arise; and in Part 3, which occupies the remainder of the book, we now explore the individual rights themselves.

Part 3 deals first, in Chapter 10, with ownership itself. This is a particularly important chapter. Not only is ownership a right in rem; envisioning it at all requires much thought about the very nature of 'property', which is therefore explored. After that come chapters on various more specific rights: leases (Chapter 11), mortgages (Chapter 12), easements (Chapter 13), restrictive covenants (Chapter 14) and beneficial interests under trusts (Chapters 15 and 16). The final chapter (Chapter 17) looks at licences, some of which are rights in rem, and some others of which once were, but which are otherwise in personam. The treatment of licences serves partly to illuminate the border that licences share with leases, but also as a context in which to look closely at the way in which the law answers the question whether a right should be in rem.

10

Ownership

10.1 The Idea of Ownership

10.1.1 The Paradigm of Ownership: *Dominium*

There is a paradigm idea of ownership; an idea that pops instinctively into our minds, before we stop to think about it. It supposes that an owner has rights to do anything he likes with the 'owned' asset, and can lose these rights by, but only by, his consent. That is to say, an owner has an unqualified legal power to use the asset, to exclude others from it, and to transfer it – or, in each case, not, if he so chooses.

This paradigm idea of ownership can be referred to by the Latin – Roman law – word '*dominium*'. It is unlikely, however, that any legal system, including the ancient Roman one,[1] ever did or would operate the idea in an unqualified way.[2] Certainly, as we are about to see, contemporary English law does not.[3] The concept of *dominium* is still useful to us, however, as an idea. Section 10.2 explores the way in which real-world ownership is the result of some sort

---

[1] See further P Birks, 'The Roman Law Concept of *Dominium* and the Idea of Absolute Ownership' (1986) *Acta Juridica* 1.

[2] Civil law jurisdictions operate a concept which is commonly referred to as '*dominium*', and represented as being of this kind. But of course it is not: such jurisdictions recognise the sorts of qualifications about to be discussed in the text. Differences between the civil law and English law approaches are thus in practical terms ones of degree (though they may rest on rather widely divergent conceptual foundations). (See further G Samuel, 'The Many Dimensions of Property' in J McLean (ed), *Property and the Constitution* (Oxford, 1999) ch 3.) The differences are perhaps most marked as regards the substantial fragmentation of ownership, a matter discussed in § 10.1.3. English law's experiments with this have certainly been more adventurous than the civil law's . . . but as we shall see, English law, having experimented, has now become more cautious, giving unitary ownership (ie *dominium*) greater emphasis after all.

[3] Likewise American law, to which much of the literature is directed. For references to many of the outstanding writings, leading us away from *dominium* in a number of interesting directions, see L Underkuffler, *The Idea of Property: Its Meaning and Power* (Oxford, 2003) 31 fn 77.

of balancing exercise between *dominium* and other ideas, whose claims conflict with it.

10.1.2   The Qualification of *Dominium*

Take even an uncomplicated asset like a pencil. There are few ways in which I may not use my pencil, but there are some: my ownership does not entitle me to commit a crime with it, say by using it to poke someone in the eye. I can give, sell or bequeath the pencil to someone else largely as I wish, but there are general restrictions on my power to alienate property when approaching bankruptcy, so as to protect my creditors, and on my power to neglect my family and dependants on my death. And while I will usually have the law on my side in objecting to others' behaviour tending to deprive me of the pencil, like all my assets it can be seized to pay my debts (in the organised manner known as bankruptcy), and for certain law enforcement and security reasons, and potentially by government expropriation (generally subject to the payment of compensation); and if someone does take the pencil from me, or damages or destroys it, there are certain restrictions (especially time limits) on my legal power to complain.

So while the law's construction of the ownership of a pencil does not diverge hugely from the paradigm idea, even in this simple case it certainly does not follow that idea entirely. When the asset is land, the picture is essentially similar, but with different emphases.[4] My right to recover my land from those who seek to steal it is in general better protected, for example, but there is a significantly higher chance of its being expropriated, under the standing arrangements for compulsory purchase. More restrictions arise upon what I can do with it, arising for instance from the environmental and planning regimes. It is also much more likely that other people will have individual rights demanding that the land shall, or shall not, be used in particular ways, such as a right entitling them – rather than me – to occupy it for a time, subject to paying me rent (a lease); or entitling them to cross it (an easement). It is wholly usual for my rights to the land to be qualified in such ways; yet we continue to think of me as 'owning' it.

So I may remain 'owner' while my rights actually fall short of the paradigm. Of course, the more my rights are limited in the ways described, the more difficult it becomes to view me as owner. (Section 10.3 considers whether there is a 'core' idea of ownership; a point beyond which we would stop using that term.) This difficulty is important not only linguistically, but also substantively. The limitations in question, for example, might make it impossible

---

[4] For discussion of some of the respects in which English law currently plays up and plays down the idea of unqualified ownership of land, and why, see K Gray and S Gray, 'The Rhetoric of Realty' in J Getzler (ed), *Rationalizing Property, Equity and Trusts – Essays in Honour of Edward Burn* (London, 2003) ch 10.

for me to extract full value from the land, or to sell it on terms enabling a buyer to do so. We might well see this as problematic, as diminishing liberty and damaging the market: see § 10.2.2. If we decide to accept it nonetheless, it should be because we believe that the negative effects of the relevant limitation are outweighed by countervailing advantages.

10.1.3 Fragmentation

English law allows *dominium* in an asset, especially land, to be explicitly divided between a number of different people. This phenomenon may be referred to as 'fragmentation'. It in fact occurs whenever a right in rem arises. Say for example I own a field. As things stand, you have no right to come on to it; my ownership allows me to exclude you. But if you now acquire a right of way over it, I can no longer do so. One can say that the right in question has been split off from my hitherto entitlement and passed to you; that my ownership has to that extent been fragmented. Notice that only rights in rem fragment ownership in this way. If I am obliged in personam to allow you to pass over my land, as where I contract personally with you to that effect, I have not fragmented my ownership; the entitlement I would pass to a transferee would remain unfragmented. In other words, fragmentation is controlled by the *numerus clausus* principle, so as to ensure that fragmentation is not on the whole injurious: see § 1.2.2.

So fragmentation can involve quite small fragments, such as rights of way. The details of rights such as this, and the arguments for allowing them to exist as ownership-fragments, will be reviewed in subsequent chapters. It is worth spending some time here, however, on three of the grandest instances of fragmentation; cases where the fragments are so large that we may hesitate, or even refuse, to say that there remains an 'owner' at all. These involve estates, trusts and leases.

The first of these involves – or involved: as explained below, it has now been discontinued – repackaging the ownership of the land (as opposed to the land itself), so as to make it available in a number of differently sized pieces, known as 'estates', which can then be held by different people. By this expedient, the ownership of the land (again, as opposed to the land itself) can be divided amongst a number of holders.

The largest estate corresponds to ownership itself. It is called the 'fee simple absolute in possession'.[5] So when we say that someone 'owns' some land, this can usually be translated into a statement that he holds the fee simple

---

[5] On this and associated issues, see further J Harris, 'Ownership of Land in English Law' in N MacCormick and P Birks (eds), *The Legal Mind – Essays for Tony Honoré* (Oxford, 1986) ch 9.

absolute in possession[6] in it, or, most properly of all, that 'he holds it in fee simple absolute in possession'.

An example of a smaller estate is a 'life estate'. If you have a life estate in a piece of land, it means that you have rights in it only for the duration of your life. But if smaller estates are created and held by different people in this way, these smaller estates must always add up to ownership, ie to the fee simple absolute in possession. So if I, hitherto having the fee simple absolute in possession, decide to give you a life estate, there must also be someone who has the fragment of my fee simple absolute in possession (which, comprising full ownership, goes on for ever) that will be left after your death. This might be John. John's fragment is called the 'fee simple absolute in remainder'.[7]

On your death, John becomes as much owner as I originally was (ie his fee simple absolute in remainder becomes a fee simple absolute in possession). But until then, neither you nor John straightforwardly has a full owner's rights, in the way that I did with my original fee simple absolute in possession. You are in a sense owner, but only for your life; while John is also in a sense owner, but only in waiting. Although your interest certainly allows you to do things with the land (eg live on it, farm it, rent it out), the need to think of John coming after you means that you cannot treat it straightforwardly as your own (eg cut down its trees, extract its minerals, and keep all the proceeds for yourself).

As well as dividing ownership into sequential fragments in this way, it is also possible to divide it (again, as opposed to the physical land itself) concurrently. For example, I might make you and John co-owners of the land: ie give you and John the fee simple absolute in possession to hold together.[8] Here again, obviously, neither of you alone is, or can behave as, full owner of the land.

The second major means of fragmenting ownership – which continues to form part of the law – involves the land being held on a trust. We shall look at trusts more fully in Chapters 15 and 16. But broadly speaking, a trust is 'a situation in which property is vested in someone (a trustee), who is under legally recognised obligations, at least some of which are of a proprietary kind [ie in rem], to handle it in a certain way, and to the exclusion of any personal interest'.[9] The obligations can be configured in many ways, but one of these is to benefit two or more people in a manner analogous to one of the forms of fragmentary ownership just discussed.

---

[6] Sometimes, this is abbreviated to 'fee simple'. But as we shall see, there are other kinds of 'fee simple', such as the 'fee simple absolute in remainder', so this abbreviation is imprecise.

[7] Or simply 'the remainder'; and John is called the 'remainderman'. The text has referred only to these two kinds of estate; there are various others besides. The combinations of estates, too, can be more complex than in the example given. In every case, however, it remains true that the estates must add up to a fee simple absolute in possession.

[8] Or indeed, I might use both sequential and concurrent estates simultaneously, as where I give you and John together an estate in the land for the life of the first of you to die, and give Kate and Liam jointly the fee simple absolute in remainder.

[9] S Gardner, *An Introduction to the Law of Trusts* (3rd edn, Oxford, 2011) 2.

So say I own some land. I may make myself trustee of it, or the law may impose a trust of it upon me. Then, although I technically continue to have the fee simple absolute in possession in the land, I have no rights as a result: for – as noted – the obligations I owe as trustee must be so great as to exclude all personal interest on my part.[10] The obligations may take various forms, but one could be to use the land for your benefit for your life, and thereafter for John's benefit; or for your and John's benefit concurrently – either way, then, to let you and (whether later or simultaneously) John live on the land, or receive the income it generates. Here we see a substantial fragmentation of ownership again. Although I have the fee simple absolute in possession, my lack of rights means that I myself certainly cannot be called the owner of the land. The rights which my obligations give you and John add up to something like ownership; but they are split between the two of you.[11]

It may be useful for the law to allow the ownership of land to be divided in the ways permitted in these two ways (trusts and estates): for example, so as to provide for successive generations of a family to have interests in their ancestral estate or, less exotically, for a couple to co-own their house. But there are disadvantages too. For example, on the face of it, the land's exploitability and hence marketability is damaged. Since, in our various examples, the ownership rights are divided between your and John's interests, someone wanting to exploit the land fully, and therefore to acquire it with full ownership (ie the right to do everything an owner could do with the land, and straight away), would seem to need to buy from both of you. This might be reasonably straightforward, but could easily be more difficult: as where you are amenable to sale but John is not (a possibility which obviously grows as I divide the ownership of the land among larger numbers of people), or indeed – for this is a possible version of the sequential arrangement – where John has not yet been born.

If this problem went unaddressed, we might conclude that the disadvantages could well outweigh the advantages, and so (via the *numerus clausus* principle: § 1.2.2) that such rights should not be able to exist in rem, ie as fragments at all. But the law has developed a solution. In the case of a trust, I, as trustee, have the power to sell the full ownership of the land, simultaneously 'overreaching' the rights under it, ie converting them into rights in the money I receive in exchange for the land. The idea of overreaching is considered in more detail in §§ 16.5–16.6, but the key point is that it allows ownership to be fragmented as described, *but re-assembled for the purposes of a sale*. This

---

[10] Though it is possible for me to be trustee for a group of people that includes myself, in which case I shall have rights in the latter capacity.

[11] Although the example in the text involves fragmented ownership, trusts are not always configured in this way. Sometimes, indeed, while the trustee continues to have no rights, *nobody else does either*. For example, I may hold the land on trust so as to house an art gallery. Then, ownership simply disappears. But this raises the same kind of difficulty as fragmentation, namely the prima facie destruction of the land's marketability; to which the law has responded in the same way, by the device of overreaching, described below.

device operates only where a trust is used, however. There is no equivalent to it where the ownership is divided into fragmentary estates ... except that the latter possibility was abolished (via *numerus clausus* thinking) in the last century, all such ventures being now channelled through the trust route, to which overreaching does apply.[12]

The third large-scale way in which the law allows the ownership of land to be fragmented is by creating a lease. Say I own a house, and lease it to you for 10 years. The exact nature of a lease is explained in Chapter 11, but in essence you thereby acquire, for the 10 years, the right to occupy the house and to exclude all others, including me; and you can normally transfer this right to someone else. You usually have to pay me rent, and you may have certain other obligations (especially regarding the house's upkeep) as well, but it is fair to view you as the house's owner for the 10 years, while I of course will once again be its unqualified owner thereafter. In the meantime, I, retaining the freehold in the land, may be referred to as its 'owner', but this is apt only in the sense that I continue to have the bare title to it, plus, generally, a right to your rent.

On the face of it, this arrangement is very like that which I create when I give you a life estate, then John – or more especially myself – a fee simple absolute in remainder. As we have seen, the law has concluded that the disadvantages of the latter arrangement make it unacceptable, and that it needs to take effect instead via a trust, with the latter's facility for overreaching the fragmentary interests so as to permit transfer of full ownership after all. The law continues to allow the creation of leases, however. If I have leased the house to you for 10 years, for that period I simply cannot transfer full ownership. I can of course sell my own interest, but until the 10 years have elapsed the buyer will be bound by your rights, as a sitting tenant, just as I was.

Why does the law not insist on overreaching here too? Presumably because (once again, remember *numerus clausus* thinking) the usefulness of leases in allowing temporary ownership of land, especially on a rental basis, is seen as outweighing the damage that this entails. The usual presence of rent surely makes a difference. Someone might well want to buy the land even with a sitting tenant, precisely so as to receive the income, in a way that could not occur if he acquired only a trustee's title to the land, with the trust obligations still attached: as we have seen, a trustee cannot personally benefit at all. At the same time, as we shall see in § 16.5.3, the susceptibility of trusts themselves to overreaching has varied over the years, and is nowadays less than it once was. This too is a reflection of the social value of the rights concerned: today, trusts of land commonly arise where a couple own their home, plainly a useful application. The suppression of the facility to create fragmentary estates occurred when the dynastic applications to which it was classically put ceased to be perceived as meriting the damage that it entailed.

---

[12] This is the effect of the Law of Property Act 1925 ss 1(1) (for sequential arrangements) and 34 and 36 (for concurrent ones).

10.1.4 'Anti-Property'

Now let us consider a seemingly different kind of qualification to paradigm ownership.

Say I own a house, but a colony of bats lives in its roof. I wish to turn the roof space into an extra bedroom, but I find that environmental laws forbid me from doing so. In other words, my ownership interest has been curtailed by laws that exist to protect the environment. These laws can be described as 'anti-property', as capturing the idea that they fight against my 'property' interest.[13]

Any kind of rule that affects my ability to use, exclude or transfer my property can be said to represent an 'anti-property' interest. This section will outline some of the most common types of such rules. We can loosely divide them into regulations that deprive me of my property entirely, those that constrain the use I can make of my property, and those that limit my ability to exclude people from my property. But this is merely a useful way of discussing the kinds of rule, not a conceptually significant division.

First, rules that operate to deprive me of my property entirely. My land may be subject to confiscation if it has been purchased with the proceeds of crime[14] or if I am suspected of being involved in terrorism.[15] Less dramatically, my land may be subject to expropriation in order to make way for a state-sponsored building project, such as a motorway, high-speed rail line, or even – it would seem – a golf course.[16] I may also be deprived of my property by the operation of the doctrines that we noticed in § 1.1.2. Say I have a right of way over some land.[17] My right will be curtailed if the land over which it exists is sold before my right has been registered, or has otherwise had the chance to operate as an overriding interest under the Land Registration Act 2002. If this happens my right will not affect a disponee of the land. Where applicable, the traditional doctrine of bona fide purchase without notice worked to similar effect: my right, being in rem, had the potential to bind any disponee, but failed to bind this one, because he was a bona fide purchaser of the land in question for value and without notice of the right.

Second, limitations on the way in which I can use my property. Environmental law limitations derive from a complex body of international[18]

---

[13] In discussions of this sort, 'ownership' is usually referred to as 'property'. Where this term is used, it certainly includes ownership – our present concern – but it also includes other kinds of lesser interest. For example, if I am the tenant rather than the freehold owner of the house in which the bats live, my 'property' will be my lease. The same discussion as to its curtailment by anti-property interests would ensue.

[14] Proceeds of Crime Act 2002.

[15] Terrorist Asset-Freezing etc Act 2010.

[16] See K Gray, 'Recreational Property' in S Bright (ed), *Modern Studies in Property Law, Volume 6* (Oxford, 2011) ch 1.

[17] This counting as my 'property': n 13.

[18] At a European level see for example the Environmental Impact Assessment Directive (85/337/EEC, amended and extended by 97/11/EEC and 2003/55/EC). At a global level see eg the

and national[19] rules. They may, for example, prevent me from using my land to dump waste,[20] or from harming endangered animals or their habitat on it.[21] It is this type of rule that means I may not be able to convert my roof space into an extra bedroom if this would mean disturbing the bats which live there. Similar restrictions may arise in the name of the protection of national heritage: there may be things that I cannot do to my house if it is particularly old, or is of historical or cultural interest in some defined way.[22] Even if my house is not so protected, my ability to alter it structurally may be limited by planning laws and building regulations.[23] I am also subject to wide-ranging restrictions imposed by the tort of nuisance, which prevents me from using my land in a way which unreasonably interferes with my neighbours' enjoyment of their land.[24]

Third, limitations on my ability to exclude people from my property. In Chapter 2 we saw that my right as owner to determine who may live in my property can be curtailed if someone else has a right to call my property their 'home' under ECHR Article 8. My land may also be subject to public access rights. For example, if my land includes downs, moors, heaths or coastal land the public have a 'right to roam' on it, subject to certain guarantees and exceptions.[25] Another situation where it seems that I do not have complete discretion to exclude the public from my land is where my land is 'quasi-public'. If I own a shopping mall, for example, I may not have the absolute right to exclude people from my mall. Since shopping malls are places of recreational social activity, there may be a protection from arbitrary or discriminatory exclusion. Such protection certainly exists where my right of control derives from statutory authority; an airport authority, for example, can exclude visitors only 'if the circumstances are such as fairly and reasonably to warrant it'.[26] It has been argued that a similar rule now prevails for private rights of control too.[27] It is not clear that there is sufficient authority

Convention on International Trade in Endangered Species of Wild Fauna and Flora (CITES), as supplemented at EU level by the Endangered Species Regulation (338/97).

[19] See eg the Control of Pollution Act 1974.

[20] Environmental Protection Act 1990.

[21] Wildlife and Countryside Act 1981; Conservation (Natural Habitats, &c) Regulations 1994 (SI 1994/2716). See C Rodgers, 'Reforming Property Rights for Nature Conservation' in P Jackson and D Wilde (eds), *Property Law: Current Issues and Debates* (Aldershot, 1999) ch 3.

[22] Planning (Listed Buildings and Conservation Areas) Act 1990.

[23] eg Town and Country Planning Act 1990; Building Act 1984.

[24] This prevents me from doing things on my land that unreasonably lessen my neighbours' enjoyment of their land, such as activities that make too much noise, create unpleasant smells, or generate debris, especially when these are not in keeping with the neighbourhood.

[25] Countryside and Rights of Way Act 2000. The public are only allowed to use my land for the purposes of open-air recreation and must refrain from activities that have a high impact on the land, such as horse-riding, hunting, swimming, cycling and lighting fires. Some 'qualifying' land is exempt, such as ploughed land, gardens, quarries, golf courses and racecourses. For a helpful discussion of the implications of this legislation see J Anderson, 'Countryside Access and Environmental Protection: an American View of Britain's Right to Roam' (2007) *ELR* 241.

[26] *Cinnamond v British Airports Authority* [1980] 1 WLR 582, 588 (CA).

[27] See K Gray, 'Equitable Property' (1994) 47 *CLP* 157, 180.

to state this firmly, but at the lowest an owner of a quasi-public location can-not take for granted his ability to control who enters and remains on his property.

10.1.5 Two Kinds of Qualification?

Sections 10.1.3–10.1.4 have thus discussed, under the titles of 'fragmentation' and 'anti-property', two sets of cases in which we find paradigm property to be qualified. This section asks whether we should want to speak of 'two sets of cases' in this way, or whether it is better to see the qualification of para-digm property as a more unitary phenomenon.

One might think that the distinction between the two 'sets' tracks the distinction between the limitation concerned being created consensually (ie the hitherto owner chooses, or agrees to, the limitation in question), or non-consensually (ie it is imposed on him from outside). For example, when I qualify my ownership of my house by granting you a lease over it, remaining landlord myself, I consensually create a limitation upon my ownership. When, on the other hand, I learn that I cannot build an extension to my house because planning permission rules forbid me to, the limitation is one that I have not consensually created.

We might well want to distinguish instances of limitation along these lines. It remains true that both produce qualifications to paradigm ownership, which is why they are discussed together here at all. But consensual limita-tions can simultaneously be presented as not really limitations of ownership at all, but as manifestations of the owner's ability, as a facet of his ownership, to deal with his property as he likes. (Albeit that this does, of course, diminish his ability to do as he likes with it in future ... and certainly also diminishes the ability of his successors to do as they like with it, without any question of consent on their part.) So this seems a potentially significant distinction, for at least certain purposes. But it is not the same as the distinction so far drawn here, between fragmentation and 'anti-property'. Although the example of a consensual limitation just given, involving the creation of a lease, features fragmentation, and the example of a non-consensual limitation, involving planning permission, features 'anti-property', it does not have to be thus. Some instances of fragmentation are not consensual: for example, I could end up holding my property on trust not because I choose to, but because the law says I do, for some other reason (ie under a 'constructive trust': § 9.1). Equally, some 'anti-property' effects are consensual, as where I am a farmer who voluntarily participates in a countryside protection scheme in return for payment.

So fragmentation and 'anti-property' are not to be differentiated along this axis. Their divergence is of a different kind. It is that fragmentation operates within the traditional understanding of property, while 'anti-property' operates externally to it. So far as fragmentation is concerned, this is because the *dominium* in 'my' land is here divided between myself and one or more specific other people who thus take other rights in rem over it (eg a tenant); all the various fragments thus remain the concern of the traditional understanding of property. By contrast, 'anti-property' limitations corrode *dominium* in a different way; often so as to mark some more general claim (eg the public interest behind the planning rules), but even where specific to a particular person (eg an ECHR claim), by definition not by generating additional rights in rem.

So the distinction between 'fragmentation' and 'anti-property' can certainly be described, quite intelligibly, in this way. But there seems to be no more to it than that. It does not actually seem to matter when we come to think about whether it should be possible to qualify *dominium*, and why. For the remainder of this chapter, then, we shall generally treat the two together, often under the single term 'anti-property'.

10.2 Fixing the Scope of Ownership

It is clear, then, that in the real world, while paradigm ownership – *dominium* – can certainly be identified as an idea, it never represents anyone's actual rights. We seen various ways in which, entirely routinely, it is in practice cut back to some smaller kind of entitlement, albeit that this is often called 'ownership' too.[28]

The next question is: how then is the balance between paradigm property and anti-property delineated? That is, how do we determine the line to which paradigm ownership should be cut back in reflection of countervailing demands? This group of sections addresses this question.

10.2.1 Paradigm Property's Power

Note the assumption that this question makes. Saying that paradigm property, or *dominium*, is put into a 'balance' with countervailing considerations, or that it is 'cut back' in reflection of them, suggests that it possesses weight, or occupies space, in the same way as they do. To return to the example of my

---

[28] Underkuffler (n 3) ch 3 describes this duality in the idea of 'ownership' well. She refers to the paradigm sense, or something like it, as the 'common conception' (thereby usefully capturing the fact that it is what generally springs first to mind), and to the qualified, real-world, sense as the 'operative conception'.

roof space that is home for a colony of bats: when it comes to be decided to what extent I must respect the bats' interests, it assumes that the fact of my 'ownership' of the house *counts for something*, ie gives me a claim, in opposition to the claim that it must be preserved as a bat habitat. The idea is thus that, while unqualified *dominium* is never encountered in the real world, as opposed to the realm of ideas, it is far from a straw man. On the contrary, it has dialectical power; that is, it claims respect, possesses persuasive force, against the considerations which would limit it.[29]

There are clear indicators that English law recognises and reflects this position.[30] The most obvious is the fact that property has been recognised as a human right in Article 1 of the First Protocol to the ECHR, signed and ratified by the UK and transposed into UK law in the Human Rights Act 1998.[31] A second indicator is the *numerus clausus* principle, discussed in §§ 1.2.1–1.2.2, which supposes that the paradigm of property is so important that any incursions on it must be accepted only where there is sufficient justification in their favour to outweigh the harm that they do.

A third indicator is the direction of travel of land registration. The principal vehicles for this development have been the Land Registration Acts of 1925[32] and, replacing the latter, 2002. The aim is to produce greater stability of title, by stipulating that the position regarding the title to the land is what the register says it is. The full working out of this idea has taken some time to evolve. It can certainly be seen in the 1925 Act, but in an inchoate form, with many tensions between the position under the pre-existing rules and the new logic left unresolved.[33] It is more confidently embedded in the 2002 Act, which is said (see § 3.3.1) to involve not 'registration of title' but 'title by registration'.

[29] See further J Harris, *Property and Justice* (Oxford, 1996) ch 6. (Harris focuses not on paradigm property as such, but on something a little less rarefied; but his argument is none the weaker, possibly all the stronger, for that.)

[30] For a chronicle of similar indicators in the United States, see Underkuffler (n 3) 38–46.

[31] We should not place any real significance on the fact that this right appears in a Protocol as opposed to the main body of the ECHR. This is probably a result of the politically difficult climate in which the ECHR was negotiated. It is not surprising that, in the height of the Cold War, capitalist countries on the one hand and communist countries on the other could not reach an agreement on what a right to property should look like. The important point is that rights enshrined in Protocols are of the same status and effect as rights that appear in the main body of the Convention.

[32] And before that, the Land Transfer Act 1875. For the context of these early statutes, see A Offer, *Property and Politics, 1870–1914: Landownership, Law, Ideology and Urban Development in England* (Cambridge, 1981); J Anderson, *Lawyers and the Making of English Land Law 1832–1940* (Oxford, 1992); A Offer, 'Lawyers and Land Law Revisited' (1994) 14 *OJLS* 269; J Anderson, 'The 1925 Property Legislation: Setting Contexts' in S Bright and J Dewar (eds), *Land Law – Themes and Perspectives* (Oxford, 1998) ch 4. These accounts explore the reasons why those involved in the development of the 1925 Act may have taken the positions they did. But the gist of the Act – and of other reforms made in the late 19th and early 20th centuries, eg in the area of substantially fragmented ownership (§ 10.1.3) – was to the effect described in the text.

[33] See also A Pottage, 'The Originality of Registration' (1995) 15 *OJLS* 371; and further, 'Evidencing Ownership' in Bright and Dewar (eds) *ibid*, ch 5.

The principal icon of, and vehicle for, the 'title by registration' vision is the 2002 Act's electronic conveyancing project, discussed in §§ 2.2.4 and 5.4.5, whereby (at least some, but maybe all) rights would be able to arise at all only if and when they are (electronically) entered on the register. In the same vein are the Act's changes to the rules about adverse possession. Under the 1925 Act it was still possible for the registered owner of the land to lose it to you, via the old adverse possession doctrine, if you behaved as though you owned it for 12 years. But as explained in § 7.2.2, under the 2002 Act he will lose it to you only if, in most cases, he fails to prevent this. While a vestige of the possibility of adverse possession thus remains, the emphasis is much more firmly on the idea that if someone is registered as owner, he is (therefore) secure.[34]

It is true that registration does not even guarantee security more generally: as we saw in § 3.3.2, there is always the possibility of the register being amended so as to correct a 'mistake'. But the scope of this possibility is not such as to make us hesitate about viewing a registered owner as indeed owner. This is at least partly because 'mistakes' are in practice very rare (the Registry claim that virtually all their entries are correct); the picture would be very different if registered 'owners' lost their land on a daily basis. It is partly, too, the result of the protection given to an owner in possession. A given correction would commonly injure such an owner more, because of the dimension added by the fact of possession, than the same correction would injure one not in possession. Accordingly, such correction is not permitted unless the mistake was the registered owner's own fault,[35] or it would be unjust not to correct it.[36]

A fourth indicator is that not only do the organised modes of acquiring a right over someone else's land (see Chapters 5–6) demand the latter's consent, but so arguably, to at least some degree, do the disorganised modes (Chapters 7–9).[37] This is important because where an owner consents to another taking rights over his property, we can see this as *giving effect to* his property interest (ie voluntarily giving aspects of it away is one of the very facets of his ownership), rather than curtailing it. Even if consent turns out not to be an absolute requirement, the fact that these modes of acquisition at the very least hint at it demonstrates a commitment to the respectful recognition of the owner's property.

---

[34] See Law Commission, *Land Registration for the Twenty-First Century – A Consultative Document* (Law Com No 254, London, 1998) para 10.11; *Land Registration for the Twenty-First Century – A Conveyancing Revolution* (Law Com No 271, London, 2001) para 14.3.

[35] '. . . unless . . . he has by fraud or lack of proper care caused or substantially contributed to the mistake . . .'.

[36] Land Registration Act 2002 Sch 4 paras 3(2), 6(2).

[37] There is some controversy over this point. Some people argue that consent has no role to play in prescription (see the Law Commission, *Making Land Work: Easements, Covenants and Profits à Prendre* (Law Com No 327, London, 2011), paras 3.120–3.122). It is further suggested, in §§ 9.3.8 and 8.4.5, that at least some family property constructive trusts, and one of proprietary estoppel's projects, do or should not truly require consent, but are instead founded on the moral implications of the parties' relationship – but there is a level of consent in terms of getting into the relationship in the first place.

10.2.2 The Sources of Paradigm Property's Power

So paradigm property matters: not because we encounter it on the ground (as we saw in §§ 10.1.2–10.1.4, we do not), but as an idea that possesses power, claims respect. It is important to see why this should be the case. And not just out of interest, but because when one comes to decide on the extent to which property should yield to anti-property, it is the *arguments for* each, and their relative strength, that should determine the outcome.

There is no simple answer. Ownership – or property – appears to be seen as mattering for a number of different reasons.

Perhaps the most commonly cited comes from the centre of liberalism's libertarian tradition. Ownership serves autonomy interests by maximising the freedom that people have in relation to the world around them.[38] Property maximises your freedom both by securing your basic life needs, so that you are free to pursue higher objectives, and by contributing to those higher objectives in terms of culture, aesthetics and personal space.[39] We could even view property as being one of the baseline distinguishing features between humanity and the (rest of the) animal kingdom: manipulation of the physical world to produce social life, including housing and wealth, being said to be a uniquely and universally human trait.[40]

A rival, or at least complementary, liberal perspective is the republican one, requiring freedom from the possibility of arbitrary domination, ie imposition by others. This too supports ownership. So far as my use of things is concerned, I am maximally free from arbitrary domination by others when I own them. Here, ownership is not merely a means to liberty, but an instantiation of liberty in itself, *making* it true that, in the sphere in question, I am my own master, subject to no one else's whim.

Ownership is valued also in other, more focused ways. For example, for the support it gives to an individual's moral constitution. It accords us a vehicle by which to develop and express such virtuous human characteristics as responsibility, prudence and self-reliance, and generally to exercise the capacity to make autonomous decisions about the direction of our lives.[41] These ideas can be seen in a number of more concrete arguments and policies, as diverse as the idea that developing countries are better aided by the provision of the capital wherewithal to establish their own infrastructure than by any

---

[38] 'The world around them' includes in particular, for present purposes, land, chattels and natural resources.

[39] See J Penner, *The Idea of Property in Law* (Oxford, 1997) 49.

[40] See C Gosden, *Prehistory – A Very Short Introduction* (Oxford, 2003) ch 3. But is it not more realistic to see this as at most a matter of degree? Do we not find at least a significant manifestation of the same trait in eg bowerbirds? Does it matter if humans cannot be categorically distinguished from a class comprising 'other animals' in this or any other way?

[41] See generally J Waldron, *The Right to Private Property* (Oxford, 1988), discussing previous writers such as Hegel and Kant.

form of 'dole'; the 'right to buy' scheme, allowing council tenants who have been living in their rented council house for a qualifying period of time to buy the house from the local authority at less than the market price; and the preoccupation of the law of trusts to maximise – bring as close as possible to absolute ownership – the rights of beneficiaries.[42] Such arguments and policies at least align with the view that it is degrading simply to give hand-outs, because controlling, and so owning, the means to one's own prosperity is an important aspect of self-worth.

Again, ownership can be aligned with a conception of human dignity which focuses on rank. The thesis is that whereas society used to be composed of a hierarchy of ranks (from noble to peasant to slave), we now think of there being a single rank of 'human beings'. What has occurred is in fact a levelling-up of rank – a universalisation of high rank – such that privileges historically reserved for those of high status now belong also to the common man.[43] The significance of this for our purposes is that in the past, property rights were associated uniquely with the ruling classes, whereas in modern times, to own property is an important status symbol for all. Thus, where castles were once the preserve of the nobility, now any 'Englishman's home is his castle' – or at least, we aspire for it to be. The 'right to buy' venture seems to connect with this too, as does the more general idea of a 'property-owning democracy'.

Ownership also has a profound economic importance. Being owner of a thing maximises my ability to trade it in the market and, according to utilitarian economic theory ('economic liberalism'), this maximises overall wealth. Having exclusive rights over something also provides me with the best incentive to improve it, by working on it or investing in it.[44]

Finally, however, it should be noted that at least some of these arguments for ownership also offer arguments against it, and they can also conflict among themselves. For example, in republican terms: to the extent that I am recognised as owning something in which others have an interest, I am able to exercise arbitrary domination over them. And in libertarian terms: in a world where resources and space are limited, respecting my freedom – allowing me to use, or not use, my thing however I like – will sooner or later mean disrespecting others' freedom (eg because I contaminate their water supply), and/or their interests in shaping their own lives (eg because I insist on putting them on a 'dole'), and/or the good of the market (eg because I choose not to trade, but to hoard my wealth).

What we have seen in this section carries two overall messages for us. One is that ownership's dialectical power is likely to be very considerable, given the

---

[42] See Gardner (n 9) 216–29.

[43] J Waldron, 'Dignity and Rank' (2007) 48 *Eur J Sociology* 201; J Waldron, 'Dignity, Rank, and Rights: The 2009 Tanner Lectures at UC Berkeley' (2009) New York University Public Law and Legal Theory Working Papers, Paper 151, http://lsr.nellco.org/nyu_plltwp/15.

[44] See Penner (n 39) 63.

array of different bases for it, and the rooting of apparently all of them in some very fundamental considerations. The other, however, is that since the arguments for ownership are so protean and to some extent internally conflicted, we can expect the exercise of balancing them against the counterarguments to be at least a complicated one.

10.2.3 Balancing

The previous section shows that the paradigm idea of property or ownership – *dominium* – can readily be seen as possessing weight; that is, as supported by important underlying considerations, giving it such weight. Relevant antiproperty considerations obviously have their own countervailing weight, for their own reasons, too. The configuration of 'property' or 'ownership' that we encounter in the real world is the overall product of these weights. But how exactly is this product to be arrived at?

We have already, in Chapter 2, considered one situation in which this question arises, rather explicitly: that where a human rights claim prima facie arises – a rule protecting the right is 'engaged' – but it has to be decided whether the claim is ultimately successful. For example, I am the owner of a house, but it is your home, and you decline to leave when I require you to: Article 8 of the ECHR is engaged, and it then has to be decided whether or not my move against you is justified. As regards the qualified rights to property and home that we are concerned with in the present context, the official vehicle for making this decision is 'proportionality'. As we saw at various points in Chapter 2, the proportionality exercise is not always a simple balancing between all the relevant factors (the right on one side, other legitimate considerations – including, sometimes, the calls of other relevant rights – on the other); in particular, the exercise is often pre-loaded, usually against the claimed right, so as to become rather an inquiry after *dis*proportionality. Even this, however, ultimately demands reference to the relative weights of all the relevant considerations, so as to arrive at a conclusion.

But alongside the proportionality exercise in the human rights context, there are myriad other innominate ways in which paradigm ownership, *dominium*, is cut back in reflection of some countervailing consideration. We looked at some of them in §§ 10.1.3–10.1.4. In these too, a judgement is required so as to strike the balance between the arguments in favour of *dominium* and those supporting the countervailing interest.

Sometimes, as in the vindication of a human right, this judgement involves not only an up-front acknowledgement that my ownership is qualified, but also an ad hoc assessment and balancing of the arguments' weights in the individual case. This is so, for example, with the tort of nuisance, defining the ways in which my use of my land may and may not affect your use of yours; my interference with your interests counts as an actionable nuisance only if it is 'unreasonable' in the particular circumstances.[45] Similarly, the bona fide purchaser defence, which in some contexts controls my ability to enforce my rights in rem against disponees, depends upon case-by-case evaluation ('bona fide', 'without notice'). Likewise even some land registration rules, in particular that governing whether my right in rem binds a disponee as an overriding interest, by virtue of my being in actual and apparent occupation of the land in question (§ 3.1.2).

More often than not, however, the balance is pre-ordained and structured into the rule itself. The most obvious instances of this are taxation laws, where the balance – between the arguments for preserving the taxpayer's *dominium* over the wealth in question on the one hand, and those for eroding it on the other – is in effect stated in the rule that, for example, 30 per cent of one's income is payable in such-and-such circumstances. Other types of legislation with which we are concerned involve such generic balances too. In drafting the Countryside and Rights of Way Act 2000, creating the 'right to roam', the government balanced the impact upon affected landowners against the benefit to the public. Concluding that the former was low whereas the latter was high, the government found it appropriate to provide a right to roam within limits, without providing compensation for the relevant land-owners. This judgement was embedded in an across-the-board rule, any special circumstances already having been taken into account by the provision of exceptions to that rule.[46]

But whether the balancing is done generically alone, or in part ad hoc as well, it is important to recognise the elusiveness of the mechanism by which it is carried out. Remember our observation to this effect in § 2.5, concerning proportionality in the human rights context. We found that proportionality does not provide any clear answers to difficult balancing questions, such as arise when a project to build a high-speed railway would interfere with people's prima facie rights (in present terms, would require their 'property' to be defined so as not to obstruct the project). Proportionality appears as a buzz-word, but in fact the test is spongy and outcome-orientated. The situation is certainly no better in the case of the innominate balancing exercises that we find in the other kinds of situations that we have considered in this section. The introduction of the 'right to roam', for example, implies that the balance between the arguments for and against it was responsibly judged, and the conclusion reached that it represents a net good thing. But it is far from easy to explain the process by which this exercise can have been carried out, let alone convincingly to predict or justify the answer arrived at.[47]

---

[45] *Cambridge Water Co Ltd v Eastern Counties Leather Plc* [1994] 2 AC 264 (HL).

[46] Prior to the finalisation of the map showing areas accessible to the public, landowners could appeal to the Secretary of State against the designation of their land on the map. But such appeals could be made only on the ground that the land in question did not consist wholly of downland, heathland etc, and not on the ground that the incorrect balance had been struck between the interests of the landowner and the interests of the public.

[47] See too M Lee, 'What is Private Nuisance?' (2003) 119 *LQR* 298, for a discussion of the difficulties attending the invocation of 'reasonableness' in nuisance.

10.2.4 The Theory of Balancing

This section seeks to go into more depth about what the proper approach to balancing – if indeed there is one, as opposed to a mere free-for-all – might be.

The 'proper approach' can be envisioned via more than one theoretical model. Here we will explore two.

The first – let us call it the 'conflictual model' – sees real-world property rights as the outcome of a competitive interplay between *dominium* and the 'anti-property' interests. This interplay is a competitive one because, so this vision supposes, the justifications for *dominium* and 'anti-property' are not necessarily politically aligned; they pursue different kinds of project. Say the question is whether I should be able to evict you from a house I own, which is also your home. On the one hand we would have my *dominium*, the arguments underpinning which were sketched in § 10.2.1. On the other we would have the arguments for respecting your home. To at least a large extent, the two sets of arguments appear to talk across each other, and to be antagonistic to – conflict with – each other. If we take the arguments on one side as seriously as in themselves they claim we should, we have to short-change those on the other side.

The second model – the 'concordant model' – does not subscribe to this vision of conflict. Instead, it sees the whole idea of 'property', in all its facets, as derived from and justified by a single value, probably the service of human dignity. This single value exists at a higher level than ideas such as *dominium* and 'anti-property' and the arguments that might otherwise be put for each in isolation. The configuration of real-world property (say, the answer to the question whether I should be able to evict you) is determined by reference not to those ideas, but to the single value itself (ie by asking whether human dignity will be better served, overall, if I can evict you, or if I cannot?). That is to say, the concept of property is inherently qualified, compromised, as compared with *dominium*. It necessarily represents the optimal reading of human dignity. It reflects *dominium* only ever to the extent that the service of human dignity, read optimally, implies that it should.

The concordant model can be recognised as reflecting the thinking of Ronald Dworkin.[48] According to Dworkin, the law necessarily pursues a coherent conception of justice and fairness. Already imbued within it is the latent single right answer to any question that may be asked of it. The strong (apparently Dworkin's own) version of this theory holds that no conflict between interests is, therefore, ever really possible. If we perceive a conflict, it is merely because we have not yet correctly interpreted the higher-level single value. But a weaker position seems also to be tenable, according to which it is

---

[48] See eg R Dworkin, *Law's Empire* (Cambridge MA, 1986).

possible for a conflict to arise, but the single value can always be used to resolve it.[49] Say we refer to human dignity and conclude that human dignity is better served if I cannot evict you. Speaking in terms of the strong conception, we would say I *never had* a right to property that I could oppose to your claim to your home; my right was *always* limited to the extent necessary to respect your right. On the weaker conception, we would say, more modestly, that I did have a right to property, but that it came into conflict with your right to home, and, by reference to human dignity, the conflict is resolved in your favour. So the ideas of *dominium* and 'anti-property' are intelligible to this weaker version of the model, but not to the strong version. But what unites the two versions, so that they can both claim to describe the concordant model, is that they regard there as always being a right answer. Although one may perceive the boundary that this answer produces between *dominium* and 'anti-property' as veering here in the direction of the former, there in the direction of the latter, the boundary as a whole is the product of human dignity's net requirements, and as such can rightly follow only one line.[50]

Though clearly beguiling, the concordant model is problematic. The first difficulty arises when we try to formulate the higher-level ideal that it revolves around. In the discussion so far, we have assumed it to be optimal human dignity. But this is not really satisfactory, for it cannot engage with all the issues we need it to. Say the question is not whether I can evict you, a human, from my house, but whether I can evict a colony of bats; reference to 'human dignity' provides no protocol for taking proper account of the bats' interests.[51] (Of course, one might argue that, insofar as their well-being does not root in human dignity, bats do indeed not matter. But this argument should be made for its own anthropocentric sake, rather than slipped in via an assumption that the concordant model must be right and that its higher-level

---

[49] See K Möller, *The Global Model of Constitutional Rights* (Oxford, forthcoming).

[50] A caveat is needed. The account in the text is hopefully a fair account of Dworkin's analysis regarding judgments that are the business of *the law*; in his early works, Dworkin certainly distinguished between the realms of law and *policy*. What then is his thinking about judgments that are the business of policy? Apparently, they too need to be made with 'integrity'... and this appears to invoke the concordant model too. (See R Dworkin, *Justice for Hedgehogs* (Cambridge MA, 2011). Well worth reading for contrast is K Hammond, *Human Judgment and Social Policy – Irreducible Uncertainty, Inevitable Error, Unavoidable Injustice* (New York, 1996)... the title says it all.) If there is a difference between law and policy for Dworkin, it is that in law, the set of information from which the single value has to be induced is more heavily influenced by the positions that the law has taken hitherto; ie a judge has to be careful to achieve reasonable consistency between his judgment on the occasion in question, and previous legal utterances.

[51] Or say the question involves the property of a non-human, such as a company or a public body. Arguably, in any concordant model dialectic, such entities' interests should be appreciated in terms of their significance for the human stakeholders beyond them; eg companies' shareholders, and public bodies' taxpayers and clients. (Note that companies, but not public bodies, have the same rights as humans under the ECHR. See Art 4, allowing applications from 'any person, non-governmental organisation or group of individuals'; and *Agrotexim v Greece* (1996) 21 EHRR 250 (ECtHR), which – in discussing the question of whether shareholders of a company can be victims of a violation of the ECHR – takes for granted that the company itself can be so.)

ideal must be human, *sic*, dignity.) The higher-level ideal needs to be broader, encompassing all the kinds of interests that deserve to be taken into account, both human and other. Some important 17th-century thinkers,[52] for example, thought in terms of the whole order of Creation, seeing human property rights as an emanation of this (via its implied need for an ordered, economically beneficial regime in this respect), necessarily therefore enveloping an obligation to respect and nurture all other aspects of it.

A second, and even more troublesome, difficulty with the concordant model concerns its translation into the real world. When we are faced with resolving a concrete problem, it does not seem to make much difference whether we subscribe to the strong or the weaker version of the theory: in real-world terms it is clear that we are faced with a conflict which must be resolved. It is equally clear that the higher-level ideal to which we are supposed to refer in order to deal with this conflict – even if conceived restrictively, eg in terms only of human dignity – is so abstract that it cannot sensibly be thought to indicate a single right answer to our problem. And it is *necessarily* so: it is only by making the ideal so abstract as 'human dignity' – or (better *per se*, and so for present purposes even worse) 'the order of Creation' – that we can find a single value having a message for all the questions to which we need answers. To meet this difficulty, Dworkin gives the task of interpreting the ideal, and identifying the one right answer that it entails to any given problem, to 'Hercules', who is omniscient and infinitely wise. It is difficult to escape the conclusion that this is a fairy story. In the real world, an actual person, or group of persons, has to find the answer. Dworkin defends against this objection by saying that real-world decision-makers are merely supposed to *emulate* Hercules. But it means little to say that the answer is sitting there within the higher-level ideal if it is undiscoverable by those to whom it is addressed. And remember the failure that we saw in § 10.2.3 of those using proportionality, and its innominate siblings outside the human rights context, to produce any kind of explanation that coherently explains and predicts the cases. It would seem that not only is no one able to emulate Hercules: no one is even getting off the starting blocks.

Having reached this point, we may be naturally drawn to the conflictual model, because it expects and allows for the real-world difficulties. It openly acknowledges the conflict between paradigm property and 'anti-property'. The weaker version of the concordant model does so too, but what is crucially different about the conflictual model is that it does not demand that the conflict be solvable by reference to a single higher-level ideal; nor does it suggest that there is only one right resolution to the conflict. It accepts that the interests pursued by paradigm property on the one hand and 'anti-property' on the other may well defy fair comparison. This may not need to be the case

---

[52] Especially Locke, but also Grotius, Hobbes and Pufendorf. See S Coyle and K Morrow, *The Philosophical Foundations of Environmental Law* (Oxford, 2004) ch 2.

if both the property and 'anti-property' interests in question are based in the same value (to the extent, for example, that my right to property and your right to home both serve our autonomy interest[53]), but certainly it will often be the case. When it is, there will be no single right balance between the competing interests, such as my ownership of my land and your interest in it as your home, or the public's interest in having the right to roam over it, or the interest in preserving it as a habitat for bats. In a word, the various interests (and the values underlying them) are *incommensurable*, and we cannot – as the concordant model does – pretend otherwise.

While the conflictual model may thus be realistic, it might be thought depressing; for if the competing interests cannot be married up in the way that the concordant model suggests, it is difficult to see how we are to – as in practice we must – respectably strike a balance between them, and so configure real-world property.[54] Many theorists have addressed this issue, some under the rubric of ownership, others dealing with balancing more generally.[55]

It has been suggested that incommensurability does not automatically entail incomparability: that we simply have to choose a particular 'covering value', ie metric, by reference to which the competing interests can then be compared and a choice made between them.[56] The choice of metric will be informed by what concerns us – what moves us to make a comparison at all – in the particular case in hand. The idea is simple enough to grasp: if we were asked to identify the 'best' strain of tomato, we could not do so in an all-things-considered way, but we could do so by reference to whatever qual-

---

[53] Though it is arguable that the same problem remains even then. My ownership promotes my autonomy in one way; your home promotes yours in another. It is hard to say objectively that one promotes it more than the other; they just promote it differently. *cf* J Finnis, *Natural Law and Natural Rights* (2nd edn, Oxford, 2011) 423.

[54] J Raz, *The Morality of Freedom* (Oxford, 1988) 353–4 sees a positive side to the difficulty. He suggests that our resistance to viewing different interests in terms of a common metric – so as to create commensurability between them – is a way of recognising the interests' distinctive values; that it debases an interest to regard it as legitimately subject to exchange with others. See too J Singer, *Entitlement – The Paradoxes of Property* (New Haven, 2000) 213, speaking of the 'tragedy' of property, in reference to the way it stands at the crossroads of so many valuable but irreconcilable desiderata. (Singer seems to use the word 'tragedy' in a humanely empathetic, rather than lachrymose, way.)

[55] One interesting thesis is suggested by Underkuffler (n 3). According to this, a property interest is to be balanced against a competing interest only where the two are commensurable; where they are not, the property interest should automatically prevail. This suggestion is aimed at the Fifth Amendment to the US Constitution, which can be read as giving unqualified protection to property rights, so allowing them to be compromised only to vindicate claims that can be seen as immanent within them (and hence are commensurable). Viewed from first principles, however, the thesis may be thought to lose attraction; the Fifth Amendment aside, it is hard to see why we should deal with a problem of incommensurability between a property right and a rival claim by simply preferring the former. Even in the Fifth Amendment context, moreover, the suggestion is compromised by the tendentious nature of the business of deciding whether a given conflict involves commensurables or incommensurables.

[56] V Afonso da Silva, 'Comparing the Incommensurable: Constitutional Principles, Balancing and Rational Decision' (2011) 31 *OJLS* 273.

ity particularly interested us; say sweetness of taste, or length of shelf life, or tolerance to drought. While it works fine for comparing tomatoes, however, this idea does not export particularly well to the business of adjudicating between interests, at any rate for the reason we generally have to do so, namely to decide which to uphold and which to suppress. Imagine we were trying to decide whether to give precedence to my ownership of my house, or to your, or some bats', residence in it, or to a proposal to run a high-speed rail link through or past it. If we made our decision by focusing on just one facet of the matter – say, economic benefit, or personal autonomy – while ignoring all others, we might indeed be able to reach a rational decision; but that decision would not be a legitimate one. It would not do justice to the question asked of us, as it would by definition neglect large areas of the various interests' claims to respect. It is the need to attend to the totality of such claims that principally makes the interests incommensurable in the first place; and this cannot properly be stipulated out of the way.

More promisingly, John Rawls[57] does engage with incommensurability as such. He sees the way to get past it, so as to arrive at the right balance between the competing considerations, as being to ask what balance we would agree to if the matter were put to us. But so that our answer will be not a merely selfish but a universalised one – ie one that works for the whole of society[58] – Rawls specifies that we should imagine ourselves as reaching it behind a 'veil of ignorance', ie without knowledge of the position in society that we would subsequently find ourselves in. So the question in our context would be: how would we strike the balance between, say, the advantages of the proposed high-speed rail link and its negative impact on property owners along its route, granted that we did not know whether we would turn out to be such a property owner, or someone hoping to build the line, or to travel on it, or indeed someone completely unaffected by it? Just as if for some reason there could be only one strain of tomato, we would design it by asking what we would want its qualities to be, given unawareness of whether we would turn out to be consumers, shopkeepers or growers – using this approach to figure the optimal compromise between the different qualities we would emphasise from each of those individual standpoints. The proposal thus submerges the problem of theoretical incommensurability beneath people's practical prefer-ences. It observes that, when faced with incommensurables, we nonetheless do manage to make concrete choices; and takes it that we would continue to do so even from behind a veil of ignorance. Therein, of course, lies the

---

[57] J Rawls, *A Theory of Justice* (Cambridge MA, 1971).

[58] Though apparently only human society; bats (etc) seem not to get a look in. Even if we insisted that they should, moreover, the proposal cannot be adapted to deliver this. In order for it to do so, we should have to extend the veil of ignorance to the question whether we are human at all, or a bat. But it is very arguable that we cannot (while we in fact remain human) know what it is like to be a bat, as we would need to in order to know the sort of choices we would make if we were bats. For discussion, see T Nagel, 'What Is it Like to Be a Bat?' (1974) LXXXIII *Philosophical Review* 435.

proposal's potential weakness; there is an air of fantasy about its reliance on the veil of ignorance (akin to that surrounding Dworkin's invocation of Hercules) that makes one sceptical of how well the proposal would deliver answers in practice.

The approach taken by John Finnis[59] is less ambitious, in a way that allows it – promisingly – to stay in closer touch with the messy reality of incommensurability. Unlike Rawls, whose proposal (like Dworkin's) aspires to disclose *the right choice*, Finnis's view allows for there being a range of defensible choices. He suggests that if a decision-maker acts with 'practical reasonableness', the balance that he strikes should be accepted, notwithstanding that, still compatibly with practical reasonableness, it could also have been struck in a number of other ways. There is much to be said about the content of 'practical reasonableness', but in brief it is a matter of thinking with rationality and respect, in particular trying to do as full justice as possible to the (generally incommensurable) basic values that define humanity.[60]

Finnis's treatment of practical reasonableness implies that subjective intentions are important: that a decision's damage to a relevant basic value (say, its causing, or tolerating, a person's death) can be accepted so long as this is not the decision-maker's purpose. This position may start to make us feel uncomfortable, in the way that it potentially allows idiosyncratic outcomes to be legitimately chosen; even if we have weaned ourselves away from the idea that there must be a single right choice, we may well wish for greater objectivity than this. The point merits further exploration. It might be thought that overlooking a relevant value, in the way of not factoring it into one's purpose, is actually incompatible with the precept of thinking responsibly about all relevant values. On the other hand, perhaps the latter can result too readily in paralysis. If so, the reference to subjective intention can be seen as a way of preserving the theory as a practicable vehicle for taking decisions between incommensurables, while insisting that such decisions be respectable, rather than the result simply of a free-for-all. But in that a free-for-all would pre-

---

[59] Finnis (n 53).

[60] Once again, bats etc are regrettably overlooked. But the thesis could in principle be adapted to remedy this, by widening the focus from the values that define humanity, to those that define Life, or Creation, or our Universe, or the Cosmos, as a whole. While doubtless not to be taken lightly, the exercise seems not essentially bootless; albeit that our – necessarily, the human – account of it would inevitably fall short of perfection, in terms both of the breadth of its vision and of the profundity of its wisdom. Indeed, the ethical strand of Buddhism, otherwise rather similar to Finnis's view, goes this further distance, regarding (intentional) ill-treatment of animals as to be avoided; see D Keown, *Buddhist Ethics – A Very Short Introduction* (Oxford, 2005) ch 3. To be sure, this injunction is aimed at producing a clean *karma* sheet on the part of humans dealing with animals, and so at first sight has an anthropocentric focus. Importantly, however, Buddhism (see especially the *Diamond Sutra* (translation available at www.diamond-sutra.com/diamond_sutra_translation.html)) denies the idea of 'anthropocentricity' as opposed to its opposite, at all; affirming instead the continuity of humanity with all other animate and indeed inanimate states, and for that matter non-states, via the vision of 'dependent co-origination' (or 'dependent co-arising'). See M Carrithers, *Buddha – A Very Short Introduction* (Oxford, 1983) 68–9.

sumably consist of people taking whatever decisions suited them, feeling free to neglect any relevant value they fancied – which sounds like a (pejorative, but otherwise possible) way of restating Finnis's tolerance of subjectivity – a tension evidently remains.

This feature of Finnis's account strikes a chord with elements of the discourse around the human rights concept of proportionality, itself purportedly the tool for fixing the balance between the relevant considerations in that context, notwithstanding their incommensurability. Remember the margin of appreciation and idea of deference,[61] allowing the political or executive decision-maker a considerable territory within which their choices will be respected.[62] Remember too the rendition of the proportionality judgement as more realistically an inquiry after *dis*proportionality, to similar effect. The idea that balancing judgements cannot be fully interrogated, just made, appears to have considerable real-world support.

10.3 The Essence of Ownership

So we have seen that, while there is a paradigm idea of ownership, ie *dominium*, ownership never operates in that way in practice; it is always (appropriately or not) qualified, compromised. One might ask, is there any limit to this? Is there a point beyond which the qualifications cannot extend, without the result ceasing to count as 'ownership' at all? Ultimately, how is (real-world) ownership to be defined?

10.3.1 'Ownership is Meaningless'

Some say that these questions cannot be answered. They do so on the basis that, in the real world, to speak of 'ownership', or 'property', is to say nothing meaningful at all. For example, Kevin and Susan Gray write: 'Our daily references to property ... tend to comprise a mutual conspiracy of unsophisticated semantic allusions and confusions, which we tolerate – frequently,

---

[61] See §§ 2.3.5, 2.4.4, 2.5.1.

[62] This being ascribed to their roles as such; *cf* Finnis's respect for 'authority': (n 53) 276–90. Ideas such as the margin of appreciation should not be confused with Dworkin's inclination to separate the realm of policy from that of law (see n 50). The margin of appreciation, etc, is a territory in which the judgement of the political or executive decision-maker will be more or less respected, even if regarding a matter which (otherwise) counts as law. Indeed, it appears that Dworkin ought not to accept ideas such as the margin of appreciation. In contrast to the single right answer that he posits (see at n 48), such ideas surely assume a plurality of possible answers, or at least the impossibility of discerning the single right one.

indeed, do not notice – largely because our linguistic shorthand commands a certain low-level communicative efficiency.'[63] This view sees to have originated with the American realists, in particular Wesley Hohfeld, who treated property as simply a bundle of rights, comprising nothing more than the sum of its parts, whatever this might be. Hence the definition of 'property' adopted for the American *Restatement*: 'legal relations between persons with respect to a thing'.[64] On this reckoning, there is no sense in seeking to distinguish between different sets of legal relations, or bundles of rights, so as to label some of them, but not others, as 'ownership' or 'property'.

Intellectually speaking (there may well be, or have been, a political undercurrent to it), this view seems a product of the fallacy that, because it is hard or impossible to say what ownership is, it must be nothing. It is surely clear that in reality, we often do use the words 'ownership' and 'property' to refer to entitlements quite considerably cut back from *dominium*, such as the situation where I 'own' a house but subject to a mortgage in favour of a bank; and that we would reject the suggestion that, when we do so, our words are not seriously meaningful. (Though we may err on the side of using the words more readily than we could fully defend ... perhaps in order to evoke the totemic power of *dominium*. For example, when we say that I 'own' my house despite its mortgage, we may do so in an effort to present me in that light, in order for example to justify supporting my interests against the bank's.)[65]

Taking their cue from this, then, a number of thinkers take it that the terms 'ownership' and 'property' do mean something, even when used to denote not *dominium*, but whatever it is that they refer to in the real world.[66] They therefore feel the need to engage more heavily with the questions posed at the start of § 10.3, of what that 'something' is.

There is another reason for seeking an answer to this question. Other property rights – leases, for example – are defined by the law with tight precision. This is required by the *numerus clausus* principle, so as to ensure that the rights are allowed to operate in rem, with all the harm that this can entail, only where they have the particular (beneficial) content to outweigh this. Ownership is a right in rem, and as such can likewise do harm – as where I own something, but you (purport to) sell it to John; John is hurt because he pays you, but ends up without the thing. We would expect it too, therefore, to have a justifying benefit. Doubtless it does, in the sorts of ways covered in

---

[63] K Gray and S Gray, *The Elements of Land Law* (5th edn, Oxford, 2008) ch 15 para 1.5.1. See too eg K Gray (n 27).

[64] American Law Institute, *Restatement (First) of Property* (1936) ch 1, Introductory Note. More recently, the position was reiterated most influentially by T Grey, 'The Disintegration of Property' in J Pennock and J Chapman (eds), *Property: Nomos XXII* (New York, 1980) 69–85. For an account of all this, and of the backlash against Grey's position, see J Singer, 'Democratic Estates: Property Law in a Free and Democratic Society' (2009) 94 *Cornell Law Rev* 1009.

[65] § 12.2.1 looks at the matter from the mortgages perspective.

[66] See especially Harris (n 29); 'Reason or Mumbo Jumbo: The Common Law's Approach to Property' (Maccabaean Lecture in Jurisprudence) (2001) 117 *Proceedings of the British Academy* 445.

§ 10.2.2. But obviously we cannot say so without knowing, or at any rate supposing, what 'it', ownership, actually is. And having said so, and thus accorded this 'ownership' in rem status, we need to be able to confine this status to the 'ownership' in question, rather than just any concept calling itself 'ownership'.

10.3.2 Defining 'Ownership'

Trying therefore to capture the essence of ownership, one might essay that some types of entitlement are key to ownership, whereas others are optional extras. Picking up the vision of ownership as a 'bundle of rights',[67] the suggestion would be that, whatever else the bundle might or might not include, some particular right or rights – a certain core – must remain in the bundle in order for it to be called 'ownership'. But the identity of this core is a question for debate.[68]

One might venture that an owner must be able to *make use* of his property, and/or that he must *control* whatever use is made of the property, and/or that he must be able to *exclude* others from using the property without his consent. There is certainly widespread agreement that, in a general sort of way, these are the sorts of thing that an 'owner' might need to be able to do. There is, however, also agreement that even if someone cannot do all of them, or do them all of the time, it may still be right to call him 'owner'. It seems to be enough that he can have and control *some* uses, and exclude *some* people from the property. For example, an ordinary house-owner cannot use his house in such a way as to cause nuisance to his neighbours, and cannot control his local authority's decision to designate it as appropriate (or not) for development, and cannot exclude police officers bearing a search warrant. Yet we still call him 'owner'.[69] The difficulty is to say *how far* – if that is not too linear a way of putting what seems likely to be a more complex phenomenon – this can be taken.[70]

---

[67] Harris, *ibid*, 465–6, argues that the idea of a 'bundle of rights' can be misleading as even a tool for thinking about property, because it implies that the set of rights in question is finite. He suggests that the rights that go with ownership are instead 'open-ended, prima facie use-privileges, control-powers and powers of transmission'. On the infrastructure of the 'bundle of rights' idea, see further Harris (n 29) ch 8; and for a complete rejection of it as a way of thinking about property, see J Penner, 'The Bundle of Rights Picture of Property' (1996) 43 *University of California Los Angeles Law Review* 711.

[68] There is much literature exploring the matter. See eg Harris, *ibid*; Penner (n 39); K Gray, 'Property in Thin Air' [1991] *CLJ* 252.

[69] See especially Harris, *ibid*, ch 5.

[70] We might try to side-step this difficulty by looking, rather than for a 'core', for a 'minimum weight': the idea being that it does not matter *which* entitlements are present, provided that there is a critical mass of them. But this does not answer the call of the *numerus clausus* principle, explained earlier, for rights in rem to be defined in their content. In order to satisfy this call, we need to revert to the idea of a core after all.

And it is, in the end, fair to say that this difficulty has so far defeated all attempts to solve it.[71] We may in fact need to conclude that, while there must indeed be an essential core to the idea of ownership, this core cannot be defined. It might then be interesting and fruitful to inquire why this should be so.

The reason may lie in the reflection that, precisely because 'ownership' is clearly a central feature and indeed ingredient of 'human society', it is as plastic as the latter concept necessarily is. More particularly, over human history, and otherwise varying from context to context (including, doubtless, what it is that is 'owned'), the notion of 'ownership' has been both valuable and objectionable, and for a variety of different reasons. There are very probably some broad endemic themes, notably the values of liberty, and economic considerations – as discussed in § 10.2.2 – on the positive side, versus the values of liberty again, and property's anti-communitarian tendency, on the negative. But the mix between these, and their relative compulsion, as well as the comings and goings of other considerations, will have been persistently, and (given the intrinsic restlessness of the human condition) entirely naturally, unsettled. It is hardly surprising, then, that 'ownership' should have meant somewhat different things, and had somewhat different-looking pros and cons, in, for example, the western Neolithic, from whose dynamic it may indeed have developed;[72] feudal societies; the ages of industrialisation, statism and privatisation; and societies where sharing is necessary to survival. (The list could, obviously, go on and on.) Nor that, even at a given time and place – our own no less than any other – it should always be contested and contingent.

[71] This conclusion was reached by A Honoré, *Making Law Bind* (Oxford, 1987) chs 8, 10, and Harris (n 29) ch 1, especially at 5; no more recent contribution appears to give cause to doubt it. Harris ascribes this effect substantially to what he calls the 'ownership spectrum'. By this he means that 'ownership' denotes a set of situations forming something like a continuum, in terms of their content, between 'full-blooded ownership' (sketched at 29–32; a slightly more realistic cousin to *dominium*) and 'mere property' (see at 28–29). Crucially for present purposes, while 'mere property' represents the lower limit of the continuum – and so, the core we are seeking – its content remains undefined ('something that pertains to a person is, *maybe within drastic limits*, his to use as he pleases and therefore his to permit others to use . . .'; emphasis added).

[72] The suggestion is that it was needed in order to allow the successful development of that era's key innovation, namely agriculture. This seems likely to have required ideas about the relationship between people and (especially) land more abstract and sophisticated than would have been needed in earlier periods, when possession may have been enough. It might further be suggested that, in order to make these more abstract and sophisticated ideas stick, there would also, for the first time, have been required that which we now call 'law'. And so, that 'property' and 'law' co-originated in this society. But this last proposed linkage is put under pressure by recent discoveries (especially regarding the history of Stonehenge) hinting that a previously unsuspected degree of social organisation characterised the Mesolithic, which preceded the Neolithic; perhaps requiring 'law' then too, for other purposes than to deliver ownership and hence successful agriculture. Further reflection on the matter will be rewarding.

11

Leases

11.1 The Idea of a Lease

The next right in rem for consideration is the lease. The general idea of a lease is well known: I own some land, but allow you to have it for some period, usually in return for rent. The case that springs quickest to mind may be a domestic residential lease, under which you make the land your home, but there are also many other kinds of leases, such as commercial and agricultural.

In a moment we shall look at the detailed rules defining the concept of a lease. But first we shall deal with a puzzle about the concept's very nature: the relationship between leases and ownership.

11.1.1 Leases and Ownership

If you have, say, a right of way over my land, my obligation to you is relatively specific. I must accept what would otherwise be a specified sort of trespass by you (your crossing my land), and I must refrain from using my land in particular ways (such as from building across your path). But although such obligations detract from the sum of the liberties I have in respect of my land, no one would say that they prevent me owning it, or that you own it instead.

If you have a lease of my land for some period, however, it might plausibly be said that you own the land, in my place, for that period (after which I resume ownership). This is because the rights and obligations involved in a lease are much more extensive than those involved in a right of way, making a lease something like the right to behave as the owner of the land in question for its duration. Having a lease of my land means that you can occupy it entirely, to a large extent excluding other people and even me, unless you choose to let us in. Subject to any restrictions in the lease's terms, you can also exploit the land economically, as for example by farming it, or running a shop on it, or sub-letting it to someone else, and keep the proceeds. You can also treat your lease as an asset in its own right, and transfer – 'assign' – it to someone else. Conversely, the lease may place upon you the responsibility of maintaining the land.[1]

At the same time, we may still find ourselves saying that I, as your landlord, remain the owner of the land. I am of course owner-in-waiting, entitled to full rights again after your lease has finished, and perhaps this is all that is meant; but the suggestion may be that in some sense I remain owner during the lease. As we saw in § 10.1.2, 'ownership' is an elastic concept. But it really does not capture my position as a landlord, at any rate if your lease is of any significant duration. My rights for this period are very limited. I cannot go onto the land without your permission, except for special reasons allowed by the lease, such as to make emergency repairs. I may have the right to receive rent from you, but this is not always true, and even where it is, it does not seem to make me owner of the land. You may have to maintain the land, but since it is you who enjoys the land, this benefits me little during the lease, though it may help me get the land back in good order at the end. There is really only one sense in which I 'own' the land during the period of your lease. I can still sell it to John, albeit that John will normally be bound by your lease, as it is a right in rem.

Unlike lesser rights such as rights of way, therefore, leases represent a substantial instance of fragmented ownership: you own the land for the period of the lease, and I own it thereafter, but during the lease no one has full ownership of it. We looked at the phenomenon of fragmented ownership in § 10.1.3. We saw that it is problematic, as for example impeding the sale of the land to someone wanting full ownership, and so damaging the land's marketability; and that as a result, the law has over the last century or so tended to suppress it, or create correctives to it. Leases have been excepted from this process of suppression or correction, however. In particular, they are much less damaging to the market: someone might well want to buy the landlord's interest during the lease, not only looking forward to the end of the lease but also for the sake of the rental income in the meantime. And the remaining damage seems to be outweighed by leases' usefulness. Allowing people to acquire most of an owner's rights in land for a limited period and for a pro-portionately limited investment – especially payable on a periodic basis – is valuable, particularly to businesses.

Perhaps because of difficulties of working with more ordinary words in a context of substantially fragmented ownership, the law's terminology regarding leases is more than usually specialised. Your right, a lease, is also known as a 'demise' (though this word is old fashioned), or especially as a 'term of

---

[1] See further § 11.5.1.

years absolute',[2] often shortened to a 'term of years', or simply 'term'. You are a tenant, or lessee, or 'termor'. As your landlord, I hold the land in 'fee simple absolute in possession', an expression which seems to cover my having mere title as well as it does beneficial ownership, but more specifically I have a 'reversion', a word which emphasises my resumption of beneficial rights at the end of your term. I am a lessor, or 'reversioner'.

11.1.2 Enfranchisement and 'Right to Buy'

There is a further dimension to the insight that a lease is in some sense owner-ship. It underlies the right which some tenants have to acquire the reversion of the land in question (or a new long lease over it), without the consent of the landlord and at a reduced price.

This right is the product of a number of pieces of legislation, aimed at – or at any rate applying to – a number of different contexts.[3] This has given the right a complex character, which will not be detailed here.[4]

Where the right (in this context called 'enfranchisement') is that of a private sector tenant with a substantial lease against his landlord, the underlying idea is said to be that the tenant, rather than the landlord, deserves to own the reversion: either because he has made an upfront payment for the lease (a 'premium') as great as he would have had to pay for the freehold, or because he has spent money on maintaining the leased property (and sometimes even building it), on a scale giving him a moral entitlement to that property.[5]

These arguments are not fully satisfactory, however, as they make sweep-ing, and arguably incorrect, financial assumptions.[6] If they were compelling, too, one would expect them to apply to all kinds of tenancies: yet the Acts cover only domestic, not commercial and agricultural, tenancies. In truth, at least part of the basis for the right seems to be an idea that the favoured tenants, simply because of their status as such, already 'own' the land in ques-tion, and this ownership entitles them to the reversion as well as the term.

---

[2] This is the expression used in the Law of Property Act 1925 s 1(1)(b).

[3] Principally the Leasehold Reform Act 1967; the Housing Acts 1980 and 1985; the Landlord and Tenant Act 1987; the Leasehold Reform, Housing and Urban Development Act 1993; the Commonhold and Leasehold Reform Act 2002; and the Housing Act 2004. For critical discus-sion of the current position, see J Morgan, 'Leasehold Enfranchisement: A Law of Unintended Consequences?' [2010] *Conv* 444.

[4] The various Acts take different approaches. The differences are only partly explicable by reference to the differences in context: to an extent they are the product of more general concep-tual or political experimentation.

[5] Government White Paper, *Leasehold Reform in England and Wales* (Cmnd 2916, London, 1966).

[6] The argument that the tenant's expenditure on the property entitles him to own the property does not, moreover, explain why he should also have the right to acquire the underlying *land*. The arguments were put under little pressure during their examination in *James v United Kingdom* (1986) 8 EHRR 123 (ECtHR). Nor, despite the advent of new and in some respects significantly different legislation, have they been since: see eg *Pitts v Earl Cadogan* [2010] 1 AC 226, [48] (SC).

The power of this vision – and so the definition of the tenants in question – varies, obviously, with factors such as the length of time the tenants have had the property, but arguably also with context, so explaining the different treatment of domestic as opposed to commercial or agricultural tenants. Domestic tenants can be said to 'own' their leased property in an especially deep sense precisely because it is their home, with the qualitative enhancement of attachment that that entails.

This latter insight connects the enfranchisement right as it applies in the private sector, with that operating in the public sector: the 'right to buy' one's council house.[7] The latter is certainly not ascribed to a financial investment by the tenant, and does not even require that the tenant should have a lease of substantial length, applying equally to those having, for example, yearly, monthly or weekly tenancies; its demand is rather for 5 years' *residence*.[8] As such, it is evidently founded purely on a notion that one who, albeit a tenant, in fact lives in a house for this period has a political claim to full ownership. It is the very fact that his home is such a key aspect of his life, even his identity, that creates the imperative for him to have a maximal claim – full ownership – over it.

11.2 The Legal Definition of a Lease

11.2.1 'Exclusive Possession, Payment, Term'

In *Street v Mountford*,[9] the House of Lords, led by Lord Templeman, ruled that a right over another person's land counts as a lease (with some exceptions) if:

——— it confers exclusive possession of the land;
——— in return for a rent, and/or a lump sum payment (a 'premium'); and
——— not for ever, but for a 'term'.

We shall examine these requirements in detail in a moment. The core ideas are simple, however. Exclusive possession is the right a tenant has to exclude other people, including the landlord, from the land. It is this requirement that is at the heart of the idea that the tenant owns the land in question. On the other hand, the requirements of payment[10] and especially of a term are what

---

[7] Under (principally) the Housing Act 1985.
[8] Housing Act 1985 s 119 (as amended by the Housing Act 2004).
[9] [1985] AC 809 (HL).
[10] In fact, it is doubtful whether this requirement is essential: § 11.4.1. It is nonetheless an almost universal feature of leases.

differentiate a lease from freehold ownership, showing that the land is not wholly the tenant's even during the lease, and that it will cease to be the tenant's at some point.

According to *Street v Mountford*,[11] if your right to occupy my land does not meet these criteria and so does not amount to a lease, it will be a licence.[12] Licences are described fully in Chapter 17, but the key point is that a lease, involving especially exclusive possession, makes you temporary *owner* of the land; whereas a licence, not involving exclusive possession, allows you to be on land which remains *mine*.

11.2.2 Leases and the Rent Acts

In turn, the distinction between a lease and a licence has traditionally reflected the boundaries of the Rent Acts.

'The Rent Acts' is the collective name for a series of pieces of legislation, which began in 1915, whose import is to restrict the level of rent that landlords can charge for, and the circumstances in which they can evict occupants from, residential accommodation.[13] The argument for the Acts is that, especially when something as important as residential accommodation is at stake, the law ought to restrain landlords from abusing the superior bargaining power they are thought to have: hence the regulation of the most crucial ways in which they might drive oppressive bargains. Even if one accepts the validity of this argument, however, there is also a counter-argument. There is nothing to make someone offer land for rental at all, and if the law regulates the value that landlords can extract from renting out their land to the point where they can do better by using it in some other way, they will do so: with the result that the supply of rental land will diminish, and would-be occupants will suffer simply by being unable to find accommodation at all. Hence the parallel provision of public sector rentals (especially council housing).

There have always been – must necessarily be – limits to the applicability of the Rent Acts regime. One such is the rule with which we are concerned: that, with some exceptions, the regime does not apply to the rental of a home under a licence rather than a lease. How is this rule to be accounted for?

One answer would say that it merely provides a device whereby the legislators could appear to be following the argument in favour of the Rent Acts, while in practice, mindful of the counter-argument, allowing the Acts' impact

---

[11] [1985] AC 809 (HL).

[12] This may not be quite correct. In theory, your right might alternatively be a 'tenancy at will': a right featuring exclusive possession, but terminable instantaneously by either party. The relationship between licences and tenancies at will is not well understood.

[13] Counterpart regimes have also existed for business and agricultural tenancies, though with differences of detail. In all these sectors, the law is nowadays much less protective of tenants than it once was. The current principal statute regarding residential accommodation is the Housing Act 1988.

to be avoided. On this view, it should be possible for parties – and especially landlords – to designate an arrangement which could be a lease, and so attract the Rent Acts, as a licence instead, and so opt out of the Acts.

This in fact was the position for a while. The arrangement in *Street v Mountford*[14] itself, for example, involved exclusive possession, rent and term, but described itself as a licence. The Court of Appeal, following the general understanding at the time, held that it was indeed a licence, and thus exempt from the Rent Acts.[15] When the House of Lords ruled that, having these features, the arrangement was necessarily a lease and thus attracted the Rent Acts, it gave the law a new direction. In drawing the line between leases and licences in this way, the decision inevitably accounted for the Acts' inapplicability to licences in a new way too, treating its newly established line between leases and licences as a principled boundary for the Acts. That is, it assumed that the rights it chose to define as leases deserve the application of the Acts; but that the rights it chose to define as licences do not.[16] More fundamentally, indeed, it emphasised that while leases are rights in rem, licences are in personam.[17] That is, while protected (though not with the strength afforded by the Rent Acts) against the original landlord, licences are – unlike leases – unprotected against the latter's disponees.[18]

This division between the two types of right is in fact difficult to accept. On appropriate facts, both lessees and licensees can clearly point to the land in question as their 'home', and so seek the protection of Article 8 of the ECHR.[19] Moreover, if anything, among those people who rent their homes, those with (what we now learn to be) leases, with their quality of temporary ownership, are the 'haves'; those with (what we now learn to be) licences, having no such quality, are the 'have nots'. Indeed, resort to a licence may well indicate that the occupant has a weaker bargaining position than if the chosen right were a lease. One would regard licensees, therefore, as on that account more in need of protection than tenants.[20] In fact, a reform proposal

---

[14] [1985] AC 809 (HL).

[15] (1984) 49 P & CR 324 (CA).

[16] The decision's reasoning states that the rules delineating leases and licences exist in their own right, uninfluenced by a desire to apply the Rent Acts or otherwise ([1985] AC 809, 819 (HL)). In reconfiguring these rules, however, it necessarily took a position on the correct scope of the Acts.

[17] [1985] AC 809, 814 (HL).

[18] See §§ 17.1.1, 17.3.2–17.3.3.

[19] Whether that protection would be forthcoming would depend on two further questions. First: (unless the landlord is a public body) whether the ECHR has horizontal effect: see § 2.2. Second: if so (and also in the case where the landlord is a public body), whether any limitation in the protection given is justifiable as a proportionate way of serving some proper competing end: see § 2.4.4. It is hard to see why one's answers to these questions should vary with the legal characterisation of the right in question as a lease or a licence. In a nutshell, such characterisation seems to be the problem, not the solution.

[20] On this account, one might also refer to ECHR Art 14, which requires (inter alia) rights to homes to be protected in a way which does not discriminate on grounds of (inter alia) property. The current better protection of the 'haves', with their leases, than of the 'have nots', with their licences, may be thought to involve such discrimination.

was at one point made, to apply the same protection regime without distinction to both leases and licences.[21] But it has not been acted upon.

The account given so far of the position produced by *Street v Mountford*[22] needs refinement, however. As we shall see, although the headline formula of 'exclusive possession, payment, term' – and so temporary ownership – broadly holds good, the precise concept of a lease developed in that and succeeding decisions has certain complexities. These complexities seem best explained not as necessary features of the concept, but as attempts by the judges to fine-tune the set of situations to which the Rent Acts apply.

11.3 Exclusive Possession

11.3.1 The Idea of Exclusive Possession

Say you have a right to occupy a house which I own. You have 'exclusive possession' if your right entitles you to occupy the house on your own: that is, to exclude everyone else if you wish, aside from those able to enter regardless of permission, such as the police under certain circumstances. If the right I confer on you is one which allows me to join you myself, or allows me to let others do so – even if I never take advantage of these possibilities – you do not have exclusive possession.

On this account, the question whether you have a lease turns on whether you have (the right of) exclusive possession. It does not matter whether you in fact occupy the house on your own, and so can be said to have 'exclusive occupation'. If you do have exclusive possession, you might nonetheless surround yourself with others; while if you do not have exclusive possession, you might in fact be left in peace. (Lord Templeman in *Antoniades v Villiers*[23] suggests the contrary. He asserts that someone who in fact occupies exclusively – paying rent, for a term – is ipso facto a tenant, and thus necessarily acquires a tenant's rights . . . including exclusive possession, regardless of any provisions in the agreement contradictory of this right. This view is incorrect.)

---

[21] Law Commission, *Renting Homes: The Final Report* (Law Com No 297, London, 2006) para 3.9.

[22] [1985] AC 809 (HL).

[23] [1990] 1 AC 417, 461–2 (HL). See too *Aslan v Murphy* [1990] 1 WLR 766, 775 (CA).

11.3.2 'Conferring' Exclusive Possession

There is an ambiguity in the key idea of conferring exclusive possession on you.

Normally, I shall be the owner of the land in question. Then, if I purport to confer exclusive possession on you, you will get it. That is because I myself (in my capacity as freehold owner) have such a right to give.

But sometimes I may purport to confer exclusive possession on you when I do not have it myself. This can occur in two kinds of case. One is where I am in the process of buying the land from John, its current owner, and I purport to set up a lease in your favour (ie confer exclusive possession on you) before the purchase is complete. At this point, I have no right at all in the land. The other is where I do have a right to the land, but it is a mere licence from the land's owner, John. As noted in § 11.2.1, a licence does not give me exclusive possession of the land: yet I purport to give you a lease (ie confer exclusive possession on you) beneath me. Either way, I am purporting to give you exclusive possession when I do not have that right myself.

In such cases, since I do not have exclusive possession myself, and so cannot effectively confer it on you, you do not gain it and become a tenant in the normal sense. But in purporting to confer exclusive possession on you, I have contracted with you that that is what you shall be. So while you do not acquire exclusive possession itself, you do acquire a contractual right to it. Because a contractual right operates only in personam, however, you cannot enforce this contractual right against John himself or others whom he allows to enter (as, if you had become a tenant in the normal sense, you could enforce your exclusive possession against all comers). But you can enforce it against me: so obliging me not to intrude on you, and to compensate you if John or others do so. Your interest in this kind of case is therefore sometimes called a 'contractual lease'.[24] Contractual leases have some features in common with true leases,[25] but fundamentally they are quite different. The in personam

---

[24] Alternatively, a 'non-estate lease'. In the first of our two cases, where I give you your lease in anticipation of acquiring the land myself, your right is usually called a 'tenancy by estoppel', but there seems to be no difference in the legal treatment. See generally *Bruton v London and Quadrant Housing Trust* [2000] 1 AC 406 (HL), where *X*, a licensee of land, purported to lease it to *Y*, with the consequences described in the text. (Much of the decision's reasoning is aimed at a distraction. The agreement between *X* and *Y* described the interest conferred on *Y* as itself only a 'licence'. If this description had held good, there would have been no contractual lease because *X* would not have been contracting that *Y* should be a tenant. But it did not hold good: the right that *X* purported to give *Y* was in substance a lease, and the word 'licence' was a mere misdescription, without effect. On misdescriptions, see further § 11.4.3.)

[25] For example, in *Bruton v London and Quadrant Housing Trust, ibid*, on the facts explained, the upshot was that *X* incurred in *Y*'s favour the obligations to repair the land imposed on landlords by the Landlord and Tenant Act 1985. In principle, it should be a matter of construction whether a given statutory rule about 'leases', certainly applicable to true leases, is applicable to contractual leases too. (The rules in the Land Registration Act 2002, for example, are obviously not. *Quaere* the rules imposing formality requirements.) But the decision does not explore this issue, merely assuming that the rule in question does have such an extended application.

character of their rights, especially the crucial right of exclusive possession, means that their effect falls far short of the ownership that is given by a true lease.[26]

11.3.3 Two Complications

Subject to the side-issue covered in § 11.3.2, the idea of exclusive possession given so far depicts it as a right entitling you, for the duration of your lease, to exclude everyone else. This simple picture needs further development in two respects, however: as regards shared occupancy, and as regards the significance of a stipulation entitling the landlord to enter.

First, then, the case where the landlord gives a number of people the right to occupy the same property. Self-evidently, there can be only one right exclusively to possess a given piece of property. So if each occupant has an individual right, the plurality of the rights means that they cannot be exclusive: none of the occupants has the right to exclude the others.[27] But a number of people can take a single right exclusively to possess the property, if they do so as 'joint tenants'[28] of the right.[29] This will be the case, however, only if they acquire their entitlement to the land together (not, say, at different moments,[30] or under separate agreements with the landlord[31]); and if their entitlement

---

[26] In particular, *Kay v Lambeth London Borough Council* [2006] 2 AC 465, [138]–[145] (HL) confirms that a contractual lease has no effect against the true owner of the land in question: only against the person who created it.

[27] Unless the landlord does indeed purport to grant each occupant an individual right exclusively to possess the same property, these rights therefore contradicting one another. Such a case is essentially the same as that where I purport to sell my car first to you, then to John. The solution is that the sale to you is effective, while that to John is not, because by the time I purport to make it I no longer have the car to sell. John is left with the right to sue me for breach of contract.

[28] The idea of joint tenancy is explained in detail in §§ 15.2.1–15.2.5. Two complications must be dealt with here. First, the word 'tenancy' here is not a reference to a lease: it is the old term for (in effect) ownership. So a statement that a number of people have a lease – or any other right – as joint tenants simply means that they share it. Second, the law recognises another form of co-ownership besides joint tenancy: tenancy in common. But tenants in common can only be beneficiaries under a trust, so persons sharing the legal title to a lease must do so as joint tenants.

[29] A joint tenancy is customarily said to require the presence of 'the four unities': see § 15.2.4. The following footnotes explain how the account in the text corresponds to three of these, but in essence both that account and its translation into the language of the unities simply detail the idea that joint tenants share a single right. The fourth unity is 'unity of possession', the gist of which is that the right must allow the persons in question to occupy a single piece, rather than separate pieces, of property. This unity is necessarily present in the context under discussion, which concerns the possibility that a number of persons may have exclusive possession of the same piece of land. (There is obviously no problem, for example, about a number of people separately having exclusive possession of the different flats in a block.)

[30] 'Unity of time'.

[31] 'Unity of title'. This is not negated if a group of co-owners are given individual copies of the agreement: the crucial thing is that it is a single agreement between all of them and the landlord.

provides for them to have the land for the same period, and to share a single set of rights and obligations (as opposed, for example, to having separate liabilities to pay individual sums of rent).[32] So a couple renting a house will often share the right exclusively to possess it,[33] while a number of single people doing the same will often have a collection of individual rights to occupy it non-exclusively.[34]

The second complication, concerning the significance of access by the landlord, is more problematic. It is easy to see that a landlord who retains an unrestricted right to be in the property does not confer exclusive possession of it, while a landlord who retains no right to be in it does. But what of the (very common) case where the landlord retains a limited right to enter? Landlords often have obligations to maintain or repair the leased property, and a right of access in order to do so. Even where the obligations lie on the tenant, the landlord will often have the right to enter so as to check that the tenant is complying with them. Landlords sometimes also have an obligation to provide 'attendance or services' (eg cleaning), and a right to enter in order to do this.

According to one passage in *Street v Mountford*,[35] only the landlord's retention of an unlimited right to enter will negate the conferment of exclusive possession, ie produce a licence rather than a lease. The retention of a limited right 'only serves to emphasise the fact that the grantee is entitled to exclusive possession', and so has a lease: presumably on the ground that a landlord who has not conferred exclusive possession will necessarily have the right to enter at will, and so has no need to stipulate on the subject.

This view is unsatisfactory, however. It has a Catch 22 quality: surely the presence or otherwise of exclusive possession should be deduced from the arrangements that the parties have in fact made. And it is clear that the landlord's retention of even a limited right of entry will sometimes – though not always – negate exclusive possession, and so yield a licence. While access so as to inspect or repair does not negate exclusive possession, access for the purpose of cleaning does so, even if it is further limited as to the permitted time of day.[36] Unsurprisingly therefore, the question has been recognised as one of

[32] 'Unity of interest'. Consistently with this, the members of the group can arrange between themselves who shall pay what, and the landlord may be happy to receive the rent in the shape of a number of separate payments from the individuals concerned. The key thing is that if the landlord wishes, he may call on all the members of the group to meet the entire liability.

[33] Though not always: the landlord may insist on renting to them as separate individuals, as in *Mikeover Ltd v Brady* [1989] 3 All ER 618 (CA), where in particular there were distinct liabilities to individual sums of rent. Nonetheless, a shared right to exclusive possession can be found if all such matters negating it can be dismissed as pretences: see § 11.3.5 below.

[34] As in *Stribling v Wickham* [1989] 21 HLR 381 (CA); *AG Securities v Vaughan* [1990] 1 AC 417 (HL).

[35] [1985] AC 809, 818 (HL).

[36] In *Aslan v Murphy* [1990] 1 WLR 766 (CA), where the landlord had access only to clean and only between 10.30am and noon, it was assumed that exclusive possession was denied, yielding a licence. (A lease was, however, eventually found on the basis that this access provision was a pretence: see § 11.3.5.)

degree,[37] but given these distinctions, even this rather understates its difficulty: it clearly has a qualitative as well as a quantitative dimension.

Lord Templeman in *Street v Mountford*[38] proposes a touchstone by which to address it. He asserts that an occupant lacks exclusive possession only if he is the landlord's 'lodger'. One can understand the thought: if you rent premises from me, and I have access to them for cleaning purposes, the word 'lodger' may be appropriate to describe you; while if I have access only to inspect or repair, it is not. But as a tool for giving a comprehensive answer to our question (when does limited access by the landlord negate exclusive possession?), the 'lodger' idea is inadequate. It can be applied at all only in the context of residential accommodation: there is no such person as a commercial lodger.[39] And even in the residential context, while the concept of a lodger is intelligible, it cannot be sharply defined, so resorting to it merely replaces one unclear test with another. Ultimately, then, the law seems not to have solved the problem: the answer to the question whether limited access by a landlord negates exclusive possession seems to lie with the individual judge.

11.3.4 Exceptions

According to Lord Templeman in *Street v Mountford*,[40] there are some cases in which exclusive possession is present, but there is no lease.

At least some instances of this phenomenon are explicable on the basis that, even if there is exclusive possession, there is no payment or term. Freehold ownership is a plain example. Another seems to be the case where a prospective purchaser of land is allowed to occupy the land before the purchase is completed (or even before negotiations towards it begin).[41]

On proper examination of certain other instances, too, there turns out to be no exclusive possession after all. One such instance is the case of a 'service occupier', ie an employee given particular accommodation by his employer, because living there is essential or important for his duties: a school caretaker, perhaps. Here, the employee is regarded as occupying on behalf of the employer,[42] so he plainly does not have possession exclusive of the employer. Another is the case of a person given the accommodation as an 'act of friendship or generosity'. Here the point is that the parties do not intend to enter

---

[37] *Aslan v Murphy, ibid* 770.

[38] [1985] AC 809, 817–18 (HL). See too *Aslan v Murphy, ibid* 770.

[39] *Booker Settled Estates Ltd v Ayers* [1987] 1 EGLR 50 (CA). In the commercial context, indeed, one can imagine a stipulation for the landlord to enter and clean which would not negate exclusive possession: the cleaning could be seen as a contract service packaged in with the tenancy. And if so there, why not also in the residential sphere?

[40] [1985] AC 809, 818–21 (HL).

[41] On this type of case, see *Ramnarace v Lutchman* [2001] 1 WLR 1651 (PC). It also seems questionable whether the prospective purchaser has a full right of exclusive possession: he may be able to exclude other people, but probably cannot exclude the seller.

[42] *Street v Mountford* [1985] AC 809, 818 (HL).

into obligations as between each other at all:[43] so again, exclusive possession (an obligation on the landowner not to enter his own land) cannot have been conferred.

In fact, it is unclear that there is any instance in which exclusive possession, payment and term are all present but the arrangement is not to be regarded as a lease. This is reassuring from the point of view of conceptual purity. But that in turn makes it all the more interesting that Lord Templeman should think of these cases as being, on the contrary, exceptions: cases in which the definition of a lease is satisfied but there is no lease. His taking this approach suggests that he in fact views a 'lease' as something not quite delineated by the technical definition after all.

11.3.5 Shams and Pretences

Say you and I agree that you will occupy a flat belonging to me, with me having the right to enter so as to provide you with attendance and services, or on the basis that you will share the flat with John, with whom I shall have a separate agreement. On the face of the matter, you do not have exclusive possession, so cannot have a lease.

But the law does not stop at the face of the matter. Instead, it asks whether any provisions of our agreement are 'shams', or 'pretences'. If they are, it disregards them, and considers whether our agreement without them gives you exclusive possession. So if the stipulation that I can enter the flat so as to provide you with attendance and services, or that you must share with John, is a sham or pretence, the law will disregard it. Without it, there is no reason to doubt that you have exclusive possession after all, so your right will be a lease. Equally, if your sharing with John is not a sham or pretence, but the separateness of my agreements with you both is, that separateness will be disregarded, giving you and John shared exclusive possession, and so a joint lease.

But what is a sham or pretence?

The original description of the concept, given by Lord Templeman in *Street v Mountford*,[44] reads: 'sham devices and artificial transactions whose only object is to disguise the grant of a tenancy and to exclude the Rent Acts'.[45] In applying this description in subsequent cases, the courts sometimes

---

[43] *ibid* 819–20. It is sometimes said that they do not intend 'to create legal relations', but that is inaccurate, as even a gratuitous licence involves legal relations.

[44] *ibid* 825.

[45] In fact, the sham/pretence rule is not limited to provisions calculated to avoid the Rent Acts, but applies to provisions calculated to avoid other statutory regimes too; for sight of it, or something like it, in another context, see *Autoclenz Ltd v Belcher* [2011] 4 All ER 745 (SC). The Rent Acts regime is, however, the usual target of such provisions in arrangements which might be leases of land. For some exploration of the rule's overall scope, see B McFarlane and E Simpson, 'Tackling Avoidance' in J Getzler (ed), *Rationalizing Property, Equity and Trusts, Essays in Honour of Edward Burn* (London, 2003) ch 8.

referred to earlier decisions that had used the term 'sham' in other contexts: principally *Snook v London and West Riding Investments Ltd*.[46] According to these earlier decisions, an agreement is a sham if it appears to have an effect that is different from that which the parties actually envisaged, and was intended by the parties to do so. This understanding was applied, for example, by the Court of Appeal in *Antoniades v Villiers*.[47] A couple rented a flat. The rental document contained a provision allowing the landlord to introduce an additional occupant. As the flat had only one bedroom, it would have been difficult[48] to do so. But the provision was not a sham in these terms, as it did indeed state the terms upon which the parties had agreed.[49] (It would have been a sham in this sense only if at the time of signing the document the landlord had, for example, said 'ignore that bit, it's just some window-dressing' and the couple had replied 'OK'.)

Findings of shams of this kind were rare, as a written document signed by the parties nearly always does reflect the contract they are in fact making. When *Antoniades v Villiers*[50] went to the House of Lords, however, Lord Templeman moved to escape the narrowness of this approach and allow provisions to be discarded more widely. To this end, he dropped the word 'sham' in favour of 'pretence'.[51] The judgments go on to tell us that a provision counts as a 'pretence' if it was 'never seriously intended in fact';[52] if it does not reflect 'the substance and reality' of the transaction;[53] or if the parties do not regard it as a provision 'to which any effect would be given'.[54] The provision in question, allowing the landlord to introduce an additional occupant, was such a pretence. Even though it reflected the parties' contract, it was 'never seriously intended in fact', at odds with 'the substance and reality' of

---

[46] [1967] 2 QB 786, 802 (CA). See too *Stone v Hitch* [2001] EWCA Civ 63, [63], [66], [69] (CA). If the requirement were merely that the apparent agreement be misleading as to the true contract, the question whether it is a 'sham' would merge with that whether it is susceptible to rectification. This, which would be a defensible position, would still leave the idea of 'sham' narrower than that envisaged by Lord Templeman. The further demand, that the parties *intend* their apparent agreement to be misleading, narrows the idea still further.

[47] [1990] 1 AC 417 (CA). Likewise *Hadjiloucas v Crean* [1988] 1 WLR 1006, 1013–14 (CA).

[48] Though not impossible. As well as a bedroom, there was a sofa-bed in the sitting-room, which was used for five or six weeks by a friend of the couple. But the resulting conditions seem to have been cramped and unsatisfactory.

[49] [1990] 1 AC 417, 444–7 (CA).

[50] [1990] 1 AC 417 (HL).

[51] *ibid* 462.

[52] *ibid* 469.

[53] *ibid* 466; see also 467–8.

[54] *ibid* 475; see also 462, 468, 476. Care is needed with this test, however. The question of whether effect *will be* given to the provision is not the same as the question of whether effect *has been*, or *is being*, given to it. The answer 'no' to the latter may be suggestive that the answer to the former is also 'no', making the provision a pretence, but explanations must be listened to. Say accommodation is rented to a group of people, with a provision allowing the landlord to choose replacements for those who leave. But in practice the landlord, out of reasonableness, kindness, politeness, does not insist upon the provision, instead allowing the remaining occupants to choose replacements for themselves. It should not be concluded that the provision was never intended to be exercised: *Stribling v Wickham* (1989) 21 HLR 381 (CA).

the transaction, and not destined to be put into effect. Similarly where, when I rent a house to you, our agreement provides that I will supply attendance and services, but I have no plan to do so.[55]

Consider the case where I rent a flat to you and John using two separate agreements, so that you and John have individual (and so necessarily non-exclusive) rights to occupy it. The agreements' separateness may be a pretence, as being at odds with 'the substance and reality' of the transaction: in which event it will be disregarded, leaving you and John sharing a single right of exclusive possession after all. The courts approach the matter via an inquiry into the nature of the relationship between you and John. If your relationship is close, as where you are a couple, your agreements will be seen as 'interdependent', and their separateness treated as a pretence;[56] whereas if you are no more than flatmates, your agreements are seen as 'independent', ie genuinely separate.[57] But this approach, requiring relationships to be allocated to one or the other of two categories in this way, is crude. Even if you and John are a couple, it is quite imaginable – including by yourselves – that you will split up. Say John leaves you: you may well feel it unnecessary to move out too, but instead stay in the flat and, being unable to afford the entire rent for it on your own, make the best of life with a new flatmate.[58] Equally, the fact that you and John are no more than flatmates does not mean that you are indifferent to each other's identity: on the contrary, you will each have a significant stake in the other's personality. In truth, just about all relationships have both interdependent and independent elements, in a subtle mix. It is impossible to characterise a given relationship one way or the other, and so make use of it to reveal pretences, without resorting to caricature. What emerges is that the 'substance and reality' of a transaction, on which the pretence doctrine depends, is a fragile – because ultimately impressionistic – concept.

There is a further, and more profound, difficulty with the 'substance and reality' idea, and so with the pretence doctrine.[59] It can be seen in the contrast between two sets of cases.

---

[55] *Aslan v Murphy* [1990] 1 WLR 766 (CA). But this decision blurs the distinction between the 'sham' and 'pretence' approaches again, by stating the question to be whether the provision is part of the parties' 'true bargain'. 'True' is ambiguous between 'as recognised by the law of contract' (sham in the narrow sense) and 'substantial and real' (pretence).

[56] As in *Antoniades v Villiers* [1990] 1 AC 417 (HL). See too the view taken, *ibid* 464 (and in *Street v Mountford* [1985] AC 809, 825 (HL)), of *Somma v Hazlehurst* [1978] 1 WLR 1014 (CA) and *Aldrington Garages Ltd v Fielder* (1978) 37 P & CR 461 (CA). But compare *Mikeover Ltd v Brady* [1989] 3 All ER 618, 625 (CA), where the facts may have been of this kind, but the court seems unwilling to engage with the issue.

[57] As in *AG Securities v Vaughan* [1990] 1 AC 417 (HL).

[58] In *Hadjiloucas v Crean* [1988] 1 WLR 1006 (CA), two ladies, who seem to have had a close relationship, rented accommodation under separate agreements. In *Antoniades v Villiers* [1990] 1 AC 417, 465 (HL) it is said that the ladies' relationship meant that the agreements were interdependent, ie their separateness was a pretence. But one of the two ladies had in fact left and been replaced.

[59] See further McFarlane and Simpson (n 45) ch 8.

The first set is principally represented by *Gisborne v Burton*.[60] Here, a land-lord agreed to rent land to a farmer. To avoid a statutory regime[61] that would have applied if he had leased the land directly to the farmer, the landlord leased it to his own wife, who then sub-leased it to the farmer. The court held that the inserted lease to the wife should be disregarded, inter alia as a pre-tence: it was at odds with the 'substance and reality' of the transaction.[62] So the farmer was left in effect with a lease rather than a sub-lease after all. Rather similarly, in *Bankway Properties Ltd v Pensfold-Dunsford*,[63] a landlord leased accommodation to a tenant on a basis[64] which in principle gave the tenant security of tenure, but on terms whereby, after two years, the annual rent increased more than five-fold, to £25,000. The idea was not that the ten-ant should pay this sum: on the contrary, it was that he should not, so that his failure would put him into default, depriving him of his security of tenure and entitling the landlord to eject him. The court declared the rent increase provision invalid.[65]

For the second, contrasting, set of cases, consider *Hilton v Plustitle Ltd*[66] and *Kaye v Massbetter*.[67] In these, an individual wanted to rent accommoda-tion. The landlord was willing to grant a lease, but not to the individual (in which case, the Rent Acts would have applied): only to a company (so that they did not). The individual therefore acquired a private company, specifi-cally for the purpose; the landlord granted the company a lease; and the company allowed the individual to occupy the accommodation. Asking itself whether the insertion of the company was a pretence and should be disregarded, yielding in effect a lease from the landlord to the individual after all, the court held that it was not. The 'company let' was the 'substance and reality' of the transaction.

The contrast between these two sets of decisions lies in their operating two different understandings of the idea of 'substance and reality'. Those com-prising the first set attend solely to the human story on the ground; while the assumption in the second set is that the parties' chosen legal vehicle is to be taken seriously – is itself a kind of 'substance and reality'.

---

[60] [1989] QB 390 (CA).

[61] Under the Agricultural Holdings (Notice to Quit) Act 1977.

[62] One detail, which might be thought important as corroborating this conclusion, turns out to be deceptive. The terms of the lease to the wife seemed to require her to farm the land: which she obviously was not going to do, apparently making the lease to her a pretence for this reason too. But the terms went on to provide for subleasing, something which would obviously rule out farming by the tenant: so the farming provision could not mean what it appeared to – it must be taken to contemplate subleasing on terms requiring farming, which is what in fact occurred.

[63] [2001] 1 WLR 1369 (CA).

[64] An assured tenancy, under the Housing Act 1988.

[65] The reasoning did not quite follow the pretence analysis, but it seems possible to believe that applying that analysis in the same way as it was applied in *Gisborne v Burton* [1989] QB 390 (CA) would yield the same answer.

[66] [1989] 1 WLR 149 (CA).

[67] (1990) 62 P & CR 558 (CA). *Belvedere Court Management Ltd v Frogmore Developments Ltd* [1997] QB 858 (CA) is legally similar, though has a different factual make-up.

The 'human story on the ground' approach is clearly the dominant one in the case-law as a whole. Its correctness is assumed in the treatment of provisions allowing the landlord to introduce additional occupants, or requiring him to supply attendance and services, and of arrangements involving separate agreements. As regards all of these, it could be said that the parties had, irrespective of the distance from the human story on the ground, chosen the arrangement in question as the legal vehicle governing their relationship. The courts' disregard of the latter reflection amounts to a rejection of it: to an affirmation that the 'substance and reality' to be attended to is of the 'human story on the ground' variety.

This position can be justified on the basis that, in the present context, those seeking to rent accommodation actually have little choice between the legal vehicles that might in principle be available: any such choices will in practice be made by the landlords: so the elimination of most of these vehicles is a measure properly calculated to restore renters' access to those vehicles it can be assumed they would wish to choose.[68] But the rejected view – that abstract legal concepts, and the choices that are available between them, can be just as significant (substantial, real) as more tangible phenomena in the shaping of people's lives – cannot simply be suppressed from the discourse. From time to time, especially where the parties do in fact seem to have bargained reasonably freely, it can be expected to bubble up (as it did in our second set of cases) . . . leaving the pretence doctrine, shaped around the 'human story on the ground' understanding, enduringly somewhat unstable.

11.4 Other Aspects of the Legal Definition

As we saw in § 11.2.1, a lease is defined in *Street v Mountford*[69] as an arrangement whereby (perhaps with some exceptions) I grant you exclusive possession of my land, in return for payment, for a term. We looked at the requirement of exclusive possession in § 11.3. Now we shall look at the requirements of payment and a term, and also at the significance of the label ('lease' or 'licence') that the parties themselves give the right conferred. Finally, in § 11.4.4, we shall take what we have learnt about the various rules about the make-up of a lease, and the difficulties they exhibit; and attempt to understand the role they all play in the operation of the concept as a whole.

[68] Compare *Burdis v Livsey* [2003] QB 36 (CA), favouring the 'chosen vehicle' approach . . . in a different context altogether, with the effect of *enhancing* consumer choice. See too *Autoclenz Ltd v Belcher* [2011] 4 All ER 745, [34] (SC), explaining the application of the sham/pretence idea (or something like it) in the employment context on a similar basis.
[69] [1985] AC 809 (HL).

11.4.1 Payment

Leases are normally given in return for some kind of payment. Indeed, this is part of their raison d'être: they represent a way in which freehold owners can exploit their land, by turning its use into money, while those wishing to have access to land can do so on a more limited basis – and thus at a lower price – than by acquiring the freehold. In principle, however, there seems to be no reason why I should not give you a right exclusively to possess my land, for a term, and thereby grant you a lease, even without your paying for it.

The payment can be made as a lump sum, known in this context as a 'premium' or 'fine'. Leases for substantial periods are often acquired in this way. The price of a very long lease might well be little less than that of the freehold, even though, in contrast to a freehold, its value will necessarily diminish over time, eventually reaching zero. The other main form of payment is rent, ie a series of payments made at periodic intervals (weekly, monthly, quarterly, annual) over the life of the lease. The possibility of letting for a rent is especially valuable because it allows the temporary ownership of land to be sold to and bought by those unable or unwilling to pay up front. (The possibility of buying freehold ownership with a mortgage serves the same purpose, however.)

In *Street v Mountford*,[70] although Lord Templeman states at one point that a lease requires either rent or a premium, he also says several times that there must be rent.[71] This was a curious position, given the entirely familiar possibility of a premium,[72] and the Court of Appeal subsequently refused to adopt it,[73] but Lord Templeman later reiterated it.[74]

11.4.2 Term

A lease must have a 'term': that is, it must be limited to some particular duration.[75] So an arrangement expressed to last for a certain number of years (say 5, 7, 21, 99 . . .)[76] can be a lease, while one expressed to last forever cannot.

---

[70] *ibid* 818.

[71] *ibid* 816, 817, 818, 826, 827.

[72] And indeed the definition of a term of years absolute (lease) in the Law of Property Act 1925 s 205(1)(xxvii), which explicitly states rent to be inessential.

[73] *Ashburn Anstalt v WJ Arnold & Co* [1989] Ch 1, 9 (CA).

[74] *AG Securities v Vaughan* [1990] 1 AC 417, 454, 459, 462, 463 (HL); *Westminster City Council v Clarke* [1992] 2 AC 288, 299 (HL). But compare *Prudential Assurance Co Ltd v London Residuary Body* [1992] 2 AC 386, 390 (HL), where he defines a lease in terms which do not mention rent.

[75] It may of course terminate ahead of its nominal end, eg after breach of its terms (especially non-payment of rent) by the tenant, or by the agreement of landlord and tenant that it should do so (known as 'surrender').

[76] The rights under the lease will normally be active throughout the period specified, but this need not be the case: a timeshare arrangement, giving you the right exclusively to possess my land for, say, a particular fortnight each year, is a valid lease so long as its overall duration meets the rule under discussion (say, it lasts for 21 years).

Expressed thus, this rule is readily explained. It is simply a crystalline statement of the difference between two things that we may be trying to do, it being important to say which we have done. Either I mean to keep a reversion, in which case I necessarily do not grant you my land forever: that is, I give you a lease. Or I do not mean to keep a reversion, in which case I necessarily do give you the land forever: that is, I make you its freehold owner in my place.

There is a complication, however. Intermediate cases are possible: cases where the arrangement is expressed neither to last for a definite time, nor to last forever; where it is to last for a *defined* period of time, but one of uncertain *duration*. For example, an arrangement expressed to last 'until your bankruptcy', or 'until I also acquire the adjoining property'.

It was held in *Prudential Assurance Co Ltd v London Residuary Body*[77] that an arrangement to such effect cannot be a valid lease; that for a valid lease to arise, it must be possible to know its maximum duration from the outset, which in these examples it is obviously not. However, where you are a human being, a quirk in the law allows an arrangement of this kind to be a valid lease after all. It used (before 1925) to be treated by the law as giving you a lease for the duration of your life, but with a right on my part to terminate it ahead of your death, in whatever circumstances we may have agreed: in the examples under discussion, on your bankruptcy or my acquisition of the adjoining property. And under section 149(6) of the Law of Property Act 1925, such a lease for life is turned into one for 90 years, terminable likewise, and also of course on your death.[78] So this, which is a valid term (its maximum duration, 90 years, can be known at the outset), will be the result of our arrangement. But if you are not a human being – that is, if you are a corporation, and so capable of indefinite existence – the arrangement cannot be treated (or at any rate, never has been treated) as being for your life, and is therefore not turned by section 149(6) into a 90-year term. So the rule recognised in *Prudential Assurance Co Ltd v London Residuary Body*[79] continues to obtain, and you acquire no lease.

Our explanation for the headline requirement of a 'term' does not account for this detailed rule: even where we cannot know the arrangement's maximum duration from the outset, it is clearly different from an avowedly indeterminate arrangement, ie a freehold transfer. Indeed, the rule may well have no satisfactory basis.[80]

---

[77] [1992] 2 AC 386 (HL); see especially at 396.
[78] *Mexfield Housing Co-operative Ltd v Berrisford* [2011] 3 WLR 1091 (SC).
[79] [1992] 2 AC 386 (HL).
[80] This is suggested in the leading cases themselves: *Prudential Assurance Co Ltd v London Residuary Body, ibid; Mexfield Housing Co-operative Ltd v Berrisford* [2011] 3 WLR 1091, [34], [94]–[96], [112], [119] (SC). For discussion, see S Bright, 'Uncertainty in Leases – Is it a Vice?' (1993) 13 *LS* 38. *cf* P Sparkes, 'Certainty of Leasehold Terms' (1993) 109 *LQR* 93, defending the rule, as allowing the courts to undo arrangements which the parties intended to last only a short time ('until the landlord is ready to redevelop the land', for example) but which have ossified,

Certainly, it appears far from well rooted. For one thing, before *Prudential Assurance Co Ltd v London Residuary Body*,[81] while some decisions had taken the same line,[82] others had taken the contrary position, holding the only objectionable arrangement to be one of avowedly indefinite duration.[83] For another, no one seems worried that an arrangement for the duration of your life itself falls foul of the rule (your life is as much a period of uncertain duration as is the period before your bankruptcy, or my acquisition of the adjoining land[84]), and is reconciled with the rule only by the way that section 149(6) reworks it into a term of 90 years, terminable upon your earlier death. Again, the substantive difference between arrangements that fall foul of the rule, and others that do not, can be quite minimal – this being, of course, part of the very argument for section 149(6). (Likewise for the similar statutory reworking of purported leases for the duration of the Second World War, similarly falling foul of the rule,[85] into ones for 10 years but finishing on the earlier end of the War.[86]) And of course if you are a corporation rather than a human being, even though an arrangement until some unpredictable event does not automatically give you a lease for up to 90 years in the way that it does if you are a human, there is no objection at all to your taking an express term of 90 years, previously terminable on that event.

Moreover, the law has always accepted the validity of 'periodic tenancies': yearly, monthly or weekly tenancies. If I give you such a tenancy, you remain my tenant until one of us gives appropriate notice. Periodic tenancies were traditionally understood to operate as a single lease with neither a fixed nor a maximum duration, continuing until ended by notice.[87] On this account, they flatly contradict the theory that at least the maximum duration of an arrangement

commonly with no provision for a rise in rent. (In *Prudential Assurance Co Ltd v London Residuary Body*, *ibid*, the arrangement, pending a road-widening scheme, was made in 1930 at an annual rent of £30; by the date of the case, the market rent would probably have been about £10,000.) Even making the unlikely assumption that the law should rescue landlords from their incaution in this way, however, the rule in question goes too far: it renders such arrangements invalid from the very outset.

[81]   [1992] 2 AC 386 (HL).

[82]   eg *Lace v Chantler* [1944] KB 368 (CA).

[83]   *Re Midland Railway Co's Agreement* [1971] Ch 725 (CA); *Ashburn Anstalt v WJ Arnold & Co* [1989] Ch 1 (CA).

[84]   There is of course this difference: we know your life will end, some time, whereas we do not know that you will ever become bankrupt or that I will acquire the adjoining land. If the need is – as it is said to be – to be able to know the maximum duration from the outset, this difference is unimportant. But recall the basic point of the 'term' requirement, suggested earlier: ie distinguishing leases from freeholds. In these terms, the difference may indeed matter. Given mortality, we can say that since a lease terminating upon a human death (if not upon some other earlier event) will certainly come to an end (even if we cannot predict when), it is indeed thus distinguished from a freehold, which by definition will not.

[85]   *Lace v Chantler* [1944] KB 368 (CA).

[86]   Validation of War-time Leases Act 1944.

[87]   *Gandy v Jubber* (1865) 5 B & S 15, 18 (Ex Ch); *Re Midland Railway Co's Agreement* [1971] Ch 725, 732 (CA). The latter decision overtly made this understanding of periodic tenancies the basis of its wider position that an arrangement even without a maximum period is valid, so long as it is not avowedly indefinite. This position chimes with the comment made in n 84.

must be fixed. To square them with the rule recognised in *Prudential Assurance Co Ltd v London Residuary Body*,[88] they are nowadays presented instead as comprising a series of individual leases, each for the period in question, put end to end.[89] But even if they can properly be analysed in this way, their use to create arrangements that de facto have no maximum duration, and the absence of any objection to this, once again suggests that there is no real fault to be found with such arrangements.

In that the rule can lead to the eviction of the 'tenant' from the premises in question, by revealing a purported lease to be invalid, its application can evidently represent an interference with his home, engaging Article 8 of the ECHR.[90] And if, as one certainly suspects from all this, it lacks any sensible basis, this interference cannot be justified as proportionate, ie as being an apt means of delivering a legitimate end. Subject to issues of horizontal effect (§ 2.2), therefore, the rule must be liable to rejection on human rights grounds.[91]

11.4.3 Labels

In *Street v Mountford*,[92] the parties' agreement gave the occupant the right of exclusive possession, in return for a rent, and for a term, but asserted that the resulting arrangement should be a licence. If its nature had been fixed by this label, the arrangement would have fallen outside the Rent Acts, which applied only to (certain) leases. Reversing the decision of the Court of Appeal,[93] the House of Lords held that the arrangement's nature was not fixed by the parties' label. Rather, it followed from the presence or otherwise of the key indicators of a lease: exclusive possession, etc. These being present, the parties had created a lease, regardless of the label they had given it.

Lord Templeman explained the ruling by an analogy: 'The manufacture of a five-pronged implement for manual digging results in a fork even if the manufacturer, unfamiliar with the English language, insists that he intended

[88] [1992] 2 AC 386 (HL).

[89] *ibid* 394. See also *Hammersmith and Fulham London Borough Council v Monk* [1992] 1 AC 478, 492 (HL); *Barrett v Morgan* [2000] 2 AC 264, 272 (HL).

[90] 'Home' here has a broad meaning, extending to business premises: *Niemietz v Germany* (1993) 16 EHRR 97 (ECtHR). It would not, however, include a property that the tenant held merely as an investment, renting it in turn to others.

[91] As suggested by I Loveland, 'Security of Tenure for Tenants of Fully Mutual Housing Co-operatives' [2010] *Conv* 461. One might ask whether the rule also engages ECHR First Protocol Art 1, with similar results. An argument to the contrary would point out that, whereas the rule could easily lead to the eviction from your de facto 'home', it could not deprive you of (or otherwise interfere with) your 'possession': your relevant 'possession' could only be your lease, and owing to the rule, you never had a lease in the first place. But since this argument taps into the 'inherent limitation' idea (see § 2.3.3), and since that idea is so unstable, one cannot say with assurance that it will hold.

[92] [1985] AC 809 (HL).

[93] (1985) 49 P & CR 324 (CA).

to make and has made a spade.'[94] This, however, is bad reasoning (and not only because forks generally have four, not five, prongs).

Forks do indeed differ from spades in the matter of their having prongs rather than a blade, and in no other respect. The presence or absence of prongs is indeed determinative, therefore. But it cannot be assumed that the presence or absence of exclusive possession etc is similarly determinative of the difference between leases and licences. This was the question that the court had to decide.

The court ruled in the affirmative. But the opposite answer was possible. The law might recognise a right featuring exclusive possession etc as having the potential to be either a lease or a licence, leaving the determinative factor to be something else – notably, whether the parties wish the right to be in rem (lease) or in personam (licence[95]).[96] On the latter view, the presence of exclusive possession etc equates with the presence of a handle and a usefulness for digging, features which forks and spades share; while the determinative contrast between prongs and a blade equates with the contrast between the parties' having characterised the right as in rem (lease) or as in personam (licence).

In fact, this latter view of the matter is in principle more likely than that given by the House of Lords. When parties, creating a right, give it features matching the requirements for some kind of right in rem (say, an easement), the law's standard position is that they still have a choice whether it shall be that right in rem, or whether it shall exist purely as a contractual provision between themselves.[97] The House of Lords' decision to take the opposite position as regards leases carries the surprising illiberal implication that this kind of right (one involving exclusive possession etc) comes in only one version – as it happens, in rem – as the law, not the parties, shall decide. (As if only one kind of digging implement – either the fork or the spade, as announced by the state – were allowed on the market.) The explanation for the position taken by the House of Lords is, fairly obviously, not that for some exceptional reason we should want (only) rights with exclusive possession etc always to be in rem, but an assumption by the House of Lords that, apart from any exceptional cases, they should always be caught by the Rent Acts.[98]

---

[94] [1985] AC 809, 819 (HL).

[95] For licences as rights in personam, see § 17.1.1.

[96] Or, one might inquire, whether they wish it to attract the Rent Acts? But contracting out of the Rent Acts is assumed to be impermissible.

[97] As regards easements, this was recognised in *IDC Group Ltd v Clark* (1992) 65 P & CR 179 (CA): see § 13.1.5.

[98] See further J Hill, 'Intention and the Creation of Proprietary Rights: Are Leases Different?' (1996) 16 *LS* 200.

11.4.4 An Interpretation

A right will deserve recognition as in rem only if its having that status will do enough good to outweigh the harm that it will also do.[99] Whether this is the case will depend on the right's essential content. As explained in § 11.1.1, the essential content of a lease is temporary ownership. It is plainly appropriate to see ownership as a right in rem, because it connotes the ability to use land substantially as one wishes, with the boons of liberty and commercial advantage that this entails. And it is appropriate to treat temporary ownership as in rem too, as allowing most of the benefits of ownership to be sold and bought on a partial, rather than all-or-nothing, basis: so permitting fine-tuning of variables such as risk and cost, and in consequence further enhancing land's exploitability.

From this point of view, then, it is right to allow as much flexibility as possible over the configuration of leases: their duration, their cost, the other rights and obligations that can be built into them. It is essential, though, that the core idea of temporary ownership is maintained, so as to preserve the basis on which leases deserve to be rights in rem. It is correct, therefore, to insist on exclusive possession (ownership), and a term (making the ownership temporary). Which makes it seem as though, broadly speaking, the major authorities considered above – in particular, *Street v Mountford*[100] and *Prudential Assurance Co Ltd v London Residuary Body*[101] – merely state the obvious.

One cannot take such a simple view of these authorities, however. We have already seen how, as well as affirming the importance of these headline concepts, they and the rules developed in their wake also take a number of more detailed positions about the headline concepts' content and significance. Many of these positions, rather than simply explicating the idea of temporary ownership, give it a particular, stylised shape. *Street v Mountford*[102] is especially striking in this respect, and above all the ideas propounded by Lord Templeman there and subsequently.[103] Remember the equation of de facto exclusive occupation with the right of exclusive possession; the treatment of a landlord's rights of entry, making the word 'exclusive' not so determinative after all; the idea that exclusive possession is defined (negatively) by the concept of a 'lodger'; the view that certain situations, while involving exclusive possession, payment and term, are nevertheless not leases; the rule that aspects of the parties' arrangement can be discarded as being 'pretences', together with the unstable idea that a provision is a pretence if it does not represent the 'substance and reality' of the parties' arrangement, and the use of caricatured relationships in the construction of 'substance and reality'; the

---

[99] See § 1.2.2.
[100] [1985] AC 809 (HL).
[101] [1992] 2 AC 386 (HL).
[102] [1985] AC 809 (HL).
[103] Principally in *AG Securities v Vaughan, Antoniades v Villiers* [1990] 1 AC 417 (HL). See also *Westminster City Council v Clarke* [1992] 2 AC 288 (HL).

suggestion that rent is needed, whereas it is clearly inessential to the notion of temporary ownership; and the rule that the parties' own characterisation of the right as in personam rather than in rem can be disregarded as an incorrect 'label'. And *Prudential Assurance Co Ltd v London Residuary Body*[104] (the leading opinion again being given by Lord Templeman) contributes, as we saw in § 11.4.2, a strangely narrow understanding of 'term'.

These detailed positions are best understood as elements in a project to ensure that certain social situations are covered by the Rent Acts. The concept of a lease is relevant to this project only because it largely controls the Acts' applicability. If Lord Templeman thinks a particular situation ought (or ought not) to be covered by the Acts, he therefore has to announce that it is (or is not) a lease. Hence the relative inattention to the parties' legal positions; the emphasis instead on their positions on the ground; and the stereotyping of the kinds of people who are covered (eg those with 'interdependent' relationships), or not (eg 'lodgers', 'service occupiers'), by the 'definition'.[105] The puzzling decision in *Prudential Assurance Co Ltd v London Residuary Body*,[106] while not concerned with the Rent Acts, has at least some resonance with this project: it reiterates the message that the law does not leave parties to organise their own version of temporary ownership, but insists on its own template.[107]

11.5 Obligations in Leases

11.5.1 Kinds of Obligation

If an arrangement allowing you to occupy my land is to be a lease at all, I must have an obligation not to exercise what would otherwise be my own

---

[104] [1992] 2 AC 386 (HL).

[105] For a similar treatment of relationships for the purposes of employment law, see *Autoclenz Ltd v Belcher* [2011] 4 All ER 745 (SC).

[106] [1992] 2 AC 386 (HL).

[107] McFarlane and Simpson (n 45), discussing the pretence rule, suggest seeing it as an example of a statute about '*X*' applying not to *X* as defined by the law, but to *X* as understood in some extra-legal way (as taxation statutes may sometimes do: *Macniven v Westmoreland Investments Ltd* [2003] 1 AC 311 (HL); *cf* now *Barclays Mercantile Business Finance Ltd v Mawson* [2005] 1 AC 684 (HL)). Specifically, the idea would be that the Rent Acts should be read as applying to leases in their social, rather than legal, understanding, the pretence doctrine being used to remove considerations of purely legal significance from the picture. In the end, however, the authors withdraw the suggestion, on the basis that *Street v Mountford* [1985] AC 809 (HL) gives 'lease' in the Rent Acts its legal meaning, ie exclusive possession, payment and term. But according to the argument in the text, the suggestion was right all along. While ostensibly applying the legal idea of a lease, the decision in fact constructs it by reference to the social situations which it was sought to bring under the Rent Acts.

rights over the land, so that you can have it 'exclusively', as discussed earlier in this chapter. Normally, you will also have an obligation to pay me rent, unless you paid by way of an initial lump sum (and often even then). Most leases, however, impose on their landlord and/or tenant a number of additional obligations, usually called 'covenants'. Generally, though not always, these will relate to the treatment of the leased land itself. For example, you may be required to use the land for certain purposes, or not to use it for certain others,[108] possibly even to erect a building on it;[109] and one of us may be required to carry out maintenance and repairs as necessary.

We may make our covenants by express provisions in the lease,[110] but they may also be implied. Implied covenants are mainly imposed by statute,[111] and operate principally to oblige landlords to keep domestic residential accommodation in good order, apparently on a basis of respect for basic human decency.[112] Such covenants tend to be interpreted fairly narrowly, however: in particular, a covenant requiring repair is not taken to demand improvement.[113] There are two pressures against greater intervention.[114] One is the idea that parties should be left to fix their own arrangements: if you want the option of leasing a derelict house from me, cheaply, and doing it up yourself, the law ought not to stop you; to insist that I do the work in advance, thus raising the rent, may not serve your interests. The other is the reflection that

---

[108] The point of such obligations will often be to safeguard my commercial interests. Say I own a shopping mall. I lease out the individual units in it. In order to be able to extract the maximum profit, I may control the kind of goods that can be sold in each unit, so as to be able to promise each tenant freedom from competition within the mall, and/or the likelihood of passing trade generated by the presence in the mall of a magnet, such as a supermarket.

[109] An interesting type of obligation in that, at the end of your lease, the building (forming part of the land) will be mine. Of course, the price you have to pay for the lease should be smaller as a result.

[110] Though they may of course then be subject to challenge as improper in some way. It is controversial to what extent the ordinary law of contract may be used in making such challenge (see J Morgan, 'Leases: Property, Contract or More?' in M Dixon (ed), *Modern Studies in Property Law, Volume 5* (Oxford, 2009) 425), but in *R (Khatun) v Newham London Borough Council* [2005] QB 37 (CA) a local authority landlord's standard form terms were successfully impeached under the Unfair Terms in Consumer Contracts Regulations 1999 (SI 1999/2082).

[111] Principally the Landlord and Tenant Act 1985. Sometimes, however, an obligation is implied on ordinary contractual principles because it is necessary to the fulfilment of the parties' understanding. For example, a lease of 'a furnished dwelling-house' will impliedly require the landlord to ensure that the house is fit for habitation (*Smith v Marrable* (1843) 11 M & W 5 (Ex)): the house could hardly be let as a furnished (ie ready to use) dwelling-house otherwise. And a lease of a flat in a tower block will impliedly require the landlord to provide the stairs, lifts, rubbish chutes etc without which tower blocks cannot function (*Liverpool City Council v Irwin* [1977] AC 239 (HL)). In the context of 'occupation contracts', the Law Commission has recommended a higher baseline requirement: *Renting Homes: The Final Report* (n 21) Pt 8 – but there appears to be no prospect of the recommendation being implemented.

[112] The protection for the 'home' given by ECHR Art 8 is relevant, but may not make a significant practical difference: see *Lee v Leeds City Council* [2002] 1 WLR 1488 (CA).

[113] *Wainwright v Leeds City Council* [1984] 1 EGLR 67 (CA).

[114] See especially *Southwark London Borough Council v Mills* [2001] 1 AC 1 (HL); *Lee v Leeds City Council* [2002] 1 WLR 1488 (CA).

to require more, particularly by a wide interpretation of obligations in existing leases, will have the unfortunate result, in the case especially of public sector landlords, of distorting spending priorities.

11.5.2 Enforcement

If either of us breaches one of our obligations, remedies are available to the other.[115]

The set of available remedies includes some that are familiar from other parts of the law. In particular, I can sue you for unpaid rent; and I can sue you, and you can sue me, for damages for any loss resulting from breach of other obligations. We will generally be able to claim injunctions to prevent future breaches of obligations not to do something, and, under appropriate circumstances, specific performance of obligations to do something.[116] Less familiarly, self-help is also possible: if I fail in my responsibility to carry out repairs, under certain circumstances you can carry them out in my place and charge me for them; and if you are in arrears with your rent, I can sometimes have a court-authorised enforcement agent come onto the land, seize your belongings and sell them to recoup the debt.[117]

Under certain circumstances, a breach by one of us will also allow the other to terminate the lease. Where the breach is on the part of the landlord, the relevant rules are drawn from the law of contract, so the tenant will be able to withdraw if, but only if, the breach was a repudiatory one.[118] In principle, one might expect the same rules to apply equally to a breach by the tenant, say a failure to pay rent. In the latter context, however, the law

---

[115] Perceiving that ad hoc enforcement of individual obligations by domestic tenants against private landlords may not be fully viable or efficacious in practice, the Law Commission has proposed (without prospect of implementation, however) the promotion of good standards via better regulation of landlords in this sector: *Housing: Encouraging Responsible Letting* (Law Com No 312, London, 2008).

[116] On the relatively restricted availability of specific performance, see *Co-operative Insurance Society Ltd v Argyll Stores (Holdings) Ltd* [1998] AC 1 (HL).

[117] Tribunals, Courts and Enforcement Act 2007 Pt 3.

[118] *Hussein v Mehlman* [1992] 2 EGLR 87 (County Court). This decision, and others on which it rests (especially *National Carriers Ltd v Panalpina (Northern) Ltd* [1981] AC 675 (HL) and *Hammersmith and Fulham London Borough Council v Monk* [1992] 1 AC 478 (HL)), are often said to demonstrate the 'contractualisation' of leases. Care must be taken with this suggestion. These cases certainly rule that leases can end in ways derived from the law of contract, as opposed to the ways traditionally found in the law of leases. Another implication of 'contractualisation' might however be that the parties to a lease can structure it as they wish, ultimately perhaps not having to respect the law's differentiation between leases and other kinds of right at all. Although the courts have experimented with such a departure, their current position is against it (*Street v Mountford* [1985] AC 809 (HL), *Prudential Assurance Co Ltd v London Residuary Body* [1992] 2 AC 386 (HL): §§ 11.2–11.4), and many statutory rules relating to the content of leases are incapable of variation by the parties. See generally S Bridge, 'Leases – Contract, Property and Status' in L Tee (ed), *Land Law: Issues, Debates, Policy* (Cullompton, 2002) ch 4; Morgan (n 110) ch 17.

superimposes a more specialised regime known as 'forfeiture', which is in some ways more, and in others less, favourable to the tenant.[119]

For forfeiture to be a possibility, the terms of the lease must so provide, either in so many words or by labelling the obligation in question a 'condition'. If you breach such an obligation, I cannot terminate the lease without more, as I could a contract. First, I must notify you of your position, and normally[120] give you the chance to put your breach right – by paying your rent arrears, or compensating me for the damage done, and putting matters to rights for the future.[121] Then, even if you fail to put matters right, you may seek 'relief from forfeiture', ie an order by the court that I cannot forfeit after all.[122] If I am able to forfeit, I can do so either by obtaining a court order, or, except in the case of a residential lease,[123] by 're-entry', ie physically retaking the land.[124]

The landlord's ability to proceed by re-entry without a court order may, like other self-help remedies, be incompatible with Article 6 of the ECHR, requiring determination of civil rights and obligations by judicial proceedings.[125] The remaining details of the law on forfeiture are more complex than they need be,[126] but the essential idea is clear. The law seeks to confine me to my legitimate interests, which it regards as being in the performance of your obligations under the lease in substance, even if not to the letter. If you deliver such a performance, a right to terminate the lease will give me advantages

---

[119] Note also *Reichman v Beveridge* [2005] EWCA Civ 1659 (CA), declining to apply another detail of the contractual termination rules in the case of a breach by the tenant – again, adversely to the tenant's interests.

[120] I do not have to give you this chance if your breach is 'irremediable'. The test of this is not whether the fact of the breach can be undone: that is never the case. It is whether the damage can be put right in a practical sense: *Expert Clothing Service and Sales Ltd v Hillgate House Ltd* [1986] Ch 340 (CA). Using the leased land for 'immoral purposes' is a common instance of a breach found to be irremediable: it is said that such use gives the land a 'stigma' which discontinuance and compensation cannot remove (see eg *Rugby School (Governors) v Tannahill* [1935] 1 KB 87 (CA)). This view may be doubted, however. If the 'stigma' has a tangible impact (say by making the land harder to let in future), this surely can be remedied, by the payment of monetary compensation. If it does not, it is unclear how the landlord is damaged at all.

[121] There are separate regimes for rent (governed principally by the Common Law Procedure Act 1852 s 210, together with, for long residential leases, the Commonhold and Leasehold Reform Act 2002 ss 166–7) and for other obligations (the Law of Property Act 1925 s 146(1) and, for long residential leases, the Commonhold and Leasehold Reform Act 2002 s 168).

[122] Again, there are separate regimes for rent (see principally the Common Law Procedure Act 1852 s 212) and other obligations (principally the Law of Property Act 1925 s 146(2)). Other legislative regimes create yet further variations: see eg the Housing Act 1988 s 7 and Sch 2.

[123] Protection from Eviction Act 1977 s 3(1).

[124] In this case, you can apply for relief against forfeiture after my re-entry: *Billson v Residential Apartments Ltd* [1992] 1 AC 494 (HL).

[125] The Law Commission has proposed abolition (*Termination of Tenancies for Tenant Default* (Law Com No 303, London, 2006) Pt 7), but without prospect of implementation.

[126] Albeit, again, without prospect of implementation, the Law Commission has made proposals for streamlining: *ibid*, and, in the particular case of 'occupation contracts', *Renting Homes: The Final Report* (n 21) Pts 4 and 5. See further P Sparkes, 'Towards a Structure for the Law of Landlord and Tenant' in E Cooke (ed), *Modern Studies in Property Law, Volume 1* (Oxford, 2001) ch 13.

going beyond my legitimate interests. To take a plain instance, say you lease a house from me for 21 years for a lump sum; the terms oblige you not to make alterations without my consent; after a couple of years, you break this obligation in some minor way; an untrammelled right to forfeit would allow me on that account to evict you (retaining the lump sum while I relet the property), or to induce you to pay me an additional amount (more than the mere cost of restoration) for fear that otherwise you will lose everything. To ensure that I cannot extract more than my legitimate interests in this way, forfeiture should not be not permitted in such a case. It is aimed at the case where you do not deliver a substantial performance, and my only way of enjoying my legitimate interests is to part company with you and move on.

The ideas in play here are also to be seen in the area of mortgages[127] and in further contexts involving the forfeiture of rights in land.[128] They have, however, been disavowed in most other contexts.[129] They seem to apply only to the forfeiture of a property interest, rather than to the termination of a contractual right.[130] The idea may be that only a property interest merits protection against all but a proportionate vindication of a significant competing interest; mere contractual rights being left to the play of the market. This would be intelligible, but perhaps involve an under-estimation of what is at stake in at least some contractual cases.

Subject to questions of horizontal effect in the case of private sector leases (discussed in § 2.2[131]), the termination of a lease, whether by forfeiture or otherwise, may also engage the ECHR First Protocol Article 1 (interference with possessions). It is, however, not easy to say which terminations should be seen as interfering with possessions, and which as merely picking up on an 'inherent limitation' of the lease itself (see § 2.3.3). This is due partly to the weakness of the latter concept, and partly to the lack of authority and discussion. Both categories appear to be populated, however. The simple expiry of a lease in accordance with its terms must surely be a case of 'inherent limitation';[132]

---

[127] § 12.2.2.

[128] *Shiloh Spinners Ltd v Harding* [1975] AC 691 (HL).

[129] In particular, so as not prevent the withdrawal of a ship from a time charter for late payment of hire (*Scandinavian Trading Tanker Co AB v Flota Petrolea Ecuatoriana, The Scaptrade* [1983] 2 AC 694 (HL)); nor the termination of a contractual right to be the exclusive retailer of a manufacturer's products (*Sport International Bussum BV v Inter-Footwear Ltd* [1984] 1 WLR 776 (HL)).

[130] *BICC plc v Burndy Corp* [1985] Ch 232 (CA), applying the 'legitimate interest' to the forfeiture of a patent right, which is a property interest.

[131] Note *Di Palma v United Kingdom* (1986) 10 EHRR 149 (ECommHR), where it was held (at Strasbourg) that the ECHR was inapplicable to a private sector forfeiture case, because the state had no obligation to prevent a landlord from stipulating for such an outcome and then enforcing it. This approach to the 'horizontal effect' issue is discussed, and criticised, in § 2.2.1. See too A Goymour 'Property and Housing' in D Hoffman (ed), *The Impact of the Human Rights Act on Private Law* (Cambridge, 2011) ch 12, 256–7.

[132] This is a fortiori from *Sheffield City Council v Smart* [2002] EWCA Civ 4, [46] (CA), treating a landlord's termination of a lease by notice to quit as not interfering with the tenant's First Protocol Art 1 right. See too *A v United Kingdom* (1988) 10 EHRR CD149, 155 (ECommHR).

while the loss of a particular statutory protection has been assumed to be an interference.[133] When (or if) one comes to the matter of proportionality, the landlord's ownership must obviously be part of the mix,[134] but to say this is to raise questions as well as to help answer them, given the compromised quality of 'ownership' itself.[135]

Likewise, the termination of a domestic residential lease may engage ECHR Article 8 (interference with home). Or perhaps *will* do so. For on the face of it, any such termination can be seen as an interference with the tenant's home, so requiring justification as legitimate and proportionate. This is certainly the impression given by the dominant authorities.[136] As is especially shown by the simple case of a lease expiring in accordance with its terms, however, it is not a wholly convincing perspective. The awkwardness arises from a fundamental difficulty besetting the ECHR, discussed in § 5.1.2, namely its lack of engagement with choice. If this consideration were taken seriously in the present context, it would perhaps play out into something not unlike the 'inherent limitation' idea again (ie to count as an 'interference', an event would need to be more than a product of one's own choice, in the way that a routine termination of a lease appears to be).[137] The decisions to date have not engaged with the issue. So long as it remains thus unaddressed, it will be liable to skew future decisions in an unacknowledged way. Finally: if one gets to the question of proportionality, the remarks in the previous paragraph apply here too.

11.6 Acquisition of Leases

The rules regarding the creation of leases have been examined fully in § 5.5, and will be only briefly recapitulated here.

[133] *Pennycook v Shaws (EAL) Ltd* [2004] Ch 296 (CA).

[134] This was noted (in the context of Art 8, rather than of First Protocol Art 1, but there seems no reason to differentiate) in *Manchester City Council v Pinnock* [2011] 2 AC 104, [54] (SC). It was also noted there that the particular landlord, being a public authority, had the right, or more accurately obligation, to manage its housing stock in the best interests of its stakeholders, which too entered the mix. It may in fact be doubted whether such a landlord, in contrast to a private individual or entity, has a significant 'ownership' right of any other kind than this: see § 2.4.4.

[135] See Ch 10. Though of course the factors that give ownership this compromised quality may – so far as is relevant to the present context – be exactly those which would weigh against an uncompromised idea of ownership, on the tenant's side of the proportionality balance. One must therefore be wary of double-counting these factors against the landlord.

[136] *McCann v United Kingdom* (2008) 47 EHRR 40 (ECtHR); *Kay v United Kingdom* [2011] HLR 2 (ECtHR); *Manchester City Council v Pinnock* [2011] 2 AC 104 (SC); *Hounslow London Borough Council v Powell* [2011] 2 AC 186 (SC).

[137] This position, or something like it, seems to have been taken in *Horsham Properties Group Ltd v Clark* [2009] 1 WLR 1255, [13] (Ch D), treating the legitimate sale of mortgaged property (which may be seen as an event parallel for present purposes to the termination of a lease) as not constituting an interference with the borrower's Art 8 right. See § 12.4.1.

A new lease is given, and an existing lease transferred, normally by an intentional conferral. (Leases are occasionally given as relief for proprietary estoppel claims, and can also be acquired by adverse possession, as where you squat on land of which I am already a tenant.)

A lease for a fixed or periodic term of three years or less may usually be created orally.[138] Otherwise, the conferral requires a deed.[139] Once the term goes above seven years, and in certain other cases, its conferral is not effective unless it is also registered.[140] Remember, however, that if I purport to confer a lease on you but fail to use the necessary formality, the conferral may nevertheless have some effect. If our transaction is nevertheless in writing, it will give you an 'equitable lease': not dissimilar to the lease that was meant, but in certain ways not quite so robust.[141] Or if you begin paying me rent, you will probably be found to have a periodic tenancy. When we looked at this assembly of rules in § 5.5, we found that it can be understood up to a point, but is in some major ways unjustified. The rules providing for electronic registration would produce a more coherent treatment, if that project were pursued.

11.7 Alienating Reversions and Leases

If I lease my land to you, both you and I have rights somewhat in the nature of ownership over it – I because the freehold title remains mine, you because you have your lease – in the way explored in § 11.1.1. So in principle, both of us can alienate our rights to someone else.

We might of course wish to alienate only some limited aspect of our rights. For example, I might mortgage my reversion, or you might mortgage your term; or you might grant an easement or a licence over the land, necessarily for a period not longer than the remaining duration of your lease. Such cases pose no particular problems: they do not affect our remaining respectively landlord and tenant. We need to spend a moment, however, looking at the case where I alienate my whole interest as landlord, or you alienate the core of your interest as tenant – the right of exclusive possession itself.

Such an alienation can take two different forms: *assignment* (by the landlord or the tenant), and *sub-leasing* (by the tenant). The next two sections explore these, explaining how their effects are governed by an idea known as 'privity of estate'.

---

[138] Law of Property Act 1925 s 54(2).
[139] *ibid* s 52.
[140] Land Registration Act 2002 s 27(2)(b).
[141] § 6.2.2.

11.7.1 Assignment

An assignment is a complete transfer of the interest in question. So I might transfer my reversion to John. (I could do this simply by transferring the land itself. Your lease, as a right in rem, would bind John so long as the relevant rules of the Land Registration Act 2002 were satisfied,[142] leaving him with the reversion alone.) Or you might transfer your lease to Kate.

The effect of an assignment is captured in the idea of privity of estate. This connotes that the landlord–tenant relationship exists, ie the rights and obligations contained in the lease are enforceable, between those holding the positions of landlord and tenant under it at a given time: that is, between assignees as well as original parties. The reversion and the lease are regarded as actually *comprising* the respective sets of rights and obligations, so to assign one of them is necessarily to pass those rights and obligations to the assignee. The assignee thus automatically acquires all the rights and obligations embedded in the interest assigned. So if I assign my reversion to John, John becomes your landlord in my place: henceforth, your liabilities are to him rather than me, and your rights are likewise against him rather than me. Conversely, if you assign your lease to Kate, Kate becomes my tenant in your place, and the liabilities and rights vis-à-vis me become Kate's rather than yours. And if both I and you have assigned, to John and Kate respectively, the landlord's and tenant's liabilities and rights now subsist between John and Kate.

Applying this idea requires us to say which rights and obligations are embedded in the interest assigned, ie affect the landlord and tenant in their capacities as such, as opposed to their personal capacities. The law has changed its approach to this task. Before the Landlord and Tenant (Covenants) Act 1995 came into effect in 1996, it asked whether the right or obligation was one 'touching and concerning', or 'having reference to',[143] the lease. If so, it was embedded, and thus passed on an assignment.[144] This remains the rule for leases made before 1996. It focuses on the correct issue, but uses concepts which, at the margin, are hard to pin down, generating uncertainty. The newer approach, applicable to leases made since 1996, instead treats all rights and obligations generated in the transaction creating the lease as embedded in the lease, unless they are expressed to be personal

---

[142] If the lease is one requiring registration in order to be effective at all (s 27(2)(b)), the same registration will make it bind a disponee. Otherwise, it will bind if it is registered (leases capable of oral creation cannot be registered: s 33(b); but all others can: s 34); or if it is overriding (legal leases are automatically overriding under Sch 3 para 1; an equitable lease can qualify as an overriding interest instead under Sch 3 para 2, if it is held by someone in actual and apparent occupation of the land in question).

[143] For these concepts, see *Hua Chiao Commercial Bank Ltd v Chiaphua Industries Ltd* [1987] AC 99 (PC); *P & A Swift Investments v Combined English Stores Group Plc* [1989] AC 632 (HL).

[144] Law of Property Act 1925 ss 141, 142 (assignment of the reversion); *Spencer's Case* (1583) 5 Co Rep 16a (QB) (assignment of the term).

only.[145] The essential idea remains the same, but this technique of leaving the parties to opt out is a clearer way of getting at it: leases containing covenants over whose nature there might be doubt are likely to be professionally drafted, so the opting-out rule will elicit the parties' own decision as to what is meant.

A final detail. When I lease to you, I almost certainly enter into a contract with you. So the obligations each of us has to the other are enforceable as a matter of contract . . . and remain so even if we part with our reversion or term. Say you assign your lease to Kate, and Kate fails to perform an obligation which, as already explained, she thus now owes me as my tenant. I can enforce the obligation against Kate, but the fact of the contract between me and you means in principle that I can alternatively enforce it against you. And if, for example, Kate is insolvent, I might well wish to do so. Because this seems oppressive to you (you have probably moved on and naturally pay no attention to what ensues between Kate and me), the law protects you. If our lease was made before 1996, your exposure remains, but with certain limits and compensations.[146] If it was made more recently, your liability terminates upon your assignment,[147] though you can often be made to replace it with a new obligation creating a limited exposure after all.[148]

11.7.2 Sub-leasing

As explained in § 11.7.1, assignment is a complete transfer of the interest in question. So if you are my tenant, and you assign your lease to Kate, she becomes my tenant in your place. There is another way in which you, as my tenant, can alienate: by sub-leasing.

In this case, the alienation is not outright (that would be an assignment); it is for a period shorter than the remaining duration of your own lease. Say I give you a 10 year lease, and you immediately sub-lease to Liam for five years (or even for 10 years less one day). Unlike in an assignment, you keep your lease with me – you remain my tenant, I remain your landlord – but for those five years, you become Liam's landlord, and Liam becomes your tenant: and my sub-tenant. In such an arrangement, your lease is sometimes called a 'head lease'. There is no limit to the number of times the land may be sub-leased, so Liam (my sub-tenant) may himself sub-lease, for a period shorter than five years, to Meg, who is thus my sub-sub-tenant; and so on.

Combinations of assignment and sub-leasing are possible. So, say I lease to you. You sub-lease to Liam, and Liam sub-leases to Meg. I assign my

---

[145] Landlord and Tenant (Covenants) Act 1995 ss 2, 3; *BHP Petroleum Great Britain Ltd v Chesterfield Properties Ltd* [2002] Ch 194 (CA).

[146] Landlord and Tenant (Covenants) Act 1995 ss 17, 19.

[147] *ibid* s 5. By ss 6–8, there is a similar, though less thorough, rule terminating the contractual liability of landlords who assign.

[148] *ibid* s 16.

reversion to John: he thus becomes overall landlord in my place. You assign your head lease to Kate: she thus becomes John's tenant, and Liam's landlord, in your place. (Or the chronology might be reversed: you might assign to Kate, then Kate might sub-lease to Liam.) Liam in turn sub-leases to Meg; either or both may also assign their interest.

In § 11.7.1, we saw how the effect of assignment is captured in the idea of privity of estate. The 'estate' is a given lease (such as mine to you), and the rights and obligations established in it operate between persons 'privy to' it: its original parties and their assignees. The effect of sub-leasing is likewise captured by privity of estate, but this time by its implicit connotation that the estate obtains, and its rights and obligations operate, *only* between the original parties and their assignees. That is, the landlord–tenant relationship exists, ie the lease's rights and obligations are enforceable, across only one level of letting at a time: so, between landlord (or his assign) and tenant (or his assign), and between tenant (or his assign) and sub-tenant (or his assign) . . . *but not between landlord and sub-tenant*.

To revert to our example, then, there is a landlord–tenant relationship between me (or my assignee, John) and you (or your assignee, Kate) throughout. And when you sub-lease to Liam, there is a landlord–tenant relationship between you (or Kate) and Liam (and anyone to whom he may in turn assign). But there is no such relationship between me (or John) and Liam. And when Liam sub-leases to Meg, there is likewise no such relationship between either me (or John) or you (or Kate) and Meg: only between Liam and Meg. So if I do not receive the rent which you and I agreed as a term of our lease, my only recourse is against you (or Kate): not against Liam or Meg.

11.7.3 Two Qualifications

But this account, focusing on privity of estate, does not give a true picture of the law as a whole. There exist two qualifications: two ways in which rights and obligations can after all be enforced across more than one level of letting at a time, say between landlord (eg me) and sub-tenant (eg Liam).[149]

First, by resort to forfeiture. If you are my tenant, and as a result of a breach of an obligation upon you I am able to forfeit your lease, everyone to whom you have given rights derived from that lease will lose those rights too.

---

[149] In addition, certain other more general rules can sometimes be relevant. In particular, under the Contracts (Rights of Third Parties) Act 1999, if X, in a contract with Y, undertakes an obligation in favour of Z, Z (as well as Y) can enforce it against X. Say, then, in my lease with you I undertake responsibility for repairs . . . then you sub-let to Liam. A lease will normally be a contract too, and the Act will therefore apply: so if my obligation is read as not merely for your benefit *but also for the benefit of anyone holding through or under you*, Liam (as well as you) will be able to enforce it against me. The key question, however, is whether my obligation should be read in that way. Arguably, a standard lease obligation is meant to be bounded by privity of estate, making such a reading inaccurate.

So if you have sub-leased to Liam, Liam's sub-lease will disappear, as will the sub-sub-lease that Liam later gives Meg.

At face value, indeed, this rule's effect goes beyond any idea of my 'enforcing' anything against Liam and Meg: I could be interested only in you, leaving Liam and Meg simply innocent victims of the logic of forfeiture. But the forfeiture regime permits the court, while allowing me to forfeit your lease, to protect anyone having a right derived from yours if it wishes.[150] The court will do so if it regards the person in question as not to blame for the situation precipitating the forfeiture. In practice, this allows me to put pressure on sub-tenants etc to respect the terms of the lease itself, even though they are not officially bound to me on those terms.

The second qualification consists in a special application of the rule we shall come to in Chapter 14, whereby a negative ('restrictive') covenant can, as a right in rem, bind anyone holding the land to which it applies.[151]

Say that the property which I lease to you is my house A, and that in the lease there is a covenant prohibiting the use of house A for business purposes. The rule allows this covenant, being negative ('*prohibiting*'), to operate in rem, so as to bind disponees of house A: but to do so only if it benefits another piece of land. So if I inserted it in the lease of house A so as to protect my neighbouring house B, the covenant will bind not only you (and your assignee, Kate), as a term of your lease: it will likewise bind Liam and Meg, for they are disponees of the affected land, and as such are caught by the covenant's in rem effect. This is an entirely routine application of the restrictive covenant rule, and involves no qualification to the idea of privity of estate: my right against Liam and Meg belongs to me not as landlord of house A, but as owner of house B. The rule's special application, which does qualify privity of estate, occurs when the land for whose benefit I insert the covenant in your lease of house A is not my neighbouring house B, but my reversionary (ie landlord's) interest in house A itself. The courts have decided that such an interest too qualifies as 'benefited land' for the purposes of this rule,[152] so the covenant will operate in rem in this instance as well: meaning that the covenant binds not only you (and Kate), but also Liam and Meg . . . in my favour, *as landlord*.

This special application of the restrictive covenant rule involves a radical departure from the rule's original thrust. As we shall see when we come to discuss the issue in § 14.2.3, the rule in its standard form makes obligations operate in rem if, *and because*, they protect the standard of amenity prevailing between neighbouring plots of (necessarily) physical land. By not conforming

---

[150] Law of Property Act 1925 s 146(4). A sub-tenant protected in this way becomes tenant in the original tenant's place. Equally, if the fault leading to the forfeiture lies wholly with the sub-tenant, the court can allow the forfeiture to go ahead so far as it affects the sub-tenant, but relieve the tenant.

[151] That is, the rule in *Tulk v Moxhay* (1848) 2 Ph 774 (Ch).

[152] *Hall v Ewin* (1887) 37 Ch D 74 (CA). The rule is preserved in the Landlord and Tenant (Covenants) Act 1995 s 3(5).

to that factual pattern, the special application therefore cannot rest on the same justification. It must have a basis of its own, on the lines that the distinction between assignee and sub-tenant (and sub-sub-tenant, etc) is unimportant: the protection of the landlord's reversionary interest requires that the lease's terms be effective against both. Contrary to the assumption made by the idea of privity of estate, that seems a very understandable position, resting on the idea that a tenant, on sub-leasing, should not be able to confer more (in the sense of an interest with fewer obligations to the landlord) than he himself has.

Because it is technically a special application of the restrictive covenant rule, this second qualification to privity of estate operates only on lease terms which impose a negative obligation on the tenant. Because, as we shall see in Chapter 14, the rule applies only to negative and not to positive covenants, the qualification does not apply to terms creating a positive obligation, such as a covenant to pay rent or keep the house in good repair. The reach of the latter continues to be limited by privity of estate, ie to extend across only one level of letting at a time. This limitation seems inappropriate. The negativity requirement may or may not be justified as an aspect of the rule's standard form.[153] But in the context of our special application, the requirement seems quite arbitrary. As we saw in the previous paragraph, the special application rests on the idea that a tenant should not be able to give away more than he himself has. And that idea makes as much sense for positive obligations as it does for negative ones. This lesson can best be absorbed, however, not by extending the standard rule to positive as well as negative covenants (whether or not that might be a good idea per se), but by attacking the fundamental problem – privity of estate – itself.

[153] See § 14.2.5.

Mortgages

In common speech, the expression 'a mortgage' is often used to refer to a money advance, normally taken from a building society or bank so as to buy a house. In law, it has a rather different meaning, though the two are connected. Put briefly, a mortgage is the right of resort that the building society or bank gains over the borrower's house, enabling it to repossess and sell the house so as to recoup itself if the advance is not repaid. As such, it is a right (held by the building society or bank) over (the householder's) land. It is also, as we shall discover, a right in rem. As such, it belongs in the series of rights in rem in land through which we are moving.

There are, naturally, a number of details to be looked at. On top of these, however, there are certain complications, arising from the roundabout way in which English law has evolved its current vision of a mortgage, and is continuing to shape that vision. So we shall begin by sketching the essential idea of a mortgage of land. Then we shall turn briefly to the history, before examining the current rules in detail, noting the points at which the circuitous development of these rights has given them an odd configuration.

12.1 The Essential Idea of a Land Mortgage

12.1.1 Mortgages as Security Rights

Say you lend me some money. I incur a debt to you: that is, a legal obligation to repay you, which you can enforce, if necessary by suing me. Which is fine, except if I find myself under obligations to you and other creditors for a total amount that I cannot afford to repay, even if I go beyond my ready cash and draw on my assets as a whole – meaning, essentially, that I am bankrupt. You and my other creditors will not get all your money back. Instead, you will receive only your due proportion of my available assets.

But there is a way for you to improve your position. You can insist that my debt to you be 'secured' on my assets in general, or some particular item(s) within them: very possibly, my land. The effect of this is that, if I fail to repay the loan, you can resort to the asset comprising the security: take it away from me, sell it, and repay the debt from the proceeds. By securing my debt to you in this way, you separate yourself from my other creditors, whose rights are unsecured. The latter are sometimes called 'general creditors', and your security right gives you 'priority [over them] in [my] bankruptcy'. So long as the value of the asset comprising your security is at least as great as the sum I owe you, your ability to resort to this asset means that you will now recover this sum in full, while the general creditors continue to suffer a shortfall. Indeed, their position becomes worse, for the assets available to pay them no longer include the asset securing my debt to you, except to the extent that the latter's value exceeds that of the debt.

You might be unwilling to lend to me at all without the debt being secured in this way. Overall, however, I probably could find someone who is willing ... but only in return for a higher rate of interest. The risk of a loan going unpaid, ie of the lender losing all his money, is evidently greater where the loan is unsecured than where it is secured. An actuarial reckoning of this risk is one of the factors to which the lender will attend in deciding whether to make the loan, and more especially on what terms to do so: the greater the risk, the higher his return (the interest rate) will need to be so as to cover it. So secured loans, in presenting (*ceteris paribus*) a lower risk, will be at lower rates of interest.

Your security right over my asset is called a mortgage, or alternatively a charge.[1] I, the borrower, am the 'mortgagor', while you, the lender, are the 'mortgagee'. My paying off the debt I owe you, at which point you lose your security right, is called 'redeeming'. The asset over which you have your right is often itself called your 'security'. More than one debt can be secured against the same piece of land, and in this event they can normally be recouped from its value in chronological order: meaning that the mortgagor under a first mortgage is generally in a better position than one under a second or subsequent mortgage (above all, of course, if the land's value is inadequate to cover the whole series of debts). Of first mortgages, the great majority are 'acquisition mortgages', ie used to secure a loan that the

---

[1] Strictly speaking, the two terms have different meanings. Both are security rights, but they arise in different ways. A 'charge' arises where I grant you a security right pure and simple. A 'mortgage' arises where I transfer my asset to you, on the basis that you will retransfer it to me (only) if I pay off my debt to you. § 12.1.4 explains the use English law has made of the two forms, and the current position. Where the distinction between them is not important, however, the words 'mortgage' and 'charge' are generally used as synonyms, the former being more common.

borrower takes out to help buy the land in question in the first place. A second mortgage is usually granted over land that he already owns, to secure a loan made to him for some other purpose.

12.1.2 Mortgages as Rights in Rem

A mortgage is a right in rem. Unlike the other rights in rem discussed in this book, however, we should not in practice expect a mortgage to affect a transferee of the asset to which it relates. If I have mortgaged my land to you, then I transfer the land to John, I will normally use the purchase money I receive from John to redeem the mortgage, so that John acquires the land free of it. The more important manifestation of a mortgage's status as a right in rem is the very way it operates to give you security, and especially priority in my bankruptcy. It does so on the basis that, to the extent of your right to resort to the asset in question to repay the debt, the asset is yours. So if I become bankrupt, and my assets are taken and sold to pay off my debts, the security asset is excepted: to the extent of your right, it is not mine but yours. As explained in § 1.1.2, this – 'nemo dat quod non habet' – is the basis on which rights are seen as in rem generally; effectiveness against disponees is another facet of it.

12.1.3 Mortgages of Land

So say I am negotiating to borrow a significant sum of money from you. You are willing in principle to lend it to me, but you are likely to require me to secure my obligation to repay it onto one or more of my assets. In practice, the asset on which we fix will commonly be some land that I own . . . or will own by the time I incur the debt: my very object in seeking the loan might well be to assemble the money that I need in order to buy the land.

The latter scenario represents the enormously common case where I buy a house; cannot afford to pay for it in cash; so, usually after a small cash downpayment ('deposit'), pay for the rest via a loan from a building society or bank. The picture we have of this situation may be that the lender now owns the house, until such time as I have paid all the instalments, when it becomes mine. In fact, however, the lender pays the loan money to me; I use it (together with my existing cash, whether savings or the net proceeds of selling my previous house) to buy the house, paying the seller the entire price for it up front, so that the house becomes quite literally mine;[2] then I owe the lender the sum

---

[2] Notice the way that we feel able to say that I own the house, despite the significant inroad into my rights that the mortgage entails. This is an example both of the way that 'ownership' can be qualified, and of the resilience of the idea of 'ownership', such that we continue to use the term even in the face of quite major qualifications. See §§ 10.1.2, 10.3.2.

it has loaned me, and must repay it this sum, plus whatever interest falls due over the time it takes me.[3] The lender has its mortgage over the house, securing my payment of these liabilities, because it required me to grant it such a mortgage as a condition of giving me the loan. So at a single instant, the loan comes through; I use the money so raised to pay the seller for the house; the house becomes mine; and I give the lender its mortgage.[4] The reason why we do not normally notice all these complications is that they are handled on our behalf by the solicitors acting for me, the seller and the lender, largely as a matter of routine.

In enabling the instalment-purchase of houses in this way, acquisition mortgages are of huge importance in contemporary Britain: without them, the options would be to buy the ownership of the house for cash, which very few could afford, or to rent, and so never become owner oneself, which would leave many dissatisfied.[5] But in their different way, second mortgages – where a house is mortgaged *after* purchase, so as to borrow money for spending on something else (often called 'equity release') – are also important. The 'something else' might be simple consumption: mortgages used in this way contributed to the consumer demand drive that featured prominently in the arrangement of the current British economy before the 2008 crash. Or it might be a project that empowers the borrower or those close to him in some more enduring way, such as enlarging his house or sending his children to university. Or it might be the establishment or expansion of his business, so creating employment and wealth more generally. As explained in § 12.1.1, even if loans for such purposes could be obtained without security, they would be more expensive, thus inhibiting the expenditure to which they might be devoted.

There is nothing in the abstract to say that my loan from you has to be secured on my land (nor even that a loan you give me to buy my house has to be secured on that house): in principle, any of my assets can be used. Land is commonly used, partly because it is often by far the most valuable of my assets, and hence uniquely capable of securing a large loan. Partly too because it tends to retain its value well, especially over the long term, which is important for these purposes: you would be ill advised to secure a 10-year loan for

---

[3] There is room for a variation on the theme. An arrangement whereby I make direct repayments to the lender is called a 'repayment' mortgage. Sometimes, I will instead make payments to some other financial institution, which will invest them with a view to generating a lump sum with which I can, in due course, repay the lender in one go. An 'endowment' mortgage is an example of the latter kind of arrangement. Crucially, however, the responsibility of repaying the loan remains mine in either case: the difference is merely a choice on my part between different approaches to doing so.

[4] And unless I am a first-time buyer, I simultaneously also transfer my old house to its buyer, receive his payment for it, pay off what remains of my mortgage on it, and put any remaining money into the payment I now make for my new house.

[5] For reflection on the tension between relaxed availability of mortgages, so as to fund owner-occupancy, and ensuring that mortgages are taken out only where truly affordable, see S Nield, 'Responsible Lending and Borrowing: Whereto Low-cost Home Ownership?' [2010] *LS* 610.

£1 million on my fleet of lorries, at the time worth that amount but obviously prone to depreciate over the 10 years to a small fraction of it, leaving the loan to that extent de facto unsecured. And partly because, thanks to the registration rules relating to land, I am unlikely to be able to conceal your rights in it so as to dispose of it, a move which could again otherwise leave your loan unsecured after all.

Because land is so commonly made the subject of security rights in this way, the rules on the subject can be expected to be especially detailed. And because land's other significances tend to be particularly important – above all, the piece of land in question will often be my home – these rules can be expected to exhibit an unusual degree of complexity, the result of the balance that the law has to strike between the various relevant considerations. The law fulfils these expectations. We shall look at the principal rules in §§ 12.3–12.6.[6]

12.1.4 The Current Legal Form of a Land Mortgage

Under the current law, a mortgage of registered land involves the borrower granting the lender a 'charge' over his land.[7] A charge is in principle a pure security right, as outlined thus far. But the law[8] views a charge over land as equivalent to a 3,000 year lease of the land from the borrower to the lender.

On the face of it, a security right and a lease are very different things. In particular, a lease entitles the lessee (the lender) to occupy the lessor's (borrower's) land, something not to be expected from a security right. It does not terminate when the debt is repaid. Nor, if the debt is not repaid, does it entitle the lessee to sell the freehold so as to recoup the amount outstanding, in the way that a security right demands. But by further rules, these inappropriate consequences of the lease are substantially removed, so as to produce an approximation to a pure security right after all.[9] Conceptually, however, the arrangement, with its introduction of a lease, remains grotesque. Moreover, the position today is only an *approximation* to a pure security right: there are points at which it still does not take quite the form one would expect of a pure security right. It derives from the history of the subject, prevailing – and showing these defects – today because the updating that has occurred has

---

[6] See further J Houghton and L Livesey, 'Mortgage Conditions: Old Law for a New Century?' in E Cooke (ed), *Modern Studies in Property Law, Volume 1* (Oxford, 2001) ch 10; M Oldham, 'Mortgages' in L Tee (ed), *Land Law: Issues, Debates, Policy* (Cullompton, 2002) ch 6. (These essays' references to the Consumer Credit Act 1974 are now out of date: the relevant provisions have been replaced by ss 140A–140C, introduced by the Consumer Credit Act 2006.)

[7] Land Registration Act 2002 s 23(1)(a).

[8] Law of Property Act 1925 s 87(1).

[9] As regards occupation, see § 12.5. As regards termination upon repayment, see the Law of Property Act 1925 s 85(1), to which s 87(1) refers. As regards sale of the freehold, see the Law of Property Act 1925 ss 88(1), 104(1), and § 12.4.

been insufficiently lucid. It will be necessary, therefore, to take a brief look at the history.[10]

12.2 The History of Land Mortgages

12.2.1 The Historical Development of the Legal Form

In late medieval times, the borrower leased his land to the lender; or, a little later, transferred the freehold in it to him, with a provision for transfer back to the borrower when the debt was paid. If the debt was not paid, the lender could recoup himself from the interest so granted to him – the freehold version being better from this point of view than the lease. But at least as important, having the freehold or lease also allowed the lender to possess the land in the meantime. Such a general right to possess the land is out of place in a pure security interest,[11] but was vital at this time, when usury – lending money for profit – was prohibited. Having possession of the land, the lender was able to extract an income from it ... and this income took the place of interest on the loan.

Eventually, this latter consideration fell away, as the laws against usury were first changed so as to allow the taking of interest not exceeding a certain percentage, then dropped altogether, so that it became possible straightforwardly to stipulate for interest.[12] There was then no need for the lender to have a general right to possess the land: only a pure security right was in principle required. Inertia prevailed, however, and mortgages continued to be made principally by freehold transfer. But such a mortgage could in principle be made to emulate a pure security right almost exactly. If you lent me money, the terms of our arrangement could provide, for example, that you would allow me to remain in possession; that so long as I continued to be able to repay, I would not lose the land; and that if I did lose it, you would have to make over to me any difference between its value and the amount I still owed you. But one difference would necessarily remain: until I repaid, you were the owner of the land, rather than me. This was felt to be inappropriate, and was addressed in a change made in 1925, whereby I thenceforth gave you not my

---

[10] See further A Simpson, *A History of the Land Law* (2nd edn, Oxford, 1986) 141–3, 242–7; G Watt, 'The Lie of the Land: Mortgage Law as Legal Fiction' in E Cooke (ed), *Modern Studies in Property Law, Volume 4* (Oxford, 2007) ch 4.

[11] The mortgagee's right to possess the land in today's law is examined in § 12.5.

[12] Maximum interest rates were applied in Tudor and Stuart legislation; final abolition came in the Usury Laws Repeal Act 1854.

ownership, but a 3,000-year lease of my land.[13] So that I could continue to secure my debts on the freehold value of my land, however, further provisions had to be and were simultaneously introduced, enabling you – if I defaulted – to sell not merely this lease, but my freehold ownership after all.[14]

At some point, the possibility was recognised of a mortgage of land being made by pure security interest, leaving me as owner of the land but giving you, in the event of my default, the right to sell it so as to recoup yourself. The legislation of 1925 mentioned this form of interest – a charge – as an alternative to the mortgage by way of 3,000-year lease.[15] And in 2002, further legislation produced the current rule, whereby the charge is the only form of mortgage of registered land.[16] The 1925 legislation went on to rule, however, that despite the name 'charge', such mortgages should have the same effect as mortgages by 3,000-year lease,[17] and this remains the position. Given the ability of a mortgagee by long lease nonetheless to sell the freehold[18] (as the holder of a security interest over the freehold by definition can), this rule makes no practical difference.[19] But the law's overall approach – defining a charge over a freehold in terms of a lease, itself tweaked so as once more to emulate a charge – is bizarrely confused. It ought to be possible to create a mortgage of land by, and only by, granting a pure security interest, as outlined in § 12.1.1.[20]

---

[13] Law of Property Act 1925 s 85. For the apparent importance of being able to regard the borrower as still the 'owner' of the mortgaged property, see § 10.3.1.

[14] *ibid* ss 101, 104. *Mutatis mutandis*, all this applies similarly to the mortgage of a lease. Say I am not the freehold owner of some land, but a tenant of it under a reasonably long lease (a short or periodic lease would hardly be of sufficient value to be useful as security). Before 1925, I could transfer the lease to you as security for my debt to you, on the basis that you would retransfer it when I paid. Under the Law of Property Act 1925 s 86, however, I cannot do this, but can grant you a sub-lease: not this time for 3,000 years, for that is likely to be longer than the term of my own lease, but for one day less than my own term.

[15] Law of Property Act 1925 s 85(1).

[16] Land Registration Act 2002 s 23(1)(a).

[17] Law of Property Act 1925 s 87(1); for registered land, the Land Registration Act 2002 s 51 in effect refers us back to s 87(1).

[18] Law of Property Act 1925 ss 88(1), 104(1).

[19] It might be thought to make a difference to the mortgagee's ability to possess – occupy – the land: a tenant normally can possess, without restriction, whereas we would expect the holder of a security right to be able to possess only to the extent demanded by the character of that right. On the best understanding, however, there is probably no such difference: the possession right of a mortgagee by way of lease is limited to what he requires as a mortgagee, ie to what he would have under a pure security right. But the issue is controversial: see § 12.5.3.

[20] The Law Commission has recommended that the law be reformed in this way: *Land Mortgages* (Law Com No 204, London, 1991), but no action has been taken. It is in fact already possible to create a pure security right over land, but this counts only as an equitable mortgage, as opposed to the common law mortgage being discussed in the text. Equitable mortgages have different rules, less advantageous to the lender, and are accordingly little used. The reform advocated would in effect be to merge the common law and equitable forms into a single, properly configured, pure security right.

12.2.2 Equity's Insistence that a Mortgage Give Only Security Rights

It was observed above that if I gave you a mortgage by way of freehold transfer, we could in principle structure the deal so as to emulate a pure security arrangement. Equally, though, we might not do so. In particular, our deal might provide for me to lose the land if I did not repay you in a certain way (by or on a particular date, at a particular place, in a particular currency, whatever), despite being able to repay in a more general sense. In fact, early mortgage arrangements were commonly formulated in this way, and were enforced at face value by lenders, with the assistance of the common law courts.

At some point, however, the position changed. Equity intervened, blocking the common law position and ruling that so long as I repaid in a practically sufficient way (and it was for equity to judge what this was), I could demand a retransfer of my land after all. The effect was, and was intended to be, that the parties could not bargain for a mortgage arrangement to give the lender more than a pure security right. Although it has other manifestations,[21] the idea was principally expressed as a demand that the mortgage be redeemable upon payment of the debt; that there be no 'clogs' or 'fetters' on the borrower's ability to redeem. This equitable right to redeem despite any contrary terms of the deal formed the principal element in what was called my 'equity of redemption'.[22]

It did not of course follow that I could simply withhold payment indefinitely, and still expect not to lose my land. My obligation to pay remained, and if I substantively failed to meet it, equity would retract its block, so that my land did indeed become yours. Such retraction of the block was called 'foreclosure'. The possibility of retraction was just as necessary – to ensure that mortgages did function as security rights – as the block itself, which ensured that they functioned as no more than that.

Modern mortgages achieve largely the same effect with less circumlocution. That is to say, not only the reality but also the appearance is closer to what one would expect of a pure security interest. The arrangement is unlikely to purport to allow you, if I do not repay exactly in some particular way, to take my land without further ado: modern mortgages do not normally stipulate for the legally impossible. And whatever the arrangement says on the subject,

---

[21] We shall notice three: the rules that a lender's sale powers may be used only so as to recoup the loan (§ 12.4.3); that a lender can possess the mortgaged land only where necessary for its role as security for the debt (§ 12.5.3); and that a lender cannot, in the mortgage agreement, stipulate for any other benefits (§ 12.6.1).

[22] The rule against irredeemability has another implication. If the land I mortgage to you is land that I lease, rather than own, the mortgage arrangement must allow me to redeem before the end of the lease. In *Fairclough v Swan Brewery Co Ltd* [1912] AC 565 (PC), the terms purported to disallow redemption until six weeks before the end of a 17-year lease; these terms were declared invalid. But cf *Knightsbridge Estates Trust Ltd v Byrne* [1939] Ch 441 (CA), where terms purporting to disallow redemption of a *freehold* for 40 years were upheld.

the law itself controls your ability to take my land through a detailed set of rules, allowing you to do so if, but only if, I default on my obligations *to a sufficiently serious extent*. These rules are explained in § 12.4. But the essential idea of the original equitable intervention – that a mortgage may not be made irredeemable, or, more generally, confer more than a security right – continues to be understood[23] and invoked.[24] (That said, we shall see in § 12.6.4 that there is an argument, based on freedom of contract, to the contrary, and that it seems to be in the ascendant.)

12.3 The Content of a Land Mortgage

Now we turn to look in more detail at the rules governing the operation of modern land mortgages. We shall see that in broad terms they provide appropriate fleshing out of mortgages' role as security rights, but that at certain points they remain redolent of the more tangential ways in which the law has approached the matter, and as a result appear dysfunctional.[25]

We shall focus in turn on a number of different rights enjoyed by a lender under a land mortgage: the right to sell the mortgaged land, or alternatively foreclose the mortgage and take the land for himself; the right to possess the mortgaged land; and the right to any additional benefits ('collateral advantages') stipulated for in the mortgage agreement. We should remember, too, that a mortgage gives the lender security for a debt that the borrower owes him. It thus presupposes such a debt.[26] Once the debt is repaid, there is nothing to secure, so there can be no mortgage. Likewise if the debt is vitiated so as to be ineffective or unenforceable. This possibility is examined in detail in § 12.7.

---

[23] *Knightsbridge Estates Trust Ltd v Byrne*, *ibid*, 456–7.

[24] *Quennell v Maltby* [1979] 1 WLR 318, 322, 324 (CA): see § 12.5.3.

[25] See further S Nield, 'Charges, Possession and Human Rights: A Reappraisal of s 87(1) Law of Property Act 1925' in E Cooke (ed), *Modern Studies in Property Law, Volume 3* (Oxford, 2005) ch 8. See also L Fox, *Conceptualising Home – Theories, Laws and Policies* (Oxford, 2007) and M Dixon, 'Mortgage Default and Mortgagee's Remedies' [2008] *Conv* 474, on the question whether the mortgage's identity as a security right should be balanced against other interests.

[26] In principle, a mortgage can be used to secure any form of obligation, at any rate one exigible in money, to raise which the mortgaged land is sold. But a debt arising as a result of a loan given to buy the land is the commonest such obligation.

12.4 Sale and Foreclosure

The most important element in a mortgage – the salient concrete manifestation of the security right it represents – is the fact that it allows the lender, if the borrower defaults in a substantial enough way on the loan, to take the borrower's land and sell it so as to recoup the amount outstanding.

12.4.1 The Source of the Right to Sell

If I have granted you a mortgage over the freehold ownership of my house, and you now sell, say to John, you transfer the freehold ownership to John. As explained in § 12.2.1, before 1925 you generally had the very freehold ownership, with an obligation to restore it to me upon my repayment, so your ability to transfer it required no explanation. But since 1925 you will not have the very freehold ownership: nowadays, in the case of registered land, you will have a charge, though it will emulate a 3,000-year lease. Your ability nonetheless to transfer the freehold ownership rests on two foundations. First, the very nature of a charge, which is a security interest. By definition, this allows you to have resort to the charged asset if the debt in question is not paid. Second, the detail that the relevant rules put into 'have resort to'. They might, for example, have provided that the court shall take over the asset and sell it, returning the required sum to you. As it happens (but doubtless influenced by the pre-1925 history), in the present context they provide for you yourself to sell,[27] and give meaning to this by stipulating that, although you do not hold the freehold ownership, your sale nonetheless transfers it.[28]

Subject to issues of horizontal effect (§ 2.2), your sale might be thought to engage the ECHR First Protocol Article 1 as interfering with my enjoyment of my possessions, but this has been denied, on the basis that – given what has just been said – the sale merely picks up on an 'inherent limitation' in my rights as mortgagor (§ 2.3.3).[29] Where the mortgage is of my residence, the sale might also be thought to engage Article 8 of the ECHR as interfering with my home, but this possibility too has been denied, on the basis that the

---

[27] But not if you find yourself bound by the right of a beneficiary of a trust on which I, though purporting to own the land absolutely, in fact held it. Then, you will have to go via the court, under the Trusts of Land and Appointment of Trustees Act 1996 s 14. See §§ 16.2.2–16.2.5.

[28] Law of Property Act 1925 ss 88.

[29] *Horsham Properties Group Ltd v Clark* [2009] 1 WLR 1255, [34]–[40] (Ch D).

protection given by Article 8 is (*mutatis mutandis*) co-extensive with that given by the First Protocol Article 1.[30] The latter perspective seems a sensible one, but it jars with the assumption apparently made in important decisions regarding Article 8's applicability to the termination of leases,[31] and noted in § 11.5.2: that the idea of 'interference with a home' is to be taken literally, and not qualified along 'inherent limitation' lines.

12.4.2 The Availability of the Right to Sell

Say I borrow from you, and grant you a mortgage over my land to secure my debt. Normally our arrangement will require me to make monthly payments, either to you direct, or to a financial institution which will eventually put the sum generated by these payments towards discharging my debt. If I fail to make one of these monthly payments, I will be in default. But you cannot normally move to a sale immediately: the law delays you for a short period during which I can put matters right, and if I do so the possibility of sale disappears again. The rules[32] are complex and not easy to understand.[33] But in broad terms you can sell if I have missed two months' interest payments . . . or if (as is likely) the mortgage allows you to demand immediate repayment if I default at all, and you do so, giving me three months to comply, which I do not.[34]

The rules thus give you the right to sell in the event of what may be called 'confirmed default' on my part. They are probably best regarded as concretised deductions from a more fundamental idea. As we saw in § 12.2.2, the law ensures that mortgage arrangements operate as security interests by disallowing lenders from using their rights so acquired otherwise than to deliver the payment of the relevant debt. The rules about the allowability of sale restrict

---

[30] *ibid*, [13].

[31] *McCann v United Kingdom* (2008) 47 EHRR 40 (ECtHR); *Kay v United Kingdom* [2011] HLR 2 (ECtHR); *Manchester City Council v Pinnock* [2011] 2 AC 104 (SC); *Hounslow London Borough Council v Powell* [2011] 2 AC 186 (SC).

[32] They are contained in the Law of Property Act 1925 ss 101, 103.

[33] They were formulated with an eye on a bygone form of mortgage, where apparently I was to repay you the entire debt after only six months; as explained in § 12.2.2, this was unreal, given equity's insistence on permitting me to redeem so long as I am able to do so; but my failure to comply nonetheless counted as a default of sorts, upon which the provisions delaying sale are built. Modern mortgages try to give a clearer idea of what they mean, but this in turn produces a difficult interface with the provisions.

[34] If you purport to sell despite not complying with these rules, you are liable for the wrong to me, but the sale nonetheless takes effect as such: Law of Property Act 1925 s 104(2), Land Registration Act 2002 s 52; see G Ferris and G Battersby, 'The General Principles of Overreaching and the Modern Legislative Reforms 1996–2002' (2003) 119 *LQR* 94, 122–4. This extension from the case of a proper sale is perhaps more likely to engage the protections of the ECHR; if it does, it may be justified as proportionate (as helpful to the market) or it may not (as perhaps *over-helpful*). These questions were left open in *Horsham Properties Group Ltd v Clark* [2009] 1 WLR 1255, [41] (Ch D).

the possibility of it to the cases where, in the eyes of the law, a lender really needs it so as to recoup himself.[35]

But in allowing sale as soon as the borrower is in 'confirmed default', the law nevertheless continues to bear quite sternly on the borrower. In practice, however, this sternness is mitigated in two ways. If – contrary to the prevailing judicial position, explained in § 12.4.1 – a sale were to engage the ECHR First Protocol Article 1 and where appropriate Article 8, these mitigations, in combination with the general interest in properly functioning security rights (§ 12.1.1), would probably justify the interference with the mortgagor's possessions as proportionate.

First, building societies and banks tend not to proceed to a sale by any means so quickly, preferring instead to investigate the possibility of achieving repayment after all by rescheduling the debt over the remaining mortgage period (or sometimes longer).

And second, you will find it hard to *sell* unless you first gain *possession* of the land by evicting me:[36] and, as we shall see in § 12.5, your ability to obtain possession is normally narrower than your (theoretical) right to sell. If the mortgaged land is my home, confirmed default is not enough for you to take possession. You can do so only if I cannot show a likelihood of being able to pay off the debt even if, following normal bank and building society practice, it is rescheduled over the whole remaining mortgage period.[37] Like the rule concerning sale, this rule concerning possession is calculated to ensure that the lender's rights do not exceed what he needs to recoup the debt. But it evidently embodies a different – narrower – view regarding the scope of his need. There is no good reason for this discrepancy: the rules on the availability of sale and of possession as a prelude to sale should have the same profile. We shall return to this issue in § 12.5.4, arguing that the profile of the possession rule is the more appropriate.

12.4.3 The Lender's Duties Regarding Sale

When you sell my house to John, you will receive the price John agrees to pay you for it. You have first call on this money, to recoup what I owe you plus the

---

[35] It might be asked whether, in restricting the lender's right to sell in this way, the rules interfere with his possessions in violation of ECHR First Protocol Art 1. The answer is probably no. Because they help ensure that the lender's rights truly reflect the idea of a security interest, the rules are best regarded as constitutive of his possessions, ie as picking up on an 'inherent limitation' (§ 2.3.3) in his rights. But were one to have to go further, the same reflection would surely render them justified as proportionate. *cf Wilson v First County Trust Ltd (No 2)* [2004] 1 AC 816 (HL).

[36] Otherwise, few will want to buy: under the circumstances, my lack of right to remain once the sale goes through will give a buyer little reassurance that I shall in fact leave when that time comes. The presence of the defaulting borrower is also likely to depress the price that can be got: many would recoil from bidding, only to make him, and usually his family, homeless.

[37] Administration of Justice Act 1970 s 36; *Cheltenham & Gloucester Building Society v Norgan* [1996] 1 WLR 343 (CA).

expenses of the sale. If any money remains after this, you must pay it to me.[38] So, say I buy my house for £200,000, of which £180,000 is a loan from you secured on the house, and (given my failure to keep pace with your interest charges) I owe you £190,000 when I default; at which point you sell for £225,000, with expenses of £5,000. Of the £225,000, you will keep £190,000 + £5,000 = £195,000 for yourself, and must return the remaining £30,000 to me.[39]

But compare the following example. Say once more that my house cost me £200,000, of which £180,000 came by way of a secured loan from you, and that at the point you sell I owe you £190,000 ... but that your sale of my house fetches only £175,000, with expenses again of £5,000. The £175,000 is absorbed entirely by your call for £195,000; I not only get nothing but am left still owing you £20,000. This scenario, or the prospect of it, is called 'negative equity'.

I am thus crucially affected by differences – especially falls – between the value of the house when I grant your mortgage and the sum realised by your sale; the impact on you is likely to be much less. Sometimes a fall will be the result of a drop in the basic value of the house itself, as where it falls victim to subsidence or planning blight, or where house prices decline generally. But sometimes it will occur because, in selling, you fail to take the steps that I would have taken on my own account, so as to maximise the house's sale price. You might, for example, accept the first offer you receive, despite advice that you can realistically expect a better one; or you might neglect to market the house properly; or you might sell when the market is depressed, despite reason to believe that it will shortly pick up; or you might sell without making some obvious improvements that would more than repay their cost in a higher price. In such circumstances, I – as the principal sufferer – will be aggrieved. Do I have any legal recourse against you?

The answer[40] has two elements. The first is that you, the lender, must always act in good faith. You will do so if you act genuinely so as to recoup the amount I owe you, no matter how much you harm me in the process; but not if you aim gratuitously to cause me loss.[41] The second element is that, *in your*

---

[38] Law of Property Act 1925 s 105, following plain security principles.

[39] Complications arise, however, where I have granted additional mortgages to other lenders: essentially, you must repay the sums I still owe them before returning any balance to me. Further complications arise where I purported to grant your mortgage over the full freehold ownership of the house, when in fact I held it on trust, say for myself and Kate equally. If you are bound by Kate's right, half of the £225,000 will be hers, leaving only £112,500 to meet your call for £195,000. You can sue me for the shortfall of £82,500, but probably not fruitfully. Whereas if you are not bound by Kate's right, the outcome is as explained in the text – you take your £195,000 and return £30,000 to me – and Kate must look to me (again, probably not fruitfully) for the £112,500 by which she is left down. For you and Kate, then, the question of whether you are bound by her right is an anxious one. For exploration of the way the law addresses it, see § 16.8.

[40] As given in *Downsview Nominees Ltd v First City Corporation Ltd* [1993] AC 295, 312, 315 (PC); *Silven Properties Ltd v Royal Bank of Scotland plc* [2004] 1 WLR 997, [13]–[20] (CA).

[41] *Downsview Nominees Ltd*, ibid. So long as you do act with the proper motive, it does not matter that you have other motives too: *Meretz Investments NV v ACP Ltd* [2006] 3 All ER 1029, [314] (Ch D).

conduct of the actual sale but in no other respect, you must take reasonable care to obtain a 'fair' or 'true market' or 'proper' (these seem to be synonymous) price.

In each of the examples just given, therefore, if you sell the house for less than its true value in bad faith, you must compensate me for the loss you thereby cause me. If you act in good faith but stupidly, however, you must compensate me where you inadvisably accept a poor first offer;[42] and where you neglect to market the house properly, say by failing to mention the existence of planning permission giving it development potential and thus a higher value;[43] but not where you make a damaging decision about the timing of any sale,[44] or about investing in improvements,[45] because these failures do not occur in the conduct of the actual sale.[46]

The law here is unstable, however. The courts in recent decisions have given a very confident account of it, but the confidence is misplaced.

The first element, requiring good faith, is unproblematic. Remember the law's demand (explained in § 12.2.2) that mortgage arrangements operate as security interests only, lenders being prohibited from using their rights under such arrangements otherwise than to recoup the debt. It follows that, even where sale is warranted so as to recoup the debt, a sale in fact carried out for some other end must be prohibited, and loss occasioned thereby must be made good.

The difficulty arises with the second element. It is hard to understand the distinction it requires between the actual sale and other aspects of the sale process, such as the timing of a sale and a decision not to improve the price by taking additional trouble. Indeed, it may not be possible firmly to say whether all given sets of facts count as occurring in the conduct of the actual sale or otherwise. Unsurprisingly, therefore, it is possible to find judicial assertions that care is *not* required as regards the actual sale;[47] and others, that care *is* required both as regards the actual sale and as regards other aspects of the sale process too. In *Palk v Mortgage Services Funding plc*[48] especially, the lender decided to postpone sale until the property market improved; the implication being that in the meantime, the debt would remain wholly unpaid, and would continue to generate interest liabilities for the borrower. The court

---

[42]   *Palk v Mortgage Services Funding plc* [1993] Ch 330, 337–8 (CA).

[43]   *Cuckmere Brick Co Ltd v Mutual Finance Ltd* [1971] Ch 949 (CA).

[44]   *China and South Seas Bank Ltd v Tan Soon Gin* [1990] 1 AC 536 (PC).

[45]   *Silven Properties Ltd v Royal Bank of Scotland plc* [2004] 1 WLR 997 (CA).

[46]   See too section 13.6 of the Financial Services Authority's *Mortgages: Conduct of Business* rules: http://fsahandbook.info/FSA/html/handbook/. Like the cases, the section imposes a duty to obtain the best price that might reasonably be paid. A little differently from the cases, though, at least in emphasis, it requires that the sale should take place as quickly as possible – though recognising that there may be legitimate reasons why it should not.

[47]   See eg *Warner v Jacob* (1882) 20 Ch D 220, 224 (Ch D); *Kennedy v De Trafford* [1897] AC 180 (HL).

[48]   [1993] Ch 330 (CA). See also *Standard Chartered Bank Ltd v Walker* [1982] 1 WLR 1410, 1415–16 (CA).

viewed this plan as wrongful, for taking insufficient care of the interests of the borrower.[49] By way of remedy, the court pre-empted the wrong by itself ordering an immediate sale.[50]

It seems likely, then, that the rule should be the same for both contexts, ie as regards all a mortgagee's decisions about sale. But what form should that rule in principle take? Should it require good faith alone, or reasonable care too?

Certainly, no demand for reasonable care can be deduced from the basic idea of disallowing lenders from using their mortgage rights otherwise than for security.[51] But it does not follow that reasonable care should not be demanded for some other reason. In fact, in *Cuckmere Brick Co Ltd v Mutual Finance Ltd*,[52] where the demand's existence (in respect of the conduct of an actual sale) was finally established, it was put in terms redolent of the tort of negligence: it is obvious that bad decisions regarding sale by the lender will injure the borrower, who bears the first impact of a failure to realise the property's potential value; so, following Lord Atkin's formula in *Donoghue v Stevenson*,[53] the borrower becomes the lender's 'neighbour', and the lender has to take reasonable care to avoid so injuring him. Now subsequent decisions have established that this formula is not to be applied literally; that situations can fall within its terms, but nonetheless not give rise to legal compensation rights. Nevertheless, it has clear prima facie moral force, so that if such rights are not to arise we want to know why. Why should there be an exception for bad decisions regarding sale by a mortgagee?

One might suggest: because the injury caused by such decisions will be economic, and many cases of economic injury are excepted from the application of Lord Atkin's formula. But while many such cases are excepted, some are not, so we need to decide which group the case under consideration (where a mortgagor is injured by a mortgagee's bad decisions about sale) should belong to. The excepted cases seem (though the area is difficult) to involve, and turn upon, the presence of one of two significant characteristics. One characteristic is that the wrong in question is of a kind which might cause economic injury far and wide (whereas physical injury tends to be much more restricted in its occurrence): if there were liability for such a wrong, it would be disproportionate to the scale of the wrong, and/or not economically insurable.[54] The

---

[49] This position is supported by the Financial Services Authority's *Mortgages: Conduct of Business* rules (n 46): section 13.6.1(1) envisages sales occurring as quickly as possible, unless there is a legitimate reason to the contrary.

[50] Under the Law of Property Act 1925 s 91(2). This decision is not contradicted, though its impact is complicated, by the position taken in *Cheltenham & Gloucester Building Society v Krausz* [1997] 1 WLR 1558 (CA), that if the sale would generate less than the entire sum owed, there is no jurisdiction to deny the lender *possession*: see n 74.

[51] *Downsview Nominees Ltd v First City Corporation Ltd* [1993] AC 295, 312 (PC).

[52] [1971] Ch 949, 966 (CA).

[53] [1932] AC 562, 580 (HL).

[54] This preoccupation can be seen in eg *Hedley Byrne & Co Ltd v Heller & Partners Ltd* [1964] AC 465, 483, 534, 536–7 (HL); *Spartan Steel and Alloys Ltd v Martin & Co Ltd* [1973] QB 27, 38–39 (CA).

other is that, even if in the particular situation economic injury could befall only a limited class of victims, the wrongdoer's duty is discernibly to some of these only (whereas we have a duty to virtually all whom we might physically injure), and the putative claimant is someone outside the latter class.[55] Our mortgage case displays neither of these characteristics. The class of potential victim is limited to mortgagors,[56] and there is no closer relationship with another type of victim to eclipse that between the mortgagor and mortgagee.

So one would have to explain the exception of our mortgage case on some third basis, possibly special to it. A candidate is a concern simply to minimise banks' exposure to risk, perhaps so as – by thus reducing their costs – to lower their interest rates, and thereby (at least under certain conditions) to boost the economy. There is evidence in other areas of land law for such a concern,[57] so it is no surprise to find a manifestation of it here too. But in no context can it be regarded as necessarily the dominant consideration, before which the rights of those injured must unquestionably be sacrificed.[58] The present set of rules, whereby mortgagees are required to take care on the mortgagor's behalf in the conduct of the actual sale but not in their other decisions regarding sale, unsurprisingly reflects both views of the matter, but does so in the form of an unprincipled and therefore unsatisfactory compromise.

12.4.4 Foreclosure

As explained in § 12.1.1, saying that a creditor has a security right over an asset owned by a debtor means that the creditor can have resort to that asset so as to recoup the debt. Selling the asset is the main way of doing so, as this – turning the asset into money – enables fine-tuning of the outcome: as just noted, the creditor takes what is owed to him, but any surplus is returned to the debtor. The law does however maintain another way, known as 'foreclosure'.

---

[55] See *Murphy v Brentwood District Council* [1991] 1 AC 398 (HL); *Caparo Industries plc v Dickman* [1990] 2 AC 605 (HL) (though *cf White v Jones* [1995] 2 AC 207 (HL)). Constructing a special duty owed only to a subset of those potentially affected is also used as a way of allowing liability for economic loss without running into the first kind of difficulty: as in *Hedley Byrne & Co Ltd v Heller & Partners Ltd, ibid,* itself.

[56] It is true that a mortgagee's bad decisions regarding sale might impact on persons beyond the mortgagor: his dependants, say, or those for whom he held the property as trustee. Even where the bad decisions occur in the conduct of the actual sale, the law has declined to protect such further victims: *Parker-Tweedale v Dunbar Bank plc* [1991] Ch 12 (CA). The decision puts this rule on the basis that the mortgagor's duty arises not in negligence but in equity, and so is owed – like the duty to use his rights regarding sale in good faith – only to the mortgagor. But the same answer could be expected in negligence, on the second ground identified in the text.

[57] See especially § 16.8.2, offering a similar explanation for the way the law is profiled so that banks are not commonly affected by trust rights.

[58] This of course prompts the reflection that, in thus sacrificing the rights of a borrower to the extent that it does, the law may (subject to questions of horizontal effect: § 2.2) violate ECHR First Protocol Art 1. However, *Horsham Properties Group Ltd v Clark* [2009] 1 WLR 1255 (Ch D)) treats a lender's right to sell at all as not engaging the Article, on 'inherent limitation' grounds (see § 12.4.1); very possible likewise, then, his duties regarding the conduct of the sale.

If I secure my loan from you by a mortgage of my house, but default on my repayment obligations, and you foreclose, you simply become the owner of the house in my place. If the house is worth no more than I owe you, that is unproblematic, though of course you would do no better by sale. But in the more ordinary case where the house is worth more than I owe you, while sale would give you only what you are owed and the remainder to me, foreclosure gives you the remainder too; I lose to you what would otherwise be my share. This is of course attractive to you.

To understand the idea of foreclosure, remember what we saw in § 12.2.2. Long ago, a mortgage was effected by a freehold transfer with retransfer on payment of the debt, so that failure to pay precisely as stipulated meant losing the freehold; but equity blocked that outcome so long as the debtor was able to pay in a practical sense. Foreclosure is the lifting of this block when the court is persuaded that the debtor really cannot pay, leaving the freehold to be lost after all.

Foreclosure never was, however, properly conformable with the theory underlying this equitable intervention: that a mortgage arrangement shall give you no more than you need to obtain repayment of my debt. As well as meaning that you cannot keep my land if I am really able to pay, this ought to entail that, if I do indeed fail to pay, you can resort to my land (by a sale) only for the sum I owe you.[59]

Recognising foreclosure's unsatisfactoriness, the courts decided to allow it only with the rider that it can be 'reopened' – ie the lender ordered to return the property in question to the borrower – if at some later point the borrower unexpectedly manages to pay after all. And they made the borrower's right to reopen itself a right in rem, capable of binding someone to whom the lender went on to transfer the property. These measures, however, damaged the exploitability of foreclosed land. They therefore added further unsatisfactoriness, still without meeting the point explained in the previous paragraph, that foreclosure always was a mistake. More helpful is the modern rule that, if a lender seeks to foreclose, the court can order sale instead.[60] Except in the unlikely event of being confident that the sale price would equate to the outstanding debt, it would be amazing for the court to do otherwise.[61] De facto, then, foreclosure is a dead letter. For the reasons explained, it deserves to be abolished altogether.

---

[59] Even if this objection is overlooked, foreclosure's place in the modern law is surprising for another, more technical, reason. Remember that nowadays, the mortgage arrangement gives you not the freehold in my land, but a lease over it: Law of Property Act 1925 ss 85, 87. So you would not naturally get to keep my freehold even if I did default. To preserve the possibility of foreclosure, the law has had to graft provision for it onto your rights as a lessee: *ibid* s 88(2).

[60] *ibid* s 91(2).

[61] And arguably also a disproportionate (because more draconian than warranted) interference with the borrower's possessions under ECHR First Protocol Art 1, and on appropriate facts also his home under Art 8. But *cf* § 12.4.1, noting that the current judicial stance (see *Horsham Properties Group Ltd v Clark* [2009] 1 WLR 1255 (Ch D)) treats a lender's sale as not engaging these Convention rights, on 'inherent limitation' grounds; it is hard to see why foreclosure should be treated differently.

12.5 Possession

12.5.1 The Basic Rule

If you lend me money and secure my debt by taking a mortgage over my land, you will normally have no reason not to leave me in possession of the land. This is likely to alter, however, if I fail to repay you, and you wish – as your security right allows you – to resort to the land so as to recoup yourself. In particular, if you want to sell the land so as to pay off the outstanding debt, you will very probably want to take possession of it first, evicting me so as to have no problem about offering it for sale with vacant possession. In ordinary speech, such a proceeding is often referred to – not very accurately – as 'repossession'.[62]

But according to the standard account of the topic, your legal right to possession is much more extensive than this. The basic rule is that, simply as mortgagee of my land, you immediately gain the right to possess it (and exclude me), for any purpose you like.[63]

The basic rule has one qualification: a borrower can hold on to possession if he will imminently be repaying the whole outstanding debt.[64] But two or three months is the maximum time allowed under this qualification, and if the borrower proposes to repay by selling the land, the sale will need to be at an advanced stage before a court will view the proposal as sufficiently solid. So confined, the qualification is best regarded as an almost procedural matter, designed to prevent the pointless cost and upheaval of evicting the borrower and installing the lender only for a few weeks. Aside from this qualification, the thrust of the basic rule is that as soon as you have your mortgage over my house, you can decide that you would enjoy living in it, and evict me in order to do so.

It was originally natural that the lender should possess. As explained in § 12.2.1, in the late Middle Ages, when lending money for interest was prohibited as usury, the lender made a profit on the loan instead by taking the land and exploiting it, and took either a lease or the freehold in the land so as to

---

[62] For the practice, context and political significance of repossession (and thus, in a sense, of the phenomenon of acquisition via mortgage as a whole), see L Whitehouse, 'The Right to Possession: The Need for Substantive Reform' in P Jackson and D Wilde (eds), *The Reform of Property Law* (Aldershot, 1997) ch 9, and 'The Home-owner: Citizen or Consumer?' in S Bright and J Dewar (eds), *Land Law – Themes and Perspectives* (Oxford, 1998) ch 7.

[63] *Cholmondeley (Marquis) v Clinton (Lord)* (1817) 2 Mer 171, 359 (Ch); *Four-Maids Ltd v Dudley Marshall (Properties) Ltd* [1957] Ch 317, 320 (Ch D); *Birmingham Citizens Permanent Building Society v Caunt* [1962] Ch 883 (Ch D).

[64] *Birmingham Citizens Permanent Building Society v Caunt*, ibid 912; *Royal Trust Co of Canada v Markham* [1975] 1 WLR 1416, 1420 (CA).

make this possible. But when this functional need for possession fell away, mortgages nonetheless continued to be made by a freehold transfer of the land; later, a long lease of it; and today, a charge accompanied by the rights of such a lease. These forms, by their very nature, continue to entitle the lender to possess, and this seems to be the foundation of the basic rule that the lender has an essentially unqualified right to do so.

We should, however, expect this basic rule to be subject to the usual equitable intervention, designed to ensure that a mortgage arrangement gives the lender only a security right over the borrower's property, ie that his rights under the arrangement shall give him no more than he needs to obtain repayment of the borrower's debt. In these terms, there seem to be only two reasons why a lender may need to possess the borrower's land. First, so as to maintain the land's value (eg by carrying out repairs on a house), so that it continues to secure the amount of the debt in question. (Say I borrow £200,000 from you, and grant you a mortgage over my house, which is then worth £250,000. If I neglect my house and its value falls to £150,000, it will no longer represent adequate security for my debt. So you should be able to come in and turn matters around.) And second, as a preliminary to extracting the value of the debt from it: that is, as a prelude to sale, in order to be able to sell with vacant possession.

In fact, the basic rule has two riders which partly – but only partly – align it with these principles.[65] It has also been reformulated, wholly in accordance with these principles, by the Court of Appeal in *Quennell v Maltby*,[66] but many commentators refuse to accept the authority of this decision. The following two sections consider first the riders, then *Quennell v Maltby*.[67]

Subject to issues of horizontal effect (§ 2.2), a lender's repossession of the borrower's property might be thought to engage the ECHR First Protocol Article 1, as interfering with the borrower's enjoyment of his possessions, and in appropriate circumstances also Article 8, as interfering with his home. As explained in § 12.4.1, however, the current judicial stance in the context of a lender's *sale* denies such engagement, on an 'inherent limitation' basis.[68] Although the two contexts appear to be parallel, in the present context the opposite assumption seems to have been made.[69]

---

[65] A further rider was introduced by the Mortgage Repossessions (Protection of Tenants etc) Act 2010 s 1, but this has no connection with the principles under discussion. It provides that where a borrower is about to lose possession in court proceedings, but the land in question is occupied by a tenant to whom he has let it in breach of his mortgage terms, the tenant – despite his tenancy being otherwise ineffective against the lender, and so having no defence to eviction (*Britannia Building Society v Earl* [1990] 1 WLR 422 (CA)) – may be given up to two months' grace.

[66] [1979] 1 WLR 318 (CA).

[67] *ibid.*

[68] *Horsham Properties Group Ltd v Clark* [2009] 1 WLR 1255 (Ch D).

[69] *Wood v United Kingdom* (1997) 24 EHRR CD69 (ECommHR) (dealing with both Art 8 and First Protocol Art 1); *Barclays Bank plc v Alcorn* [2002] EWHC 498 (Ch D) (dealing only with Art 8). The relevant passages are extremely short, however, and precede an acceptance of the respective repossessions as justified by proportionality anyway.

12.5.2 The Two Riders

The first rider to the basic rule of an essentially unqualified right to possession is this. A modern lender can and will charge interest, so does not need possession in order to generate a return on his loan. If he nonetheless takes possession, he is not allowed to keep (he must 'account to the borrower for') the financial benefits of doing so. Instead, he must pay the borrower the profit he makes, or could make, from it (eg by renting the land out).[70] This rule does not, however, seek in any case actually to prohibit possession.

The second rider is established by the Administration of Justice Act 1970, section 36.[71] By this provision, the court should normally refuse possession if the borrower[72] seems likely to be able to pay the debt over a period up to the planned term,[73] and the land's value is sufficient to secure the outstanding debt in the meantime.[74] (If the lender is denied possession under this rule, any further lapses by the borrower will normally result in immediate eviction.[75]) This rule is probably of little practical value to borrowers, for a lender will normally go to the trouble of seeking possession only if it has already become clear that the borrower's problems cannot be solved by rescheduling. But the rule is of some doctrinal importance: it seems to proceed on the theory that a lender can possess only if he needs to, in order to obtain repayment of his loan. It is prevented from giving full effect to that theory, however, by the statutory terms in which it is put.[76] It is confined to mortgages of a 'dwelling-

[70] See *Robertson v Norris* (1859) 1 Giff 428 (Ch); *White v City of London Brewery Co* (1889) 42 Ch D 237 (CA). Nowadays, lenders normally take possession only as a prelude to sale, and keep it for such a short time that this liability is only theoretical.

[71] For discussion, see N Bamforth, 'Lord Macnaghten's Puzzle: The Mortgage of Real Property in English Law' [1996] *CLP* Pt II 207, 231–43. An earlier judicial experiment on similar lines had ended in *Birmingham Citizens Permanent Building Society v Caunt* [1962] Ch 883 (Ch D), reaffirming the idea that a lender's right to possession is unqualified save in the respects already discussed.

[72] Or another member of his family. Payments by such a person must be accepted by the lender as if made by the borrower personally (s 30(3)), and he has the right to be made a party to proceedings against the borrower (ss 55, 56) – in particular if his contribution might be expected to impact on the position under the Administration of Justice Act (s 55(3)(c)(ii)).

[73] *Cheltenham & Gloucester Building Society v Norgan* [1996] 1 WLR 343 (CA); but see L Whitehouse, 'A Longitudinal Analysis of the Mortgage Repossession Process 1995–2010: Stability, Regulation and Reform' in S Bright (ed), *Modern Studies in Property Law, Volume 6* (Oxford, 2011) ch 7, 16–18, reporting that in practice, periods of up to only five years are used. In any event, note that the borrower's liabilities are not simply suspended for the period allowed, in the hope that something may turn up. To refuse possession, the court must be satisfied that the *whole* debt is *likely to be paid* in this time. (Mortgage arrangements often stipulate that if the borrower defaults, the whole debt becomes repayable immediately, but the Administration of Justice Act 1973 s 8 instructs courts to disregard such stipulations in assessing the likelihood of repayment.)

[74] *Cheltenham & Gloucester Building Society v Krausz* [1997] 1 WLR 1558 (CA). So a lender is not denied possession where the borrower has a scheme (however sensible) to sell the mortgaged land and, from the proceeds, repay only part of the debt, leaving the remainder unsecured.

[75] *Cheltenham & Gloucester Building Society v Norgan, ibid.*

[76] In addition to the features noted in the text, the rule's drafting has spawned a number of other problems, particularly regarding its applicability to different kinds of mortgages (see

house', ie a domestic residence. And it applies only where the lender *sues* for possession, not where he enters in the borrower's absence, then prevents the borrower from returning; nor where he sells, leaving the purchaser to take possession.[77] In terms of aligning the lender's right to possession with the principle that mortgage rights should be usable only to obtain payment of the debt, these are arbitrary limitations.[78]

With these two riders, then, the law regarding the lender's ability to possess moves closer to the position we should expect[79] . . . but not so far as to be in exact conformity with it.[80] Especially the second of them may well also ensure that a lender's repossession of a borrower's home will always be proportionate, assuming it engages ECHR rights at all (see § 12.5.1),[81] but the same cannot necessarily be said of mortgages of other kinds of property, falling as they do outside the scope of the second rider.

Centrax Trustee Ltd v Ross [1979] 2 All ER 952 (Ch D); *Habib Bank Ltd v Tailor* [1982] 1 WLR 1218 (CA); *Bank of Scotland v Grimes* [1985] QB 1179 (CA)), and to cases where the lender seeks possession otherwise than after default by the borrower (*Western Bank Ltd v Schindler* [1977] Ch 1 (CA)).

[77] *Ropaigealach v Barclays Bank plc* [2000] QB 263 (CA); *Horsham Properties Group Ltd v Clark* [2009] 1 WLR 1255 (Ch D). The law as stated by the latter decision has been the subject of a consultation by the Ministry of Justice (see http://www.justice.gov.uk/consultations/mortgages-power-sale.htm), and resort to it has been generally disavowed by the Council of Mortgage Lenders (see http://www.cml.org.uk/cml/policy/issues/4707). The self-help approach that the decisions involve might be thought to infringe the borrower's right to a fair trial under ECHR Art 6. But it is (puzzlingly) implied in *Horsham Properties Group Ltd v Clark* at [13] that the protection given by Art 6 does not extend beyond that given by Art 8 and First Protocol Art 1 to the borrower's home and possessions themselves.

[78] In the case of a mortgage regulated under the Consumer Credit Act 1974 (see § 12.7.1), possession can be taken only by order of the court (s 126), and the court, in considering the making of the order, has the power to alleviate the position of the borrower in various ways (ss 129, 135, 136). The principle(s) by reference to which the court should exercise this power are unclear, however.

[79] It might be asked whether, in qualifying the lender's right to possess, the riders interfere with his 'possessions' contrary to ECHR First Protocol Art 1; but the answer is probably no. Rather, in helping produce conformity between that right and the essential quality of a security interest, the riders are better seen as *defining* his 'possessions', ie as reflecting an 'inherent limitation' (§ 2.3.3) in the latter. In any event, their solicitude for the ECHR interests of the borrower is surely defensible, justifying them as proportionate.

[80] In addition to the two riders, in October 2008 – in the context of the economic crisis then prevailing – the Civil Justice Council introduced a new Pre-Action Protocol, 'Pre-Action Protocol for Possession Claims based on Mortgage or Home Purchase Plan Arrears in Respect of Residential Property' (see www.justice.gov.uk/civil/procrules_fin/contents/protocols/prot_mha.htm). The Protocol declares that courts will normally expect lenders to have considered rescheduling before moving to repossess; but this was probably the position already. For discussion, see L Whitehouse, 'The Mortgage Arrears Pre-Action Protocol: An Opportunity Lost' (2009) 72 *MLR* 793.

[81] This view was taken in *Barclays Bank plc v Alcorn* [2002] EWHC 498 (Ch D), dealing with ECHR Art 8. The repossession in *Wood v United Kingdom* (1997) 24 EHRR CD69 (ECommHR) was held proportionate too, as regards both Art 8 and First Protocol Art 1; no reference was made to the second rider, but the repossession was unproblematic on the individual facts.

12.5.3 *Quennell v Maltby*

One judicial statement has been made, however, which would deliver such exact conformity with the position we should expect, and in so doing align the law more satisfactorily also with the ECHR. It consists in the decision of the Court of Appeal in *Quennell v Maltby*.[82]

A lender wished to take possession of the mortgaged land for reasons unconnected with obtaining repayment of the debt. The court refused to allow her to do so, referring to the overarching equitable principle and on that basis asserting that possession can be had only where it is sought for that purpose, and represents a reasonable way of delivering it.[83] Although not germane to the case itself, the latter element could be the more important. It would mean that, even where a lender sought to recoup his loan, he could nonetheless not take possession unless this was a proportionate means to that end.

But this decision is rather isolated, and its rejection of the basic rule, and the latter's essentially unqualified right to possess, has been generally disparaged by commentators. This is odd: given the argument above, the decision seems undeniably correct, and the resilience of the basic rule is unexpected.[84] How are we to explain this resilience? Perhaps as tending, when lenders do seek properly to enforce their security rights, to remove obstacles from their path. It is not as if they will in practice commonly (ever?) want possession for any other reason: so maybe the idea is to regard that as sufficient reassurance, in the interests of allowing them to claim possession when they wish to do so without having to justify themselves in court.

If this is the explanation, however, it is not good enough.[85] It leaves the law not only in essential conflict with the overarching equitable principle, but also inconsistent with the borrower's human rights. As explained in § 12.5.1, a lender's taking possession may engage the borrower's rights under the ECHR

---

[82] [1979] 1 WLR 318 (CA); followed, with further reference to the general equitable principle, in *Albany Home Loans Ltd v Massey* [1997] 2 All ER 609, 612–13 (CA).

[83] Lord Denning MR put it, *ibid* 322: 'A mortgagee will be restrained from getting possession except where it is sought bona fide and reasonably for the purpose of enforcing the security and then only subject to such conditions as the court thinks fit to impose.' The reference to conditions is a little speculative, but sound in principle as allowing the court to ensure that a mortgagee, having been granted a possession order, can use it only for the approved purpose. Templeman LJ put the same idea, *ibid* 324: 'The estate, rights and powers of a mortgagee . . . are only vested in a mortgagee to protect his position as a mortgagee and to enable him to obtain repayment. Subject to this, the property belongs in equity to the mortgagor.'

[84] Even, it seems, within the industry. The Financial Services Authority's *Mortgages: Conduct of Business* rules (n 46) require lenders to 'deal fairly with' customers in arrears, and treat it as an aspect of this that repossession should be used only as a last resort: section 13.3.2.

[85] For a critical review of the current possession rules *except* as taken in *Quennell v Maltby* [1979] 1 WLR 318 (CA), see L Whitehouse, 'A Longitudinal Analysis of the Mortgage Repossession Process 1995-2010: Stability, Regulation and Reform' in S Bright (ed), *Modern Studies in Property Law, Volume 6* (Oxford, 2011) ch 7.

First Protocol Article 1, and on appropriate facts (ie where the property in question is his home) Article 8. If the possession is calculated to assist the lender to recoup his loan, it will presumably be justified, as a proportionate means of achieving a proper purpose.[86] But if it is to any other end – as the law permits, if one rejects *Quennell v Maltby*[87] – its purpose seems not to be a proper one, so cannot be justified.

12.5.4 Connecting Possession and Sale

To revert to an observation made in § 12.4.2: the law's rules about possession do not mesh with its rules about sale. This is problematic, given the intimate linkage between possession and sale, the former normally being of interest only as a prelude to the latter, and the two being combined in the idea of 'repossession'.

As explained in § 12.5.2, the provision in section 36 of the Administration of Justice Act 1970 partially tracks the idea that rights conferred by mortgage arrangements can be used only so as to recoup the debt. Even if the lender seeks possession with this motive, he can have it (where the land in question is a 'dwelling-house') only if the law regards it as necessary that he should, and it does not take this view if the borrower seems likely to be able to repay over the mortgage period.

This construction of what is necessary for the recoupment of the debt is noticeably different from – narrower, more favourable to the borrower, than – the construction implicit in the rules indicating when the lender can *sell*. As explained in § 12.4.2, the latter treat sale as warranted as soon as the borrower is in 'confirmed default', regardless of the possibility of obtaining repayment after all, by rescheduling. The law thus declares that the lender can sell more often than he can claim possession in order to do so: an absurd position.[88] The rules about sale and possession need to be aligned.[89] And the alignment should be on the lines of the possession rule. This rule's construction of what

---

[86] So held in *Wood v United Kingdom* (1997) 24 EHRR CD 69 (ECommHR).

[87] [1979] 1 WLR 318 (CA).

[88] Hence the result in, and the disquiet about, *Horsham Properties Group Ltd v Clark* [2009] 1 WLR 1255 (Ch D). There the lender – rather than seeking possession, and only selling after acquiring it – sold the house without taking possession, leaving the purchaser then to take possession, unaffected by the constraints of the Administration of Justice Act 1970 s 36: see § 12.5.2. This essentially self-help style of proceeding might be thought to infringe the borrower's right to a fair trial under ECHR Art 6, but in *Horsham Properties Group Ltd v Clark* [2009] 1 WLR 1255, [13] (Ch D), it is implied – *quaere* why – that the protection given by Art 6 is no greater than that given by ECHR First Protocol Art 1 to the borrower's 'possessions' themselves. For the treatment of the latter, see § 12.4.1.

[89] In the case of mortgages regulated under the Consumer Credit Act 1974 (see § 12.7.1), this appears to be already the position, or at least potentially so. By s 126, the lender's rights under the mortgage can be enforced only via a court order; and by ss 129, 135 and 136 that order can diverge in various ways from the nominal rights themselves. There seems no reason why these provisions should be used differentially as between possession and sale.

is necessary for the recoupment of the debt is explicitly designed to reflect the view that banks and building societies take of their own needs.[90] Nothing wider can be justified.

In one context, the two constructions diverge in a different way. Where a borrower defaults on his repayments but there is negative equity, ie the house's value is below that of the outstanding debt, the borrower may want a quick sale (so as to reduce the amount of the debt on which interest liabilities would continue to accrue), while the lender may prefer to delay (in the hope that land values may rise, thus improving the chances of a sale eventually recouping the whole debt). On this sale issue alone, authority is in favour of the borrower, on the ground that the lender's approach shows insufficient care for the borrower's interest.[91] But given the negative equity, the present rules leave the lender entitled to possession,[92] effectively preventing the borrower from selling after all.[93] Evidently, again, embedded in these positions are two different constructions of what is 'necessary for the recoupment of the debt', one (that taken over possession) allowing the lender to transfer the effects of negative equity as far as possible to the borrower, the other (that taken over sale) requiring them to be shared. An argument could be made for both views, but the Financial Services Authority's *Mortgages: Conduct of Business* rules[94] favour the latter, requiring lenders to consider allowing the borrower to remain in possession and conduct his own sale. Once again, this position should therefore be adopted as regards both possession and sale.

12.6 Collateral Advantages

In our review of the different rights comprising a land mortgage, we have so far looked at those rights that are automatically present: the lender's debt against the borrower, and his rights to sell or foreclose, and to possess. Now, finally, we look at the possibility that the parties may agree to give the lender other rights in addition. Such additional rights are known as 'collateral advantages'.

---

[90] *Cheltenham & Gloucester Building Society v Norgan* [1996] 1 WLR 343, 353, 356–7 (CA), referring to the statement of the Council of Mortgage Lenders regarding the handling of borrowers who fall into arrears with their repayments.

[91] *Palk v Mortgage Services Funding plc* [1993] Ch 330 (CA): see at nn 48–50.

[92] *Cheltenham & Gloucester Building Society v Krausz* [1997] 1 WLR 1558 (CA): see n 74. For discussion, see M Dixon, 'Combating the Mortgagee's Right to Possession: New Hope for the Mortgagor in Chains?' (1998) 18 *LS* 279.

[93] Though it should not prevent the court from ordering sale, under the Law of Property Act 1925 s 91(2). This was the relief given in *Palk v Mortgage Services Funding plc* [1993] Ch 330 (CA).

[94] (n 46) section 13.3.2(1)(e).

12.6.1 Collateral Advantages and their Evolving Treatment

Say I own a petrol station. To raise finance to modernise it, I make a deal with your oil company that you will lend me the money I need, my debt being secured by a mortgage over the land in question, in return for interest ... and additionally a stipulation – a 'solus tie' – that I buy all my petrol from you.[95] This solus tie would be a collateral advantage. The law of mortgages may disallow it.[96]

Section 12.2.2 explained how, if a mortgage arrangement purports to give the lender more than security – say, if it allows him to keep the mortgaged asset on a technicality, when the borrower is in substance able to pay – the additional rights will be unenforceable. From the late 17th to the turn of the 20th century, this position was taken with full rigour (give or take the aberrant rule about possession). A collateral advantage is an additional right: so it was struck down.[97]

But since the turn of the 20th century, collateral advantages have sometimes been upheld after all.[98] There has been no overt abandonment of the idea that a mortgage must give no more than security, but the courts have sometimes recognised collateral advantages as valid despite this seeming to have just that effect.[99] The (alleged) justifications for the shift cluster into essentially two approaches.

12.6.2 The First Approach

The first approach involves saying that the law of mortgages is applicable, but that, after all, the particular collateral advantage in question contravenes none of its principles.

The principle against which this approach measures collateral advantages is the principle (§ 12.2.2) requiring that the security must always be redeemable:

[95] Likewise if you, a brewery, lend me money to buy a pub, requiring me to buy all my beer from you (creating a 'tied house', as opposed to the 'free house' that it would be if I had no such obligation to a beer company); or if you, a bank, lend me money to buy my house, requiring me to buy other financial products, eg insurance, from you. Likewise too a converse arrangement, say where you, a cheese manufacturer, lend me money to buy a farm, requiring me to *sell* you all the milk I produce.

[96] As well as being disallowed under the law of mortgages as discussed here, some forms of collateral advantage – especially solus ties – may also run into problems with competition law.

[97] *Jennings v Ward* (1705) 2 Vern 520 (Rolls). Likewise certain decisions dating from a time when this straightforward approach had begun to be challenged: *Noakes & Co Ltd v Rice* [1902] AC 24 (HL); *Bradley v Carritt* [1903] AC 253 (HL).

[98] For early indications of the shift, see especially *Santley v Wilde* [1899] 2 Ch 474 (CA); Lord Lindley's dissent in *Bradley v Carritt* [1903] AC 253 (HL); and the expressions of dissatisfaction with the old position in *Samuel v Jarrah Timber and Wood Paving Corporation Ltd* [1904] AC 323 (HL). The shift was put beyond doubt in *Kreglinger v New Patagonia Meat and Cold Storage Co Ltd* [1914] AC 25 (HL).

[99] For further discussion, see Bamforth (n 71) 213–31; Watt (n 10) ch 4.

ie that the lender's security interest (right to resort to the mortgaged asset) must come to an end when the borrower repays the debt.

It has accordingly been held that a collateral advantage is valid if it is expressed to end not later than the date when the loan is repaid.[100] Ending then, it cannot prevent redemption. It has also been held that a collateral advantage, even if expressed to extend beyond redemption, is valid if the security interest can nonetheless lift from the land. A distinction is necessary. Some collateral advantages do prevent the security interest from being lifted. Say, with your mortgage, I give you an option over my land (ie a right to demand that I sell the land to you on your demand). Continuing beyond redemption, such an option effectively extends your right of resort to my land: by exercising the option, you can still take the land, even though I have paid off the debt.[101] The option must therefore be invalid.[102] Other collateral advantages, however, do not prevent the lifting of the security interest from the land in this way. This is especially the case if, with your mortgage, I give you a solus tie. Your rights under this tie are not rights to resort to my land, ie to take it or sell it as your own. So even when the tie continues after my repayment of the loan, it does not prevent your right of resort from ending upon my repayment. The tie is therefore valid.[103]

In its own terms, this approach makes sense. But it has a weakness. The principle that it uses as its benchmark – the demand that the security must always be redeemable – while certainly not simply erroneous, is put too narrowly. When we discussed it in § 12.2.2, we depicted it in terms of a broader idea, that a mortgage must give only security rights. The existence of this broader idea is shown by the rule that a lender's sale powers cannot be used for other purposes than to recoup the debt (§ 12.4.3), and generates the argument that a lender's right to possession of the mortgaged land is similarly confined (§ 12.5.3). In the present context, it should entail that collateral advantages are unacceptable not merely when they impede redemption, but for the very fact that they – necessarily – mean the lender getting more from

[100] *Biggs v Hoddinott* [1898] 2 Ch 307 (CA).

[101] Or at any rate, it does so if the price that the option requires you to pay for the land is below the market value. If it is the market value, the option certainly extends your right of resort to my land in the sense that you can insist on having it (even after repayment) despite my opposition. But in another sense, it falls short of doing so: resort despite repayment is objectionable because it gives you wealth to which you have no proper claim, and if you must pay the market value this is not the case.

[102] *Samuel v Jarrah Timber and Wood Paving Corporation Ltd* [1904] AC 323, 328–9 (HL); *Kreglinger v New Patagonia Meat and Cold Storage Co Ltd* [1914] AC 25, 50–51 (HL); *Lewis v Frank Love Ltd* [1961] 1 WLR 261 (Ch D).

[103] *Kreglinger v New Patagonia Meat and Cold Storage Co Ltd, ibid.* (See in particular the inquiries, *ibid* 39, 41, as to whether the collateral advantage is 'outside and clear' of the mortgage, or 'outside the security . . . independent of it'. These are aimed precisely at this question of whether the collateral advantage connects with the lender's right to resort to the borrower's asset.) For earlier statements of this approach, see *Santley v Wilde* [1899] 2 Ch 474, 474–5 (CA); *Bradley v Carritt* [1903] AC 253, 276 (HL).

the mortgage than security alone. As noted in § 12.6.1, this was the view that was originally taken of them.

12.6.3 The Second Approach

The second approach to allowing collateral advantages involves saying that, in appropriate circumstances, the parties' deal for the collateral advantage does not form part of a mortgage transaction at all: so no matter what the law of mortgages has to say about collateral advantages within mortgage transactions, this particular collateral advantage is unaffected.

This approach is obviously sound in the abstract. If I grant you a solus tie over my petrol station (say, in return for certain pricing guarantees), then a decade later also borrow from you and secure my debt by a mortgage of my petrol station, the solus tie is plainly unconnected with the mortgage and will not be invalidated for inconsistency with the law of mortgages. What requires attention is the courts' use of this approach when the lack of connection between the collateral advantage and the mortgage is much less clear.

Some decisions indicate that a collateral advantage is unconnected with our mortgage, and so (in terms of mortgage law) good, if we establish it on a different day from the mortgage itself, however close the two days may be; or perhaps even if we establish both on the same day but in separate documents.[104] This deployment of the approach is wholly technical; it uses distinctions of no substantive merit.[105]

Other decisions assert that a transaction may place me under a debt to you, and give you a right of resort to my land for the recoupment of that debt, *and yet not be (or count for this purpose as) a mortgage ...* so that the mortgage rules do not apply, and a collateral advantage also conferred by the transaction will therefore be untroubled by those rules.[106] These decisions treat the classification of such a transaction, as a mortgage or not, as a matter for the parties' intentions. And they seem to regard the parties' intentions in this respect as indicated by the 'emphasis' of the transaction: if it centres on the loan, it will be a mortgage; while if it centres on the collateral advantage, it will not. (So on this approach, even an option in the lender's favour over the borrower's land will not necessarily be invalid.[107]) These decisions seem quite unstable. They in effect invite parties to opt into or out of the law of

---

[104] *Reeve v Lisle* [1902] AC 461 (HL); *Samuel v Jarrah Timber and Wood Paving Corporation Ltd* [1904] AC 323, 325 (HL).

[105] So in *Lewis v Frank Love Ltd* [1961] 1 WLR 261 (Ch D) an argument on these lines was rejected, and a collateral advantage held invalid despite separation in this way.

[106] *Kreglinger v New Patagonia Meat and Cold Storage Co Ltd* [1914] AC 25, 52–54 (HL); *Jones v Morgan* [2001] EWCA Civ 995, [55] (CA); *Warnborough Ltd v Garmite Ltd* [2003] EWCA Civ 1544, [69] (CA); *Brighton and Hove City Council v Audus* [2009] EWHC 340 (Ch D).

[107] *Warnborough Ltd v Garmite Ltd, ibid* [73].

mortgages; and, in the idea of 'emphasis', use a highly subjective tool to discern the choice made.[108]

12.6.4 The Key

The first approach thus accepts the applicability of mortgage principles, but takes too narrow a view of them. The second denies the applicability of mortgage principles, on unsatisfactory grounds. Both approaches are therefore unconvincing.

The root of the problem is the tension that exists between the proposition that a mortgage cannot give the lender more than a security right, and the idea of freedom of contract, whereby parties should be able to make whatever agreements they like. The judges themselves have noted this tension, and have criticised the rule against collateral advantages for its inconsistency with freedom of contract.[109]

To address the problem, we need to regard freedom of contract as given (it is a very general idea, and rests on a liberal moral and political foundation which we find compelling). We need to regard it as likewise given that there should be, and are, exceptions to it (because its liberal foundation is either falsified or outgunned). We need to focus on the case for treating collateral advantages in mortgage transactions as one of these exceptions. Historically, two arguments for doing so have been advanced.

One lies in the old rules against usury, ie lending money in return for interest (later, excessive interest). A lender wanting to evade those rules might stipulate for a return in a different form – a collateral advantage – only for the courts, wishing to enforce the spirit of the rules, to declare this invalid.[110] This argument was certainly sustainable when the usury rules were in force, but their abolition by the Usury Laws Repeal Act 1854 has left it untenable since that time.

The other argument takes the line that if a borrower is vulnerable, a bargain for more than pure security will amount to an exploitation of that vulnerability, and so merits suppression as involving unconscionability on the part of the lender;[111] and continues that borrowers are so nearly always vulnerable that it is hardly worthwhile inquiring into the facts of the individual

---

[108] See further A Tanney, 'Worn Out Clogs? [2009] *Conv* 490.

[109] See especially *Samuel v Jarrah Timber and Wood Paving Corporation Ltd* [1904] AC 323, 325, 327 (HL); *Kreglinger v New Patagonia Meat and Cold Storage Co Ltd* [1914] AC 25, 46–47 (HL). The rule is disparaged also, on less precise grounds, in *Jones v Morgan* [2001] EWCA Civ 995, [86] (CA).

[110] The illegality of collateral advantages is explained in this way in *Kreglinger v New Patagonia Meat and Cold Storage Co Ltd* [1914] AC 25, 54–55, 58 (HL), citing *Chambers v Goldwin* (1802, 1803, 1804) 9 Ves Jun 254, 271 (Ch).

[111] For unconscionability, see § 12.7.1.

case: unconscionability can be presumed.[112] Freedom of contract should certainly yield in the face of the exploitation of vulnerability. But the argument's perception of borrowers as always vulnerable, so that lenders bargaining for more than security necessarily act unconscionably, is problematic. Perhaps when this position was originally taken, in the 17th century, it was backed by sound empirical observation, and/or a proportionate use of presumption in the prevailing forensic context. (An alternative hypothesis might be that, even then, it sprang from a prejudiced view of lenders.) Today, however, mortgage lenders operate in an environment that is both competitive and regulated,[113] and while most borrowers probably do remain at a disadvantage, factors such as the availability of independent advice limit its extent, and the possibilities for its exploitation. Where exploitation does occur, it can be dealt with ad hoc. This argument for generically suppressing collateral advantages is therefore untenable too.

So far as concerns the relationship between collateral advantages and freedom of contract, there seems to be no other argument. It might therefore be concluded that the law should allow mortgage arrangements to contain stipulations for collateral advantages after all – the courts' decisions narrowing the scope of the rule against collateral advantages being, for all their instability, steps towards this position. A caveat must be entered, however. Freedom of contract is a proposition only about what can be included in a contract. It does not mean that parties should or do have similar freedom to create rights in rem: the *numerus clausus* principle, discussed in §§ 1.2.1–1.2.2, insists that, on the contrary, rights can be given in rem status only where they fit a template that the law maintains for this purpose. As a right in rem, a mortgage can therefore have only the content that the law allows: essentially, as we have seen, it must be – only – a security right. Collateral advantages are, by definition, not security rights. So they cannot properly be given in rem effect merely by virtue of their attachment to a security right. But if the idea is that they shall operate only as between the original parties, ie in personam, there seems no reason not to revert to the conclusion that, in principle,[114] they should be free to do so.

---

[112] This explanation for the illegality of collateral advantages is given in *Samuel v Jarrah Timber and Wood Paving Corporation Ltd* [1904] AC 323, 326 (HL), citing *Vernon v Bethell* (1761) 2 Eden 110, 113 (Ch).

[113] See especially the Financial Services Authority's *Mortgages: Conduct of Business* rules (n 46).

[114] Arguably their freedom should be curtailed (in particular) where the land is a family home, as there is a paramount social interest in safeguarding homes.

12.7 The Creation of Mortgages

Mortgages are in practice always created by intentional conferral. In the case of registered land, such a conferral must (as we would expect: § 5.4) be effected by deed,[115] and completed by registration.[116]

It is, however, unnecessary for a mortgage to announce itself as such. If I grant you an interest in my land de facto as security for an obligation I owe you, the law recognises it as a mortgage. And if I give it features inconsistent with the law's idea of a mortgage, the law adjusts it so as to fit the perception of a mortgage as a security right. For example, there will be an insistence on redeemability. There will also be an insistence on the required legal form, as explained in § 12.1.4. So if I purport to secure my debt to you by transferring my freehold to you, as was possible in the past, the transaction will be translated (if the land is registered) into one creating a charge.[117]

12.7.1 Vitiation

A mortgage may of course be vitiated, so as to be ineffective or unenforceable. Since a mortgage must exist to secure – and so presupposes – a loan,[118] it will also have no effect if the loan it purports to secure is itself so vitiated.

The ways in which a loan or mortgage may be vitiated include the commonplace ones such as duress, undue influence, mistake and misrepresentation, about which little further will be said here: details can be found in books on the law of contract. Another such way, however, is unconscionability, and this requires special mention, as its profile for mortgages[119] may differ from that for other kinds of contract.

---

[115] Law of Property Act 1925 s 52(1).

[116] Land Registration Act 2002 s 27(2)(f). This, however, goes only for legal mortgages, on which this chapter has focused. A mortgage may also be created in equity, either deliberately or as a fall-back from failure to use the formalities required for a legal mortgage (as explained in § 6.2.4). An equitable mortgage requires writing (Law of Property Act 1925 s 53(1)(a); Law of Property (Miscellaneous Provisions) Act 1989 s 2). Equitable mortgages do, however, also behave differently in certain respects, especially as regards the lender's right to sell.

[117] At one time, the law explicitly provided for such translation: Law of Property Act 1925 s 85(2), ruling that a mortgage purportedly by freehold transfer should take effect instead by a 3,000-year lease, that being the then prevailing form. There seems to be no corresponding provision translating a freehold transfer into the now prevailing form of a charge (Land Registration Act 2002 s 23(1)(a)), but it is assumed that the translation will occur nonetheless. There is a difficulty at a formal level, however. The register will necessarily show the freehold transfer, and not the charge. Presumably it will have to be altered so as to reflect the true substantive position.

[118] Or some other kind of liability (n 26): this section applies *mutatis mutandis*, but note that many of the vitiation rules, especially the statutory ones, are aimed at loans in particular.

[119] See *Knightsbridge Estates Trust Ltd v Byrne* [1939] Ch 441, 457 (CA); *Multiservice Bookbinding Ltd v Marden* [1979] Ch 84 (Ch D).

In the abstract, a stipulation is unconscionable if the promisee procured it 'in a morally reprehensible manner, that is to say, in a way which affects his conscience'.[120] As regards contracts generally, this is apparently seen as occurring only where one party exploits some especial weakness from which the other suffers;[121] the straightforward exploitation of superior bargaining power is not enough.[122] In the mortgage context, however, it seems that the straightforward exploitation of superior bargaining power may be sufficient.[123] There seems to be no warrant for this difference (perhaps it is a throwback to the idea that borrowers are conclusively presumed to be in desperate straits?), and the rules should be assimilated. Unconscionability in its mortgage variant (whether or not otherwise too) also differs from duress, undue influence and so on in another way. They operate in an 'all-or-nothing' way: if an obligation is affected by one of them, it is bad in toto, rather than rewritten into an acceptable form. But where a mortgage or its underlying loan is affected by unconscionability, it seems that a court can rewrite it in this way.[124]

A transaction can also be rewritten where it infringes the Unfair Contract Terms Act 1977 or the Unfair Terms in Consumer Contracts Regulations 1999.[125] The 1977 Act, while inapplicable to land mortgages,[126] appears to apply to loans as such, so long as to consumers; but it attacks only exclusion or indemnity clauses.[127] The 1999 Regulations, again limited to consumer transactions,[128] apply to mortgages as well as to loans,[129] and to their terms in

---

[120] *Multiservice Bookbinding Ltd v Marden, ibid* 110.

[121] *Fry v Lane* (1888) 40 Ch D 312 (Ch D); *Cresswell v Potter* [1978] 1 WLR 255n (Ch D); *Alec Lobb (Garages) Ltd v Total Oil (Great Britain) Ltd* [1983] 1 WLR 87, 94–5 (Ch D); *Boustany v Piggott* (1995) 69 P & CR 298, 303 (PC).

[122] *National Westminster Bank plc v Morgan* [1985] AC 686, 708 (HL) (denying the contrary view expressed in *Lloyds Bank Ltd v Bundy* [1975] QB 326, 336 (CA)).

[123] So, in the mortgage decision *Multiservice Bookbinding Ltd v Marden* [1979] Ch 84 (Ch D), the judge declares (*ibid* 110) that unconscionability is not limited to situations of especial weakness, and that 'the court can and should intervene where a bargain has been procured by unfair means'; before going on (*ibid* 111) to assess this in terms of the parties' relative bargaining strengths.

[124] Thus, in *Cityland and Property (Holdings) Ltd v Dabrah* [1968] Ch 166 (Ch D) an excessive interest rate was replaced by a proper one. (The judge rejected the stipulated interest rate as being 'unreasonable', but *Multiservice Bookbinding Ltd v Marden* [1979] Ch 84 (Ch D), reflecting *Knightsbridge Estates Trust Ltd v Byrne* [1939] Ch 441 (CA), confirms that the correct test is unconscionability.) It is unclear how the substitute rate was, or should be, fixed. Other terms of a debt may be altered in this way too. So, for example, if you lend me money, unconscionably stipulating that I cannot repay for a certain time – forcing me to continue paying you interest all the while – this prolongation may be set aside. In *Knightsbridge Estates Trust Ltd v Byrne, ibid*, a 40-year debt term was attacked on this ground (among others), but was upheld because on the facts there was no unconscionability: the borrower was a business entity, adequately capable of looking after its own interests.

[125] SI 1999/2083.

[126] Sch 1(1)(b).

[127] Sections 3, 4. Such clauses are unenforceable if they are 'unreasonable'.

[128] Reg 4(1).

[129] *R (Khatun) v Newham London Borough Council* [2005] QB 37, [77]–[83] (CA) holds that the Regulations extend to land transactions (there, leases), and there appears no reason to exclude mortgages.

general, but with the exception, very importantly, of the obligation to repay and the interest rate.[130] Probably more usefully as regards mortgage transactions in particular, therefore, rewriting is also possible via the Consumer Credit Act 1974. Under sections 140A and 140B of this Act, a court can rewrite the transaction where otherwise it would leave a relationship between lender and borrower that is unfair to the borrower, having regard either to its terms in the abstract, or to the way in which the lender is operating it. Under other provisions of the Act, lenders must comply with the numerous regulatory rules constituting the bulk of the Act itself and also established by the Office of Fair Trading,[131] and, if they fail to do so, will be unable to enforce what would otherwise be their rights except to the extent that a court allows them to.[132] The effect of an objectionable mortgage transaction can also be adjusted through an order of the Financial Ombudsman.[133] The Act has a limited scope, however. As well as being restricted to consumer transactions,[134] it does not apply[135] to a first mortgage of land at least 40 per cent of which is used 'as or in connection with' a dwelling.[136] Mortgages of the latter kind – that is, most ordinary domestic mortgages – are instead the concern of the Financial Services and Markets Act 2000. Under this Act, the Financial Services Authority's *Mortgages: Conduct of Business* ('MCOB') rules[137] require financial institutions to undertake retail lending in a 'responsible' way, taking proper account of the customer's ability to repay, and treating him 'fairly': so, ensuring that the loan's interest rate is not excessive as compared with others available in the market.[138] Here too an offensive transaction's effect can be altered through an order of the Financial Ombudsman,[139] though this time not by a court.

The main impact of the MCOB rules and the regulatory rules under the Consumer Credit Act 1974 – as well as of the activities of the Office of Fair Trading under the Unfair Terms in Consumer Contracts Regulations 1999[140] – is prophylactic, however. That is, they operate to police lenders (albeit sometimes by punishing them after they have transgressed), so that problem-

---

[130] Reg 6(2) – except that even the interest rate must be clearly expressed. Where the Regulations do apply, they render unenforceable (reg 8) a standard-form term that is 'unfair' to the consumer (where 'it causes a significant imbalance in the parties' rights and obligations arising under the contract, to the detriment of the consumer'): reg 5(1).

[131] See www.oft.gov.uk/OFTwork/credit/.

[132] Consumer Credit Act 1974 ss 55(2), 61B(3), 65(1), 105(7), 111(2), 124, 127, 135, 136.

[133] *ibid* ss 59–61; Financial Services and Markets Act 2000 ss 228, 229. For the Financial Ombudsman Service see http://www.financial-ombudsman.org.uk.

[134] Consumer Credit Act 1974 s 8.

[135] *ibid* s 16(6C).

[136] Financial Services and Markets Act 2000 (Regulated Activities) Order 2001 (SI 2001/544).

[137] See n 46.

[138] Sections 11.3, 12.2.5. Section 12.2 further prohibits other kinds of charge (for early redemption, or for falling into arrears) from rising above the actual costs in question.

[139] Financial Services and Markets Act 2000 ss 228, 229.

[140] Regs 10–15.

atic loans are not made in the first place.[141] But it is fair to say that the 2008 crash showed these provisions to be deficient. It revealed that many borrowers had been permitted (indeed, encouraged?) to undertake loans which they could very decidedly not afford.[142] The complexity of the overall picture is striking, and may be regarded as unwarranted and indeed unfortunate. This may be particularly the case as regards the division of territory between the Consumer Credit Act 1974 and the Financial Services and Markets Act 2000, with their different – but not so very different, and anyway different for no apparent reason – regimes;[143] and also as regards the relationship between these regimes, and between the regimes and the traditional doctrines whereby mortgage transactions are controlled, in particular unconscionability.

12.7.2 Vitiation and Third Parties

A mortgage or its loan may be thus vitiated by reference to the dealings between the mortgagee and mortgagor themselves. But it may also be vitiated by reference to problems in the dealings between a third person and the mortgagor. In this event, the vitiation will nonetheless affect the mortgagee if he has notice of the problems.[144]

Say I am married to John, and together we own a house. John wants to mortgage it to you, so as to secure a loan, perhaps in order to raise funds for his business. You demand that his debt be secured on our house, but since we own it jointly, John cannot mortgage it to you without my participation.[145] In

[141] Also relevant, and likewise prophylactic, are the Consumer Protection from Unfair Trading Regulations 2008 (SI 2008/1277).

[142] Nield (n 5) strikingly depicts the welter of lesson-learning, and new-initiative-introduction, in the wake of the crash. It is hard not to view all this activity as uncoordinated, and also, as Nield points out, in an (as yet unexplored) tension with the perennial policy aim of ensuring affordable home-ownership.

[143] The government announced on 26 March 2010 that it intends to put all mortgage regulation into the hands of the Financial Services Authority ('FSA'), which currently deals only with the mortgages covered by the Financial Services and Markets Act 2000, the remainder, covered by the Consumer Credit Act 1974, being the concern of the Office of Fair Trading ('OFT'). See www.hm-treasury.gov.uk/consult_mortgage_regulation.htm, following upon HM Treasury, *Mortgage Regulation: A Consultation* (2009) (www.hm-treasury.gov.uk/d/consult_mortgage_regulation.pdf). Para 2.25 of the latter implies (as one might expect) that not only will the FSA become the sole regulator, but the 2000 Act will become the sole relevant legislation. Remember, however, that only the 1974 Act, not the 2000 one, allows judicial modification of an objectionable transaction . . . and then compare para 2.29, which states that 'The Government considers the level of consumer protection offered by the OFT's regime vital, and is determined that should any transfer of regulation occur, it should not result in a lower level of protection for consumers.' Clarification is awaited; *cf* Nield (n 5) 612–16.

[144] *Barclays Bank plc v O'Brien* [1994] 1 AC 180 (HL); *Royal Bank of Scotland plc v Etridge (No 2)* [2002] 2 AC 773 (HL). For a fuller account, see eg M Chen-Wishart, *Contract Law* (4th edn, Oxford, 2012) 345–51. For discussion, see M Thompson, 'Mortgages and Undue Influence' in E Cooke (ed), *Modern Studies in Property Law, Volume 2* (Oxford, 2003) ch 7.

[145] The same issues arise if the house is solely in my name, as in *Castle Phillips Finance v Piddington* [1995] 1 FLR 783 (CA). Alternatively, the house may be registered in John's name

securing my participation, he tells me lies about what is afoot. So there is mis-representation between him and me. But this does not directly affect the validity of the mortgage as between me and you. It does so, however, if you have notice of it. This will be the case if you should realise the risk of John not behaving properly (generally from the nature of the deal and the relation-ship between John and me), and fail to insist that I obtain independent legal advice.

It is clear that this doctrine applies in the case of misrepresentation or undue influence between John and myself, and presumably also duress or unconscionability. It is, however, not obviously relevant where the transaction is objectionable by reference to the various statutory rules discussed above, since these rules are aimed at problems arising in the transaction between the borrower and lender themselves.

12.8 Mortgages' Effectiveness against Disponees

As explained in § 12.1.2, although a mortgage is a right in rem, we do not expect it in practice to bind a transferee of the land in question. Instead, we expect it to be redeemed using the purchase money, so that the transferee takes the land free from it. Its status as a right in rem is more significant as giving it priority in the borrower's bankruptcy. It does, however, also mean that the mortgage takes precedence over a disposition of the land short of a transfer.

Say, for example, I buy a house with a loan from you, mortgaging the house to you so as to secure my debt. Some time later, but before I have redeemed, I agree with John – with whom I am in a family relationship – that he shall have a share in the house. As explained in § 9.3, I thenceforth hold the house on trust for John and myself. But John's beneficial interest will be in the house subject to the mortgage. If you have occasion to repossess, John will not be able to prevent you doing so by pointing to his interest; and if you sell, John will have no claim against you to a share of the proceeds (though he will have a claim against me, to a share of the balance that you pay me after deducting what is due to you).[146]

alone, but he holds it on trust for himself and me, so that he may be able to give you a mortgage taking precedence over my beneficial right only if he obtains my consent. The same issues again arise with regard to his doing so: *Scottish Equitable Life plc v Virdee* [1999] 1 FLR 863 (CA): see §§ 4.2.3–4.2.4, where the idea of 'notice' for these purposes is discussed more fully.

[146] Contrast the situation where John's beneficial interest arises *before* I grant you the mort-gage. In principle, John's interest then takes precedence over the mortgage. But the law maintains a number of rules which, in practice, produce the opposite effect. See § 16.8.

As a right in rem, a mortgage is capable of binding a disponee in this way. For it actually to do so, the rules on this subject in the Land Registration Act 2002 must be observed. As explained in § 12.7, a mortgage has to be registered in order to exist at all.[147] This registration serves to make it bind,[148] but the requirement for it means that the mortgage cannot operate as an overriding interest.[149] This is as one would expect: mortgages are quintessentially rights created only in an organised way.

---

[147] Land Registration Act 2002 s 27(2)(f).

[148] *ibid* s 29(2)(a)(i).

[149] Except that, if not completed by registration under the Land Registration Act 2002 s 27(2) (f), it can still take effect as an equitable mortgage (assuming that writing has been used: Law of Property (Miscellaneous Provisions) Act 1989 s 2), and as such could operate as an overriding interest . . . though only in the unlikely event that you, the mortgagee, are in actual and apparent occupation of the land, so as to bring the case within the Land Registration Act 2002 Sch 3 para 2.

13

Easements

13.1 What is an Easement?

The label 'easement' covers an assortment of rights in land, whose content varies but which are covered by the formula in *Re Ellenborough Park*,[1] explored below. Important examples are rights of way (entitling you to cross my land, on a particular route, going to and from your own land); rights of water (entitling you to the water flowing through a channel or pipe which crosses my land before reaching yours, meaning that I must not divert the water away from you); rights of light (entitling you to the supply of light that reaches your windows via my land, meaning that I may not build on my land so as to block them); and rights of support (entitling you to the support my land gives your buildings; I must not do anything to my land that compromises that support).[2]

Lest the possibility of there being such rights against my land should seem simply unfair on me, it should be understood that in principle they arise when I grant them to you (commonly for money), or my predecessor did so and, as I acquire the land, I am bound by them as the rights in rem they are (which will be reflected in my paying a lower price than I would have paid if there were no such disadvantage to me). We shall look at the issues of grant, and operation in rem, in §§ 13.2 and 13.3.

---

[1] [1956] Ch 131, 163, 170 (CA).
[2] Cousins to easements are profits à prendre (profits, for short), which differ from easements in entitling you to take something from my land, which until that moment counted as part of my land. Examples of profits are thus the right to excavate (and remove for your own benefit) the stone in my quarry or the coal in my mine . . . and, because these things also count as 'land', to cut the trees in my wood or to graze your cattle on my grass, or to catch the fish in my lake or the game in my forest.

13.1.1 The Rule in *Re Ellenborough Park*

The instances of easements given above are not regarded as a series of individual rights in rem. They are treated as particular manifestations of a generalised concept.

The concept's most famous formulation was induced from earlier case-law by a commentator,[3] and adopted by the court in *Re Ellenborough Park*.[4] According to this formulation, for a right to qualify as an easement:

> (1) there must be a dominant and a servient tenement: (2) an easement must 'accommodate' the dominant tenement: (3) dominant and servient owners must be different persons, and (4) a right over land cannot amount to an easement, unless it is capable of forming the subject-matter of a grant.

Although this formula is so inadequate that a fresh start might be preferable, its privileged status means that we must continue to pay attention to it. What follows is an attempt to describe the rules defining easements which follows the formula in *Re Ellenborough Park*,[5] but challenges this where necessary.

13.1.2 Elements (1) and (3): Two Pieces of Land, Two Owners

The formula demands two pieces of land, with different owners. Although the formula leaves it unexplained, the point behind this is that an easement is a right:

—— requiring that one piece of land (the 'servient tenement': my land, in the examples above) be used in a certain way, and
—— belonging to another piece of land (the 'dominant tenement': your land, in the examples).

That you and I must be different people is obvious: unless it existed between two people, giving one (you) entitlements against the other (me), an easement could not be a right at all. But we need to take a closer look at the two points just isolated.

First, the demand that an easement relate to the use of my land. In the abstract, your right against me could be a right that I behave in a certain way *in my personal capacity*. To be an easement, however, the right must control not merely what I do in my personal capacity, but what I do *on my land*. Otherwise, it could not rationally be attached to the land, as rights in rem regarding land necessarily are, so as to be capable of binding disponees of the land. Say I am a builder, and I undertake to do work to shore up your

---

[3] G Cheshire, *The Modern Law of Real Property* (7th edn, London, 1954) 456 ff.
[4] [1956] Ch 131, 163, 170 (CA).
[5] *ibid.*

buildings. My obligation does not affect my use of my own house or builder's yard, several miles away, and will not bind someone to whom I sell that house or yard. So there is no easement in this case: merely a contract. Whereas if I live next door to you, and my obligation is not to take away the support that my land gives your buildings, my obligation does connect with my use of my land, and so can be an easement. Hence the formula's statement 'there must be . . . a servient tenement'.

Then, the demand that an easement must belong to your land. In the abstract, again, a right dictating what I do on my land could belong to you personally. Some rights in rem over land are like this: for instance, leases and mortgages. But to qualify as an easement, your right must (we shall explore this further in § 13.1.3) belong to you *in your capacity as owner of your land*. And to do this, it must benefit you in this capacity, ie connect with the use you make of your land: as where it is a right for you to cross my land, *so as to access your adjoining land*. And that in turn presupposes that you have some such land: 'there must be a dominant . . . tenement'.

The idea that an easement 'belongs' to the dominant land (or 'appertains' to that land; so an easement is an 'appurtenant right') is of course a figure, since English law supposes that rights can only belong to humans. But it stands for the truth that, when you have an easement in your capacity as owner of some piece of land, and you transfer that land to John, the ease-ment will automatically pass to John with it.[6]

13.1.3 Element (2): 'Accommodating' the Dominant Land

As we have just seen, not only must you have some land: in addition, and as the reason for this rule, the right (if it is to be an easement) must benefit you in your capacity as that land's owner. The formula in *Re Ellenborough Park*[7] records this requirement in its separate assertion that 'an easement must "accommodate" the dominant tenement'. This section looks more closely at this requirement.[8]

Say you have the right to come onto my land so as to enjoy the views. This right benefits you in your personal capacity: the views are equally valuable to you regardless of whether, or where, you have land of your own. So, even if you live adjacent to me, it cannot be an easement: it can only be a licence. Licences are looked at in Chapter 17. Essentially, whereas easements are rights in rem, licences are only in personam. By contrast, a right to cross my

---

[6] For a complication, see *Wall v Collins* [2007] Ch 390 (CA); E Cooke, 'The Genetics of Appurtenant Interests' in S Bright (ed), *Modern Studies in Property Law, Volume 6* (Oxford, 2011) ch 9; *cf* Law Commission, *Making Land Work: Easements, Covenants and Profits à Prendre* (Law Com No 327, London, 2011) paras 3.232–3.263.

[7] [1956] Ch 131, 163, 170 (CA).

[8] See further M Sturley, 'Easements in Gross' (1980) 96 *LQR* 557.

land *so as to access yours* benefits you in your capacity as owner of your land,[9] because you would have no reason to cross my land if you did not live on the adjoining land. So it can be an easement. Easements of this kind – rights of way – are very common. Other rights benefiting you in your capacity as owner of your land, and so capable of existing as easements, include those where you run a pub, and have the right to erect your sign on my nearby wall;[10] or where you have a farm, and have the right to a supply of water piped through my land to your farm, so as to irrigate your crops; or where you live in a house, and have the right to make use of my neighbouring garden.[11]

This requirement that the right benefit you as owner of your land is, however, often paraphrased, or glossed, in ways which make it more exacting. The effect is that rights which otherwise could be easements – they benefit you as owner of your land, and fulfil the other requirements – are prevented from existing as easements after all, meaning that they must be only licences. Several examples of this can be found.[12]

First, some accounts demand that your land should be *close to* mine. Most easements are put under no pressure by this view, but it would rule out a right entitling you to let clients coming to your city-centre hotel land their helicopters in my field at the edge of the city, even though this right certainly benefits you in your capacity as owner of your hotel. Essentially, the effect is to privilege the more down-to-earth, traditional ways in which a right over my land can benefit you as the owner of yours.

Second, in the *Re Ellenborough Park*[13] formula itself, the requirement that you benefit as owner of your land is put in the form of the demand that the right 'must "accommodate" the dominant land'. This is a bad choice of paraphrase. In our culture,[14] to speak of benefiting the land itself is fundamentally unintelligible. The 'accommodation' – that is, benefit – has to be to the human who has the land, rather than to the land itself. But it is possible to make some sense of the idea. Farmers, especially, speak of some practice or happening as being good for the land. What they mean is that the practice or happening assists the work which some or all humans think the land should

---

[9] For this as the meaning of 'accommodate' (though with a reminder not to read too much into 'benefit'), see *Polo Woods Foundation v Shelton-Agar* [2010] 1 All ER 539, [32]–[60], [90]–[91] (Ch D).

[10] *Moody v Steggles* (1879) 12 Ch D 261 (Ch D).

[11] This was the situation in *Re Ellenborough Park* [1956] Ch 131 (CA) itself.

[12] A further example is a statement, *ibid*, 169, that the alleged easement must be 'reasonably necessary' for the better enjoyment of the dominant land. If this were taken seriously as a requirement additional to that of 'accommodation', it would seriously limit the instances in which a right could be an easement. But it is actually regarded as adding nothing: *Polo Woods Foundation v Shelton-Agar* [2010] 1 All ER 539, [37]–[39] (Ch D).

[13] [1956] Ch 131 (CA).

[14] Contrast cultures, such as the native American, which ascribe animate quality to a wider range of natural entities and phenomena. Some, too, ascribe animate quality to man-made entities such as buildings, but perhaps this is no more than a metaphor.

do. So salvaged, however, the rule that the right 'must "accommodate" the dominant land' makes it easiest to find easements in agricultural and similar contexts, where the focus is on working the land itself. Our original statement, that the right must benefit you in your capacity as owner of your land, is wider, allowing the easement to engage with any use to which you may put your land.

The difference can be seen in *Hill v Tupper*.[15] The claimant had a small piece of land on the bank of a canal. This was the base for his business, running pleasure boats on the canal. The canal company gave him the exclusive right to do this. The court held that this right was not an easement over the canal. The boat business did not 'accommodate' the claimant's land in the sense of 'facilitate a working of the very soil of the land'. But it did benefit the claimant in his capacity as owner of the land, for this was the place which he in fact used to bring his boats to shore.

Third, further passages in the judgment in *Re Ellenborough Park*[16] assert that a right cannot be an easement unless it is 'connected with the normal enjoyment' of your land. Say your land is a farm, but you bought it not to farm it, but because you are a Druid and the land contains part of a Neolithic henge where you wish to perform rituals. The remainder of the henge is on my adjoining land. You buy from me the right to come onto my land so as to visit all parts of the henge during your rituals. The right benefits you in your capacity as owner of your land, but it is not connected with the 'normal enjoyment' of that land.

This 'normal enjoyment' gloss is ambiguous. It could mean that the alleged easement must connect with the use to which the dominant land is in fact normally, ie usually, put – farming, in the example. Or it could mean that, on top of the requirement that the alleged easement should connect with the use to which the dominant land is put, that use must be 'normal', in the sense of 'ordinary (at least for land of that kind)' – so that even if, in the example, the farm were normally used for the pursuit of Druidism, there could be no easement of access to the neighbouring henge, since the pursuit of Druidism is not an ordinary use for land. The former, less demanding, reading is probably the authentic one,[17] but the latter is sometimes espoused. Moreover, the demand for normality is sometimes surreptitiously relocated. Instead of referring to the use of the dominant land, it is made to refer instead to the benefit offered by the alleged easement, so as to require this to be a normal adjunct to land (of the relevant kind). On this understanding, it is sometimes said that there cannot be an easement allowing the owner of a house to use the neighbouring swimming pool or tennis court (as opposed to garden).

---

[15] (1863) 2 H & C 121 (Ex).

[16] [1956] Ch 131, 170, 173, 174 (CA).

[17] See *Polo Woods Foundation v Shelton-Agar* [2010] 1 All ER 539, [90] (Ch D). Both readings are consistent with the decision in *Re Ellenborough Park* [1956] Ch 131 (CA) itself: the dominant land was usually used for housing, and housing is an ordinary user.

Although the dominant land is usually used as a house, and use as a house is entirely ordinary, and access to the pool or court would certainly benefit the house, such access is not normal (whereas access to a garden is). There is no warrant in *Re Ellenborough Park*[18] for this reading of the gloss, but it is presumably attractive to those who espouse it.

A fourth gloss is a view that a right cannot be an easement if the benefit it gives you is in the nature of 'mere recreation and amusement'. This view was raised as an argument against the possibility of an easement over a garden in *Re Ellenborough Park*.[19] The argument was rejected, making it hard to see what purchase the alleged rule could have, but the court stopped short of denying the rule itself.

In comparison with the demand simply that you benefit as owner of your land, these various paraphrases and glosses (and understandings thereof) allow your right to count as an easement in a restricted range of cases. As we have seen, they tend to privilege rights that are traditional, ordinary ('normal'), agricultural, and about business rather than recreation, over those benefiting you in other ways. But their juridical status and precise meaning are far from clear. It can reasonably be said, however, that they are played down, rather than up, by the decision in *Re Ellenborough Park*.[20]

13.1.4 Element (4): A Right 'Capable of Forming the Subject-matter of a Grant'

The formula in *Re Ellenborough Park*[21] ends with the statement that 'a right over land cannot amount to an easement, unless it is capable of forming the subject-matter of a grant'.

The mention of a 'grant' refers to the possibility of your acquiring an easement by my conferring it on you, using a deed. For this to be possible, you must be clearly enough identified, but that has nothing to do with the quality of the right, which is the focus of element (4). The right's content must also be clearly enough identified, but that is not confined to acquisition in this way rather than otherwise, or indeed to easements: it is intrinsic to your being recognised by the law as having any kind of right.

---

[18] [1956] Ch 131 (CA).

[19] *ibid*, 177–9. See too *Polo Woods Foundation v Shelton-Agar* [2010] 1 All ER 539, [94] (Ch D), denying the possibility of an easement to 'wander or exercise'. This rule can to some extent be sidestepped, in that your right to amenity can be established instead as a 'restrictive covenant' (see Ch 14). You can certainly thus secure, say, an uninterrupted pleasant outlook across my land, even though this may be purely of recreational value: indeed, it is the very point of restrictive covenants to allow the establishment of such a right (§ 14.2.3). Perhaps you could equally secure a right to wander or exercise recreationally on my land. Such active rather than passive rights over servient land seem never to have been created as restrictive covenants, but there appears to be nothing in the rules about the latter to prevent it.

[20] [1956] Ch 131 (CA).

[21] *ibid*.

In truth, element (4) is an inept shorthand for three rules which impose further restrictions on the rights, of all those acceptable under the rules as explained so far, that are allowed to count as easements. These rules bar from existence as an easement rights that otherwise satisfy the law's requirements, but which:

—— *require me actively to do something*, except to maintain a fence between our two pieces of land; or

—— *benefit you without activity on your part* ('negative easements'), except those requiring me not to remove the support that my land gives your buildings, or not to impede a flow across my land of water through an artificial channel to your land, or of air or light to a particular aperture on your land; or

—— *give you excessively extensive rights over my land*, rather than allow you to use it in some more restricted way.

As to the first of these rules, the law recognises as an easement the obligation on me to maintain a fence between my land and yours.[22] But that apart, the traditional view is that an obligation requiring me actively to do something for you (even assuming it needs to be done on my land, and benefits you in your capacity as owner of your land) cannot be an easement.[23] So a right allowing you to take water through a pipe crossing my land cannot be an easement if, the pipe being metered as it enters my land, I have to pay for what you use.[24] This traditional view cannot be altogether right, however. If you foreseeably come onto my land, I owe a duty of care under the Occupiers' Liability Acts 1957 and 1984 to save you from injury. The discharge of this duty may well oblige me to take active steps. And this obligation is not merely a quite general one, having no particular association with easements: on the contrary, your having a right to enter my land – such as an easement – makes it particularly foreseeable that you will do so. Yet no one suggests that, on account of my obligation, your right cannot be an easement after all.[25]

The second rule limits the existence of 'negative easements'. A positive easement is one whose enjoyment involves you encroaching on my land, as for example by coming onto it yourself, or allowing fumes from your land to blow over mine. (So positive easements are those affording you a defence to trespass or nuisance against me.) A negative easement, on the other hand, is one which does not involve you encroaching on my land. Four kinds of negative easement are well established: those obliging me (i) not to impede a flow

---

[22] *Jones v Price* [1965] 2 QB 618 (CA); *Crow v Wood* [1971] 1 QB 77 (CA).

[23] *Moncrieff v Jamieson* [2007] 1 WLR 2620, [47] (HL). If the easement requires upkeep, this is your responsibility. So if you have a right of way along my track, but the track has become boggy, you have the right to enter and do the necessary work, at *your* expense.

[24] *Rance v Elvin* (1985) 50 P & CR 9, 13 (CA). The principle was distinguished, perhaps questionably, on the facts.

[25] See further A Waite, 'Easements: Positive Duties on the Servient Owner?' [1985] *CLJ* 458.

of water through an artificial channel[26] from my land to yours, or (ii) a flow of air or (iii) one of light across my land to a particular aperture[27] on your land; and (iv) not to remove the support that my land gives your buildings.[28] In *Phipps v Pears*[29] it was held that no other kinds of negative easement can exist. There cannot, therefore, be an easement not to remove the protection from the weather that my building gives yours.[30]

This rule is not what it seems, however. An obligation which it prevents from being a negative easement can be created instead as a 'restrictive covenant'.[31] But restrictive covenants can be created only by conferral, whereas easements can arise alternatively by prescription: broadly, from the mere fact that you have behaved as though you had the easement in question for the past 20 years.[32] So the real effect of *Phipps v Pears*[33] is that although further rights in the nature of negative easements can be acquired by conferral (as restrictive covenants), they cannot be acquired by prescription. This makes sense. As explained in § 7.3, prescription cannot be an acceptable basis for the generation of rights unless I have the opportunity to prevent the usage on which it is based. In the nature of things, I normally do have that opportunity in the case of a positive easement, where you encroach on my land in some way. But the reverse is true in the case of a negative easement, where you do not encroach on my land. You merely arrange matters on your own

[26] You are entitled to the water in a natural river or stream as a 'natural right': that is, your entitlement comes automatically with your ownership of your land, and you do not need to point to an additional right – easement – against me.

[27] There is no natural right to the flow of light or air to your land over mine (as opposed to vertically down). The only rights of this kind are easements, and they can exist only in respect of light or air entering your land through a particular aperture such as a window, located on the boundary between your land and mine, which I would otherwise be free to block, say by building on my land. A particular aperture is required because otherwise, an easement could arise against me by prescription (§§ 7.3, 13.2.7) without my having a proper chance to prevent it.

[28] You are entitled to have my land support your bare land as a natural right. But this right does not entitle you to the additional support you may need for the buildings on your land. To obtain the latter, you need an easement against me.

[29] [1965] 1 QB 76 (CA); likewise *Hunter v Canary Wharf Ltd* [1997] AC 655 (HL). The two decisions (at 83 and 726 respectively) explain that further negative easements are embargoed because negative easements unduly restrict what I can do on my own land. This cannot be the point, however, because positive easements are no different from negative ones in this respect (I cannot build across your right of way any more than I can across your window), and because preventing me from doing things on what is otherwise my own land is the very raison d'être of easements.

[30] *ibid*. But you apparently can have easements obliging me to allow your electricity, gas and so on to come through my cables, pipes etc up to your boundary, and such easements are negative too. Presumably they are analogous to the undoubted easement obliging me to allow your water to come through my land. Moreover, I can certainly have an easement to send my drainage out through your land, because it is positive: it would be bizarre if I could not have one to bring these other utilities in. Perhaps the point is that, unlike the negative easements discussed in the text, those noted here are highly unlikely to arise by prescription, in the way the text below identifies as the true source of the embargo on further negative easements.

[31] For restrictive covenants, see Ch 14.

[32] For prescription, see §§ 7.3, 13.2.7.

[33] [1965] 1 QB 76 (CA).

land in a manner dependent on the configuration of mine – say, you build your house so that its windows' source of light and ventilation is across an open area of my adjoining land. I might well not even realise that I have any reason to react, and even if I do, the means of doing so will be awkward and possibly even detrimental to me: I might, say, have to build an otherwise unwanted wall purely so as to block your windows.[34] In truth, this problem is an argument against allowing any rights in the nature of negative easements to be acquirable by prescription. Yet *Phipps v Pears*[35] applied its embargo only to such rights beyond the established four. Presumably, the law's recognition of those four was too firmly entrenched to be reversed.

The third rule withholds the status of easement from an obligation giving you excessively extensive rights over my land, rather than allowing you to use it in some more restricted way.[36] Obviously, the question arises 'What counts as excessively extensive?' The familiar kinds of easement, such as a right to cross my land, evidently do not infringe this rule: many of them certainly allow you some use of my land, but their familiarity tells us that this use does not count as excessively extensive. At the other extreme, if you and I own adjoining farms and I give you the sole right to use mine, everyone agrees that it is not an easement that I have created: as explained in § 11.2.1, it is a lease. Between these well-established instances, however, lies a considerable area of doubt. In particular, the judges have struggled to decide whether – or in what circumstances – your right to store things on my land, or to park vehicles there, can be an easement.

It seems to be accepted as clear that a right to occupy a specified part of my land, say to park in a particular space in my car park, excluding all others *including myself*, cannot be an easement. Such a right could be conferred, but since it would thus confer a right of exclusive possession, it would have to be a lease[37] ... and so be exposed to the rules about the conferment and behaviour of leases, as opposed to easements. At the other extreme, a right allowing you only the non-exclusive use of an unspecified part of my land – as where you have the right to park one car, in no particular space, in my car park – is accepted as a viable easement.[38] At issue is the area between these two cases:

[34] In the case of light, however, the Rights of Light Act 1959 allows me to 'obstruct' your windows by registering a notice against you.

[35] [1965] 1 QB 76 (CA).

[36] The rule is examined by P Luther, 'Easements and Exclusive Possession' (1996) 16 *LS* 51; but this pre-dates a number of important cases.

[37] Or, if given for an indefinite time, a transfer of ownership. For exclusive possession as a component of leases, see § 11.3. By way of exception to this rule, it appears that a right to the exclusive use of a pipe running through another's land can be an easement: see Law Commission: *Making Land Work: Easements, Covenants and Profits à Prendre* (n 6) para 3.211. This exception is probably best understood as putting further pressure on the assertion that exclusive possession is truly a doctrinal characteristic of leases, as opposed to an aspect of a political position: *cf* §§ 11.3.4, 11.4.4.

[38] *London & Blenheim Estates Ltd v Ladbroke Retail Parks Ltd* [1992] 1 WLR 1278 (Ch D); *Batchelor v Marlow* [2003] 1 WLR 764 (CA); *Moncrieff v Jamieson* [2007] 1 WLR 2620, [137]–[138] (HL).

for example, the case of a right to park in a particular space, excluding all others ... with the exception of myself, in that I may come into the space during the time when your car is not there.

The currently dominant view seems to be that the right can exist as a valid easement so long as it does not leave me 'without any reasonable use', or with only an 'illusory' use, of my land.[39] This formulation, however, leaves much in the eye of the beholder. One could interpret it as differing very little, if at all, from the rule that an easement cannot amount to a lease, allowing you to have, as a valid easement, more or less any right that allows you to occupy my land without completely excluding me. Or one could place more emphasis on the word 'use', and, reading this with an eye on the nature of the land in question and the sort of use that I might realistically be expected to want to make of that land, conclude that your right cannot after all qualify as an easement if it seriously interferes with this 'use'. A right to park in a particular space for as long as you like would appear to be acceptable in terms of the former understanding (in the nature of things, you would not be there permanently, so there would come a moment when I could enter once more). But it would probably not be acceptable in terms of the latter understanding (it would seriously interfere with my own ability to use the space in question for parking or other occupation). So the rule's ambiguity means that the law cannot be regarded as clear and stable.[40]

13.1.5 Intention to Create a Right in Rem

Say we have created a right that satisfies the above rules. It will still not be an easement unless we want it to be. The *Re Ellenborough Park*[41] formula makes no reference to this point.

The presumption is probably that we do want such a right to be an easement, and usually we will. But if we prefer, we can make it a licence instead.[42] The difference is that an easement is a right in rem, and so capable of binding disponees of my land, whereas a licence is a right in personam, and so effective only between you and me.

---

[39] *London & Blenheim Estates Ltd v Ladbroke Retail Parks Ltd, ibid; Batchelor v Marlow, ibid,* [15], [18] (CA). See too *Virdi v Chana* [2008] EWHC 2901 (Ch D); *Polo Woods Foundation v Shelton-Agar* [2010] 1 All ER 539, [121] (Ch D).

[40] The law is reviewed by the Law Commission: *Making Land Work: Easements, Covenants and Profits à Prendre* (n 6) paras 3.188–3.211. The Commission's recommendation (para 3.209) is for a rule whereby 'a right to use another's land in a way that [while not amounting to exclusive possession of the land] prevents that other from making any reasonable use of it will not for that reason fail to be an easement'. The phrase 'any reasonable use', and the surrounding text, suggests that the Commission sees this as closer to the first than to the second of the understandings discussed in the text.

[41] [1956] Ch 131 (CA).

[42] *IDC Group Ltd v Clark* (1992) 65 P & CR 179 (CA).

In allowing us to choose whether or not our right should be in rem, the law takes a position different from that which it takes when the right is in the nature of a lease.[43] As explained in § 11.4.3, there we have no option to make it an in personam licence instead. But the rule for leases rests on a consideration special to them, namely a desire to prevent exclusion of the Rent Acts, which apply to leases but not licences.

13.1.6 Why do Easements Take this Form?

Summarising the foregoing sections: to be an easement, a right must therefore:

—— not normally require me to do anything active; merely limit the use I can make of my land . . .

—— . . . though not too extensively (certainly, it must not give you exclusive possession of the land, and perhaps it must stop some way short of that); and

—— be for your benefit, in your capacity as owner of your land . . . though perhaps only in certain (traditional, ordinary, agricultural, business) ways.

Why should the law insist on this delineation?

Remember the *numerus clausus* principle, considered in § 1.2.2. As we saw there, in order to decide whether a right should be in rem, we need to see whether the damage this would do is outweighed by the good that would follow in other respects. And this links with the question whether your enjoyment of the right ought to be protected *in specie*, or whether it is good enough that you lose the right and have to accept compensation instead. After I have alienated the land in question to John, a right in personam will still deliver the latter, but only a right in rem will deliver the former.

The footing on which easements exist as rights in rem should therefore be that their delineation gives them a nature requiring in rem status in this way. The core idea is for you, in doing what you do on your land, to be able to take limited advantage of my land too. Why should we regard this as meriting protection *in specie*, so as to affect someone to whom I transfer my land? Because it allows the exploitation of land to have the best of both worlds between division into sealed packets – mine and yours – and a more communal approach.

Division into sealed packets has a great merit: at a basic level, it gives the owner of each packet the maximum opportunity and incentive to exploit his own packet to the full. But a given packet of land may in practice not be self-

---

[43] See J Hill, 'Intention and the Creation of Proprietary Rights: Are Leases Different?' (1996) 16 *LS* 200.

sufficient in the things required for its optimal exploitation. It may lack efficient access, for example. Greater benefit can be extracted by running the land in question co-operatively with neighbouring packets, from which such additional requirements can be sourced. Say you decide that you can best exploit your land by growing crops, but your land lacks water to irrigate them when necessary: the solution could be to pipe water in from my nearby lake. Or say you want to build houses, but cannot come right to the edge of your land, for fear that I will block your houses' light and air by building right to the edge of my land too: the problem is solved if you can rely on my not doing so.

You could contract with me for a water supply or against activity inimical to the houses on your land. But a contract alone, being in personam, will not affect John, to whom I soon transfer my land: if John refuses to repeat my deal with you, you will be left with parched fields or uninhabitable houses. As you will be entitled to compensation (damages for breach of contract) from me, you yourself may emerge reasonably unscathed. But the common good will suffer: that food, or those houses, which would otherwise have become available for further use by others, will become unavailable after all. To allow your exploitation of your land to stick, therefore, you need to be able to secure what you need in a way that is enforceable not only against me, but also against John after me: that is, in the form of a right in rem – an easement.

The English law on easements thus developed most during the 19th century.[44] In a movement dating from the late 18th century, English agricultural land came to be divided into sealed packets, a process known as 'enclosure'. Previously, the land had been operated much more communally. Enclosure was born of a perception that the old communal approach impeded the land's maximal exploitation. (The classic argument was that, as a communal approach meant the land's yield being shared between its several users, none of them had a straightforward incentive to invest in it, eg by fertilising or draining it. Enclosure, by giving the yield to a particular individual, offered this incentive to that individual.[45]) But easements were developed out of a perception, in turn, that even greater exploitation was possible if one could have it both ways.[46] At about the same period, too, intensive building was

---

[44] The leading specialist book on the subject, *Gale on Easements*, was first published in 1839. Its preface speaks of both the need for, and the dearth of, law on the area. The overall history of easements is much longer, shaped by such other phenomena as the urbanisation of the 16th century. For an overview, see J Getzler, 'Easements' in S Katz (ed), *The Oxford International Encyclopedia of Legal History* (New York, 2009).

[45] See eg A Young, *Political Arithmetic* (London, 1774) 787–88.

[46] See generally A Simpson, *A History of the Land Law* (2nd edn, Oxford, 1986) 261–4. The connection between easements and enclosure may explain the possibility of creating an easement requiring me to maintain a fence (see at n 22 above). An earlier bout of enclosure occurred during the late medieval and early modern period. This was aimed principally at establishing exclusive hunting parks for the aristocracy. By contrast, the kind of enclosure that occurred in the 18th and 19th centuries, by packaging up what had previously been manorial common land,

taking place, centred on the mills, factories and so on which were perceived as the most effective tools by which to exploit downstream resources. Maximum intensity was achieved by introducing easements to allow the collaborative use of neighbouring plots of land.

Care is needed, of course. Cross-exploitation does harm as well as good, for it erodes the benefits to be had from dividing land into sealed packets. The less *my* land becomes simply 'mine' because there are obligations such as easements affecting its use, the further *I* shall be from having the maximum opportunity and incentive to exploit it, by most effectively growing crops myself, or building houses, or whatever.[47] So the establishment of easements needs to be restricted to the situations in which unsealing the packets does more good than harm. The law does this with its rules that limit the forms of benefit that can be associated with easements, favouring those that are traditional, ordinary, agricultural, and a matter of business rather than recreation, and its rule limiting easements to rights that do not intrude excessively into my own rights over my land. But the situations where unsealing the packets does more good than harm can be only imprecisely identified, so it comes as no surprise that we found the courts lacking in confidence as to the status and exact meaning of these rules.[48]

All this goes only to show the argument that does exist for having rights in rem in the shape of easements. It is by no means an argument against having rights in rem of other shapes. One such right is worth mentioning here, for it is a sister to the easement.

Individual feeds of water, electricity, gas, data and so on to individual properties, if they have to cross other people's land, will count as easements. But the companies supplying these utilities also need to run their main distribution pipes and cables through other people's land,[49] and the rights under which they do so cannot be easements, because they do not benefit the company in its capacity as owner of its own land.[50] Nor can they easily be leases: these could arise only if the company had exclusive possession of the area in question,[51] and it would be hard satisfactorily to define the precise 'area' of

(potentially) collided with the hunting privileges that the lords of that land had hitherto enjoyed over it. At least part of the development of easements took the form of a discourse regarding the proper treatment of this issue, which of course additionally had its own particular dynamics. See J Getzler, 'Judges and Hunters: Law and Economic Conflict in the English Countryside, 1800–1860' in C Brooks and M Lobban (eds), *Communities and Courts* (London, 1997) ch 12.

[47] This was explicitly noticed in some of the hunting cases: see eg *Lord Leconfield v Dixon* (1867) LR 2 Ex 202, 205 (Ex); *Sowerby v Smith* (1874) LR 9 CP 524, 532–38, 539–40 (Ex Ch).

[48] The Law Commission (*Easements, Covenants and Profits à Prendre: A Consultation Paper* (Consultation Paper No 186, London, 2008)) is similarly confused. At times it seems to think that only certain kinds of rights can be easements (eg paras 3.11, 15.12–15.13, 15.32); at other times, it seems to demand only that they should not be 'capricious and personal benefits' (paras 3.20–3.33).

[49] Or airspace, which counts as land.

[50] Though this statement may assume that the dominant and servient land must be adjacent, and that the idea of 'benefit' is limited as held in *Hill v Tupper* (1863) 2 H & C 121 (Ex) (see at n 15). As explained in § 13.1.3, neither of these assumptions is unchallengeable.

[51] See § 11.2.1.

the pipe or cable.[52] These rights clearly need to be in rem: the nation's utility distribution arrangements would collapse unless protected *in specie* through changes in ownership of the land over which they run: another facet of the truth that land cannot be maximally exploited if it is literally divided into sealed packets. But there is no other common law type of right in rem that these rights can be.[53] Instead, however, they are established as in rem in their own right, under statutory provisions aimed specifically at their context.[54]

13.2 The Creation of Easements

In principle, we should expect it to be possible to acquire easements in the sorts of organised and disorganised ways discussed in Part 2 of this book, and at one level that is the case: they can, in particular, certainly be acquired by conferral, prescription and proprietary estoppel.

In this context, however, 'conferral' is not a straightforward idea. It can be implied as well as express. Nevertheless, one might suppose that both forms depended on consent. As we shall see, however, only express conferral depends purely on consent, while implied conferral depends, like prescription, on a blend of an argument from utility and an attenuated form of consent. We shall see too that in some cases, the basis on which the easement arises provides insufficient justification for its doing so.

13.2.1 Express and Implied Conferral

If I intend to confer an easement on you, there are fewest problems if I do so expressly. Express conferral could occur in an ad hoc transaction. You and I are neighbours: you would like an easement over my land: you obtain my agreement, usually in return for payment: and I give you the easement. Often, though, conferral occurs when I own a piece of land and, splitting it in two, sell one part to you, keeping the other for myself. Reckoning that your part will be more attractive (so, I can demand a higher price for it) if it has some

---

[52] Whereas a road or railway can be put across my land using a lease, or (more usually) a purchase, for these require a more definable area.

[53] They can certainly be licences, for these can take any shape the parties wish, but they operate only in personam, not in rem: see § 17.1.1.

[54] For example, the Electricity Act 1989 Sch 4 para 6. They are described as 'wayleaves', though that word can probably also be used for rights to pipes and cables which are easements.

right over mine, I 'grant'[55] you an easement over my part as a term of the transfer to you of the land itself. Or – conversely – I might reckon that I want a right over your part, for the benefit of the part I keep (at the cost of being able to charge you less): as a term of the transfer of your part to you, I will 'reserve' an easement for myself.

But as well as being an express term of a transfer in this way, a conferral or reservation can be implied into the transfer. An argument can be made that this should not be possible, especially for the sake of certainty. But that position would sacrifice deserving cases.

The law might have sought to detect an implied easement merely by asking whether its creation was probably intended by the parties, as a matter of fact. This does seem to be one of its approaches,[56] but additionally, it allows implication to be found through a number of special rules.[57] We shall explore the details of these in a moment, but in outline they will generate an easement on the basis that it is 'necessary'; that it is needed for the use of the land in a way which the parties commonly intended when making the transfer; or that it reflects a pre-existing usage of the two pieces of land in question, via the 'rule in *Wheeldon v Burrows*'[58] or section 62 of the Law of Property Act 1925.[59]

Where the facts needed to trigger one of these special rules are present, the law does not ask whether the parties probably meant to create the easement. Rather, it *imputes* the easement: that is, it finds the easement automatically, unless the parties have decided and stipulated against creating it. (In other words, the law presumes the easement's creation, leaving it to me to rebut this presumption.) When you acquire an easement under one of these rules, therefore, you do so not simply for the reason that I intend you to. Nor do these

---

[55] The word 'grant' is strictly applicable only to the valid conferment of a legal easement, using the formalities that the law requires for this. See § 13.2.8.

[56] *Re Webb's Lease* [1951] Ch 808 (CA); *Moncrieff v Jamieson* [2007] 1 WLR 2620, [52] (HL); but very few cases seem to have been decided on this basis. The Law Commission would discontinue it: *Making Land Work: Easements, Covenants and Profits à Prendre* (n 6) paras 3.37–3.41.

[57] For discussion, see A Lawson, 'Easements' in L Tee (ed), *Land Law: Issues, Debates, Policy* (Cullompton, 2002) 74–96. The Law Commission proposes abolishing all the existing implication rules, and replacing them with a single rule whereby implication should occur where, but only where, the easement in question is necessary for the future reasonable use of the dominant land: *Making Land Work: Easements, Covenants and Profits à Prendre, ibid*, paras 3.11–3.70.

[58] (1879) 12 Ch D 31 (CA).

[59] Some commentators – and the Law Commission: *Making Land Work: Easements, Covenants and Profits à Prendre* (n 6) para 3.58 – depict easements created by s 62 as expressly granted, in that the section operates by inserting words apt to create an easement into a transfer (see § 13.2.5). This, however, is a good description of implied grant: the word 'inserting' can without alteration of meaning be changed to 'implying', making the point exactly. Functionally, too, easements created by s 62 are relatives not of those created expressly, but of those created by (other) implied grant rules: the key point being that expressly granted easements are organised rights, while those created by s 62 and (other) implied grant rules are disorganised. So when the Land Registration Act 2002 s 27(2)(d) rules that the express grant of an easement must be completed by registration, but naturally does not apply this rule to easements created by implied grant, it goes on (s 27(7)) to include easements created by s 62 with the latter. It follows too that, like (other) impliedly granted easements, those created by s 62 can operate as overriding interests under Sch 3 para 3: see § 13.3.

rules connect to any corrective issue between us.[60] In fact, they seem to reflect a desire in legal policy, for utilitarian reasons, to achieve the most effective use of the resource that is land, by actively promoting the kind of cross-exploitation identified in § 13.1.6 as easements' raison d'être.[61]

Since implied easements depend on utility in this way, should they not be imposed wherever utility so indicates, rather than by imputation into my transfer of part of my land to you? The usefulness of cross-exploitation between two pieces of land could be just as great when their respective owners have had no dealings as when they have. In fact, easements do sometimes arise outside a transaction in this way, under statutory schemes in the nature of compulsory purchase.[62] It remains the case, however, that imputation into a transfer is privileged as a mode of creation on grounds of utility, if only because it involves no question of compensation. This is probably defensible[63] on the basis that in such cases, utility does not operate alone. There is at least a degree of consent, in the sense that if I wish to prevent an easement from being imputed into the transfer, I can always have the terms of the transfer so stipulate. This creates a close similarity between implied grant and prescription, which likewise operates on the basis of a combination of utility and low-grade consent.[64]

The approach to finding that an easement has been impliedly *granted* is somewhat different from that to finding that one has been impliedly *reserved*. We shall look at the former first, then, in § 13.2.6, consider the differences.

13.2.2 Necessity and Common Intention

The first two implication rules look at the situation that has come about as a result of my transferring part of my land to you, deduce from it that you should have an easement against me, and 'discover' the conferral of that easement as an implied term of the transfer.

---

[60] Where, however, there is such an issue, it may yield an easement under the doctrine of proprietary estoppel (Ch 8). *Crabb v Arun District Council* [1976] Ch 179 (CA) may be an example of this.

[61] *Moncrieff v Jamieson* [2007] 1 WLR 2620, [113] (HL) may take insufficient account of what the special rules owe to utilitarian considerations when they are identified with the general principle 'that the law will imply a term into a contract, where, in the light of the terms of the contract and the facts known to the parties at the time of the contract, such a term would have been regarded as reasonably necessary or obvious to the parties' (see too *ibid* [130]).

[62] On this and analogous phenomena, see further S Grattan, 'Proprietarian Conceptions of Statutory Access Rights' in E Cooke (ed), *Modern Studies in Property Law, Volume 2* (Oxford, 2003) ch 18.

[63] Subject usually to questions of horizontal effect (§ 2.2), defence is required not only in principle, but also under the ECHR First Protocol Art 1, since in granting you the easement, the law interferes with my possessions (though *quaere* which type of 'interference' is involved: see § 2.3.4). This can be defended if the grant is a proportionate means of implementing a proper public interest. Given what has been said about utility, and the (albeit attenuated) ingredient of consent, a proper public interest may at least be present. Though this is more questionable as regards Law of Property Act 1925 s 62, where only a lesser degree of utility is needed: see n 105.

[64] See §§ 7.3, 13.2.7.

The first rule operates where the piece of land I have transferred to you is landlocked, and – unless excluded by contrary intention[65] – finds an easement over my retained land so as to give you access to it. So an easement will not be found on this basis if there is a footpath, or even access by water, to your land.[66] Easements arising in this way are called 'easements of necessity'.

The second rule operates where we made the transfer with a common intention that you should use the transferred land for a particular purpose, and that purpose is feasible only if you have an easement over the land I retain. That easement will be found.[67] (You are *not* required to produce direct evidence that we commonly intended the easement itself: that is what the law infers from the fact of our commonly intending the *purpose*.) Say I own a building, and lease you the basement to use as a restaurant, retaining the higher floors. We never considered the issue, but it turns out that you cannot have a restaurant there without a ventilation duct, and that this will have to run up the outside wall of the higher floors. It will be inferred that the transfer (lease) contains an implied term giving you the easement you need in order to do so,[68] unless it stipulates to the contrary.[69]

The two rules operate only cautiously. Easements of necessity are used only so as to give you the bare minimum of access to your land,[70] and easements arise under the common intention rule only where they are essential to the sole use(s) to which we contemplated you would put the land.[71] Given this, the rules will generate an easement only where there is a high degree of utility. When this high degree of utility is combined with the element of consent that the rules also demand (in their limitation to a transfer from me to you, as part of which I can exclude the easement), the rules' effect in generating the easement seems justified.

13.2.3 Implication on the Basis of Prior Usage

The third and fourth rules by which implied easements are found are the rule in *Wheeldon v Burrows*,[72] and that arising under section 62 of the Law of Property Act 1925.

[65] *Nickerson v Barraclough* [1980] Ch 325 (CA).
[66] *MRA Engineering Ltd v Trimster Co Ltd* (1988) 56 P & CR 1 (CA); *Manjang v Drammeh* (1991) 61 P & CR 194 (PC). The courts seem not yet to have considered whether the possibility of access by air (eg by helicopter) likewise rules out an easement of necessity. In *Sweet v Sommer* [2004] 4 All ER 288n (Ch D), affirmed [2005] 2 All ER 64 (CA), however, a piece of land was regarded as landlocked even though its owner could have accessed it from his adjoining land by demolishing a building forming the boundary between the two.
[67] *Pwllbach Colliery Co Ltd v Woodman* [1915] AC 634 (HL).
[68] *Wong v Beaumont Property Trust Ltd* [1965] 1 QB 173 (CA). The court confuses matters by speaking, incorrectly, in terms of an 'easement of necessity'.
[69] *Pwllbach Colliery Co Ltd v Woodman* [1915] AC 634 (HL).
[70] *Corporation of London v Riggs* (1880) 13 Ch D 798 (Ch D).
[71] *Pwllbach Colliery Co Ltd v Woodman* [1915] AC 634 (HL).
[72] (1879) 12 Ch D 31 (CA).

Like the first and second rules, these two rules operate to discover an easement implied in my transfer of part of my land to you. But the first and second rules focus on the present and future, generating an easement where this seems right in the situation that the transfer has created. The third and fourth rules, by contrast, primarily look back to the situation before the transfer. They see whether, at that time, the land was used in a way suggestive of an easement; and treat this as a basis on which to say that the transfer impliedly gives an easement allowing the use to continue after it.

Under these two rules, the new easement will have the shape of the prior usage. It follows that the prior usage must itself have been easement-shaped. This means, in particular, that the prior situation involved the use of one piece of land (that which will now become the dominant land) *identifiably for the benefit of another* (which will now become the servient land). Reproducing this situation, the new easement will – as it must – 'accommodate' the dominant land.

The two rules thus both demand a prior situation of this kind. Beyond this, however, they diverge. The rule in *Wheeldon v Burrows*[73] deals with the case where, before the transfer which is alleged to contain the implied easement, I both owned and occupied the two pieces of land in question (ie there was 'unity of occupation'); while that in section 62 deals with the case where I owned both but occupied only one (ie there was 'diversity of occupation').[74] If in other respects the two rules were the same, this would be merely a technical dividing up of the territory, and we could nonetheless discuss them together. But as we shall see, there are other differences too, so we shall need to consider them individually, and compare their approaches.

13.2.4 *Wheeldon v Burrows*

By the rule in *Wheeldon v Burrows*,[75] where I own two pieces of land, and transfer one to you, an easement over the piece I retain is implied into the transfer of the other piece to you where:

—— before the transfer, there was a quasi-easement over the retained piece in favour of the transferred piece, in the shape of the easement that you now argue should be implied;

---

[73] *ibid.*

[74] *Kent v Kavanagh* [2006] 2 All ER 645, [45]–[46] (CA).

[75] (1879) 12 Ch D 31, 49 (CA): '[O]n the grant by the owner of a tenement of part of that tenement as it is then used and enjoyed, there will pass to the grantee all those continuous and apparent easements (by which, of course, I mean quasi-easements), or, in other words, all those easements which are necessary to the reasonable enjoyment of the property granted, and which have been and are at the time of the grant used by the owners of the entirety for the benefit of the part granted.' For the provenance of this rule, see A Simpson, 'The Rule in *Wheeldon v Burrows* and the Code Civile' (1967) 83 *LQR* 240.

—— at the time of the transfer, this quasi-easement was 'continuous and apparent'; and[76]

—— it is 'necessary for the reasonable enjoyment' of the transferred piece that you now have an easement in the shape of this earlier quasi-easement.

The first of these requirements is that, before the transfer, there was a 'quasi-easement' corresponding to the easement that you now claim. A 'quasi-easement' is an easement-shaped practice that I have, as both owner and occupant of two pieces of land.[77]

Say I own and occupy a farm, which includes fields *A* and *B*. I keep cows in field *A*. When I need to bring cows in or out by road, I take them through field *B*. (Field *A* has road access of its own, but of a more dangerous nature.) This use of field *B* is easement-shaped. In particular, it benefits me as owner of field *A*. At this stage, as I own and occupy both fields, it cannot be an actual easement. But, being thus easement-shaped, it counts as a 'quasi-easement'. (Field *A* is called the 'quasi-dominant land', and field *B* is the 'quasi-servient land'.) Now I transfer field *A* to you, retaining field *B*. If my usage of field *B* before the transfer was also 'continuous and apparent', and if the ability to continue with it is 'necessary for the reasonable enjoyment' of field *A* after its transfer to you, this rule will imply into that transfer an easement entitling you too to cross my retained field *B* with your cows.

By contrast, say that before the transfer I move my cows using the route through field *B* purely because I enjoy the exercise. Or that I operate fields *A* and *B* as a single unit, leaving the gate between them open and letting my cows roam across both fields as they will. In these instances, in different ways, my use of field *B* does not benefit me in my capacity as owner of field *A*. It therefore does not count as a quasi-easement, and the rule will not give you an easement to do likewise when I transfer field *A* to you.

The rule's second requirement, that the quasi-easement must have been 'continuous and apparent', is undemanding. It seems to mean merely 'always discoverable', often – though not necessarily – from permanent clues on the land rather than from the quasi-easement's actual exercise. The use of a made-up road will therefore count, even if the use itself is intermittent,[78] as

---

[76] This 'and' is controversial, however, as explained below.

[77] *Kent v Kavanagh* [2006] 2 All ER 645, [45], [73] (CA). The term 'quasi-easement' has in the past also been used to describe an easement-shaped usage of one piece of land for the benefit of another, where I own both but occupy only one (renting the other to a tenant): see eg *Hansford v Jago* [1921] 1 Ch 322 (Ch D). According to the account given here, however, that situation is addressed not by the rule in *Wheeldon v Burrows* but by the Law of Property Act 1925 s 62 (§ 13.2.5). If the account given here is wrong, so that a quasi-easement can exist also where there is diversity of occupation, it should make little difference: *Wheeldon v Burrows* will not normally be relied on in that situation, for s 62 applies to it, and involves less demanding requirements than *Wheeldon v Burrows*.

[78] *Borman v Griffith* [1930] 1 Ch 493 (Ch D).

will the use of drains beneath the quasi-servient land.[79] So my use of field *B* to take my cows to and from the road will count as 'continuous and apparent' if the cows' passage has worn a discernible track,[80] or perhaps even on the strength of the presence of gates at either end of the field. Taken thus, the requirement helps to ensure that an easement can arise under this rule only from a rather clearly identifiable quasi-easement. That is useful: without it, so that any quasi-easement existing before the transfer could yield an easement after it, arguments might proliferate over what quasi-easements there had been.

The rule's third requirement is that the easement in question be necessary for the reasonable enjoyment of the land transferred – field *A* in our example. This requirement is more exigent than the demand that, to be an easement at all, the right must 'accommodate' the land, ie benefit the transferee in his capacity as the land's owner. So in one case,[81] the court held that it was *not* necessary for the reasonable enjoyment of a business annexe at the back of a house for the transferees of the annexe to have access to it through the house, as well as by a path down the side of the house. On the other hand, a right can be 'necessary' for the land's 'reasonable enjoyment' without being 'necessary' in the way that an easement of necessity is: so the existence of alternative means of access will not always preclude an easement arising under the present rule.[82] This requirement attaches significance to the situation that has arisen since the transfer. It thus parts company with the first two requirements, which relate to the state of affairs existing before the transfer. On their own, they would generate an easement purely so as to replicate a usage that had previously gone on between the two pieces of land in question. The third requirement means that such replication occurs only where the right in question is now *needed*.

The third requirement is welcome. The previous existence of a continuous and apparent quasi-easement alone can provide evidence of a genuine implied intention to confer the easement, though it will only rarely suffice to prove it on the balance of probabilities. But that is not how the rule in *Wheeldon v Burrows*[83] operates. Instead, as explained in § 13.2.1, it actually creates the easement, by imputing an intention to confer it. And the existence of a continuous and apparent quasi-easement alone is an inadequate basis on which

[79] *Schwann v Cotton* [1916] 2 Ch 120 (Ch D).

[80] A track made by human traffic was accepted in *Hansford v Jago* [1921] 1 Ch 322 (Ch D). Such a case would be excluded by the formulation adopted in *Ward v Kirkland* [1967] Ch 194, 225 (Ch D), that there must be 'a continuous and apparent feature *designed or appropriate for* the exercise of the easement on the servient tenement' (emphasis added). But this seems too narrow.

[81] *Goldberg v Edwards* [1950] Ch 247 (CA).

[82] An easement was found in *Borman v Griffith* [1930] 1 Ch 493 (Ch D), where the alternative access was inadequate for heavy traffic, including that associated with the transferee's business as a poultry farmer. Compare *Wheeler v JJ Saunders Ltd* [1996] Ch 19 (CA), where an easement was not found, because the route in question was only 10 cm wider than the alternative access available.

[83] (1879) 12 Ch D 31 (CA).

to do this. The imputation is acceptable only when the additional utilitarian argument for it is sufficiently powerful. The fact that I visibly did something in the past may contribute to the making of such an argument, by giving a prima facie indication that the alleged easement would be useful. But to complete the argument, the easement must be positively needed: as the law has it, 'necessary for the reasonable enjoyment' of the land transferred. Perhaps for this reason, although the relevant case-law is in disarray,[84] the majority of commentators agree that this third requirement is essential.

13.2.5 Law of Property Act 1925 Section 62

We now turn to the final rule whereby the law discovers the implication of an easement into a transfer. This rule is rooted in section 62 of the Law of Property Act 1925.[85]

Like the rule in *Wheeldon v Burrows*,[86] this rule applies where I used to own an area of land, and have now transferred part of it to you, retaining the other part myself: and operates to imply into that transfer, as an easement in your favour over my retained land, a right modelled on the way in which the two pieces of land were used before the transfer. But there are two ways in which section 62 differs from *Wheeldon v Burrows*.[87]

First, as noted in § 13.2.4, *Wheeldon v Burrows*[88] applies only where there was unity of occupation before the transfer, as in the example of fields *A* and *B*. Section 62, on the other hand, applies only where there was diversity of occupation.[89] That is to say, although I owned both the pieces of land in question,[90]

---

[84] The statement of the rule in *Wheeldon v Burrows*, *ibid*, itself (see n 75 above) treats the demands that the quasi-easement be continuous and apparent, and that the alleged easement be necessary for the reasonable enjoyment of your land, as synonymous. That is an impossible position, but it was repeated in *Wheeler v JJ Saunders Ltd* [1996] Ch 19, 31 (CA). *Ward v Kirkland* [1967] Ch 194 (Ch D) is sometimes read as asserting that the third requirement is part of the rule, but it in fact seems to take that for granted. Its insistence is rather on the second requirement, which, given the original statement, could hardly have been in doubt. *Kent v Kavanagh* [2006] 2 All ER 645, [43] (CA) firmly demands the third requirement, but does so without discussion.

[85] s 62(1) reads: 'A conveyance of land shall be deemed to include and shall by virtue of this Act operate to convey, with the land, all buildings, erections, fixtures, commons, hedges, ditches, fences, ways, waters, watercourses, liberties, privileges, easements, rights, and advantages whatsoever, appertaining or reputed to appertain to the land, or any part thereof, or, at the time of the conveyance, demised, occupied, or enjoyed with, or reputed or known as part and parcel of or appurtenant to the land or any part thereof.'

[86] (1879) 12 Ch D 31 (CA).

[87] *ibid*.

[88] *ibid*.

[89] *Long v Gowlett* [1923] 2 Ch 177 (Ch D); *Sovmots Investments Ltd v Secretary of State for the Environment* [1979] AC 144 (HL). The rule was overlooked in *P & S Platt Ltd v Crouch* [2004] 1 P & CR 18, [42], [59] (CA), suggesting that s 62 applies in both situations, but reaffirmed in *Kent v Kavanagh* [2006] 2 All ER 645, [46], [73] (CA).

[90] The rule is sometimes expressed as a requirement for diversity of occupation *or ownership*. That is incorrect. Unless I owned both pieces of land at the moment of the transfer, I could not

I occupied only the piece that I now retain: the piece that I have transferred to you was occupied by someone else (possibly you, as my tenant). The required prior use accordingly takes the form of a licence which I allowed that person over my retained land.[91] This difference merely means that the two rules divide the relevant territory between them. Second, however, *Wheeldon v Burrows*[92] demands additionally that the prior use be 'continuous and apparent' and that the easement now claimed be 'necessary for the reasonable enjoyment' of the transferred land. Section 62 does not make these demands, and indeed has no further requirements at all. This difference is more striking, and will be discussed further once we have a firmer idea of how section 62 operates.

So, say I own two adjoining houses, *C* and *D*. I rent *C* to a tenant – let us say you, but it might be someone else – while continuing to occupy *D* myself. *C* is heated by a wood-burning stove. Since *C* has no shed, however, I allow you (give you a licence) to keep your wood in a shed attached to *D*. I then transfer[93] *C* to you. By virtue of section 62, and regardless of whether your previous use of the shed was 'continuous and apparent' and whether it is nec-essary for your future enjoyment of *C* for this use to continue, the law regards the transfer as conferring on you an easement to that effect.[94]

Section 62 produces this effect in the following way.[95] By section 62, 'all ... rights ... appertaining ... to the land' are included in the transfer of the land, unless a contrary intention appears.[96] Your licence to use the shed attached to *D* was a 'right appertaining to' *C*, ie belonging to you in your capacity as the tenant of *C*. Applying section 62, it is therefore included in, and thus reiter-ated by, the transfer of *C* to you. No problem so far, but also no mention of an easement. The crucial step comes next. The supposition is that an ease-ment-shaped licence is an easement *manqué*, in the sense of an easement in substance, lacking only the formality of a deed that (§ 13.2.8) is needed for its valid creation as such. Then, the reasoning continues, the transfer of *C* is (necessarily) made by deed (§ 5.4.1); when section 62 reiterates the licence, it

---

simultaneously transfer the one to you and grant you an easement over the other. The reference to ownership must refer only to the possibility that the diversity of occupation arose through your having (not strictly ownership but) a lease from me.

[91] For licences, see Ch 17.

[92] (1879) 12 Ch D 31 (CA).

[93] Sell or give you the freehold ownership, or a new lease.

[94] The example given is similar to the leading decision on this rule, *Wright v Macadam* [1949] 2 KB 744 (CA). The other main authority is *International Tea Stores Co v Hobbs* [1903] 2 Ch 165 (Ch D) (concerning not the Law of Property Act 1925 s 62 but its similarly worded predecessor, the Conveyancing Act 1881 s 6).

[95] See further L Tee, 'Metamorphoses and Section 62 of the Law of Property Act 1925' [1998] *Conv* 115.

[96] s 62(4). The provision seems to require that the contrary intention be expressed, but *Birmingham, Dudley and District Banking Co v Ross* (1888) 38 Ch D 295 (CA) holds that it can be implied from the circumstances prevailing at the time of the transfer.

therefore implies this into that deed; so the lack of a deed is repaired, and the easement *manqué* blossoms into an easement proper.[97]

This reasoning could work. It does so if the licence was easement-shaped *in every particular*, including that it was intended by us to be an easement (§ 13.1.5), so that the lack of a deed was truly the only reason for its not taking effect as such. Otherwise, and even if the licence had all the other characteristics of an easement, putting it in a deed should make it not an easement, but simply a licence in a deed. But in practice, the courts seem not to restrict section 62 in this way, to licences that are easement-shaped *in every particular*. They apply it to licences which, while having some of an easement's characteristics, fall short of easements by more than just the lack of a deed. They may not be intended to be easements, or even not be easement-shaped in some other way.

Unsurprisingly, there is no explicit dissension from the proposition that, to be turned into an easement by section 62, the licence must be easement-shaped. But there is certainly a degree of carelessness over ensuring this to be the case. So, for example, to become an easement, the right over my land given by the previous licence must not be too extensive (§ 13.1.4). But the leading case on section 62[98] fails even to consider the issue, despite having facts which certainly made it relevant. Likewise, to be easement-shaped, the licence must benefit the prior occupant of the dominant land in his capacity as owner of that land, rather than in his personal capacity.[99] So, if I let you use the shed attached to *D*, not to store wood for your stove but to play your drum kit, an easement should not arise. But the cases have apparently treated section 62 as operating where, although the usage might by its nature have been for the benefit of the future dominant land, it was in fact enjoyed in a personal capacity: as where, say, I allow you to use my shed to keep your wood, but only because I want to do you a favour as an individual.[100] Again, a licence is not easement-shaped unless it is intended to be irrevocable.[101] So if

---

[97] *Wright v Macadam* [1949] 2 KB 744, 751 (CA). There is a similarity with the reasoning in *Wood v Leadbitter* (1845) 13 M & W 838 (Ex): see § 17.3.2. In this decision, the court held that a licence could be terminated ahead of its promised duration. It seemed to ascribe this conclusion to the fact that the licence was not a legal property right, such as an easement or lease, and proved this by pointing out that it had not been granted by deed. The implication seems to be that, if it had been granted by deed, it would have been such a property right, and could not be terminated.

[98] *Wright v Macadam, ibid.* The facts involved the use of a shed, on similar lines to those of the example used in this section.

[99] § 13.1.3. There is another reason why s 62 should not turn such a usage into an easement. The section implies into the conveyance only rights that 'appertain to' the land being conveyed. A usage that benefits only in a personal capacity does not 'appertain' to the land, and so should not be implied into the conveyance *even to be reiterated as a licence*.

[100] The issue might have been relevant, but was ignored, in *International Tea Stores Co v Hobbs* [1903] 2 Ch 165 (Ch D); *Wright v Macadam* [1949] 2 KB 744 (CA); *Green v Ashco Horticulturist Ltd* [1966] 1 WLR 889 (Ch D).

[101] The important point is the intention. Unless given by contract, a licence is necessarily revocable (§ 17.2.2), but this would not prevent its being easement-shaped if it was nonetheless intended to be irrevocable.

I give you permission to use my shed on an open-ended but not necessarily permanent basis, this ought not to be enough. But the courts have expressly held section 62 to apply on such facts.[102] The breadth that this approach gives section 62 has been criticised as unfair,[103] but the more fundamental objection is that it is unprincipled.

But even if section 62 were applied properly, ie to fully easement-shaped licences alone, it would be problematic. As we saw in § 13.2.1, the implied grant rules in fact operate to *impute* easements, rather than on the basis of a genuine implicit intention, and section 62 is certainly no exception. To justify the imputation requires a utilitarian argument for the easement in question, bolstered by the degree of consent discernible in my failure to stipulate against it. Even given the prior usage, the rule in *Wheeldon v Burrows*[104] demands that the claimed easement be 'necessary for the reasonable enjoyment' of the transferred land, but section 62 has no such requirement, nor anything equivalent. Without such a requirement, the section demands only a lesser degree of utility in order to operate. That degree is surely insufficient, even given the element of consent.[105]

There is less difficulty, however, about the fact that section 62 has no requirement that the prior usage be 'continuous and apparent', ie always discoverable, in the way that *Wheeldon v Burrows*[106] does. Such a requirement is in principle useful, as it enables the parties to the transfer to identify the rights that the transfer will create. But as we have seen, for section 62 to apply, the two pieces of land in question must previously have been occupied by different people, with a licence for one over the other. Under these circumstances, the right is likely to be discoverable in its very nature.

13.2.6 Implied Reservation

So far, the discussion has been about the four rules operating to impliedly *grant* you an easement, ie to give you an easement over the land that I retain, for your benefit as owner (or tenant) of the land that I have transferred to you. The question addressed in the present section is: do the same rules

---

[102] *International Tea Stores Co v Hobbs* [1903] 2 Ch 165, 172 (Ch D); *Wright v Macadam* [1949] 2 KB 744, 751–2 (CA); *Green v Ashco Horticulturist Ltd* [1966] 1 WLR 889, 896 (Ch D). But a distinction is drawn, so that s 62 does not apply, if I make my permission explicitly temporary (*Wright v Macadam* at 751), or conditional on its exercise not inconveniencing me (*Green v Ashco Horticulturist Ltd* at 897). It is correct to regard s 62 as inapplicable in the latter cases, as such licences are clearly not easement-shaped. But the distinction between them and the open-ended case, to which s 62 does apply, is unsustainable.

[103] *Wright v Macadam, ibid* 755; *Green v Ashco Horticulturist Ltd, ibid.*

[104] (1879) 12 Ch D 31 (CA): § 13.2.4.

[105] This form of implied grant is therefore more vulnerable than the others to challenge under ECHR First Protocol Art 1, since the interference it apparently involves with my possessions is aimed at a weaker public interest, and so less likely to be proportionate. See n 63 above.

[106] (1879) 12 Ch D 31 (CA): § 13.2.4.

operate also to *reserve* an easement – to create an easement over the land that I have transferred to you, for my benefit as owner of my retained land?

The rule arising from section 62 of the Law of Property Act 1925 cannot operate to reserve an easement. This follows from the section's wording: it applies where I transfer some land to you, to give you the rights – not the obligations – belonging to that land.

The other three rules involve no statutory text. As we have seen, they depend principally on the existence of a utilitarian case for an easement. As a matter of principle, such a case can arise as much for reserving as for granting an easement. So if my transfer to you leaves me with a piece of land that is inaccessible, there is an argument for creating a right of way for me across your piece. Likewise if I lease you the upper part of my building, keeping the basement for myself so as to open a restaurant, and discover that I need to fix a ventilation duct to your part; or if I used to take my cows to and from field *A* over field *B*, and after transferring field *B* to you it is necessary for the reasonable enjoyment of field *A* that I should continue to be able to do so.

As we have seen, however, the law does not treat the argument from utility as sufficient to generate easements in these ways. Instead, it additionally requires a degree of consent. In the case of implied grant, this degree of consent is found in my transferring the dominant land to you without ruling out the easement, as I could have done. And there is a difference between grant and reservation in this respect. The person most in control of the transfer is me, the transferor. From my previous ownership of the two pieces of land, I will also have the greater sense of what easements might be useful between them. Your lack of previous acquaintance with the two pieces of land leaves you in the converse position. So your failure to rule the easement out does not so clearly bespeak a degree of consent to it on your part. The argument for implied reservation is thus weaker than that for implied grant.

According to the cases, the law will reserve as well as grant an easement where it is necessary[107] and where the parties commonly intended that the reserved land be used for a particular purpose and the easement is needed for this to occur;[108] but only grant, not reservation, is possible under the rule in *Wheeldon v Burrows*.[109] This division between the rules is understandable. The utilitarian case for an easement is stronger under the first two rules, with their requirement of necessity, than under *Wheeldon v Burrows*,[110] which accepts the lower standard of 'necessary for the reasonable enjoyment' of the land, together with a visible prior usage. It is right that the difficulty in pointing to

---

[107] *Corporation of London v Riggs* (1880) 13 Ch D 798 (Ch D).
[108] *Pwllbach Colliery Co Ltd v Woodman* [1915] AC 634, 646 (HL).
[109] (1879) 12 Ch D 31, 49 (CA); *Kent v Kavanagh* [2006] 2 All ER 645, [47] (CA).
[110] (1879) 12 Ch D 31 (CA).

consent on the transferee's part in a reservation case should fatally undermine the generation of an easement under the latter rule.[111]

13.2.7 Prescription

Prescription is a means of acquiring an easement on the basis, broadly speaking, that for 20 years you have acted as though you already had it. For example, if you have gone across my land to and from your own for 20 years, you will generally acquire an easement against me entitling you to continue to do so.

The law about prescription was explained in § 7.3. For present purposes, recall that this method of acquisition is founded on a combination of utility and consent. However, it runs into the same criticism as is to be made of the imputation of easements under section 62 of the Law of Property Act 1925 (§ 13.2.5). Unlike the other grounds for imputing easements, section 62 does not require the easement to be in any way necessary, and nor does prescription. Instead, these grounds look to the prior usage alone. Their basis in utility is thus relatively weak. Even with the help of my consent, it may not be enough to warrant depriving me of my rights by giving you an easement.[112]

13.2.8 Formalities

The express grant or reservation of an easement has to be made using the correct formalities. Formalities in general are discussed in Chapters 5 and 6. Briefly, to create a legal easement (ie a right recognised by the common law as an easement[113]), the grant or reservation has to be effected using a deed,[114] and (since it counts as a registrable disposition) has to be registered.[115] To expressly create an equitable easement (ie a right recognised by equity, though

---

[111] The Law Commission has recommended that, in future, implied reservation should be dealt with exactly like implied grant (ie that in both cases, implication should occur where, but only where, the easement in question is necessary for the future reasonable use of the dominant land): *Making Land Work: Easements, Covenants and Profits à Prendre* (n 6) para 3.29.

[112] The Law Commission has nonetheless not recommended the abolition of prescription (only its rationalisation): ibid, paras 3.71–3.187; see § 7.3. The Commission's account of its reasoning on the matter (paras 3.74–3.81) is not analytically profound, however.

[113] Another condition must be satisfied before an easement can be recognised by the common law: the easement must be equivalent in duration to either a freehold or a lease: ie be either indefinite or for a 'term', as that concept is understood in the context of leases (see § 11.4.2). Most easements meet this requirement (an easement for life would not, for example, but is uncommon), so in practice the distinction between legal and equitable easements usually depends on the formality issue.

[114] Law of Property Act 1925 s 52(1).

[115] Land Registration Act 2002 s 27(2)(d).

not the common law, as an easement), writing must be used:[116] there is no requirement of registration.[117]

An implied grant or reservation, though dependent on utilitarian considerations, is regarded as a deemed express grant or reservation, and so attracts the same formality requirements. At first sight, it fails to meet them. But the implication is into the transfer,[118] and the easement is seen as having been made with the formality that was used for the transfer. In particular, the transfer will usually be made by deed, so an easement implied into it will be regarded as made by deed too.[119] It is unclear whether the registration of the transfer[120] would likewise count as the registration of an easement implied into it. But the issue is avoided thanks to a rule – reflecting the utilitarian flavour of implied easements – lifting the requirement of registration from the creation of implied easements.[121]

The prescription rules generate easements by imagining (fictitiously, of course) that these easements were originally conferred by an express grant, which can no longer be discovered. That grant would need to have been made using the appropriate formalities. If there were any reason why the imagined grant *could not* have validly occurred, prescription under these rules will fail.[122] But although it is sometimes possible to point to other reasons why there could not have been a proper grant, it is hard to see any reason why the supposed grantor could not have used the relevant formalities. So the issue is unlikely to pose a problem in practice. That is as it should be, for prescription is, as we have seen, based not on intention, but on utility, subject to exclusion: it is therefore a disorganised way of generating the easement: so a formality requirement is counter-indicated, as explained in § 7.1.2.

The other main method of acquiring an easement is proprietary estoppel (described in Chapter 8). The formality rules are simply inapplicable to this method: it does not even pretend to rest purely on an intentional conferral, so, again, any requirement of formality would be misplaced.

---

[116] Law of Property Act 1925 s 53(1)(a); or, if the equitable easement is the result of conversion (§ 6.2), Law of Property (Miscellaneous Provisions) Act 1989 s 2.

[117] But as equitable easements are not normally overriding interests (§ 13.3), they will have to be registered if they are to bind disponees.

[118] Implication under the Law of Property Act 1925 s 62 is specifically into a 'conveyance', which is the transfer of a legal estate. This rule cannot therefore imply an easement into an estate contract: *Borman v Griffith* [1930] 1 Ch D 493 (Ch D).

[119] The trick seems not to work, however, where an easement is implied in an oral lease for three years or less. Such a lease is itself valid: Law of Property Act 1925 s 54(2). But an easement implied into it has not been granted by deed.

[120] Under the Land Registration Act 2002 s 27. By s 27(2)(b), a lease need not be registered if it is for seven years or less, so an easement implied in such a lease would be in difficulties if it were not for the rule explained next.

[121] Land Registration Act 2002 s 27(2)(d).

[122] *Dalton v Angus & Co* (1881) 6 App Cas 740 (HL); *Tehidy Minerals Ltd v Norman* [1971] 2 QB 528, 552 (CA); *Oakley v Boston* [1976] QB 270 (CA).

13.3 Easements' Effectiveness against Disponees

Say you have acquired an easement over my land. Will your easement bind a disponee of the land from me? Easements are rights in rem, so it is certainly capable of doing so. Whether it actually does, in the case of registered land, depends on the rules in the Land Registration Act 2002. It can bind either through registration or as an overriding interest. The details are, however, complex.

The rules distinguish between legal and equitable easements. An easement will be legal – ie recognised by the common law – if it is expressly or impliedly granted or reserved by deed, or created by prescription.[123] Otherwise it will be equitable. Equitable easements thus arise where the easement is expressly or impliedly given or reserved in a transaction that is recognised by equity but not the common law, such as an estate contract (§ 6.2). Easements generated by proprietary estoppel are also equitable, as this is an equitable doctrine. Then:

——The *express* grant or reservation of a *legal* easement is a registrable disposition, so an easement created in such a way must be registered, in order to exist as a legal easement at all.[124] Being registered, it will necessarily then bind a disponee of the servient land. (If an easement would otherwise be legal but is not registered in this way, it becomes an equitable easement: for it is given by a transaction which equity recognises, but the common law does not.)

——A *legal* easement arising in any other way (ie by implied grant or reservation, or prescription) does not have to be registered in order to exist as a legal easement at all. However, it can be registered, so as to bind disponees of the servient land.[125] It can also operate as an overriding interest. But it will do so only if, at the time of the disposition, (i) the disponee knows of it; or (ii) it would have been obvious on a reasonably careful inspection of the land; or (iii) it has been exercised in the past year.[126]

——An *equitable* easement need not be registered in order to exist at all, but can be in order to bind a disponee.[127] It cannot, however, operate as an overriding interest.[128]

---

[123] The easement must also be equivalent in duration to either a freehold or a lease: see n 113.
[124] Land Registration Act 2002 s 27(2)(d).
[125] *ibid* s 34.
[126] *ibid* Sch 3 para 3.
[127] *ibid* s 34.
[128] The overriding interest provision relating to easements (Sch 3 para 3) is limited to legal easements, as detailed above. An equitable easement could nevertheless count as an overriding

As explained in § 3.2, the general approach of the Land Registration Act 2002 is to require registration, except where it is 'neither reasonable to expect nor sensible to require' registration and the right is, despite not being registered, readily discoverable by a disponee.

The rules regarding legal easements broadly track this approach. Where an easement is created expressly, it will have arisen in an organised way, so it will be reasonable to expect and sensible to require its registration. Otherwise, it will have arisen in a disorganised way. It would therefore not be reasonable to expect or sensible to require its registration, so it is a candidate for overriding interest status. But the further desideratum of ready discoverability by the disponee is covered by the Act's insistence that one of the three conditions explained above be present. (Or is it? The third condition, that the easement has been exercised in the past year, does not quite secure its discoverability, and may reflect a loss of confidence in the Act's overall approach.)

The position regarding equitable easements – the rule that these cannot be overriding interests – is however ill judged. These easements too will often have arisen in a disorganised way, so that it is not reasonable to expect or sensible to require their registration. And they should be no less readily discoverable by a disponee than their legal counterparts. So their inability to operate as overriding interests cannot be ascribed to the Act's own values. Rather, they seem to have been sacrificed so that the Act can be *portrayed* as lubricating trade in land by sweeping away a number of kinds of overriding interests entirely.[129] The new position may therefore breach the ECHR First Protocol Article 1, as an unjustified interference with a possession.

The very distinction between legal and equitable easements is an unnecessary complication, moreover. It arises principally from the fact that the two systems historically applied different formality rules. The resulting situation is criticised in § 5.4.2.

interest under the provision relating to rights in rem generally (Sch 3 para 2), but only if the person entitled to the easement – the dominant owner – is in actual and apparent occupation of the servient land, which (in the nature of easements) is unlikely. *cf Chaudhary v Yavuz* [2011] EWCA Civ 1314, [28]–[35] (CA).

[129] Under the 2002 Act's predecessor, the Land Registration Act 1925, equitable easements (as well legal easements) could operate as overriding interests: *Celsteel Ltd v Alton House Holdings* [1985] 1 WLR 204 (Ch D) (though the relevant statutory wording itself was garbled).

Restrictive Covenants

The next kind of right in rem over land we shall consider is that known as a 'restrictive covenant'.

14.1 The Idea of a Restrictive Covenant

Say you and I have next-door houses. The law automatically imposes certain obligations on me requiring me to respect your amenity as my neighbour. It will be a tort of nuisance, for example, if I inflict an excessive amount of noise or smoke on you. On top of these automatic obligations, we can create additional ones as we wish. So we can oblige me not to use my house for business purposes (which might lead to annoyance for you), or not to erect further buildings on its garden (which might interrupt your view), or to keep my hedge trimmed to a certain height (again, so as to preserve your view).

We can create such additional obligations as contractual duties. In this case they will bind only me, as contractual obligations are only in personam; the benefit could in theory be personal to you too, but in practice will usually be extended to others living in your house (with you or after you) under the Contracts (Rights of Third Parties) Act 1999, or be capable of assignment. Alternatively, we can create such obligations as rights in rem. In this case, they will bind not only me, but also (so long as the relevant rules in the Land Registration Act 2002 are satisfied) disponees of my land from me; and the benefit of them will in principle belong first to you, but then to your successors in your house. More than one type of right in rem can be used for such purposes, but the principal type is the 'restrictive covenant'.

Restrictive covenants were developed by the Court of Chancery, and so are equitable rights. That is, the common law continues to assert that there are no such rights in rem, but they obtain because equity says the contrary, and equity takes precedence over the common law.[1] As rights in rem go, they are also relatively young. They emerged only in the 1840s,[2] and even then only with the benefit of hindsight: early accounts tended to say that disponees were bound not by the covenant's own power, but because they took the land with notice:[3] assertions that the covenant itself has in rem status are made confidently only from 1882.[4]

Perhaps for these reasons, treatments of the subject often present the relevant common law rules first, then go on to explain the difference that restrictive covenants make. This approach is confusing, however, and gives an unrealistic impression of the law (just as if one talked in this way about trusts, which likewise do not form part of the common law). It is better to focus primarily on the law's main right in rem of this kind, namely the restrictive covenant.

Let us familiarise ourselves with the terminology: the person first undertaking the obligation (me, in our example) is called the 'covenantor'; the person first holding the right (you) is the 'covenantee'; my land is the 'servient' or 'burdened' land, and yours is the 'dominant' or 'benefited' land.[5]

14.2 What Counts as a Restrictive Covenant?

A restrictive covenant is an obligation that I undertake in your favour and which:

---

[1] See § 1.3.1. As equitable rights, it has been argued (see B McFarlane and R Stevens, 'The Nature of Equitable Property' (2010) 4 *Journal of Equity* 1, 13–14) that restrictive covenants should be not rights in rem, but 'persistent rights'. For discussion (and rejection) of this argument, and in any event its unimportance, see § 1.3.2.

[2] The earliest traces of the relevant rules seem to be in *Whatman v Gibson* (1838) 9 Sim 196 (Ch) and *Mann v Stephens* (1846) 15 Sim 377 (Ch), followed by the better-known *Tulk v Moxhay* (1848) 2 Ph 774 (Ch).

[3] See especially *Tulk v Moxhay* (1848) 2 Ph 774, 777–8 (Ch). The idea seemed to be that this generated a new obligation against the disponee, in the manner canvassed, though not accepted, in § 9.2.4.

[4] See *London & South Western Railway v Gomm* (1882) 20 Ch D 562, 583 (CA), followed by *Rogers v Hosegood* [1900] 2 Ch 388, 407 (CA), *Formby v Barker* [1903] 2 Ch 539 (CA) and *Re Nisbet and Potts' Contract* [1905] 1 Ch 391 (Ch D), affirmed [1906] 1 Ch 386 (CA). Earlier examples can be found, however: eg *Coles v Sims* (1854) 5 De G M & G 1, 7–8 (LJJ).

[5] Though, as explained in the context of easements (§ 13.1.3), the idea of 'benefited land' cannot be taken literally: the benefit must necessarily be to humans' use of the land.

—— 'touches and concerns' *my* (the servient) land: ie affects the use I make of my land, and is intended to bind not only me, but also disponees of my land;

—— 'touches and concerns' *your* (the dominant) land: ie is, and is intended to be, beneficial to you in your capacity as the owner of your land, rather than your personal capacity; and

—— operates in a *negative* way: ie limits the things I may do on my land, rather than requiring activity from me.

14.2.1 The First Requirement: 'Touching and Concerning' the Servient Land

The first requirement – that the obligation must 'touch and concern' my land – has two aspects.

The first is that the duties created by the obligation must affect me *as regards the use I make of my land*. For example, an undertaking requiring me to refrain from competing with your business at all does not meet this requirement; but one requiring me *not to use my land* so as to compete with your business does. You and I can of course make a contract requiring me to refrain from competition with you at all,[6] but this cannot be a right in rem, in the way that an undertaking not to use my land so as to compete with you thus can.

But even if an obligation does apply to the use of particular land in this way, it does not follow that the obligation must be in rem. The second aspect of the requirement that the obligation must 'touch and concern' is that we should additionally *intend* it to be in rem, rather than operating only in personam. But if the first aspect is present – that is, if the undertaking does in fact relate to the use of my land – the law presumes that the second is too, ie that the undertaking is intended to operate in rem, unless the contrary intention appears.[7]

14.2.2 The Second Requirement: 'Touching and Concerning' the Dominant Land

So the first requirement is that the undertaking must 'touch and concern' the servient land. The second requirement[8] is that it must also 'touch and concern' the dominant land. This requirement likewise has two aspects: the undertaking must benefit you in your capacity as owner of your (the dominant, or benefited) land, rather than in your personal capacity; and we must create it with the intention that it should do so.

---

[6] Subject to the allowability of such a contract under competition law.

[7] Law of Property Act 1925 s 79.

[8] Definitively recognised in *Formby v Barker* [1903] 2 Ch 539 (CA) and *London County Council v Allen* [1914] 3 KB 642 (CA).

Say I contract with you not to erect a religious building on my land. This undertaking touches and concerns my land. But it cannot qualify as a restrictive covenant, so as to operate in rem and bind John to whom I transfer my land, if it merely benefits you personally. Even if you live next door to my land, for example, you might want the undertaking because you yourself are a fervent atheist, and wish not to live cheek by jowl with the faithful. But it can qualify if it benefits you in your capacity as owner of your land (for example, if your aim is to preserve your house's access against the parking of churchgoers' cars, or its tranquility against the ringing of bells), and if we intend it to do so (ie if we intend it to benefit not merely you, but also your successors: those who take the land in question after you).

It will sometimes be obvious whether an undertaking touches and concerns the covenantee's land in this way; but sometimes less so.[9] But if it is clear (either from the words in which we make the covenant, or from the circumstances[10]) that we intend the covenant to benefit you as owner of your land, the law assumes that it also does so in fact, unless this seems unbelievable.[11] Equally, if an undertaking in fact benefits you as owner of your land, it is a likely inference that it is also intended to benefit you in that capacity.

A scenario in which this inference is especially easy is that known as a 'building scheme', or 'scheme of development'. Here, I sell a number of properties, and as I sell each property, I impose obligations regarding its use. The nature of the properties is such that they form an overall entity, such as a square, or terrace, or close, so that the use made of each property affects the others: the obligations regarding each property will thus benefit the others de facto.[12] The sale documents will probably say that the obligations are also *intended* to benefit the other properties, in which case this point too will be established. But even if there is no such statement, that is the natural inference, and the courts will draw it.[13]

---

[9] And careful thought will also be needed where, some time after the covenant is made, the covenantee's land is split up. The fact that it originally touched and concerned that land as a whole does not mean that it will necessarily touch and concern every one of the parts into which it has now been divided.

[10] *Renals v Cowlishaw* (1878) 9 Ch D 125 (Ch D); *Rogers v Hosegood* [1900] 2 Ch 388 (Ch D and CA). See too *Nottingham Patent Brick and Tile Co v Butler* (1885) 15 QBD 261, 268–70 (QBD) and (1886) 16 QBD 778, 784 (CA).

[11] *Marten v Flight Refuelling Ltd* [1962] Ch 115 (Ch D); *Earl of Leicester v Wells-next-the-Sea Urban District Council* [1973] Ch 110 (Ch D).

[12] The expression 'building scheme' originally referred specifically to the case where the properties are empty lots, the plan being for each purchaser to build his own house on the property he purchases. In that case, each purchaser's covenant contributes to the overall scheme by controlling the very design of the houses. But the expression has been extended to the case where the properties are sold with houses already built on them, and the covenants operate to maintain the overall entity in other respects, eg by preventing further building. The legal significance, as described in the text, is the same either way.

[13] In *Elliston v Reacher* [1908] 2 Ch 374, 385 (Ch D) inference from a building scheme was said to be possible only when the scheme has certain characteristics. Taken together, the list of these characteristics amounts to little more than a long-winded statement of the obvious ('there is a building scheme when there seems to be a building scheme'), but the details can occasionally

14.2.3 The Role of the First and Second Requirements

These first two requirements, that the covenant should touch and concern land owned by the covenantor and by the covenantee, reflect the context in which these covenants began to be made, and their legal effectiveness urged and accepted.[14] It is such covenants' usefulness in this context that provides the argument for their acceptance by the law as rights in rem.

They date from the first half of the 19th century, a time of rapid growth of English towns.[15] Many inhabitants were poor, but there was also an affluent urban middle class, which aspired to a high standard of living. The prevailing environment of slum housing, factories and so on was inimical to this: even if a middle class family's home was inwardly agreeable, stepping outside the front door could entail a quite different experience. Things could be improved, however, by creating enclaves of middle class housing, producing a more pleasant external as well as internal environment. The techniques by which this was done included the architectural (eg the terrace; and the square was an especially useful way of creating such an enclave, especially if the rear rooms of the houses, facing the squalor beyond, were made the servants' quarters), and the horticultural (eg creating a pleasant garden in the middle of the square, a larger space than each individual house could command, and a place for socialising with persons similarly circumstanced[16]).

But the trick would work only if it was possible to secure the enclave's integrity over time, ie to ensure that those inhabiting the enclave respected its standards. This was a task for the law. Restrictive covenants are best understood as the new rights in rem developed to perform it.

So, those buying houses in the enclaves were placed under obligations in this respect, requiring them not to use their premises for 'noxious trades', etc. It was essential – part of their job specification – that these obligations should operate in rem: the enclaves would not have been secured by obligations against the original inhabitants personally, ineffective against their

---

pinch: *Lund v Taylor* (1975) 31 P & CR 167 (CA); *Emile Elias & Co Ltd v Pine Groves Ltd* [1993] 1 WLR 305 (PC). To approach the matter in this formulaic way, however, is to lose sight of the essential point: we are seeking evidence that the covenant is intended to benefit you as owner of your land rather than personally, and this evidence can come from any source: see at n 10 above. The latter approach was favoured in *Baxter v Four Oaks Properties Ltd* [1965] Ch 816 (Ch D); *Re Dolphin's Conveyance* [1970] Ch 654 (Ch D); *Brunner v Greenslade* [1971] Ch 993, 1006 (Ch D); *Whitgift v Stocks* [2001] EWCA 1732, [85]–[87] (CA).

[14] *Tulk v Moxhay* (1848) 2 Ph 774 (Ch) itself involved facts of the kind about to be described, as did its precursors (*Whatman v Gibson* (1838) 9 Sim 196 (Ch); *Mann v Stephens* (1846) 15 Sim 377 (Ch)), and very many of its successors.

[15] Census data show the population of London rising from 957,000 in 1801 to 2,362,000 in 1851.

[16] It may be no coincidence that the case in which the concept of an easement was restated and applied in a rather relaxed way, *Re Ellenborough Park* [1956] Ch 131 (CA) (see especially § 13.1.3), also concerned rights over a shared garden.

successors. Hence the first requirement, that such covenants should touch and concern land owned by the covenantor.

And it was equally part of such covenants' job specification that they should touch and concern land owned by the covenantee, as demanded by the second requirement. This is because their very raison d'être was to secure the integrity of the enclave *as between its inhabitants at a given time* – specifically, between a claimant occupying one of its houses and a defendant occupying another. Their effect on these lines was described at the time as 'local law'. So it is no coincidence that the law treats the existence of a building scheme as almost conclusively probative of this requirement's elements. The idea of a building scheme captures the very project for which this kind of right in rem was created: the establishment and preservation of an agreeable enclave for the mutual benefit of its inhabitants.

So the first two requirements reflect restrictive covenants' alignment to a certain social task, the perceived importance of which justifies their acceptance into the *numerus clausus* of rights in rem.[17] But in principle, there might be other social tasks, of equal importance, to which restrictive covenants might also be applied. The first requirement, that the obligation should touch and concern servient land, would remain: regardless of context, the restrictive covenant could not exist as a right in rem without it. (It does not make sense for the undertaking to affect a disponee of my land – this being the significance of its being a right in rem – unless it relates to the use of that land, rather than to my personal activities.) But the second requirement, that it should touch and concern dominant land, is a different matter. This requirement fits restrictive covenants to the task just described. But it might disable covenants from other tasks, also meriting admission to the *numerus clausus*. If so, covenants should be applicable to such other tasks without the second requirement.

Restrictive covenants have in fact been used for other tasks, and in the course of this the requirement for dominant land has indeed been questioned. One such task has been to protect you against business competition. The idea might be to prevent me and my successors from doing business with your competitors, by imposing on us an undertaking known as a 'solus tie'. In this case, I (say, a pub landlord) agree to buy my supplies exclusively from you (a brewery company).[18] The benefit of such an agreement is evidently to you yourself, not you as owner of your land. So if the law is to count such an agreement as a restrictive covenant (so as to bind not only me, but also disponees of my pub), it needs in this context to drop the demand for dominant

---

[17] For the *numerus clausus* – the idea that a type of right cannot exist in rem unless the good involved in its doing so outweighs the harm – see § 1.2.2.

[18] Solus ties upon pubs were normally imposed in a *lease* of the pub by the brewery to the landlord. In that context, they were certainly in rem, and remain so. The development discussed in the text concerned some unusual cases in which such ties were created independently of a leasehold relationship.

land. The courts experimented with using restrictive covenants in this way,[19] before ending the experiment by affirming that demand as a universal requirement.[20]

While preventing solus ties from operating in rem, however, this affirmation did not prevent the use of restrictive covenants for all business protection purposes. Say you and I own nearby shops, you run yours as a baker's, and I agree with you not to run mine as a baker's too. Here, the demand for dominant land is met, in the shape of your shop, so my undertaking can count as a restrictive covenant.[21] But this is not a sensible state of affairs. Whereas dominant land is crucial to the project of preserving urban enclaves, and so demanded in that context, it is essentially irrelevant to business protection. So the law needs to ask itself whether the task of business protection is so valuable as to warrant in rem status for agreements undertaking it;[22] and to give effect to its answer regardless of the presence or absence of dominant land.[23, 24]

14.2.4 The Third Requirement: The Obligation Must be Negative

The remaining requirement is that the obligation must be negative, or 'restrictive' (hence the name, 'restrictive covenant').[25] So an obligation requiring me not to erect buildings on my land can qualify as in rem in the present manner,

---

[19] While solus ties were initially in personam only (*Keppell v Bailey* (1834) 2 My & K 517 (Ch)), they were later held to operate in rem (*Catt v Tourle* (1869) 4 Ch App 654 (CA in Ch); *Luker v Dennis* (1877) 7 Ch D 227 (Ch D)).

[20] *London County Council v Allen* [1914] 3 KB 642 (CA).

[21] See eg *Jay v Richardson* (1862) 30 Beav 563 (Rolls); *Stuart v Diplock* (1889) 43 Ch D 343 (Ch D and CA) (though the Court of Appeal expresses doubts); *Wilkes v Spooner* [1911] 2 KB 473 (KBD and CA); *Newton Abbott Co-operative Society Ltd v Williamson & Treadgold Ltd* [1952] Ch 286 (Ch D).

[22] This question arises, of course, only if such agreements are acceptable in themselves (ie in personam), as a matter of competition law.

[23] As explained in § 11.7.3, there is a further distinct task to which the courts have applied restrictive covenants. Where a lease contains a negative obligation against the tenant for the benefit of the landlord, this obligation binds all those deriving their interests from the tenant (assignees and sub-tenants) on a restrictive covenant basis: *Hall v Ewin* (1887) 37 Ch D 74 (CA). Nominally, this application complies with the requirement for dominant land, the landlord's freehold title to the leased property being regarded as that land. But this is unconvincing (the landlord's freehold title is quite different from the physical dominant land intrinsic to the original context of restrictive covenants), and either way, this application likewise requires its own justification. If it exists, that justification lies in considerations within the realm of leases.

[24] The Law Commission (*Easements, Covenants and Profits à Prendre: A Consultation Paper* (Consultation Paper No 186, London, 2008)) regards it as proper for parties to be able to make rights in rem of any content they like, so long as they are appurtenant to dominant land (paras 8.16–8.24, 8.64. 8.71–8.73). Although the Commission seems to deny it (para 15.14), this view would have the startling result of allowing a contractual licence, a right only in personam (§ 17.3.3), to be made as a right in rem, so long as it was for the benefit of neighbouring land. The Commission offers no argument for its view.

[25] *Haywood v Brunswick Permanent Benefit Building Society* (1881) 8 QBD 403 (CA); *London & South Western Railway Co v Gomm* (1882) 20 Ch D 562 (CA); *Austerberry v Corporation of Oldham* (1885) 29 Ch D 750 (CA); *Rhone v Stephens* [1994] 2 AC 310 (HL).

for it is negative; whereas one requiring me to cut my hedge cannot, as it is positive.

Whether an obligation is positive or negative depends on its effect (whether it requires me to do something, including spend money), not on its wording. So, a covenant 'not to let my wall fall into disrepair' is as positive as one 'to keep my wall in good repair'; while one 'to keep my field as an open space' is as negative as one 'not to build on my field'. Sometimes a covenant has both positive and negative elements, for example 'to maintain the area in front of my house as a garden', which obliges me both to refrain from using the area for any other purpose and to keep it in good shape. Then, the law treats the negative aspect as a right in rem, leaving the positive aspect in personam (as a contractual obligation) only.

14.2.5 The Role of the Third Requirement

The requirement that the obligation be negative was established in *Haywood v Brunswick Permanent Benefit Building Society*.[26] The judgments offer little by way of argument for it, but perhaps do convey a sense that to allow disponees to be affected by positive as well as negative obligations would be to burden them excessively.

That disponees would be *burdened* is self-evident: it is the whole point of a right in rem. Why the burden would necessarily be *excessive* is less clear. In economic terms, an individual disponee should have nothing to complain about, for he will be bound only if the obligation is registered (§ 14.4), making it easily discoverable by him; and the price he pays for the land should reflect the obligations encumbering it, so the greater the burden, the lower the price. The worry may be at the level of the land market in general: not so much on the basis that such burdens would make land unsellable (the price correction mechanism should prevent this), as that they would chill its subsequent enjoyment and exploitation. This concern, however, seems as relevant to negative covenants, regarding which it is evidently seen as outweighed.[27] But perhaps the focus of the concern was not economic at all, but rather a reluctance to countenance too great an erosion of the liberty – in the republican sense of freedom from domination – taken to be a key characteristic of 'ownership'. Negative covenants represent such an erosion, of course; but the suggestion would be that positive ones represent a greater erosion. This seems an intelligible perspective, but notice its class dimension. Positive covenants

---

[26] (1881) 8 QBD 403 (CA). The later decision confirming the requirement, *Rhone v Stephens* [1994] 2 AC 310 (HL), asserts that it is *doctrinally impossible* to recognise positive covenants as rights in rem, but this is a baseless view: see S Gardner, 'Two Maxims of Equity' [1995] *CLJ* 60.

[27] For a thoughtful treatment of the possible difference between negative and positive covenants in this respect (arguing that positive covenants pose considerably greater problems), see, however, P O'Connor, 'Careful What You Wish For: Positive Freehold Covenants' [2011] *Conv* 191.

were entirely familiar, and seen as fully acceptable, in leases, where they affected tenants. The argument would have to have been that freeholders could not be expected to render service in the same way, except on an in personam basis, ie with their personal consent. In other words, whereas freeholders deserve and so have (or have and so deserve – there seems to be a circularity about this) relative freedom from domination, tenants do not. Although one can recognise the picture,[28] however, it is surely an unacceptable one, certainly to modern eyes, given its implication that, apparently by nature, citizens can and should be so divided into 'haves' and 'have nots'.[29]

The alleged drawbacks to positive covenants thus seem illusory. Indeed, positive covenants may sometimes actually benefit those who are subject to them, as with the garden in the centre of the square described in § 14.2.3. The ban on positive covenants means that covenants cannot be used to require the householders around the square to contribute to its upkeep: so it is the more likely to degenerate, to the householders' detriment. Applied thus, the ban seems perverse. We saw in § 14.2.3 how negative covenants were appropriately admitted to the *numerus clausus* precisely because they were aimed at the preservation of such squares and the like. Similarly aimed positive covenants should have been admitted for exactly the same reason.[30] It is no accident, therefore, that the law has introduced alternative ways of giving in rem effect to positive obligations *calculated to secure communal facilities*. The most notable[31] of these is 'commonhold'.[32] Say a set of flats, houses or other units has communal areas, such as the entrance, stairs, lifts and roof of a block of flats – or the garden in the middle of a square of houses. The units (flats, houses etc) can be sold to their individual owners on the basis that the communal areas are vested in a 'commonhold association' (a form of company, whose members are the owners of the units), having the duty to look after them for the unit-holders. The commonhold association's work is financed by

[28] Its most celebrated icon is the hymn 'All Things Bright and Beautiful' (lyric C Alexander, 1848), with its verse 'The rich man in his castle,/ The poor man at his gate,/ He made them, high or lowly,/ And ordered their estate./ All things bright and beautiful,/ All creatures great and small,/ All things wise and wonderful:/ The Lord God made them all.'

[29] Moreover, to the extent that there are two groups in this way, the boundary between them is settled not at all by nature, but more contingently, by politics and economics. The 'right to buy' policies of the 1980s took substantial numbers of people from 'have nots', tenants, to 'haves', freeholders. One effect of the 2008 financial crash seems likely to be to move similarly substantial numbers in the opposite direction.

[30] For other reflections concerning positive covenants and the *numerus clausus*, see B McFarlane, 'The *Numerus Clausus* Principle and Covenants Relating to Land' in S Bright (ed), *Modern Studies in Property Law, Volume 6* (Oxford, 2011) ch 15.

[31] But as regards gardens in squares, see the Town Gardens Protection Act 1863 (and certain similar legislation), allowing a garden committee, elected by the square's residents, to levy a charge on the residents in order to maintain the garden.

[32] Commonhold was introduced by the Commonhold and Leasehold Reform Act 2002. This additionally provides for sets of units currently held on a leasehold basis, with their communal parts vested in the landlord, to be moved onto a commonhold basis. For discussion, see C van der Merwe and P Smith, 'Commonhold – A Critical Appraisal' in E Cooke (ed), *Modern Studies in Property Law, Volume 3* (Oxford, 2005) ch 11.

contributions from the unit-holders. The unit-holders each have an obligation to make these contributions. These obligations are inherent in their ownership of their unit: in traditional terms, they are effective in rem. Commonhold associations are however controlled by arrangements that are bureaucratic, but even then arguably fail to give the unit-holders sufficient protection.

But a commonhold arrangement makes sense only where there are communal facilities in this way. Otherwise – for example, where the owners of two semi-detached houses each covenant with the other to maintain their roof, against the damage that incoming rain could otherwise do to the other house – the need is for a facility to undertake a positive obligation, pure and simple.[33] Despite its distance from the context in and for which in rem covenants were introduced, this application seems fully worthy of admission to the *numerus clausus*.[34]

14.3 The Creation of Restrictive Covenants

14.3.1 General

Restrictive covenants normally arise from an intentional conferral.

They are often created as part of a transaction whereby I transfer a piece of my land to you, retaining another piece for myself. Sometimes it is I who undertake the obligation, restricting the use to which the retained land can in future be put, for the benefit of you and your successors as owners of the land transferred. This will enable me to charge you a higher price for the transfer, as the benefit of my covenant will make the transferred land more valuable. Alternatively, I may (in what in the context of easements is called a 'reservation') extract the obligation from you, restricting the use of the transferred land, for the benefit of me and my successors as owners of the retained land. This will mean a lower price for the transfer, as the transferred land, burdened with the obligation, will be less valuable.

---

[33] The Law Commission proposes allowing the creation of positive covenants ('land obligations') in appropriate cases: *Making Land Work: Easements, Covenants and Profits à Prendre* (Law Com No 327, London, 2011) paras 5.12–5.62. The Commission recognises the need to justify their acceptance into the *numerus clausus*: ibid paras 5.29–5.38, 5.60. The account of that justification is unimpressive, however. It consists only in the observation that people do in fact desire to create such rights. Without such desire, the *numerus clausus* would of course be unnecessary. It exists to police the gratification of the desire.

[34] It is essentially akin to the negative easement of support, which is certainly in rem.

Equally, however, the covenant could be made not in the context of a transfer, but ad hoc. For example, we are neighbours; you, seeking to secure the view from your house, ask me to enter into a covenant not to erect further buildings on my land; and I agree, usually for a price.

An undertaking generating a restrictive covenant is normally express. Presumably, it could in principle be implied, for example an implied term of a transfer of one piece of my land to you. But such a thing is rarely, if ever, encountered in practice. There is no evidence of implied covenants being found in the way that implied easements are, for predominantly utilitarian reasons (§ 13.2.1). Nor can covenants arise via anything in the nature of prescription, on a similar predominantly utilitarian basis.[35] Given restrictive covenants' usefulness, such a thing might be contemplated in principle. But it would be rare for a covenant to be *needed*, to the degree required so as to warrant its creation on such a basis. It is, however, possible to imagine a restrictive covenant arising via proprietary estoppel.

14.3.2 Conferral on a Third Party

So a restrictive covenant will normally arise from an intentional conferral. In the examples just given, I conferred a covenant on you, or vice versa, in a transaction between the two of us. But a covenant can also be conferred *in* a transaction between two people, but *on* a third person.

It is in fact very common for covenants to be created in this way. Say I build a pair of houses – call them *A* and *B* – and plan to sell each of them with a restrictive covenant in favour of the other. First I sell *A* to John, who undertakes the covenant. John's covenant is for the benefit of *B*, which I still own. So when I later sell *B* to you, you in turn acquire that benefit.[36] At the same time, you undertake your covenant, for the benefit of *A*. But I no longer own *A*: John already does, and you have no direct dealing with him. Nonetheless, he acquires the right to your covenant.

John can acquire the right to your obligation in this way because the rights and duties involved in restrictive covenants are not merely contractual.[37] As explained in § 14.3.1, and as seen in the example of you undertaking your covenant in buying house *B* from me, they are often created in contractual

---

[35] That is why the law is content to allow obligations to be created as restrictive covenants which it will not allow to arise as easements. If they could be easements, they could arise by prescription, and that is regarded as unsatisfactory. See the discussion of *Phipps v Pears* [1965] 1 QB 76 (CA) in § 13.1.4.

[36] The benefit of a restrictive covenant normally 'runs with' the benefited land: § 14.5.

[37] The Contracts (Rights of Third Parties) Act 1999 allows you to enforce a contract John makes with me but for your benefit. The Law of Property Act 1925 s 56 operates somewhat similarly. But these provisions operate only to widen the class of people (from me alone, to you too) having the right to John's *contractual* obligation. They have nothing to say about rights to obligations in rem, which are our concern.

transactions; but that does not constrain their own essential nature.[38] One aspect of this is familiar: the fact that the obligation is in rem, so that the duties can bind not only you but also your successors in *B* (contractual obligations operate only in personam). The phenomenon currently under discussion is less familiar, but it is another aspect of the same point. Despite your obligation being created in a contract between you and me, the right to that obligation belongs to the person(s) at whom it is aimed: namely John and his successors in *A*.[39]

It is a question of fact whether the covenant you make with me is meant for some third person such as John in this way, or whether it is meant merely as a contract between you and me. But it is essentially the same question as that whether, when you covenant with me in a case where I retain the benefited land myself, your obligation is meant to benefit me in my capacity as owner of my retained land, or merely in my personal capacity. As we saw in § 14.2.2, only if the former is the case does the covenant take effect as a right in rem between the two pieces of land, rather than as a mere contract between the two of us personally. Like the intention to benefit me in my capacity as owner of my retained land, the intention to benefit third persons can be shown by the terms of the documentation,[40] or from the surrounding circumstances, especially the existence of a building scheme.[41]

14.3.3 Formalities

The making of a restrictive covenant by intentional conferral attracts a formality requirement of writing,[42] which – this being an organised mode of creation – is unproblematic and indeed appropriate (§ 5.2).

Strictly speaking, the word 'covenant' denotes an undertaking given by deed: a reflection of the fact that, as explained in § 14.3.1, these obligations

---

[38] The Law Commission has a different vision, depicting restrictive covenants very much as fundamentally contractual: *Making Land Work: Easements, Covenants and Profits à Prendre* (Law Com No 327, London, 2011) paras 2.39, 2.42, 5.4–5.11. Regarding this as unsatisfactory, the Commission proceeds to propose their supersession by a new form of right in rem, analogous to easements, to be known as 'land obligations' (see paras 5.68–5.70, and Pt 6). But the bases for the vision are overstated, and the difficulties with it overlooked. Substantively, however, there is no real issue. All agree that covenants should be analogous to easements; to a large extent, they already are; the question is simply whether to deal with the few respects in which they differ by addressing these ad hoc, or (as the Commission proposes) by attaching covenants to easements' coat-tails.

[39] Other rights in rem can be created in the same way. Say John, in a contract with me, makes himself trustee of some property for you. The contract with me is irrelevant: John has thereby created an obligation in rem in your favour.

[40] *Rogers v Hosegood* [1900] 2 Ch 388 (Ch D and CA); *Baxter v Four Oaks Properties Ltd* [1965] Ch 816 (Ch D); *Re Dolphin's Conveyance* [1970] Ch 654 (Ch D).

[41] *Nottingham Patent Brick and Tile Co v Butler* (1885) 15 QBD 261, 268–70 (QBD); (1886) 16 QBD 778, 784 (CA).

[42] Law of Property Act 1925 s 53(1)(a).

are often created by the terms of a transfer, and transfers do have to be made by deed.[43] But the rule for restrictive covenants themselves requires only writing – not a deed or registration – because, as noted in § 14.1, restrictive covenants are equitable rights. In § 5.4.2, however, we criticised this differentiation between legal and equitable rights.

But intentionally made restrictive covenants would make good candidates for electronic conveyancing, ie the proposed system (see § 5.4.5) allowing the rights to which it applies to be made solely by electronic entry on the register.

14.4 Restrictive Covenants' Effectiveness against Disponees

The obligation arising under a restrictive covenant is in rem, and so capable of binding disponees of the servient land. Under the Land Registration Act 2002, it will bind if it is registered.[44] There is no provision for restrictive covenants to operate as overriding interests.[45] That is broadly as it should be: as we have seen, restrictive covenants normally arise only in an organised way, so it is sensible to expect them to be registered.

14.5 The Passing of the Benefit

If you have rights against me under a restrictive covenant, these rights can be enforced not only by you, but also by your successors on the land that the covenant benefits.[46] Unlike the parallel issue in easements (where the right passes to the successor automatically), this is a matter of some complexity.

---

[43] *ibid* s 52.

[44] Restrictive covenants can be registered under s 34.

[45] Your restrictive covenant against my land would bind my disponee as an overriding interest under Sch 3 para 2, if you were in actual and apparent occupation of my land. But that is unlikely.

[46] This account deals only with the passing of the benefit of a restrictive covenant, as part of our consideration of restrictive covenants as rights in rem. If I give you an undertaking that does not satisfy the requirements explained in § 14.2, and so counts not as such a right in rem but only as a contractual obligation (as for example a positive undertaking), the benefit of it may nonetheless enure to others besides you, especially by assignment or under the Contracts (Rights of Third Parties) Act 1999.

First we shall absorb the standard account of it, but then we shall criticise that account, seeing that its complexity is in fact unwarranted.

14.5.1 The Standard Account

According to the standard account, if I enter into a covenant in favour of you, then you transfer the land it benefits to Kate, Kate will acquire the covenant rights if one of three conditions is satisfied:

—— the original transaction between me and you *annexed* the covenant to your (dominant) land; or

—— while it was not originally annexed to your land, you *assigned* the benefit of the covenant to Kate when you transferred the land to her (and Kate assigned it to anyone to whom she in turn transferred the land, and so on down to the present owner); or

—— I entered into the covenant in your favour in the context of a *building scheme*.

Take first *annexation*. There are said to be two kinds. The first, 'express annexation', occurs if the original transaction not only creates the covenant, but additionally states – whether in express words or by necessary implication[47] – that the covenant is for the benefit not merely of you,[48] but of you in your capacity as owner of the land in question, or of you and your successors in that land.[49] Then, the right becomes fixed to your land, so when Kate acquires your land, she automatically acquires the covenant right too.[50]

The second kind of annexation, 'statutory annexation', was recognised in *Federated Homes Ltd v Mill Lodge Properties Ltd*,[51] which points – controver-

---

[47] See *Re Union of London and Smith's Bank's Conveyance, Miles v Easter* [1933] Ch 611, 628 (CA) and especially *J Sainsbury plc v Enfield London Borough Council* [1989] 1 WLR 590, 595–7 (Ch D). Even this extension is somewhat controversial: *Reid v Bickerstaff* [1909] 2 Ch 305, 329 (CA) and *Re Pinewood Estate, Farnborough* [1958] Ch 280, 286 (Ch D) seem to require express words. But according to the standard account, 'annexation' certainly cannot be found by reference purely to surrounding circumstances (*ibid*) . . . except via 'statutory annexation', described below.

[48] 'You and your assigns' is also insufficient to annex: *Renals v Cowlishaw* (1878) 9 Ch D 125 (Ch D), affirmed (1879) 11 Ch D 866 (CA). The problem is that 'assigns' is ambiguous. It could mean 'persons to whom you transfer the land', in which case it is synonymous with 'successors in the land', a phrase which is sufficient to annex. But it could mean 'persons to whom you pass the right', which contemplates a separation between right and land, and so cannot annex.

[49] As in *Rogers v Hosegood* [1900] 2 Ch 388 (Ch D and CA).

[50] If the annexation is to land *A*, and you divide *A* into parts – say *A1* and *A2* – the question arises of whether the annexation survives the division. The annexing words can supply either answer (though if the answer is yes, the covenant, which must formerly have in fact benefited the whole, must now in fact benefit the newly created parts). If the words are ambiguous (eg simply 'to *A*'), they are assumed to mean that annexation should survive the division: *Federated Homes Ltd v Mill Lodge Properties Ltd* [1980] 1 WLR 594, 606–7 (CA).

[51] [1980] 1 WLR 594 (CA).

sially[52] – to section 78 of the Law of Property Act 1925[53] as implying into the covenant the words which the express annexation rules present as necessary to effect an annexation. For the section to apply, the covenant must in fact benefit you in your capacity as owner of your land, and must be intended to do so (which can apparently be evidenced in any way). But this demand simply reproduces the second requirement for the existence of a restrictive covenant, discussed in § 14.2.2. This, and the first and third requirements, will necessarily have been met for the agreement to have qualified as a restrictive covenant in the first place. The result is that annexation occurs in this way *whenever the agreement exists as a restrictive covenant at all*. So whenever a restrictive covenant arises, its benefit is automatically annexed, and will pass likewise automatically, like that of an easement. Except, the courts have ruled,[54] such annexation does not occur unless the covenant document also identifies the dominant land;[55] or if the document shows an intention *against* annexing the rights.[56]

Assignment occurs when the rights are not annexed, but are passed with the dominant land by you to Kate. Given the wide scope of statutory annexation, it should hardly ever be relevant; it will apply only in the exceptions to statutory annexation, and in the absence also of express annexation. For assignment to be possible, the dominant land must be identifiable, but not necessarily from the terms of the covenant document: common sense inferences will suffice.[57]

A covenant right will remain enforceable on the basis of assignment only if it remains with the dominant land through the sequence of transfers of the land.[58] Say I covenant with you regarding the use of my land and so as to benefit you as owner of your land. Then I transfer my land to John. Assuming the covenant obligation is registered, you can enforce it against John, as it operates in rem. If you transfer your land to Kate, and simultaneously assign

---

[52] See especially G Newsom, 'Universal Annexation?' (1981) 97 *LQR* 32.

[53] 'A covenant relating to any land of the covenantee shall be deemed to be made with the covenantee and his successors in title and the persons deriving title under him or them . . .'.

[54] *Crest Nicholson Residential (South) Ltd v McAllister* [2004] 1 WLR 2409 (CA).

[55] This ruling, which cannot be ascribed to the wording of s 78, aims to ensure that the person under the obligation can discover who is entitled to enforce it (eg so as to facilitate negotiations towards having it removed). But in this it fails, for it apparently tolerates a covenant such as 'for the benefit of the covenantee's nearby land': a formula which tells the covenantor and his successors rather little.

[56] s 78 appears not to allow for opting out of its effect in this way. The ruling seeks to meet the problem by reading a statement that a covenant is not to be annexed as one that it is not intended to benefit the covenantee as owner of his land at all. From the latter it would indeed follow, as explained in the text, that the covenant is not annexed by s 78. Unfortunately, however, the reasoning proves too much. It should also mean that the covenant's benefit cannot pass at all, even by assignment; and indeed that the agreement cannot even qualify as a restrictive covenant in the first place.

[57] *Newton Abbott Co-operative Society Ltd v Williamson & Treadgold Ltd* [1952] Ch 286, 297 (Ch D).

[58] *Chambers v Randall* [1923] 1 Ch 149 (Ch D); *Re Union of London and Smith's Bank Ltd's Conveyance, Miles v Easter* [1933] Ch 611, 629–34 (CA).

your covenant rights with it, Kate now has the right to John's obligation. But if you transfer your land to Kate and do not simultaneously assign your covenant rights with it (even if you assign them to her later), John is no longer liable to either you or Kate.[59]

The benefit of a covenant passes under a *building scheme* when the two pieces of land in question are contained within such a scheme, as described in § 14.2.2. Then, there is no need to show annexation or assignment: the benefit passes with the dominant land quite automatically. On the standard account, this is the closest the restrictive covenant rules come to their easement counterparts.

14.5.2 A Critique

The standard account thus presents this area of law as governed by a complex set of rules. It is prone to criticism on this account. But the complexity is the result of a failure properly to grasp the topic's key ideas.

Essentially, the standard account depicts the benefit of a covenant as 'running' according to this set of rules, while its burden 'runs' under the circumstances described in §§ 14.2 and 10.4. But this is a fundamentally incorrect way of seeing the matter. The correct vision is as follows.

When I create a restrictive covenant in your favour, I attach its obligation to my land, whose use it controls. So if I transfer my land to John, the obligation will bind him, so long as it is registered (§ 14.4). All this is what we mean when we say that it is in rem.[60] We can if we wish put the point in a metaphor, using the figure of 'running'. But we should not say that the obligation runs: rather, it stays with the land, while I, John and so on run. Similarly with the covenant's benefit, or right. As explained in § 14.2.2, it is intrinsic to the make-up of a restrictive covenant that it benefits you – you have the right – in your capacity as owner of your land, rather than in your personal capacity. It follows that when you and the land part company, as when you transfer the land to Kate, it is the land with which the right should remain; Kate should acquire the right as part of the transfer. Like the obligation, then, the right does not run: it stays with the dominant land, and any running is done by you, Kate and so on. Hence the idea that restrictive covenants establish 'local law' between the pieces of land concerned: both obligations and rights are incurred simply by being there.

On this view, then, the trigger for covenant rights to pass should simply be the fact that the rights do and are intended to benefit you as owner of your land. This is in fact simply the second requirement that must be met for an agreement to take effect as a restrictive covenant at all (§ 14.2.2). It follows

---

[59] If I have not transferred to John, however, Kate can enforce against me, for this is purely a matter of contract.

[60] *Re Nisbet and Potts' Contract* [1905] 1 Ch 391 (Ch D), affirmed [1906] 1 Ch 386 (CA).

that whenever an agreement does take effect as a restrictive covenant (meaning that the second requirement, along with the first and the third, has been satisfied), the covenant right should automatically pass with the covenantee's land. Now we can grasp the essential difference between this view and the standard account. While this view treats the satisfaction of the second requirement as *sufficient* to make the right pass, the standard account treats it as only *necessary*, ruling (as explained in § 14.5.1) that the right will pass only if certain additional facts are shown.

The view for which we are arguing is in fact the same as that arrived at in *Federated Homes Ltd v Mill Lodge Properties Ltd*,[61] on the basis of section 78 of the Law of Property Act 1925. Though this is less commonly understood, it was also taken, as a matter of basic principle, in *Rogers v Hosegood*,[62] the original leading case on the issue.

The judgments in the latter hold that, so long as the agreement both does and is intended to benefit you as owner of your land, the right it generates is 'annexed to' your land (and the obligation is likewise 'annexed to' my land).[63] Notice how this word is used: not (as in the standard account) to describe a step taken in order to *make* the right belong to your land, but to describe the situation where the right *does* belong to your land. Notice too how the judgments treat this approach's key question of whether, as well as in fact benefiting you as owner of your land, the agreement is intended to do so. The required intention can, according to the judgments,[64] be discovered either from the documents creating the covenant, or from the surrounding circumstances. On this view, then, 'express annexation' is simply annexation occurring when the evidence of the necessary intention happens to consist in the content of the covenant document. The judgments[65] present the existence of a building scheme as another (rather good) type of evidence for the same crucial intention, so it would be as logical to speak of 'building scheme annexation'. There is no ruling that the evidence cannot also take the form of other surrounding circumstances.[66] In principle, then, it should be possible to infer the necessary intention simply from the covenant's being in fact beneficial to you as owner of your land. All this is – as we should expect – identical with what we found in § 14.2.2, when looking at the same question (was the agreement intended to benefit you as owner of your land?) in its role as the

---

[61] [1980] 1 WLR 594 (CA). See at n 51 above. It is also the position that would be produced by the Law Commission's alignment of future covenants – 'land obligations' – with easements (see n 38 above).

[62] [1900] 2 Ch 388, 396–7 (Ch D), 404–8 (CA).

[63] *ibid* 406–7.

[64] *ibid* 396–7 (Ch D), 408 (CA).

[65] *ibid*.

[66] The standard account treats the earlier decision in *Renals v Cowlishaw* (1878) 9 Ch D 125 (Ch D), affirmed (1879) 11 Ch D 866 (CA) as establishing such a rule. But *Rogers v Hosegood* [1900] 2 Ch 388, 407–8 (CA) treats that case merely as a decision on its facts, in which the required intention could be discovered from neither the documentary words nor the surrounding circumstances.

second requirement for an agreement to take effect as a restrictive covenant at all.

This view thus integrates what the standard account calls 'express annexation' and the 'building scheme' rule into a single understanding of the circumstances in which a restrictive covenant right will pass with the covenantee's land: namely that it will do so whenever – as will necessarily be the case, if such a covenant right has arisen at all – the right does, and is found (for these or other reasons) to be intended to, benefit the covenantee as owner of his land. 'Statutory annexation' largely reproduces the effect of this view, but the reference to section 78 turns out to be unnecessary.

This view leaves assignment rather out in the cold. Assignment cannot be for cases where the conditions for annexation are not met, for on this view, the covenant would then not qualify as a restrictive covenant at all. An agreement could on the one hand qualify as a restrictive covenant, but on the other hand *not* have its rights automatically attach themselves to the covenantee's land and so pass only if assigned, only if the law positively allows opting out from such attachment. Although introducing a complication, there is no essential reason why the law should not do so, if there is a demand for it.

14.6 A Comparison with Easements

Restrictive covenants have a basic similarity with easements (explored in Chapter 13),[67] in the sense that both are obligations in rem with 'appurtenant rights': that is, they can exist against me only if the rights to them benefit you not in your personal capacity but as owner of your land. Is there any reason why they should not be merged? To assess the possibility we need to take stock of their present differences. These are to be found principally on two points.[68]

One relates to the obligation's content. Easements were developed in and for one application (the cross-exploitation of agricultural properties in the context of enclosure, and of town properties in the context of urbanisation), while covenants were developed in and for another (as a corrective to the discomforts of urbanisation). Each has, however, been applied more widely, to the extent possible without transgressing the rules reflecting the original

[67] The link was made explicitly in *London & South Western Railway Co v Gomm* (1882) 20 Ch D 562, 583 (CA).

[68] At one time there might have been a third. Easement rights are regarded as belonging to the land that they benefit, and are transferred automatically with it; but on the standard account (criticised in § 14.5.2, however), this was not the case for restrictive covenants . . . until *Federated Homes Ltd v Mill Lodge Properties Ltd* [1980] 1 WLR 594 (CA) made it so.

applications, especially the requirement of dominant land. But in easements, there has been an attempt, albeit not a wholly thorough one, to limit the range of application, in the shape of the bias towards rights of a traditional, ordinary, agricultural, business nature, as we saw in § 13.1.6. There is no counterpart to this in the law of covenants, though in practice few novel applications seem to have been essayed for them.[69]

The reason why content matters is that obligations in rem are acceptable only if their usefulness outweighs the harm they necessarily do;[70] and their usefulness is a function of their content. The original applications of covenants and easements were evidently felt at the time to make them, on the whole, appropriate rights in rem – probably rightly – and that probably remains the balance of advantage today too. But novel applications require justification in the light of their own content, so the law on easements is right to be wary of them, and that on covenants wrong to give the appearance of insouciance on the point. If the two kinds of obligation were to be merged, then, it should not be on a basis which allows people to create appurtenant rights of whatever content they choose.

The other key difference between easements and covenants is in respect of the ways in which they can be created. It boils down to the issue whether it is right for the law to generate such obligations on the basis of utility (backed up by a weak element of consent), as it has traditionally done with easements but not with covenants. Where a right is not merely useful enough to merit acceptance as in rem, but exceptionally useful, there will be a case for allowing it to arise on that very basis. The law of easements reflects this point well in accepting non-intentional conferral in case of necessity, but misses it with its rule arising under section 62 of the Law of Property Act 1925 and its institution of prescription.[71] The law of covenants seems right not to contemplate non-intentional conferral, in that rights of the content to which it caters surely cannot be necessary. If the two kinds of obligation were to be merged, it should be on the basis that non-intentional conferral remains possible, but only where the right in question is in some sense necessary.

---

[69] For those that have, see § 14.2.3.
[70] This is the *numerus clausus* principle: see § 1.2.2.
[71] §§ 13.2.5, 7.3, 13.2.7 respectively.

Trust Rights 1

Our next right in rem is a beneficial interest under a trust. The topic is large and difficult, so our consideration of it will be divided between two chapters, this and Chapter 16.

15.1 The Basic Concepts

Trusts involve deep and complex ideas, many of which this book will not attempt to explore. But broadly speaking, a trust is

a situation in which property is vested in someone (a trustee), who is under legally recognised obligations, at least some of which are of a proprietary kind [ie in rem], to handle it in a certain way, and to the exclusion of any personal interest. These obligations may arise either by conscious creation by the previous owner of the property (the settlor), or because some other legally significant circumstances are present.[1]

Commonly,[2] the trustee owes his obligations to another person, a 'beneficiary',[3] who thus has rights to their performance. These rights comprise the beneficiary's 'beneficial interest'. Commonly, too, the property vested in the trustee is a legal estate:[4] in the case of land, usually the freehold ownership,

[1] S Gardner, *An Introduction to the Law of Trusts* (3rd edn, Oxford, 2011) 2.
[2] Though not necessarily. Some trusts involve only obligations, not rights, which is why the description given focuses on obligations alone. See Gardner, *ibid* ch 12.
[3] Sometimes called by the old Law French name, '*cestui que trust*' (pronounced 'settee key trust').
[4] The alternative is that the property vested in the trustee, and held on trust for the beneficiaries, is itself an equitable interest. In broad terms, this makes no difference. But it could entail

sometimes a lease, or some other legal interest such as a mortgage. Especially where it is the freehold ownership, the trustee is often therefore referred to as the 'legal owner', while the beneficiaries' rights under the trust are necessarily (because the trust concept was developed in the equity jurisdiction) equitable.

So, I might transfer a farm to you, on the basis that you will hold it on trust for John. This creates a trust, of which John is the beneficiary, you are the trustee, and I am the settlor. You are required to use the farm for John's benefit. Your doing so might take the form of renting it out to a tenant farmer and paying over the incoming rent to John (though it might take some other form instead). John has rights that you shall do so, which collectively add up to his beneficial interest. In this case, the trust arises because I create it. A trust arising in this way is called an 'express' trust.

Alternatively, I might own our family home, but agree with you that we will share it equally. The upshot (§ 9.3) is that a trust arises against me in your favour, requiring me to treat the house as 50 per cent mine, 50 per cent yours. I am the trustee, and, with our 50 per cent interests, you and I are the beneficiaries. This trust arises not because I (unilaterally) create it, but because our agreement amounts to a 'legally significant circumstance' leading the law to impose it. A trust arising on the basis of some 'legally significant circumstance' other than a settlor's wish in this way is usually, as in this example, a 'constructive' trust; sometimes, a 'resulting' trust.[5]

15.2 Where a Trust has More than One Beneficiary

15.2.1 Concurrent and Consecutive Interests

Sometimes, a trust will have only one beneficiary: such as John, in the first example given above. Often, though, it will have two or more: such as you and me, in the second example. If it has two or more, their interests can either be concurrent (simultaneous) or successive (consecutive). In the second example above, you and I have concurrent interests: we are both entitled immediately and indefinitely, but alongside one another. An instance of consecutive interests would occur if, say, I transfer land to you on trust for John for his life, and thereafter for Kate. In such an arrangement, John is a 'tenant for life' (or 'life tenant'), and Kate is a 'remainderman'.

differences of detail regarding such things as formality, and, depending on their precise wording, the applicability of particular statutory provisions.

[5] See Gardner (n 1) ch 16 for the cases in which the trust is labelled 'resulting', and discussion of the (not universally accepted) view that such trusts arise, like constructive trusts, for reasons other than that a settlor intends them to.

There can be any number of successive interests, and any kind of event (so long as its occurrence will be sufficiently clear) can act as the boundary between one and another. A common arrangement is that already instanced, 'for John for his life, then for Kate', but I could make a trust 'for John until he dies, or is married, or reaches the age of 21, or becomes a student, or goes to live abroad, or is made bankrupt,' etc, 'then for Kate'; and I could limit Kate's interest in similar ways, providing that after her shall come Liam; and so on. The law's principal restriction on the creation of consecutive interests is a set of rules, collectively known as 'the rule against perpetuities', whereby (above all) I can stipulate for new beneficial interests to come into existence in this way only for a certain distance into the future. These rules are complicated, and a detailed treatment of them will not be attempted here.[6]

So far as concurrent interests are concerned, there can once again be any number, as where I make a trust of land 'for John, Kate, Liam, Meg', and so on down the alphabet. But such interests can take two forms, and it must be decided which of these forms a given interest takes. Concurrent beneficiaries may either have a *shared single interest* in the particular piece of property, or a *set of separate interests* in it. (But not a set of interests in separate pieces of property, as say if I transferred house *A* to you on trust for John, and house *B* on trust for Kate. Then, John and Kate would not have beneficial rights in the same property at all, even if for example the two houses are a semi-detached pair.) Where concurrent beneficiaries have a shared single interest, they are called 'joint tenants'. Where they have separate interests, they are called 'tenants in common'.[7] Tenants in common are sometimes said to have 'undivided shares': this is another way of saying that they have separate interests ('shares'), but in the same property ('undivided').[8]

15.2.2 Joint Tenancies and Tenancies in Common

The principal difference between the two kinds of concurrent interest relates to the situation when one of the beneficiaries dies. Say I give you a house to hold on trust for John and Kate, then John dies. If John and Kate were *tenants in common*, John had a separate interest, which now devolves in the usual way, in accordance with his will or, if he has not left a will, under the intestacy rules. So say he leaves a will bequeathing all his property to Liam: you now hold the house for Kate and Liam.[9] But if John and Kate were *joint tenants*,

---

[6] For an outline treatment, see Gardner, *ibid*, 45–8.

[7] The word 'tenant' in these expressions is not a synonym for 'lessee'. It is used in its etymological sense of 'holder'. (In the same way, someone who has the freehold to a piece of land is called, in technical language, a 'tenant in fee simple absolute in possession'.)

[8] On the two forms of concurrent interest, and their implications, see further L Tee, 'Co-ownership and Trusts' in L Tee (ed), *Land Law: Issues, Debates, Policy* (Cullompton, 2002) 132–48; R Smith, *Plural Ownership* (Oxford, 2005) Pt II.

[9] Who are likewise tenants in common: so if Kate dies, her interest will devolve in the same way, and so on.

you now hold the house on trust for Kate alone. John and Kate previously shared a single interest, so upon John's death, Kate is simply left as sole owner of that interest. Liam does not inherit, because John did not have a separate interest upon which his will or the intestacy rules could operate. This expression of the nature of a joint tenancy is known as '(the right of) survivorship'.[10]

15.2.3 Should Joint Tenancy be Abolished?

It can be argued that joint tenancy is nowadays insupportable, and that it should therefore be abolished, leaving tenancy in common as the only possibility.[11]

The case against joint tenancy is that the difference between it and tenancy in common, namely survivorship, does harm, and no countervailing good. The harm occurs when a joint tenant dies unaware of his status as such, or of its implications. He probably assumes that his right will pass under an apparently relevant provision in his will (eg 'all my property to . . .', or 'my share in the house to . . .'), or under the intestate succession rules. But survivorship confounds his assumption, thus frustrating his wishes.

There is no such objection if our joint tenant is aware of his status as a joint tenant, and of its implications: he has the choice of becoming a tenant in common by severance (explained in § 15.2.6), and if he fails to do so he presumably wants survivorship to occur at his death. But the fact that it offers him the option of precipitating survivorship in this way, if he understands the position and wants this, is not an argument *in favour of* the joint tenancy. For he can achieve the same effect under a tenancy in common, by bequeathing his share to his fellow tenant(s) in common.

The following argument for the joint tenancy is sometimes made. Conceding the truth of the previous paragraph in general, it asserts that in certain circumstances, survivorship is beneficent as reflecting the way in which a deceased co-owner, dying intestate, would have wished to leave his right; or in which, regardless of his wishes, he ought to have left it. The 'certain circumstances' are, circularly, those where the co-owners' relationship is such that the one would or should have left his right to the other in this way . . . above all, where the two were married, or civil partners, or had a similarly close but informal relationship.

This counter-argument fails, however, as once again survivorship is not the only way in which such work can be done; nor indeed is it the best way. The law has other rules specifically designed for these purposes,[12] and these will

---

[10] Sometimes the Latin is used: '*ius accrescendi*'.

[11] For further exploration, see M Thompson, 'Beneficial Joint Tenancies: A Case for Abolition?' [1987] *Conv* 29; A Pritchard, 'Beneficial Joint Tenancies: A Riposte' [1987] *Conv* 273; M Thompson, 'Beneficial Joint Tenancies: A Reply to Professor Pritchard' [1987] *Conv* 275.

[12] Intestates' Estates Act 1952; Inheritance (Provision for Family and Dependants) Act 1975. Of course, these rules may themselves be capable of improvement. In particular, in their current forms, they are not well adapted to informal relationships. For reform proposals, see Law

apply where a concurrent owner dies a tenant in common. Moreover, these rules operate in a subtler way than survivorship: they also benefit children of the relationship, and – above all – they operate on the basis of the relationship as it prevails at the time of death. By contrast, survivorship occurs on the strength of the joint tenancy that was established when the parties initially acquired their interests, regardless (unless there has been a severance) of supervening changes in their relationship making survivorship inappropriate. In an era when a relationship's closeness cannot be predicted to make it also enduring, this feature of the joint tenancy is especially damaging.

It may be concluded that joint tenancy, with its characteristic of survivorship, should be abolished, leaving tenancy in common as the only platform for concurrent beneficial rights.

15.2.4 The Four Unities

As the law stands, however, concurrent interests may exist under either a tenancy in common or a joint tenancy, and we need to be able to say which.

To capture the key idea that a joint tenancy is a shared single interest, it is commonly said that, if John and Kate are to be joint tenants, their concurrent rights must exhibit 'the four unities'. These are:

—— *Possession*, meaning that their rights must be in the same piece of property (say, the house you hold on trust for them, rather than two separate houses, one apiece).

—— *Time*, meaning that their rights must vest at the same time (this would not be satisfied, for example, if I transferred the house to you to hold on trust 'for John, and for Kate too if and when John marries her').

—— *Title*, meaning that their rights must arise immediately from the same transaction (as where I establish them under the trust on which I give you the house; contrast the case where John later alienates his right to Liam, whereupon Kate and Liam are the beneficiaries but with rights which do not arise immediately from the same transaction).

—— *Interest*, meaning that their rights must be of the same extent (eg both indefinite, or both for the duration of a certain lease) and size (ie, necessarily, equal; rather than say John's right being double Kate's).

Unity of possession is indeed essential if John and Kate are to have a shared single interest, but only because it is essential if they are to have concurrent rights in the same property at all: that is, it necessarily characterises a tenancy in common as much as it does a joint tenancy. It is the other three unities that are supposedly crucial to the question whether concurrent rights are shares in a single interest, rather than a set of separate interests.

Commission, *Intestacy and Family Provision Claims on Death* (Law Com No 331, London, 2011), especially Pt 8.

Plainly, John and Kate can have separate concurrent interests in the same property notwithstanding that these arise at different times, under different transactions, and are of different extents or sizes, and it follows that these unities are not required of tenancies in common. But equally plainly, they cannot share a single interest unless that interest was made at one time, under one transaction, and with a certain extent and size. In principle, however, the same need not be true of their *shares in* the single interest: in the abstract, there is no reason why these should not be of different relative sizes, or be acquired independently of one another. In particular, the idea of survivorship – that if John and Kate share a single interest, it becomes solely Kate's on John's death – makes as good sense regardless of the way in which their shares arose or of their relative sizes. Unsurprisingly, therefore, the idea that these three unities are essential to a joint tenancy has come under pressure.[13]

Moreover, the rights in question can exhibit the three unities (as well as unity of possession) and nevertheless amount to a tenancy in common rather than a joint tenancy. That is, they can arise at the same time, under the same transaction, and be identical in extent and size, and still be separate interests in the property, as opposed to shares in a single interest. So the unities do not, as might have been thought, actually *constitute* the single interest. They are (or perhaps are not quite, if the previous paragraph is right) necessary to the existence of such an interest, but not sufficient: those controlling the rights concerned must further intend them to exist in a combined state.[14] Where the unities are present, such an intention is presumed, but can be displaced by contrary evidence, showing either an intention at the outset that the rights should be separate, or a later intention that they should be separated ('severed'). These two possibilities are respectively considered in §§ 15.2.5 and 15.2.6.

15.2.5 Separation at the Outset

So beneficial rights, exhibiting all four unities, will nonetheless be held in common rather than jointly if they are created with that intention. Such an intention can be discovered from the language in which the rights are created. If I create a trust 'for John and Kate', adding nothing, they will probably be found

---

[13] See especially Smith (n 8) 27–30 (querying indeed whether today's law requires unity of time at all), 44–6. On the other hand, it seems correct to say that joint tenants of a lease must have a single responsibility for the rent (as held in *Mikeover Ltd v Brady* [1989] 3 All ER 618 (CA); *AG Securities v Vaughan* [1990] 1 AC 417 (CA and HL)): the single responsibility is the counterpart of the single interest which, to be joint tenants, they must share.

[14] Or should one see the question, less metaphysically, as whether survivorship is intended? If so, is there the further implication that those with concurrent rights lacking the three unities can nonetheless opt into survivorship? This possibility would close the circle with the observation in the previous paragraph, that the three unities may not in fact be crucial to a joint tenancy anyway.

to be joint tenants. But if I add more or less anything – say, 'equally', or 'in equal shares' – the cases show that John and Kate will probably be found to be tenants in common.[15] Such additions are known as 'words of severance'.

The intention can alternatively be surmised from the surrounding circumstances. Say John and Kate have beneficial rights exhibiting all four unities in a house. If their relationship is of a business nature – for instance, they are dentists sharing surgery premises – it will be inferred that they do not intend to share a single interest (so that if John dies, Kate alone will take that interest, rather than John's share going to his estate: an inappropriate outcome in the circumstances).[16] Such an intention should also be found if John and Kate are friends who bought the house together because they wanted to 'get on the property ladder' and could not afford to do so separately. But not if they are a couple: then, survivorship is not contraindicated.

The law's readiness to find especially words of severance suggests that it is not neutral on the question whether a joint tenancy or a tenancy in common has been created: that it has a preference for the latter answer. This is probably a reflection of the feeling, explored in § 15.2.3, that joint tenancies are an embarrassment, and that the law should cease to recognise them.

15.2.6 Subsequent Severance

An initial joint tenancy can be turned into a tenancy in common by subsequent severance.[17] Severance can occur in a number of ways:[18]

—— by written notice from one joint tenant to the other(s);[19]
—— by agreement between the joint tenants concerned, or a 'course of dealing' (ie a set of pieces of behaviour) showing that they in fact regard the joint tenancy as having been severed;

---

[15] See eg *Robertson v Fraser* (1871) LR 6 Ch App 696 (CA in Ch).

[16] *Malayan Credit Ltd v Jack Chia-MPH Ltd* [1986] AC 549 (PC).

[17] If there are only two joint tenants, say John and Kate, a severance necessarily leaves both as tenants in common. But say there are three – John, Kate, Liam – or more, and that John severs. John becomes tenant in common vis-à-vis Kate and Liam, so John's death will not benefit Kate and Liam by survivorship, nor will Kate's or Liam's death benefit John by survivorship. But (*ceteris paribus*) Kate and Liam remain joint tenants between themselves, so Kate's death will still benefit Liam by survivorship, and vice versa.

[18] Law of Property Act 1925 s 36(2); *Williams v Hensman* (1861) 1 J & H 546, 557–8 (Ch). In addition to those listed, perhaps also by the criminal killing of one joint tenant by another. Certainly, the killer does not take (unless relieved under the Forfeiture Act 1982), but this may alternatively be because survivorship does operate in the killer's favour, but the resulting gain is caught by a constructive trust for his victim's estate. See *Re K* [1985] Ch 85, 100 (Ch D).

[19] This method of severance was established by the Law of Property Act 1925 s 36(2). On a literal reading of s 36, it applies solely where the people concerned not only have concurrent beneficial rights as joint tenants, but also are trustees of the trust in question ('where a legal estate . . . is vested in joint tenants beneficially . . .'). This restriction is, however, unprincipled: severance affects only the relationship of the beneficial rights between themselves, not in any way the position of the trustees: so the identity of the trustees ought to be irrelevant.

—— by 'an act operating on' one joint tenant's share,[20] such as where John, hitherto joint tenant with Kate, transfers[21] his right to Liam.[22]

In § 15.2.5, we saw that in deciding whether concurrent rights exhibiting all four unities are initially established under a joint tenancy or a tenancy in common, the law shows a preference for the latter answer, ascribable to the unwelcome implications of the former. Unsurprisingly – all the more so given that changes in the parties' relationship may well make survivorship even less appropriate as time goes on – there are signs of the same tendency in the law's approach to discovering that a joint tenancy has subsequently been severed.

In particular, the courts are ready to find severance by written notice despite the piece of writing in question saying nothing about severance. A written document of any kind, passing from one joint tenant to another, will count as a notice of severance so long as the writer's desire to sever can be discovered by reflecting upon its content. Say land is currently held for John and Kate – perhaps brother and sister – as joint tenants. John, wishing to realise his share, applies to court[23] for an order that the land be sold and the proceeds divided between them. This application will necessarily be made in writing, and a copy of it served on Kate. Here then we have some writing passing from John to Kate … and, although there is no mention of severance, it will count as a *notice of severance* because it plainly shows John as not wanting survivorship to continue to apply between himself and Kate.[24] In the same vein, an *agreement to sever* has been found despite those concerned making no reference to the issue, on the basis that they were negotiating to split the land in question between them.[25] And some judges have held that there is a severance by *course of dealing* if one joint tenant merely tells the other (orally is enough) of a desire on his part that is inconsistent with a continued joint tenancy:[26] a mere request to negotiate for a split would suffice.

---

[20] Severance by an act operating on one's own share is sometimes presented as logically inevitable: since Liam acquires his right from John, there is no unity of title between his right and Kate's, so they cannot be joint tenants. But in *allowing* a joint tenant to split his right out of a single interest in this way, the rule presupposes – like the other methods of severance – that the preservation of the single interest is optional, to be ended if those concerned so choose.

[21] Transfer of one's interest certainly counts as an act operating on it and thus severs. A mortgage of it probably does too. It is unclear whether the same is true of a lease of it.

[22] Or where John's right is taken from him, eg upon his bankruptcy, or where he and Kate are joint tenants of their family home, and Kate becomes entitled to a larger than 50% share, under the rules discussed in § 9.3.

[23] Under the Trusts of Land and Appointment of Trustees Act 1996 s 14: see §§ 16.2.2–16.2.5.

[24] *Re Draper's Conveyance* [1969] 1 Ch 486 (Ch D), approved in *Burgess v Rawnsley* [1975] Ch 429 (CA) and *Harris v Goddard* [1983] 1 WLR 1203 (CA). If the order that John seeks is made and carried out, the division of the money will end the unity of possession necessary for John and Kate to have concurrent rights in the same property at all: that is, they will at that point cease even to be tenants in common.

[25] *Burgess v Rawnsley, ibid.*

[26] See *Re Draper's Conveyance* [1969] 1 Ch 486, 490–2 (Ch D); *Burgess v Rawnsley, ibid* 439–40; perhaps also *Harris v Goddard* [1983] 1 WLR 1203, 1210–11 (CA).

But the cases also show a contrary tendency, sometimes taking a much narrower view of severance. The idea that unilateral oral notice amounts to a course of dealing has been disapproved:[27] a position that can certainly be supported on technical grounds,[28] but over which the judges concerned seem to shed no tears. Some decisions have declined to discern an agreement to sever, or even a shared treatment of the joint tenancy as severed, in unfinished negotiations towards a split.[29] And while there currently seems to be no doubt that a piece of writing need show only an implicit intention to sever, it has been held[30] that the intention must be for an immediate severance, a position for which there is no basis;[31] and that an intention to sever cannot be read into an application for a court order to reallocate a couple's property in the context of their divorce, a view which surely overlooks the significance of the applicant's desire for divorce itself. Finally, it might be thought that a generally distant relationship between joint tenants, either all along or evolving from something closer, should constitute a course of dealings showing that survivorship is not wanted; but the idea seems not even to have been argued, let alone judicially adopted.[32]

How are these narrower treatments of severance to be explained? It is understandable that the judges should worry about joint tenancies being severed in nebulous circumstances. The effect of a severance, aborting survivorship, will generally not matter until one of the people concerned dies, possibly years or even decades later. If the law defines severance in such a way that it is hard to discern at such a distance, it will have created a recipe for undesirable litigation. From this point of view, it would be right to require that severance be by explicit writing alone (that is, if the law continues to maintain joint tenancies, and so have a place for severance, at all). But this argument seems not to account for the positions that the judges have in fact taken against easy severance: though relatively narrow, they do not especially promote certainty.

Perhaps these positions are ascribable instead to a sense that, in an individual context, the survivor of two joint tenants positively ought to have the whole interest. Say John lives with Kate, who is separated but not divorced

---

[27] *Burgess v Rawnsley, ibid* 447; *Harris v Goddard, ibid* 1211.

[28] If severance could occur by unilateral *oral* notice, there would be no need for the rule (Law of Property Act 1925 s 36(2)) specifically stating that it can occur by unilateral *written* notice.

[29] This view was taken in *Nielson-Jones v Fedden* [1975] Ch 222 (Ch D). That decision was criticised in *Burgess v Rawnsley* [1975] Ch 429 (CA), but the same view was again taken in *Gore and Snell v Carpenter* (1990) 60 P & CR 456 (Ch D).

[30] *Harris v Goddard* [1983] 1 WLR 1203, 1209 (CA).

[31] Severance by written notice is made possible by the Law of Property Act 1925 s 36(2), but the wording of this says nothing on the issue of immediacy.

[32] One might think to detect it, for example, in the context of a family property case (§ 9.3), where the house is held in joint names and so impliedly for the parties as joint tenants, but they then drift apart. There will certainly be a severance if the evolving circumstances mean that their shares move from 50:50 to some unequal ratio, but that will be for the different reason of an act operating on their shares, negating the unities.

from her husband, in a house in which they have beneficial interests as joint tenants. Kate then dies intestate. A judge who finds severance will cause Kate's right to devolve to her estranged husband rather than to John. In these terms, even if the relationship between John and Kate had become troubled, it may remain more appropriate to treat the joint tenancy as remaining unsevered, so as to precipitate survivorship in John's favour. The same could be true even if John and Kate had parted, or indeed if Kate had recently found a new partner and made a will in the latter's favour: the basis of John's claim seems to lie less in the quasi-formal fact of his being Kate's partner than, substantively, in his having made his life with her over a significant and at any rate not too distant period. In their present forms, however, the intestacy and family provision regimes do not respond satisfactorily to this claim,[33] a deficiency which a judge can correct by refusing to find severance.

It is hard to say whether thinking of this kind was influential in the principal cases taking a narrow approach to severance,[34] as their facts are not fully enough reported. But they do seem to have involved a husband who, in the very throes of a divorce from his wife, dies, leaving his property elsewhere. So it is certainly possible that the court's perception of the wife's deserts, in terms of her role within the marriage, may have guided its treatment of the severance issue.[35] But such manipulation of the severance issue is ultimately an inappropriate tool for such work. It is available only where the parties were joint tenants in the first place, a point which is irrelevant to the true character of John's or the wife's claim; and where severance has not occurred beyond doubt (eg by an unequivocal written notice),[36] also an essentially irrelevant consideration.

---

[33] As Kate's unmarried partner, John will have no rights under the intestacy rules. He will have rights under the Inheritance (Provision for Family and Dependants) Act 1975 only if he still lived with Kate when she died, and then only to the extent of providing him with reasonable maintenance. For reform proposals, see Law Commission, *Intestacy and Family Provision Claims on Death* (n 8) Pt 8.

[34] *Nielson-Jones v Fedden* [1975] Ch 222 (Ch D); *Harris v Goddard* [1983] 1 WLR 1203 (CA); *Gore and Snell v Carpenter* (1990) 60 P & CR 456 (Ch D).

[35] Though the fact of the parties' marriage certainly creates a difficulty for this argument. The Inheritance (Provision for Family and Dependants) Act 1975 is more generous to bereaved spouses than to other kinds of family member or dependants, approaching quantum in a way similar to the regime applicable upon divorce (Matrimonial Causes Act 1973 s 24). So (except in *Nielson-Jones v Fedden* [1975] Ch 222 (Ch D), which pre-dated the 1975 Act) the court could have used the 1975 Act to treat the wife as well as she would have been treated had the divorce gone through before her husband's death. In comparison, a tendentious refusal to recognise severance of the joint tenancy would have been a very blunt instrument.

[36] Perhaps aiming to neutralise this difficulty, Lord Denning MR in *Bedson v Bedson* [1965] 2 QB 666, 678 (CA) asserted that persons (or he may have meant specifically spouses) having concurrent beneficial interests in property as joint tenants may not sever their joint tenancy so long as one of them is in possession of the property in question. But, as Russell LJ observed *ibid*, at 690, there is no foundation for this position; and Russell LJ's view was accepted in *Re Draper's Conveyance* [1969] 1 Ch 486, 494 (Ch D) and *Harris v Goddard* [1983] 1 WLR 1203, 1208 (CA).

15.3 The Creation of Trust Rights in Land

15.3.1 Express and Constructive Trusts

As explained in the outline given in § 15.1, a trust can arise in two ways. First, because a settlor intends it to. The settlor may either transfer the property in question to the trustee on this basis, or keep it and declare himself trustee of it.[37] A trust arising in this way is an express trust. Second, because 'some other legally significant circumstances are present', in which case it is a constructive trust (or a resulting trust). The law operates a substantial number of sets of 'other legally significant circumstances'. Details of the rules concerning these can be found in books about trusts.[38] In most cases, the fact that the property in question is land rather than something else (eg money, stocks and shares) makes little or no difference, and so the rules merit no particular attention in a book about land law. This book will focus only on those rules to which it matters that the property is land, or whose exploration has occurred substantially in cases involving land.

One such type of constructive trust is that instanced in § 15.1, arising when I own our family home, and we agree that you should have at least a share in it.[39] This type is discussed fully in § 9.3. Another type arises when I own some land and transfer it to you, stipulating that you should hold it on what would be an express trust, except that I fail to put this stipulation in writing, as I have to in order to create a valid express trust of land.[40] As explained in § 9.2, you hold the land on constructive trust instead.[41] A third type allegedly arises when I transfer property to you, you having promised to use it in a certain way (many of the relevant decisions involve land, though in fact the nature of the property seems inessential).[42] An obligation arises against you: the authorities label it a constructive trust, though in truth it seems not to have to be a trust at all. This type too is explored in § 9.2.

---

[37] It almost goes without saying that the finding of the required intention can be manipulated to serve other policy ends. See generally Gardner (n 1) chs 2, 3.

[38] See eg *ibid* chs 15–18.

[39] *Gissing v Gissing* [1971] AC 889 (HL); *Lloyds Bank plc v Rosset* [1991] 1 AC 107 (HL); *Stack v Dowden* [2007] 2 AC 432 (HL); *Abbott v Abbott* [2008] 1 FLR 1451 (PC); *Jones v Kernott* [2011] 3 WLR 1121 (SC).

[40] Law of Property Act 1925 s 53(1)(b).

[41] *Rochefoucauld v Boustead* [1897] 1 Ch 196 (CA); *Bannister v Bannister* [1948] 2 All ER 133 (CA).

[42] *Binions v Evans* [1972] Ch 359 (CA); *Swiss Bank Corporation v Lloyds Bank Ltd* [1979] Ch 548 (Ch D); *Lyus v Prowsa Developments Ltd* [1982] 1 WLR 1044 (Ch D); *Ashburn Anstalt v WJ Arnold & Co* [1989] Ch 1 (CA).

15.3.2 A Complication regarding Tenancies in Common

Certain statutory provisions, read literally, appear to dictate that beneficial rights to be enjoyed by tenants in common can arise under an express trust,[43] but cannot arise under a constructive trust.

The ensuing gap would be substantial. In particular, consider the constructive trust that takes effect when I own our family home, but we agree that you should have a share in it (§ 9.3). Unless your share is to be 100 per cent, so that I hold the land on a bare trust for you alone, you and I must emerge with concurrent beneficial rights. And we cannot be joint tenants (this is true even if we are each to have a 50 per cent share), as unity of title is absent: your share derives from the fact that the rule in play here imposes an obligation on me in your favour, while my share is my original entire ownership, minus what this obligation takes away from me.[44] If this rule is to generate beneficial rights at all, then, those holding them must do so as tenants in common. But the trust containing these rights is a constructive trust, and the statutory provisions referred to in the last paragraph say that a tenancy in common cannot arise under a constructive trust. It ought to follow that the rule under discussion cannot generate beneficial rights at all.

That is unthinkable, however. These trusts provide the law's principal way of allowing family members to acquire a greater share in their home than the title specifies, and if they are neither married to nor civil partners with the other party, this will in turn be their principal means of sharing in the family's assets in the event of a breakdown. At the level of principle, moreover, there seems to be no reason why beneficial rights created via an express trust[45] can be held under a tenancy in common while those arising under a constructive trust cannot. Unsurprisingly, then, the courts have rejected this reading of the statutory provisions, and do allow beneficial rights created by constructive trusts to take effect under a tenancy in common after all.[46]

15.3.3 Formalities for Express and Constructive Trusts

An express trust of land needs to be created in writing.[47] (If it involves a transfer from the settlor to the trustee of the interest to be held on trust, the

---

[43] Settled Land Act 1925 s 36(4) . . . or under a statutory trust (§ 15.4) arising when I purport simply to transfer land to people as tenants in common, either *inter vivos* (Law of Property Act 1925 s 34(2)) or in my will (s 34(3)).

[44] The contrary is however asserted in *Hurst v Supperstone* [2005] EWHC 1309, [11] (Ch D).

[45] Or statutory trust: § 15.4.

[46] This position is implicit in, for example, *Bull v Bull* [1955] 1 QB 234 (CA); *Williams & Glyn's Bank Ltd v Boland* [1981] AC 487 (HL); *City of London Building Society v Flegg* [1988] AC 54, 74 (HL); *Abbey National Building Society v Cann* [1991] 1 AC 56 (HL). It is unclear how it is to be reconciled with the statutory wording.

[47] Law of Property Act 1925 s 53(1)(b).

formalities appropriate to the interest concerned must also be used. In the ordinary case, the settlor transfers the freehold ownership of the land to the trustee, and this requires a deed and registration.[48])

No formality is required in order for there to be a constructive or resulting trust.[49] Unlike an express trust, such trusts are not based on someone's intention to create them, and so can and commonly do arise without anybody intending them to. Any demand for formality would therefore not be complied with, and thus would normally prevent the trust from arising after all, frustrating the reasons why the law seeks its imposition (see § 7.1.2).

15.3.4 Trustees

If land is to be held on trust, so as to establish beneficial interests, there must be one or more trustees. The trustees are the people in whom the property that is the subject-matter of the trust[50] is vested; as the outline given in § 15.1 explains, they then owe obligations to the beneficiaries, so generating the beneficiaries' rights. To complete our account of how trust rights are created, we need therefore to understand how people become trustees.

Say I wish to make an express trust, for John, of land that I have owned hitherto. I can transfer it to you as trustee for John. Usually, however, I will make the transfer to you and at least one other trustee, up to a maximum of four.[51] It is hard to find a direct authoritative statement on the point, but it appears that a trust of land ought to have a minimum of two trustees. As will be seen in § 16.6, two are required in order for the beneficial interests to be overreached from the land in the event of a disposition,[52] and the standard explanation is that this rule aims to reduce the risk of the proceeds being embezzled[53] ... implying that, if there is only a single trustee, it is his duty to seek the appointment of at least one colleague, at any rate before attempting to dispose of the land.

There is an alternative way in which I can create an express trust: by 'declaring' it, ie retaining the land and making myself trustee of it. In this case, the need for at least two trustees will entail that I should seek the appointment of a second trustee alongside me. Likewise, if I own land and a constructive (or resulting) trust of it arises in John's favour, I again retain it, becoming trustee

---

[48] *ibid* s 52(1), Land Registration Act 2002 s 27: § 5.4.1.

[49] Law of Property Act 1925 s 53(2).

[50] Often, the very freehold ownership of the relevant land, but it could be some other interest, such as a lease, or a mortgage, or indeed the trustee's own right as beneficiary of another trust.

[51] Trustee Act 1925 s 34.

[52] Law of Property Act 1925 s 27(2). But a single trustee will suffice if it is a 'trust corporation', eg the trustee department of a bank.

[53] *City of London Building Society v Flegg* [1988] AC 54, 74 (HL). This explanation is shaky, however. If a trust holds assets other than land all along, the danger of embezzlement seems at least as great, yet there is no rule against its being run by a single trustee.

myself, and should find a second trustee. In this case especially, though, the likelihood is that I will not do so. I shall probably not realise that I hold the land on trust at all, let alone the need for such a trust to have at least two trustees. As we shall see in §§ 16.6 and 16.8.1, considerable problems follow when I, as a sole trustee, then purport to make a disposition of the land.

15.3.5 Multiple Trustees as 'Legal Joint Tenants'

When there are – as there should be – multiple trustees (ie two, three or four of them), they are said to hold the land as 'legal joint tenants'.

This statement makes use of the joint tenancy concept, discussed in §§ 15.2.1–15.2.6. There, the discussion was of the possible ways in which a trust's *beneficiaries* could have concurrent beneficial interests under it, these being as joint tenants or as tenants in common. When two or more people hold the legal title to the land as *trustees*, however, they cannot do so as tenants in common: legal estates cannot be co-owned under a tenancy in common, either from the outset or as a result of later severance.[54] Only the other alternative, a joint tenancy, is allowed.

Say, therefore, that a settlor transfers land to you and me on trust for John and Kate. No matter whether the settlor uses words of severance in the transfer (eg to you and me 'equally'), or whether the relationship between you and me is one that would ordinarily yield a tenancy in common (eg we are business partners): in taking the land as trustees, we necessarily do so as 'legal joint tenants'.

Because our positions as trustees cannot be held under a tenancy in common, they are incapable of severance and so of alienation – we cannot simply transfer them to others in our place. All either of us can do is die (or 'release', ie resign, our position), in which case survivorship takes effect in favour of the other. This indeed is the point of the rule. It ensures that the number of trustees of a given piece of land certainly does not rise, and tends to fall; and that the trustees probably remain a relatively close group. This in turn limits the number of obstacles potentially facing someone wishing to buy the land, which would otherwise reduce its marketability.[55] (The purchaser can

---

[54] Law of Property Act 1925 ss 1(6), 34(1), 36(2).

[55] Even if the group is limited and close, however, the need for the trustees to number at least two introduces an obstacle which would be absent if the prospective buyer had to deal only with a single owner. But further rules are calculated to diminish this obstacle's size. Although in principle the trustees have to be unanimous in deciding to sell, their duty is to act in the beneficiaries' (collective) best interests, so removing at least some of the reasons why unanimity might otherwise elude them; and where one or more vetoes a proposed disposition, the court can be asked (though of course it may not agree) to authorise it anyway (Trusts of Land and Appointment of Trustees Act 1996 s 14). In fact, a sale is effective and overreaches the beneficial interests even if the buyer deals with only two of the trustees (Law of Property Act 1925 s 27(2)), but if these two have gone against the wishes of their colleagues and have not obtained court approval they will generally be liable for breach of trust.

normally disregard the beneficial rights under the trust, for these will be 'overreached', as explained in § 16.5.)

However: while this is the traditional account, it is not quite accurate. It is certainly correct to say that trustees cannot hold their positions as tenants in common, and that (therefore) these positions cannot be transferred, and that survivorship operates on death. But it is actually incorrect to say that trustees hold as joint tenants. If it were correct, the effect of death (or release) would be that a group of up to four trustees would, over time, dwindle to a single trustee: there would be no way of introducing new ones. The law could not allow that: as we have seen, trusts of land need at least two trustees. In fact, trustees of land can – unsurprisingly – be replaced (and, for that matter, removed), and additional ones appointed, in the same way as trustees of any other kind of property.[56] It is better, therefore, to regard those who hold property as trustees as doing so in a unique way: simply as co-trustees, under the rules explained in this section.

15.4 Statutory Trusts

15.4.1 The Nature of Statutory Trusts

As we have seen, concurrent beneficial interests in land can be created under an express trust, as where I transfer land to you on trust for John and Kate.

In the distant past, as we saw in § 10.1.3, it used to be possible for me alternatively to transfer land directly to John and Kate as concurrent owners: that is, without creating a trust. But nowadays, if I purport to do so, the law[57] interjects a trust, to like effect as if I had made an express trust: so if I try simply to transfer my house 'to John and Kate', without mention of a trust, the result will nonetheless be that the house is held on trust for them, their rights being as beneficiaries of this trust. Because the rule responsible for this is to be found in the Law of Property Act 1925, this trust is referred to as a 'statutory' trust.

If I establish an express trust, I will normally name its trustee(s). But if I thought I was making a simple transfer, I will not have done so. The law goes on to provide that the trustees of a purported transfer to concurrent owners will be the purported transferees themselves (or, if there are more than four

---

[56] The relevant rules are quite complex. See principally the Trustee Act 1925 Pt III, together with the Trusts of Land and Appointment of Trustees Act 1996 Pt II.

[57] Law of Property Act 1925 ss 34(2) and (3), 36(1).

of them, the first four named in the transfer).[58] My purported transfer 'to John and Kate', therefore, will take effect as a transfer to John and Kate as trustees, holding on trust for themselves as beneficiaries.[59]

15.4.2 The Rights in a Statutory Trust

Where I purport to transfer land to John and Kate, and a statutory trust thus arises for John and Kate as its beneficiaries, their beneficial interests can exist under either a joint tenancy or a tenancy in common (and, if under a tenancy in common, in any proportions), in the usual way.

To decide their precise nature, we make use of the rules about the four unities and about initial separation, as explained in §§ 15.2.4–15.2.5. The task is assisted, however, by a Land Registry procedure. When land is transferred to multiple owners, the Registry, realising that the transferees must necessarily hold it on trust, requires that the trust's terms be expressly announced. So if land is transferred 'to John and Kate', its registration in their name will be accompanied by a statement telling us whether their beneficial interests are to be joint or in common, and if in common, in what proportions.

There is no question about the transferees' position as trustees, however. As explained in § 15.3.5, co-trusteeship can take only one form, traditionally (though not quite accurately) described as 'legal joint tenancy'. This rule's impact is especially noticeable in the case of a statutory trust. Say I purport to transfer land 'to John and Kate in equal shares'. Such a purported transfer has to take effect as a transfer to John and Kate on trust for themselves (§ 15.4.1). Containing words of severance, it is calculated to create a tenancy in common. It certainly does so in respect of John's and Kate's beneficial interests; but in their capacity as trustees, they necessarily hold as 'legal joint tenants'. So they can transfer their beneficial rights to others, whether during their lifetime or on death, as they please. But they cannot behave in this way with their positions as trustees. If, then, Kate sells her share in the house to Liam, Liam becomes beneficiary alongside John (as tenants in common), but (unless she also releases) Kate remains John's co-trustee.

---

[58] *ibid* ss 34(2) (for purported transfers to tenants in common), 36(1) (for purported transfers to joint tenants). Children, however, cannot own legal estates in land (s 1(6)), so cannot become trustees in this way. So if I purport to transfer land to a group of people which includes children, the children will be disregarded in identifying the first four named, who will become the trustees.

[59] Parallel rules apply to two further cases where the law forbids a purported transfer of land from taking effect as expressed: where it is to a child (Law of Property Act 1925 ss 1(6), 4), or to transferees in succession (eg 'to John for life, then to Kate') (ss 1(1), 4). The approach to the location of trustees is necessarily different in such cases, however.

15.4.3 The Point of Statutory Trusts

Why should the law read a purported transfer 'to John and Kate' as a transfer to John and Kate as trustees, on trust for themselves as beneficiaries, in this way? Anything that John and Kate might have wanted to do as outright transferees they can still do, in one or other of their two capacities (trustee and beneficiary): so why separate these?

The explanation is that interjecting a trust in this way preserves the land's future marketability, as explained in § 10.1.3: essentially, because a putative purchaser will need to deal only with the trustees, rather than with all those who would otherwise have been co-owners but who, under the statutory trust, are instead beneficiaries. While there can be any number of beneficiaries, and the number can grow over time through alienation (even an original joint tenancy can be severed and so treated in this way), we saw in §§ 15.3.4–15.3.5 how there can be no more than four trustees, and how trusteeships cannot be alienated.

The advantage is invisible so long as the trustees and beneficiaries remain the same people: John and Kate in our example. Here, the statutory trust seems a pointless complication. But the advantage becomes clearer if John and Kate (if necessary, sever and) alienate their beneficial interests, further fragmenting them in the process, so that by the time someone wishes to buy the land, the beneficiaries – ie, if there were no statutory trust, the owners – have become a large and diffuse group. Likewise if the purported transfer is to more than four people concurrently from the outset.

Where trustees and beneficiaries are non-identical groups in this way, however, there is also a disadvantage. Although trustees must act in the interests of their beneficiaries, in practice this still leaves them considerable latitude. Those who are merely beneficiaries are correspondingly disempowered, as compared with people who are owners in their own right. This is the price of the statutory trust device. It is of course in principle no larger a problem than is intrinsic to an express or constructive trust (where the beneficiaries are necessarily no more than beneficiaries) anyway. And it is modulated by a further set of rules, discussed in §§ 16.2–16.3, which restrict the latitude enjoyed by trustees of land, giving (some) beneficiaries of such trusts of land an unusually large say in what should happen.

15.4.4 Statutory Trusts and Formalities

For formality purposes, a statutory trust counts as a constructive trust, and as such (§ 15.3.3) requires no formality. My purported outright transfer to John and Kate takes effect (assuming of course that any formalities needed for the transfer itself have been used[60]), after which the statutory trust rule makes John and Kate trustees for themselves, regardless of my, or their, intentions.

15.5 A Worked Example

This chapter has looked at the main rules regarding the nature and creation of trust rights. These rules are complex. It may be helpful to illustrate their operation. The illustration will focus on a case involving the transfer of land to multiple transferees, as this scenario in particular can create confusion.

Say I am selling my house to John, Kate and Liam; let us imagine that they are three adult siblings who wish to live together. If I purport, literally, to transfer it 'to John, Kate and Liam', a statutory trust will arise, whereby John, Kate and Liam will hold the house on trust for themselves. More probably, John, Kate and Liam will have me transfer it to the three of them on an express trust for themselves. Either way, the upshot is that John, Kate and Liam become co-trustees ('legal joint tenants') of the house. The beneficiaries of the trust are themselves. On these facts – there being no words of severance or circumstances pointing to a tenancy in common – they hold their beneficial rights as joint tenants.

Some time later, John dies, leaving a will bequeathing all his property to Meg. What happens now depends on whether, before his death, the joint tenancy between John and Kate and Liam in respect of their beneficial interests had been severed, according to the rules explained in § 15.2.6, so that by the time of his death John was a tenant in common with Kate and Liam. If it had, John's rights as beneficiary of the trust will pass under his will to Meg. Otherwise, survivorship will occur, leaving Kate and Liam as the trust's sole beneficiaries.

But either way, the trustees are now Kate and Liam. Even if Meg inherits John's beneficial interest, she does not become a trustee in his place. The severance that led to her inheriting does not affect trusteeship; to put it another way, there cannot be a legal tenancy in common, only a legal joint tenancy, to which survivorship applies. (Meg can, however, be appointed a trustee alongside Kate and Liam in John's place.)

---

[60] Normally a deed (Law of Property Act 1925 s 52(1)), and registration (Land Registration Act 2002 s 27): § 5.4.1.

In the end, then, the house is held on trust by Kate and Liam. If the joint tenancy between his beneficial right and the others had been severed before John's death, the trust's beneficiaries are Kate, Liam and Meg.[61] Otherwise, the beneficiaries are Kate and Liam alone.

---

[61] Although Meg certainly holds her interest as a tenant in common with Kate and Liam, as between themselves Kate and Liam may be either joint tenants or tenants in common. It depends on whether severance has occurred between them. If John's severance was unilateral, eg effected by written notice, there is no reason to doubt that Kate and Liam remain joint tenants; but if it was by agreement or course of dealings, the same agreement or course of dealings may (though it need not) show a severance between Kate and Liam too.

Trust Rights 2

In Chapter 15 we looked at the basic nature of the rights that exist under a trust of land, and at how they come into being. In this chapter, we go on to consider first the content of such rights, and then their impact on a disponee of the land.

16.1 The Possible Variety of Beneficial Rights

Beneficial interests can exist in a wide variety of sizes.

Sometimes they can be said to amount to ownership. Say you hold land on trust 'for John'. John is the only beneficiary; he is entitled indefinitely (so his interest continues to exist after his death, passing say under his will); and no other restrictions on his entitlement are mentioned. The land's legal title is vested in you as trustee, but in the nature of trusts, you must derive no benefit from this. So it is reasonable to regard John as in effect owning the land; reflecting the fact that trust rights are equitable, he is commonly described as having equitable ownership.[1] Or say you are trustee 'for John and Kate'. In this case, John and Kate once more have unrestricted and indefinite rights, such as we decided amounted to ownership in the first example. But here, they have concurrent interests, so the ownership entitlement is shared between

---

[1] We encounter here another example of 'ownership' being used in a way denoting less than full *dominium*, on account of the title remaining with the trustee: *cf* § 10.1.2. However, assuming he is an adult and not suffering from mental incapacity, John can in fact require you to transfer the legal title to him, so as to make him owner of the full freehold estate, under the doctrine in *Saunders v Vautier* (1841) 1 Cr & Ph 240 (Ch). See S Gardner, *An Introduction to the Law of Trusts* (3rd edn, Oxford, 2011) 179–81.

them.[2] Or again, say you are trustee 'for John for life, then for Kate'. Here, the overall ownership entitlement is again shared between John and Kate, but this time in a successive fashion, so that each has a distinct tranche. John's rights are for his life only, and Kate's, though indefinite, begin (in the sense of being available for direct enjoyment) only with John's death. So neither John's nor Kate's interest amounts to ownership in the way that John's interest in the first example did.[3] But for the time that each prevails it confers quite a full set of rights, making it possible to regard John and Kate each as owner for a time, rather as lessees are, and in the manner discussed in § 10.1.3. Of course, John's rights cannot allow him to damage what Kate gets after his death. In this respect, his position is again similar to that of a lessee, who must not damage the reversion.

Other examples can be given, however, featuring beneficial rights clearly *not* amounting to ownership. For instance, say you (more probably, you and a group of colleagues) are the trustee of a large benevolent scheme, and you hold your investments, including land (farms, shops, offices, blocks of flats), on terms requiring you to pay the income to the scheme's members, but in amounts decided by you. A trust of this kind is called a 'discretionary trust'. The members are beneficiaries of the trust, ie have rights to the performance of your obligations, but since each member will receive only what you decide, he cannot sensibly be described as owning the trust's land and other investments.[4]

16.2 Access to Particular Benefits 1: General Principles

16.2.1 The Ordinary Law of Trusts

The main ways in which the beneficiaries of a trust of land may wish to enjoy their rights are by occupying the land, and by taking its financial value. In turn, there are a number of ways in which the beneficiaries could take the land's financial value. In principle, the land might, for example, be sold and

---

[2] The doctrine in *Saunders v Vautier, ibid*, applies again, but requires John and Kate to agree on demanding the legal title.

[3] Nonetheless, John and Kate can once more combine to demand the legal title from you under the doctrine in *Saunders v Vautier, ibid*.

[4] In theory, the doctrine in *Saunders v Vautier, ibid*, applies here too, so that if all the members agree, they can demand the trust's assets. (The assets would have to be divided between them in such a way that they would also have to agree.) But when a trust has many beneficiaries, as here, this is unlikely to be feasible.

the proceeds simply paid over to the beneficiaries, ending the trust; or sold and the proceeds reinvested in other assets so as to produce an income for the beneficiaries; or retained but rented out to tenants, again producing an income; or retained but mortgaged to secure a loan, itself used, say, to enhance the land's profitability (improving a farm, for instance), or to benefit one or more of the beneficiaries in some other way, perhaps by providing finance to set up or develop a business. But given this range of possibilities, how do we determine the way in which a beneficial right is in fact to be enjoyed?

In this section, we will review the general principles applicable to answering this question. These principles are, however, to some extent set aside in the situation where a beneficiary wishes to occupy the trust land. We shall look at the rules regarding that situation, and their relationship with these general principles, in § 16.3.

The dominant power to decide how a beneficial right is to be enjoyed lies with the beneficiaries, though they have this power only if they are all of full capacity and are unanimous about what they want. In this case, they can in the last resort remove their trustees, make themselves owners of the trust assets and so take their own decisions.[5] So if you hold land on trust for John alone, John can choose the way in which he wants to enjoy his interest. Likewise if your trust is for John for life, then Kate, or for John and Kate concurrently: John and Kate, if they agree, can choose how to enjoy their rights.

In English law, the beneficiaries' invocation of this rule prevails over even a settlor's explicit contrary instructions. But if the beneficiaries are not unanimous, or do not wish to go so far as to dismantle the trust, the next resort is to the settlor's stipulations. So if the terms of your trust indicate that the land must be used in a certain way, or cannot be used in some other way, and the beneficiaries do not agree to dissolve the trust, you must abide by this.[6]

Where, however, the mode of enjoyment is not determined by the beneficiaries or the settlor in these ways, it becomes a matter for the trustees' discretion. But the ordinary law of trusts stipulates two requirements regarding the exercise of this discretion:[7]

—— In making your choices under it, you, as trustee, must conduct yourself in your beneficiaries' interests.[8] Where there are two or more beneficiaries,

---

[5] This is the doctrine in *Saunders v Vautier*, *ibid*, again. If the known beneficiaries of full capacity all agree, but some of the beneficiaries are unable to agree because, eg, they are still children (or even not yet born), the provisions of the Variation of Trusts Act 1958 may allow the court to agree on behalf of the latter. See Gardner (n 1) 181–3.

[6] This is confirmed for trusts of land by the Trusts of Land and Appointment of Trustees Act 1996 s 8. There is an exception, however: the settlor cannot stipulate that the trustees must sell the land: s 4 gives trustees a power to delay sale indefinitely.

[7] On both requirements, see Gardner (n 1) ch 7.

[8] *Cowan v Scargill* [1985] Ch 270 (Ch D); *Hayim v Citibank NA* [1987] AC 730 (PC).

this duty to serve the beneficiaries' interests requires you to be even-handed as between them.[9]

—— You must act with the degree of prudence, care and skill that the law requires of trustees.[10]

These rules seem to apply equally to trusts of land,[11] together with an additional requirement to, 'so far as practicable', consult the adult beneficiaries with immediate interests, and follow the wishes of the majority by value, 'so far as consistent with the general interest of the trust'.[12] A settlor can, however, exclude this additional requirement,[13] and will often do so, in order to spare his trustees what could well be a headache; though the qualifications just quoted must in any case deprive the requirement of much force, so the contrast with the ordinary law of trusts, which has no such requirement, is less marked than at first appears.

16.2.2 The Trusts of Land and Appointment of Trustees Act 1996 Section 14

The ordinary law of trusts continues to say that if you are not the only trustee, you and your colleagues will have to be unanimous in choosing what to do (a rule which in theory could produce paralysis, but in practice seems to pose few problems); but that, so long as you have complied with the rules in making it, your choice of what to do will stand: a judge will not normally substitute some other choice on the basis that, while yours is tenable, his is preferable.[14]

[9] *Raby v Ridehalgh* (1855) 7 De GM & G 104 (CA in Ch). In *Nestle v National Westminster Bank plc* [1993] 1 WLR 1260, 1279 (CA), the duty to be even-handed between beneficiaries was reformulated as a duty to be 'fair'. For consideration of this, see n 59.

[10] By *Re Whiteley* (1886) 33 Ch D 347, 355 (CA), 'the duty of a trustee is . . . to take such care as an ordinary prudent man would take if he were minded to [act] for the benefit of other people for whom he felt morally bound to provide'. By the Trustee Act 2000 s 1(1), a trustee must exhibit 'such care and skill as is reasonable in the circumstances, having regard in particular – (a) to any special knowledge or experience that [the trustee] has or holds himself out as having, and (b) if he acts as trustee in the course of a business or profession, to any special knowledge or experience that it is reasonable to expect of a person acting in the course of that kind of business or profession'. These duties can, however, be excluded by the terms of an express trust: *Armitage v Nurse* [1998] Ch 241 (CA); Trustee Act 2000 Sch 1 para 7.

[11] The Trusts of Land and Appointment of Trustees Act 1996 s 6(1) confirms the trustees' discretion to choose the mode of enjoyment, by giving them the power to do anything with the trust land that an absolute owner might do. The text's two requirements regarding the exercise of the discretion are confirmed by s 6(5)–(8), requiring the trustees to 'have regard to the rights of the beneficiaries' and to act lawfully, including in compliance with the rules of equity; and by s 6(9), requiring them to act with the degree of care and skill demanded by the Trustee Act 2000 s 1(1). But there is an exception. In respect of a discretionary decision not to sell the land, trustees are exempted from the two requirements (they are not to be 'liable in any way': Trusts of Land and Appointment of Trustees Act 1996 s 4). This exemption apparently allows them, in this particular, to be self-interested, biased, careless and incompetent: an extraordinary rule.

[12] Trusts of Land and Appointment of Trustees Act 1996 s 11(1).

[13] ibid, s 11(2).

[14] *Tempest v Lord Camoys* (1882) 21 Ch D 571 (CA).

In these respects, however, the law is quite different where the trust is one of land. By the Trusts of Land and Appointment of Trustees Act 1996, section 14, it allows the court to take decisions regarding the management of the trust in lieu of the trustees.[15] So if trustees are divided over what to do, they can ask the court to adjudicate. And if a beneficiary, or any other person having a right in the trust land, does not like what the trustees are proposing to do or not do, he can ask the court – if it is persuaded of his view – to over-rule them in favour of his preferred course.

16.2.3 The Justification for Section 14

Why does the law thus provide for judicial micromanagement of trusts where, but only where, they are trusts of land?

The ordinary rule, disavowing judicial micromanagement, is probably ascribable to a concern not to overload available judicial resources; and to a view of trusts as autonomous enclaves, into whose life judges should be slow to intrude.[16] These considerations are as relevant to trusts of land as to other kinds of trust, but in the case of trusts of land there is another, countervailing, pair of points which perhaps explain section 14.

First, groups of trustees are normally detached from the beneficiaries (that is usually one of the reasons for having a trust), and close knit among themselves, so that irresolvable disagreements are rare. But the trustees of a trust of land are often the same people as the beneficiaries, most commonly a couple who have bought a house together.[17] If their personal relationship breaks down, they may well disagree over what should be done with the house, one perhaps wishing to continue living in it (maybe with their children), the other wishing to sell so as to be able to buy somewhere new.

Second, where a trust does not involve land, it is very probable that all concerned will regard its assets simply as investments. Where the trust holds land, however, occupation is quite likely to be an issue. In the former case, there may be differences of opinion over the choice of investments, but these will normally be less difficult than the arguments between rivals wishing to occupy, or between those wishing to occupy and those wishing to see the land used for financial gain.

On both counts, disagreements in trusts of land are likely to be more than usually heated. There is therefore some basis for supposing it appropriate for a court to be able to manage matters over the trustees' heads, as provided for under section 14. On the other hand, the fact that the decisions will then be judicial ones does not make them necessarily, or even usually, unproblematic.

---

[15] It also allows the court to dispense trustees from a need to consult beneficiaries or to obtain consents.

[16] On the latter, see further Gardner (n 1) 234–5.

[17] This generates a statutory trust of the land, as explained in § 15.4.

On the contrary, the fact that they are thus given a public, official, state-sanctified quality makes them in some sense more problematic. It also means that they must be formed so as to respect the rights of those affected under the ECHR.[18]

16.2.4 The Operation of Section 14: the Statutory Considerations

So far we have thought of section 14 as putting the trustees' discretions into the hands of the court. The implication has perhaps been that, in exercising these discretions in the trustees' place, the court should proceed as trustees should do, ie as described in § 16.2.1. But that is not quite how section 14 is configured. To be sure, section 14 seems not generally[19] to allow the court to order outcomes not available to the trustees.[20] For example, if the settlor has stipulated that the land shall not be sold before a certain date, section 14 does not allow the court to order otherwise. But in exercising its (or rather, the trustees') discretions under section 14, the court is required to take into account a set of considerations that are different from those to which the trustees are required, or indeed allowed, to attend.

By section 15 of the 1996 Act, the court must ordinarily[21] take into account:[22]

—— The intentions of the person(s) who created the trust (at the time they created it[23]).[24] This ought to refer only to the intentions of the settlor(s) of an *express* trust: constructive trusts are not 'created' by people (rather, they are made by the law, in reaction to what people have done), and the same is true of statutory trusts. But the general assumption is that, on the contrary, the intentions of those acquiring land as co-owners are indeed to be considered too. The intentions may be well documented,

---

[18] A court, as a public authority, is required to act in accordance with the ECHR (eg with due respect for the family life of those affected: Art 8): Human Rights Act 1998 s 6. This requirement was acknowledged, and the approach to the decision shaped accordingly (though not noticeably differently from the approach that would have been taken anyway), in *C Putnam & Sons v Taylor* [2009] EWHC 317, [27]–[38] (Ch D). This is not to say, however, that ordinary trustees' decisions, and/or the rules of law (otherwise) permitting them, are necessarily unaffected by the ECHR. It is a question of the latter's horizontal effect, on which see § 2.2.

[19] It does specifically allow the court to override an obligation not to act without consultation or consent: s 14(2)(a).

[20] See eg R Smith, *Plural Ownership* (Oxford, 2005) 156, referring to the Law Commission report which preceded the 1996 Act; but note the contradictory view, regarding occupation, discussed in § 16.3.3. Other jurisdictions exist to this effect, however: notably the Trustee Act 1925 s 57.

[21] It is quite different where sale of the trust land is sought by an insolvent beneficiary's trustee in bankruptcy (seeking to realise the beneficiary's assets so as to distribute the proceeds among his creditors). Then, the case is governed by the Insolvency Act 1986 s 335A. See § 16.2.6.

[22] See further Smith (n 20) ch 8.

[23] *White v White* [2004] 2 FLR 321, [23] (CA).

[24] Trusts of Land and Appointment of Trustees Act 1996 s 15(1)(a).

but are more often inferred. A frequently encountered intention is that the land, a house, should provide a family home for a couple. Such an intention is rarely influential, however, as litigation under section 14 will not normally occur at all unless the couple are now estranged, so that the aim of providing them with a family home is no longer feasible.

—— The purposes for which the trust's land is held (at the time of the litigation[25]).[26] It is the trustees who 'hold' the land, so the purposes must presumably be theirs. (In most statutory trusts, of course, the trustees and the beneficiaries will be the same people.) The fact that land is *used* in a particular way is neither necessary nor sufficient to show a *purpose* for which the land is held, however: the crucial thing is a sense, on the part of all the trustees, that the land *should* be used or usable in the particular way.[27] Finding such a sense will often be a matter of inference, however.

—— The welfare of any children who occupy or might occupy the trust land[28] – most often, the children of the couple whose home the land is. Note 'welfare': it cannot be assumed, merely because there are children, that their welfare will be (significantly) affected by the relief being sought, eg the sale of the house:[29] children move house all the time, and usually without lasting bad effects, at any rate of a kind that weighs with adults. Something particular is needed, such as disruption of the child's education in the period immediately before public examinations . . . though perhaps suffering not only the estrangement of his parents but also the loss of a familiar environment would, or should, count too.

—— The interests of any beneficiary's secured creditors:[30] notably, of a bank which has loaned the beneficiary money, taking a mortgage over his interest in the land. So long as the mortgage payments are being made and the security remains adequate, the creditor will not normally have an interest in any particular outcome, but if payments are in arrears, it may be asking for a sale.[31]

---

[25] *White v White* [2004] 2 FLR 321, [24] (CA).

[26] Trusts of Land and Appointment of Trustees Act 1996 s 15(1)(b).

[27] *White v White* [2004] 2 FLR 321, [24] (CA).

[28] Trusts of Land and Appointment of Trustees Act 1996 s 15(1)(c). Note the resulting exclusion of, for example, children of a new relationship into which one of the beneficiaries has now entered, leaving his former partner and the children of that relationship in the house. Since s 15 is non-exhaustive, the judge could nonetheless attend to their interests. And a failure to do so might constitute a neglect of their, and/or their parents', rights under ECHR Art 8. Under the Human Rights Act 1998 s 6, courts (as public authorities) are required to act consistently with the ECHR, so should avoid such neglect.

[29] *First National Bank plc v Achampong* [2004] 1 FCR 18, [2003] EWCA Civ 487, [65] (CA).

[30] Trusts of Land and Appointment of Trustees Act 1996 s 15(1)(d).

[31] A creditor will need to seek a sale of the land under s 14 in this way, moreover, only where the mortgage security does not comprise the entire beneficial entitlement to the land. Say John and Kate hold a house on trust for themselves and their parents, and mortgage it to a bank. Because in this case the loan money will be paid to two trustees, *all* the beneficial interests will be overreached (§ 16.5.1). That is to say, the bank will be unconcerned with them, so if it later seeks

——The circumstances and wishes of the majority (by value) of adult beneficiaries with immediate rights.[32] Note the inattention to future beneficiaries, like Kate in the case of a trust for John for his life, thereafter for Kate.

These five considerations are however non-exhaustive. So the court could, for example, view a house as a fund of wealth, available (via an order for sale) to help an estranged couple move on, even if this was neither the intention with which the couple acquired the house nor a purpose to which they subsequently put it. It is noticeable, however, that this consideration is commonly treated as somehow less relevant, or positively important, than those privileged by section 15.

16.2.5 The Operation of Section 14: the Aim of the Jurisdiction

When, in operating section 14, reference is made to a consideration, it is not enough to say that the consideration is indeed a live issue in the individual circumstances: thought must be given to its weight. For example, the mere presence of children is irrelevant. A threat to their welfare is relevant, but inconclusive. To arrive at an outcome, a value must be put on the threat, and be entered into a calculus alongside the values put on all other relevant considerations.[33] But how is this to be done?

We could simply acknowledge that the various relevant considerations are incommensurable (or, while theoretically commensurable, impossible in practice to treat in that way, which comes to the same thing); and leave the judges to make the best of this, using the sorts of approaches explored in § 10.2.4. Or we could try to tap into the idea, mentioned there, of identifying a specific 'covering value' that we are interested in, and measuring and balancing the considerations in terms of their reflection of this covering value. This covering value would be the common meta-consideration that is the *aim* of the section 14 jurisdiction. The statutory scheme, however, does not explicitly

to repossess and sell the house to recoup the debt, it can do so without needing to enter into arguments under s 14 with beneficiaries who oppose sale. But say John alone is the trustee. Here, the beneficial interests will *not* be overreached, and so may bind the bank. (They will do so if the beneficiary was in actual and apparent occupation at the time the mortgage was created, and did not consent to it. If they do not bind the bank, the bank will be unconcerned by them, just as if they had been overreached.) Beneficial interests thus binding upon the bank will rank at the same level as the mortgage; so in order to sell (if the beneficiaries oppose this), the bank will need to obtain an order under s 14. See further § 16.8.1.

[32] Trusts of Land and Appointment of Trustees Act 1996 s 15(3).

[33] *Mortgage Corporation v Shaire* [2001] Ch 743 (Ch D). *White v White* [2004] 2 FLR 321 (CA) involved a couple who had separated. The woman wanted the house to be sold, so as to realise her share of the capital tied up in it, while the man wished to retain the house for occupation by himself and the children. Sale was ordered despite the consequence of requiring the man to find a cheaper and smaller house for himself and the children, perhaps obliging them to share a bedroom.

identify any such common meta-consideration or aim, so in order to pursue this idea, we have to work it out for ourselves.

According to the ordinary principles of the law of trusts, as noted in § 16.2.1, the aim ought to be even-handedly to maximise the trust's benefit to its beneficiaries. The statutory scheme does not work in this way, however. The direction to attend to the circumstances and wishes of adult beneficiaries with immediate rights,[34] no mention being made of others, reads as an invitation not to be even-handed; and the statutory scheme's foci – the intention of the trust's creator(s)[35] (save as embedded in the specification of the beneficial interests), its purpose,[36] and the welfare of children[37] – seem at best tangential to this consideration. Nor does the key lie in viewing the aim as even-handedly to maximise the trust's benefit to its beneficiaries, *but not necessarily in financial terms* (albeit that even-handedness cannot easily be judged otherwise than in financial terms). The same evidence defeats this possibility too.

Indeed, for the most part, the statutory considerations invite the court to step outside the thinking required or allowed by the ordinary law of trusts, and indeed this seems to be the very reason for the Act's mention of them. They can, however, plausibly be read as calculated to deliver family welfare among the beneficiaries and their dependants.[38] Hence the preference for immediate beneficiaries over remoter ones; the attention to non-beneficiary children, alone among those persons not recognised by the ordinary law of trusts itself. Hence too a visible tendency to think of intentions and purposes predominantly in domestic terms; where the property in question is a family home, the idea that it also has a role as a fund of wealth is, as we noted in § 16.2.4, treated as rather a Cinderella.

For the scheme to aim to deliver family welfare certainly seems defensible as a matter of principle, moreover. As we have seen, a trust is needed for land to be concurrently owned, and doubtless land is concurrently owned most commonly when it is a family home. Looking at the jurisdiction in these terms, too, decisions taken under it stand a good chance of being inoffensive to the ECHR.[39]

So far, so good … but difficulties remain. First, 'family welfare' is not itself a single idea: it can be viewed in a number of ways. Since the considerations

---

[34] Trusts of Land and Appointment of Trustees Act 1996 s 15(3).

[35] s 15(1)(a).

[36] s 15(1)(b).

[37] s 15(1)(c).

[38] See further J Dewar, 'Land, Law, and the Family Home' in S Bright and J Dewar (eds), *Land Law – Themes and Perspectives* (Oxford, 1998) ch 13.

[39] Of course, in every case there will be a loser as well as a winner, and the decision in the winner's favour may engage ECHR First Protocol Art 1, and sometimes Art 8 too, as representing an interference with the loser's rights under these provisions. Though it may not: the 'interference' could be seen as merely picking up on an 'inherent limitation' in at any rate his First Protocol Art 1 rights (see § 2.3.3). In any event, all the considerations likely to be taken into account in the decision can be seen as proper ends to which (proportionate) preference can legitimately be given, so as commonly to justify any interference there may be.

in section 15 are relatively unspecific in content and in any event non-exhaustive, we cannot say just which idea the scheme adopts. Further, it is far from clear how we would in practice calibrate opposing considerations' promotion (or otherwise) of family welfare. They will surely often promote it (or not) in, simply, different – and incomparable – ways.[40]

Further, it is odd to make delivering family welfare the aim of a rule of trust law in this way. If we are seriously out to promote family welfare, we surely ought to go about this quite generally, rather than specifically targeting the trusts context: the welfare needs are the same, whether the home is concurrently owned or not.[41] At the same time, if the focus of the present jurisdiction is indeed family welfare, the jurisdiction is left having nothing to say about the many cases in which there is a trust of land, but the land held on trust is not a family home, so there is nothing at stake in terms of family welfare either way.

Moreover, if family welfare is the scheme's aim, it is hard to see how it can refer us – as it does – to the interests of secured creditors. The vindication of such interests, normally by selling the land, is likely to be categorically inimical to family welfare, at least in an immediate perspective. Yet such interests must inevitably enter into the calculus, otherwise credit could not realistically be secured on beneficial interests in land in the first place, with injurious effects on its availability and/or cost. For such interests to be (therefore) included in the calculus, the jurisdiction's focus must be set at a higher level of abstraction, to which both they and the family welfare considerations are germane. In *Mortgage Corporation v Shaire*,[42] it was correctly held that the Act requires the interests of secured creditors to be weighed against all other relevant considerations, thus positing the existence of such a focus, but no guidance was given as to its nature. In the individual case, no such guidance was necessary: sale was refused on the basis that the beneficiary opposing it bought out the secured interest, so that both she and the creditor should have been happy ... it is hard to see why the case came to court. Guidance is however needed for the more usual sort of litigated case where the beneficiary cannot afford such a solution and a choice has to be made. But the guidance has never been given; it is simply observable that secured creditors are normally awarded sale.[43]

---

[40] *cf* J Finnis, *Natural Law and Natural Rights* (2nd edn, Oxford, 2011) 423.

[41] So, where both the Trusts of Land and Appointment of Trustees Act 1996 and the Matrimonial Causes Act 1973 apply, the latter takes precedence: *Tee v Tee* [1999] 2 FLR 613 (CA). Likewise presumably the Children Act 1989.

[42] [2001] Ch 743 (Ch D).

[43] See eg *Bank of Ireland Home Mortgages Ltd v Bell* [2001] 2 FLR 809 (CA). In *C Putnam & Sons v Taylor* [2009] EWHC 317, [27]–[38] (Ch D), such an outcome was presented as possible notwithstanding its (assumed: *cf* n 39) interference with the opposing parties' ECHR interests (notably, under Art 8), as a proportionate means of delivering a proper end. The invocation of 'proportionality' gives a spurious appearance of rationality to the judgment: *cf* § 2.5.

In the end, then, we seem to have to abandon the hope of being able to make the judgements required by section 14 by calibrating considerations in terms of an aim of family welfare, or indeed anything else. We are returned to the thought that the jurisdiction requires the handling of incommensurables, as considered in § 10.2.4.[44]

16.2.6 The Special Case of Insolvency

The law deals separately with the case where one of the beneficiaries has become insolvent, and the court is asked by the bankruptcy authorities to order sale of the trust land so as to pay his creditors. Because the need to weigh the creditors' interests against other relevant considerations is evidently the very crux of this case, we might expect greater transparency about how the Act proposes the weighing be done. But again, it is elusive.

For the first year after the bankruptcy, the court has a task – and a problem – similar to that discussed above. It is required to take into account not only the claims of the creditors, but also all the other circumstances of the case (other than the needs of the bankrupt), including in particular, if the land in question is their home, the claims of the bankrupt's spouse or civil partner and children;[45] but the law does not declare the basis on which these various interests are to be compared. (Bizarrely from the viewpoint of the ordinary law of trusts, the provision makes no reference at all to the claims of other beneficiaries under the trust.) Thereafter, the court must order sale 'unless the circumstances of the case are exceptional'.[46] Even then, there is a choice. The court should still order sale unless the 'exceptional' circumstances are compelling enough to demand otherwise, reviving the same conundrum.[47]

---

[44] See further R Probert, '(Mis)interpreting the Trusts of Land and Appointment of Trustees Act 1996' in M Dixon and G Griffiths (eds), *Contemporary Perspectives on Property, Equity and Trusts Law* (Oxford, 2007) ch 4; L Fox, *Conceptualising Home – Theories, Laws and Policies* (Oxford, 2007); M Dixon, 'To Sell or Not To Sell: That is the Question' [2011] *CLJ* 579.

[45] Insolvency Act 1986 s 335A(2).

[46] s 335A(3). The courts have treated 'exceptional' as meaning 'unusual'. Exceptional circumstances were found, and sale refused, in *Claughton v Charalamabous* [1999] 1 FLR 740 (Ch D), where the bankrupt's spouse was severely disabled and the house had been adapted accordingly (see too *Judd v Brown* [1998] 2 FLR 360 (Ch D); *Re Rave* [1998] 2 FLR 718 (Ch D)). But the hardship to the bankrupt's family routinely associated with insolvency is (therefore) not 'exceptional', and not taken into consideration: *Re Citro* [1991] Ch 142 (CA). However, this reading of 'exceptional', which is not required by s 335A(3) itself, may well on appropriate facts lead a court to infringe ECHR Art 8, requiring respect for family life and homes except as proportionately required for, inter alia, the protection of the rights of others (here, the creditors' rights to the money owed them) – a calculation to which the 'usualness' of the circumstances seems irrelevant. In order to comply with their duty, as public authorities, to respect Art 8 (Human Rights Act 1998 s 6), courts should therefore abandon 'usualness' and conduct a more ad hoc examination of the rival (relevant) considerations and their strength in the individual case. See *Barca v Mears* [2004] EWHC 2170, [38]–[42] (Ch D); *Donohoe v Ingram* [2006] EWHC 282, [20]–[22] (Ch D).

[47] See further Fox (n 44).

16.3 Access to Particular Benefits 2: the Right to Occupy Trust Land

16.3.1 The Rules

Say you hold land on trust for John and Kate. Under certain circumstances, John and/or Kate will have a right to occupy it. This right is established by sections 12 and 13 of the Trusts of Land and Appointment of Trustees Act 1996.[48]

Under section 12, a beneficiary of a trust of land is 'entitled' to occupy that land if this is one of 'the purposes of the trust', or 'the land is held by the trustees so as to be' available for occupation by him, so long as it is in fact available and suitable. This rule evidently cuts back the discretion that, as we saw in § 16.2.1, the trustees otherwise have to decide the form in which the beneficiaries shall enjoy their interests. That said, the 'entitlement' to occupy is less solid than at first appears. The concepts in which the provisions' requirements are expressed ('purposes', 'held ... so as to be', 'available', 'suitable') lack conceptual clarity, and the facts at which they are aimed will often be disputable. So in practice, a significant degree of discretion creeps back in after all.

This is all the more so where section 12 gives two or more beneficiaries simultaneous 'entitlements' to occupy the same piece of land, but they cannot realistically do so. In such a case, the trustees must choose which of the beneficiaries shall occupy.[49] In making their choice, the trustees must act reasonably,[50] and have regard to, alongside possible other considerations, the intentions with which the trust was made; the purposes for which they currently hold the land; and the circumstances and wishes of the entitled beneficiaries.[51] However, a beneficiary already occupying the trust land cannot be removed except by a court order.[52]

16.3.2 An Objection

There is a major objection to these provisions. Contrary to the law's ordinary thinking, as explained in § 16.2.1, they may require outcomes that are not even-handed among the beneficiaries.

[48] See further Smith (n 20) ch 7, and other contributions reviewed there; S Pascoe, 'Right to Occupy under a Trust of Land: Muddled Legislative Logic' [2006] *Conv* 54.
[49] s 13(1).
[50] s 13(2).
[51] s 13(4).
[52] s 13(7).

Where their requirements are (held to be) satisfied, the provisions allow one beneficiary to occupy the trust land despite the loss this may cause other beneficiaries, relative to the land being treated as an investment. Say you hold the land on trust for John and Kate concurrently. If you rent the land out, the resulting income will go to John and Kate in their due shares. But if John occupies, and if as a result Kate gets nothing, they will not have been treated even-handedly.

At first sight, there seems to be an answer to this complaint, in the shape of a set of rules whereby the beneficiary who is chosen to occupy can be made to pay compensation to his fellow beneficiaries.[53] The compensation that John will thus pay Kate will restore even-handedness after all. But the compensation rules are organised in such a way that even-handedness may not in fact always be secured.

The first problem is that the rules give no real guidance as to how this compensation's quantum should be fixed. Here too, the trustees must have regard to, inter alia, the intentions with which the trust was made, the purposes for which they currently hold the land, and the circumstances and wishes of the entitled beneficiaries.[54] To the extent that this tells us anything of relevance at all, it clearly suggests that even-handedness among the beneficiaries is not the sole, or even the dominant, consideration. It is commonly assumed that, in practice, the main consideration will be the market rental value of the house in question,[55] which sounds more promising, but even this yardstick can be problematic. Say the house is modest in itself, so that its rental value is unremarkable, but it is strategically placed in redevelopment terms, so that it has a high sale (and hence reinvestment) value. Kate will not be treated even-handedly – on the contrary, she will subsidise John – if you choose John to occupy and require him to pay Kate no more than the rental value.

Moreover, the rules do not provide for John to compensate Kate at all unless Kate too is entitled to occupy the house under the Act's scheme, but you have 'excluded' her entitlement,[56] subordinating it to John's. Yet Kate is nonetheless a beneficiary, and the absence of compensation will mean that she is not treated even-handedly. Say John and Kate have successive interests, as in a trust 'for John for life, then for Kate'. John has the right to occupy during his lifetime, so you must allow him to do so, but Kate does not,[57] so John cannot be made to compensate her.

---

[53] s 13(6); see S Bright, 'Occupation Rents and the Trusts of Land and Appointment of Trustees Act 1996: From Property to Welfare?' [2009] *Conv* 378. The trustees may impose other kinds of condition too, including a requirement that the occupying beneficiary pays the outgoings on the land: s 13(3), (5).

[54] s 13(4).

[55] Compare *Stack v Dowden* [2007] 2 AC 432, [154], [157] (HL), depicting this as the usual yardstick where compensation is assessed by a court.

[56] s 13(6).

[57] Her interest is not 'in possession', as required for an entitlement to occupy under s 12(1).

All should be well if the trust property is the freehold ownership of the house, as, even though in the meantime you retain it for John's occupation, it will meet Kate's essential need for an investment asset that at least maintains its real value over John's life. Not so, however, if the trust property is for example a 99-year lease of the house, for this will diminish in value over John's life. To safeguard Kate's interest in succeeding to capital whose real worth is at least as great as when the trust begins, your natural course would be to sell the lease, and invest the proceeds so as to secure their real capital value for Kate and also to pay an income to John. If the house is to be retained for John's use, John should have to pay such sums as will produce an equivalent result for Kate. But given Kate's lack of an entitlement to occupy, the Act does not provide for you to require him to do so.

Equally, say John and Kate have concurrent interests, but the house you hold for them is a multi-storey house, which is suitable for occupation by John . . . but not by Kate, who is disabled and needs a bungalow. Under the Act, the fact that the house is unsuitable for Kate means that she is not entitled to occupy it, which in turn means that, although you must allow John to occupy it, there is no provision for requiring him to pay compensation to Kate. She is therefore not treated even-handedly. Likewise if the house was suitable for occupation by Kate as much as by John, but you did not 'exclude' her from occupying, because she was reticent about even asking to do so. Further, you must not require John to compensate Kate if, or to the extent that, he is likely not to be able to afford to do so, and therefore have to forego his own occupancy.[58]

So, in its provisions giving beneficiaries a right to occupy trust land, the 1996 Act derogates from the ordinary law's requirement that trust assets be managed in a manner that is even-handed as between beneficiaries. Is there a principled basis for this derogation? Presumably, the right to occupy can be ascribed to a concern to vindicate people's rights to their home. That is a proper project for the law. But so is the even-handed treatment of beneficiaries: a departure from this principle is in effect a confiscation of one beneficiary's rights for the benefit of another. If the two principles conflict, the law can legitimately treat the former as capable of taking precedence over the latter, but to treat it as automatically doing so, as the 1996 Act largely does, is objectionable because so crude.[59] And not only in general terms, but also from the point of view of the ECHR. Any departure from even-handedness

---

[58] s 13(7).

[59] In *Nestle v National Westminster Bank plc* [1993] 1 WLR 1260, 1279 (CA), the duty to treat beneficiaries even-handedly was reformulated as a duty to be 'fair', and was said to allow trustees to favour one beneficiary over another so as to redress an imbalance between the two beneficiaries' other wealth. Even if it were uncontroversial in itself (which it is not), this position would not justify the approach of the Trusts of Land and Appointment of Trustees Act 1996. The 'fairness' rule requires the trustees to consider the relative claims of the individual beneficiaries involved, whereas the Act discriminates against classes of beneficiary defined without reference to their deserts.

appears to be an interference with the detrimentally affected beneficiary's possessions, engaging Article 1 of the First Protocol. A particular departure may nonetheless be justified if it represents the proportionate pursuit of some other appropriate goal. But it is unlikely that one could say that of a blanket rule such as that under discussion.[60]

There may be a partial answer to this objection to the 1996 Act. Remember that the problem arises from the combination, in the Act, of a right allowing one beneficiary (John) to occupy, to the financial disadvantage of another (Kate), without sufficient provision for redressing that disadvantage. Outside the Act, however, there exists a wider mechanism, known as 'accounting', which may be usable to redress the disadvantage in at least some cases. Accounting was commonly used before 1996, in cases where two beneficiaries had once lived together in the same house, but one had moved out as it was no longer realistic for them to cohabit,[61] to require the other to pay 'rent' for having the house to himself. Some of its territory – the case where both parties have a right to occupy under the 1996 Act and the trustees choose one of them over the other – has now been taken over by the Act's own compensation provision.[62] But accounting remains available in all other cases where parties have concurrent interests in land but cannot realistically be expected to occupy it together.[63] It would, then, avail Kate in the case where she and John have concurrent interests, but due to her disability she has no statutory right to occupy, and so no statutory claim to compensation. It would not, however, avail her in the case we took first, where her interest is successive to John's. In this case, she could not expect to occupy at all during John's life: so neither the statutory provision, nor accounting, can help her. Our objection to the approach taken by the 1996 Act thus remains.

16.3.3 Intervention by the Court

In the event of dissatisfaction with the trustees' decisions under sections 12 and 13, the court can be asked to substitute decisions of its own, under the jurisdiction conferred by section 14 of the 1996 Act, discussed in §§ 16.2.2–

---

[60] Whether this objection could in practice be brought home might be thought to depend on whether the Human Rights Act 1998 gives 'horizontal effect' to ECHR rights; see § 2.2. Since the objectionable departure from even-handedness is less *permitted to* trustees than, by the terms of the 1996 Act, *required of* them, this may be thought a case of positive interference with the detrimentally affected beneficiary's possessions on the part of the state itself, susceptible to attack under ss 3, 4 of the 1998 Act. There is of course the further possible difficulty that the impact on the detrimentally affected beneficiary may be seen as picking up on an 'inherent limitation' in his right (§ 2.3.3).

[61] As where their relationship had broken down: *Dennis v McDonald* [1982] Fam 63 (Fam D and CA); *Bernard v Josephs* [1982] Ch 391 (CA).

[62] In this case, the old accounting mechanism has been superseded by the statutory provision: *Stack v Dowden* [2007] 2 AC 432, [94], [150] (HL).

[63] *Byford v Butler* [2003] EWHC 1267 (Ch D); *French v Barcham* [2008] EWHC 1505 (Ch D).

16.2.5. So the court can overrule the trustees' judgements about whether the conditions under which a right of occupation arises are satisfied, and about which of two or more entitled beneficiaries shall occupy, and about the terms upon which he shall do so.

In exercising this jurisdiction, the court is once again required (under section 15) to have regard to a set of considerations wider than that to which sections 12 and 13 explicitly direct the trustees themselves. The principal extension is that the court must attend to the welfare of minor children who live in the house or might reasonably be expected to do so.[64] The pattern identified and discussed in §§ 16.2.4–16.2.5 is thus found again here. Bearing in mind the reference to children's welfare, we may be inclined once more to think of the discretion as one aimed at delivering family welfare. We reviewed the strengths and weaknesses of such a vision in § 16.2.5, but at all events it ought to count as an appropriate goal in which to interfere with the detrimentally affected beneficiaries' possessions for the purposes of the ECHR. There is a snag in the present context, however. Here the court is standing in for the trustees under sections 12 and 13. As we have seen, these sections largely *require* an interference with beneficiaries' rights. So even if the interference is aimed at achieving (what is regarded as) an appropriate goal, it is likely at times not to represent a proportionate means of doing so, and will thus be open to challenge in the way discussed in § 16.3.2.[65]

Although, as we have seen,[66] section 14 appears to address the exercise by the court of functions *possessed by the trustees*, not to give the court additional powers, it is generally viewed as going further in one very important respect relating to occupation. If it only allowed the court to exercise functions possessed by the trustees, it would not allow the court to override a right to occupy – to say that, despite the requirements of section 12 being satisfied, no beneficiary is to occupy the land.[67] The commentators, however, appear to think, on the contrary, that the court *can* order sale in such cases.[68] The issue seems not to have been explicitly litigated so far. In certain cases, notably *Mortgage Corporation v Shaire*,[69] it logically should have been, but was not: although the court seems to have assumed, with the commentators, that it can order sale despite an occupation right.

Although apparently excluded by its wording, this view certainly makes the best sense of section 14. Most section 14 disputes will be over the question

---

[64]   s 15(1)(c); omitted (but *quaere* why) from s 13(4).

[65]   Here, moreover, the challenge may be put under the Human Rights Act 1998 s 6, as being to the act of a public authority, namely the court.

[66]   At nn 19–20 above.

[67]   Such a possibility might seem to be contemplated by s 13(7), providing that, if a beneficiary currently occupies the trust land, the trustees can evict him *if the court so approves*. But s 13(7) makes it clear that the eviction (if the court approves it) occurs under the trustees' s 13(1) power to choose which of two beneficiaries, each entitled to occupy, may do so. Section 13(7) does not, therefore, allow the court – any more than the trustees – to exclude both, in order to sell.

[68]   See eg Smith (n 20) 157.

[69]   [2001] Ch 743 (Ch D).

whether the land should be sold, and the party opposing sale will very often have a right to occupy. So unless section 14 allows the court to override that right, the practical scope of section 14 is small.

This view is also the more desirable stance for the law in terms of substantive justice, as allowing the court to address the concerns expressed in § 16.3.2 regarding the absolute right of occupation.[70] Even-handedness may well require the land to be sold. So may considerations of family welfare: as where a house is held for a couple; their relationship having broken down, they need to find separate accommodation; to this end, at least one of them needs to take their entitlement in the form of money; and this cannot be delivered without selling the existing house. The court should therefore be able to order sale despite a beneficiary having a right to occupy, and insisting on it. Better still, of course, the occupation 'entitlement' should itself be abolished, so that in any case, trustees and courts can allow occupation outside the circumstances determined by the ordinary law of trusts only as a matter of discretion, where to do so represents a proportionate means of achieving some other appropriate goal.[71]

16.4 Trust Rights' Effectiveness against Disponees

At least some[72] of the obligations and rights arising under every trust are in rem, and thus capable of binding disponees of the land or other property to

---

[70] Provisions regarding occupation and allowing the various considerations to be weighed against each other in this way are to be found in the Family Law Act 1996. Commentators assume that even where the land in question is the subject of a trust, thus attracting the Trusts of Land and Appointment of Trustees Act 1996, it is the Family Law Act that takes precedence. This may matter even if the former allows the court to order sale despite a right to occupy, as the considerations to be taken into account differ a little between the two Acts. But it certainly matters if this is not the case, for then the right to occupy, if absolute under the Trusts of Land and Appointment of Trustees Act, turns out not to be absolute after all. The Acts themselves, however, say nothing about their interrelationship.

[71] It might be argued, contrary to the position taken in the text, that s 12 already has this shape. Say you hold a house for John and Kate, and that at first sight, the s 12 requirements are satisfied, giving John a right to occupy, even though your duty to treat your beneficiaries even-handedly, or the court's family welfare responsibilities under s 14, would otherwise indicate selling the house. The argument is that the factors indicating sale make the house 'unavailable' for occupation, with the result that the s 12 requirements are not satisfied after all, and that John has no right to occupy. The problem with the argument, however, is that it leaves the 'right' to occupy surprisingly narrow. On this reading, the right would arise and make a difference only where, although Kate does not agree that John should occupy, her reasons are subjective, rather than justified complaints in terms of even-handedness or family welfare.

[72] For the point that only some trust obligations and rights are in rem, while others are in personam, see R Nolan, 'Equitable Property' (2006) 122 *LQR* 232; Gardner (n 1) 214–5.) The

which they relate.[73] So if you hold land on trust for John, then you transfer the land to Liam, Liam may in principle be bound by John's interest. As compared to the question whether a disponee is bound by any other kind of right in rem, however, the question whether Liam is in fact bound by John's trust right is an unusually complex one.

There are two principal issues, though each of them has a number of detailed aspects.

One of these issues is that to which we are by now accustomed: the message of the rules, mainly to be found in the Land Registration Act 2002, stating the circumstances in which a right that is capable of binding Liam will actually do so. This issue will be covered in § 16.7.

Before that, however, we need to explore the other issue: the possibility that John's right, while in principle a right in rem capable of binding Liam as a right affecting the land which Liam acquires, may become detached from the land ('overreached') as part of your transfer to Liam. If this occurs, John's right ceases to be capable of binding Liam after all, so we do not need to continue to the issue of whether Liam is in fact bound: he simply cannot be. We look at this issue next, therefore, in §§ 16.5–16.6.

Finally, in § 16.8 we shall come to a worked example, covering the various aspects of both issues, and offering a perspective on the topic as a whole.

16.5 Overreaching 1: the Key Ideas

The present group of sections looks at the idea of trust rights being overreached by a disposition, explaining what happens when they are, and giving an evaluation. When the disposition involves an impropriety, however, the rights may not be overreached after all (and so may endure to bind the disponee). We shall look at this complication in § 16.6.

---

point is important in establishing that trust rights conform with the *numerus clausus* principle. It does so by showing that such rights impact on a disponee only to the extent that the latter must recognise that the property in question is trust property and probably at some fairly low level look after it; if the trust's full performance requires anything more (which is usually the case, and where their variety becomes visible), the disponee is not called upon to deliver this, but must simply transfer the land to a proper trustee (whether the original trustee or one newly appointed for this purpose).The principal concern of this book is with those obligations and rights that are in rem.

[73] For the argument that, being equitable, trust rights and obligations must be 'persistent' rather than in rem, see § 1.3.

16.5.1 The Idea of Overreaching

When trustees dispose – properly – of a piece of property that they hold on trust, the beneficial rights, which would otherwise remain with the property, instead detach themselves from it, so that the disponee cannot be affected by them. Then the rights re-attach themselves, once more as rights in rem, to the replacement property (usually money) that the trustees receive from the disponee: it becomes the trust property instead.

This phenomenon is called 'overreaching'.[74] Overreaching is thus a device by which rights in rem are made, temporarily (ie in favour of a disponee under a proper disposition), to behave as though they were rights only in personam. On the strength of their susceptibility to overreaching, beneficial rights in land are sometimes said to lie behind a 'curtain', so that a disponee of the trust land cannot be affected by them.[75]

16.5.2 The Value of Overreaching

Trustees of land have a power to dispose of the land.[76] This enables them to deal with it in various ways that are potentially advantageous to their beneficiaries: to exchange it for other land, or turn it into cash, or rent it out, or secure loans against it. But the power to dispose would be valueless without overreaching.

By definition (as explained in § 15.1), trustees can have no beneficial interest in the trust property themselves: their obligations to the beneficiaries must be so exhaustive as to deny them any such interest. So if they sought to dispose of the property with these obligations (in other words, the beneficiaries' rights) still attached, so that the disponee became bound by them, the disponee could acquire nothing of value to him: he would become a mere trustee in turn. No one would want to take (buy, rent, accept a security right over) property from trustees in such circumstances. Coupling the power to dispose with overreaching transforms the picture, enabling a disposition of trust property to confer its full value on the disponee, and so opening up the possibility that someone might indeed want to take the property after all.

This matters not only for the story of an individual trust. By making it feasible for trustees to sell trust property, the combination of a power to dispose and overreaching also exposes trust property to the market, so benefiting the

---

[74] See too § 10.1.3.

[75] In the case of trusts of land, overreaching is provided for by the Law of Property Act 1925 s 2.

[76] As an aspect of their power to do anything that an ordinary owner can do, conferred by the Trusts of Land and Appointment of Trustees Act 1996 s 6(1). As explained in § 16.2, however, this power can be withdrawn or subjected to conditions by the settlor (s 8), and overridden by a court order (s 14), as well as by the agreement of the beneficiaries.

economy. Remember an inherent disadvantage of rights in rem: that they damage the economy by making the property to which they apply less exploitable, and therefore less valuable.[77] The ability to overreach beneficial interests on a disposition of trust property enables their in rem effect to be temporarily cancelled, undoing its capacity to do such damage.

The law's interjection of a statutory trust whenever I purport simply to transfer land to two or more people, as explained in § 15.4, springs from the same considerations. Without such a trust, the ownership of the land in question would be shared between the transferees, rather than held by trustees. This in turn would make the land less readily marketable, as someone wishing to buy it outright (and buying a lesser interest would not often be worthwhile) would need to deal with all the sharers: a relatively time-consuming and expensive task at best, and perhaps a fruitless one (an awkward individual could block the whole transaction, or at best hold it to ransom). The difficulty is exacerbated by the possibility of the sharers' interests being alienated to new owners. The interjection of a trust means that the title to the land is instead held by the trustees, and that the sharers' fragmentary interests take effect as beneficial rights. Adding a power for the trustees to dispose of the land and overreach the sharers' beneficial rights, the law allows the would-be disponee to acquire the land outright without dealing with the sharers – only with the trustees – after all.

16.5.3 The Settlor's and Beneficiaries' Perspective

For their part, a trust's settlor (if any) and beneficiaries will welcome a power to dispose and overreach if they see the – or a – point of the trust as being to provide money benefits. Say a farm is held on trust, and rented out so as to produce an income which the trustees then pay over to the beneficiary. The farm is essentially an investment, and it could be as valuable to the beneficiary to receive the profits from another piece of land, or indeed some other form of asset. A power to dispose and overreach enables the trustees to trade between assets so as to maximise the return to the beneficiary. *Mutatis mutandis*, a similar account can be given if the aim is to provide a residence for the beneficiary. It may benefit the beneficiary for the trust to be able to switch from one property to another, so as to gain a nicer home, or to take a new job in a different part of the country, or in response to a change in the make-up of his family.

But not all settlors and beneficiaries will want their trust's land to be tradable in this way. To take an extreme case, say a family's ancestral estate is held on trust for the members of the family. They may see the particular land in question as important in its own right and to be retained, rather than as to be

---

[77] § 1.2.2.

held only until something different is needed or wanted. Or take the more mundane case of an ordinary home held on trust because it is co-owned by a couple. While the couple will value the ability to dispose and overreach in principle, under particular circumstances at least one of them may prefer to be able to insist on the house being retained: above all, where they separate and, while one wants a sale so as to liquidate his share, the other wants to continue living in the same house.

At one time – before the late 19th century – the law did not insist on disposal and overreaching where these were unwelcome to the settlor and beneficiaries, and indeed did little to provide for them even where they were wanted. During this period, land was put in trust principally to secure its retention within a family in a dynastic fashion, something once seen as valuable. But eventually there emerged a political movement, with several bases, seeking to make land more exposed to the market.[78] To this end, the law (especially the Settled Land Act 1882) went to the other extreme, making rather rigorous provision for disposal and overreaching even where the settlor and beneficiaries did not want it. In effect, the law chose to conceive the dynastic trusts on which these new rules operated as about wealth rather than specifically land, and imposed this choice on settlors and beneficiaries.

Today, however, the law's position is different again. It has swung away from an insistence on disposal and overreaching. This is unsurprising, given how commonly ordinary homes will nowadays be held on trust. As we have seen (§ 15.4), in today's law, land owned by more than one person must be held on trust … and a very common case of this is where a couple co-own their home.

Under the current rules, then, there is full provision for disposal and overreaching where the beneficiaries do want it, but a preference to the contrary will be given respect, though it will sometimes be outweighed. The default rule remains that trustees have a power to dispose of the trust land and to overreach the beneficial interests.[79] But settlors can exclude this power,[80] or (normally a wiser course) allow it to stand but stipulate that it cannot be exercised without the consent of one or more identified individuals.[81] For their part, unless they are unanimous,[82] beneficiaries are unable to say that the land shall never be disposed of, or to veto a particular impending disposition; but they may be able to block it by asserting an occupation right inconsistent

[78] See H Perkin, 'Land Reform and Class Conflict in Victorian Britain' in J Butt and I Clarke (eds), *The Victorians and Social Protest* (Newton Abbott, 1973) 177; F Thompson, 'Land and Politics in England in the Nineteenth Century' (1965) *Transactions of the Royal Historical Society* 5th series, vol 15, 23.

[79] Trusts of Land and Appointment of Trustees Act 1996 s 6(1); Law of Property Act 1925 s 2(1).

[80] Trusts of Land and Appointment of Trustees Act 1996 s 8(1).

[81] *ibid.* If a required consent is withheld, however, the court has a discretion to supply it instead: s 14(2)(a).

[82] In which case they can invoke the rule in *Saunders v Vautier* (1841) 1 Cr & Ph 240 (Ch), enabling them to take control of the land and do what they like with it: see at nn 1–5 above.

with the proposed disposition, or by persuading the court to order against it. We reviewed the latter possibilities in §§ 16.2–16.3. The overall effect is that, while overreaching itself is not compromised, the underlying power to dispose is heavily qualified, presumably on the basis that the market advantages of a wider power are often outweighed by other considerations.[83]

16.5.4 Why does Overreaching Apply Only to Trust Interests?

Why does overreaching apply only to trust interests, and not to other kinds of right in rem? Say you own land that is subject to a lease or an easement in favour of John. When you transfer the land to Liam, why should not John's lease or easement, instead of binding Liam, likewise be converted into a right against the money Liam pays you?

One might answer, 'Because a right to occupy a specific piece of land, or to cross it, can exist only in respect of that specific piece of land. It cannot sensibly be turned into a right in money.' That is not correct, however. Rendition into money is possible: it happens whenever a lease or easement exists over land which is compulsorily purchased, and is itself bought out in the process. The key is rather the degree of usefulness that the law perceives in the particular type of right, relative to the damage that its attachment to the land will do.

In not applying overreaching to non-trust rights – leases, easements, etc – the law seems to have been persuaded of their net usefulness. This is no surprise. Each chapter in this Part has explored the reasons why such rights are allowed in rem status at all, despite the ensuing damage: these are also the reasons why the rights are not to be overreached. The same cannot necessarily be said for trusts, however. In their case, the question depends on the use to which they are in fact put. This explains the variable extent to which the law has in fact subjected them to overreaching. When they were used to service dynasties and this was thought to be all-important, overreaching was

---

[83]   Subject to issues of horizontal effect (§ 2.2), overreaching may represent a potential infringement of ECHR Art 8, as (in appropriate cases) depriving a beneficiary of his home, and First Protocol Art 1, as interfering with his 'possessions' in the shape of his right more generally to enjoy the trust property in its original form. But at least the latter proposition is contentious, in that overreaching could be seen as picking up on an 'inherent limitation' in the beneficial interest (§ 2.3.3). In any event, however, the effect described in the text – whereby, at any rate so far as trusts of land are concerned, the power to dispose is heavily qualified – means that overreaching stands a fair chance of being in practice justified, as operating in the proportionate promotion of an appropriate goal. Nonetheless, the material generating that effect could usefully be given a more transparent alignment with these considerations. (At one time, it was proposed that the interest of a beneficiary in occupation of the trust land should not be overreached without his consent, or judicial permission: Law Commission, *Overreaching: Beneficiaries in Occupation* (Law Com No 188, London, 1989). But this proposal was not reflected in the subsequent legislation, namely the Trusts of Land and Appointment of Trustees Act 1996.) On all this, see A Goymour, 'Property and Housing' in D Hoffman (ed) *The Impact of the UK Human Rights Act on Private Law* (Cambridge, 2011) ch 12, 281, 288, 297.

not emphasised. When the priority became the exposure of land to the market, it was. With their contemporary role of allowing the co-ownership of family homes, the balance has changed again, and, as we have seen, over-reaching has once more been de-emphasised.

16.6 Overreaching 2: the Effect of Impropriety

At the start of § 16.5.1, it was explained that overreaching occurs when trustees 'properly' dispose of land that they hold on trust. The word 'properly' requires some attention, to see when a disposition counts as improper. We also need to explore what happens if trustees make (or purport to make) such an improper disposition.

16.6.1 'Impropriety'

A number of duties bind trustees as they make a disposition of trust land. For example, if the terms of a trust require the trustees to obtain a certain person's consent before making the disposition in question, the trustees have a duty to do so.[84] The trustees must act only in the interests of the beneficiaries:[85] so they will act wrongfully if, for example, they mortgage the land to secure a loan which they plan to spend on themselves. Trustees of land are often required to consult their beneficiaries before making a disposition of it.[86] And in making the disposition, they must exercise appropriate care and skill (say, in negotiating the price).[87] The most celebrated among these duties is, however, that of ensuring that any money produced by the disposition – eg the price for which the land is sold – is paid to at least two trustees.[88] This duty is known as the 'two-trustee rule', and is said to exist to protect the beneficiaries, by lessening the chances of the purchase money being embezzled.[89]

If the trustees act contrary to such duties, they will certainly be in breach of trust, entitling their beneficiaries to sue them for an injunction to prevent the behaviour in question, or for financial relief against its consequences.

---

[84] Trusts of Land and Appointment of Trustees Act 1996 s 8(2).

[85] *Cowan v Scargill* [1985] Ch D 270 (Ch); *Hayim v Citibank NA* [1987] AC 730 (PC), applied to trusts of land by the Trusts of Land and Appointment of Trustees Act 1996 s 6(5) and (6).

[86] *ibid* s 11. 'Often', because this section lists a number of exceptions.

[87] *ibid* s 6(9).

[88] Law of Property Act 1925 s 27.

[89] *City of London Building Society v Flegg* [1988] AC 54, 73–4 (HL).

There may also be implications for the disponee. Our focus is on the latter issue. It needs to be considered in terms of two contrasting scenarios: where the duty in question is noted on the register by means of a 'restriction' (§ 16.6.3), and where it is not (§§ 16.6.4–16.6.5).[90]

16.6.2 Restrictions

A 'restriction' is an entry on the register recording the duty.[91] The law allows such an entry to be made precisely so as to help ensure that the duty is obeyed. But it seems that not all duties relevant to dispositions of trust land can be recorded by a restriction. A restriction can be entered only if, in the nature of the duty, obedience can be easily verified by the Registry staff.[92]

This will be so, and a restriction can therefore be entered, in the case of the duty to pay two trustees, and a duty to obtain someone's consent before making a disposition. It will be plain whether or not these duties have been obeyed. But it is otherwise in the case of the duty to act solely in the beneficiaries' interests, or to exercise due care and skill. It is impossible for the Registry staff to verify whether these duties have been obeyed: even if the staff can discover all the relevant facts, deciding whether these amount to obedience involves applying the relevant rule, and that requires the exercise of judgement, which is vested solely in a court with appropriate jurisdiction.

So in terms of our two scenarios, the first (where the duty is noted by a restriction on the register) will involve duties which are of the former kind and which have been registered. The second scenario (where the duty is not noted by a restriction on the register) will involve duties which are of the former kind and so could have been registered, but have not been; together with duties of the latter kind, which simply cannot be registered.

16.6.3 The First Scenario: Where there is a Restriction

If a restriction has been entered and the duty to which it refers is obeyed, the disposition of course goes through, and the trust rights are overreached, as explained in § 16.5.1. However, if a restriction has been entered but (the Registry staff conclude) the duty to which it refers is *not* obeyed, the disposition is generally blocked.[93] There will then be no question of overreaching:

---

[90] The rules discussed are those for registered land. The position of unregistered land is not dissimilar in overall effect, but different techniques are used to achieve this. See principally the Trusts of Land and Appointment of Trustees Act 1996 s 16.

[91] Land Registration Act 2002 s 42.

[92] *ibid* s 43 forbids the entering of restrictions unless checking on compliance 'would . . . be straightforward, and . . . not place an unreasonable burden on [Registry staff]'.

[93] *ibid* s 41. Specifically, the disposition cannot be registered. But (s 27) in the case of freehold transfers, leases for more than seven years and ordinary mortgages, registration is required for the disposition to take effect at all.

the land will remain with the trustees, and beneficial rights will continue to bind it in their hands.

Say you and I are trustees of a piece of land for John, and are in the course of transferring it to Liam. If the register contains a restriction noting that a disponee of this piece of land must pay two trustees, and Liam pays us both, the transfer will be successful: Liam will acquire the land, and John's interest will be overreached. But if there is such a restriction but Liam pays only one of us, Liam will not acquire the land at all, and John's interest will continue to bind it in our hands. Likewise if there is a restriction noting that John's consent is required before we can make the transfer. If John does consent, the transfer will be successful and will overreach John's interest; but otherwise, the transfer will simply fail, and there will be no question of overreaching.

16.6.4 The Second Scenario: Where there is No Restriction

The second scenario is that where the duty has *not* been recorded by a restriction, no matter whether or not it could have been.

If the duty is obeyed, the lack of a restriction is irrelevant: the disposition goes through and the beneficial interests are overreached. It is where the duty is not obeyed that the complications start. The relevant law was changed in 2002. But the new rules appear not simply to replace the old ones, so we need to look at both.

Before 2002, when an improperly made disposition of trust land was not prevented by a restriction, the disposition took effect; but sometimes without overreaching the beneficial rights. Say you and I held land on trust for John, and had a duty not to dispose of it without John's consent, but this duty was not registered. Say then that, without obtaining John's consent, we purported to transfer the land to Liam. The transfer to Liam succeeded, but John's right was not overreached (and so could go on to bind Liam). The icon of this set of rules was the decision of the House of Lords in *Williams & Glyn's Bank Ltd v Boland*,[94] where overreaching was blocked by a breach of the two-trustee rule (and the unoverreached right went on to bind the disponee). But while we know that improprieties of these two kinds – failure to obtain consent, and breach of the two-trustee rule – blocked overreaching, we are less sure about others, such as failure by the trustees to act solely in the beneficiaries' interests, or to exercise due care and skill, in making the disposition. It is possible that in these cases, the impropriety had no impact on the disposition

---

[94] [1981] AC 487 (HL). For a challenge to the decision's correctness, however, see N Jackson, 'Overreaching in Registered Land Law' (2006) 69 *MLR* 214 (and 'Overreaching and Unauthorised Dispositions of Registered Land' [2007] *Conv* 120). For more on the relationship between the two-trustee rule and overreaching, see *City of London Building Society v Flegg* [1988] AC 54 (HL).

at all: that the disposition not only took effect, but also overreached the beneficial interests, notwithstanding the impropriety.[95]

The change that occurred in 2002 was the arrival of section 26 of the Land Registration Act 2002. By this section (with the possible, but enormous, exception addressed in a moment), the previous law's blocks on overreaching are lifted. The section achieves this by ruling that a duty unprotected by a restriction is to be treated, vis-à-vis a disponee,[96] as if it never existed.

So: (there being no restriction) the disposition continues to take effect, as before, but now the beneficial interests are always overreached, despite the impropriety. In other words, a breach of a duty regarding the disposition of trust land *cannot* result in the disposition taking effect but without the beneficial interests being overreached, so that the disponee is bound by them. If the duty is protected by a restriction, its breach means that the disposition will fail altogether. If the duty is not protected by a restriction, then, notwithstanding the breach, section 26 ensures that the disposition takes effect and that the beneficial interests are overreached after all.

Except, perhaps, where the impropriety is of one particular, but very important, kind: a breach of the two-trustee rule. The relationship between section 26 and this rule has not yet received attention from the courts, but has been much discussed by commentators.[97] There is a consensus among the latter that the section does not apply to such a breach. If this is right, the pre-2002 position – that such a breach blocks overreaching – continues to prevail: the law continues to be as it was stated by the pre-2002 decision in *Williams & Glyn's Bank Ltd v Boland*,[98] which itself involved a breach of the two-trustee rule. That is, (there being no restriction) the disposition takes effect, but the

---

[95] In theory, the effect of such other improprieties could be gathered from the wording of the relevant provisions of the Trusts of Land and Appointment of Trustees Act 1996, but in practice the wording gave no clear indication. For an effort to quarry answers nonetheless, see G Ferris and G Battersby, 'The General Principles of Overreaching and the Modern Legislative Reforms 1996–2002' (2003) 119 *LQR* 94, 95–108; but the arguments used there often seem strained.

[96] The duty continues to apply between the trustee(s) and the beneficiaries, so disobeying it continues to operate as a breach of trust by the trustee(s), who can be sued for this by the beneficiaries. Moreover, if the disponee helps the trustee(s) to break the duty (perhaps even simply by taking the transfer of the land), and does so 'dishonestly', he can be sued for the breach alongside the trustee(s), in 'dishonest assistance': see Gardner (n 1) 260–4. It is additionally possible that a disponee who acquires the land with an 'unconscionable' awareness or lack of awareness of the beneficial interests will also be liable to the beneficiaries for the loss arising from the interests' failure to affect him as rights in rem, in 'knowing receipt'. But the nature of this liability is controversial. The preferable understanding (*ibid* 281–2; S Gardner, 'Moment of Truth for Knowing Receipt?' (2009) 125 *LQR* 20) is that it reacts to losses arising from breaches of trust on the part of those who, receiving trust property from trustees, are bound by the beneficial interests as rights in rem. Disponees protected by s 26 are precisely not so bound, for on the section's assumption that the duty in question never existed, the disposition takes effect and the beneficial interests are overreached. See further M Conaglen and A Goymour, 'Knowing Receipt and Registered Land' in C Mitchell (ed), *Constructive and Resulting Trusts* (Oxford, 2010) ch 5.

[97] The fullest account is G Ferris, 'Making Sense of Section 26 of the Land Registration Act 2002' in E Cooke (ed), *Modern Studies in Property Law, Volume 2* (Oxford, 2003) ch 6.

[98] [1981] AC 487 (HL).

beneficial rights are not overreached: they remain with the land as rights in rem capable of binding the disponee.[99]

16.6.5 Does, and Should, Section 26 Apply Where there is a Breach of the Two-trustee Rule?

The wording of section 26 gives little or no support to the view that it does not apply to breaches of the two-trustee rule.[100] Beyond that, however, *ought* such breaches to remain – as the consensus has it – outside section 26, so that, in this case (alone), the beneficial interests can survive the impropriety and be capable of binding the disponee? Arguably so. The argument runs as follows.

As we saw in § 16.6.4, under the pre-2002 law (as exemplified by *Williams & Glyn's Bank Ltd v Boland*[101]), a disponee could be affected by an impropriety, by taking the land but with the beneficial interests still attached. This was objectionable in that, the duty in question not being recorded by a restriction, the disponee might not have been able to anticipate the problem and avert this damaging outcome. The issue of the two-trustee rule apart, section 26 means that this can no longer occur. Either the duty in question will be recorded by a restriction, in which case a breach of it will block the disposition itself, but the disponee will have every opportunity to anticipate the problem and avert this outcome by noticing the restriction and complying with it to ensure that there is no breach. Or there will be no restriction, in which case a breach will not affect the disponee at all: the disposition will take effect and the beneficial interests will be overreached.

It might be asked, 'Why do we need section 26 to ensure that a disponee can anticipate difficulty over an impropriety? Under the pre-2002 rule, even if the impropriety meant the beneficial interest not being overreached, the

---

[99] This position was argued in *National Westminster Bank plc v Malhan* [2004] EWHC 847 (Ch D) to mean that where beneficial rights *are* overreached, as a result of compliance with the two-trustee rule, there is an infringement of ECHR Art 14. Art 14 proscribes unwarrantable discrimination in respect of Convention rights: here, the beneficiary's rights to enjoyment of his possessions (the trust property in its original form), and his home (if he lives in the trust property) (ECHR First Protocol Art 1, and Art 8, respectively.) The unwarrantable discrimination was said to lie in the way that a beneficiary suffers overreaching only if payment is made to two trustees, not if it is made to one. The judgment (at [45]–[49]) records the argument, but (at [53]) appears unenthused by it.

[100] See Ferris and Battersby(n 95) 120–2; Smith (n 20) 192–8. Perhaps the best argument is as follows. Under s 26, a disponee is unaffected by any (unregistered) 'limitation' upon the disponor, ie the trustee. The word 'limitation' is apt to refer to duties of the trustee, such as a duty to obtain a certain consent. But it is not apt to refer to the two-trustee rule, which operates as a demand upon the disponee rather than as a duty of the trustee. This argument seems unsuccessful, however, for two reasons. First, because the two-trustee rule probably does involve a duty of the trustee (if you are a single trustee, you may not try to make a disposition without securing the appointment of a colleague). Second, even if that is wrong, because the word 'limitation' is capable of referring not only to duties of the trustee, but also to rules otherwise controlling the effect of a trustee's disposition . . . notably the two-trustee rule.

[101] [1981] AC 487 (HL).

interest did not actually bind the disponee unless the beneficiary was in actual and apparent[102] occupation of the land,[103] and surely this alerted the disponee to the potential problem?'

For most improprieties, however, this was not the case. Certainly, the disponee could discover the beneficiary's *occupation*, and so his interest, in the manner described. But this did not normally alert the disponee to the risk of an *impropriety*, and so to the risk of that interest actually *binding* him, rather than being harmlessly overreached. (Some duties apply only to some trusts: such as a duty to obtain a consent. Other duties apply to all trusts, but the disponee would not know whether the trustees were in breach: such as the duties to act solely in the beneficiaries' interests, and to exercise due care and skill.) Section 26 was needed, therefore, so as to protect the disponee against surprise, in the manner described.

Breaches of the two-trustee rule are different, however. Unlike other duties, not only does this rule apply to nearly[104] every disposition of trust land, but a breach of it will also be obvious to the disponee. So in this instance, the disponee, aware of the beneficial interest itself, can also anticipate the risk of being bound by it, and act to avert this risk. The additional protection of section 26 is unnecessary.

Indeed, not only is it unnecessary: it would be positively inappropriate. If the disponee can (despite the absence of a restriction) anticipate the impropriety in this way, it is right to expect him to play his part in averting it, for the sake of the beneficiary, whom the duty exists to protect. Applying section 26 in such circumstances would relieve him of that responsibility.

In this way, then, the consensus view – that section 26 does not apply to breaches of the two-trustee rule, and that the pre-2002 decision in *Williams & Glyn's Bank Ltd v Boland*[105] remains, on its (two-trustee rule) facts, good law – can be supported.

16.7 Binding Disponees

As a result of the rules about restrictions and section 26, then, if a disposition of trust land takes effect at all, the beneficial rights will at least normally be

---

[102] In fact, the pre-2002 rule required only actual occupation, but its counterpart today requires the occupation also to be apparent (Land Registration Act 2002 Sch 3 para 2). The question is whether this was the only adjustment needed, leaving s 26 unnecessary.

[103] Thereby allowing the unoverreached interest to bind the disponee as an overriding interest: see further § 16.7.

[104] It does not apply if the disposition does not produce purchase money, as for example where the land is exchanged for other land: *State Bank of India v Sood* [1997] Ch 276 (CA).

[105] [1981] AC 487 (HL).

overreached and so be incapable of affecting the disponee. But the position may be different where the disponee pays the purchase money to only one trustee. If there was no restriction requiring payment to two trustees, the disposition will take effect. And if breaches of the two-trustee rule lie outside the scope of section 26 (as the commentators think, but it is far from certain), overreaching will be blocked. So in this case (alone), the beneficial rights will remain attached to the land and capable, as rights in rem, of binding the disponee.

Whether, in such a case, the beneficial rights actually do bind the disponee depends on the usual rules regarding the operation of rights in rem. Two issues require attention. First (§ 16.7.1), how do the relevant rules in the Land Registration Act 2002 apply to such rights? Then (§ 16.7.2), how does the consent principle described in Chapter 4 (that if the holder of a right consents to its not binding the disponee, it will not do so) apply to these rights?

16.7.1 Unoverreached Beneficial Rights as Overriding Interests

There is no question of the beneficial rights binding through registration. They cannot be registered by notice.[106] This is because, if a right is protected by a notice, it necessarily binds a disponee. In the case of a trust right, as we saw in § 16.5.2, the preferred outcome is that the right is overreached, so that the disponee is not bound. If those involved with the trust are able to register it, therefore, they must do so by a restriction,[107] the effect of which is – as explained in § 16.6.3 – to ensure that, if a disposition of the trust land occurs at all, the rights under the trust will be overreached. But if the rights are overreached, there will, by definition, be no question of them binding the disponee. So in thinking about whether unoverreached beneficial rights will bind a disponee, we are necessarily concerned with the case where there is no registration. The remaining question, then, is whether the rights operate as overriding interests.

This question is answered by reference to schedule 3 of the Land Registration Act 2002. The schedule makes no specific mention of beneficial rights, but they can qualify under paragraph 2, which gives overriding effect to a right in rem if (with some exceptions) its owner is in actual and apparent occupation of the land in question at the time of the disposition. If the beneficiary is in actual and apparent occupation of the trust land when the trustees dispose of it, his unoverreached right will therefore generally operate as an overriding interest to bind the disponee.

This is appropriate. A breach of the two-trustee rule is most likely to occur when the trust in question has only one trustee. This is in turn likely to be

---

[106] Land Registration Act 2002 s 33(a).
[107] *ibid*, s 42.

where the trust is a constructive (or resulting) one: as for example where you are the registered owner of your and John's family home, and agree with John that he should have a share in it, which creates a constructive trust under the doctrine explored in § 9.3. Beneficial rights under constructive (or resulting) trusts clearly arise in a disorganised way. As a result, it is neither reasonable to expect nor sensible to require their registration (in this case, via a restriction). As explained in §§ 3.2.2–3.2.3, therefore, it is right that they should be able to operate instead as overriding interests, at any rate where actual and apparent occupation makes them discoverable.

In a case of this kind, too, it is extremely common for John to live in the house. The possibility of a disponee being bound by John's right, on account of a breach of the two-trustee rule together with John's being in actual and apparent occupation, is therefore a routine one.

16.7.2 The Consent Principle

One final issue. Say you hold land on trust for John, then transfer it (on your own, and therefore in breach of the two-trustee rule) to Liam. Assuming that section 26 of the Land Registration Act 2002 does not apply and that the transfer therefore takes effect without John's beneficial right being overreached (§§ 16.6.4–16.6.5), and that John is in actual and apparent occupation of the land (§ 16.7.1), John's right will bind Liam as an overriding interest … unless John has consented to its not doing so.

The rule that an interest that would otherwise bind a disponee can be 'postponed' by consent in this way[108] is explained in detail in Chapter 4.

Although in principle this rule can apply to any kind of right in rem, it is especially associated with trust rights. It will normally be possible to find an *implied* consent only where you (the disponor) and John (the owner of the right) are closely connected, in such a way that Liam (the disponee) will understandably read the disposition as a shared project between you and John (§ 4.2.1). This will be the case almost exclusively where the land is your and John's shared home, and, given this, the right in question (John's right in the land, whose postponement to Liam's right John assents to) will most commonly be a beneficial interest. In fact, a putative disponee will commonly seek the safety of an *express* consent, by proceeding with the transaction only when all occupants of the land in question have signed a form postponing their rights (if any) to his. Again, it is only where the disponor (you) and the owner of the right (John) are closely connected in this way that such a signature is likely to be forthcoming: someone whose interests were not aligned with the disponor's would have no reason to supply it.

---

[108] *Bristol and West Building Society v Henning* [1985] 1 WLR 778 (CA); *Paddington Building Society v Mendelsohn* (1985) 50 P & CR 244 (CA).

16.8 A Worked Example, and an Appraisal

16.8.1 A Worked Example

Sections 16.5–16.7 show that beneficial rights under trusts thus affect disponees of the land in question according to more complex rules than other
rights in rem in land. It may be helpful to work through an illustration covering the issue as a whole, together with its possible consequences.

In our discussions so far, the disposition has tended to be instanced as a
transfer of the trust land. But for the present example, let us make it instead
a mortgage of the land, by the trustee. The rules are essentially the same, but
it is in mortgage cases that their difficulties appear in the most practically
acute form.

So: say you are registered as the owner of a house, and you mortgage it to
a bank. In due course, however, you fail to keep up the payments, and the
bank wishes to repossess the house and sell it. At this point John intervenes,
saying that you held the house on trust for yourself and him in equal shares,
by virtue of a common intention to that effect (§ 9.3). The register contained
no restriction reflecting such an interest, however. Our task is to assess John's
intervention, and determine its impact on you and, especially, the bank. To
perform this task, we need to ask and answer seven separate questions.

—— *Question 1: did John indeed have a beneficial interest in the house?* So
long as John can substantiate his assertion of a common intention, in
terms of the law set out in § 9.3, the answer should be yes.
—— *Question 2: did John acquire his beneficial interest before the bank took its
mortgage?* If he did not, the bank cannot be affected by his interest.[109]
Sometimes this rule is easy to apply. Say you acquired the house with
money the bank lent you, so that the mortgage arose at the moment the
house became yours . . . but it was five years later that you met John and
his interest came into being: the mortgage obviously pre-dates John's
interest. Conversely, say you acquired the house on the basis of your
agreement with John, so that his interest in the house arose at the
moment the house became yours . . . and you mortgaged it to the bank,
maybe to raise funds for your business, only five years later: John's interest obviously pre-dates the mortgage. The hard case is the very common
one where you acquired the house *both* with money the bank lent you,
and on the basis of your agreement with John: so that, seemingly, the
mortgage and John's interest arose simultaneously, at the moment the

---

[109] *Abbey National Building Society v Cann* [1991] 1 AC 56 (HL).

house became yours. In this situation, the law – for no sufficient reason[110] – treats the mortgage as having arisen first, with the result that it cannot be affected by John's interest. It can be affected by John's interest only in the case of a post-acquisition mortgage. In many cases, the possibility of John's right binding the bank will therefore proceed no further.

—— *Question 3: was John's interest overreached by the mortgage disposition?* On the given facts, you being the only trustee, there has been a breach of the two-trustee rule. Since there was no restriction requiring compliance with the rule, the mortgage nonetheless takes effect: § 16.6.4. But assuming that breaches of the two-trustee rule are not within the scope of section 26 of the Land Registration Act 2002,[111] John's interest was not overreached by the mortgage, and so remained attached to the land, capable of binding the bank.[112]

If these three questions are answered in John's favour, John had, at the time you mortgaged the house, a right in rem in it, capable of binding the bank. Questions 4 and 5 tell us whether it actually did bind the bank.

—— *Question 4: did John's unoverreached right qualify as an overriding interest?* This question has to be addressed by reference to the terms of schedule 3 paragraph 2 of the Land Registration Act 2002: see § 16.7.1. The answer depends principally on whether, at the time you granted the mortgage, John was in actual and apparent occupation of the house. Given that (as explained in answer to question 2) the mortgage will need to have been a post-acquisition mortgage, there is a good chance that he was, but of course everything will depend on the particular facts.[113]

If John's right does qualify as an overriding interest in this way, the bank is bound by it[114] ... unless the answer to question 5 dictates otherwise.

---

[110] *Abbey National Building Society v Cann, ibid*, offers two justifications. First, John's interest did not pre-date the bank's; so the bank's must have pre-dated John's. Wrong: it is correct to say that John's interest did not pre-date the bank's because they arose simultaneously, so the bank's interest did not pre-date John's either. Second, even if the bank's interest did not in fact arise first, it *deserves* to be treated as though it did, because you could not have bought the house without the bank's help. Again, wrong: it may be true that you needed the bank's help, but if so you probably needed John's help (eg his contribution to repaying the mortgage) too.

[111] §§ 16.6.4–16.6.5. If this is wrong, and breaches of the two-trustee rule *are* within the scope of s 26, we must instead pretend in the bank's favour that two trustees were not required, leaving no reason why the bank should be affected by John's interest. In this event, John's claim against the bank can proceed no further. (Just as if John's argument against overreaching was any other kind of impropriety in the mortgage, such as your having taken the loan for yourself alone: s 26 certainly applies then.) John could however proceed against you, to recover his share of the mortgage money.

[112] As in *Williams & Glyn's Bank Ltd v Boland* [1981] AC 487 (HL).

[113] For the meaning of 'actual occupation', see § 3.1.2.

[114] As the bank was bound by Mrs Boland's right, operating as an overriding interest on the basis of her actual occupation, in *Williams & Glyn's Bank Ltd v Boland* [1981] AC 487 (HL).

—— *Question 5: can the bank say that John consented to the mortgage?* If so, he loses[115] the ability to assert his right against the bank: § 16.7.2. The meaning of 'consent' in this context is discussed fully in §§ 4.2–4.3, but, in brief, it is wide. John will probably be found to have consented so long as he was aware that you were creating a mortgage and did not oppose you, or even so long as he consented in this way to an earlier mortgage, which this one (perhaps quite unknown to him) replaced.[116] However, if John appeared to consent, but his consent was vitiated by the manner in which you obtained it, the bank may not be able to rely on it: §§ 4.2.3–4.2.4.

If questions 4 and 5 are answered in John's favour, his right actually does affect the bank. That is to say, the mortgage binds your interest in the house, but not John's. It remains to be seen where this leaves John in practice.

—— *Question 6: if you default on the mortgage repayments, and the bank (naturally enough) wishes the house to be sold so as to recoup its loan, can John prevent this?* The answer lies in the court's discretion, under section 14 of the Trusts of Land and Appointment of Trustees Act 1996 (see §§ 16.2.2–16.2.6, 16.3.3). In brief, if you have been bankrupt for a year or more, the house will almost certainly have to be sold;[117] otherwise, it will probably have to be sold,[118] unless John is able to take the mortgage over himself.[119] So while John's beneficial right does (if the previous five questions have been answered in his favour) bind the bank, it is unlikely that he can on this account simply ignore the mortgage. He may well have to leave the house, and be content with a substitute entitlement.

—— *Question 7: if the house is sold, what rights does John have?* If the bank succeeds in its request for a sale, the proceeds of that sale will be divided in the same proportions as the beneficial interests: if you and John had equal rights, 50:50. Your share will go to the bank so as to pay off your debt and any sale expenses (you will receive any surplus, of course), and John's share will go to him. Contrast the position if John's right had *not* bound the bank, so that the bank could repossess the house and sell it without regard to John. Then, the bank would have been entitled to retain as much of the proceeds as it needed to pay off the loan, before paying any surplus to you. John would still have been entitled to half the sale price, but his claim for it would have been only against you, his trustee. In theory, then, John is entitled to half the sale price of the house either way. But in practice, his chances of actually getting his hands on

---

[115] As in *Bristol and West Building Society v Henning* [1985] 1 WLR 778 (CA); *Paddington Building Society v Mendelsohn* (1985) 50 P & CR 244 (CA). In *Williams & Glyn's Bank Ltd v Boland, ibid*, the bank did not argue that Mrs Boland had consented to the mortgage: presumably because there was no evidence that she even knew about it at the time her husband was granting it.

[116] *Equity and Law Home Loans v Prestidge* [1992] 1 WLR 137 (CA).

[117] Insolvency Act 1986 s 335A; *Re Citro* [1991] Ch 142 (CA).

[118] *Bank of Ireland Home Mortgages Ltd v Bell* [2001] 2 FLR 809 (CA).

[119] *Mortgage Corporation v Shaire* [2001] Ch 743 (Ch D).

this money are far greater if he has a right against the bank (because it is a bank) than if he does not, and has to resort to claiming from you (who by definition – since the bank wants a sale – are over your head in debt).

The ability to claim money from the bank rather than from you is the real-time advantage John can hope to gain from asserting that he has a beneficial right in the house, binding on the bank. From the bank's point of view, of course, the difference between the two outcomes is even greater: if it is bound by John's right it can take only half the proceeds of sale, while otherwise it can keep all the proceeds up to the value of your debt.

The difference both to you and to the bank is most acute if, as is likely, the bank, taking you to have full rights in the house, loaned you a sum greater than the value of the 50 per cent share you actually had. Say, for example, the house was worth £200,000; the bank loaned you £180,000; £160,000 is outstanding; and the house is now sold, for £240,000 (net of expenses). If the bank is *not* bound by John's interest, it takes its £160,000 first, then pays the remaining £80,000 of the sale money to you, leaving John with the unpromising prospect of claiming his half share of the sale money – £120,000 – from you. But if the bank *is* bound by John's interest, the £240,000 will go £120,000 to John and £120,000 to the bank: the bank will not recover the whole outstanding debt, there will be no surplus to come to you, but John will receive his full entitlement.

16.8.2 An Appraisal

The law embedded in § 16.8.1's seven questions (especially the first five of them) gives John a rather slim chance of being able to look to the bank, rather than you, in this way. This is probably no accident. Not merely overreaching (§ 16.5), but the whole set of rules regulating the impact of trust rights on disponees of land can be seen as calculated to ensure that trust rights remain 'behind the curtain', ie that a disponee is not normally affected, and need not normally fear being affected, by such rights.[120]

This is an intelligible position for the law to adopt (though one would wish to think carefully about its compatibility with the ECHR). It enhances land's commerciability, and so lubricates the economy; and if we focus especially on the question whether beneficial rights should bind mortgagee banks,[121] it

---

[120] Discussing the leading authority on Question 2, *Abbey National Building Society v Cann* [1991] 1 AC 56 (HL), R Smith, 'Mortgagees and Trust Beneficiaries' (1990) 106 *LQR* 545, 548 observes that it 'comes perilously close to a simple assertion that a mortgagee wins because he is a mortgagee'. See further M Dixon, 'Equitable Co-Ownership: Proprietary Rights in Name Only?' in E Cooke (ed), *Modern Studies in Property Law, Volume 4* (Oxford, 2007) ch 2; Fox (n 44).

[121] On this, see further C Sawyer, 'A World Safe for Mortgagees? – Registering a Scintilla of Doubt' in E Cooke (ed), *Modern Studies in Property Law, Volume 1* (Oxford, 2001) ch 12.

reduces the bank's risk, and so facilitates a lower interest rate, and fuels the economy in that way. The position is by no means unavoidable, however: one could see banks as having social responsibilities in respect of the damage that can occur (to persons such as beneficiaries) in transactions involving them, because of their position as 'gate-keepers' of such transactions.[122] Moreover, even the position in fact adopted by the law does not quite imply a disregard for the protection of beneficiaries, even where their desire to stay with the land leaves them unhappy with overreaching: rather, it involves seeing their protection as the responsibility normally of their trustees alone, and not of outsiders taking a disposition of the land.

This position would, however, be more simply expressed by a rule that (at least in the case of land) trust rights operate in personam only. As the law stands, there is considerable conceptual overkill. It treats such rights as in principle in rem, but then cuts back the significance of this to almost zero, by the multifarious and tortuous rules described in this chapter. So we find rules to the effect that the right in rem may be overreached ... but that overreaching will in principle be blocked by certain, but not all clearly identified, improprieties in the disposition ... but that in fact the block is lifted by pretending that the impropriety was not an impropriety, though it is unclear whether in every case ... and so on.

If trust rights are viewed as essentially in personam, the implication is that, after a disposition, a beneficiary will need to be content to enjoy his right in a money form.[123] To be sure, this may conflict with his actual preference, which may well involve enjoying – and continuing to enjoy – his right against the physical trust land itself, usually by occupying it. The vision treating trust rights as essentially in personam has no quarrel with this as a preference, but regards it as a matter solely between the beneficiary and his trustees, to be addressed *prior to* a proposed disposition. Although (as we saw in §§ 16.2–16.3) they are configured in an unsatisfactory way, the provisions of the Trusts of Land and Appointment of Trustees Act 1996 – giving a right to occupy, and allowing trustees' proposals for the operation of the trust to be challenged in court – are in a broad way organised along these lines: see § 16.5.3. On this view, the beneficiary's preference should not be capable of impinging on a disponee at all, let alone doing so via issues that essentially have no relevance to that preference, such as whether the money arising upon a disposition was paid to two trustees rather than one.

---

[122] Some of the rhetoric in *Barclays Bank plc v O'Brien* [1994] 1 AC 180 (HL) views banks in this way, though the detail of that decision and especially of its successor, *Royal Bank of Scotland plc v Etridge (No 2)* [2002] 2 AC 773 (HL), is aimed more at allowing banks to discharge these responsibilities with minimum effort.

[123] This is obvious where the disposition is a sale or a lease; where it is a mortgage, he may be able to occupy so long as the mortgage is being repaid, but in the event of default he will have to go. The key point is whether his presence is compatible with the rights conferred on the disponee.

Licences

17.1 What is a Licence?

17.1.1 Licences as Residual Consensual Rights in Personam to Be on Another's Land

Given the general liberal suppositions of English land law, you gain a right to be on my land only if I consent to you doing so, or if the law contains a specific rule requiring it in particular circumstances. That is, you can acquire such a right without my consent only in a finite number of specified ways, and then only in a form that the way in question allows.[1] But if I consent to your having a right to be on my land, I can in principle give that right any form I like.

Of the infinite variety of rights over my land that I can therefore create by consent, however, only some are allowed to operate in rem. This is because of the *numerus clausus* principle: the phenomenon explained in § 1.2.2 whereby, because a right in rem is always harmful in some ways, the law allows it to arise only where some stronger consideration indicates that it should. This argument will be a function of the right's nature, as reflected in its definition. (An easement, for example, is a right in rem because a right with the characteristics required for an easement deserves to operate in rem, despite the harm that this does: § 13.1.6.) Of the infinite variety of possible consensual rights over land, the residue thus operates in personam only.

And within this residue of consensual rights in personam over land, certain ones are referred to as 'licences'. The term is normally applied only to rights

---

[1] Rights of this non-consensual kind include, for example, your right to enter my land under certain circumstances so as to search it; a right arising from my responsibilities towards you as a member of my family, under the Family Law Act 1996 Pt IV; or your 'right to roam' or right of coastal access over my land, under the Countryside and Rights of Way Act 2000 and the Marine and Coastal Access Act 2009.

of this kind that allow you to *be on* my land. Say, by contrast, I agree to use my land on your behalf in some other way: perhaps to grow flowers there, for you to sell in your shop. Your right regarding my land is of the residual kind: ie consensual, and, as it does not match the specification of any right in rem, in personam only. But as it does not involve your actually being on my land, it is not called a licence. While not referred to as licences, however, rights of this latter kind (which have no generic name of their own) seem to give rise to essentially the same issues, and to attract essentially the same rules, as licences.

It is possible to give instances of licences by contrasting them with rights in rem (arising by my consent, and allowing you to be on my land) to which they bear some, but necessarily not a full, resemblance. For example, if we have an agreement entitling you to occupy my house, but in one way or another your right is not exclusive, you do not have a lease[2] ... but you do have a licence. Or if you rent a cottage on my large country estate, and I give you, but only you, a right to ride your horse around the estate, you do not have an easement[3] ... but you do have a licence.

At the same time, we can notice certain very common kinds of right that are in fact licences. If you come and visit me at my house, for example, the reason you are not a trespasser is because you have a licence (a right, arising from my consent) to be on my land. Likewise if you go into a shop, or a restaurant, or a theatre or cinema or museum or gym or sports ground ... Likewise too if you are a guest in my hotel, or a lodger in my house. (In none of these cases do you have the exclusive possession of my land needed for your right to be a lease; nor does your right accommodate other land owned by you, so as to be a potential easement.)

In all these examples, you are known to the law as a 'licensee'; I am a 'licensor'.

17.1.2 Kinds of Licence

It is usual to discern three different kinds of licence: bare licences, contractual licences and licences coupled with an interest (or with a grant). We shall examine each kind in turn. As we do so, we shall discover certain departures from the position we have just worked out, that a licence over another's land is necessarily a right in personam. These departures will need careful consideration.

---

[2] *Street v Mountford* [1985] AC 809 (HL); § 11.2.1. For the question whether this line of distinction between leases and licences fully conforms with the ECHR, see § 11.2.2.

[3] § 13.1.3.

17.2 Bare Licences

17.2.1 The Nature of a Bare Licence

If I give you a bare licence to be on my land, I merely give you permission to do so. The permission can of course be explicit (as where I make you a formal invitation to visit me), or tacit (as with the permission I extend to all comers – or at any rate all bona fide comers – to walk up my garden path so as to ring at my front door). But it is no more than a voluntary permission. It is in this respect that bare licences differ from especially contractual licences. If I give you a contractual licence to be on my land, I still give you permission to do so . . . but it is not simply a voluntary permission: I am obliged to give you it because I have entered into a contract to that effect. For example, say I have sold you a ticket to visit my stately home: we have a contract obliging me to allow you to do so. A bare licence is one that lacks this obligatory element.

17.2.2 Duration

The fact that you have a licence – my permission to be on my land – means that you are not a trespasser when you are there. (Another way of speaking of your licence is to say that you have the defence of *volenti non fit iniuria* to the tort of trespass that you would otherwise commit against me.[4])

If I state a limit to my permission, therefore, you become a trespasser if you stay on my land past that limit. So if I say that you can remain only until midnight, you do not (unless I extend the licence) have permission to remain beyond midnight. If you are still on my land a moment after midnight, you are trespassing: it is your responsibility to ensure that you do whatever it takes to get yourself away before the clock strikes twelve.[5]

But my saying that you can remain until midnight does not mean that you can certainly stay even that long. Promises made without consideration are not binding: so I can change my mind and revoke my permission. Similarly if my permission is open-ended: whether or not you have the impression that this means you can stay permanently, I can revoke it.[6]

---

[4] *Winter Garden Theatre (London) Ltd v Millennium Productions Ltd* [1948] AC 173, 188 (HL).

[5] I may also limit your licence in other ways, express or implied. Say I permit you to come into my house: if you in fact enter with the object of stealing from me, you will be a trespasser because you are acting outside the terms on which I surely gave that permission: *R v Jones and Smith* [1976] 1 WLR 672 (CA).

[6] If the land in question is your home, you might (subject where relevant to the question of horizontal effect: § 2.2) invoke ECHR Art 8 and argue that my revocation – or even the ending of

I cannot, however, simply announce, 'your licence is now over' and instantly make you a trespasser. After my announcement, you certainly have enough time to take yourself and where relevant your belongings off my land before you commit trespass. This rule is surely intrinsic to the idea of trespass, confining your liability to the case where your presence on my land can properly be ascribed to your agency at all.

But the relevant law is surprisingly confused,[7] and contains some support for two further propositions. The first is that I must express my announcement so that it takes effect only after a reasonable delay (eg 'your licence will be over in 24 hours' time'). This may simply be another way of couching your basic right to enough time to leave, making it inoffensive unless misunderstood, and cumulated with that basic right: there seems no reason why you should have both. The second proposition assumes that the first does indeed represent the law, then goes on to assert that its requirement of 'a reasonable delay' means enough time not merely to leave, but also to make alternative arrangements. This seems dubious: it is hard to see why your future needs are my concern, rather than something for you to consider before setting so much store by a mere gratuitous permission.[8]

17.2.3 Effect on Disponees

The authorities on bare licences are fully aligned with the idea that licences operate in personam only.[9] Given the ease with which such licences can be revoked, the question will rarely require attention, let alone litigation . . . unless it is true that you can claim enough time to make other arrangements, for this could be considerable.

your licence under its own terms, discussed in the previous paragraph – is an interference with your home, requiring justification as proportionate (which might of course be readily established, by pointing to my own rights in the matter). As explained in § 11.5.2, however, it seems odd to think of a product of your own choice as an 'interference' in this way.

[7] See J Hill, 'The Termination of Bare Licences' [2001] *CLJ* 89. The principal authorities are *Canadian Pacific Railway Co v R* [1931] AC 414 (PC); *Winter Garden Theatre (London) Ltd v Millennium Productions Ltd* [1948] AC 173 (HL); *Governing Body of Henrietta Barnett School v Hampstead Garden Suburb Institute* (1995) 93 LGR 470 (Ch D). Each contains unreconciled traces of all the ideas referred to in the text.

[8] Unless, by coming or staying on my land rather than making other arrangements, you have acted in detrimental reliance on an assurance from me that *you can stay*. Then you have an estoppel right, which may entitle you to remain on my land in this way. But care is needed in deciding whether I have indeed assured you that you can stay: it may not be right to read a bare revocable permission in that way.

[9] The point is made in a passage from an antique case in another context (*Thomas v Sorrell* (1673) Vaugh 330, 351 (Ex Ch)), adopted for the present context in *Winter Garden Theatre (London) Ltd v Millennium Productions Ltd* [1948] AC 173, 188 (HL). Once again, if the land in question is your home, this rule might be challenged under ECHR Art 8: *cf* n 6.

17.3 Contractual Licences

17.3.1 The Nature of a Contractual Licence

As said in § 17.2.1, if I give you a contractual licence to be on my land, I give you permission to do so ... but this time I am obliged to give you this permission, because I have entered into a contract to that effect.

The obligation to let you be on my land may be an express term of the contract (as where I sell you a ticket to visit my stately home), or an implied term, implied normally so as to give business efficacy to the more explicit aim of the contract (as where you visit my restaurant; our contract focuses on your meal, but impliedly obliges me to allow you to sit at a table to eat it).[10] The contract may give you a right alone (in neither of the foregoing examples do you have to enter or remain on my land, if you change your mind), or it may give you a right enabling you to perform an obligation which the contract simultaneously imposes on you (as where you are my employee; our contract obliges you to work on my farm; so it necessarily also obliges me to let you be on my farm for that purpose).[11]

17.3.2 Duration

As with a bare licence, it is your responsibility to keep within the confines of your licence. So if you book a room in my hotel for one week, but then refuse to leave and stay for another, during this second week you will be a trespasser. Also as with a bare licence, if I have given you an open-ended permission, I can terminate it; in which event, I must certainly allow you enough time to remove yourself and your belongings, and perhaps also give you reasonable notice beforehand, and/or enough time to make other arrangements.[12] But in

---

[10] In *Tanner v Tanner* [1975] 1 WLR 1346 (CA), the very contract seems to have been invented, so as to allow the court to give protection in the name of a contractual licence. On very similar facts, no contract – and so no contractual licence – was found in *Horrocks v Forray* [1976] 1 WLR 230 (CA). In these cases, a woman had a close relationship with a man, and was in some degree materially dependent on him. He provided her with a home, but later sought to evict her. She could probably be said to have relied on an understanding between them that he would house her, giving her an estoppel claim (Ch 8). Even if the estoppel requirements are not truly present, moreover, the courts will often invent them so as to enforce what are perceived as the defendant's family responsibilities: § 8.4.5.

[11] The contract may be between me and you, or between me and someone else for your benefit – as where you attend my theatre, but your father buys your ticket. In such a case you will normally be able to enforce your father's contract against me, under the Contracts (Rights of Third Parties) Act 1999.

[12] *Winter Garden Theatre (London) Ltd v Millennium Productions Ltd* [1948] AC 173 (HL). Such a possibility of revocation tends to be found even if the contract seems to allow you to stay

the case of a contractual licence, this default rule may be overlain by more specific arrangements (usually more generous to you) required by the express or implied terms of the contract: in particular, the contract may state your licence to be terminable on, say, a month's notice.[13]

The most important difference between bare and contractual licences arises, however, where I purport to end your licence prematurely, ie inconsistently with my promise. Say I promise that you can stay for a year. If my promise is gratuitous, I can legitimately revoke it any time, and you must leave (though I must give you at least a reasonable time in which to do so). But if my promise is in a contract, I cannot legitimately revoke it.[14] You can insist on staying;[15] and if I use force to eject you – even no more force than I can lawfully use against someone who really is a trespasser – I therefore commit an assault on you, as you are not a trespasser.[16]

Given the contractual quality of the licence, an account of this rule needs to begin with the ordinary law of contract. In these terms, my purported revocation counts as a repudiation. Two possibilities follow. One is that you accept my repudiation (ie accept that the licence is over, and take yourself away), and, if you suffer loss, claim this from me as damages for breach of contract. The other is that you affirm the contract, so that we are both obliged to continue performing it (ie I must let you stay on my land for the remainder of the year after all). But you do not have a free choice between the two possibilities. The former is always available, but you can opt for the latter only in two situations. First, if you can claim specific performance – an equitable order for the performance of the contract – against me. This is only exceptionally the case. And second, without specific performance, only if you can keep the contract going by your own activities alone, and the law allows you to do so. This is not always the case. In particular, it is not if, to continue, you need my cooperation; and you are seen as needing my co-operation if keeping the contract going will involve your using my property.[17] Affirming your

---

forever: *Staffordshire Area Health Authority v South Staffordshire Waterworks Co* [1978] 1 WLR 1307 (CA) (in a different context). In theory, it follows that a contract apparently permitting you to stay for some *fixed* time could likewise be read as allowing earlier termination on notice. But in general such a reading would be surprising.

[13] Once again (see n 6), if the land in question is your home, you might (subject where relevant to the question of horizontal effect: § 2.2) invoke ECHR Art 8 in order to resist the ending of your licence in this way, and also in the way that the text goes on to consider.

[14] Unless my revocation is an acceptance by *me* of an earlier repudiatory breach on *your* part: eg if you have abused your licence by harassing me. *Thompson v Park* [1944] KB 408 (CA), where the licensor's termination was held to render the licensee a trespasser, is commonly explained in this way.

[15] *Winter Garden Theatre (London) Ltd v Millennium Productions Ltd* [1948] AC 173 (HL); *Hounslow London Borough Council v Twickenham Garden Developments Ltd* [1971] Ch 233 (Ch D).

[16] *Hurst v Picture Theatres Ltd* [1915] 1 KB 1 (CA); approved, *Winter Garden Theatre (London) Ltd*, ibid 191, 193–4, 202–3; accepted as the law, *Hounslow London Borough Council v Twickenham Garden Developments Ltd*, ibid 254–5.

[17] *Hounslow London Borough Council v Twickenham Garden Developments Ltd*, ibid 252–4, discussing *White & Carter (Councils) Ltd v McGregor* [1962] AC 413 (HL).

contractual licence and continuing to enjoy it will plainly involve your using my land. Affirming and continuing to enjoy your licence will not, therefore, be possible unless you can claim specific performance of our contract against me.

This, then, is the position we should expect under the ordinary law of contract. The cases about the revocability of contractual licences are broadly consonant with it; but, as we shall see, they also display certain unexpected features.

The story begins with *Wood v Leadbitter*.[18] In this early decision, the court treated a contractual licensee as not surviving a purported revocation by the licensor. It is often therefore taken as a decision that contractual licences are revocable. In truth, however, it may not say so much. Its reasoning is rather to the effect that a licensee – even a contractual licensee – cannot have the same sort of right to be on the land as someone who has the benefit of a properly conferred right in rem entitling him to be there. This is obviously correct: by definition, as explained in § 17.1.1, licences are not rights in rem. It notices the possibility of thinking matters through, quite separately, in terms of the parties' rights and duties under the law of contract, as the account above does, but does not pursue the matter.[19]

In time, however, the contractual dimension did receive attention, in decisions concluding on the strength of it that a contractual licence normally will survive its purported termination by the licensor. They held that the licensee can demand specific performance[20] of the contract, obliging the licensor to let him stay on the land if he is currently there,[21] or to let him enter if he is not.[22] And further that, even if the licensee has no opportunity to obtain specific performance, the *theoretical availability* of specific performance means that

---

[18] (1845) 13 M & W 838 (Ex). This decision did, however, disapprove some even earlier authority to the contrary, especially *Tayler v Waters* (1817) 7 Taunt 374 (CP). The basis of the latter is unclear.

[19] (1845) 13 M & W 838, 855 (Ex).

[20] The discussion in *Winter Garden Theatre (London) Ltd v Millennium Productions Ltd* [1946] 1 All ER 678, 685 (CA) speaks not of specific performance of my promise to let you be on my land, but of an injunction enforcing my promise not to revoke my permission for you to be on my land. The latter is an odd way of approaching the matter (treating the permission – licence – as one entity, and the required promise not to revoke it as another: an analysis which the judgment, at 680, rejects), and one which fails to acknowledge that to enforce the licence is, by whatever name it is called, in effect to grant specific performance of the contract. The language of specific performance is used in *Hounslow London Borough Council v Twickenham Garden Developments Ltd* [1971] Ch 233, 254–5 (Ch D); see also *Hurst v Picture Theatres Ltd* [1915] 1 KB 1, 9, 14, 15 (CA).

[21] *Winter Garden Theatre (London) Ltd v Millennium Productions Ltd* [1946] 1 All ER 678, 685 (CA); approved, [1948] AC 173, 202–3 (HL); accepted as the law, *Hounslow London Borough Council v Twickenham Garden Developments Ltd, ibid* 247, 254–5 (Ch D).

[22] As in *Verrall v Great Yarmouth Borough Council* [1981] QB 202 (CA). In that case, there was an additional reason for granting specific performance: to protect the licensee's right of free speech (he had hired the licensor's conference centre for a political event which the licensor no longer wished to see happen). But the logic of the surrounding law suggests that specific performance should be granted even without such a special factor.

he can again treat the licence as still operative. So if the licensor, having unsuccessfully asked the licensee to leave, goes on to evict the licensee by force in the same way as he would a trespasser, the licensee is seen as entitled to be on the land, meaning that the force is an assault.[23] These propositions represent the prevailing law.

The theme of this treatment – its focus on specific performance as making all the difference – is fundamentally correct. As explained above, in a context like this, it is only by claiming specific performance that a licensee can affirm the contract, and so keep the licence in being. But the treatment has two surprising aspects.

First, it seems to suppose that a licensee, faced with a licensor's repudiation, can always claim specific performance. But this remedy is usually seen as obtainable only where damages for breach of contract would not be adequate. Why should that always be the case where a licence is involved? Say you hire space to keep your (quite ordinary) goods in my (quite ordinary) warehouse for a year, and after six months I ask you to remove them. Surely your interests are adequately covered by my liability to pay you your removal expenses, plus any amount by which equivalent replacement accommodation costs you more. The notion that specific performance is always available in licence cases seems rather to be aimed at teeing up the further proposition that a licensee can treat the licence as still operative, even without obtaining an order of specific performance.

The second surprise is that further proposition: the idea that, even if specific performance is available, a licensee need not actually obtain it, but can simply proceed on the basis that the licence remains operative. This idea depends on the doctrine 'equity looks upon as done that which ought to be done', as applied to the specific performance of the licence contract. That is, because specific performance would (let us assume) be given if it were sought, we pretend that it has been given and complied with: and therefore that the licensor's permission still stands, making the licensee not a trespasser. But this doctrine's pedigree is as a rule about contracts to confer interests, operating in the fashion described in § 6.2.1. To apply it to a contract to permit what would otherwise be a trespass is clearly to take it outside this pedigree.[24] Viewed substantively, however, the resulting rule perhaps represents an effort to discourage licensors from, at all events, using force to evict their licensees. That is intelligible, resonating with a more general perception that self-help is an undesirable way for a landowner to deal even with an undoubted trespasser.[25]

[23] *Hurst v Picture Theatres Ltd* [1915] 1 KB 1 (CA); approved, *Winter Garden Theatre (London) Ltd v Millennium Productions Ltd* [1948] AC 173, 191, 193–4, 202–3 (HL); accepted as the law, *Hounslow London Borough Council v Twickenham Garden Developments Ltd* [1971] Ch 233, 254–5 (Ch D).

[24] And so was declared impossible in Phillimore LJ's dissenting judgment in *Hurst v Picture Theatres Ltd, ibid* 18–19 (CA).

[25] *McPhail v Persons (Names Unknown)* [1973] Ch 447, 456 (CA).

If this suggestion is right, it would be possible to disentangle the law by adopting a general rule against the forcible eviction by landowners even of trespassers, and leaving the subsistence of contractual licences in the face of a licensor's repudiation to the ordinary law of contract: meaning that the licensee can always have damages for breach of contract, and specific performance in appropriate cases. But a general rule against forcible eviction of trespassers seems politically unachievable, so the law is likely to remain in its present analytically unsatisfactory state.

17.3.3 Are Contractual Licences Rights in Personam or in Rem?

In § 17.1.1, we saw that licences comprise those consensual rights to be on land that are not rights in rem, and as such must be in personam. The prevailing view regarding contractual licences is that they are indeed in personam.

The cases have not all told the same story, however. To be sure, in *King v David Allen & Sons Billposting Ltd*[26] *and Clore v Theatrical Properties Ltd*,[27] the House of Lords and Court of Appeal respectively treated contractual licences as rights in personam. But in *Errington v Errington*,[28] the Court of Appeal (or some of its members) subsequently treated such licences as rights in rem. The House of Lords in *National Provincial Bank Ltd v Ainsworth*[29] discouraged this development when it once again drew attention to the earlier decisions, though without quite disapproving the development as a matter of substance;[30] it did not pursue the issue further, however, as it was not relevant to the case in hand. Certain later decisions of the lower courts[31] nevertheless continued to treat such licences as in rem, though the explanations given for this position, and especially for its ability to co-exist with *King v David Allen & Sons Billposting Ltd*[32] and *Clore v Theatrical Properties Ltd*,[33] lacked clarity.[34] Eventually, the Court of Appeal in *Ashburn Anstalt v WJ Arnold &*

---

[26] [1916] 2 AC 54 (HL).

[27] [1936] 3 All ER 483 (CA).

[28] [1952] 1 KB 290 (CA).

[29] [1965] AC 1175 (HL).

[30] *ibid* 1239–40, 1254.

[31] *Binions v Evans* [1972] Ch 359 (CA) (the judgment of Lord Denning MR); *DHN Food Distributors Ltd v Tower Hamlets London Borough Council* [1976] 1 WLR 852 (CA); *Re Sharpe (a bankrupt)* [1980] 1 WLR 219 (Ch D); *Midland Bank Ltd v Farmpride Hatcheries Ltd* (1980) 260 EG 493 (CA).

[32] [1916] 2 AC 54 (HL).

[33] [1936] 3 All ER 483 (CA).

[34] The key statement is that by Lord Denning MR in *Binions v Evans* [1972] Ch 359 (CA). He appears to reach the conclusion that the licence operates in rem on two grounds. First (at 367), on the facts there the licence was for the duration of the licensee's life, and older authority treated licences for life as rights in rem. This is correct, but: (i) the older authority proceeded on the basis that a 'licence for life' in fact amounted to a beneficial interest for life under a trust, which is a right in rem (§ 16.4); (ii) Lord Denning MR had already (at 366) rejected that analysis (for insufficient reasons, though in the end correctly: *Dent v Dent* [1996] 1 WLR 683 (Ch D)); (iii) in any case, such reasoning did not apply to licences other than for life. Second (at 368), because if the

Co^{35} declared the in rem view unsupportable, and since then contractual licences have been accepted as operating in personam only.[36] (The court did, however, draw attention to the rule – examined in § 9.2 – whereby a disponee who promises to honour the licence will be obliged to do so, under a 'constructive trust'.)

As a matter of principle, however, is there anything to be said in favour of the experiment with in rem status?

A number of arguments seem possible, but most of them are unconvincing. First, it has been said that contractual licences deserve in rem status – and have been given it – (only) when they are identical in substance to a recognised right in rem, which is absent only because of a want of formality.[37] The supposed identification with another kind of right in rem is often dubious, however, and the want of formality certainly cannot be dismissed as unimportant. It is easier to say, secondly, that where a contractual licence is present, there is (almost always) a proprietary estoppel claim too,[38] which may yield the same (expectation) response;[39] and that since an estoppel claim operates in rem,[40] it is therefore only sensible that the contractual licence should too – otherwise the outcome in this respect depends on the choice between two equally correct labels. This argument, however, overlooks the fact that proprietary estoppel is a (disorganised) method of generating rights. Where the right is itself in rem, it makes sense for the estoppel claim to be

---

land is transferred to someone who promises to honour the licence, the latter is bound by a 'constructive trust' to do so (§ 9.2) . . . such a promise can be implied . . . and, according to Lord Denning MR (at 369), apparently always is implied where the licensee is in actual occupation of the land. But (i) it is fanciful to think that the required promise is always given in such circumstances; (ii) when it is given, the transferee is necessarily bound by it – not, as with a right in rem, only if the relevant detailed rules are satisfied (ie the right is registered or qualifies as an overriding interest); (iii) the 'constructive trust' obligation can arise only upon the transfer, whereas a right in rem operates as such from its very creation, which can make a difference to its behaviour even before any transfer occurs (as in *DHN Food Distributors Ltd v Tower Hamlets London Borough Council* [1976] 1 WLR 852 (CA) and *Re Sharpe (a bankrupt)* [1980] 1 WLR 219 (Ch D)).

[35] [1989] Ch 1 (CA).

[36] It is sometimes suggested that, in registered land, contractual licences have become in rem as a result of the Land Registration Act 2002 s 116(b), declaring 'a mere equity' to be a right in rem. 'A mere equity', however, is a very different kind of right from a contractual licence. If I transfer land to you under a contract vitiated by misrepresentation, undue influence, etc, the law allows me to rescind the contract and so regain my land. My (as yet unexercised) right to do so is a 'mere equity', which s 116(b) declares to be a full right in rem, making it capable of binding John, to whom you have transferred the land in the meantime.

[37] S Moriarty, 'Licences and Land Law: Legal Principles and Public Policies' (1984) 100 *LQR* 376.

[38] For proprietary estoppel, see Ch 8. The offer, acceptance and consideration needed for the contract are a fortiori to the claimant's belief and reliance, ascribable to the defendant, needed for estoppel (unless the consideration remains wholly executory). Estoppel is wider, however: belief and reliance, ascribable to the defendant, may exist without amounting to offer, acceptance and consideration.

[39] Though it may not. For estoppel relief, see § 8.3.

[40] This is now established (for registered land) by the Land Registration Act 2002 s 116(a), but was probably the law all along. See § 8.5.2.

likewise in rem; but where the right is itself in personam (as a contractual licence is), the estoppel claim ought to be in personam too. Thirdly, it might be said that the law's vindication of contractual licences always (as we saw in § 17.3.2) by specific performance demonstrates a view that it is important to protect such licences *in specie*, rather than see them dissolve into a right to damages against the original licensor: and after a disposition, protecting them *in specie* requires that they be capable of binding the disponee, ie operate in rem. There is merit in this argument,[41] but it starts from a weak premise, for as we saw in § 17.3.2, specific performance's role in the protection of contractual licences is essentially technical, aimed at securing them against premature termination by the licensor.

These arguments, moreover, fail to engage with the central question, ie whether contractual licences – seen simply as themselves – ought to be rights in rem rather than in personam.

As we saw in § 17.1.1, in principle 'licences' comprise all consensual rights allowing you to be on my land, but not amounting to established rights in rem. By definition, then, they are in personam. This does not mean, however, that they necessarily *should be* in personam. The class of rights deserving to operate in rem is not static.[42] As social conditions change, the arguments for allowing a given kind of right to operate in rem will fluctuate in strength. As a result, the balance between these arguments and the harm done to the market can alter too. Sometimes the balance regarding an existing right in rem will change to the point where it ought to be reclassified as in personam;[43] sometimes the movement will be the other way, so that a right hitherto in personam should be reclassified as in rem.

It is, however, highly unlikely to be the case that all rights in personam regarding land – or even those to be on land – ought simultaneously to become rights in rem in this way. Rather, some such rights, defined by their content, may merit reclassification, while the remainder do not. The selective

[41] More merit than is recognised in *National Provincial Bank Ltd v Ainsworth* [1965] AC 1175, 1253–4 (HL). It is certainly true that the availability of specific performance to enforce a contract does not automatically entail its operation in rem, but, as explained in the text, the information it ought to give us about the right is also relevant to the question of whether it should be in rem.

[42] Note that the text says, 'the class of rights *deserving to* operate in rem is not static'. Arguably, the class of rights (over land) actually *allowed to* operate in rem is indeed static, or at any rate not to be added to, for the Law of Property Act 1925 s 4(1) appears to rule that only those rights recognised as in rem in 1925 can have that status. Such a rule can be defended if, although reclassifying a particular right in personam as a right in rem would in itself promote the greater good, the process of reclassification would create so much upset (to the market) that it would at least cancel this out. This is, however, unlikely to be true of all such reclassifications, as a matter of principle; the law ought therefore to retain the flexibility to make them, taking the ensuing upset into account in effecting the required calculus. Section 4(1) has accordingly been largely ignored by commentators, and even more markedly by the courts: even when arguing against a new right in rem (as in *Ashburn Anstalt v WJ Arnold & Co* [1989] Ch 1 (CA)), the judges tend to speak ad hoc, avoiding reference to the absolutism of s 4(1).

[43] The law's current treatment of trust rights, supposedly in rem but in reality closer to in personam (§ 16.8.2), may be seen as reflecting such an adjustment.

nature of the phenomenon should not be obscured by the fact that, while in personam, all such rights are called 'licences'. Those deserving to become in rem need to be identified, by reference to their characteristics, and, for clarity's sake, given an appropriate name. That name will then join the series 'lease, easement, etc', representing the class of rights which, on account of their nature, it is right to except from the normal in personam rule, and make operate in rem. Those not deserving to be in rem will remain 'licences': that is to say, rights in personam. In short, the identity between licences and rights in personam does not entail that a given kind of right, currently classified as a licence, alias in personam, is properly so classified.

So, when some judges said that 'contractual licences' were, or ought to be, rights in rem, they probably meant that *a particular set* of licences – not simply all those covered by a contract, but those also possessing particular substantive characteristics – merited identification and recognition as a new right in rem in this way. Those substantive characteristics were never sharply identified, but the licences at issue in the cases favouring in rem status mostly fit a certain pattern. They are nearly all domestic residential licences.[44] The cases disfavouring in rem status,[45] on the other hand, involve commercial licences.

The idea that domestic residential contractual licences should be in rem is certainly defensible. It aligns with the treatment of respect for people's homes as a fundamental human right.[46] In large measure, the law has already absorbed this argument. More recently than the decisions depicting such licences as in rem, and before the confirmation that they are only in personam, *Street v Mountford*[47] declared (as we saw in § 11.4.3) that 'licences' conferring exclusive possession of land must be seen instead as leases. Many domestic residential 'licences' are caught by this ruling, and translated by it (as leases) into rights in rem. It would be wrong, however, to think that the case for regarding domestic residential contractual licences as in rem has thereby been completely addressed. Those arrangements not conferring exclusive possession are left as licences: including the situations where the landlord has access to the premises in question so as to provide services (the cases of lodgers, then, and of elderly people living in residential care), and where two or more people occupy the premises but do not share a single right

---

[44] This is true of *Errington v Errington* [1952] 1 KB 290 (CA), *Binions v Evans* [1972] Ch 359 (CA), *Re Sharpe (a bankrupt)* [1980] 1 WLR 219 (Ch D) and *Midland Bank Ltd v Farmpride Hatcheries Ltd* (1980) 260 EG 493 (CA). It is not true of *DHN Food Distributors Ltd v Tower Hamlets London Borough Council* [1976] 1 WLR 852 (CA). There, the licence was over a commercial warehouse. A local authority compulsorily purchased the warehouse in order to redevelop the site for housing, destroying the licensee's business. Under the relevant rules, the licensee could demand compensation for this if, but only if, its right was in rem. The court's decision in its favour can be understood as aimed at this specific outcome.

[45] *King v David Allen & Sons Billposting Ltd* [1916] 2 AC 54 (HL), *Clore v Theatrical Properties Ltd* [1936] 3 All ER 483 (CA) and *Ashburn Anstalt v WJ Arnold & Co* [1989] Ch 1 (CA).

[46] ECHR Art 8.

[47] [1985] AC 809 (HL).

to do so (as is true of many flatmates). While these situations fall outside the law's definition of a lease, the premises concerned may easily (as in these examples) be the occupant's home. And this returns us to the argument that, even if it is a contractual licence rather than a lease, the occupant's right to it merits in rem status.

17.4 Licences Coupled with an Interest

17.4.1 Characteristics

Say I sell you the right to shoot – and keep – game from my wood. My wood is in the middle of my estate, so in order to enjoy this right you additionally need the right to be on my land. The right to do so may be given expressly with the shooting right, but otherwise it will be given impliedly, so as to ensure that you can take advantage of the shooting right.

A right of this kind is commonly called a 'licence coupled with an interest', or (meaning the same thing) a 'licence coupled with a grant'. This denotes that it is a licence (ie a permission on my part allowing you to be on my land), but a licence with legal characteristics different from bare and contractual licences.

Unlike a bare licence, though like a contractual licence, I cannot terminate it prematurely – that is, while you are still entitled to enjoy your 'interest'.[48] If your shooting right is for 12 months, therefore, the licence coupled with it will be for 12 months too. So I may not treat you as a trespasser during that time.

And, it is said, unlike a bare or contractual licence, a licence coupled with an interest operates in rem.[49] So if, during the 12 months, I transfer the land containing the wood to John, your right to access the wood (as well as your right to take the game[50]) will be capable of binding John.

17.4.2 What Counts as a Licence Coupled with an Interest?

Your right to be on my land counts as a licence coupled with an interest if you have an 'interest', to enjoy which you need to be on my land. But what counts as the required 'interest'?

---

[48] *Wood v Leadbitter* (1845) 13 M & W 838, 845–6 (Ex).

[49] The only authority for this, however, seems to be *Webb v Paternoster* (1619) Poph 151 (KB), which cannot be definitively seen as concerning a licence coupled with an interest at all: see n 61.

[50] This is a profit à prendre, a recognised type of right in rem.

Two sorts of right are firmly recognised as 'interests' for this purpose. One is a right in rem in my land. Your right to take my game is a right of this kind: it is a profit à prendre, a kind of right entitling you to take something from my land, which until that moment counted as part of my land. The right to take my game – or my fish – counts because the law regards the animals or birds or fish, before you take them, as part of my land. Other instances are the right to excavate my gravel or coal or stone, or to cut my meadow-grass or my trees.[51] Another kind of right in rem in my land, with which a licence might be coupled in this way, is presumably a lease, as where I lease you a barn situated in my field: the access right you need in order to reach it can be regarded as a licence coupled with the 'interest' which it represents.

The other firmly recognised type of 'interest' is a right in rem in chattels (ie property other than land) situated on my land. In such cases, the right in question is usually ownership. So if I sell you some logs that are in my yard, leaving you to come and fetch them, you necessarily have the right to be on my land so as to do so: and this right counts as a licence coupled with an interest, the 'interest' being the ownership of the logs given to you by the sale.[52]

There is some authority for a third type of 'interest', consisting in a right of any other kind, to enjoy which you need to be on my land: as where you buy a ticket to watch the film being shown in my cinema, to do which you need to enter and remain in the cinema.[53] The prevailing view, however, is that there is no such third kind of 'interest': only the two described above.[54] This seems correct. As already noted, a licence coupled with an interest is thought to operate in rem, ie to be capable of binding a disponee of the land in question. It can hardly do so unless the interest in question, which the licence exists to support, is itself in rem. The alleged third type of 'interest' is by definition (by virtue of the contrast between it and the other two types) a right only in personam: usually a contractual right, which is prevented from affecting a disponee of the land in question by the doctrine of privity. So for a licence associated with it to operate in rem would be absurd.

---

[51] *James Jones & Sons Ltd v Earl of Tankerville* [1909] 2 Ch 440 (Ch D). *Frogley v Earl of Lovelace* (1859) John 333 (Ch) also involved an interest of this kind, and is commonly regarded as likewise exhibiting a licence coupled with it.

[52] The authority for this is said to be *Wood v Manley* (1839) 11 Ad & El 34 (QB), holding a buyer of hay entitled to collect it from the seller's land despite the seller's refusal to allow this. Once something growing in or on the land is harvested – for example, once a tree or a field of hay is cut – it ceases to count as land, so a right to it is not a profit à prendre.

[53] *Hurst v Picture Theatres Ltd* [1915] 1 KB 1, 7 (CA). This decision also treated your right on these facts as a contractual licence, and reached the same conclusion – that I cannot prematurely terminate it – on that basis: see at n 23.

[54] *Hounslow London Borough Council v Twickenham Garden Developments Ltd* [1971] Ch 233, 243–5 (Ch D). There, a construction firm contracted to build on the council's land. This was held to give the firm the access it needed to do so as a contractual licence, but not as a licence coupled with an interest: ie its right to perform the contract did not count as an 'interest'.

17.4.3 Does this Concept Exist?

An argument can be made that there is little reason, and no need, to think that the law maintains the concept of a licence coupled with an interest at all.

As a matter of authority, the concept has no great support. A key decision exemplifying it is said to be *Wood v Manley*.[55] There, a buyer of some cut hay was to collect it from the seller's land, and the court held that the seller could not revoke the buyer's licence to do so. This licence could have been seen simply as a contractual licence (an implied term of the contract selling the hay, obliging the seller to let the buyer enter and collect it). Then, the case would have decided that contractual licences are irrevocable. A few years later, however, the court in *Wood v Leadbitter*,[56] dealing with contractual licences and holding them revocable, distinguished *Wood v Manley*,[57] treating the latter as dealing instead with 'licences coupled with an interest'. But the reasoning in *Wood v Manley*[58] makes no reference to this concept, whether by name or by unmistakable allusion,[59] and it is arguable that *Wood v Leadbitter*[60] identified it solely for this purpose.[61] Its genuineness has subsequently been assumed, but in a set of authority which is neither large nor powerful.[62]

Do we need the concept of a licence coupled with an interest? Consider how the cases in question would be handled without it.

So far as revocability goes, the absence of the concept would make little difference. Usually, I will give you your interest – the right to catch my game, or the ownership of my crop of hay – via a contract. If I do, you will have an access right in the form of an implied contractual licence. And in the modern law (as it has developed since *Wood v Leadbitter*[63]), a contractual licence is irrevocable, just as a licence coupled with an interest is. At the same time, if

[55] (1839) 11 Ad & El 34 (QB).
[56] (1845) 13 M & W 838 (Ex).
[57] (1839) 11 Ad & El 34 (QB).
[58] *ibid.*
[59] The reasoning raises the possibility that the licence was irrevocable simply because of the sale contract (ie a contractual licence), though apparently without conviction; but firmly asserts the licence's irrevocability on the ground that the buyer acted upon it: ie on the faith of the seller's promise to allow collection of the hay, the buyer contracted to buy it and indeed paid for it. This idea of a 'licence acted upon' has had a sporadic and not always comprehensible existence in the law. It may be best regarded as subsumed in the doctrine of proprietary estoppel (Ch 8).
[60] (1845) 13 M & W 838 (Ex).
[61] The judgment seems to ascribe the concept to two earlier decisions, *Webb v Paternoster* (1619) Poph 151 (KB) and *Thomas v Sorrell* (1673) Vaugh 330 (Ex Ch), but neither refers to it by name, or describes it in terms leaving it clearly distinct from other possible analyses. Likewise other old decisions sometimes referred to as exemplifying it, both before and after *Wood v Leadbitter* (1845) 13 M & W 838 (Ex): eg *Doe d Hanley v Wood* (1819) 2 B & Ald 724 (KB), *Muskett v Hill* (1839) 5 Bing NC 694 (CP), and *Frogley v Earl of Lovelace* (1859) John 333 (Ch).
[62] See principally *James Jones & Sons Ltd v Earl of Tankerville* [1909] 2 Ch 440 (Ch D) and *Hurst v Picture Theatres Ltd* [1915] 1 KB 1, 7 (CA): considered at nn 51 and 53.
[63] (1845) 13 M & W 838 (Ex).

the interest I give you (via a contract or otherwise) is itself a right in my land – a profit or a lease – your access right can take the form of an easement.[64] And easements too are irrevocable. The remaining case is where I give you a chattel interest without using a contract. In this case, your access right can only be a bare licence. So here there would be a difference: unlike a licence coupled with an interest, a bare licence is revocable. But, as explained in § 17.2.2, I cannot revoke even a bare licence without giving you at least enough time to take yourself and your belongings off my land. So where you have a bare licence so as to access your chattel that is on my land, I must still allow you to collect the chattel.

The absence of licences coupled with an interest would make a greater difference to the question whether your access right would affect a disponee of my land. Where your interest is a right in my land, again, you can claim an easement. An easement is a right in rem, so there is no difference there. But in other cases, claiming a contractual or bare licence, you have only a right in personam. So if I sell or give you some logs stacked in my yard, on the basis that you are to collect them, and before you do so I transfer my land to John, your having only a contractual or bare licence would mean you could no longer enter and take them: whereas if we reintroduce the concept of a licence coupled with an interest, it seems that you may be able to do so.

In the end, then, the question whether or not to acknowledge the concept of a licence coupled with an interest largely resolves into the question whether access rights associated with chattel interests should, against the background of the *numerus clausus* principle, be accepted as rights in rem. It is very arguable that they should not. Even though you cannot demand entry to John's land to collect your logs, they remain yours, and if you are prevented from retrieving them, you can still sue me and/or John for their value. That is probably protection enough.

17.5 Creation of Licences, and their Operation against Disponees

As things stand, no formalities are required to establish a bare or a contractual licence. The formality rules relevant to dealings with land focus solely on

---

[64] As explained in § 13.1.2, an easement requires a dominant tenement. A lease counts as a dominant tenement, as does a profit (*Hanbury v Jenkins* [1901] 2 Ch 401, 422–3 (Ch D)). A chattel right, of course, does not. The easement would be impliedly granted as part of the grant of the interest, on the principles described in § 13.2.2.

the conferral of a right in rem in the land, or a contract to confer such a right.[65] And as we have seen, bare and contractual licences are not rights in rem.

Similarly, bare and contractual licences have no engagement with the Land Registration Act 2002. As explained in Chapter 3, the rules in this Act detail the precise circumstances in which a right in rem, ie capable of binding a disponee, will actually do so. They have nothing to say about a right which is simply *not* capable of binding a disponee. So a bare or contractual licence cannot be registered.[66] And even if the licensee is in actual and apparent occupation of the land in question at the time of the disposition, his licence will not affect the disponee as an overriding interest.[67]

If there is such a concept as a licence coupled with an interest, however, it seems to be (as we saw in § 17.4.1) a right in rem. As such, the formality rules should apply, meaning that writing must certainly be used,[68] and in certain circumstances arguably a deed.[69] In some cases, the same requirements will apply also to the conferral of the interest with which the licence is associated, and the valid conferral of the interest will therefore automatically entail the valid creation of the licence, on the basis that the latter is implied into the former. This is true in particular where the interest in question is a profit. (To validly grant you your profit, I will have to use a deed;[70] and the same deed will suffice to confer the licence coupled with the profit.) But where the interest is in a chattel such as the logs in our illustration, no formalities will normally be required for its conferral, or used in practice. So the apparent need for formality so as to establish the associated licence becomes more of a problem, and one which has not been addressed by the courts.

As rights in rem, licences coupled with an interest should qualify for registration, and for operation as overriding interests. In practice, they will not normally be registered, so the latter possibility is the important one. Since a licence coupled with an interest is by its nature merely an access right, however, the licensee will not normally occupy the land concerned, so such a right will not normally qualify as an overriding interest on that particular basis . . . and the only other basis on which it might do so is that it can be regarded also

---

[65] Law of Property Act 1925 ss 52, 53; Law of Property (Miscellaneous Provisions) Act 1989 s 2.

[66] Land Registration Act 2002 s 32(1), allowing registration by notice only of 'an interest affecting' the land in question: this being code for a right in rem relating to it.

[67] To qualify as an overriding interest under the Land Registration Act 2002 Sch 3 para 2, a right must be an 'interest': again, code for a right in rem.

[68] Law of Property Act 1925 s 53(1)(a); Law of Property (Miscellaneous Provisions) Act 1989 s 2.

[69] If the licence is indefinite or for a term of years, it appears to count as a legal estate (Law of Property Act 1925 s 1(2)(a), (4)), and as such must be conferred by deed (s 52). It also requires registration under the Land Registration Act 2002 s 27(2)(d) . . . unless it is implied, as such licences commonly are.

[70] Law of Property Act 1925 s 52: profits are analogous to easements, whose formality requirements are discussed in § 13.2.8.

(as explained in § 17.4.3) as an easement, implied into a grant of a profit or lease over the land in question.[71]

The confused and probably unsatisfactory picture regarding licences coupled with an interest is a further reason to suspect that the concept does not actually exist.

---

[71] Such an easement can operate as an overriding interest under the Land Registration Act 2002 sch 3 para 3: see § 13.3.

Index